MW01168888

The Evolution of Social Systems

The Evolution of Social Systems

edited by
J. FRIEDMAN and
M.J. ROWLANDS

Proceedings of a meeting of the
Research Seminar in Archaeology and Related Subjects
held at the Institute of Archaeology, London University

University of Pittsburgh Press

First published in 1978 by
Gerald Duckworth and Co. Ltd.
Published in the U.S.A. in 1978 by the
University of Pittsburgh Press,
Pittsburgh, PA 15260

Designed by Derek Doyle

Photoset by
Specialised Offset Services Limited, Liverpool
and printed in Great Britain

Library of Congress Catalogue Card Number 77-90941
ISBN 0-8229-1133-7

CONTENTS

Section Three: *Evolution and political differentiation*

Section Four: *Demography, trade and technology in evolution*

Contributors

J. Allen, Research School of Pacific Studies, Australian National University.
M. Bloch, Department of Anthropology, London School of Economics.
P. Bonte, Laboratoire d'Anthropologie Sociale, Ecole des Hautes Etudes, Paris.
W. Bray, Department of Prehistoric Archaeology, Institute of Archaeology, London.
K. Ekholm, Institute for Social Anthropology, University of Lund.
C. Friedberg, Laboratoire d'Ethnobotanique, Muséum National d'Histoire Naturelle, Paris.
J. Friedman, Institut for Etnologi og Antropologi, University of Copenhagen.
M. Godelier, Laboratoire d'Anthropologie Sociale, Ecole des Hautes Etudes, Paris.
J. Goody, Department of Social Anthropology, Cambridge.
D.R. Harris, Department of Geography, University College London.
S.C. Humpreys, Department of Anthropology, University College London.
J. Oates, Girton College, Cambridge.
R.A. Rappaport, Department of Anthropology, University of Michigan.
C. Renfrew, Department of Archaeology, Southampton University.
M.J. Rowlands, Department of Anthropology, University College London.
M.G. Smith, Department of Anthropology, University College London.
E. Terray, University of Paris, Vincennes, Paris VIIIe.
A. Whyte, Department of Geography, University of Toronto.
I. Wilks, Program of African Studies, Northwestern University, Illinois.

Introduction

The following papers were presented at a seminar on the 'Evolution of Social Systems', the fifth meeting of the Research Seminar on Archaeology and Related Subjects, held at the Institute of Archaeology, University of London. In spite of the title, we should say from the outset that this is not a book about traditional problems of cultural evolution as they have been treated in general works on the subject. The papers do not, by and large, concentrate on the kinds of problems which occupied Sahlins (in his early work), Service, Fried et al., i.e. the typology of evolutionary stages. Rather they deal with more specific aspects of evolutionary processes. This is primarily a book about the nature of such processes rather than an abstract history or survey of the development of the great civilisations.

Little can be claimed for this volume in the way of theoretical unity. A number of very different, often mutually incompatible, approaches are represented. This we do not consider to be a drawback; on the contrary it has proved to be the most stimulating and productive aspect of the seminar. At this stage in theoretical discussion it has been both necessary and fruitful to present the results of very different major approaches.

The study of social evolution in the past twenty-five years has been more or less confined to several institutions in the United States. Students of Steward and White, a great number of whom work with archaeological data, have developed, refined and explored the implications of their teachers' early schemes. The great majority of these researchers were and are concerned primarily with the identification of stages and with the technological and demographic correlates presumed to be the most causally significant. Rarely, however, has the nature of the process of transformation been explored in any systematic way. Some evolutionists, Adams and more recently Flannery, have been critical of their colleagues and have stressed the need to develop an approach that specifies the social determinants in evolution.[1] Adams was one of the first severely to criticise what he felt to be a clear rejection of the role of social structure itself in social evolution. This was brought out most forcefully in his attack on the simpleminded technological determinism of Wittfogel and his followers.[2] His suggestive analyses in *The Evolution of Urban Society* and more recent works have stressed a more multifactorial approach to evolution, but he has not been able, we feel, to follow through his own programmatic proposals, often falling back on typical cultural materialist explanations which stress population growth or more general environmental adaptation as instrumental causes. The problem here seems to have been that no models of the social formation were ever developed in which it was clearly indicated how social structures were linked to the extraction, transformation and distribution of energy from nature. No specifically social dynamic was postulated and so the causes of evolution had to be sought outside the social framework. Flannery's recent article[3] in which he systematically rejects the cultural materialist position provides a more thoroughgoing theoretical attempt to construct a framework for analysing evolutionary change. Using the notion of control hierarchy applied to societies (immediate production process at the lowest level, the goals of production and distribution at the next level, administrative and ideological maintenance at a third level), he describes a number of ways in which control can shift from one level to another. Thus, a special purpose institution may be promoted to a higher general purpose subsystem, as when a war leader becomes head of state, a change which may alter the operating goals of the system. While this model of functional hierarchy does clearly show the inadequacies of the mechanical materialist approach by demonstrating that evolution can be directed 'from above', it does not in itself contain the social properties that would account for the actual forms of control and their evolution. The fact that the brain coordinates a number of lower order functions does not help us explain its structure, i.e. the *particular way* in which it performs its function. What evolves, after all, is structure and not functional hierarchies which are, as Flannery seems to assume, more or less constant in time. While this kind of model is extremely illuminating for the study of particular functional aspects of evolving systems it would have to be combined with a social structural model in order to explain evolutionary change. A new kind of framework will, perhaps, be needed in order to combine social-structural and material-functional (hierarchical) properties in a way that enables us to account for evolution as a systemic process.

The papers in this volume, the majority of which deal with developmental processes in specific social formations, should contribute to the elaboration of a more complete evolutionary theory. Some of the papers, especially those of the first part, do, of course, deal with more general aspects of evolution. They do not address themselves, however, to the question of social typology but instead focus on particular problems, such as the changing functions of institutions in different forms of social reproduction (Godelier), the nature of structural change in stratification systems (Smith), or the way in which maladaptive structures have emerged in social evolution (Rappaport). Most of the papers deal with particular periods of history, with particular regions and societies, attempting to delineate the mechanisms and processes of evolution that occur in these limited cases.

The papers in the second section dealing with transformational models are the clearest example of this kind of analysis. Transformational models are those that attempt to account for a variety of social forms in terms of a single underlying structure. Two of the papers, those by Ekholm and Friedberg, demonstrate the way in which particular kinds of exchange system and kinship structure articulate with trade in order to produce varying degrees of political hierarchy and specific variations in the kinship form of that hierarchy. Ekholm's paper, especially, shows most explicitly how an underlying structure can generate a series of variants which are superficially very unlike one another, but where the evolution of particular variants can only be understood in terms of the larger context of a regional or 'international' system. Bonte's discussion of East African societies demonstrates that technological as well as social variation can be best understood in terms of a single transformational model. He analyses a number of societies with economies ranging from pure pastoralism to more mixed technologies. Significant variations in lineage, alliance and age class structures are accounted for all in terms of a cycle of expansion and contraction. Our own paper attempts to apply this kind of transformational model to the archaeological and historical data on the evolution of the major early civilisations.

The third section deals with problems of political and other forms of institutional differentiation in social evolution. Terray discusses the way in which formerly connected elements are recombined to form new structures as well as the interplay of local conditions or events and systemic responses. Bloch analyses the particular way in which ritual and political power are articulated in Merina society in order to develop an hypothesis about the formation of the kingdom which unified Madagascar. He tries to connect the specific economic conditions of expansion to the ideological processes articulating ritual and secular authority which account for the caste-like nature of the system that emerges. The paper by Humphreys analyses processes of institutional differentiation in ancient Athens using a notion of social structure based on concepts of role and corporate group. She attempts, in this way, to link macro-structural change to individual behaviour and the interaction between social groups. She also attempts to connect institutional differentiation to the elaboration of more complex forms of communication including the development of philosophical discourse. Bray's paper provides a very interesting analysis of the nature of Aztec development and expansion which uses evidence from local mythology and historical documents as well as archaeological data. He shows how Aztec development was not a response to technological change or population growth, the latter, in particular, being a more likely result of immigration – a political and not a material phenomenon. He demonstrates that the development of that society can only be understood as part of a complex larger system of already existing states where shifts in dominant centres were linked to structural transformation in an economy in which expansion was necessary for survival.

The last section deals with problems of demography, technology, ecology and trade in evolution. The paper by Harris provides a model which reveals the relations among a number of material and social factors in the transition from mobile hunting and gathering to sedentary communities. He examines these relationships in terms of a complex feedback structure which predicts a number of necessary alterations in social relations as well as rapid population increase. The paper by Allen examines the increasing specialisation of communities over an extended period of time within a larger system of societies occupying zones with different ecological potentials. Allen demonstrates very well a point made in some other papers, that the reproductive base of a society need not be equivalent to its productive base. Thus, regional exchange provides the basis for local population densities that increase well beyond the limits of local carrying capacity. Most interesting here is Allen's time depth perspective which shows how this situation evolved from a much less integrated state. The paper by Oates is a complete survey of the archaeological data from Mesopotamia in which she carefully evaluates the indicators of types of social organisation and the explanatory force of numerous factors such as population growth, technological change, and most importantly, such phenomena as the economic function of cult activity and their development effects. A good deal of her discussion is levelled against the simple imposition of ethnographic analogues on archaeological data. Wilks, in a very thoroughly documented and argued paper, demonstrates the role of long distance trade on the formation of early Akan forest kingdoms, showing the precise connection between trade, the accumulation of labour, the expansion of agriculture and the development of political hierarchy. Goody offers a critique of Stevenson's population density theory of African state formation by demonstrating, at least for West Africa, an inverse correlation between high density and the existence of the state. He argues for a more systemic regional analysis which accounts for political variation in terms of competitive state economies based on raiding and the 'complementary' development of high density refuge areas between such states.

The more general papers of the first section deal with major problems of causality, function and structure. Godelier's papers are concerned with the definition of dominant structures of reproduction and with changes of dominance that occur in evolution. The first paper compares the function of religion in a set of societies placed on a scale of increasing hierarchy in an attempt to determine the relations between religion, political power and relations of production in increasingly stratified societies. He suggests that religion in certain societies can only be understood when seen, not as ideological reflection, but as part of the relations of production themselves. Similarly, the second paper shows how political relations function as relations of production in Classical Greece, and how this fact determines the particular form of development of these states as well as the nature of the internal class struggle. Smith critically reviews what he feels to be the inadequacies of Marx's economic theory of class structure as well as the theories advanced by Parsons and the American functionalists. He offers a formulation which seems to develop the more radical side of Weber's notion of the role of political power in social systems and their evolution. His tightly argued hypotheses attempt to establish the abstract-formal conditions for structural change in stratified societies in terms of the nature of the social units involved; their relative autonomy, their resources, their 'range' of control, and the 'scope' of their action. Rappaport's paper deals with the problem of the maladaptiveness of social systems using a control hierarchy model derived from cybernetic systems. He discusses the problem in terms of the determinate goals set by systems where the purpose is other than simple survival (the most adaptive general program). He tries to show how structures evolve in which lower order sub-systems replace higher order more inclusive sub-systems and lead thus to non-adaptive behaviour. He specifies a number of structural hierarchical anomalies that can lead to such maladaptation and argues that these anomalies tend to increase over time – a phenomenon which he ultimately links to the 'linearity' of conscious purpose confronted by the 'circularity' of the ecosystem to which it must adapt. Thus, the goals of human social systems tend to become increasingly incompatible with the long run survival of those systems. The ensuing critique by and discussion with Whyte centres on the problem of the sufficiency of Rappaport's definition of adaptation in terms of general survival where it is not specified precisely *what* it is that is to survive, nor what the nature of survival activity should entail. The whole question of the utility of the notion of homeostasis in such an approach is also raised. Renfrew presents a critique of Service's evolutionary classification of band, tribe, chiefdom and state with reference to the utility of such a scheme for archaeological data. He offers instead a spatial analysis of social structure that might fit autonomously generated patterns in archaeological material that would not rely on ethnographic analogue for their interpretation.

As we have said, the approaches represented here are quite varied and often diametrically opposed. A number of common mechanisms seemed to have received attention as instrumental in the diverse cases of specific evolution. The papers by Ekholm, Friedberg, and Wilks all demonstrate the necessity of considering the articulation of internal and external relations in the development of state structures, and Allen gives a specific example that should make us quite aware that the energy base of a society may depend on a larger system than that of the local 'evolving' unit. This represents an important criticism of local production and technological models that have characterised most stage theory in evolution. The importance of considering the relation between the internal structure and goals of a social system and its external 'objective' reality is brought out clearly in the papers by Godelier, Rappaport and Bloch. This relation is crucial for an understanding of a system's evolutionary capacity as well as the very form of its behaviour. A number of the papers attempt to discuss evolution in terms of the differentiation and/or transformation of institutional structures. This is true for Bloch and Humphreys and applies most emphatically to the papers in the section on transformational models. Among the more general issues that arose with respect to all of the papers which dealt with the development of specific social formations was the question of the relation between internal dynamics and the expansionist nature of social systems. This question appears to be especially relevant to the development of a new approach to social evolution, one which concentrates on social reproductive totalities rather than on the simple correlation of 'factors'. The so-called 'processual' archaeology as well as neo-evolutionary anthropology has singularly ignored the actual processes involved in evolution in favour of the juxtaposition of social types and supposedly external or environmental factors. It is hoped that this volume will draw attention to those social processes, and to the need for more complete explanatory models of the evolution of social systems.

NOTES

1 Adams, R. McC. (1965), *The Evolution of Urban Society*, London, p. 12; Flannery, K. (1973), 'Archaeology with a capital S', *in* Redman, C.L. (ed.), *Research and Theory in Current Archaeology*, New York.

2 Adams, R. McC. (1960), 'Early civilisations, subsistence and environment', *in* Kraeling, C.H. and Adams, R. McC. (ed.), *City Invincible: an Oriental Institute Symposium*, Chicago.

3 Flannery, K. (1972), 'The cultural evolution of civilisations', *Annual Review of Ecology and Systematics*, 3, pp. 399-426.

Acknowledgments

We should like to express our gratitude here to the Director of the Institute of Archaeology, University of London, Professor J.D. Evans, for the support and encouragement he offered us in organising and holding the seminar, and to members of the staff of the Institute, in particular Margery Hunt and Penny Wyatt, for helping with many of the arrangements.

The success of individual sessions relied very largely on the efforts of the chairmen. We should therefore like to express our thanks to Professor H.C. Brookfield, Professor S. Falk-Moore, Dr. M. Gilsenan, Mrs. S.C. Humphreys, Dr. A. Whyte and Dr. R.D. Martin for so ably performing this function.

Finally, our thanks go to Susan Frankenstein who did much to make the organisation of the seminar run smoothly and helped subsequently in the editing of this volume.

J. Friedman
M.J. Rowlands

SECTION I

General problems in evolutionary theory

MAURICE GODELIER

Economy and religion: an evolutionary optical illusion

It is not our purpose to indulge in an exegesis of Marx's and Engels' work on religion in the following pages.[1] Not that such a task is without utility, but it would seem preferable to give an account of how a Marxist anthropologist might analyse the religious element in the societies he studies.

We shall, however, briefly review Marx's principal views on religion. For Marx, religion is the imaginary reflection of reality in men's minds. In a spontaneous and unconscious fashion, primitive thought treats nature as a world of persons and treats the subjective world of this personified reality as an objective, transcendent reality independent of man and his thought. In *Capital*, Marx stressed the analogy between religious forms of ideology and men's spontaneous representations of the origin and nature of the value of commodities. Marx used the term 'fetishism of commodities' to describe their enigmatic character and to refer to the fact that the value of commodities which is made up of congealed social labour, i.e. a relation between people, is spontaneously represented in human consciousness as a property or a secret, mysterious quality of the objects themselves. Every category of a market economy experiences some aspects of this fetishism culminating in the notion of capital i.e. money that produces money, value which creates new value, surplus-value:

> In truth, however, value is here the active factor in a process, in which, while constantly assuming the form in turn of money and commodities, it at the same time changes in magnitude, differentiates itself by throwing off surplus-value from itself; the original value, in other words, expands spontaneously. For the movement, in the course of which it adds surplus-value, is its own movement, its expansion, therefore its automatic expansion. Because it is value, it has acquired the occult quality of being able to add value to itself. It brings forth living offspring, or, at the least, lays golden eggs.[2]

The internal, hidden structure of social relations, the mechanism by which surplus-value is formed, the fact that wages are not equal to the value created by the worker and the fact that profit is unpaid labour, all remain hidden from the spontaneously-formed consciousness of individuals taking part in the capitalist mode of production. Their conscious mind is presented with an inversion of this deep, unseen reality. Value, a social relation, is presented as a property of things. The phantasmic nature of this representation consists therefore in the reification of relations of production and the personification of things.

To sum up, for Marx, religion appeared to be a phantasmic aspect of social life, an illusionary representation of the internal structure of social relations and nature as well as a sphere in which man is alienated, i.e. where he represents himself in an imaginary way and his behaviour toward this reality is based upon an illusion. For Marx, religious thought and practice are the product of specific social relations and can only change with the transformation of these social relations. Therefore, it is not consciousness that is alienated; reality is such that it conceals its internal structure from consciousness. Marx does not expect religion to disappear as a result of a theoretical critique or struggle of ideas. The disappearance of religion can only result from the transformation of society itself and the establishment of new social relations founded on the abolition of class exploitation, when producers take control of the production process and social organisation.

These are the basic points in Marx. However, we should remember that he considered that the greater part of a scientific analysis and critique remained to be carried out:

> It is, in reality, much easier to discover by analysis the earthly core of the misty creations of religion, than, conversely, it is to develop from the actual relations of life the corresponding celestial forms of those relations.[3]

Few Marxists to our knowledge have embarked upon this difficult theoretical endeavour. However, such an analysis is necessary if we are to develop a scientific theory of ideologies and of the rôle that social representations play in social practice. Such an analysis is all the more necessary if we are to develop a scientific explanation of the mechanism through which man is spontaneously alienated in the development of his social relations. The following pages are dedicated to the analysis of a few examples of religious representations and practices in pre-capitalist societies.

Religious practices in a hunting and gathering society

We begin with the example of the Mbuti Pygmies, a hunting and gathering people who live in the heart of the Congolese rain-forest.[4] The Mbuti are organised into bands of limited numbers (from 7 to 30 nuclear families each with an average of 4 or 5 individuals). Each band hunts and gathers free-growing species within a defined territory, the boundaries of which are recognised by other bands. The internal organisation of bands is highly fluid. A family always has the possibility of leaving one band and joining another where they can find friends and relatives ready to take them in. No individual or family as such holds rights over land. They must belong to a band if they are to reproduce themselves materially. The band, a community of nuclear families temporarily joined together, is the social unit appropriating the means of production and natural resources. Within each band, individuals, assigned tasks specific to their age and sex, cooperate in the production process. Any individual who attempts to transform his prestige into power is criticised and ridiculed. In hunting, nets belonging to the individual hunters are set out end to end. Women and young people beat the game into the nets. The game caught is divided among all the members of the band; the collected foodstuffs are redistributed among members of the nuclear family. Every morning as they set out for the hunt, the Pygmies light a fire at the foot of a tree in tribute to the forest. They pass by this fire as they leave their camp and often sing to the forest to send them game. In the evening on their way home, they divide up the game at the foot of this same tree and proceed to sing a song thanking the forest for its kindness. Thus, for the Pygmies, the forest is an omnipresent, omniscient and omnipotent divine presence. When addressing it they use the kin terms which in their language mean 'father', 'mother', 'friend' and even 'lover'. However, it would be incorrect to assume that the Mbuti conceive of the forest as a reality entirely separate from themselves. For them, the forest is everything that exists: trees, plants, animals, sun, moon and the Mbuti themselves. When a Mbuti dies, his breath leaves him and mingles with the wind, the forest's breath. Thus men are a part of *this totality which also exists as an omnipresent and omnipotent person*.

To sum up briefly, religious activity among the Mbuti occurs at two levels and in two forms: at the level of daily life, in the rituals associated with hunting and other routine tasks in the camp's everyday life; and on exceptional occasions in the life of the individual or group. At the level of the individual, rituals are carried out at birth, at puberty for girls, at marriage, death or in times of illness. At the band level, collective rituals are held at puberty and death (*elima* rituals for puberty and *molimo* for death). When disease chronically affects a band a 'small *molimo* ritual' is organised to call on the forest to watch over them and protect them. Thus religion is both an everyday activity and one occurring at all critical moments in an individual's development and in the reproduction of the band as a whole, as the organic social unit.

Positive action on social reality

We shall briefly describe the most important ritual in Mbuti religious life, the *molimo* ceremony, held to honour a respected adult who had died. This ritual first of all involves an intensification of hunting or economic activity. More than the usual amount of game is captured and reciprocity in the sharing of game is intensified. The evening meal is transformed into a feast which is followed by special dances and songs honouring the forest. These songs are appeals to the forest to come and visit its children. In the morning, the young people enter the camp carrying horns. The sounds they play on these horns are the 'voice' of the forest who thus replies to its children and comes to visit them. Any person found asleep when the voice of the forest arrives is banished, naked and unarmed, since he has interrupted men's communion with the forest.

There are no priests among the Mbuti. Every person is priest and layman and everyone acknowledges their common dependence upon the forest. If we think about these religious practices, we see that the Mbuti are taking positive action on their social reality. By hunting more and in sharing more game, they intensify their solidarity and strengthen the unity of band members; they are taking action on the conflicts which build up in every day life. In this way they are acting both physically and symbolically upon the contradictions in their social relations while not actually eliminating them. They amplify all the positive aspects of their social life and every aspect of their social organisation is called into play in these religious practices. From one perspective, these religious practices represent the limit of all political activity directed at the system's contadictions. Initiated in grief over an adult's death, the ritual ends in the positive exaltation of solidarity among all Mbuti and between them and the forest. The Mbuti celebrate the *molimo* ritual not as individuals or specific families or even as members of a specific local band. They do so as Mbuti i.e. as men living a certain way of life within a specific natural context.

Now if we consider more closely the elements of this religious activity, we can see that it consists of both real and symbolic action upon the actual and imaginary conditions of the reproduction of their social system. But simultaneously, there is a process of inversion at work: by intensifying their hunting, sharing out more game and joining together in dance, song and musical and aesthetic emotion, the Mbuti are actually producing certain effects themselves, even though they think that their new feelings of unity are the effect of the forest being nearer and kinder to them. Here, perhaps, is an example of what Marx meant by the 'camera obscura' mechanism of ideological representations.

Real and imaginary causes

In religious representations imaginary causes are substituted for real causes. Or at least the actual causes become the effects of imaginary, transcendent causes personified by an omnipresent being requiring all their loves and gratitude. And if tomorrow the hunt is as successful or even more successful, it proves that the forest is closer to them and more attentive to their needs. Thus there is no possible doubt that can disturb the evidence based on faith. There is a circularity in religious thinking.

Finally, it would seem that the raw material of the sacred lies in this hidden articulation of social relations and the conditions for the reproduction of the social system within a specific natural environment. In the representation of this articulation, the sacred is immanent to the system in the form of a cause transcending society and this articulation is an *unintentional reality* depicted as a causal force endowed with consciousness, will and intention i.e. it takes the form of an anthropomorphic reality, a god.

What then are the components of religious alienation? The immanent is represented as transcendent, the unintentional as intentional causality and the non-human is represented in the larger than life human form of an omnipresent, omnipotent and omniscient being i.e. one possessing all the attributes of man in an exaggerated form.

The transition of the religious and the development of social classes and the state

Taking the Mbuti case as a starting point, we should like to sketch the profound transformations of religion which occur with the development of social classes and the appearance of the State. Within certain other hunting and gathering societies we find an individual with superior status, the shaman, who monopolises the means of access to the divine. He can influence the imaginary conditions of the system's reproduction better than any other man, causing the rain to come when it is lacking or the game to return in periods of scarcity. This man enjoys greater status than others; he has begun to penetrate the space separating men from gods and already stands somewhat above other men since he is that bit closer to the gods. He is already superior to ordinary men since the latter acknowledge their dependence upon him. Now, we know that the other side of a relation of dependence is one of obligation. Thus, among the Eskimo for example, the shaman appears in the role of 'priest' with specialised duties to intercede with the supernatural powers that control the reproduction of nature and culture. In exchange for his services, this priest receives a few gifts and additional portions of game, etc. Here we can see the beginnings of surplus-labour aimed at securing the existence of a ritual specialist. In some cases the latter has ceased to be a direct producer. Economic, religious, political and symbolic inequalities find their traces within these primitive communities.

The foundations of a non-violent form of violence

If we turn to another example – the Pawnees, Wichita and other Caddoan groups living in great permanent villages in the Mississippi Valley before the whites arrived in North America – we find a far more advanced development of political and religious inequality.[5] The chief inherited in his mother's line a magical packet of antelope skin containing a few sacred teeth and other sacred objects. This packet possessed the property of insuring the fertility of the earth and maize and controlled the annual return of the buffalo in the summer. The chief owned the talismans that guaranteed the intercession of the supernatural powers for the general well-being of the community. Tradition had it that if the magical packet were stolen or destroyed, the entire tribe would split up, be torn apart, and disappear as a society. Everyone would leave and attach himself to another group. Here religious ideology can be seen as functioning as the basis and legitimation of dependence upon an aristocracy formed by the chiefly and priestly lineages. At the same time, this dependence can be seen to be agreed upon and accepted since the ideology is shared by the dominant and the dominated. In religion we find the foundation of a non-violent form of violence, the ideal material for a relation of exploitation of man by man. However, among the Caddoans, the chief was still man's representative to the gods and economic and even political inequality remained limited.

An internal element in the relations of production

The case is altogether different among the Incas. The Inca, the son of the Sun, is no longer the representative of men before the gods, but represents the gods in the world of men.[6] In order to understand this qualitative change i.e. the deification of social forces, one must realise that Inca society was a class society and that the dominant class, the Inca ethnic group, monopolised the State apparatus. In this case we are presented with one of the early forms of class society still based upon tribal forms of community.

But, in this context, we see that religious ideology is not merely the superficial, phantasmic reflection of social relations. It is an element internal to the social relations of production; it functions as one of the internal components of the politico-economic relation of exploitation

Table 1 **The evolution of "Religious Facts" represented in the form of an optical illusion.**

Classless societies		*Societies with ranking and hereditary statuses*	*State class societies*
Mbuti Pygmies (Hunters and gatherers)	Eskimo (Hunters and gatherers)	Pawnee (Hunters and cultivators)	Inca (Cultivators and herders)
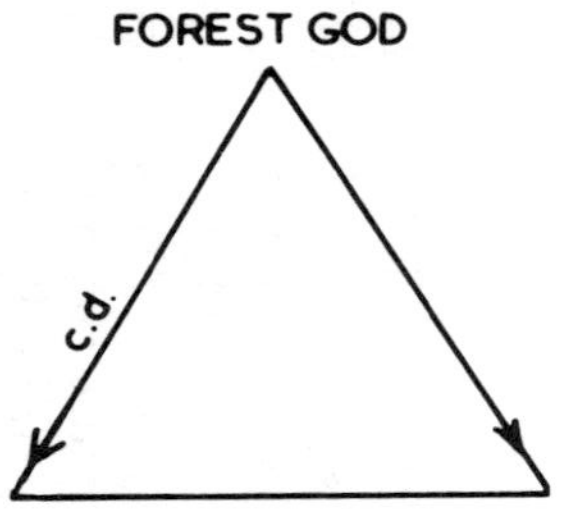 FOREST GOD c.d.	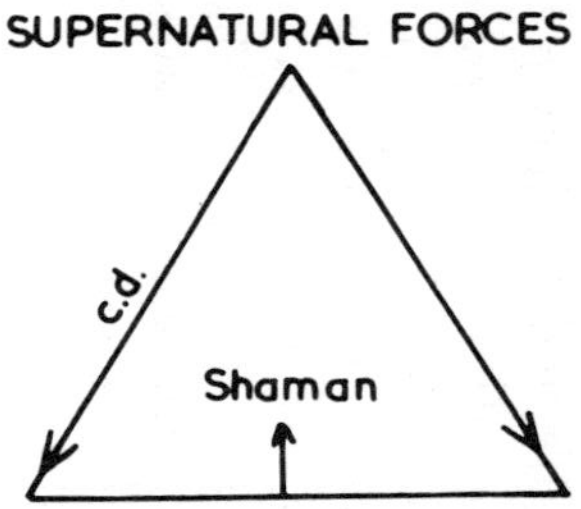 SUPERNATURAL FORCES c.d. Shaman	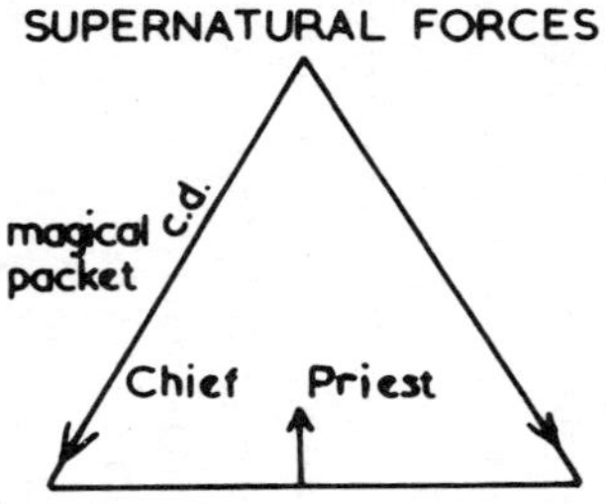 SUPERNATURAL FORCES magical packet c.d. Chief Priest	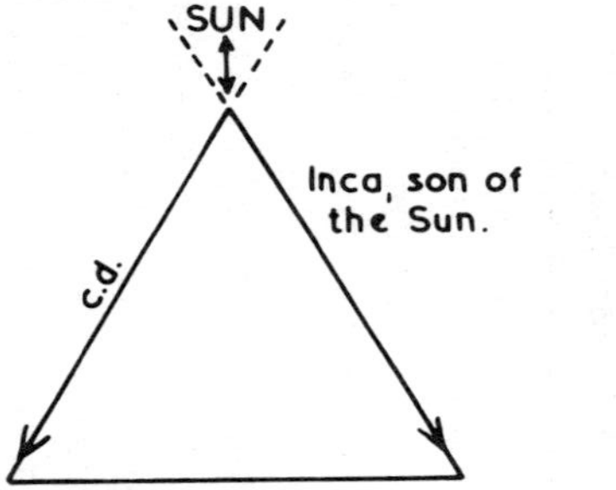 SUN c.d. Inca, son of the Sun.
	(The developing process of the divinisation of a section of humanity)		
(c.d. = common dependence of individuals and local groups in their relationship to the (imaginary) conditions for the reproduction of nature and society. Every person is priest and layman. Additional labour to glorify the divine.)	The shaman (priest) is privileged in his ability to communicate with the gods; he stands closer to the gods, thus above men. A fraction of additional labour becomes surplus labour to compensate for the good works and services of the shaman. Status is individual and non-hereditary.	The chief possesses the magical packet responsible for hunting and agricultural success. He and the priests carry out the ceremonies Surplus labour, chief and priest perform little productive labour. Collective and hereditary status.	Qualitative change. The Inca represents the gods in the world of men. Corvee for the Inca, his father, the Sun-God, and for the palaces and for the palaces and temples. A state class.
	(The development of social inequality, class opposition and the State: the exploitation of man by man)		
MAN EXPLOITS NATURE		MAN TRANSFORMS NATURE	

between the peasantry and an aristocracy holding State power. This belief in the Inca's supernatural abilities, a belief shared by the dominated peasantry and the dominant class alike, was not merely a legitimising ideology, after the fact, for the relations of production; *it was a part of the internal armature of these relations of production.* Once each individual or local community thought that they owed their existence and their women's and field's fertility to the Inca's supernatural power, they found themselves dependent upon him and obliged to provide him with labour and goods. The latter were destined to celebrate this glorious, transcendent reality and to repay partially all the Inca's efforts, which to us are merely symbolic and imaginary efforts, to maintain the general welfare. Thus, for the Inca religion functions from within as a relation of production and this fact determines the sort of information about the working and reproduction of their system which the members of Inca society possessed. This information determined in turn the actual direction of the action undertaken by groups and individuals to maintain or to change this social system. For instance, the response of the citizens of the Inca Empire in the face of a drought-caused crisis necessarily included an intensification of religious sacrifice. Large quantities of luxury and ordinary cloth were burned on *huacas*, the sacred dwelling places of the ancestors and the gods; llamas were sacrificed and maize beer poured out. Thus, given the form of their social relations – (domination by a politico-religious class) the Indians' response to these extraordinary occurrences consisted of an immense amount of symbolic labour dedicated to the supernatural powers represented by the dead and the gods. Vast quantities of material resources and labour power available to the society were consumed in this manner.

By placing these four examples in succession – the Mbuti, the Eskimo shaman, the Pawnee chief and the Inca, son of the Sun – we have created *an optical illusion as a theoretical effect* (Table 1). We have created the impression that this entire development was already in embryonic form in the hunting and gathering Mbuti society, in a community where the only inequalities are based on sex and age, and that this embryo would necessarily develop and give rise to different stages and forms of increasing inequality. Actually, let's be clear on this point: Marxism is not evolutionism and history does not consist in the development of an embryo. To understand the multiple forms of social evolution as well as the status and content of religion which differs in each case, a specific theory of the conditions for the appearance of these social relations on the basis of specific modes of production must be constructed in each case. We are therefore faced with the task of *developing* a theory of the relations between economy and society that would simultaneously explain the aspects and phantasmic forms that envelop social relations throughout history. This theory has yet to be constructed; in the very terms of Marx, the balance of work remains to be done.

Regardless of this fact, this theory is sufficiently advanced for a Marxist to realise there can be no final solution for the critique of religion at the level of ideas; it will depend upon the actual transformation of social relations. Thus, only by joining in the pursuit of this transformation will the true value of these theories be established.

(*Translated by Anne Bailey*)

NOTES

1 See Marx, K. and Engels, F. (1960), *Sur la religion*, Paris; Marx, K. and Engels, F. (1970), *Sur les sociétés précapitalistes*, Paris.

2 Marx, K. (1973), *Capital*, New York, Vol. I, pp. 153-4.

3 Marx (1973), pp. 372-3.

4 Turnbull, C. (1966), *Wayward Servants*, London, p. 390.

5 Holder, P. (1970), *The Hoe and the Horse on the Plains: a study of cultural development among North American Indians*, p. 176.

6 Godelier, M. (1973), 'Fétichisme, religion et théorie générale de l'idéologie chez Marx', *in* Godelier, M., *Horizon, trajets marxistes en anthropologie*, Paris.

MAURICE GODELIER

Politics as 'infrastructure': an anthropologist's thoughts on the example of classical Greece and the notions of relations of production and economic determination

To defend or reject the notion of economic determinism: several ways of understanding this notion

In the previous paper[1] I tried to show how, in at least one example, i.e. Inca society, religion was not merely an ideology legitimising the existing relations of production (after the fact) but constituted an essential part of the internal armature of these relations of production. Belief in the divinity of the Inca, the son of the Sun, and in the supernatural efficacy of his powers, a belief shared alike by the dominated peasantry and the dominating aristocracy, was not merely a surface or phantasmic reflection to the social relations. It was an internal part of the exploitative politico-economic relations endured by this peasantry. This belief could not have been a mere legitimation after the fact of an existing state which could have existed and developed without this belief. The belief itself was a source of the peasants' obligation to the Inca and therefore a source of their consent to his domination and to a form of subjection which did not necessarily require physical coercion by an army or police force to be accepted. Thus, the belief must have been originally present in the very content of the peasants' relationship of subjection to the 'class' representing the Inca and exercising power in his name.

This brief summary makes it possible to offer two theoretical remarks of a wider scope:

1. Ideology is not merely the expression or the more or less distorted reflection of social relations – the superstructure of superstructures built upon the foundation of various 'modes of production', to use the expression of certain 'new' Marxists who take Althusser as their authority. These recent 'revolutionary' theorists might be surprised to be presented with the fact that

this extremely 'mechanistic' and reductionist view of the relations between economy and ideology is shared by many old and new styled functionalists (for instance Marvin Harris) whom they would contemptuously banish to the realms of empiricism or vulgar materialism. Ideology exists at all levels or at least there are no social structures without an ideology internal to them.

2. The distinction between infrastructure and superstructure is not a distinction between institutions but one between functions. Anthropologists can no doubt provide all sorts of examples confirming this point and one has only to consult their research to show how kinship and political relations (or rather social relations which to *us* seem only to derive from *the* categories of kinship, politics or religion) function as relations of production, as infrastructure. Furthermore, these data provided Polanyi and the substantivists with their original ammunition for a critique of the formalism of neo-marginalist economists and the Marxist economists' often simplistic determinist positions. Given the empirical data, Polanyi was no doubt correct in reminding us that the economic can occupy quite distinct places, present itself in different forms and experience varied modes of development depending on the society or the period in question. But he comes up against the very same obstacle which confronts all empiricist 'explanations' whether by historians, anthropologists or sociologists. For once one has concluded that in a given society at a given time, kinship or political relations of religious relations play a dominant role in the social organisation and thinking of the groups and individuals making up these societies, the reasons for this dominance still remain to be explained. Furthermore, for Polanyi, the fact that kinship or politics is dominant suffices to dismiss the Marxist hypothesis of the role of the economy as determinant in the last instance. Every time the economy is not dominant as in capitalist society, it is dominated i.e. it only plays a subordinate role in social life.

For Marxists, the problem remains more difficult since they must explain how the dominance of kinship or politics is combined with and 'is explained' by the determination in the last instance by the economic. Some authors get around this problem by stating that within society the economy in some way *selects* from among the other social 'instances' (i.e. structural levels) the one which will play a dominant role in the overall structure of the society. Thus determination in the last instance by the economy would consist of a *selective mechanism and the placing of a non-economic structure in the dominant position.* This is the path taken by Terray, Meillassoux and other anthropologists inspired by Althusser's 'reading' of Marx.

In my view, such a solution or path fails since once again determination in the last instance by the economy is conceived of as a relationship between distinct *institutions*. Determination in the last instance by the economic should be understood as the hypothesis that a social structure dominates the functioning of a society as a whole, and organises its reproduction over time, if and only if it simultaneously functions as social relations of production – if it constitutes the social matrix of this society's infrastructure. This is only a hypothesis, not an act of faith. To verify it, we must analyse in greater detail, or rather reconstruct, since we have no other alternative, the conditions and reasons which act as constraints upon social relations, especially kinship relations and the political relations between men, requiring that these social relations take on the function of relations of production as well, and socially organise the conditions for the material existence of the society, its infrastructure. Therefore what is taken as a solution (no doubt a deceptive one) for the empiricists (i.e. the fact that religion, kinship or politics is dominant) is to be considered a problem. But this is not a case of constructing a 'general' theory of economic 'causality' or of treating the relations between infrastructure and superstructure as separate institutions and not as distinct functions in a hierarchical relationship which may be assumed by the same institution.

There can be no *a priori*, abstract and general solution to these sorts of questions. It is for the anthropologist and historian to pose and answer these questions. In this way a science of societies, simultaneously a science of their history and of the appearance, evolution and disappearance of social relations, will be possible. Without this rather long preamble setting out the theoretical context, the following text might at best have seemed unusual, at worst unbecoming to an anthropologist. For if it is becoming fairly frequent for historians to use anthropology to clarify the data of ancient or medieval history (a development in which we should take some pride: examples are the works of Moses Finley, J.P. Vernant, S.C. Humphreys in ancient history and Georges Duby and Jacques Le Goff in medieval history) it is quite unusual for an anthropologist to do the inverse and use history to advance his discipline. Furthermore, why choose ancient Greece and classical Athens, a difficult example since we know so little about them, and dangerous to handle since they continue to nourish certain ethnocentric predjudices, haunting the European anthropologist's conscience by presenting him with the steadfast paradigm of *the* civilisation?

I have chosen 'classical' Athens principally because it seemed to me to offer an example of a society where politics functions *from within* as relations of production. Politics here is not just any sort of politics, but a form of politics which has become distinct from relations of kinship and largely freed from relations of religion and priestly hierarchies. We no longer have a case of kinship relations functioning as relations of production as among the Australian Aborigines[2] or one where a politico-religious power organises the society's infrastructure as among the Incas. In these various research projects, the goal is not simply to make a systematic inventory of the various forms of relations of production encountered in history, i.e. to construct a typology. While such a typology should be attempted elsewhere, what I principally hoped to see here was whether this reading of the Greek data offered any theoretical advantages and allowed certain insights into the original logic of the functioning and development of Greek society. Everyone recalls the debate between the advocates of a 'primitive' Greek economy and the proponents of a 'modern' capitalist view of this society. Today this controversy seems to have been put to rest. However, even for a specialist as eminent as Edouard Will, who did so much to settle this controversy, the idea that there could have been one or several Greek economic systems seems to have been rejected as historical ethnocentrism, the product of a non-critical viewpoint. Our reading of the data brings us to an opposite conclusion. However – and this is a measure of the drawback in presenting these pages out of the context in which they are to be presented in their final form – in order to carry out our analysis we were obliged to pose again the question of the existence of classes in ancient Greece and Rome, i.e. the old 'order' and/or 'classes' debate which anthropologists who have dealt with African, pre-Columbian and Asiatic state societies know only too well. This led me to seek the origins of the concept of class in the eighteenth century, and to the discovery that historians' or anthropologists' difficulties, in taking up or totally rejecting the concept of class to characterise the dominant groups in the state societies they were analysing, were due to their ignorance of the origins of the concept and its epistemological functions. But this point, a fundamental one for the scientific interpretation of the evolution of social systems, will be treated elsewhere.

I have reduced bibliographical references to a bare minimum, but historians will readily recognise my debt to the works of Edouard Will, Moses Finley, Jean-Pierre Vernant, P. Vidal-Naquet, Pierre Leveque, Charles Parain, etc. as well as the selective use made of their works.

The Greek example

Social relations of production are those social relations that determine the use and control of the means of production and the social product, and the division of social labour power between various productive and non-productive activities. Among the Australian Aborigines for example, we find that relations of kinship between groups and individuals served as a framework for the control and use of territory and natural resources and for organising the labour process based on a division between the sexes and generations and for the redistribution of products. Thus kinship relations functioned as relations of production and belonged to both the 'infrastructure' and the superstructure of the society, providing the general framework or dominant aspect of its organisation.

Even though their effects are different, the productive forces and the relations of production never exist separately. They are always articulated and united within a single whole. The productive forces among hunters and gatherers partially explain the differential valuation and division of productive work between men (hunting, etc.) and women (gathering) and between the old and the young. Among the Murngin for example, old men no longer take part in productive work, even though they enjoy all forms of social power. On the one hand, they control the circulation of women between the kin groups they represent and in this way control the reproduction of the social systems of production. On the other hand, only they have access to the supernatural powers believed to control the reproduction of nature and the society. It is thus as representatives of their own kin groups (moieties, sections or sub-sections) that they cooperate in all ritual and insure their own survival and that of all the other members of the tribe through their symbolic labour. Thus in this case the nature of the productive forces and the relations of production explains why social power cannot be separated from religion and kinship and is a masculine privilege.

If we turn our attention to the example of a Greek city like Athens in the fifth century B.C., we find that political power, from the time of Solon's and Kleisthenes' reforms, was largely divorced from the functioning of previously existing kin groups and the religious or priestly privileges that continued to protect the 'well-born' families. Of course we still know little about developments in the forces of production which may have occurred during the seventh and sixth centuries B.C. in Ionia and continental Greece, but we do find that the social relations which functioned as relations of production from that time onward were the political relations between citizens and non-citizens, between free men and slaves. To be a citizen was to own a piece of land in the City and vice versa; only landowners were citizens. Granting the status of landowner to someone from outside the City was always an exception and a privilege. To be a citizen, i.e. a man enjoying *all* the rights associated with freedom meant that one owned land, was eligible for political and judicial offices, took part in the cult of the City's gods and had the honour of taking up arms in her defence. The manner in which the political functioned as relations of production thus determined a specific division of labour. Free men foreign to the community or *politeia* (and slaves *a fortiori*) were simultaneously excluded from agricultural activity, political office, ritual activities and protecting the City gods. Handicrafts, commerce and banking were confined to the metics. Here we find an initial characteristic of the economic, social and intellectual development of a Greek city. However, in addition to this opposition between foreigner and citizen, we encounter another in the fact that all free men, be they citizens or metics, could, depending on their wealth, work their own land or have it worked by slaves, work themselves or make slaves work for them. This is a second characteristics of a Greek city. While indispensable to the functioning and prosperity of Greek society, metics and slaves were excluded to varying degrees from the administration of the community or *politeia*.

Thus, it seems that something along the lines of an economic 'system' of Classical Greek city-states becomes apparent. The original characteristics and specific 'logic' of these city-states derive from the very nature of the two components of their infrastructure. These two components were, on the one hand, the fact that the productive base was a rural economy, but one becoming more and more open to production for the market and a monetary economy, and secondly and above all, the fact that the social relations organising and orienting this material base were from within i.e. the political relations. For this reason, because of the original nature of these relations of production, the Greek economy was neither 'primitive' nor 'modern' and undoubtedly had the capacity to reproduce itself as a 'system' or totality, but only in so far as these political relations were reproduced. Here we find a challenge to modern thinking which can only spontaneously envision the political, the economic, kinship or religion in an anachronistic and ethnocentric fashion as different institutions (such as they 'appear' in our industrial capitalist society) and not as different functions that may be assumed by the same institutions or social relations.

Thus we can see the error in these opposing viewpoints and the futility of the debate which has divided 'primitivists' and 'modernists', Karl Rodbertus' disciples and followers of Edward Meyer and Rostovtseff since the end of the last century. For the former, the Greek economy remained 'primitive' since it was essentially based on agricultural production organised within the framework of the *oikos* i.e. a family group, including slaves of course, but remaining largely self-sufficient. For the latter, on the other hand, this economy was far more 'modern' than primitive since only the commercial aspects of its production, the existence of international trade and the more and more generalised use of money – characteristics later found in modern industrial capitalism – could explain both the prosperity and hegemony of Athens. Although after Hasebroeck's work, which was far more thorough-going than that of Rodbertus or Karl Bucher, E. Meyer's 'modernist' theses have lost much of their impact so that today the 'primitivist' position appears closer to the truth, it would seem that this debate was at the outset a dead end. Marx, the only person of his day not to be led into this vacuous debate, has enabled many other scholars to avoid this trap (e.g. E. Will, Moses Finley, J.P. Vernant, P. Vidal-Naquet and others).

For an economy to be characterised as a 'primitive economic system' it is not enough for it to be organised within a framework of domestic units of production. At least one further condition must be satisfied; that the social relations governing access to resources and allocating social labour power are the kinship relations linking these family units of production. After the reforms of Solon and Kleisthenes, we no longer have such a situation. Nor is it sufficient that an economy be oriented toward a distant international market and employ large amounts of money for it to be 'modern' i.e. similar to the capitalism governing our own societies. To be considered modern, another condition must be met: production in all sectors including agriculture should have an industrial character and the producers should be wage labourers, personally free, but constrained to sell their own 'labour power'. Now even in Athens, production for export never became 'industrialised', but continued to remain in the hands of artisans; wage labour by free men played only a minor role compared with that of slave labour.

Thus, the Greek economy was a 'political economy' in the literal sense. This determined its fundamental character, its unity and the conditions for its reproduction, in other words, its characteristics of a system having a specific 'rationality' of functioning, its own conditions of appearance and disappearance. Therefore we cannot agree with the following statement of Edouard Will over-riding his previous correct and well-supported assertions that the 'principles governing the economy of the Greek cities cannot in any way be reduced to those elaborated by modern economic theorists':

> Thus, the underlying tendency is not toward a rational allocation of the 'productive forces' but toward an *irrational division of social labour* by virtue of *the dignity attributed to man*.[3]

Here Will is making a value judgment, using a norm of what 'should' be a 'rational' allocation of the productive forces, a norm external to Greek society and history, but one which in fact reflects the (actual or illusive) principles of the functioning of contemporary capitalist economy. However, Will himself has shown that given the fact that landownership was the exclusive right of citizens, 'working of the land was the most honourable form of work, that which involved him to the bone',[4] and thus was more than just work, but 'the essential basis of a person who "lived well", of civic virtue and of man's relationship to the gods'.[5] Landownership was reserved exclusively for citizens in order to prevent them from losing their freedom, from having to become subservient to others in order to survive, i.e. by enabling them to exist *socially*. Thus, this intimate connection between political relations, landownership and the dignity attributed to agriculture explains, the forms and conditions of the allocation of social labour power in the case of citizens as well as that of metics and slaves. It also explains the conditions and forms of the employment of productive forces in the various 'sectors' (agriculture for export, handicrafts, mining, commerce and banking) which must have expanded with the development of the city. And it was due to the fact that such activities like commerce, handicrafts and mining rendered the free individual engaging in them dependent on others that these activities were considered beneath the dignity of a citizen and were quite willingly left to slaves and foreigners. This situation was not in the least 'irrational'.

However, Will's remark has the merit of drawing our attention to the problems and contradictions encountered and developed by such a system and which lead to its eventual disappearance. We can understand why the struggle for *land* and the stuggle for *political equality* were only two sides of the *same struggle* by the very nature of the relations of production. Thus, we can also understand why the political struggles amongst citizens for the maintenance and expansion of 'democracy' were a strategic element in the reproduction of the material basis of their social existence, of their society and played such a decisive role not only in Greek ideology but also in the actions of the Greeks. We can understand why the concentration of landed property, or the accumulation of transferable wealth, in short, any form of development toward differences in wealth between free men, threatened the empoverished and often landless citizens with becoming dependent upon the wealthy or the State and thus losing the very basis of their existence as citizens. 'The condition for a man to be free' said Aristotle, 'is that he is not dependent on another' (Rhetoric 1367:32). Now what was true of the individual was true of the whole city. The individual's desire to continue to exist in *autarkeia* parallels the city's desire and need to intervene in international trade and in the freely practised commerce of citizens and metics of other cities. But this intervention was only at the level of the importation of staple goods which contributed to the poor citizens' subsistence and strategic goods necessary to the city's military power.

Of course in a society largely governed by private property (even if it remains family land as in the case of the *kleros* which was inalienable for a long period), the State can only intervene within certain limits. But the Greek state possessed perhaps more extensive means of intervention than did the State in the most advanced industrial capitalist nations of the nineteenth century. The leasing of its *ager publicus* brought in revenues and heavily taxed the wealthy metics and slaves. Even the wealthy citizens could hardly refuse the State when it asked them to subsidise liturgies and other ceremonial or military expenses of the city. Furthermore, they had an interest in making such contributions since they brought political honour and prestige. In this way, the poor could live thanks in part to the State subsidies that enabled them to retain their status and take public office. For a long time, they could also expatriate themselves and establish colonies in distant, but fertile barbarian lands or along strategic trade routes. But despite all these possible outlets, the very expansion of the system made continued equality between citizens, and even more so equality between cities, increasingly difficult and threatened the very foundations of the economy and society.

Thus, we come to see the structural reasons – those having their basis in the properties of social relations rather than in the will and intentions of individuals – why the conflict between rich and poor citizens would almost entirely prevail over that between free men and slaves in the history and minds of the Classical Greeks. For the same reasons, the second and perhaps the more decisive conflict (free men/slaves) for the society's eventual fate and for the long term reproduction of this economy and way of life did not have the same possibility of becoming politically evident, and thereby assuming equal importance in the social consciousness of the time, or reaching the same level of development in political practice. However, the development of the Greek cities, occasionally a very rapid and profound development as in Athens during the sixth century, resulted in the increasingly extensive use of slave labour in agriculture as well as in all other sectors including finance. In the fifth and sixth centuries B.C., given the nature of productive technology, slave manpower was necessarily the main productive force.

Why, except on very rare occasions, did this fundamental conflict never occupy the centre stage in the political life, consciousness and social struggles of the Greek cities? First of all, we should begin by remembering that for the Greeks (as well as the Romans) slavery was taken for granted as part of the 'natural basis' of society and that the institution as such was never seriously challenged by either free men or by slaves. In fact, among the essential elements of a free man's 'liberty' was the freedom to enslave other men.[6] But the possession of slaves was not merely an abstract quality of the status of free man because the slave was an integral and essential part of every free man's *oikos*, his family and his home, and was explicitly acknowledged as such.

> Now the Household, when complete, consists of slaves and free persons . . . the first and smallest elements of the household are master and slave, husband and wife, father and children.[7]

Moreover, according to Aristotle's vivid expression, 'the slave is really a part of the master, being a sort of animate but unattached part of his body'.[8] Separate like the oxen, also part of the family, but different in that while the slave, like the oxen, is an 'animate tool', he is 'endowed with speech'. Above all, he is a living body, a 'corporal force' at his master's service, subject to his command or to that of an overseer taking his place. This living body 'only reasons in order to fulfil some vague emotion'. It is the body of a human being deprived of any of the qualities of the human personality. The slave is a nobody. He 'belongs' to his masters as part of the latter's 'possessions'.

> But of property, the first and most necessary part is that which is best and chiefest; and this is man. Hence it is necessary to obtain worthy slaves. But there are two kinds of slaves, a steward and a drudge.[9]

This piece of advice was expressed by the author of *Economics*, a work so lacking in originality that some scholars have attributed it to Aristotle. These slaves were so indispensable to the lives of every individual and city that a poor, sick Athenian around 400 B.C., seeing himself deprived of any form of State aid on the pretext that he was too poor to be eligible for any office, 'appealed formally to the Council for reconsideration of his case. One of his arguments was that he could not yet afford to buy a slave who would support him, though he hoped eventually to do so'.[10] This anecdote shows once more that only the existence of slavery made the maintenance of an extremely relative equality between citizens possible. Thus the two conflicts, between rich and poor and between free men and slaves, tightly enmeshed with each other in a complex and original way, combining the effects of inequality of wealth with those of inequality in status. To be a wealthy citizen meant that one possessed large quantities of the two 'true' forms of wealth, land and slaves.

In Athens after Solon's reforms a citizen could no longer be reduced to slavery except for a serious crime. From that time on debt bondage was ablished and the poor were protected by the law. Slaves could only be imported. They could only be foreigners, preferably Barbarians bought on the market or whose capture was left to other Barbarians, Scythian, Phrygians or other 'native' tribes specialising in and profiting from this activity. Without pressing the point further, we simply note that war was a necessary element in the reproduction of these relations of production and to some extent determined the relations between the Greeks and Barbarians and amongst the Barbarians themselves.

But to be a slave is not simply to be a man living in a foreign city working in a disabled profession willingly relegated to him. Reduced to the state of an animate tool, but one that speaks, the slave is completely eliminated from the human order and is no longer a part of culture but is a part of nature. The slave is emprisoned within society and the community of free men since he lives in the intimacy of his master's family. He is simultaneously an integral and indispensable part of the latter's *oikos* and its social and material substance. He is completely devoid of any human quality. Only the free man living in *his* city, owning and working his own land or having it worked by his slaves is fully a man. As a landowner and a slaveowner, the citizen 'represents' the society, the existing human order. Political relations function as relations of production because they give access to the two essential means of production: land and labour.

The specific nature of these relations of production or their political essence placed the slave, in contrast to the free foreigner, the metic, beyond *any* polity, and prevented him from becoming politically conscious of his lot, and from uniting with other slaves in order to take their place in history, and collectively leading the political struggles which could have one day put an end to their common exploitation. To have organised such struggles and to have had the possibility of imposing a solution ending their oppression, two conditions, excluded by the very nature of the relations of production, would have had to be met: the slaves would have had, first, to become conscious of themselves as an exploited class and, secondly, to extend their consciousness through various forms of struggle and elaborate a viable, all-embracing long term solution – i.e. one that not only seemed to satisfy their own interests but satisfied those of the whole society. Such a situation would have presupposed a much stronger consciousness and struggle than that which enabled the poor citizens to obtain the final abolition of debt bondage in the face of resistence from the wealthy. However, even in the latter case the possibility of redress pre-existed in the society. This possibility was provided by slavery, slavery which from then on would be confined to foreigners and Barbarians whose enslavement could only take on greater proportions.

Let us elaborate on these two points, i.e. the impossibility of imagining a way of ending their oppression, and the impossibility of becoming conscious of themselves as a 'class'. As far as the first is concerned, some criticism of slavery did occur amongst *free* men in Greece. The sophist, Antiphon, proclaimed that all men are naturally identical and, that all things considered, one was not 'genetically' determined to be free or enslaved. We can understand Aristotle's determination to refute such theses which were so contrary to his own. Xenophon tells us that even before the rule of the 'thirty', some citizens went as far as maintaining that there would be no 'true' democracy before the slaves took part in the governing of the city. And we witnessed how Agathocles in Sicily at the end of the fourth century emancipated all his armed slaves in order to create a better *esprit de corps* between slaves and citizens and thus strengthen his city's military potential. However, we know little of the opinions of the slaves themselves. In any case as Moses Finley has reminded us, proposing the slaves' participation in a city's government and proposing the abolition of slavery itself, an institution acknowledged to be necessary to material and intellectual life, are not at all the same thing.

Therefore the second point, the impossibility of slaves becoming conscious of themselves as an exploited class, was more decisive and can be explained by the same structural reasons. First of all, the fact that their masters allowed them to hope for their eventual emancipation was sufficient for many to accept their lot. Resistance by others was principally in a passive or semi-active form, when it was accompanied by acts of sabotage. But above all, most slaves chose to escape either individually or collectively when the external situation permitted. Some slaves even dared to go as far as an armed uprising but were always mercilessly suppressed. Thus, as J.P. Vernant has pointed out, the opposition between the slaves and their owners, which was unable to assume the form of a concerted struggle at the level of social and political structures, at another level played a decisive role in the evolution of ancient Greek society:

> The resistance of slaves – as an entire social group – to their masters was manifested at the level of the productive forces, for given the techno-economic context of ancient Greece, slaves in fact were the essential part of these productive forces. At this level of the productive forces, as the employment of slave labour became generalised, the opposition between slaves and their owners would take the nature of the fundamental contradiction of the slave system of production. Effectively, in this system where technical progress as a whole was obstructed or at least extremely slow, the extension of slavery appeared to be the only means of developing the productive forces. Simultaneously, the slaves' opposition and resistance to their masters, their inevitable lack of enthusiasm in carrying out their appointed tasks, was directly opposed to such progress and increasingly limited yields.
>
> Thus, in terms of the intensification of productive forces, the number of slaves could not go on increasing indefinitely without threatening the equilibrium of the social system. Therefore, we can see that at a certain stage, the opposition between slaves and those employing them becomes the fundamental contradiction of the system, even if, as has been stated,[11] it does not appear as the principal contradiction.[12]

Here again we find the same structural reason, i.e. the fact that the relations of production are internal to the political relations. This fact had two distinct effects and determined two complementary but opposing modes of development in the contradictions of the system: on the one hand, the contradictions between free men were directly visible at the political level and could be the object of explicit political action and change; on the other hand, the contradictions between slaves and free men could only appear on the political level indirectly and could not become the object of political action and change for the slaves. However, J.P. Vernant's analysis enables us to point out the existence of another fundamental structural relation, a special relationship between the 'mode' of development of the productive forces, both material and intellectual, and the nature of the social relations which function as relations of production. We find that in the case of Greece, the development of the productive forces took a specific form and occurred within certain limits set by the position, content and form of the social relations that functioned as relations of production within the cities. Recognised by many historians of ancient times, this special relationship has been clearly outlined by Will when he states that in Greece 'production was never governed by worries about productivity in any branch of activity since it was paralysed by archaic conceptions of a religious and moral nature . . . The non-productive spirit of the individual worker found its corollary in the cities' policy of handling, often indirectly, economic matters.'[13]

In Greece, the thought of free men, men having the means and time to cultivate themselves, was drawn more to 'pure' knowledge, the theoretical and speculative sciences, rather than to applied science and technical innovation which could have enabled 'the production of more by producing differently', and could in the long run have changed the material and intellectual relationship with nature, the relationship which Marx spoke of as a 'generator of myth'. It is perhaps too much to speak of a 'technological stagnation' of Greek society in the fourth century, but the expression draws our attention to the general fact that in the long run it is the development of the productive forces which is the condition for the reproduction of the society's material base, given population growth, etc. Without such development, a society risks becoming gradually and unwittingly stagnant and turning in on itself, becoming less able to cope with the effects of internal conflicts or the attacks of neighbouring and more dynamic societies. Thus we come to the basic idea of the existence of an internal relationship of structural order between the nature of the social relations functioning as relations of production, and the content, form and intensity of the development of the productive forces elicited by these social relations. This gives rise to a relationship of 'reciprocal dependence' which is complex and cannot be analysed in an exhaustive fashion by proceeding in a single direction. Through this analysis of a specific case, it has already become possible to suggest that, within the infrastructure of any society, there exists a network of unintentional causalities between the productive forces and the social relations of production constituting the infrastructure, which acts upon all the other levels and aspects of social reality.

To be more exact about what we mean by 'unintentional causality', we should recall that these relations of order are based on the inherent properties of the relations of production and productive forces. These properties, being properties of 'relations', exist whether or not the individuals living within them are conscious of them. Such objective properties of social relations constitute the 'unintentional' content of social reality, but this unintentional content is not socially inactive or passive. It 'acts'. It determines a range of causes and effects which neither originate from nor are based on the consciousness or will of social actors, be they individuals or collectivities. These unintentional properties, depending on neither consciousness nor will for their existence, can never cease existing and acting as long as the social relations which they express continue to exist. In no way does this mean that these relations do not evolve under the influence of men's conscious actions or that the understanding of these relations has no bearing on the process of evolution. It only means that when these modes of consciousness and action produce changes in the social relations, they do so by transforming their properties, not by 'creating' them.

A society is not a subject, and social actors are always in determined relations. If some actors within a society are in some way or to some extent aware of the existence and nature of the inherent properties of their social relations, they can confront at least certain of the effects more or less successfully, but they can only abolish these effects by abolishing the social relations which cause them, i.e. only by transforming their society. The analysis of these networks of unintentional causalities has sometimes been called the 'analysis of structural causality'. However, these concepts are often enveloped in an air of mystery by creating the impression that social structures have the capabilities or power to act without any form of human action. Social structures only act by virtue of and through the individual and collective actions daily carried out by men to reproduce or change their material and social conditions of existence. The properties of these structures are the invisible and unintentional foundation of social reality, the basis of necessity in which the actions of men acquire their ultimate meaning, find the objective measure of their efficacy and encounter the multitude of their social effects.

These general theoretical remarks inspired by our analysis of classical Greek economy and society have provided a useful detour. In the case of Greek society we are confronted with a veritable network of the distinct effects of the productive forces and the relations of production which cross-cut, converge and mutually reinforce one another. We have already seen that the very nature of the relations of production makes it impossible for the slaves to become conscious of themselves as a class and to organise an all-out political and economic struggle for the abolition of slavery. But if we follow another causal chain within the infrastructure of this society, we find another supplementary reason why the slaves (as well as the free men) could not work out a basic, all-embracing solution to the problem of slavery, i.e. a solution permitting a conscious and actual elimination of this social institution without bringing about a general stagnation of society. The effect of the same relations of production on the development of the forces of production can be found in the lack of real interest by the dominant classes, and trained minds amongst them, in the search for technological innovations which could have increased the productivity of labour and offered a real possibility of employing fewer slaves for an identical amount of work.

Had the Greek slaves wanted and attempted[14] to free themselves through revolt, the only objective conditions for the abolition of slavery they would have found in their society at that time would have been ephemeral and glorious dreams, ideas without the means of becoming reality, a utopian vision. Marc Bloch, Verlinden, and George Duby have shown that there were still many slaves throughout the European countryside during the seventh and eighth centuries A.D. and that they played an important role in the domestic economy and in agricultural production. Incapable of being imposed through the struggles of a revolutionary class conscious of itself, the disappearance of slavery within western society could only be an extremely slow, 'unending' process. And it is not in the least surprising to find that its disappearance often stemmed from initiatives on the part of the masters themselves who suppressed slavery in their own interest, in order to substitute more profitable and less brutal forms of personal dependance, since the latter required less effort to control individuals and organise their labour, even though it induced them to work and cooperate to a greater degree. This only appears paradoxical to those who project anachronistic and ethnocentric images of the bourgeois revolution of 1789 or of the Bolshevik revolution on to the resistance against their masters by the slaves of antiquity. Such projections have no bearing on an understanding of the logic of the 'political economy of slavery'.

In conclusion, the economy of a Greek city during the Classical period was a coherent whole, even in its contradictions. For us the source both of this coherence and these contradictions was the same and was to be found in the fact that political relations functioned as relations of production giving this system its original form and structure as a totality capable of reproduction within only certain limits. The ambiguity of Will's proposition which confuses the level of consciousness and intention with that of objective, unintentional realities can be appreciated when he writes:

> When the modern historian tries to reconstruct 'the Greek economy' or less ambitiously that of a *polis*, he has set himself an arbitrary task, since this economy, if conceived of as a totality, was non-existent, as it was but a sum of the activities performed in the various sectors and not a coherent organism conceived of as such.[15]

(*Translated by Anne Bailey*)

NOTES

1 See this volume, p. 3.

2 See Godelier, M. (1975), 'Modes of production, kinship and demographic structures', *in* Bloch, M. (ed.), *Marxist Analyses and Social Anthropology*, London.

3 Will, E. (1972), *Le monde grec et l'orient*, Paris. Chapter 'Le Ve Siècle, 510-403', p. 633, Will's italics.

4 Will (1972), p. 632.

5 Will (1972), p. 671.

6 Finley, M.I. (1964), 'Between slavery and freedom', *Comparative Studies in Society and History*, VI, 3.

7 Aristotle (1877), *Politics*, London (trans. Bolland), p. 115.

8 Aristotle, *Politics*, p. 126.

9 Aristotle (1871), *The Politics and Economics*, London, p. 293.

10 Lysias, cf. Finley (1964), p. 245.

11 See Charles Parain's remarkable article, to which we are greatly endebted: Parain, C. (1963), 'Les caractères spécifiques de la lutte des classes dans l'antiquité classique', *La Pensée*, 108, pp. 3-25.

12 Vernant, J. (1965), 'La lutte des classes', *EIRENE, Studia Graeca et Latina*, IV, pp. 5-19. (Republished in Vernant, J. (1974), *Mythe et société en Grèce ancienne*, Paris, pp. 28-9.)

13 Will (1972), p. 672.

14 As the Roman slaves did several times in 217, 199, 196, 185, 139, 104, until Spartacus' famous revolt of 73-71 B.C. These revolts ceased during the period of the Empire.

15 Will (1972), p. 631.

M.G. SMITH

Conditions of change in social stratification

Social stratification is present wherever an objectively differential distribution of life chances and situations obtains among categories or groups of persons ranked as superior and inferior within the social aggregate. Where present, such stratification normally encompasses the total society, and accordingly subsumes a multitude of diverse features, conditions and processes of social organisation in some more or less integrated and inclusive structure or structures which observers and actors alike regard as 'real' and for which they devise models to apprehend and interpret the facts. In the nature of the case, such models can rarely represent exactly the facts with which they deal, since these are multi-dimensional and situational, and obscurely related. Moreover, social stratification is both a state of affairs, a process of ordering relations, a condition of that and other social processes, and the product of many social processes, factors and relations which differ greatly in their particulars and significance for the stratification as a whole. For these reasons I cannot follow those scholars who conceptualise stratification as a system, since these conceptions imply a precise knowledge of the components and relations within the system. Moreover, no single system model, however generalised, can be equally valid for all differing forms of stratification; nor is it likely that a given model will be equally appropriate for a particular stratification at different moments in time. With these reservations, I shall treat stratifications as structures or orders whose conditions and properties are imperfectly known, especially as regards their dynamics and foundations. Accordingly, to grasp the conditions of change in social stratification we need first to understand their nature and foundations.

Stratified distributions of differential life chances entail corresponding differences in the life situations and life cycles typical of the ranked strata, and commonly in their modal life spans as well. Such stratified differences of life chances indicate the differential distributions of opportunities, advantages, sanctions and resources of all kinds, material, cultural, social and other, relevant to the stratification. In stratified societies these relevant variables commonly include location, sex, age, occupation and income, education, political and legal status, wealth and descent. In societies that are ethnically or radically heterogeneous, ethnicity and race are normally relevant and frequently critical for the stratification. Nonetheless, though many scholars study ethnic stratification, race relations, occupational and economic stratification, and although much has been written about ruling classes and elites, we have relatively few studies of social stratification as politically ordered structure, and fewer that examine the place of location, age and sex in empirical stratifications. While each of these deficiencies may have a different base, they both reflect the 'Westocentric' biases of stratification studies.

Like sociology and much else, the study of social stratification is a product of modern western societies, the fruit of a specific period in which the rigid, politically regulated strata of these societies eroded rapidly as the rate and scale of social (vertical) and geographical mobility increased, within as well as between generations. Partly for these reasons, Marx, who though by no means the first was by far the most influential early student of social stratification, oriented his studies towards their economic aspect and defined classes as strata in terms of their relations with the mode of production. Marx also argued in various places that these economic relations were the foci and motive forces of the social and political order. He thus directed those who shared or opposed his views to consider social stratification in its relation to the economic order of society; and following Marx, many sociologists have regarded the economic order as the primary condition of social stratification.

I believe that this is a serious error for which Marx is responsible. On leaving Germany for Paris and finally London, Marx also broke with his early philosophical self and determined to master and relativise the theory of classical economics. He thus unwittingly dedicated himself to an economistic view of society, albeit one which corrected the 'errors' of classical economics by situating economies fully and firmly in their social matrices.[1] Yet even to pursue these aims, Marx had first to view the world of societies in terms of economic relations and categories. He was thus predisposed to recognise and delineate social categories as classes by reference to their economic roles, and never fully escaped from this perspective. However, those differing relations to the mode of production by which Marx distinguished classes had already been determined and institutionalised for these strata by their differing relations to the political order; while some strata ruled, others were ruled; and of the rulers, some where dominant by virtue of various conditions, including descent, while others, including most of the enfranchised bourgeoisie of Marx's day, had at best secondary or tertiary roles in selecting or electing, with restricted choices, some of those who were already eligible to compete for the power to rule. Of the ruled, among whom the rulers promoted useful distinctions, some had various means and degrees of influence over others in various contexts, while most probably had little or none. The latter were thus fully disenfranchised, formally and substantively, while the former, even though formally disenfranchised, had some substantive power. Marx, given his economistic predilections, distinguished and identified these politically differentiated strata solely in economic terms as categories distinguished by their relations with the prevailing mode of production. The ruling strata, that is the rulers and their auxiliaries, he curiously labelled the 'bourgeoisie', although these rulers throughout the nineteenth century were mainly nobles and landed gentry.[2] Bourgeois who, although enfranchised, were ineligible to compete for high office, were treated as 'intermediate strata' and sometimes referred to as professionals and 'petit bourgeois'. Politically disenfranchised strata were likewise classified by him as petit bourgeois, proletarians and peasants. It appears then that Marx employed two significantly different conceptions of classes, one which distinguished 'wage labourers, capitalists and land owners' as 'three big classes of modern society based upon the capitalist mode of production'[3] while the second discriminated various intermediate strata relevant for the discussion of concrete historical situations such as Louis Napoleon's seizure of power in 1848.[4] While Marxists would disagree, the unresolved differences of these conceptual schemes suggest that Marx, despite his economistic bias, hovered between an economic and a political definition of classes and other ranked categories of social stratification; and it is clear that the economic strata identified by Marx were politically instituted, distinguished and ordered by explicitly political means for political ends and in political terms, for example by reference to the franchise. Nonetheless, in supporting, applying, amending or rebutting Marx's hypotheses, subsequent writers on social stratification have perhaps inevitably and unwittingly treated the subject in explicitly economic terms, despite the influential work of Max Weber.

To refine and supplement Marx's monofactorial classification, Weber distinguished classes, status groups and parties as strata based respectively on objective criteria of market position, association, prestige and style of life, and on relative power.[5] He stressed that the nature and concordance of these scales were problems for empirical investigation in any society. Nonetheless, conservative sociologists who adopted Weber's ideas obscured the nature of social stratification for several years by defining this solely in terms of prestige, as relative evaluation of social roles or units on some collective scale of worth. Talcott Parsons, Kingsley Davis, Wilbert Moore and other 'structural-functionalists' or 'action-theorists' were especially prominent in promoting and expounding this diversion of interest from objective distributions of differential life changes to subjective distributions of differential prestige, and described such disembodied abstractions as occupational roles.[6] Meanwhile other students who followed Weber and Marx distinguished caste, slavery, estates and 'classes' as significantly different units and structures of stratification. Some, especially the structural-functionalists, proclaimed on implausible theoretical grounds that stratification was a necessary and universal feature of human societies, even in the absence of ranked social strata.[7] Gradually, however, it has been accepted that stratification, however important and prevalent, is neither necessary nor universal in human societies, and that many societies in which ranking obtains lack social strata, while others with varied types of social differentiation may lack ranking and stratificational together. Normally societies of the latter type are acephalous, weakly differentiated in their economies and technologically poor, while those that institutionalise rank without stratification have better developed technologies and diversified economic and social organisations.[8]

It is not within the scope of this paper to discuss unstratified societies, nor even those that emphasise rank but lack social strata. Instead we are here concerned only with the dynamics of evident stratifications, that is with changes in the stratification of those societies already divided in ranked strata which are characterised by differential life situations and chances of their members. By dynamics here I understand three distinct but closely related processes: (i) Processes of development and institutionalisation of distinct positions, roles and relations within a social order; (ii) Processes of differential allocation of these positions and roles within the stratified population; and (iii) Processes by which a given stratified distribution of positions and roles are maintained or modified. It is convenient to review briefly some of these processes in order to identify their necessary and sufficient conditions, and thereby hopefully to isolate the foundations of social stratification.

Over the past two centuries social scientists have increasingly identified the differentiated role structures of modern societies with their divisions of labour and, despite the work of Millar, Ferguson, Spencer and Durkheim among others,[9] these divisions of labour have been increasingly treated as social structures generated and patterned by techno-economic and demographic forces. For many writers the division of labour is indeed the primary and formative structure of social stratification, to which all others, such as kinship or law, are secondary.[10] In consequence, many sociologists virtually identify stratification with the prevailing prestige scale of occupations and equate social with occupational mobility.[11] However, such conceptions are tenable only if it can be shown that occupational hierarchies always emerge, crystallise, develop and modify or transform themselves autonomously, or in direct response to 'demo-techno-economic' pressures,[12] of their own gestation. Should these occupational structures be thus auto-productive and self-determining, such stratifications as they entail or illustrate would indeed correspond closely with that of the society as a whole and so demonstrate the primacy of the occupational order. However, this is clearly not the case. As Ferguson and Millar both stressed, the antecedent 'differentiation of ranks' conditions the development of differentiated occupational roles and their allocations within societies. Slaves recruited by purchase, capture, birth or by other means are commonly employed in servile work and heavy labour or in roles requiring special qualities of confidentiality and skill for which eunuchs are often preferred. Serfs, likewise, held their typical occupations by virtue of their political and legal status. Even in India, although Hinduism defines its caste components occupationally and otherwise, as the number of these castes greatly exceeded the number of distinctive occupations in Indian society, while members of the same caste often practised different occupations, members of many different castes sometimes practised the same occupation without undergoing any changes in social status. In practise the apparent autonomy of techno-economic conditions to proliferate new occupations and to modify the occupational structure is a relatively recent phenomenon which correlates with the development of industrial societies in the West; but western sociologists, having chosen to ignore the specificity of these industrial developments and structures on the one hand, and their political and legal preconditions and correlates on the other, have abstracted some of their features for extrapolation as a general theory and evolutionary model of the forms and processes of stratification valid for all societies. Yet even Durkheim was obliged to admit the decisive influence of political factors in directing the development of functional specialisation from its earliest stage up to the anomic phase of late Victorian Europe.[13] Certainly for pre-industrial societies at all developmental levels, as reflected in the differentiation of their occupational role systems, we have abundant evidence that such occupational differentiations were guided, promoted, repressed or otherwise regulated by political means, that is by exercises of juridical authority and power, as illustrated, for example, by the prohibitions on interest in medieval Catholicism and Islam, the occupational specialisations of medieval Jewry, of merchants and craftsmen, by the restrictions on production, commerce and banking that distinguished Mercantilism, the divisions of labour in imperial China, ancient Athens and Rome, and other instances too numerous to list.

The reduction of such political repression and direction of the occupation order which proceeded in western Europe from the fourteenth century at accelerating pace, and thus permitted progressively autonomous growth of the division of labour, was equally political in its source and character and decisive for the radical development of European science, technology and economy on which elaboration of the occupational structures rested. Unfortunately these political developments have been so much taken for granted by social scientists that their significance is overlooked, perhaps because scholars have been preoccupied rather with the validity of Marxist theses and Weber's alternatives in tracing the genesis of modern capitalism. However no one disputes the centrality of the three successive political revolutions, that of the Puritans in seventeenth-century Britain, of the American colonists in 1776 and of the French in 1789, in destroying the political-juridical structures that had hitherto enchained and subordinated to a stratification essentially anchored in estate feudalism, those burgeoning techno-economic forces and interests that have since precipitated the modern occupational order of industrial societies. To detail the principal political and legal developments which made possible this great transformation is patently inappropriate here, nor is that necessary, since we can demonstrate elliptically the decisive role of these political conditions in establishing the central pre-requisites for modern industrial capitalism simply by scrutinising Max Weber's list of eight features or conditions necessary to constitute modern industrial capitalism as a pure type.

These are, respectively:

1. 'The complete appropriation of all the non-human means of production by owners, and the complete absence of all formal appropriation of opportunities of profit in the market; that is, market freedom' – a juridical condition which obviously requires political action and which inspired all three revolutions mentioned above.
2. 'Complete autonomy in the selection of management by the owners, thus absence of formal appropriation of rights to managerial functions', another condition that presupposes political dissolution and abolition of those managerial arrangements and models typical of feudalism in the manor and the towns, and of the colonial regime in the American states.
3. 'The complete absence of the appropriation of jobs and of opportunities for earning by workers, and, conversely, absence of appropriation of workers by owners. This involves free labour, freedom of the labour market, and freedom in the selection of workers;' – the political preconditions and processes of such liberalisation from feudal forms of labour control are too obvious and familiar to need attention.
4. 'Complete absence of substantive regulation of consumption, production and prices, or of other forms of regulation which limit freedom of contract or specify conditions of exchange. This may be called substantive freedom of contract.' This is also clearly a juridical condition that assumes the establishment and continued efficacy of requisite political and legal arrangements. To establish such freedom of contract, political action to destroy the feudal restrictions was obviously necessary.

5. 'Maximum of calculability of the technical conditions of the productive process; that is, a mechanically rational technology' – the development of which likewise presupposed and proceeded with the establishment of appropriate political conditions in Protestant countries to free science and technology from ecclesiastical and monarchic controls.
6. 'Complete calculability of the functioning of public administration and the legal order, and the reliable formal guarantee of all contracts by the political authority. This is formally rational administration and law.' This condition assumes the efficient implementation of the doctrines of separation of powers as propounded notably by Locke and by Montesquieu before the British revolution of 1688 and the American revolution of 1776 respectively.
7. 'The most complete possible separation of the enterprise and its conditions of success and failure from the household or private budgetary unit and its property interests.' Though superficially indifferent to juridical facts, as expressed in joint stock limited liability companies or in modern multi-national corporations having similar bases, this condition likewise assumes specific political and juridical arrangements.
8. 'A monetary system with the highest possible degree of formal rationality' – which obviously presupposes a formally rational political administration that regulates currency as one of the routine affairs of a centralised state.[14]

Of course, with these eight conditions Weber merely intended to specify the minimal prerequisites of an industrial capitalism characterised by perfect competition and maximum formal rationality in its operations. Such an economy has perhaps rarely if ever existed in any period and place. Yet insofar as various empirical economies depart from this model, they can only be made to approximate it more closely through specific measures of explicitly political and juridical kind. Contemporary South Africa is only the most familiar and striking demonstration in the western world of the combination of regulated labour with an expanding industrial economy; and clearly the restrictions and disabilities of coloured labour in South Africa are politically determined and enforced, even against the rational economic interests of those who dominate the regime.[15] In like fashion, West Indian planters opposed the abolition of slavery by Britain in 1834 although the institution had become increasingly uneconomic since the abolition of the slave trade in 1808.[16] There are, of course, numberless cases in which specifically economic interests have been set aside or overruled by other considerations, normally of a political and social kind, always by explicitly political or juridical means. Clearly also, as history affirms, the institution, maintenance, modification or dissolution of servile stratifications such as slavery, serfdom, peonage, helotage and characteristically colonial structures, all assume, reflect and proceed by specific applications of political power. Caste in India is singular only in so far as the ritual ranking of categories on the scale of purity and pollution which correlates broadly with the distribution of political power in many areas, provides the medium or object of this distribution, though never its decisive means or base. Accordingly in all major varieties of social stratification, we find that the distribution of power is decisive and central to their form, range and scope. It is thus not surprising that the differential allocations of positions, prestige and roles within a given division of labour should be governed by principles and factors, the validity of which directly or indirectly illustrates political bases and conditions. Neither can a political order persist or develop in flagrant contradiction to the order of social stratification; nor is the reverse conceivable. Accordingly in those regions of India dominated by low-ranking castes, the latter rapidly acquire higher ritual status appropriate to their secular roles. In less elaborately ritualised societies, if the traditional stratification loses its former validity, dynamic strata assert their predominance by political means, and on occasion by violent action. We may therefore ask whether, in any single instance a stable or persisting order of stratification inverts or controverts the distribution of power among the social strata; and I believe that even in India we shall find no exception.

This conclusion may be tested further by detailed study of the processes by which empirical orders of stratification have historically been maintained or modified; but no such examination will be attempted here. The preceding discussion of the three sets of processes that together provide the dynamics of stratification illustrates their necessarily close and constant association with the distribution of power, of which they are simultaneously the product, the object and an important condition. Accordingly, to investigate further the dynamics of stratification, we should examine the relations between different kinds of stratification and distributions of political power.

For clarity, specifically political power is manifested in the regulation of public affairs, that is, the collective affairs, however defined, of a continuing social aggregate organised as a public or corporate group. There are of course many modalities of power and influence besides the explicitly political, for example religious, economic, military, social and industrial power; these and other categories alike refer to activities and relations which are specific to some distinct segment of the collectivity rather than to the inclusive aggregate that forms the public as a unit. Moreover, in so far as such segmentally based power is employed to regulate the public and its affairs, it acquires by this fact an explicitly political character and relevance. However, political power has diverse bases and components, which include individual and collective prestige, ritual, military, economic, technical, intellectual, administrative, demographic and other resources, and a variety of situationally relevant social capacities and cultural skills including control of communication channels, of relevant organisations, symbolic and ideological structures, capacities for self-discipline, solidarity and much else. The distribution of power that decides which side prevails in any confrontation is thus a situationally specific combination of many variable components. Thus as power is the ability to secure compliance to one's will, and as the situations, subjects and objects of such compliance vary widely in time and place, any individual or group that seeks to regulate a public's affairs has first to mobilise sufficient resources and support to secure its preponderance, and then to establish an effective organisation of these resources to stabilise its rule by controlling most or all of the requisites just listed. Inevitably such efforts to stabilise a favourable distribution of power rarely succeed in full for, as indicated above, power as a product of many labile factors is highly conditional, contingent, and for its stabilisation it therefore requires an appropriate regulation of all relevant conditions which can rarely be achieved as an integrated structure. Such stability also presupposes that the predominant power in question should be accepted as legitimate and authoritative by the public it regulates and by other bodies with whom it deals externally. This assumption of authority is not equally feasible for all politically oriented or dominant groups, as the constitutional norms of public organisation, which themselves enshrine the outcomes of earlier political action, often restrict acceptable solutions. For example, in African chiefdoms, only princes of the ruling house are eligible to succeed; in Melanesia only those who have demonstrated their charisma could become 'big men'. In America the presidency must be won by a direct national election; but in Britain the Prime Ministership reflects electoral results less directly and may pass by other means. Such variable constitutional norms define conditions of eligibility for authoritative positions and establish frameworks within which mobilisations and deployments of power to regulate public affairs normally proceed. Naturally, despite the sanctity that often clothes them, constitutions are frequently the instruments and targets of political action.

While authority is the appropriate mode in which power to regulate a public's affairs is institutionalised as legitimate, without the power necessary to enforce its procedures and rules, authority is ineffective, and those who hold power will regulate the public affairs proportionately in their own interests, as in the various Japanese shogunates. Conversely in certain situations, although the rulers may be able to enforce their orders, and may thus claim to exercise authority, their rule may be regarded as illegitimate or even illegal by the majority they govern, so that empirically their regulation exhibits power without legitimacy. Both alternatives indicate that while authority is the normal and most appropriate medium of public regulation, and while its forms, organisation and ideology clearly influence the distribution and exercise of power within collectivities, the efficacy and forms of authoritative regulation ultimately depend on the balance of power among the structures that support and oppose it.

In unstratified acephalous societies, authority and power are either diffuse and labile, or are frequently combined as coincident ritual and secular capacities. In some societies lineage heads and patriarchs symbolise and exercise both; in others, while shamans and priests exercise ritual authority, warriors, leaders in men's associations, and other secular figures wield personal power. In many weakly differentiated societies priests or priest-chiefs who uphold and symbolise the authority of collective norms take precedence over war leaders and secular chiefs concerned with mundane administration. Normally these contrasting types of leadership are recruited and exercised by differing means.

Despite its greater scale, complexity and elaborate stratification, Hindu society, which is modally polycephalous, illustrates this pattern in the ritual superiority it accords Brahmans over Kshatriya and other Varna or castes. The resulting social structure is highly flexible, adaptive and resilient; it offers insecure and shifting bases for any extensive indigenous centralised state. By virtue of their ritual pre-eminence and collective immunities, Brahmans personify and hold the ultimate keys of authority, even where Kshatriyas or others dominate; and in those regions governed by Brahmans, their secular dominance is reinforced and overlaid by their ritual status. In consequence at different times and places, India illustrates a variety of unstable political alignments among high-ranking castes whose ritual stratification corresponds variably with the secular order based on prevailing distributions of power and wealth.

The feudal society of western Christendom in medieval Europe offers intriguing parallels and contrasts with this Hindu order. As with Hindu caste rankings of Brahman, Kshatriya, Vaisya, Sudra, so in the European estate system, clergy claimed precedence over secular nobles, who ranked above the merchants, the freemen and serfs. However, unlike the Brahmans, European clergy were forbidden to marry, and they were also organised and controlled by a powerful central head. Thus, unlike the Brahman caste, the clerical estate in Europe was not self-reproducing and recruited its members from other strata. The centralised monarchic organisation also brought this order into prolonged and direct conflict for supremacy and dominance with secular states; and when the clergy finally lost the struggle in the fourteenth and fifteenth centuries, the road to the Reformation was open, and thereafter, by religious wars and other processes, secularisation and the development of modern society advanced together.

Islamic societies, founded originally by the Prophet as an

indissoluble integration of ritual authority and secular power, illustrate in different ways other variants of this pattern. So does imperial China, through the differing interpretations of the doctrine that rulers, including rebels, usurpers and dowagers, governed by 'the mandate of Heaven'. These and other outcomes of the familiar struggles between ritual and secular authorities in most extensive and complex pre-industrial societies together indicate that the instability and persistence of social structures based on such accommodations depend firstly on the distribution of power among the supporters of these competing institutions, and secondly on their ability to avoid direct mutual confrontations. In medieval Europe the centralisation of secular and ritual authorities, coupled with proscription of marriage for clerics, promoted and encouraged direct struggles that destroyed the basic accommodation on which the estate organisation of feudal society rested. By contrast, the diffuse and flexible fragmented accommodations of Kshatriyas and Brahmans endowed Hinduism and Indian society with a fundamental resilience and adaptivity that secured its prepetuation, while the Chinese imperium owed its security as much to religious divisions of the people among Taoism, Buddhism, Confucianism as to the overwhelming concentration of power in Peking.

Such observations enable us to treat these societies together with due attention to their differing stratifications. They likewise justify the attempt to treat them with other societies such as ancient Rome and Athens, Ruanda, Mossi, Uganda or modern metropolitan and colonial societies that lack such ideological bifurcations of authority and power in ritual and secular scales within a single framework, provided we recognise first that, like other forms of subordination, stratification assumes regulation and that regulation combines power, defined as the ability to secure compliance, and authority, identified as the right and responsibility to order certain affairs in particular ways and situations for a given aggregate. It is clear that all forms of stratified societies and all strata within these alike derive and depend upon the evolution of their distributions of regulatory power for their form and development. However, as we have seen, such regulation always combines authority, which may be purely secular, narrowly ritual, or mixed, and political power, which has many modalities, official and unofficial, collective and individual, military, economic, social, religious, etc. Thus where ritual rulers, structures and strata regulate collectivities by virtue of their ritual status and by ritual means, the predominance of ritual authority and power over alternative forms is clear. In other cases we are confronted with predominantly secular modes of regulation, even where, as in Hindu India, in Islam, China and medieval Europe, ritual support and legitimation are necessary to establish the ruler's authority. An essentially similar situation arises in expressly secular modern states which oblige their most powerful leaders to fulfil constitutional norms in order to legitimise their authority; and it is this identity that allows us to treat all these variably ritualised stratification structures together, as equally dependent on the distribution of regulative power, despite variable bases and composition. As we have seen, even the most heavily ritualised and resilient structure, that of Hindu caste, developed and persists by successive adjustments that adapt its ritual hierarchy to the changing distributions of power in space and time. Accordingly, to penetrate the dynamics of stratification structures, given that their legitimacy corresponds with public recognition of the authority of the ruling groups or strata, we have now to specify the various forms which ruling groups may take, and the essential requisites of their regulation. Clearly, in so far as rulers or social stratifications lack public acceptance as legitimate, their regulative capacities express naked power, that is, power without corresponding moral or religious support. This situation, illustrated by the subservience of Roman and Japanese emperors to their powerful subjects, illustrates once again the role and ultimate primacy of power distributions in structures of public regulation, however heavily embedded these may be in ritual, moral and juridical norms. Accordingly, to determine the conditions of such public regulation, we must examine the basic forms and conditions of the distribution of power.

Public regulation, as already remarked, involves the administration of routine or emergency affairs for a definite collectivity organised as a corporate group, that is, one presumed to be perpetual, which thus has clear rules of closure and recruitment, a unique identity, a determinate membership, a set of common but exclusive affairs, and the organisation, procedures and autonomy required to manage these. Such properties are necessary and sufficient to define in the simplest and most general terms all publics and units involved in their routine positive regulation, such as councils (colleges) and offices.[17] To stabilise the constitutional frameworks for orderly legitimate regulation, such regulatory units and agencies as corporate groups require are normally themselves constituted as corporations and presumed to be perpetual. However, corporate groups in many simple societies lack such differentiated regulatory organs as councils or offices.

In other small-scale societies, corporate groups may be regulated directly by offices and councils embedded in them, with minimal administrative staffs; but in larger aggregates, adequate administrative provisions are needed to enforce orders and rules on those beyond direct reach of the chief and his councillors. An informal but flexible stratification accordingly emerges based on differences of political and juridical status and roles between the chief, the ruling house, officials, his councillors, their staffs, and the commoners who compose the majority of the public. Clearly priests, diviners and ritual experts of various kinds may be included in the ruler's staff and/or council; and the ruler is often himself primarily a ritual figure. But in so far as these and other official positions on the council and staff are filled by hereditary recruitment from most or all descent groups within the community, as for example among the Yoruba,[18] the distinction between commoners and their rulers will not establish strata, since all lineages will participate in the regulatory structure, albeit in differing ways and times. Only when the stratum of rulers and their assistants is effectively cut off by its modes of recruitment from other parts of the public do we find an evident stratification; and in such situations it is rarely the case that the public consists of two strata only, the rulers and the ruled. Normally each of these strata is further subdivided, as for example, rulers into the dynasty and/or aristocracy of birth on the one hand, their patrimonial staffs, the nobles of office, on the other, and their subjects who may include free native commoners, resident aliens, free people of differing ethnic stock, and unfree persons such as pawns, eunuchs, slaves, serfs and bondsmen. It is evident that the status differences of these various subject strata are political in their institution and juridical in kind; and also that their closure or crystallisation, their elaboration or differentiation, and persistence or dissolution, alike depend upon the effective exercise of political power by those strata privileged to rule. It is also evident, as we pass from aggregates that distribute regulatory roles widely and equally throughout the free elements of their communities to those that do not, that the bases and character of the corporations in which these regulatory functions and powers reside undergo signal change. In the first case, illustrated to a degree by the Ibo, Yoruba and Kikuyu, the public as a whole constitutes the ruling corporate group, even though at any time only some elements of that public may exercise regulatory power. In the latter case, regulatory power and functions vest in a stratum which is characteristically organised as a corporate group which remains pre-occupied with the regulation of collective affairs, including its relations with other strata, whether these be its ritual superiors, as were the Hindu Brahmans or the medieval clergy, or its inferiors in ritual and secular status alike, as is commonly the case.

It is surely significant that these alternative forms of ruling group between them divide the two alternative forms of corporation aggregate, the corporate category and the corporate group, and equally significant that in pre-industrial societies social strata should commonly appear as corporate categories, even within such graded secret societies as the Mende Poro, Yoruba Ogboni or the Efik Ekpe. In East Africa and elsewhere, graded age-sets reproduce this pattern even though they fail to establish valid stratification. In ancient Rome and Athens, patricians constituted strata which were closed equally against the demos, plebs and against clients, bondsmen and slaves. In medieval Europe the strata of nobles, clergy, merchants, free villeins and serfs were likewise closed and ordered categorically; so too in

Japan the orders of *daimyo, samurai,* serfs and the caste of *eta*. The categorical status of the ranked Hindu castes has already been noted. In the eighteenth-century Caribbean slave societies a relatively small number of freemen were divided as strata first by colour or race as free coloured, free blacks and whites, and finally within the last category, by political status as those ineligible to vote, those eligible to vote only, and those who could vote and contest elections for the local assembly. Rhodesia and South Africa parallel this pattern today. It is of course instructive to find in the relatively fluid and complex stratifications of industrial societies that folk models assert the corporate nature of social strata, despite overwhelming contrary evidence.

Of course within a ruling stratum such as dominant whites in Caribbean slave societies or Muslims in Muslim conquest states, we commonly find institutional features that distinguish the 'ruling class' or 'political elite' from others of the same broad strata. Rarely shall we find such crisp distinctions as those in the post-bellum South or post-emancipation Caribbean colonies between *petit blancs*, the poor whites, and *grand blancs*, their masters, or those that emphasised ethnicity in ranking, as between Fulani and Hausa in Northern Nigeria or Osmanli Arabs, Asians, Shirazi and mainland Africans in pre-revolutionary Zanzibar. Moreover, even with such subdivided strata, that division which furnishes the ruling group generally consists of one or at most a very small number of competing or co-operating groups which either operate as if they are corporate units, or already hold that status. In such societies, once again power and responsibility to preserve or modify the social stratification reside in the corporate group or stratum that regulates the whole by virtue of its preponderant power.

History shows that despite internal conflicts and struggles for power, certain stratifications last longer than others, are more resilient, and develop or adapt rather than collapse. In such situations as those that followed emancipation in the southern U.S.A., independence in Mauritius and the Caribbean, or the dissolution of feudalism in Britain and France, adaptations and readjustments of the old status structure yielded dissimilar results as equally rational responses to diverse conditions. Such comparisons suggest that to determine the dynamics of stratification in general terms, we should look more closely at those features that distinguish the ruling stratum from others, before considering particulars.

As corporations, ruling strata or those components endowed with regulatory power and responsibilities need first to regulate their relations with other strata and with foreign bodies, that is, to ensure satisfactory *external articulations*. Secondly they have inevitably to regulate all those relations among their members and components which could possibly impair or subvert their collective status and power. These latter I group together as their *internal articulations*. Certain minimally adequate internal and external articulations are requisite, that is, necessary conditions for the effective regulation of collective relations and affairs by the ruling group. How to determine these minima in any given case will be indicated briefly after other minimal conditions or requisites for the adequate operation of the regulatory structure have been reviewed.

The first of these substantive requisites is adequate *autonomy* – that is freedom and power to actively uphold and pursue the unit's indispensable interests, for without adequate autonomy no social unit can regulate any interest for itself or any other. The second substantive requisite for effective regulation is the necessary *resources*. Resources may be classified as material, i.e. technical, fiscal and other properties; as ideological, that is moral, ritual, cognitive, affectual and symbolic resources, and as social, by which I mean the situationally and individually variable combinations of kin, affines, clients, friends, dependents and others that a social unit may mobilise in times of need. A group may of course possess all the *resources* it needs for self-regulation but lack the *autonomy* to employ them, and vice versa.

The third requisite of any regulative unit is determinate *range*. By a unit's range I mean here the area and/or population for which its regulation is or should be valid and effective at any given instant. Clearly the validity of a regulatory relation may alter territorially or demographically, separately or together, thereby changing the unit's *range*. For example, under Western norms, relations of marriage bind couples absolutely with respect to distance in space but not in time; on the other hand, by conquest or otherwise, a political unit's regulatory authority may expand or contract in area and/or population; and normally, though its boundaries may escape change, the unit's population will normally change over time.

Fourthly, these requisites of range, resources and autonomy alike assume a definite *scope*, that is, a set of affairs and relations which are subject to regulation by a specific unit. It is therefore necessary to define the minimal scope of such regulatory units, irrespective of their bases, form and size, in order to determine the conditions under which regulation and stratification may alter.

A final condition, though not a requisite but an implication or product of the preceding is, like them, an intrinsic attribute of all concrete social units, whether corporate or other. This is the *capacity* or ability of each unit either to regulate its current scope more efficiently, that is with increased effectiveness, precision, speed, etc., or at lower cost with fewer staff; or alternatively, to regulate the same affairs over an expanded range, or to expand its scope and thus to regulate additional affairs efficiently within the given range. Thus the capacity of social units, regulatory or other, derives from their external and internal articulations, their autonomy, resources, scope and range. Capacity, in short, is a derivative implication or product of the preceding properties together, and though an intrinsic attribute of all social units, is not a requisite but an implication.

Clearly while scope and range serve to define precisely the regulatory unit's sphere of operations, resources and autonomy together likewise define its ability to regulate these affairs effectively within the specified range. Likewise, the unit's external and internal articulations, that is, its actual organisation and relations with other units of the same or different kind, and the order it enforces among its members, together define the scope and autonomy at its disposal. Thus these structural conditions of external and internal articulation operatively determine the autonomy and resources the unit enjoys, and thus define its actual and maximal scope, and its capacity, given determinate resources and range.

To specify the minimal scope of regulatory structures of any kind is thus the immediate task; for this known, we can then indicate certain requisite conditions of its autonomy and external articulation. Fortunately, despite their great variety, the minimal scope of all corporations is always prescribed by two sets of conditions, namely the criteria or principles that govern their recruitment of members, and the form or nature of the corporation itself, which define in turn its positive capacities. Those principles that regulate the recruitment and differentiation of members in a corporation or other social unit constitute the basis of the unit concerned; they also define those minimal interests and affairs that the corporation or unit has to regulate in order that it may continue effectively as a unit whose members are recruited and organised on the prescribed lines. Thus, in so far as these relate to collective interests and corporate affairs, the conduct of all members, including the leader and his staff where these are present, are essential objects of corporate regulation, as institutional norms illustrate. Further, as regards the factor of form, for brevity there are two main types of corporations aggregate – that is, those with plural memberships. One, illustrated by corporate categories, lacks the attributes requisite for any positive corporate action, including those of a self-regulatory kind; the corporate category is therefore imperfect. Perfect corporations of any type, which include the corporate group, the college (that is, permanent councils, certain standing committees, etc.) and the office, a variety of corporation sole, have the attributes requisite for positive corporate action, namely inclusive or representative organisation, a set of legitimate procedures, a body of exclusive though common, that is, corporate, affairs, and the autonomy requisite to regulate them by positive corporate action. For present purposes we may ignore councils and offices, since both are always lodged within corporate groups; but in doing so we should distinguish two features that they have in common, firstly, that all are organs and members of some corporate group, and secondly, that in many situations they regulate collectivities which are excluded from the corporate group to which these organs belong.

We have to deal then with three kinds of corporation aggregate:

(i) those that are self-regulating, solely and always;
(ii) those that are not self-regulating and must therefore be regulated from outside – these are always corporate categories;
(iii) those that regulate others as well as themselves – these are always corporate groups.

Clearly corporations of class (iii) presume the presence of class (ii) corporations; and clearly their association institutes an overt stratification explicitly in political-juridical terms and implicitly in other scales such as wealth, prestige, knowledge and style of life. Thus at the minimum, besides regulating the actions and corporate interests of their members, corporations concerned to regulate a stratified order have simultaneously by various means and agencies so to regulate the interests and conduct of the corporate categories or groups subordinate to them as to ensure that they conform to all those conditions that are requisite for the maintenance of the social order and/or the enhancement of the interests of the ruling corporation. These regulatory foci of inter-corporate relations include, *inter alia*; (1) the distribution of technological and economic assets, opportunities and disabilities; (2) the distribution of ritual, moral, theological and cognitive assets, opportunities and disabilities; (3) the distribution of facilities, opportunities and obstacles for social communication, mobility (geographical and social), and especially for collective organisation; and finally (4) effective monopoly or control of all societally relevant political, administrative, military and juridical resources, opportunities and autonomies.

It will be immediately apparent that besides organised justice, government and force, the dominant stratum or its inner ruling core in a hierarchically ordered society must also regulate the social economy, religion, ideology, education and communication structures of the aggregate, together with all opportunities for mobility and organisation among subordinates. Contemporary South Africa illustrates one attempt at such total regulation, the USSR and China some others. In pursuing such regulation, the ruling group seeks to protect and promote the collective interests of its members, and to regulate their individual conduct. Accordingly by these means, and as the decisive condition of their achievement, it seeks to ensure the persistence of the social order with which it is identified. Thus the persistence of any form of social stratification presupposes an effective regulation by the inner core of its ruling stratum organised as a corporate group, not only of relations among its members, relations within the ruling stratum, but also of relations between that stratum and all others, as the objective and condition of an effective and appropriate regulation of the economic, demographic, ritual, ideological, military, organisational, communication and juridical resources and structures of the total soceity; and to this end it requires either a monopoly or effective control of the public political and administrative structures. In consequence, should any ruling group or stratum fail adequately to control or direct any of these strategic institutional sectors or the strata they serve to subordinate, its supremacy will be correspondingly weakened by that loss of resources, autonomy, scope, capacity and perhaps by a loss of range as well. However, any substantive change of this kind presupposes some structural change in the articulations of the ruling and subordinate strata; and even though such structural shifts may themselves follow antecedent shifts in the substance or content of the rulers' power, ultimately we can always trace these sequences of substantive change that crystallise, elaborate or destabilise a regulatory order and the stratification over which it presides, either to some prior modification of internal articulations within the ruling group or stratum which altered its external articulations in some significant way, thereby modifying its autonomy, resources, scope and range; or, in the absence of any internal changes among the rulers, we shall find some significant change in the external articulation of the ruling stratum which modified its position and capacities. Clearly such changing external articulations may be initiated by autonomous actions of the ruling or subject strata.

From this it follows that if we seek to study the dynamics of any social stratification, we should first determine its form, scope and range as precisely as we may, and then seek to isolate the requisites of that order, and especially those requisites that define together the minimal properties and conditions of its ruling stratum. With the aid of these principles, we can then specify the precise conditions which are necessary for the persistence of the regime by detailing the requisites for the maintenance of the form and position of the ruling group without change in terms of its appropriate internal and external articulations, scope, autonomy, resources, range and capacity. This done, we may then proceed to translate prevailing distributions of differential privilege and control of the relevant societal structures in the empirical instance under study into these structural and substantive categories; and with these data we may easily distinguish those internal changes which reflect exogenous stimuli from others generated internally.

It will at once be evident, given the many complex conditions the ruling stratum has to control and direct appropriately to perpetuate its position, that we shall only rarely and in very special circumstances find situations in which given strata preserve the stratification without significant change for any period of time. The ideal of a changeless stratification is surely a limiting case, however commonly selected as the goal of ruling strata. On the other hand, we shall rarely encounter such radical reversals or realignments of a stratification as the structuralist notion of transformation requires; and even then such partial transformations normally proceed by violent collective action. Unfortunately for structural theorists, social change, including changes of social stratification, proceeds diachronically and vertically by chronologically successive modifications of the requisite conditions of empirical structures, and not horizontally or reversibly by some mysterious rearrangements of central components in a common basic model that illustrates the human mind.

NOTES

1 Marx, K. (1959), *Capital*, Moscow, vol. III, pp. 862-3; Marx, K. (1963), *The Eighteenth Brumaire of Louis Bonaparte*, New York; Marx, K. and Engels, F. (1948), *The Communist Manifesto*, London. See also Bendix, R. and Lipset, S.M. (1953), 'Karl Marx's theory of social classes', *in* Bendix, R. and Lipset, S.M. (eds.), *Class, Status and Power*, Glencoe, Ill., pp. 26-34.

2 Schumpeter, Joseph A. (1950), *Capitalism, Socialism and Democracy*, New York, pp. 134-9.

3 Marx (1959), Vol. III, Ch. 52.

4 Weber, Max (1947), *The Theory of Social and Economic Organisation*, trans. A.R. Henderson and T. Parsons, London, pp. 390-5; Gerth, H. and Mills, C.W. (1948), *From Max Weber: Essays in Sociology*, London, pp. 180-195.

5 Parsons, T. (1940), 'An analytical approach to the theory of social stratification', *American Journal of Sociology,* XLV, no. 6; Parsons, T. (1953), 'A revised analytical approach to the theory of social stratification', *in* Bendix and Lipset (eds.) (1953).

6 Parsons (1940); Parsons (1953); Davis, Kingsley and Moore, W.E. (1945), 'Some principles of stratification', *American Sociological Review*, 10; Aberle, D.F. *et al.* (1950), 'The functional prerequisites of a society', *Ethics*, 60, January.

7 For representative contributions to this debate, see Bendix, R. and Lipset, S.M. (1967), *Class, Status and Power: Social Stratification in Comparative Perspective* (2nd edition), London, pp. 47-96; and Heller, Celia S. (1969), *Structured Social Inequality: A Reader in Comparative Social Stratification,* London, pp. 479-531.

8 Smith, M.G. (1966), 'Pre-industrial stratification systems', *in* Smelser, Neil J. and Lipset, S.M. (eds.), *Social Structure and Mobility in Economic Development*, Chicago, pp. 141-76.

9 Ferguson, Adam (1966), *Essay on the History of Civil Society, 1767,* Edinburgh; Millar, John (1973), *Observations on the Distinctions of Ranks,* London; Spencer, Herbert (1969), *Principles of Sociology*, ed. Stanislav Andreski, London; Durkheim, Emile (1947), *The Division of Labour in Society*, trans. George Simpson, Glencoe, Ill.

10 Fallers, Lloyd (1963), 'Equality, modernity and democracy in the new states', *in* Geertz, Clifford (ed.), *Old Societies and New States*, Glencoe, Ill., pp. 162-8; also Smith, R.T. (1970), 'Social stratification in the Caribbean', *in* Plotnicov, L. and Tuden, A. (eds.), *Essays in Comparative Social Stratification*, Pittsburgh, pp. 46 ff.

11 v. Glass, David (ed.) (1954), *Social Mobility in Britain,* London; and Reiss, Albert J. Jr. (1961), *Occupations and Social Status*, Glencoe, Ill. For conflicting data, see Smith, M.G. (1965), *Stratification in Grenada*, Berkeley and Los Angeles, Ch. 4.

12 For this hybrid conception, v. Harris, Marvin (1969), 'Monistic determinism: anti-Service', *S. West. J. Anthrop.*, 25, pp. 198-206.

13 cf. Durkheim (1947). For comments, v. Barnes, J.A. (1966), 'Durkheim's division of labour in society', *Man n.s.* 1, no. 2, June; and Smith, M.G. (1974), 'The comparative study of complex societies', in Smith, M.G., *Corporations and Society*, London.

14 Weber (1947), pp. 252 ff.

15 Blumer, Herbert (1965), 'Industrialization and race relations', *in* Hunter, Guy (ed.) *Industrialization and Race Relations*, London, pp. 220-53; Kuper, Leo (1965),

An African Bourgeoisie, New Haven; and Kuper, Leo (1970), 'Stratification in plural societies: focus on white settler societies in Africa', in Plotnicov and Tuden (eds.) (1970); van den Berghe, Pierre L. (1965), *South Africa: A Study in Conflict*, Middletown.

16 Smith, M.G. (1965), *The Plural Society in the British West Indies*, Berkeley and Los Angeles, pp. 113-15, 140-5.

17 For further discussion, see Smith (1974).

18 Lloyd, Peter (1971), *The Political Development of Yoruba Kingdoms in the Eighteenth and Nineteenth Centuries*, R.A.I. Occasional Papers no. 31; London; Lloyd, Peter (1962), *Yoruba Land Law*, London, Ch. 3.

ROY A. RAPPAPORT

Maladaptation in social systems

I shall be concerned in this essay with maladaptation and its evolution. The notion of maladaptation is, of course, contingent upon the concept of adaptation, a concept central to much biological and anthropological thought. Like most central concepts, that of adaptation is not entirely clear, and perhaps it should not be. In remaining vague it itself remains adaptive. Be that as it may, usage and understanding varies, and before approaching maladaption it is necessary for me to make my understanding of adaptation explicit, even at the risk of rehearsing some elementary matters.

I take the term 'adaptation' to refer to the processes by which living systems maintain homeostasis in the face of both short term environmental fluctuations and, by transforming their own structures, through long-term nonreversing changes in the composition and structure of their environments as well. I take living systems to include (1) organisms, (2) single species assemblages such as populations, troops, tribes and states, and (3) the multispecies associations of ecosystemic communities. Systemic homeostasis may be given specific, if not always precise meaning if it is conceived as a set of ranges of viability on a corresponding set of variables abstracted from what, for independently established empirical or theoretical reasons, are taken to be conditions vital to the survival of the system. This is to say that any process, physiological, behavioural, cultural or genetic which tends to keep the states of crucial variables (e.g. body temperature, population size, protein intake, energy flux) within ranges of viability or tends to return them to such ranges should they depart from them may be taken, other things being equal, to be adaptive. Later it will be necessary to consider difficulties in the association of adaptiveness with particular variables, but this preliminary formulation may stand for the present, because it underlines certain features of adaptive process and structure. These are:

First, adaptation is basically cybernetic. In response to signals of system endangering change in the state of a component or an aspect of the environment, actions tending to ameliorate those changes are initiated. Corrective actions may eliminate the stressor, make compensatory adjustments or even involve changes – genetic, constitutional, structural – in the system's organisation. Adaptation in this view includes both the self-regulatory processes through which living systems maintain themselves in fluctuating environments and the self-organising processes by which they transform themselves in response to directional environmental changes. These two classes of processes have generally been distinguished in anthropology and have formed the foci of two distinct modes of analysis: 'functional' on the one hand, and 'evolutionary' on the other. But the distinction has surely been overdrawn. In a changing universe, after all, the maintenance of organisation is likely to demand its continual modification. The connecting generalisation is what Hockett and Ascher called 'Romer's Rule' after the zoologist who first enunciated it in a discussion of the emergence of the amphibia.[1] The lobe-finned fish, Romer argued, did not come onto dry land to take advantage of the terrestrial habitat. Rather, relatively minor modification of their fins and other subsystems made them better able to migrate from one drying up stream or pond to another still containing water during the intermittent periods of desiccation presumed to have characterised the Devonian era. Such changes, this is to say, made it possible for these creatures to maintain their general aquatic organisation during a period of marked environmental change. In slightly different terms, self-organising or evolutionary changes in components of systems are functions of the self-regulatory process of the more inclusive systems of which they are parts. Thus, structural or evolutionary changes, such as fin to leg, although on some grounds they may be distinguished from 'functional' changes or 'systemic adjustments' are not separated from them in the larger more inclusive scheme of adaptive process. Together they form ordered series of responses to perturbations.

Several comments are in order before discussing adaptive response sequences. First, it is worth making explicit because there seems to be considerable confusion surrounding this matter, that the view of adaptation proposed here suggests that there is no contradiction between the maintenance of homeostasis and evolutionary change. Indeed, the most salient question to ask concerning any structural change is 'What does this change maintain unchanged?'. Second, insofar as adaptive processes are cybernetic they are possessed of a characteristic structure because cybernetic systems have a characteristic structure, namely that of the closed causal loop. In a cybernetic system a deviation from a reference value itself initiates the process which attempts to correct it. Third, while adaptive processes may have cybernetic characteristics all that is cybernetic is *not* adaptive in the sense outlined in the first paragraphs of this essay. In the most general terms cybernetic systems attempt to maintain the truth value of propositions about themselves in the face of perturbations tending to falsify them.[2] In systems dominated by humans at least, the propositions so maintained (and the physical states represented by such propositions) may not correspond to, or may even contradict, homeostasis biologically or even socially defined.

Adaptive response sequences have certain important properties that can be noted only briefly here.[3] The responses most quickly mobilised are likely to be energetically expensive, but they have the advantage of being easily reversible should the stress cease, and they can hold the line, so to speak, until relieved by slower acting, less energetically expensive, less easily reversible changes should the stress not cease. Thus responses to high altitudes start with panting and racing of the heart, which are immediate, and continue through a series of circulatory and other changes, to, after a year or so, irreversible changes in lung capacity and in the size of the heart's right ventricle.[4] The ultimate change in such sequences would be genetic, although this seems not to have been necessary in high altitude adaptation. Similarly, the initial response of a town to very heavy traffic loads during peak periods may be transitory redeployment of police. But if this response is inadequate or itself causes an intolerable strain a series of less reversible actions may be initiated, the ultimate perhaps being the construction of a highway by-pass, a change which is virtually irreversible.

It is of note that the earlier responses deprive the system of immediate behavioural flexibility while they continue – the organism when it first moves to 15,000 feet can do little except aerate itself; the police force while it is taking care of peak traffic is not free to attend to emergencies. But while they continue, the structure of the system remains unchanged; thus they conserve the long run flexibility of the system. In contrast, while the later responses do alleviate the strain of the earlier, they are likely to reduce long-range flexibility. There is in such series a continual and graduated trade-off of adaptive flexibility for adapted efficiency. To the extent that the perturbations to which the system will be subjected in the future are unpredictable it is good evolutionary strategy to give up as little long-range flexibility as possible, and evolutionary wisdom seems to be intrinsic to the graduated structure of adaptive response sequences, at least in biological systems. Social systems, on the other hand can make mistakes of which biological systems may be incapable.

A second general point, related to the first, is that adaptive processes are not only cybernetic, sequential and graduated. The adaptive structure of any living system is not merely a collection of more or less distinct feedback loops. Special adaptations must be related to each other in structured ways and general adaptations, human or otherwise, biological or cultural, must take the form of enormously complex sets of interlocking correcting loops, roughly and generally hierarchically arranged and including not only mechanisms regulating material variables, but regulators regulating relations between regulators and so on.[5] Adaptive structures are *structured sets of processes*, and regulatory hierarchies, whether or not they are embodied in particular organs or institutions are found in *all* biological and social systems. However, it is important to issue a caveat here: to say that regulatory structure is hierarchical is not to say that it is centralised, nor does it imply social stratification. For instance, among some egalitarian societies, components of regulatory hierarchies are embedded in ritual cycles; in others in segmentary kinship organisation.[6]

Another aspect of the hierarchical organisation of adaptation is the relationship of parts to wholes. This was implied in Romer's discussion of the emergence of the amphibia. Modifications in certain of the special purpose *subsystems* of the lobe-finned fish made it possible to maintain unchanged the general systemic characteristics of those organisms. Now whole living systems – organisms and assemblages of organisms – are what Pask[7] has called 'general purpose systems', for they do not have special goals or outputs. Their only purpose or goal is that most general of purposes or goals (or if you prefer, non-purposes or non-goals): survival. They are, as Slobodkin[8] has put it, 'players of the existential game', one in which there are no pay-offs external to the game because the player can't leave the table, one in which, therefore, the only reward for successful play is to be allowed to continue playing. But they are made up of subsystems which do have special goals or outputs valuable, presumably, to the larger systems of which they are parts. The increasing differentiation, in the course of evolution, of special purpose subsystems in organisms, societies and ecosystems has been called 'progressive segregation',[9] and it is often accompanied in organisms and social systems, but not ecosystems, by increasing centralisation of regulatory operation, or 'progressive centralisation'. In organisms we note the elaboration of central nervous systems, in societies the development of administrative structures. This contrast between the development of ecological and other systems may rest upon their contrasting bases for order maintenance. The basis of orderliness in ecosystems seems to shift in the course of successions from a reliance upon the resilience of individual organisms not to central regulation, but to a reliance upon the increasing redundancy of matter and energy pathways resulting from increasing species diversity. These contrasting bases of order maintenance, in turn, reflect differences in the degrees of coherence that these different classes of systems require and can tolerate. By 'coherence' I refer to the extent to which a change in one system component affects changes in others; in a fully coherent system any change results in immediate and proportional changes in all components.[10] As no living system can be totally incoherent neither could it be totally coherent, for in a fully coherent system disruptions anywhere would immediately spread everywhere. Whereas anthropologists traditionally have been concerned with the ways in which the various components of socio-cultural systems are bound together – the jargon is 'integrated' – they have generally ignored the ways in which the parts and processes of such systems are buffered from each other and each other's disruptions.

Organisms are, and in their nature must be, more coherent than social systems, and social systems are more coherent than ecosystems. As a rule of thumb, the more inclusive the system, and the greater the degree of relative autonomy inhering in its subsystems, the less coherent it must be. The less inclusive the system the more its internal orderliness and the effectiveness of its activities depends upon the fine coordination of its parts. An organism requires and can tolerate closer coordination of the activities of its parts than societies and societies more, at least from time to time, than ecosystems. Coordination depends upon centralisation, hence progressive centralisation in organisms and societies, but not ecosystems. Whereas the adaptive structures of all living systems have certain fundamental features in common they also differ in certain ways, probably related most importantly to differences in their coherence and in the relative autonomy of their subsystems.

I shall now make explicit what I think may be some of the salient features of orderly adaptive structure in social systems as a preliminary to noting the ways in which they may be disrupted. For the sake of brevity and clarity the suggestions that follow will be expressed more simply and certainly than they should be. Empirical research and further conceptualisation is badly needed; what follows is to be taken to be suggestive. I shall be concerned mainly with the hierarchical organisation of adaptive structure, and shall follow the convention of referring to more inclusive systems and regulation as 'higher order', less inclusive as 'lower order'. Certain of the features of orderly adaptive structures have already been implied, and some seem to be logically necessary, but it is well to make them explicit.

1. Lowest order regulators are concerned with the regulation of specific material or behavioural variables. The regulation of, say, a garden is concerned with a complex of material variables – soil moisture, weed density, insect infestation – that are likely to fluctuate or change in value very quickly and that require more or less constant attention. Lower order regulators – like factory foremen or gardeners – operate more or less continuously, reacting very quickly to slight changes in conditions. The directives of low order regulators are, typically, highly specific commands relating to immediate states of affairs. In sum, low order regulation is concerned with specific operations in special purpose subsystems. However, such operations are typically guided by goals or considerations established from 'above', either by directive or by such mechanisms as demand in market economies.
2. As a rule, the responses of lower order regulators in social

systems are more easily reversible than those of higher order. (They may differ in this regard from biological systems in which early response – such as easily reversible panting upon first entering high altitude – may mobilise much of the resources of the system as a whole, and which may radically affect the behaviour of the system as a whole. This possible difference between biological and social systems is, perhaps, related to their differences in coherence, and in the ability of social systems to develop rather easily special purpose subsystems, like the Red Cross and the fire department, specifically for dealing with emergencies.) Moreover, being closer to possibly perturbing changes in the states of variables, and being in a position to take highly specific actions, or to issue highly specific commands very quickly, lower order regulators are likely to respond more delicately to perturbations than are regulators of higher order.

3. Higher order regulators are, as a rule, not so much concerned with the correction of minor deviations in the states of particular variables as they are with regulating the relations among lower order regulators and relations among the outputs, requirements, or special purposes of the several subsystems subordinate to them. They often operate in terms of highly aggregated variables (such as monetary values), and they become directly concerned with affairs usually managed by lower order regulators only when the lower order regulators experience difficulty. Several comments should be made here.

   First, it is clear that higher order regulators do not 'know', nor do they need to know, everything known by the lower order regulators subordinate to them. In fact it is perhaps better that they don't, for economy of information processing capacity is an important aspect of regulatory hierarchies. Too much detailed information concerning the states of low order variables could overload the capacities of higher order regulators.

   Second, in technologically simple and relatively undifferentiated societies in which a domestic mode of production prevails,[11] high order regulation is likely to be simpler and operate less continuously than that of low order. For instance, in the horticultural societies of New Guinea the regulation of gardening is typically located in individual households and is continuous. The regulation of the dispersion of the population over land so that they *can* garden, a matter concerning relations among households, is 'embedded' in the segmentary organisation of more inclusive groups and in some cases in ritual cycles,[12] and operates only occasionally.

   Third, whereas higher order regulators do issue specific commands, other sorts of directives are also likely to emanate from them. There are, first, rules, which differ from commands in that they are not situation-specific. They specify what is to be done or not to be done under specified categories of circumstances. This is to say that they are less specific, or more general, than commands. Yet higher order regulation enunciates yet more general directives which may be called policy statements or principles, like 'All men are entitled to life, liberty and the pursuit of happiness.' It is presumably to define the vague terms of such principles, and to fulfill them, that rules are encoded, and it is in conformity to rules that commands are issued. In sum, from highest order regulation, associated with the general purpose system as a whole, to lowest, associated with the operation of special purpose subsystems, there is a progress from regulatory sentences which are high in generality and vagueness to sentences high in specificity and concreteness.

Fourth, although obvious it is nevertheless worth making explicit that this account implies that the hierarchical relations outlined here include authority relations. Higher order regulators are 'higher' authorities. It is important to note that higher order authorities need not be discrete, living individuals. Highest authority may be vested in documents such as constitutions, in the conventions of ritual cycles, in immemorial tradition or in supernaturals.

4. In proceeding from lower to higher order the degree to which regulatory operation is directly determined by environmental or other material factors seems to diminish. That is, high order regulation may be more arbitrary or more affected by conventional considerations than that of lower order. For instance, the ways in which a particular inventory of crops may be grown in a particular region may be rather narrowly determined by soil conditions and climate. The ways in which the harvests are distributed, a function of a higher order system, 'an economic system', of which 'the agricultural system' is only a part, are probably not as narrowly determined. There are likely to be, therefore, more ways to distribute the crop than to grow it. The relations of production, this is to say, are likely to be more arbitrary than the means of production.
5. Possibly correlated with the increasing arbitrariness of higher order regulation is an increase in the value laden terms surrounding higher order regulation. For example, the discourse concerning both Soviet and American wheat farming is highly concrete. It concerns seed, soil, water, tractors, fuel and autoparts. The fundamental agricultural assumptions of a Soviet wheat farmer would probably be acceptable to his American counterpart. Differences of opinion would be, for the most part, slight and technical. But when economics are discussed phrases like 'free enterprise' and 'from each what he can give, to each what he needs' begin to appear. The difference between what are connoted by these phrases is not technical but ideological: both

are taken by those subscribing to them to be highly moral, and yet higher order regulation is bolstered by such notions as honour, freedom, righteousness and patriotism. At the highest levels of regulation divinity is likely to be invoked. This was patent in such archaic states as Egypt in which the Pharaoh was the living Horus, but remains even in modern societies in which there is an ostensible separation of church and state. United States takes itself to be 'One nation under God'. To summarise, the higher order the regulator the more it is associated with values and the more support it receives from sanctification, or even from association with the ultimately sacred: God Himself. This may be correlated with, or even a function of, the increasing arbitrariness, or at least increasingly conventional nature, of higher and higher order regulation, and it also seems to correlate with the hierarchical ordering of authority relations.

6. The general structure of adaptive processes outlined here implies that there are included in the repertories of higher order regulators rules and procedures for modifying or changing the goals of lower order regulators, or even replacing both them and the special purpose subsystems over which they preside with others. This is to say that adaptive structures may transform themselves in more or less orderly ways in response to changes in environmental or historical circumstances. As noted earlier, the maintenance of general purpose systems may require their more or less continual modification in response to non-reversing environmental changes, as well as in response to reversible environmental fluctuations.
7. Throughout this account certain temporal relations between levels have been noted in passing or merely implied. These temporal relations may themselves imply qualities other than temporal, and it would be well to make them explicit and remark upon them here.

   First, it was suggested that the response times of low order regulators are faster than those of higher order. It may be suggested that their rapidity is correlated with their reversibility, and also with their position in what Simon[13] calls 'nearly decomposable systems'. A qualification is, however, necessary here. In the fact of strong perturbation from outside the system – for instance, in response to imminent attack – higher order regulators may respond more quickly than those of lower order. Complex systems may include mechanisms for calibrating the level of responses to the strength and pervasiveness of perturbations.

   Second, that a typical relationship of longevity prevails between systems and their subsystems or components was also implied by the observation that included among programs of higher order regulators are programs for changing or even replacing lower order regulators or subsystems. This suggests that as a rule general purpose systems are more enduring than are their subsystems or components. It is well to make clear that I refer here to particular living systems located in time and space and *not* to principles of organisation. For instance, clans are longer lived than any of the conjugal families of which they are composed, tribes endure through the extinction and replacement of their clans. However, the conjugal family as a mode of organisation, it is safe to say, was operative before clanship appeared and it survives in societies, organised as states, from which clanship has disappeared.

Third, there also seem to be differences in the temporal qualities of the sentences concerned with regulation at different levels. The sentences typical of low order regulation – commands – are situation specific and thus emphemeral. Rules, which are typical of middle range regulation, are more or less enduring, and the principles characteristic of highest order regulation may be conceived to reflect timeless aspects of nature. Indeed, higher order regulation is likely to be associated with propositions concerning Gods conceived to be outside of time altogether. We move from the quick to the eternal. These relations of duration seem to correspond to the continuum from the specific, concrete, pragmatic and materially determined to the conventionally determined, value-laden, general, vague and sacred.

8. Although it has already been noted it is well to reiterate here that terms like 'higher' and 'lower order', 'systems' and 'subsystems' and 'hierarchy' should not be taken to indicate that adaptive structure in human societies is necessarily incorporated in discrete bureaucracies, well-defined administrative structures or special purpose subsystems to which are assigned special personnel. Regulatory hierarchies are sets of responses to perturbation ordered along axes of specificity, concreteness, reversibility, authority, time, sanctity and perhaps other dimensions as well. While in some societies administrative structures are clearly defined, in others, notably the small, technologically simple and relatively undifferentiated societies that form the subject matter of traditional anthropoligical studies, adaptive structure is intrinsic to segmentary organisation, exchange relations, ritual cycles and other aspects of the general social organisation. The emergence of well-defined administrative structures with special offices and officers is an aspect of progressive centralisation, a process that seems to be characteristic of evolution generally. In the evolution of human societies a high degree of centralisation is found only in some state organised societies.

However, it should not be assumed that even in modern state societies adaptive structure is completely embedded in

> administration structure. Individuals, private firms and voluntary organisations, 'grass roots movements' and revitalistic cults may also participate in the cybernetics of social and ecological correction, and are, thus, also to be included in any account of adaptive structure. There is a dialectic, so to speak, between formal organisation and 'spontaneous' adaptive responses, the latter modifying the former and even, perhaps, redefining systemic boundaries from time to time. Indeed, it is at least as correct to say that adaptive processes define, discriminate or establish living systems and their limits as it is to say that they 'inhere in' living systems. We should not be bemused by the apparently immutable boundaries of the living systems most easily observed, namely organisms, or the enduring frontiers of some societies, into taking living systems to be 'things' when they are better regarded as dynamic processes organising matter, energy and information.

The adaptive structures of living systems of different classes (ecosystems, societies, organisms) surely differ in important respects, possibly related to differences in the coherence they require and can tolerate. There are also, surely, important differences to be discerned among the adaptive structures of members of the same class, such as different human societies. I have suggested, however, that orderly adaptive structure has certain universal characteristics, and that we may expect to find important structural similarities underlying apparently great differences. Orderly adapative structure, I have argued, is both cybernetic and hierarchical, and I have made some suggestions – they are no more than that – concerning features or dimensions that may be organised hierarchically. These suggestions may be of some use in guiding investigations leading to more refined formulations. For now they may serve as the basis for further suggestions concerning the nature of maladaptation.

If adaptive processes are those which tend to maintain homeostasis in crucial variables in the fact of perturbation, maladaptations are factors internal to systems interfering with their homeostatic responses. They reduce the survival chances of a system not, in the first instance, by subjecting the system to stress, but by impeding the effectiveness of its responses to stress. Maladaptations are not to be confused with stressors, or perturbing factors, although they themselves can produce stress. This view of maladaptation, it may be noted, is similar to the concept of disease (dis-ease) proposed by Young and Rowley.[14]

If the maintenance of homeostasis depends upon hierarchically ordered sequences of cybernetic responses, it should be possible to describe maladaptation structurally. That is, maladaptations may be conceived as anomalies in the hierarchical and cybernetic features we have taken to be characteristic of orderly adaptive structure. If the feedback of information to regulators concerning the states of systemic variables and the effects of their operations upon those variables is faulty, trouble is likely to ensue. The simplest forms of maladaptation are such cybernetic difficulties as impedence to the detection of deviation of variables from crucial ranges, breaks in feedback loops, or even excessive delay of information transmissions concerning variable states to system regulators, loss or distortion of information in transit and the failure of regulators to understand the signals they are receiving. These and other difficulties to which we shall attend are exacerbated by scale. For instance, the more nodes through which it must pass, the more subject is information to distortion or loss. Other things equal, the higher the administrator the less accurate and adequate his information is likely to be, and the more diverse the subsystems he is regulating the more likely he is to misunderstand the signals upon which he must act. Loss, distortion and misunderstanding of information are likely to result in erroneous or inappropriate regulatory responses.

We note here what may seem an inconsistency in argument but is rather, I think, a problem in the real world. It was suggested earlier that high order regulators do not need to 'know', indeed, cannot afford to 'know' all that the lower order regulators subordinate to them 'know'. Now it is claimed that distortion, or even simple loss of information, can lead high order regulators into error. Complex living systems, especially human social systems, are faced with the problem, perhaps never fully resolved, of balancing comprehensiveness of information against information processing efficiency. Intrinsic to the reduction of information required by limited information processing facilities is the danger of faulty, distorting or self-serving editing. There is perhaps no way for such a danger to be avoided completely, but it can perhaps be minimised by maximising the autonomy of low order regulators, thus reducing the amount of information that must be processed by those of higher order.

Much more remains to be said about cybernetic problems *per se*, but they are relatively well-known and in the interest of brevity we may turn now to hierarchical anomalies. Their likelihood too is increased with scale, and some of them are closely related to the cybernetic disorders we have been discussing. For instance, the deeper the regulatory hierarchy the more likely are time aberrations. Excessive time lag between the onset of a perturbation and response to it may sometimes be a problem, but so may the opposite – too rapid a response by a high order regulator. Excessively fast response by high order regulators may destroy those of lower order by continuously overriding them. The destruction of the lower order regulator may then throw an additional burden upon that which overrode it, with error and possibly breakdown resulting. The likelihood of excessively rapid high order response – let us call it 'premature override' – is increased, of course, by high speed communication, which may put information concerning perturbations into the hands of higher authorities as quickly as it informs the lower.

'Over-response' is related to, and may even be entailed by, premature over-ride. The responses of higher order regulators are not likely to be as delicate or as reversible as those of lower order, and if they are initiated too quickly they may be more massive than may be required. Since they may not be easily reversible they commit the system's future more than necessary. That is to say they reduce its evolutionary flexibility. Over-response, it may be suggested, is impossible, or at least highly unlikely, in biological systems, for in strictly biological processes the sequencing of adaptive responses to perturbation is ordered not by conscious purpose but by non-conscious somatic and genetic organisation. Over-response may be a product of intelligence, particularly human intelligence with its great powers of foresight and imagination. It becomes more serious, of course, as that intelligence comes to control ever more powerful means for effecting its ends.

We are led here to several more general interrelated trends that seem to be common aspects of the increased scale of social systems. First there is what may be called 'over-segregation', the extreme differentiation of special purpose subsystems. Oversegregation may be expressed geographically, with serious ecological consequences. Increasingly large areas become increasingly specialised. Whole regions are turned into wheat fields, whole countries into sugar plantations. But with increasing regional specialisation there is decreasing ecological stability, for monocrop fields, particularly those planted in high yield varieties, are among the most delicate ecosystems ever to have appeared on the face of the earth. Part of this decrease in ecological stability is an aspect of the reduction of self-sufficiency, for modern monocrop agriculture depends upon fuel, machinery, pesticides and herbicides that usually travel through far flung and complicated networks, and distant disruptions in such networks, as well as local problems, can disrupt local activities. With loss of local self-sufficiency there is also loss of local regulatory autonomy, and the homeostatic capacity lost from the local system is not adequately replaced by increasingly remote centralised regulators responding to increasingly aggregated and simplified variables (like the dollar values of crops) through operations increasingly subject to simple cybernetic impedences and time aberrations. Moreover, the regulatory responses of these distant regulators are often to factors extraneous to some of the local systems they affect. For instance, the effect of market response to increased vanilla production in Madagascar may be decreased cash in Tahiti. We recognise here a consequence of over-segregation and 'over-centralisation' that has elsewhere been called 'hyper-coherence' or 'hyper-integration'.[15] The coherence of the world system increases to dangerous levels as the self-sufficiency of local systems is reduced and their autonomy destroyed.

Disruptions occurring anywhere may now spread everywhere. A local war in the Middle East leads to increased starvation in India, for India relies upon Japanese fertiliser, which requires Middle Eastern oil for its manufacture. As Geoffrey Vickers has put it, 'The trouble is not that we are not one world, but that we are'.[16]

Over-segregation and over-centralisation taken together are complementary aspects of a more general structural anomaly that I have mentioned elsewhere,[17] and which may be called the 'hierarchical maldistribution of organisation'. 'Organisation' is notoriously difficult to define; I take the term to refer to complexity and the means for maintaining order within it, and have been suggesting that organisation at more inclusive levels seems to be increasing at the expense of organisation at local levels. Increasing organisation at the world level is based upon decreasingly organised local, regional, and even national social and ecological systems. It seems doubtful that a worldwide human organisation can persist and elaborate itself indefinitely at the expense of its local infrastructures, and it may be suggested that the ability of the world system to withstand perturbation would be increased by returning to its local subsystems some of the autonomy and diversity that they have lost, as China may be doing. This is not to advocate fracturing the world system into smaller, autonomous self-sufficient systems, as undesirable a programme as it would be impossible to achieve. It is to suggest that redistribution of organisation among the levels of the world system, with somewhat greater autonomy and self-sufficiency vested in localities, regions and even nations than presently is the case, would serve well the world system as a whole.

There is another general class of maladaptations, combining with those discussed so far in complex evolutionary sequences. The basic form has elsewhere been called 'usurpation', 'escalation', and 'overspecification'.[18] I speak here of special purpose subsystems coming to dominate the larger general purpose systems of which they are parts. When particular individuals become identified with special purpose systems they tend to identify the special purposes of those sub-systems with their own general purposes, i.e. with their own survival, and attempt to promote those purposes to positions of predominance in the larger systems of which they are parts. As they become increasingly powerful they are increasingly able to succeed. The logical end is for a subsystem, or cluster of subsystems, such as a group of industrial firms, financial institutions and a military establishment, to come to dominate a society. This eventually is nicely summed up in the deathless phrase 'What's good for General Motors is good for America'. But no matter how public spirited or benign General Motors might be, what is good for it cannot in the long run be good for America. General purpose systems have – or should have – as their goals nothing more specific than survival. For a general purpose system, like the United States, to commit itself to what may be good for one of its subsystems is for it to overspecify or narrow the range of the conditions under which it can survive, that is, it is for it to sacrifice evolutionary flexibility.

We may note that this trend may lead to aberrations of sanctification. It is of importance in this regard that ultimate sacred propositions – propositions about gods and the like – are typically without material terms. As such they themselves specify no particular social arrangements or instutitions. Being without material or social specificity they are well suited to be associated with the general goal of general purpose systems, i.e. the non-specific goal of survival, for they can sanctify changing social arrangements while they themselves, remaining inviolate and unchanged, provide continuity through change.

The typically mysterious nature of ultimate sacred propositions is also of importance. The association of mysterious propositions concerning ultimate reality with the immediate reality of contemporary institutions and events is a matter of interpretation. That which is a matter of interpretation allows or even demands reinterpretation, but reinterpretation does not challenge ultimate sacred propositions themselves. It merely challenges previous interpretations of them. Thus, if any proposition is to be taken to be unquestionable, it is important that no one understands it. It is of interest that the very qualities of such propositions that lead positivists to take them to be without sense or even to be nonsense – that they are devoid of logical necessity or empirical referents – are those that make them adaptively valid.

Sanctification, however, can become maladaptive through the process we are calling usurpation. As the specific material goals of lower order systems usurp the places of those of higher order systems they may lay claim to their sanctity. To use a crude example, if the United States is 'One nation under God', and if, as Coolidge said, 'the business of America is business', then business becomes highly sanctified. What is highly sanctified is resistant to change, and thus to oversanctify the specific and material is to reduce evolutionary flexibility. It is of interest that the theologian Paul Tillich[19] used the term 'idolatry' to refer to the 'absolutising of the relative' and the 'relativising of the absolute'. What he took to be a form of evil we may take to be a form of maladaptation.

Another trend seems to be related to the elevation of the goals of lower order systems to positions of predominance in higher order systems. As industrial subsystems become increasingly large and powerful the quality and utility of their products are likely to deteriorate, for the subsystem's contribution to the society becomes less its product and more its mere operation, which provides wages to some, profits to others, and a market for yet others. Arms, which are both expensive and immediately obsolete, and automobiles into which obsolescence is built are ideal products, nor is there anything wrong with products that serve no useful purpose whatsoever. The product tends to become a by-, or even waste product of what might be called the 'industrial metabolism' which is, ultimately, simply the operation of machines. (To use a bald analogy, products come to be related to the firms producing them as faeces are related to the organisms excreting them, and 'consumers' are transformed into coprophages.) Neither competition nor an independently established demand serves to regulate or limit industrial metabolism effectively because large industries are usually not very competitive and they can exercise considerable control over the demand to which they are supposed to be subject.[20]

With the escalation of low order goals to positions of predominance in higher order systems it becomes increasingly possible for ancient and complex systems, particularly ecological systems, to be disrupted by ever smaller groups with ever more narrowly defined interests. But the ultimate consequence of the promotion of the low order goals of industrialised subsystems to predominant positions in societies is not merely that the short-run interests of a few powerful men or institutions come to prevail, but that the 'interests' of machines that even powerful men serve are ultimately dominant. Needless to say, the interests of machines and organisms do not coincide. They do not have the same needs for pure air or water, and being blind and deaf, machines have no need at all for quiet, or for landscapes that refresh the eye. And whereas organisms have need of uncounted numbers of subtle compounds, the needs of machines are few, simple and voracious. It is in accordance with the logic of a world dominated by the gargantuan and simple appetites of machines to tear the tops off complex systems like the states of West Virginia and Colorado to extract a few simple substances like coal and oil.

We have been led beyond structural anomaly to substantive problems, and we may return here to a question raised but not answered earlier. What are the variables to be maintained in homeostasis if a living system is to be adaptive? Some, after all, may be maintained at the expense of others. When highest order regulation is directed toward economic goals it may impede the maintenance of biological variables – organic, demographic and ecosystemic – within their ranges of viability. We may ask, even if the cybernetics of the system seem to be in good order, whether this may be properly regarded as adaptive.

If the goal of general purpose systems is simply survival the question of what is ultimately to be maintained in homeostasis is reduced to the question of what the term 'survival' minimally implies. Here we may be reminded that the term 'adaptation' is basically a biological term, and that the systems with which we are concerned have living components. This is to say that 'survival', although difficult to specify has, minimally, a biological meaning, and that the adaptiveness of aspects of culture may ultimately be assessed in terms of their effects upon the biological components of the systems in which they occur. This is further to say, as we noted earlier when distinguishing adaptive processes from cybernetic processes in general, that what is called 'cultural adaptation', the processes through which social structures or institutions maintain themselves in the face of perturbation, may contradict or defeat the general or biological adaptation of which culture in its emergence must have been a part. But, since survival is nothing if not biological, evolutionary changes perpetuating economic or political institutions at the expense of the biological well being of man, societies and ecosystems may be considered maladaptive. This assertion is not arbitrary for it reflects the way contingency is structured. There are no particular institutions with which a society could not dispense, but obviously, if man perished culture would cease to exist.

There are problems, however. For one thing, given the 'counter-intuitive' nature of complex systems it is difficult or impossible to assess the long-run effects of any aspect of culture on particular biological variables. For a second, it does not seem possible to specify any paticular feature of biological structure or function that will always contribute to survival chances.[21] Although particular variables are, and must be, maintained within ranges of viability at particular times, these ranges, and even the systemic components of which they are states, may be changed by evolution. Thus, adaptiveness is not to be identified with particular variables, even biological variables, but with the maintenance of a general homeostasis in living systems, systems with biological components.

The notion of a general homeostasis is not fully operational but neither is it mystical. One of the implications of the argument presented here is that it is intrinsic to adaptive structure, to a certain ordering of processes and the systemic components in which they may occur, with respect to time, reversibility, specificity, sanctity, and contingency. If such an order is maintained, general homeostasis, it is suggested, prevails. This is a claim that the *formal* or *structural* characteristics of adaptive processes have *substantive* implications. The primacy of biological considerations is implicit in the structure, for the escalation of non-biological variables to positions of predominance violates adaptive order with respect to specificity, contingency and possibly sanctity as well.

In light of possible contradictions between cultural and biological adaptation it seems reasonable to search for the factors impelling maladaptive trends among those that have been taken to be advances in cultural evolution. In the world of events cause is seldom simple. The discussion that follows, which implicates increases in energy capture, money and the division of labour does not purport to represent a general theory. It is intended to do no more than suggest, briefly and tentatively, a few of the many factors that could be adduced.

Some suggestions have already been made about energy capture in this regard. It is important to remember, however, that energy capture has sometimes been taken to be the metric of cultural evolution. A quarter of a century ago Leslie White, following Ostwald, proclaimed what he called 'The Basic Law of Cultural Evolution' as follows:

> Other factors remaining constant, culture evolves as the amount of energy harnessed per capita per year is increased, or as the efficiency of the instrumental means of putting energy to work is increased.[22]

There can be no denying the first clause[23] of this formulation. Large technologically developed states appearing late in history surely do harness more energy per capita per day or year than do the small 'primitive' societies which appeared earlier. One recent estimate would place daily energy consumption in contemporary United States at 230,000 kilocalories, and in hunting and gathering societies as 2,000-3,000.[24]

Contemporary United States has a population of 200,000,000 people, the bushmen bands seldom include more than a score or two of people, and increases in energy capture have made possible much larger and more sedentary social systems. But some, if not all, of the maladaptive trends I have suggested here are related to increased scale. Moreover, high energy technology itself frees those operating in local ecosystems from the limits imposed upon them by the need to derive energy from the contemporary biological processes of those systems. Gasoline, pipelines, bulldozers, high voltage electrical transmission permit virtually unlimited amounts of energy to be focused upon very small systems, and the ecological disruption of those systems can be tolerated – at least for a time – because of the increased specialisation of other local systems. I have argued, however, that in the long run the increasing specialisation of larger and larger regions – itself made possible by a technology that provides means for moving even bulky commodities long distances inexpensively, and for transmitting information long distances instantaneously, is unstable.

The increasing specialisation of increasingly large geographical regions is simply one aspect of increasing internal differentiation of social systems. Progressive segregation and progressive centralisation were, of course, encouraged by the emergence of plant and animal cultivation 10,000 or so years ago, for plant and animal cultivation provided significant opportunities for full time division of labour. By 4,000 B.C., if not earlier, subsistence, craft, religious and administrative specialisation was well developed. But the emergence of high energy technology based upon fossil fuels has accelerated and exaggerated this trend and the maladaptations associated with it.

These include not only over-segregation and over-centralisation, with their concommitants of ecological instability and hypercoherence. High energy technology is differentially distributed among the subsystems of societies and it permits or encourages the promotion of the special purposes of the more powerful to positions of dominance in systems of higher order than their degree of specialisation warrants.

High energy technology is, of course, not alone in impelling maladaptive trends. All-purpose money has also played a part. In addition to its obvious contribution to the concentration of real wealth and regulatory prerogative, it flows through virtually all barriers increasing the coherence of the world system enormously. Its ability to penetrate whatever barriers may have protected previously autonomous systems against outside disruption rests upon its most peculiar and interesting property: it annihilates distinctions. It tends to dissolve the differences between all things by providing a simple metric against which virtually all things can be assessed, and in terms of which decisions concerning them can be made. But the world upon which this metric is imposed is not as simple as this metric. Living systems – plants, animals, societies, ecosystems – are very diverse and each requires a great variety of particular materials to remain healthy. Monetisation, however, forces the great ranges of unique and distinct materials and processes that together sustain or even constitute life into an arbitrary and specious equivalence and decisions informed by these terms are likely to simplify, that is, to degrade and to disrupt, the ecological systems in which they are effective. Needless to say the application of large amounts of mindless energy under the guidance of the simplified or even simple-minded and often selfish considerations that all-purpose money makes virtually omnipotent and, when united with a capitalist ideology, even sacred, is in its nature stupid, brutal, and almost bound to be destructive.

With increases in the amounts of energy harnessed, with increases in the internal differentiation of social systems, with the monetisation of larger and larger portions of life, the disparity between the direction of cultural change and the goal of biological survival has surely become greater. We are led to ask whether civilisation, the elaborate stage of culture with which are associated money and banking, high energy technology, and social stratification and specialisation, is not maladaptive. It is, after all, in civilised societies that we can observe most clearly over-segregation, over-centralisation, over-sanctification, hypercoherence, the domination of higher by lower order systems, and the destruction of ecosystems. Civilisation has emerged only recently – in the past six thousand or so years – and it may yet prove to be an unsuccessful experiment.

If civilisation is an inevitable outcome of culture it may be asked if culture itself is in the long run adaptive. To the extent that cultural conventions are arbitrary men may devise aberrant regulatory structures, and to the extent that their activities are freed from limitation by the capacities of the ecosystems in which they occur to provide the energy they require, they may maintain their aberrant regulatory structures in the face of mounting difficulties for protracted periods of time. This does not seem possible for other creatures whose activity is dependent upon energy derived from the contemporary biological processes of the systems in which it occurs, and whose adaptive structures are much more narrowly specified by their biological characteristics. Nor could others with less powerful intellects develop ideologies that not only mask from themselves the maladaptiveness of their institutions but sanctify those aspects of them that are most maladaptive. Although the adaptive structures of other creatures may sometimes prove inadequate to cope with some environmental changes it is perhaps only in cultural populations that maladaptations can develop, for conscious logic and foresight may have to be brought into play to violate the logic of adaptive structure. And it is hard to imagine how the truth value of adaptively false propositions could be maintained in the absence of some abstract notion of truth.

We are led to a yet more radical question. If civilisation with its maladaptive regulatory hierarchies and misguiding ideologies is an inevitable outcome of culture, and culture in turn an inevitable outcome of the human level and type of intelligence, and if human intelligence is capable of violating adaptive logic, we may ask if human intelligence is in the long run adaptive, or if it is merely an evolutionary anomaly bound finally to be destroyed by its own contradictions or the contradictions of its cultural products. Gregory Bateson[25] has recently addressed this problem. He argues that purposefulness is the salient characteristic of human reason, a plausible suggestion, for purposefulness, subsuming both foresight and concentration, must have been strongly selected for during man's two or three million years on earth (and even earlier among man's pre-human forbears and other animals). But, located in the conscious minds of individuals and serving in the first instance their separate survivals, purposefulness must incline toward self-interest or even selfishness. (Indeed the philosopher Bergson[26] in recognising this problem took religion to be society's defense against the 'dissolving power' of the human mind.)

That some human purposes are selfish cannot be gainsaid. But Bateson suggests that the problem of purposefulness is more profound. Purposefulness, he argues, has a linear structure. A man at point A with goal D takes actions B and C, and with the achievement of D considers the process to be completed. Thus, the structure of purposeful action is linear – A→ B→ C→ D. But the world is not constructed in linear fashion. We have already discussed the circular structure of cybernetic, that is, self correcting, systems and it is well known that ecosystems are roughly circular in plan, with materials being cycled and recycled through the soil, the air, and organisms of many species. Moreover, the circularity of both cybernetic and ecosystemic structure blurs the distinction between cause and effect, or rather suggests to us that simple linear notions of causality, which lead us to think of actors, objects upon which they act and the transformation of such objects, are inadequate, for purposeful behaviour seldom affects only a single object, here designated D, but usually many other objects as well, often in complex and ramifying ways. Among those being affected in unforeseen and possibly unpleasant ways may be the actor himself.

It may be suggested, however, that linear, purposeful thought is adequate to the needs of simple hunters and gatherers, and not very destructive to the ecological systems in which they live, because both the scope and power of their activities are limited. It is when linear thought comes to guide the operations of an increasingly powerful technology over domains of ever increasing scope that disruption may become inevitable.

Bateson argues that the problem is not only to make men aware of the ramifying and circular structure of the universe, but to make the imperatives of this structure more compelling than their own linearly defined goals. He believes that this requires that more of their minds than their conscious reason be engaged. It is also necessary, be believes, to engage their primary processes, their emotions. He suggests that such engagement is achieved through art and religion. I would agree with this, and elsewhere[27] I have written about the role of the sacred and the numinous in adaptive structure. But to argue that more than reason is to be engaged in the restoration of adaptiveness to a system which seems beset by maladaptations is not to argue for the banishment of reason or its replacement by either mysticism or commitment. That our reason causes us difficulties does not mean that it should, or could possibly be, excluded from the solution of the difficulties to which it itself has contributed. Conscious reason has entered into evolutionary processes for better or worse. It cannot be ignored and should, obviously, be put to the task of ameliorating adaptive difficulties. An apparent paradox may be that attempts to solve problems of adaptation are likely to cause further problems, perhaps because 'problem solving' is in its nature linear. Moreover, the systems in which men participate are so complex that we cannot now, and probably never shall be, able to analyse them in sufficient detail to predict with precision the outcome of many of our own actions within them. We must, therefore, investigate the possibilities for developing theories of action which, although based upon incomplete knowledge, will permit us to participate in systems without destroying them and ourselves along with them. This task is not hopeless. To say that the complexity of living systems is so great as to confound prediction is not to say that we cannot apprehend the salient characteristics of their structures. It is, I think, the task of anthropologists, among others, to analyse the structures of social systems in terms of their adaptive characteristics, to develop theories of what the structures of healthy adaptive systems may be like, and also to develop theories of maladaptation and its amelioration. Some crude suggestions have been made here, but the necessary empirical and theoretical work has hardly begun.

NOTES

1 Hockett, C.F. and Ascher, R. (1964), 'The human revolution', *Current Anthropology*, 5, pp. 135-68; Romer, Alfred S. (1954), *Man and the Vertebrates*, Harmondsworth (First published in 1933).

2 Bateson, Gregory (1972a), 'Cybernetic explanation', *in* Bateson, Gregory, *Steps to an Ecology of Mind*, New York.

3 Bateson, Gregory (1963), 'The role of somatic change in evolution', *Evolution*, 17, pp. 529-39; Slobodkin, L.B. (1968), 'Toward a predictive theory of evolution', *in* Slobodkin, L.B., *Population, Biology and Evolution*, Syracuse.

4 Bateson (1963); Frisancho, Roberto (1975), 'Functional adaptation to high altitude hypoxia', *Science*, 187, pp. 313-19; Hurtado, Alberto (1964), 'Animals in high altitudes: resident man', *in* Dill, D.B. (ed.) *Adaptation to the Environment, Handbook of Physiology, Section 4*, Washington, pp. 843-60; Leake, Chauncey (1964), 'Perspectives on adaptation: historical background', *in* Dill, pp. 11-26; Slobodkin, L.B. (1968).

5 Kalmus, H. (1966), 'Control hierarchies', *in* Kalmus, H. (ed.) *Regulation and Control of Living Systems*, New York; Miller, James A. (1965a), 'Living systems: basic concepts', *Behavioral Science*, 10, pp. 193-257; Miller, James A. (1965b), 'Living systems: structure and process', *Behavioral Science*, 10, pp. 337-79; Pattee, Howard H. (ed.) (1973), *Hierarchy Theory*, International Library of Systems Theory and Philosophy; Powers, W.T., Clarke, R.K. and McFarland, R.L. (1960), 'A general feedback theory of human behavior', *Perceptual and Motor Skills*, 11, pp. 71-88, reprinted in Smith, Alfred G. (ed.) (1966), *Communication and Culture*, New York; Rappaport, R.A. (1969), 'Sanctity and adaptation', paper presented for Wenner-Gren symposium no. 44, *The Moral and Aesthetic Structure of Human Adaptation*, reprint in *Io* no. 7, Feb. 1970, and *Coevolution Quarterly*, 1, no. 2, 1974; Rappaport, R.A. (1971a), 'Nature culture and ecological anthropology', *in* Shapiro, Harry (ed.), *Man, Culture and Society* (revised edition), New York and Oxford; Rappaport, R.A. (1971b), 'The flow of energy in an agricultural society', *Scientific American*, 225, Sept., pp. 116-32; Simon, Herbert (1969), *The Sciences of the Artificial*, Boston.

6 Brookfield, H. and Brown, Paula (1963), *Struggle for Land*, Melbourne; Meggitt, M.J. (1965), *The Lineage System of the Mae Enga*, London; Meggitt, M.J. (1972), 'Understanding Australian Aboriginal society: kinship systems or cultural categories', *in* Reining, Priscilla (ed.) *Kinship Studies in the Morgan Centennial Year*, Washington; Ortiz, Alphonso (1970), *The Tewa World*, Chicago; Rappaport, R.A. (1968), *Pigs for the Ancestors*, New Haven and London; Sahlins, M. (1961), 'The segmentary lineage: an organisation of predatory expansion', *American Anthropologist*, 63, pp. 322-45.

7 Pask, Gordon (1968), 'Some mechanical concepts of goals, individuals, consciousness and symbolic evolution', Paper presented to Wenner-Gren Symposium on the Effects of Conscious Purpose on Human Adaptation.

8 Slobodkin (1968).

9 Hall, A.D. and Fagen, R.E. (1956), 'Definition of system', *General Systems Yearbook*, 1, pp. 18-28; Von Bertalanffy, L. (1969), *General Systems Theory*, Braziller, N.Y.

10 Hall and Fagen (1956).
11 See Sahlins, M. (1967), *The Tribesmen*, Englewood Cliffs.
12 Rappaport (1968).
13 Simon, Herbert (1969), *The Sciences of the Artificial*, Boston.
14 Young, I.J. and Rowley, W.F. (1967), 'The logic of disease', *International Journal of Neuropsychiatry*.
15 Flannery, Kent (1972), 'The cultural evolution of civilizations', *Annual Review of Ecology and Systematics*, III: Rappaport (1969).
16 Vickers, G. (1968), 'A theory of reflexive consciousness', Paper presented to Wenner-Gren Symposium on the Effects of Conscious Purpose on Human Adaptation.
17 Rappaport (1971b).
18 Flannery (1972); Rappaport (1969) and (1971a).
19 Tillich, Paul (1957), *Dynamics of Faith*, New York.
20 Galbraith, J.C. (1967), *The New Industrial State*, New York.
21 Slobodkin, L. and Rapoport, A. (1974), 'An optimal strategy of evolution', *The Quarterly Review of Biology*, 49, pp. 181-200.
22 White, Leslie (1949), *The Science of Culture,* New York, pp. 368-9; Ostwald, Wilhelm (1907), 'The modern theory of energetics', *The Monist*, 17, pp. 481-515.
23 The second clause of White's Law seems to be in error, for high energy technology, as suggested in 'The flow of energy in an agricultural society', seems to decrease efficiency. First, high energy technology decreases the thermodynamic efficiency of human subsistence activities. Hannon has recently estimated the slash and burn horticulture of the Maring of New Guinea, in which the only sources of energy are the gardeners themselves, to be forty times as efficient as 'modern food delivery systems' (Hannon, Bruce (1973), *Man in the Ecosystem*. Mss. Centre for Advanced Computation, University of Illinois at Urbana-Champaign). Whereas he estimates that the Maring produce ten units of food energy for every unit of energy input (my own estimate is closer to 20:1, Rappaport (1968)), he claims, following Herendeen, that in modern agriculture and food processing 45 units of fossil fuel are used to deliver 10 units to the supermarket (Herendeen, Robert A. (1973), *An Energy Input-Output Matrix for the United States*, 1963: Users Guide CAC Document No. 69, Centre for Advanced Computation, University of Illinois at Urbana-Champaign). Heichel has observed that in the more efficient modern systems such as maize cultivation, the return of food energy for energy input approaches 5:1, but in the less efficient systems like rice, sugarbeet and peanut cultivation, it sometimes is less than 1:1, and he further notes that in a 'surprising number of modern cropping systems a 10 to 50 fold increase in cultural energy has only doubled or tripled the digestible energy yield compared with the more primitive systems using substantially less technology' (Heichel, G.H. (1973), 'Comparative efficiency of energy use in crop production: Connecticut Agricultural Experiment Station', *New Haven: Bull.* 739, November, p. 18ff).

A more general index of the decreasing thermodynamic efficiency of contemporary industrial societies is implicit in the first part of 'White's Law' itself. If a figure already cited is correct, South African bushmen and Australian aborigines are able to support a person on 1/75 to 1/100 of what it takes to support an American. That is, from the standpoint of the ratio of energy flux per unit of standing biomass, hunters and gatherers are 75 to 100 times more efficient than we are. Or, to put it a little differently, modern societies, on a per capita basis, are entropising the world 75 to 100 times faster than are primitive hunting societies. We note in passing, an inconsistency between the two criteria of 'White's Law'.

It may be objected, of course, that the use of ever increasing amounts of fossil and hydroelectric energy has increased the efficiency of the ratio of biological energy input to food energy return, and this is undoubtedly true. But fossil energy is not without its costs, and neither is hydroelectric power, and, as it has been argued here, their use may encourage maladaptive trends.

24 Cook, Earl (1971), 'The flow of energy in an industrial society', *Energy and Power*, edited by *Scientific American*, pp. 83-94.

25 Bateson, G. (1972b), 'Effects of conscious purpose on human adaptation', *in Steps to an Ecology of Mind;* New York.

26 Bergson, Henri (1935), *The Two Sources of Morality and Religion*, trans. by R. Ashley Audra and Cloudsley Breveton with the assistance of W. Horsfall Carter, New York.

27 Rappaport (1969), (1971a); Rappaport, R.A. (1974), 'The obvious aspects of ritual', *Cambridge Anthropology*, 2, 1; Rappaport, R.A. (1975), 'Liturgies and lies', *International Yearbook for the Sociology of Religion and Knowledge*, 10 (in press).

ANNE WHYTE*

Systems as perceived: a discussion of 'Maladaptation in social systems'

In his paper on 'Maladaptation in social systems' Rappaport[1] extends his cybernetic approach to social systems by considering the evolution of systems in the context of 'maladaptation'. Maladaptation is the obverse of adaptation. It is an interference with the ability of systems to modulate their own processes and to change their structures in order to maintain homeostasis with their environment. The former changes are usually reversible whereas the latter are not. Maladaptive responses, like adaptive responses, arise within the system itself. They presuppose the existence of a definable system and an environment outside it which can generate stimuli to which the system responds internally.

Rappaport concentrates on the *structural* qualities of maladaptation because the systems with which he is principally concerned – social systems and ecosystems – are characterised by hierarchical and complex organisation of their structures and process links that are rarely simple. He identifies three classes of maladaptive responses: (a) cybernetic difficulties; (b) hierarchial anomalies; and (c) system domination by one of its parts.

Cybernetic difficulties interfere directly with the processes linking and organising the system. They are classically problems in information transmission between system elements. Hierarchial anomalies are structural characteristics of the arrangement of elements which *predispose* the system to cybernetic difficulties. Systems which are highly centralised or highly diversified are thus vulnerable to excessive time lags in response, and conversely also to over-response, because their organisational circuits are more complex and more sensitive to breakdown. System domination by one of its parts is maladaptive because it reduces the flexibility of the higher order system to respond to environmental changes. Maximum flexibility is maintained when a general system has only the general goal of

* Formerly Anne Kirkby.

survival. Lower-order systems have more specific goals and hence more rigidity in their range of adaptation. Thus 'over-specification' of a general system leads to maladaptation.

In the paper, Rappaport is concerned with 'living systems' including single organisms, groups of single species, and multi-species associations. He distinguishes between social systems and ecosystems – both of which I take to be multi-species associations – on the criterion of conscious purpose. This he defines as characteristic only of man. Conscious purpose, Rappaport argues, can set cultural evolution at odds with biological evolution so that 'cultural advance' is not system adaptation but ultimately may be biological *maladaptation*. Furthermore, he suggests that culture may not only be maladaptive, but that only in cultural systems can maladaptations develop.

The paper is a very stimulating exploration of new ideas. It raises two interesting questions. These concern first, the concepts of malaptation and adaptation; and second, the larger issue of the way we use and interpret systems models in explaining human behaviour and social organisation. Central to both questions is the problem of defining terms and concepts without attaching to them the constraints of our own values. Systems are subjective models and Kuhn's notion of the paradigm[2] as conventional scientific wisdom can also be applied to 'systems thinking'.

The use of the terms 'adaptation' and 'maladaptation' in systems analysis is usually made in the context of *adaptive systems* rather than *homeostatic systems*. The difference between the two types of systems is that whereas a homeostatic system maintains a constant operating environment in the face of random external fluctuations and will thus return to a stationary or 'steady state', an adaptive .system is one which has a 'preferred state' and 'if the system is not initially in a preferred state, the system will so act as to alter its state until one of the preferred ones is achieved'.[3]

Adaptive systems are thus usually thought of as 'goal-seeking' or teleological. They are difficult to analyse because they require that the 'preferred state' is identified. Furthermore, adaptation does not necessarily arise through changes in the processes and structure of the system, but is commonly modelled as feedback *from* the system producing modification *in the environment* until the inputs are modulated to achieve the desired response. Thus it is the environment that is adapting to the system rather than necessarily the other way round.

Rappaport postulates that adaptation occurs in homeostatic systems whose only goal is that of 'survival'. In his terms, adaptation can involve not just modulation of internal processes but irreversible structural changes in the system. There is therefore no clear way to distinguish survival from non-survival. When faced with a real-world social system that has radically altered its structure, it becomes a matter of opinion whether it is the same system that has survived through adaptive response, or has perished through maladaptation and been replaced by a new system. Even if one avoids the notion of 'preferred states' and their teleological implications, the 'steady state' to which homeostatic responses tend, need to be more rigorously defined than simply 'survival'.

The argument here is that 'maladaptation' is not an axiomatic term but a contextual one. It depends heavily on the scale of system chosen and where the system is 'closed' or bounded in relation to its environment; on the time scales considered; and on the criteria accepted for 'survival'. These provide the minimum *text* (in Nagel's terms)[4] by which the concept of maladaptation can be linked to empirical systems. Without such a context, maladaptations can become adaptations and vice versa. Rappaport himself stresses the importance of time scales for distinguishing between adaptive and maladaptive responses. The *same set of responses* (e.g. agriculture and irrigation leading to intensive crop specialisation) can be evaluated as 'adaptive' on the time scale of social development from nomadic hunting and gathering bands to the centralised state; and as 'maladaptive' viewed on a geological time scale. From this second perspective, the modification of diverse ecosystems to monocultures leads to a maladaptive state in which man, like Samson in the temple, destroys his supporting ecosystems and himself with them.

Similarly, 'maladaptation' is very dependent upon the closing of one's system. Since all the systems with which we are concerned are open-systems, the closing of a system, or the imposing of boundaries, is a matter of judgment made in the context of our experience of real-world phenomena and the objectives of our analysis. What is defined as 'inside' the system and what remains 'outside' to form its environment obviously has significant implications for the results of systems analysis. Input-output analysis and definition of 'adaptive' and 'maladaptive' response both depend on where the boundaries of the system are drawn. In his paper, Rappaport sometimes draws the line around *both* Man and Nature so that man becomes the agent of conscious intelligence for a general biological system. At other points in the argument, he sets Man and Nature apart as two contrasting systems in which Nature adapts through non-conscious and genetic organisation and Man 'maladapts' through his capacity for violating adaptive logic by conscious purpose.

That 'survival' is a necessary, but not sufficient, condition for defining adaption and maladaption is evident from both systems theory and from our experience of real social systems. Systems tend to elaborate and to enlarge themselves. To return to Slobodkin's metaphor,[5] they may be 'players of the existential game' in which the only reward for successful play is to be allowed to continue playing, because the player cannot leave the table. But they can play in more or less comfort, and get more or less satisfaction from playing an elaborate, elegant or devious game.

The dependence of 'maladaptation' on its context and its tendency to be confused with teleological systems produce difficulties in trying to state a general model for the evolution of social systems. Furthermore, the term emphasises a Stimulus-Response view of social evolution rather than either a learning model or one in which *creativity* is a quality of the system itself. I would prefer to substitute *system-change* or *system-enlargement* as a central notion for 'adaptation' and 'maladaptation'. The concept of system-change is neutral in that it does not specify whether the change is responsive or creative within the system. The changes with which we are almost exclusively concerned in studying social systems are those inherent in system-enlargement.

The main processes associated with increasing scale of social systems and thus with their evolution include:

1. *Greater differentiation and greater integration*; as the scale of a system enlarges to incorporate other systems as its sub-systems, its parts will become more specialised (e.g. economic production and social relations). At the same time the system will *create* new forms of organisation (including hierarchies) to integrate and manage the wider differentiation of its parts which each become more dependent upon the total enlarging system.
2. *Increased rate of change*; wider organisations facilitate the diffusion of innovations and the generation of more innovations so that the potential *rate* of change is accelerated – a process which is shown historically.
3. *Increased generation of conflicts*; it follows from an increased differentation and rate of change that the generation of conflicts also increases. Their resolution is a major part of the learning process of system integration.
4. *Reduction in the efficiency of energy use*; the enlargement of scale, together with specialisation of the system's parts, lead to a reduction in the diversity of systems and a greater expenditure of energy on communication and organisation. Consequently there is less output in return for input in energy terms.
5. *Division of labour and social institutions.*
6. *Codifying of social responsibility and social relations*; as systems enlarge, roles and institutions become more specialised and more sharply delimited, and conflicts become more acute so that more formal codes are necessary for regulating social relations.

The emphasis here is on analysis of these processes of system enlargement without reference to a specific datum of 'steady state' or 'preferred state'. The suggested model of evolution is dynamic rather than homeostatic or adaptive. Thus the social system moves through a sequence of states that are not repeated but follow a line of the system's 'trajectory'[6] as it elaborates and enlarges itself. The trajectory of the system is determined not only by feedback from the environment but by the system itself identifying new preferred states (i.e. learning) and by its own accelerating capacity to produce innovations and conflicts – both of which generate system, and social, change.

In suggesting a systems model that reduces the difficulty I have with a 'maladaptive' one, I am retaining the present paradigm of 'systems thinking'. That is to say, systems models may be used as straightforward heuristic devices to 'picture' and organise complex data; or as more sophisticated analogue models to extend the domain of the theory to some part of reality; or they may be regarded as providing explanation in themselves. As such, they remain however an external view of the social system that does not necessarily match up with what we know about human behaviour. They are weakest where social change is occuring most rapidly, because the dimensions of change are less the stimulus-response, input-output transactions between the social system and its environment, and more the perceptual context in which decisions are made within the system.

A perception paradigm is thus a necessary corrollary to a cybernetic systems one. It emphasises that for every element and process (times n individuals); and for every transaction between the system and the environment there is a perceived transaction. And it is within this perceived system that human behaviour takes place. Viewed from within the system, change is brought about not by adaptive response to environmental stimuli, for that implies more perfect knowledge and steadfastness of 'conscious purpose' than most of us possess. It is achieved through a series of choices and errors made in the context of risk and uncertainty. Social systems construct perceptual models of themselves which provide a major input to the direction of their choices, and thus of the system's trajectory.

In such a decision-making systems approach, Rappaport's analysis of the structural anomalies of hierarchies which lead to maladaptation would be modelled as a set of choice relationships. These choices are made at different levels of decision-making within the system (which is itself nested) and each provide contextual parameters for the other. Thus the relationship is not uni-directional and linear, but forms a network. Higher-order regulators (in Rappaport's terms) make choices which facilitate, regulate or mandate the choices of lower-order regulators. Similarly, lower order regulators constrain and open up the choices available to higher-order decision-makers. Thus, central government can ban, by decree, or regulate and encourage by tax and subsidy arrangements the production of certain crops, or the activities of specific institutions. But they are not operating in a vaccum or with knowledge that is *systematically* superior or inferior to that of others. They are faced with the past, ongoing and expected future correct choices and errors being made by lower-order regulators. Similarly, each higher and lower order regulator makes choices with regard to what others at his own level are doing, and each decision-maker will act as a higher and lower order regulator as his role shifts within different parts of the system and through time.

The resulting social system looks less like a well-defined cybernetic system than a shifting network of perceptions, choices and roles; whose limits are described by the time and space horizons of the actors. Its evolution depends upon their subjective probabilities and subjective utilities. Cybernetic systems and subjective decision-making models used together provide powerful tools for analysing social systems. The cybernetic model stands in some sense as a normative one implying full rationality and knowledge, against which the behavioural one charts the trajectory and the 'wobbles' of the enlarging social system. Their integration becomes more possible in the investigation of real social systems as field techniques are improved for the behavioural analysis of perception and decision-making. But that leads on to another discussion.

NOTES

1 Rappaport, R.A., in this volume, pp. 49-71.
2 Kuhn, T.S. (1962), *The Structure of Scientific Revolutions*, Chicago.
3 Rosen, R. (1967), *Optimality Principles in Biology*, London.
4 Nagel, E. (1961), *The Structure of Science*, New York.
5 Slobodkin, L.B. (1968), 'Toward a predictive theory of evolution', *in* Slobodkin, L.B., *Population, Biology and Evolution*, Syracuse.
6 Ashby, W.R. (1963), *An Introduction to Cybernetics*, New York.

R.A. RAPPAPORT

Normative models of adaptive processes: a response to Anne Whyte[1]

In her discussion of 'Maladaptation in social systems'[2] Dr. Whyte raises a number of points that merit more extended discussion than the present context allows. It is important, however, that I do respond now, if only relatively briefly, both to clarify my position and to increase the likelihood of further consideration of the general problems being approached by more scholars than are presently considering them. I shall take up a number of Whyte's points in roughly the order that she raised them.

Whyte adopts a traditional distinction between homeostatic systems and adaptive systems, the former maintaining 'steady states', the latter seeking 'preferred states'. I do not think that this distinction can boast either verisimilitude or utility, and in my paper I attempted to dissolve it. I take living systems to be hierarchically organised complexes of sub-systems, sub-sub-systems, and so on, in which even structural changes in lower order systems (i.e. sub-systems) may maintain more inclusive systems (i.e. relations among the lower order systems) unchanged. Rather than define adaptive systems as those which seek a preferred state (I agree with Whyte concerning the difficulties of specifying preferred states, the more so because I take identifiable preferred states to be more or less ephemeral and because I take the ultimate goal of relatively autonomous living systems, simply to keep functioning, to be low in specificity) I take them to be systems which can respond homeostatically to perturbation, through structural changes in themselves if necessary. It seems to me that the distinction between what is connoted by the terms 'preferred state' and 'steady state' are not radical. Both terms may be taken to refer to reference values in cybernetic mechanisms.

Whyte's point, made later in the course of her remarks, that the model I proposed emphasises, perhaps unduly, response to perturbation or stress (i.e. response to dangerous stimulus) and virtually ignores learning and creativity is well taken, and any further development of the model should give much more attention to these factors. This does not, however, obviate the possibility, and in my view the desirability, of regarding preferred as well as steady state values as cybernetic reference values – as indeed they are in the two classic examples of mechanical cybernetic mechanisms, thermostats and automated gun-sights. Furthermore, since reversible responses to fluctuating perturbations and structural modification in response to more or less enduring environmental changes seem to be organised into ordered sequence in nature I can see no reason to separate them radically, although they can, of course, be distinguished formally.

Whyte further notes in her discussion of adaptive versus homeostatic systems that adaptation 'is commonly modelled as feedback *from* the system producing modification *in the environment* until the inputs are modulated to achieve the desired responses, thus it is the environment that is adapting to the system rather than necessarily the other way round'. Now it is surely true that in some instances the response to stress is the elimination of the stressing factor, a possibility I recognised in the paper. I would simply note that this is not always the case and, second, that there are obviously limits to the environmental alterations that can be accomplished or, if accomplished, gotten away with. Environmental alterations, it is hardly necessary to point out, especially when they are massive, in the long or even not so-long-run may be maladaptive in either the structural sense emphasised in the paper or in the material sense of degrading the ecosystems upon which the actors depend.

An important problem recognised by Whyte is that of the meaning of the term 'survival'. She argues that since, in my terms, 'adaptation can involve not just modulation of internal processes but irreversible structural changes . . . there is no clear way to distinguish survival from non-survival' and that 'when faced with a real-world social system that has radically altered its structure, it becomes a matter of opinion whether it is the same system that has survived through adaptive response, or has perished through maladaptation and been replaced by a new system'.

Such difficulties are not to be minimised. We should not be mislead by the fact that the distinction between survival and non-survival is relatively clearcut in one sub-class of living systems, the higher organisms, which are either alive or dead. It might seem, analogously, that populations and species are either extant or extinct. But, as Slobodkin and Rapoport[3] have pointed out, there are two ways for populations or species to cease to exist. Simplifying their argument: First, 'when there no longer exist any descendants of a population we [may] say that it is extinct.' The evolutionary processes that it embodied have come to an end. On the other hand, a species may be said to cease to exist when 'enough evolutionary change [has occurred] in its descendants so that they may be called [a new] species'. The evolutionary processes that it had embodied continue. 'From our standpoint, a population that has descendants, even if they are called by a different species name, is evolutionarily successful . . .'[4] In light of Slobodkin and Rapoport's discussion it seems to me that the question is not whether or not there have been structural transformations but whether or not there has been processual continuity. In my view an ecosystem which has replaced all or nearly all of its constituent species several times through the course of a succession in which the later stages are contingent upon the earlier survives (that is, is 'the same system'), for its processual continuity has been orderly and unbroken. Similarly, in my view, England as *a* system has survived from the fifth century until the present.[5] Survival, I am arguing is, in the first instance, to be understood as the persistence of processes rather than of entities defined in terms of particular constituents or particular arrangements, genetic or institutional, of constituents. (What we discriminate as discrete entities – organisms, states, ecosystems, even pre-Cambrian rocks – are, of course, organised by, the product of, or even the summation of such processes).

In a changing world processual continuity must entail structural (evolutionary) change as well as reversible compensatory change. In 'Maladaptation in social systems' I argued that processual continuity requires a certain hierarchical ordering of the constituent processes, and I made some suggestions concerning what these orderly relations might be with respect to operating time, longevity, reversibility, sanctity, specificity of goals and directives, material determination and contingency. I argued that anomalies among these relations threaten processual continuity by themselves impeding responses to stress (and, to follow Whyte's suggestion, opportunity) and by producing responses the material and social effects of which – loss of local autonomy, hypercoherence, environmental degradation and the like – also endanger processual continuity. I argued, this is to say, for a structural conception of maladaptation, but I further suggested that the structural characteristics of adaptive processes do have substantive implications. Because of the hierarchical ordering of contingency and specificity, biological (including ecosystemic) considerations must take precedence over institutional ones in adaptive processes.

Conceptual problems – and serious ones at that – remain, and I do not pretend to have solutions for them. For one thing, the criteria of continuity and discontinuity may not always be easy to apply and some residuum of ambiguity may always remain. Whyte's insistence on the specification of the systemic levels under consideration is important. I agree with her entirely, but it is important to understand that such specification does not itself solve the problems of relations between levels, of the relations, that is to say, between processual continuities and discontinuities on different systemic levels, and how to speak of them. For instance, is it proper – or even if proper, useful – to say in a particular case that the population survives but that the social order (I take the term 'social order' to refer to an arrangement of regulators, regulations and regulated entities or processes prevailing during a particular period among a particular people), or some level of the social order, has become extinct? I have argued that in conformity to the structure of contingency, processual continuity among the biological components of systems takes precedence and, following this argument, it may be suggested that the term 'survival' should be reserved for reference to biological (including ecological) continuity. This usage not only may increase clarity somewhat, but may also emphasise the possibility that discontinuities in other aspects of systems may serve the continuity of their biological components. Even violent revolutions destroying existing social orders may, at least in some instances, be regarded as ultimate attempts to correct living systems so beset by structural anomaly as to make less radical cures seem hopelessly difficult or impossible. The continuity of general purpose living systems, this is to say, may require the termination of particular subsystemic processes and their replacement by others, and the necessity for such change may effect very high order – even highest order – regulation. Conversely, as the paper emphasised, the perpetuation of particular regulatory arrangements may threaten the survival of the more inclusive systems in which they occur.

In the terms proposed here instances of non-survival or extinction in systems dominated by men are rare, but instances of more or less sharp discontinuities in regulatory processes and of the replacement of one set of regulatory arrangements by another are relatively common. Structural anomalies of the sort discussed in the paper may be so stressful that they may often provoke attempts to correct themselves. This is a seemingly less gloomy view of history than emphasised in the paper and, I would note, it is in general agreement with Flannery,[6] who argues that attempts to correct structural anomalies through massive and sometimes deliberate transformative action seem important in social evolution. It should not be forgotten, however, that radical correction, as through revolution, is costly in matter, energy, wealth, blood, time, emotion and trust, among other things, and revolutions may actually reduce the amount of information systems contain, at least for a while: libraries and records may be destroyed, knowledgable men killed or driven into exile. They often fail to correct what they aim to correct while succeeding in establishing structures that are, or soon become, as maladaptive as those they replace. Nothing short of revolutionary transformations may be sufficient to deal with the problems of some social systems; however, it is important to note that Slobodkin and Rapoport[7] have demonstrated mathematically that, other things being equal, transformation through continuous small, incremental changes serves processual continuity more effectively than occasional, massive and radical changes.

Thus, while I am in general agreement with Whyte's discussion of the context-specific nature of maladaptation, she and I also agree, I think, that there is much more to be said than, simply, that which is maladaptive for systems at one level may be adaptive for more inclusive, higher level systems, or vice versa. Systems at various levels of inclusiveness are, of course, often at odds. It is surely beyond dispute that the immediate interests of men and of the societies of which they are parts do not always coincide, nor do those of societies and ecosystems. This is indubitable, and specification of the systemic levels implicated in any such contradiction or conflict is surely necessary. However, as I tried to point out in the paper, relations of precedence pertain between the goals and needs of systems of different degrees of inclusiveness and longevity. Thus, for the narrowly defined short-run special interests of some individuals to prevail over the long-run requirements of the societies and ecosystems *of which they are parts* is, it seems to me, maladaptive *per se.* It violates what I take to be orderly relations of specificity and time and, more importantly, contingency as well. Contingency, it seems to me, is *most immediately* of the part upon that of which it is a part. Less immediately, the persistence of the whole is itself contingent upon the persistence of at least some of its constituents. This is to say that contingency is *ultimately* circular.

Whyte points out that 'What is defined as "inside" the system and what remains "outside" to form its environment obviously has significant implications for the results of systems analysis'. With this there can be no argument. However, I attempted to make a somewhat different point, namely that this is not simply a problem of analysis. It is also – and most importantly – a real-world problem. Men impose conceptual and physical boundaries upon the world in ways which do not necessarily, or even usually, correspond to the continuities and discontinuities of nature. They make their worlds with words. Indeed, many creation myths are quite explicit about this, deriving the world from creative Word. Be this as it may, it is, if not inevitable, at least highly likely that, in imposing distinctions upon the world, men will pit themselves against the nature of which they are parts and upon which their lives are in fact contingent. This, of course, becomes increasingly problematic as men become increasingly powerful and thus increasingly capable of transforming their understandings of the world into physical reality. Therefore, as Whyte notes, at some points in my argument I 'drew the line around both Man and Nature so that man becomes the conscious intelligence for a general biological system' (certainly the case in instances in which man is an ecological dominant), and at other points set them apart as 'two contrasting' – and, I would say, often opposed systems. To put this a little differently, as an ecological dominant Man is the conscious intelligence of general biological systems, but his perceived interests may set him against those systems. I take this to be an aspect of the human condition and not simply an analytic problem, although, of course, it produces analytic problems.

We come here to Whyte's assertion that a 'perception paradigm is . . . a necessary corrollary to a cybernetic system one'. I would go further. A cognition-perception paradigm is not simply a corrollary of cybernetic paradigms. It is intrinsic to them. Cybernetic mechanisms do not generally respond to changes in the states of variables directly, but to *information*, to *signals*, concerning such changes. Changes must be *detected*, and in system with living regulators signals concerning changes must be *interpreted* by the regulators. Such interpretation can only proceed in accordance with their *understandings,* which include their *values*. For me, although it was perhaps not made sufficiently clear in the paper,. the very idea of a regulator entails perception, cognition, and evaluation, at least when we are dealing with human regulators, but processes that are at least analogous to perception, cognition and evaluation are to be observed even in mechanical and electronic systems.

In a number of earlier publications[8] I have contrasted what I have called 'cognised' and 'operational' models. Cognised models are descriptions of the knowledge and beliefs concerning their environment entertained by a people. They are intrinsic to whatever regulatory processes prevail among the group. Operational models are descriptions of approximately the same domains prepared in accordance with the assumptions and methods proposed by some scientific theory – ecology, systems theory, structural theory. The two models are overlapping but not necessarily isomorphic. Operational models may include elements of which the actors are unaware, such as micro-organisms, cognised models may include elements which scientific theories do not generally recognise to exist, such as spirits.

While it is in terms of the cognised model that men act in nature it is upon nature herself (as represented as best we can by an operational model) that men do act, and it is nature herself that acts upon men, nurturing them, impoverishing them or even destroying them. Now it seems to me that disparities between men's images of nature (including society) and the actual structure of nature are inevitable. Men are, surely, gifted learners and may continually enlarge and correct their knowledge of their environments. But their images of nature are always simpler than nature herself, and often incorrect, for the ecological and social systems within which men act are complex and subtle beyond full comprehension. In short, people can, and frequently do, 'get it wrong'.

This may seem arrogant. To say that 'they' often 'get it wrong' suggests that 'we' (perhaps in our operational models) usually 'get it right'. We must keep in mind that the operational models of social and ecological systems that we prepare are simplified, crude, and at best only relatively accurate. More important, it should not be imagined that a people's cognised model is merely a less accurate or more ignorant view of the world than is represented by an analyst's operational model. Cognised models are not to be understood as descriptive models. That is, their goal, function or purpose is not primarily to describe the world. They should be taken to be aspects or components of the regulatory mechanisms through which populations adapt. That is to say they are intrinsic to the adaptive structure of human populations. Therefore the important question concerning a cognised model is not the extent to which it resembles what the analyst, in accordance with his theory and method, takes to be reality (i.e. the operational model), but the extent to which it elicits adaptive responses. Analysis consists of an integration of cognised and operational models so that the effects of behaviour undertaken with respect to cognised models on the ecosystems and social systems within which the behaviour is undertaken can be described and assessed.

It might seem that the closer a cognised model resembles a rigorously developed operational model corresponding to it the more effective it will be. However, there does not seem to be any simple or direct relationship between the amount of testable empirical knowledge included in a cognised model and the adaptiveness of the behaviour it elicits. As I have suggested elsewhere, it is by no means certain that scientific representations of nature are more adaptive than the images of worlds inhabited by spirits and unknowable forces that guide the actions of men in some 'primitive' societies. Indeed, our 'more accurate', cognised models may be less adaptive than the 'less accurate', cognised models of some 'primitives'. To invest nature with the supernatural is to provide her with some protection against human parochialism, greed and destructiveness. On the other hand, parochialism, greed and destructiveness may be encouraged, or at least not strongly discouraged, by a rational, naturalistic view of nature.

Getting it wrong, then, is not a matter of simple empirical inaccuracy, nor does increase in empirical accuracy necessarily correct errors which are not errors of fact but of act. The rational empirical models of nature that are available to contemporary western society do not seem to have reduced errors of act. Needless to say, with ever larger numbers of people and ever more powerful technologies acting in or on systems of ever increasing scope and coherence the consequences of error become ever more serious.

This leads to my final points. I do not at all disagree with the suggestions Whyte makes concerning aspects of 'system-change'. They are hardly new and they seem to me to be patent. But they do not serve as an alternative to my suggestions, or at least what was intended by my suggestions, concerning the structure of adaptation and maladaptation. It was not my intention to propose 'a general model for the evolution of social systems' much less a neutral one, nor even to propose a descriptive model of adaptive social structure that could be substantiated by a single historical case. It was, rather, my intention to propose a *normative* model in terms of which the adaptiveness of historical systems might be *assessed* and their difficulties diagnosed.

The notion of assessing cultural systems may also seem arrogant and may require justification. It must be kept in mind that the criterion proposed, adaptiveness, while a general one, is not comprehensive. It probably has little or nothing to say about much of culture content. Moreover, it should also be kept in mind that our theories and the operational models we develop through their application are bound to be imperfect and may well be erroneous, without value or even misleading. Assessment also runs counter to a strong tradition in anthropology. This tradition, which rebelled against a yet older tradition that made invidious comparisons between 'the west' and 'the savages' on the grounds of progress disguised as evolution, holds that societies and cultures are to be understood, but not judged, at least not in terms alien to themselves. I would surely agree that we should not judge other cultures and societies by the values of our own, and I recognise that it would be naive to assert that the concepts of adaptation and maladaptation are culture-free. They come out of western scientific tradition (as do such other concepts as structure, system, function, culture and society), and surely we must guard as best we can against covert ethnocentrism, but to say that the concepts of adaptation and maladaptation come out of a particular intellectual tradition is not to say that they, or their application to other traditions, are ethnocentric. In my view they are not. Their terms are, it seems to me, as neutral as it is possible to be in dealing with matters of life, death and extinction. But the consequences of applying these terms to historical systems are not neutral. Some, I think, can be shown to be more or less adaptive, or more or less maladaptive than others. Our own culture would, I think, fare very badly in any such rigorous assessment. If this is ethnocentrism it is inverted ethnocentrism.

It is important to note here that the concepts of adaptation and adaptive structure are more inclusive than are the concepts of culture or society: they apply to all living systems. The suggestion is, then, that we assess the specifics of cultural structures in terms of the structural characteristics of a universal phenomenon. That cultures and organisms are ontologically distinct does not make it illegitimate to do so. The emergence of culture among our earliest hominid forebears must have been a consequence of normal adaptive processes occurring among particular populations of organisms, and surely must have contributed importantly to the persistence of their evolutionary line. Moreover, the persistence of all cultural processes is contingent upon the survival of the organisms that they organise. As I noted in the paper, there are no particular institutions which any population of humans could not replace or even abolish, but if the humans perished the culture would cease to exist. It is sometimes said that cultures 'have lives of their own', but this is only a figure of speech. Men must given them breath. Of course it is true that cultures and the societies they organise follow imperatives of their own. Not all cultural or social facts are to be accounted for by reference to physiological, demographic or ecological processes, and the exigencies of cultures can lead men to violate the nature from which they and their cultures sprang and of which they remain parts. But that is the real-world problem with which I am concerned and to which 'Maladaptation in social systems' is addressed. I reiterate in closing that the formulation I have offered is crude, tentative, incomplete and no doubt wrong in some or many particulars. It may even be so wrong that it could contribute to the very problems it addresses. But I will under any circumstances insist that the problems with which it grapples are real. Adequate means for conceptualising them and for conceiving how they may be corrected have, in my view, been lacking. I have made some suggestions concerning these matters in 'Maladaptation in social systems' in the hope that they might serve as a basis for discussion, and I am grateful to Dr Whyte both for the attention she has given them and for the opportunity she has given me to consider them further in these comments. That they prove ultimately 'correct' matters less than that they stimulate others to think about the problems with which they are concerned.

NOTES

1 Whyte, Anne, in this volume, pp. 73-8.
2 Rappaport, R.A., in this volume, pp. 49-71.
3 Slobodkin, L.B. and Rapoport, Anatol (1974), 'An optimal strategy of evolution', *The Quarterly Review of Biology*, 49, pp. 181-200.
4 All citations from p. 183.
5 See Cadwallader, Mervyn L. (1959), 'The cybernetic analysis of change in complex social organisations', *American Journal of Sociology*, 65, pp. 154-7, on 'ultra-stable systems'.
6 Flannery, Kent (1972), 'The cultural evolution of civilisations', *Annual Review of Ecology and Systematics*, 3, pp. 399-426.
7 Slobodkin and Rapoport (1974).
8 Rappaport, R.A. (1963). 'Aspects of man's influence on island ecosystems: Alteration and control', *in* Fosberg, F.R. (ed.), *Man's Place in the Island Ecosystem*. Honolulu; Rappaport, R.A. (1968), *Pigs for the Ancestors*, New Haven; Rappaport, R.A. (1969), 'Sanctity and adaptation', Paper prepared for the Wenner-Gren symposium, *The Moral and Aesthetic Structure of Human Adaptation*. Reprinted 1970 in *Io*, no. 7, 1974; in *Co-evolution Quarterly*, 1, no. 2. Rappaport, R.A. (1971), 'Nature culture and ecological anthropology', *in* Shapiro, Harry (ed.), *Man, Culture and Society* (revised edition), New York and Oxford.

COLIN RENFREW

Space, time and polity

How can the archaeologist reconstruct the social organisation of prehistoric communities? Can we hope to trace the evolution of societies from the palaeolithic hunting group to the modern state from archaeological data by the use of logically tenable procedures of reasoning, or must any statement about the social organisation of an early society be based upon a facile and ultimately untenable 'analogy' with some entirely unrelated modern community? In this article I hope to approach this problem in terms of spatial organisation – not because the notion of 'territoriality' has recently been fashionable in anthropology, but because the insights of the modern human geographer into spatial organisation offer many potential applications to archaeology which we are only just beginning to explore. In general the geographer, with a frequently simplified model of modern economising man blindly obeying a Law of Least Effort or a Principle of Least Action, is no more concerned with the social organisation of non-market societies than is the structural anthropologist with a Christaller hexagonal lattice. Yet, as I hope to show, the evolution of human society can profitably be considered in terms of spatial patterning. To do so, however, inevitably implies for the archaeologist the final abandonment of the simple notion of 'culture', with its counterpart of 'people' as a fundamental unit of discussion, for these impose upon the data, and hence upon our vision of the past, categories of thought which seem today of doubtful value or validity, obscuring just those questions which we may hope to answer. A further factor contributing to the failure of archaeology to arrive at a coherent view of the development of social organisation may be the sometimes uncritical use of ready-made anthropological concepts, which are validated by reference to data different from those of archaeology. It is our task to formulate concepts and ideas which can operate upon archaeological data, but which do at the same time have real meaning and interest when applied to living societies.

Social anthropology and social archaeology: a distinction

The prospects of reconstructing prehistoric social organisation has been regarded by some anthropologists with pessimism.[1] Given the limited range of ethnographic reporting before the accounts of Cook and Forster, the view that 'The belief that something significant about the sociology of a remotely antique human society can be inferred from a study of its material residues is similar to supposing that if we had a random selection of the utterances of unknown meaning from some dozens of unknown and now disused languages we could use this evidence to validate useful general propositions about the nature of human language'[2] effectively abandons the hope of studying non-literate societies prior to about 1700 A.D.

In order to counter this claim, it is necessary to bring out the rather special interpretation of social organisation which underlies it. Leach is so mesmerised by the variety in human communities, by the intriguing uniqueness of each, that no suspicion of discernible order or pattern emerges: 'in archaeology the accumulation of more and more evidence increases our information about historical artefacts; it does not increase the probability of our sociological guesswork, since the whole range of contemporary ethnographic variety still needs to be taken into account for each new sample of evidence'.[3] The image which this statement conjures up of social anthropology as a disordered thesaurus of anecdotal observations, entirely lacking in structure, may not be what Leach intends. The dissociation between 'material residues' and 'sociology' does establish, however, a curious polarisation between mind and matter which the best of recent anthropological work, including Leach's own earlier writings, has managed to avoid.

The crux of the matter may well indeed be language, as Leach's analogy perhaps betrays. For the social anthropologist invariably proceeds by learning the language of the community which he is studying, seeking to perceive the world as his informants perceived it, working towards a shared perception, a shared cognition, which he can then interpret. From this cognised model which he forms of the society (and the world) as its members see it, he proceeds to an analysis of the society as it operates 'in reality', that is to say from the standpoint of the modern anthropoligical observer. The focus of study shifts as follows;

Whether dealing with kinship, myth or religion the social anthropologist has traditionally worked in this way, the functionalist school focussing upon the relation between the cognitive and operational aspects within specific societies, the structuralists comparing the cognitive perceptions in different societies. To the outsider it often seems that the social anthropologist is more concerned with what people think than with what they actually do, which perhaps partly explains the comparative neglect into which ethnography has fallen.

The prehistoric archaeologist has no access to direct verbal testimony, and testimony of any kind – in the form of visual representations of the world or other explicit symbols – forms only a small part of his material of study. His progression must therefore be from the data – the artefacts and associated materials in their contexts – as relics of past actions, towards a knowledge of these actions (whether individually or in aggregate) and hence of the operation of certain aspects of the society. In certain cases it may be legitimate to infer or propose aspects of the world picture, the working of the society as recognised by that society, from such operational data:

I suggest that it is a failure adequately to distinguish these very different procedures, to distinguish between the actions of a society as interpreted by its members and as analysed by the modern anthropologist, which has recently darkened counsel. The distinction has been made to very good effect in practice by Rappaport.[4] And it is, of course, precisely that which some anthropologists seek to convey by those infelicitous and synthetic terms 'emic' (i.e. cognitive) and 'etic' (i.e. operational).[5] Harris's words indeed offer the archaeologist comfort and encouragement: 'You are relatively free from the mystifications which arise from the emic approach . . . Your operationally defined categories and processes are superior to the unoperational definitions and categories of much of contemporary cultural anthropology . . . Archaeologists, shrive yourselves of the notion that the units which you seek to reconstruct must match the units in social organisation which contemporary ethnographers have attempted to tell you exist.'[6]

But what then are the effective units of social organisation, these 'operationally defined categories of the archaeologist?' Elman Service, after offering us a hierarchy of band, tribe, chiefdom and state, increasingly used by the archaeologist, dramatically lost his nerve, suggesting instead 'Three aboriginal types which might represent evolutionary stages: (1) the Egalitarian Society out of which grew (2) the Hierarchical Society, which was replaced in only a few instances in the world by the Empire-State that was the basis of the next stage (3) the Archaic Civilisation or Classical Empire'.[7] This offers an alternative so imprecisely formulated that even the initial capitals can do little to recommend it. Are the other existing archaeological categories and procedures for dealing with social organisation as 'superior' as Harris flatteringly suggests?

The archaeological conundrum: what is a social group?

For fifty years archaeologists have imagined that they knew the answer to this question. In Europe it was most clearly expressed by Gordon Childe, who introduced the concept of a culture as an entity with extension in space and time.[8] He wrote:

> We find certain types of remains – pots, implements, ornaments, burial sites, house forms – constantly recurring together. Such a complex of regularly associated traits we shall term a 'cultural group' or just a 'culture'. We assume that such a complex is the material expression of what today would be called a people.
>
> The same complex may be found with relatively negligible diminutions over a wide area. In such cases of the total and bodily transferance of a complete culture from one place to another we think ourselves justified in assuming a 'movement of people'.

Precisely this view, which has been stigmatised in recent years as the 'normative approach',[9] has been lucidly reasserted recently by Rouse:[10] 'Prehistorians start with the archaeological facts and from them synthesise a picture of ethnic groups and their distribution, nature and development, using an inductive strategy . . . [There are] four questions that the prehistorian attempts to answer by means of his research: (1) Who produced the archaeological remains under study, that is to which ethnic groups did the producers belong? (2) Where and when did each group live? (3) What was each group like in its culture, morphology, social structure, or language, as the case may be? (4) How and why did each group become that way?'

On this view the archaeologist makes two important implicit assertions, neither of which is explicitly questioned. First that the archaeological record contains homogeneous assemblages of objects (i.e. cultures) which may be distinguished as entities from other assemblages. And second that these homogeneous distributions are the material expression of a social reality, the ethnic group. This term, 'ethnic group', is rarely defined with precision, but does not necessarily have racial implications. Rouse[11] uses the term 'in a general sense to refer collectively' to four different kinds of groups: cultural, morphological (i.e., racial), social, and linguistic: 'A people and its culture are but sides of the same coin, the term "people" referring to the individuals who compose the group, and the term "culture" to the activities that distinguish the group.'

Already in 1958, Willey and Phillips[12] recognised the difficulties in such a view, and admitted that 'phase' (which in their special terminology is analogous to Childe's term 'culture' with its specific and often restricted spatial distribution) cannot be directly equated with 'society'. In their words:

> The equivalent of phase, then, ought to be 'society', and in a good many cases it probably is . . . Unfortunately in practice it does not work. We have no means of knowing whether the components we group together into a phase are the same communities an ethnographer . . . would group into a society. We cannot be sure that the individual members of these communities would recognise themselves as belong to the same 'people' . . . In sum, it looks as though the present chances are against archaeological phases having much if any social reality, but this does not prevent us from maintaining that they can have and that in the meantime we may act as if they did have.

The normative approach has been criticised to good effect by Binford[13] on the appropriate ground that 'change in the total cultural system must be viewed in an adaptive context, both social and environmental, not whimsically viewed as the result of "influences", "stimuli", or even "migrations" between and among geographically defined units'. In a subsequent article, Binford[14] carries the discussion much further, suggesting that 'culture be viewed as a system composed of subsystems', advocating the separate study of the subsystems within specific culture systems, so as to avoid the holistic simplicities of the normative approach. A distinction is made between adaptive areas – within which similar techniques for exploiting the environment are used, whatever the stylistic variation – and interaction spheres, large areas within which social interactions occur. The problem of identifying the geographical extent of the specific culture systems to be studied is not considered – indeed the article does not rule out the possibility that this decision might be an arbitrary one. In any case the question of recognising social units is not specifically considered.

Ironically too it is a problem which the increasing taxonomic sophistication of the archaeologist has obscured rather than clarified. For in practice, in specific cases, it has often been dificult to define the boundaries or extent of particular archaeological cultures, and this might have led to doubts about the validity of the concept itself. But instead a willingness to consider at once the differing distributions of the various artefacts which go together to make up the 'recurring assemblage' which defines the 'culture', – a polythetic approach, in other words – serves to overcome the difficulty. David Clarke[15] has discussed the problem in some detail, and finally establishes a hierarchy of attribute, artefact, assemblage, culture, culture-group and technocomplex. Ultimately, however, and with some sophistication, culture as an entity (as defined and established by the archaeologist) is equated by Clarke with social groups as formulated by the ethnographer:

> An archaeological cultural assemblage is not identical in space or time distribution with a tribal group, a language, or a subrace and these sets themselves share different boundaries. Nevertheless, archaeological culture is most likely to have been the product of a group of people with a largely homogeneous tribal organisation, language system and breeding population – whether the people themselves recognised the set or not. The archaeological culture maps a real entity that really existed, marking real interconnection – that this entity is not identical to historical, political, linguistic or racial entities does not make it the less real or important. The archaeological entities reflect realities as important as those recognised by the traditional classifications of other disciplines; the entities in all these fields are equally real, equally arbitrary and simply different.

I suggest that the only solution is the total abandonment of the notion of the culture (and the 'phase' of the Midwestern taxonomic system) as recognisable archaeological units. For very often, while imagining that we are allowing real patterns to emerge from the archaeological data – patterns which must, it is thought, betoken some social reality – we are instead imposing taxonomic categories upon the data which are purely constructs of our own devising. Of course we are at liberty to classify the material remains of the past in any way we choose, but the inference should be avoided that such arbitrary categories mean anything in terms of 'peoples' or 'societies', if these themselves are conceived as more than the arbitrary creations of the modern archaeologist.

For it is easy to show how spatial distributions, equivalent to the traditional cultural entities, can be generated by the archaeologist out of a continuum of change. If uniformities and similarities in artefact assemblage are viewed as the result of interactions between individuals, and if such interactions decrease in intensity uniformly with distance, each point will be most like its close neighbours. Consider the point P lying in a uniform plain, with its neighbours fairly regularly spaced around it. Similarity in terms of trait C decreases with distance r from P. At the same time the variables A and B vary uniformly across the plain with distance along the axes x and y. If the excavator first digs at P and recovers its assemblage, he will subsequently learn that adjacent points have a broadly similar assemblage, which he will call 'the P culture'. Gradually its boundaries will be set up by further research, with the criterion that only those assemblages which attain a given threshold level of similarity with the finds from P qualify for inclusion. So a 'culture' is born, centring on P, the type site, whose bounds are entirely arbitrary, depending solely on the threshold level of similarity and the initial, fortuitous choice of P as the point of reference.

If the plain is not homogeneous, but there are in fact barriers to interaction, for instance mountains or water, the rate of change of similarity with distance will be modified, so that similarity clines will emerge. To the archaeologist the real (that is, taxonomically real) entities so observed will serve to confirm his definition of 'culture' and its equation with 'people' or 'society'. Of course it does not follow, simply because archaeologists can create arbitrary taxonomic units, that less arbitrary units may not be found. But if the question is firmly posed, it is clear that such entities could only maintain their unity or homogeneity through the persistence of interactions operating preferentially among their members. These interactions would not in general be operating with comparable intensity between one entity and its neighbour. Some of the archaeological units termed 'culture' are so large in extent that this intense sharing is questionable. One would wish to be assured that the differences observed between the archaeological remains found at points P and Q are more than the result simply of diminished interaction resulting from distance or limited accessibility. Ian Hodder at Cambridge has been the first, I believe, to study archaeological distributions from this standpoint,[16] and his approach is clearly a very fruitful one.

The archaeologist's interest clearly is not – or at least should not be – limited simply to the attenuating effects of distance upon human interactions. In attempting to say something more about human society, his interest must centre upon specially patterned interactions which are indicative of organisation, or the membership of some society or group.

Seen in this rather sceptical perspective, the notion of social group is seen urgently to require definition: it cannot be allowed to emerge from the archaeological data as an uncritical distribution of similar artefacts. And the idea of 'people' as deriving from social group begins to look a very doubtful one. One might well enquire, indeed, whether the notion of 'people' in the sense of a large group of broadly similar and related individuals and greater in size than individual community groups, is not itself dependent upon the existence in the world of large political units. The notion of 'one people', familiar from the modern nation state, can perhaps be traced back to the Romans, but it may not be necessary to take it very much further. Both Binford[17] and Isaac[18] have asked at what point in human development did 'ethnicity' come into the world. And very possibly social groups beyond the band level, with special interactions within them, may have developed during the palaeolithic. But to take this further, to suggest widespread, homogenous units of distinct and distinguishable 'peoples' prior to the emergence of very large political units or 'empires' may not be warranted. What is a people if it is not a political unit? The anthropologists who speak of 'tribes' may have the answer, but the archaeologist will ask what is the essential unitary nature of the tribe, if it is not a political unit.[19] The observed 'culture' defined by the archaeologist may arise from special interactions at the time in question due to social affiliation. It may even be observable as a result of past interactions within the area, even though that social affiliation has now broken down – this is what some writers mean by 'tradition'. But often it is no more than a reflection of diminishing interaction with distance.

The moral to be drawn from this discussion is not necessarily a pessimistic one, even if the taxonomic manipulation of artefact distributions can no longer be expected automatically to yield social or ethnic information. It is rather that to produce social answers we must formulate social questions. When we go ahead and do so the problem emerges in a very different light. We have to ask ourselves what we mean by social organisation – or rather what we choose to mean by it, since the discussion in the first section indicated that our choice may be something very different from that of the social anthropologist, and it is at this point in the discussion that the possibility arises of breaking new ground, with the realisation that the traditional archaeological notion of social organisation may be as invalid as the traditional anthropological one is inappropriate.

The archaeologist may well be concerned to establish many things about early societies which the anthropologist will take entirely for granted. And the first of these could be, indeed should be, to identify units of analysis. The social anthropologist can avoid this problem on arrival to conduct his fieldwork by (a) asking 'Who are you? To what group do you belong?', and (b) requesting 'Take me to your leader'. Few anthropologists or archaeologists have recognised the fundamental nature of the assumptions which these procedures entail.

Is there in fact any area of administrative or 'ethnic' unity, beyond that of the individual settlement unit? What is its size? Does it occupy a specific territory? With boundaries? Is the community sedentary – over one year, over many years? Can it be subdivided into smaller social units? Is settlement dispersed or aggregated? What hierarchies of power, of prestige and of wealth exist within it? Is the administration – political, religious or economic – centralised at all? Do these functions overlap in a single place or person? What investment of labour and produce is devoted to the organisational and religious centres? By what means are status, power, wealth and sanctity expressed or symbolised? What degree of specialisation is there in these fields, as well as in agriculture and technology? What other kinds of interaction take place within it? Is the group affiliated with neighbouring groups by joint membership of any kind of association? Is it related to neighbouring groups by any position of dominance? What interactions take place with neighbouring groups outside the territory?

These indicate the kind of question which the archaeologist will wish to ask – and of course many of the answers would be self-evident to the field worker in a living society. In framing them it was no longer possible to avoid the idea of the group as in some sense an entity – the term is meaningless otherwise. This implies the assumption that, at least among living communities, societies or groups can be recognised that are not merely the product of interactions varying in intensity with distance yet otherwise unstructured. Because human beings are acutely aware of many social relationships I suggest that they will be explicitly aware of membership of such groups – these are therefore cognised entities, and in any given case a specific individual is either a member of a group or he is not. Clearly an individual can belong to several groups, but not without being aware of it. The kind of social group we are speaking of here is relevant to the notion of identity, to the 'Who are you?' question. So that operative groups, visible to the modern observer but not to the participant (e.g., 'middle income group', or group sharing a specific blood type) are not relevant. But for once we are not defeated by the evanescent, irrecoverable nature of past cognitive categories. For *it is precisely the recognition of the group that governs group behaviour.* When we are dealing with social groups their cognitive existence, recognised by those included and those excluded, reinforces their operational existence or may indeed create it. And the distinctive group behaviour – the differential nature of interactions with members of the group in distinction to those outside it – reinforces its cognitive recognition. It is this feedback mechanism that gives social groups their distinctiveness – for the group does not count as such if you cannot recognise it. (Even secret societies are no exception – considerable care is taken that their members should be mutually recognisable). This being so, we ought to be able to see them, in favourable cases, in the archaeological record.

Social organisation and social groups

In what I have written so far there has perhaps been a preoccupation with the definition and reality of entities of supposed 'social groups'. The social anthropologist will remark that there is more to social anthropology than this, and may find the foregoing critique of the entities traditionally used by the archaeologist altogether unsurprising. Indeed it could be argued that many of the social aspects studied by the anthropologist could function without the recognition of groups at all.

The whole web of kinship relations, for instance, is often studied in terms of *rules* of behaviour operating within the specific area under discussion. There is no reason here why its bounds need be defined. We can envisage a network of local kin relationships extending indefinitely in all directions, accompanied by a gradual and fairly continuous change with distance in the rules of exchange. We could then contrast the practices in operation at points A and B without any need to consider the definition of entities.

This brings us right back to a fundamental question which should perhaps have been posed earlier: just what do we mean by 'social organisation' in the context of a study of its evolution? Clearly the term entails consideration of the whole field of human interactions – of languages and symbolic systems, of kinship, or resource allocation between individuals, of government and war, and of other forms of exchange. In each of these fields, entities or groups may be defined: language groups, kin groups, economic units, polities, sodalities, etc. Or in each of them the discussion may well proceed without any definition of such entities.

I would suggest that, in studying the evolution of social organisation, what we are in the broadest sense concerned with is the emergence of inhomogeneity. It is true that in the case of the hypothetical network mentioned above, there can be complete continuity, with one individual acting much like another, and we may nonetheless be concerned with the rules of behaviour, that is to say, with the social organisation of the system. But in a certain sense, however elaborate the rules of interaction may be, the lack of specialisation and differentiation of this network would lead us to regard it as existing at a low level of organisation. When we think of higher levels of organisation we are certainly thinking in terms of *differential interactions* among the individuals participating in the organisation. Of course these interactions can be of many different kinds, so that two individuals may interact strongly in one subsystem of society, as it were, and hardly at all in another. It is precisely when a number of individuals do interact fairly strongly in a number of different ways, and less strongly with others outside that number, that we can begin to speak in terms of a social group. I would suggest that it is difficult to imagine a social hierarchy of any kind without the effective fulfilment of this condition.

It remains to ask just what kind of group the archaeologist is likely to be interested in. And here the material nature of the archaeologist's finds does impose some restrictions. For we can only legitimately speak, as archaeologists, of activities which leave at least some discernible trace in the material record. Prehistoric linguistic groups, for instance, cannot be recovered archaeologically unless there is some kind of correlation between language and the material world. One aspect of organisation which is very pertinent here is administration: it implies both government (with the exercise of power) and resource allocation. Both imply some partition of the world into persons and resources governed or allocated, and those which fall out of the control of the administration, and hence by their very nature some kind of delineation of an entity, the polity.

An increasing number of archaeologists has come to rely on the 'neoevolutionary' classification of social organisation in order to consider human societies. The hierarchy of band, tribe, chiefdom and state[20] has recommended itself to many workers concerned to make generalisations of some kind about culture change, or to fit specific societies under study into some more general perspective. The notion of chiefdom in particular has helped to fill the gap in the workings of earlier anthropologists between the tribe and the state.

These classificatory terms have been criticised by some, either because they are not observable from the archaeological record[21] or because they have no real existence[22] or again because the hierarchy is thought to imply some evolutionary necessity,[23] an implication which those who have used these terms would reject. Like the terms in any classificatory scheme they are constructs which are justified if found useful in practice. And their application to the prehistoric past is greatly strengthened by the effectiveness with which they have been applied to living societies. Certainly they appear less regularly sequential than classifications with a strong chronological component such as Palaeolithic, Neolithic, Bronze Age, etc., or Formative, Classic, Florescent, Decadent, etc. They certainly supersede the older social categories of savagery, barbarism and civilisation, which later took on both chronological and economic/technological overtones in a confusing way. Childe sometimes used barbarism as the equivalent of Neolithic-to-Bronze Age where today we find it convenient to speak of hunter/gatherer bands and agricultural tribes.

The real operational difficulty of recognising these forms of society in many cases should not be underestimated, however – which is not the same as Leach's assertion that to do so is logically not possible. And it should not be overlooked that increasingly they are being distinguished in terms of settlement pattern. For the sake of argument, and to stimulate discussion, I would like to suggest here that tighter and more effective definitions can be obtained by replacing the band/tribe/chiefdom/state hierarchy *in toto* with a classification based on the spatial arrangement of society.

The term band, for instance, is recognisable by its small size – normally less than 100 persons – and by the impermanence of its place of residence. (For some reason no one calls a sedentary village of the same number of persons, living in complete isolation, a band – it is automatically considered 'tribal', generally without the application of any positive criteria to justify that term.)

And at the other end of the spectrum the term state has always proved almost impossible to define – just as difficult indeed as 'city' and 'civilisation', with which it generally overlaps. At a recent conference in Santa Fe it proved very difficult to hit on any criteria which can be recognised archaeologically, since the one clear criterion proposed by Service is not a practicable one, 'the presence of that special form of control, the consistent threat of force by a body of persons legitimately constituted to use it'.[24] Instead both Wright[25] and

Johnson[26] suggested that the most characteristic feature was a three-tier hierarchy of control, which is best seen archaeologically in the trimodal settlement size distribution of city, town and village.

Turning now to chiefdoms, I suggest that their most distinctive feature in the archaeological record is the presence of central places. For the central person who is the permanent chief is generally situated at a central place, even if this may be a periodic one, either in the sense of rotating (i.e., changing regularly in location) or in the sense of operating only for part of the year. Most of the Polynesian chiefdoms were of the latter kind. But the central place was usually dignified by special buildings pertaining to the chief, and sometimes by monumental ones relating to ceremonies of life or death. As Service remarks, chiefdoms are distinguished from tribal societies 'by the presence of centres which co-ordinate economic, social and religious activities'.[27]

One cannot go so far as to assert that those societies which are not organised as chiefdoms or states, or with comparable complexity, entirely lack central places. But it is difficult to point to permanent central places with a permanent population which do not, in fact, exercise a central administrative authority over the territory which they serve.

As for the tribe, the concept remains archaeologically undefined. Steward[28] has stigmatised 'tribal society' as an 'ill-defined catchall', and Service's definition is perhaps the least satisfactory of any in his hierarchy. It gives little clue as to how the limits of the tribe in space might be ascertained: 'Pan-tribal sodalities make a tribe a tribe, for if they did not exist then there is nothing but a series of bands, more affluent than hunters and gatherers, but still bands, with only intermarriage between certain ones providing any unity.'[29] Nowhere do we find a clear picture of the nature of those interactions, taking place within the tribe but not across its boundaries, which work to maintain and enhance its unity and homogeneity. Until we have some inkling of what we are searching for in the archaeological record we shall not find it, for, as I have indicated above, the simple fall-off in interaction with distance is sufficient to allow the generation of 'cultures' by the archaeological taxonomist which need have no cognitive meaning.

Fried's criticisms of the concept of tribe have not been adequately answered, and his suggestion that 'most tribes seem to be secondary phenomena ... the product of processes stimulated by the appearances of relatively highly organised societies amidst other societies which are organised much more simply',[30] is paralleled by the suggestion above that the notion of 'a people' is largely the product of modern (or early imperial) nationalist thought.

Goody's discussion in *The Social Organisation of the LoWiili*[31] is particularly useful here, for he makes it clear that the recognition of tribal entities among the Dagari-speaking peoples is largely the act of outside observers taking relative terms as fixed, tribal designations: the diffuseness of the political organisation gives rise to the lack of distinct tribal nomenclature. Such designations as exist, however, arise not primarily from a consciousness of unity, which would surely lead to a recognised name within the tribe itself, but 'from a consciousness of the differences between their own institutions and those of neighbouring peoples'.[32] Goody shows clearly (chapter 5) that the basic territorial division of the land in the region is the 'parish', the ritual area associated with a particular earth shrine. The inhabitants of this area may be described as a political group, and it is clear that in any discussion of social organisation the 'parish' must be a fundamental unit of discussion, although the members of several parishes can meet at a market for purposes of exchange. The case of the LoWiili is a particularly interesting one for the archaeologist, illustrating as it does the diffuse nature of a supposed social grouping above that of the operative and cognised territorial units. The 'tribe' is a dangerous concept for the archaeologist.

This critique is not offered in a negative sense however, since the 'evolutionary' hierarchy at least gives us something to compensate for the failure of archaeology to talk about social organisation at all until very recently. A discussion in spatial terms is operationally more convenient and perhaps no less apposite for social description. For is not the most important feature of a chiefdom the existence of a central person, resident at a central place, whether this be periodic or permanent? And is not the distinguishing feature of the state generally accepted as the existence of a permanent hierarchical structure of administration and authority – a structure generally reflected in a hierarchy of central places, so that between the major centre (or state capital) and the minor residence unit (or village) there is at least one intermediate settlement and administrative unit, the regional centre?

Polity and space

The spatial structure of society has never been adequately explored. Locational analysts have developed sophisticated techniques in modern geography for investigating settlement distributions, but their implications in terms of social organisation have not been investigated. Anthropologists have written of territoriality, but focussed upon the behavioural analogy between non-human primate behaviour and the most closely analogous human societies, generally choosing non-sedentary socities. And thinkers such as Eliade[33] have commented on the symbolic aspects of space without, however, using it in the study of society as a whole.

I suggest that there is a whole range of generalisations to be made, many of them exceedingly obvious (and no doubt formulated in isolation often enough) which together might lay the foundations for a general study of human social organisation in a manner that is operationally explicit, so that it can, in favourable cases, be applied to past societies as well as to living ones.[34]

The presentation offered here, like the whole of this paper, is provisional. But I hope it may serve as a basis for discussion.

1. The basic social group is defined by the habitual association of persons within a territory. These are the persons who live together throughout the year, what Murdock terms the community, 'the maximal group of persons who normally reside together in face-to-face association'.[35] Among hunters this may be a group of families who normally camp together, i.e., a 'band'. Among sedentary communities with fairly aggregate settlement it will be a village, or in some areas such as south Italy without villages, a town. With a dispersed settlement pattern it may even be a household. It is often possible to subdivide the group into families or households, but these live at the same location: if they split up for part of the year the smaller units so formed would be regarded as the basic social group.

This definition implies two statements about human behaviour. First that there are such habitual associations. And second that human behaviour is territorially organised. This operational assertion carries with it cognitive implications: 'L'installation dans un territoire équivaut à la fondation d'un monde.'[36]

Perhaps the most fundamental assumption of all, however, is that the individual can belong to only one such basic social group at a time, whatever his affiliations to groups of other kinds.

2. Human social organisation is segmentary in nature: human spatial organisation is therefore cellular and modular. This is to say that the basic social group, with its territory, is repeated in space, so that a simple cellular pattern is generated. The boundaries of the units need not, however, be particularly well defined: the territory may rather consist of a 'core area' with a 'development of a territorial gradient from the "core" to the "periphery" of their home range'.[37] What is being asserted here, however, is that the essential unit, the basic group, whatever its precise nature, is repeated spatially. There is, of course, no *a priori* reason why this should be so – an entire range of different kinds of such basic groups could live in juxtaposition, each quite unlike the others in its scale or internal structure. But this is not the way it works in practice. The adjacent units do have comparable organisation and also comparable size – which is the implication of the term modular.

This modular feature of the segments, that in a given region the territories are of approximately the same size is a feature not generally discussed, but appears in fact to be one of the most fundamental features of human social and spatial organisation. It has been demonstrated for the Australian Aborigines by Birdsell[38] who has shown that the modular size of 'hordes' in Australia correlated with rainfall in a regular way.

Binford (personal communication) is at present working on more general regularities in the territorial group sizes of hunters and gatherers. But clearly the concept bears investigation in more general terms, since a modular arrangement is evident among sedentary village societies likewise, and the idea is inherent in most Central Place studies, although rarely brought out explicitly.

Archaeologically the important aspect of this observation is that it can in fact be investigated. Studies of settlement spacing of basic groups have in fact been undertaken[39] although clearly there is a risk of error when the settlements considered are not precisely contemporary.[40]

Birdsell's work promotes the thought that we may be dealing not primarily with a territorial module but a population one – that is to say that it is the size of population of the groups which remains stable rather than the area they occupy. The two will be the same only when ecological conditions are constant. There may be underlying social reasons for such modular sizes, that is to say thresholds beyond which the group population cannot grow without a change in the nature and structure of the group.[41]

Alternatively there may be mechanisms which tend to keep the territories and population sizes of groups in a given region at about the same size one-to-another, without discriminating in favour of a particular size range. Rowlands[42] has discussed the relation between territoriality and defence, and one can envisage factors which might work toward parity among the social units (and hence for a *local* modular size).

Archaeologically this pattern is a very frequently recurring one, discernible in almost every case where there are sedentary communities. When the settlement is aggregated into villages, their spacing and placing can be viewed in these terms. Such a patterning may certainly be discerned, for example, over much of prehistoric Europe. The notion of modular organisation, for what has been termed the Early State Module (ESM) has been discussed further in a recent paper.[43]

3. Basic social groups do not exist in isolation, but affiliate into larger groups, meeting together at periodic intervals. The affiliated groups are generally adjacent to each other, so that their territories, taken together, may be regarded as forming a larger, continuous and uninterrupted territory.

Among hunting groups the meeting place itself may vary from time to time.[44] Among sedentary communities the place of meeting may move in rotation (cf the Kyaka). Often it is a permanent meeting place, however – that is to say the meeting always takes place at the same location, and it must then rank as a central place. (If the meeting takes place only on specific occasions through the year it can be regarded as a periodic central place.) Moreover it is a feature of many societies that they express the uniqueness of this location by symbolic means, sometimes by monumental construction, since the location may have a religious significance as well as expressing the affiliation of groups itself. Once again the observed operational reality has further cognitive overtones: 'Notre monde se situe toujours autour d'un centre.'[45]

This is precisely the situation described in detail for the LoWiili by Goody,[46] where the Earth Shrine is the focal point of the polity, and the principal feature of its territory. In archaeologically favourable cases these constructions are of a durable nature – in the Tuamotu islands of Polynesia the *marae* is the focal point of the lineage territory,[47] and archaeological research has produced patterns in location[48] which even without the ethnographic observations available would have been suggestive of a cellular and modular territorial arrangement and social partitioning.

Analogous spatial patterning has been noted among the collective tombs of Neolithic northern Europe,[49] and a segmentary social grouping suggested in consequence. The monuments are there viewed as the traditional ceremonial focal point in a territory where household location is either dispersed or shifting every few years. The modular aspect of the patterning is reflected in the approximately equal size of territories, or more often in the approximately equal area of arable land within each, suggesting approximate equality of population. In some cases, as Fleming has pointed out[50] the interior division of the tombs is itself cellular, reflecting perhaps the division of the territory into several households, or other sub-division, each of which would have access to one part of the tomb.

4. Human society is often hierarchical in nature: human spatial organisation is therefore stratified. This generalisation effectively follows from the cellular pattern discussed above. Once the cells are contiguous, sharing common boundaries, they can no longer all expand territorially simply by increasing in size. It would, of course, be possible for some to expand at the expense of others, so that there would be fewer, larger cells, each organised just as before. And no doubt examples can be found of such aggrandisement without further organisation or complexity.

Instead, however, development occurs by the union of a number of basic cells or segments into the kind of affiliation indicated above, with the emergence of a new and (in the sense of our stratification) higher organisation to deal with the consequences of union, *while retaining elements of the former cellular pattern.* These observations hold whether the union occurs by direct conquest, in which case the conqueror takes over the central administrative functions of the conquered group, or by peaceful assimilation or symbiosis. In each case the union of a number of cells into a higher order cell implies the emergence of a higher order centre, but the lower order centres normally survive.

And growth continues in this way in stratified order, the cellular units at each level of organisation together forming the sub-units for the next with the emergence of a higher order centre, usually located at the traditional centre of one of the constituent subunits.

Already this process is seen in operation in embryo among the Tiv,[51] an example worth citing because it has been described in explicitly spatial terms. Evidently the process of urbanisation, although it is conventionally considered primarily in terms of the urban centre itself, can perhaps be seen as appropriately in terms of territorial amalgamation of this kind, although the importance of increasing population density should not be overlooked in any discussion of territorial size.

5. The effective polity, the highest order social unit, may be identified by the scale and distribution of central places. In the stratified ordering of cellular territories, the individual person has allegiance at a number of levels – to the basic group (the community), to the local region focussed on its main town, and to the higher order realm comprised of several regions, focussed upon its capital. He is a member of each, but he is a *citizen* of the highest order polity. For it is the central organisation of this polity, usually its central person, who wields supreme power. This is the highest level of society, in M.A. Smith's words: 'A group of people acknowledging a single political authority, obedient to a single system of law, and in some degree organised to resist attack from other such societies.'[52] This is the highest social unit effective in political terms, which means in military terms.

Now in order to recognise such a unit archaeologically, one approach is certainly to study the symbolism which the central authority employs to express its power. For instance the extent of the Roman Empire, if it were not known to archaeologists, could be established by plotting the distribution of monumental Imperial inscriptions. This is certainly more effective than trying to follow boundaries (which may not always be delineated by a Hadrian's Wall) or attempting to follow artefact uniformities. For we saw in the last section how archaeologists can create 'cultures' where no social group need have existed. And equally the boundaries of existing social groups may be blurred by interactions, notably trade, across them.

A feasible alternative is to study the hierarchy of central places, establishing first the approximate size of the highest order centres. Assuming these can safely be indentified as such (and here the symbolic evidence may be required as corroboration) their distribution marks the centres of the highest order cellular territories, that is of the polities. And some attempt can be made at reconstructing the subsidiary cells of this stratified arrangement.

Precisely such a study has been undertaken by Johnson in

Mesopotamia, with this underlying implication that spatial organisation is the counterpart of social organisation. Spatial hierarchy has been examined in Britain by Hodder and Hassall,[53] although the social implications were less obvious since the centre of the polity was by then outside the British Isles, in Rome. It was clearly brought out in the Tehuacan valley by MacNeish in a pioneering study,[54] and in the Maya lowlands by Flannery, Hammond and Marcus.[55] The existence of a social hierarchy in Neolithic south Britain has been postulated on the basis of a hierarchy of places.[56]

The modular arrangement is apparently reproduced at each level in the hierarchy, including the highest, so that for each polity, with its centre (or 'capital'), there will be an analogous one with a contiguous territorial boundary, until the polity is so large that it occupies all the available land of the land mass (i.e. continent) or island group where it is situated.

In asserting the widespread nature of the modular arrangement it is not of course claimed that all the neighbours of a polity need be unified into territories of a comparably higher order – this would be to assert the worldwide nature of a specific social organisation at a given time. But this is, nonetheless, a general tendency over fairly large regions.

The social and political aspects of spatial hierarchy are frequently overlooked by geographers, but it does seem broadly true that the polities of the world each boast a capital city, and that within broad regions these capitals could be recognised by their size and relation to subsidiary centres, as well as by the attendant symbolism, without prior information about national boundaries. (Artificial capitals such as Canberra or Washington D.C. clearly present a specific problem, foreshadowed by the summer palaces of early emperors, but again it is a problem which a consideration of symbolism would help to solve).

6. Special interactions between polities undoubtedly take place, creating uniformities in artefact distribution, and require closer study: such uniformities in themselves do not document societies or 'peoples'. This is a re-statement of the critique of the normative approach discussed in section 2. Generalisation 3, above, contains the germ of an idea, however, that the highest units of the social hierarchy (i.e., the polities) sometimes enter some kind of affiliation without losing any element of their autonomy. This may have been the case in the early Greek city leagues,[57] and at a lower level may be true of tribes which are recognised as such without sharing any central tribal organisation whatever.

Clearly the tribe still presents a problem, which the archaeologist alone cannot be expected to solve if the anthropologist remains in doubt about precisely what a tribe is. I suggest, however, that the concrete approach outlined here, of considering first effective polities and territories, together with their hierarchical arrangement socially and spatially, may be useful, since it is an approach which has meaning both for the archaeologist and the anthropologist. This will leave for further examination the nature of the 'tribal' links across and between polities and territories – the sodalities and other affiliations and the linguistic affinities. It may be that in some cases the symbolism used to express such affiliations may offer the hope of archaeological interpretation.

The procedure adopted here has been to risk certain generalisations about the spatial behaviour of social groups – that is to say as groups recognised as such by their participant members, and recognised as operational by external observers. The consideration has been limited to groups whose members are spatially contiguous, so that the group can be delimited spatially. Clearly other kinds of group could be considered, but they are less easy to approach archaeologically, and in any case it is suggested that polities are indeed bounded units of this kind. If these generalisations can be accepted as holding – broad as they are – for human societies as a whole, then they do offer the possibility for the archaeologist of proceeding from observations of spatial organisation to conclusions about social organisation.

No doubt these specific formulations can be questioned on a number of grounds. But unless some such formulations as these can be made, I see little hope of using archaeological data to suggest conclusions which would interest the anthropologist. Of course it may be argued that the kind of conclusions suggested here are altogether unremarkable, and the generalisations attempted above highly banal. Nonetheless, if they are accepted, they can lead to a clear and simple picture of the growth of some aspects of social organisation, a picture which so far has been outlined only in a few specific areas of study, especially Mesoamerica and Mesopatamia.

Nor should the practical difficulties be overlooked that are inherent in the eliciting of spatial patterning from archaeological data. Incomplete survey evidence, and the difficulties of setting up a chronology sufficiently exact to identify settlements occupied contemporaneously present real problems. And some of the necessary procedures have hardly yet been worked out: there is so far no general treatment of the problems involved in the ordering of places into a hierarchy from archaeological evidence. This may be effected by a consideration of size,[58] of labour invested in their construction, of functional aspects such as defences (e.g. Romano-British walled towns),[59] of monumental ceremonial centres (e.g. Maya centres[60]) of the finding of artefacts interpreted as symbolically relevant (e.g. clay nails in Mesopotamia),[61] and no doubt in other ways. A strict analysis by size will generally begin with a frequency distribution, which if non-random in terms of size (i.e. stratified) may allow of positive conclusions.

Systems in space

In the discussion so far social organisation has been considered primarily in terms of its spatial structure, an essentially static approach. Whatever descriptive clarity it may claim, as a framework for the explanation of culture change it is incomplete.

The formulation has been conceived, however, with a systemic approach very much in mind. That is to say that a human society is conveniently regarded as a system, whose components are the human individuals within that society, the artefacts which they use, and those elements of the environment with which the men and artefacts interact.

The first and fundamental observation here is that we are interested in man-environment interactions, since it is a fundamental of any ecological approach that the impact of man on his environment cannot be divorced from the impact of the environment on him. And the second and equally fundamental point is that we are interested too in man-man interactions, since the way in which the activities in that society are patterned determines both its nature and the way it exploits the environment.

The bounds of our system include relevant aspects of the environment, then – the model does not suggest that culture alone be bounded and interactions with the environment seen as input or output of that culture system.

Evidently the man-environment system is an open one, but how shall its bounds be selected? Naturally that is purely a matter of choice, but the choice is an important one. It is not, however, one that has been much discussed in the literature; neither Binford, who introduced the systems approach to archaeology,[62] nor Clarke, who has discussed it instructively, deal with this question. Indeed, Clarke, with his image of the trajectory of the system, with its successive system states,[63] uses the dimensions of space for his exposition to represent time and sub-system relationships. In my own discussion of cultures as systems,[64] I stressed that the choice of the spatial boundaries for the system is an arbitrary decision. I now feel, however, that explicit definition is important, and that for many purposes the appropriate systemic units are the polities discussed above. For some purposes it may be convenient to lump several autonomous polities together within the bounds of a single system – for instance when ecological variation within large regions is considered – but in general the polity is often the natural unit.

For some purposes it may be subdivided spatially into subsystems, and the cellular structure may facilitate this. But in general the division into sub-systems is more appropriately defined by human activities. Each individual operates simultaneously in several subsystems. The following sub-systems have been used for an analysis of culture change in the early Aegean, and they are of general applicability:[62]

1. The subsistence sub-system. Defined by interactions relating to the acquisition and distribution of food resources. Man and the food resources and the food units themselves are components of the sub-system and interrelated by these specifically subsistence-oriented activities.
2. The technological sub-system. Defined by the activities of man which result in the production of material artefacts.
3. The social sub-system. A system of behaviour patterns where the defining activities are those which take place between men. It would be possible to distinguish an economic sub-system from the social sub-system, but it is more profitable to regard the movement of goods as much in terms of social relations as of procurement.
4. Projective or symbolic sub-system. Defined by those activities, earlier termed cognitive, in which man gives formal expression to his understanding of and reaction to the world. His thoughts and feelings are projected, given symbolic form.
5. Trade and communication sub-system. Defined by the interactions which take place with areas outside the bounds of the system.

It should be noted that population and population density do not constitute a sub-system: they are basic parameters of the system, which determine its size and other features. In this perspective settlement pattern does not constitute a sub-system (for we are defining sub-systems by their different kinds of activities): it is merely one feature of the system.

These categories bear some relation to Binford's discussion of technomic, sociotechnic and ideotechnic artefacts.[66] However, just as men operate in several sub-systems at once, so do artefacts, and the distinction proposed here is in terms of activities – although they too can operate in several sub-systems at once.

The stable persistence of the system through time, with limited change in the values of the state variables of the sub-system, is the consequence of negative feedback. Stability may be described in terms of homeostasis.

Growth and change cannot adequately be described in these terms, however, as homeostatic responses to change outside the system. Culture change involves fundamental and irreversible changes of structure, and the process of morphogenesis cannot be explained simply by means of negative feedback: it needs positive feedback so that growth is sustained. The term 'multiplier effect' has been proposed for the positive mutual interactions between sub-systems, which can promote sustained growth and the basic changes which accompany them. Growth can be analysed and explained, therefore, by the detailed analysis of the interactions between sub-systems – the impact of changing technology on the social organisation for instance, or of the projective system on subsistence production (for instance through the agency of the temple organisation) – and it is these which will repay detailed analysis.

This may serve as a convenient framework for the investigation of the changes implied in the development of the different forms of spatial organisation described above, and in particular for the specific size, in area or population, of the modular units. The role of external trade in stimulating the growth of urban centres and a pronounced social hierarchy, to take one example, has been stressed by workers in Mesoamerica,[67] in Africa[68] and in Europe.[69] This process has to be studied in terms of the impact of changes in the external exchange sub-system upon other sub-systems of the society. Clearly if one of the results is a marked increase in the size of polities (and territorial units) with a marked decreased in their number, we shall wish to understand this transformation in systemic terms.

NOTES

1 Leach, E.R. (1973), Concluding address, *in* Renfrew, C. (ed.), *The Explanation of Culture Change: Models in Prehistory,* London.

2 Leach, E.R. (1974), 'Reply to Dr Mellor', *Cambridge Opinion*, 95, February 1974, p. 73.

3 Leach (1974).

4 Rappaport, R.A. (1969), 'Sanctity and adaptation', paper presented at the Wenner-Gren Symposium no. 44, *The Moral and Aesthetic Structure of Human Adaptation.*

5 Harris, M. (1968), *The Rise of Anthropological Theory,* London, pp. 571 ff.

6 Harris, M. (1968), 'Comments', *in* Binford L.R. and S.R. (eds.), *New Perspectives in Archaeology*, Chicago, pp. 360-1.

7 Service, E.R. (1971), *Cultural Evolutionism*, New York, p. 157.

8 Childe, V.G. (1929), *The Danube in Prehistory*, Oxford, pp. v-vi.

9 Binford, L.R. (1962), 'Archaeology as anthropology', *American Antiquity*, 28, pp. 217-25.

10 Rouse, I. (1972), *A Systematic Approach to Prehistory*, New York, p. 62.

11 Rouse (1972), p. 6.

12 Willey, G.R. and Phillips, P. (1958), *Method and Theory in American Archaeology*, Chicago, p. 49.

13 Binford (1962).

14 Binford, L.R. (1965), 'Archaeological systematics and the study of culture process', *American Antiquity*, 31, pp. 203-10.

15 Clarke, D.L. (1968), *Analytical Archaeology*, London, pp. 358-65.

16 Hodder, I.R. and Orton, C. (1976), *Spatial Analysis in Archaeology,* Cambridge.

17 Binford, L.R. (1972), 'Paradigms and the current state of Palaeolithic research', *in* Clarke, D.L. (ed.), *Models in Archaeology*, London.

18 Isaac, G.Ll. (1972), 'Early phases of human behaviour', *in* Clarke (ed.), (1972).

19 Fried, M. (1968), 'On the concept of "Tribe" and "Tribal Society" ', *in* Helm, J. (ed.), *Essays on the Problem of the Tribe*, American Ethnological Society.

20 Service, E.R. (1962), *Primitive Social Organisation*, New York.

21 e.g. Leach (1973).

22 Fried (1968).

23 Tringham, R. (1974), Comments on Prof. Renfrew's paper, *in* Moore, C.B. (ed.), *Reconstructing Complex Societies*, p. 88.

24 Service (1962), p. 171.

25 Wright, H.T., in press.

26 Johnson, G. (1975), 'Locational analysis and the investigation of Vruk local exchange systems', *in* Sabloff J.A. *and* Lamberg-Karlovsky C. (eds.), *Ancient Civilisation and Trade*, Albuquerque, pp. 285-340.

27 Service (1962), p. 143.

28 Steward, J.H. (1955), *Theory of Culture Change*, Urbana, pp. 44 and 53.

29 Service (1962), p. 115.

30 Fried (1968), p. 15.

31 Goody, J. (1967), *The Social Organisation of the Lo Wiili*, Oxford.

32 Goody (1967), p. 113.

33 Eliade, M. (1965), *Le sacré et le profane*, Paris.

34 Some of these possibilities have been indicated in a number of useful articles by Trigger, notably: Trigger, B. (1972), 'Determinants of urban growth in pre-industrial societies', *in* Ucko, P.J., Tringham, R. and Dimbleby, G.W. (eds.), *Man, Settlement and Urbanism*, London, pp. 575-99; Trigger, B. (1974), 'The archaeology of government', *World Archaeology*, 6, pp. 95-106.

35 Murdock, G.P. (1949), *Social Structure*, New York, p. 79.

36 Eliade (1965), p. 43.

37 Flannery, K. (1972), 'The origins of the village as a settlement type in Mesoamerica and the Near East', in Ucko, Tringham and Dimbleby (eds.) (1972), p. 28.

38 Birdsell, J.B. (1973), 'A basic demographic unit', *Current Anthropology*, 14, pp. 337-56.

39 e.g. MacNeish, R.S. (1964), 'Ancient Mesoamerican civilisation', *Science*, 143, pp. 531-7.

40 cf. Ellison, A. and Harriss, J. (1972), 'Settlement and land use in the prehistory and early history of southern England', *in* Clarke (ed.) (1972).

41 cf. Forge, A. (1972), 'Normative factors in the settlement size of neolithic cultivators', *in* Ucko, Tringham and Dimbleby (eds.) (1972).

42 Rowlands, M.J. (1972), 'Defence – a factor in the organisation of settlements', *in* Ucko, Tringham and Dimbleby (eds.) (1972).

43 Renfrew, C. (1975), Trade as action at a distance, *in* Sabloff and Lamberg-Karlovsky (eds.), p. 12.

44 Birdsell (1973).

45 Eliade (1965).

46 Goody (1967), Ch. 5 and Fig. 6.

47 Ottino, P. (1967), 'Early Ati of the Western Tuamotus', *in* Highland, G.A. *et al.* (eds.), *Polynesian Culture History*, Honolulu, pp. 451-82.

48 Garanger, J. (1966), 'Recherches archéologiques à Rangiroa', *Journal de la Société des Océanistes*, 22, Fig. 1.

49 Renfrew, C. (1973a). 'Monuments, mobilisation and social organisation in neolithic Wessex', *in* Renfrew, C. (ed.), *The Explanation of Culture Change: Models in Prehistory*, London, pp. 545, fig. 1; Renfrew, C. (1973b), *Before Civilisation*, London, figs. 29 and 30.

50 Fleming, A. (1972), 'Vision and design: approaches to ceremonial monument typology', *Man*, 7, 57-72.

51 Bohannan, P. (1954), 'The migration and expansion of the Tiv', *Africa*, II, p. 4, Fig. 1.

52 Smith, M.A. (1955), 'The limitations of inference in archaeology', *Archaeological Newsletter*, 6, 3-7.

53 Hodder, I. and Hassall, M. (1971), 'The non-random spacing of Romano-British walled towns', *Man*. 6.

54 MacNeish (1964).

55 Flannery, K.V. (1972), 'The cultural evolution of civilisations', *Annual Review of Ecology and Systematics*, 3, p. 399; Hammond, N.D.C. (1972), 'Locational models and the site of Lubaantun', *in*, Clarke, D.L. (ed.), *Models in Archaeology*, London; Marcus, J. (1973), 'Territorial organisation of the Lowland Classic Maya', *Science*, 180, pp. 911-16.

56 Renfrew (1973a).

57 Fustel de Coulanges, N.D. (1873), *The Ancient City*, London.

58 Johnson, G. (1972), 'A test of central place theory in archaeology', *in* Ucko, Tringham and Dimbleby (eds.) (1972).

59 Hodder and Hassall (1972).

60 Marcus (1973).

61 Wright, H.T. (1972), 'A consideration of interregional exchange in Greater Mesopotamia: 4000-3000 BC', *in* Wilmsen, E.N. (ed.), *Social Exchange and Interaction*, Ann Arbor; Johnson (1975).

62 Binford (1965).

63 Clarke (1968), p. 104.

64 Renfrew, C. (1972), *The Emergence of Civilisation: The Cyclades and the Aegean in the Third Millennium BC*, London, pp. 19 ff.

65 Renfrew (1972).

66 Binford (1962).

67 Flannery, K.V. (1968), 'The Olmec and the valley of Oaxaca', *in* Benson, E.P. (ed.), *Dumbarton Oaks Conference on the Olmec*, Washington.

68 Meillassoux, C. (ed.) (1971), *The Development of Indigenous Trade and Markets in West Africa*, Oxford.

69 Rowlands, M.J. (1973), 'Modes of exchange and the incentives for trade with reference to later European prehistory', *in* Renfrew (ed.) (1973), pp. 589-600.

SECTION II

Transformational models in evolution

KAJSA EKHOLM

External exchange and the transformation of centr al African social systems

The problem: patriliny/matriliny

The question of the development of matrilineal as opposed to patrilineal societies is one which has never been satisfactorily answered in the anthropological literature. In his article 'Patrilineal and matrilineal succession',[1] Radcliffe-Brown asserts that social anthropology lacks sufficient 'knowledge and understanding' to ask the question 'what general factors determine the selection by some people of the matrilineal and by others of the patrilineal principle in determining status of succession'.[2]

Anthropologists have generally assumed the social structure to be 'given' and have thus been content merely to describe the relations among its parts. An example of this approach is *Matrilineal Kinship* where Schneider points out that his co-authors 'for the most part . . . have chosen to take matrilineal systems as given',[3] and instead of asking the question 'why' have analysed the 'where' and the 'how' (e.g. in matrilineal societies the bond between brother and sister is strong while that between husband and wife is weak; children belong not to their father's but to their mother's kin group; children inherit from their mother's kin group and not from their father's group; the father has only limited authority over them).

It is only the materialists who have specifically addressed themselves to the question 'why',[4] and their position is, briefly, that matriliny and patriliny are simply ideological reflections of more objective conditions such as residence patterns. A society in which co-operation among men in production and military activities is more important than women's co-operation becomes virilocal and therefore patrilineal, since members of such groups tend to be patrilineally related. Conversely, in a society in which co-operation among women is more important, matrilocal residence and matriliny will follow. Local groups will consist of matrilineally related women (mothers and daughters) and attached men. Service, for example, concludes that matriliny will be found in a very specific socio-economic situation:

> One notes first that uxorilocal-matrilineal tribes are widely scattered in the primitive world – in parts of North and South America, Melanesia, South East Asia, and Africa – but also that they are found typically in one kind of socio-economic situation: rainfall horticulture with the gardening done by women.[5]

The materialist approach might be said to supply us with one set of possible explanations for the existence of matrilineal-matrilocal societies, but societies like the Kongo, with matrilineal descent and *avunculocal* residence do not fit this model since the local segment of the matriline consists not of mothers and daughters but of mothers' brothers and sisters' sons i.e. a group of brothers in the oldest generation plus adult sisters' sons in the following generation. In Kongo, sisters remained members of their own descent group throughout life, but upon marriage moved to their husband's village where their children resided until the day they left their father to take up residence with their mother's brother.[6]

This situation clearly contradicts the materialist theory, and, as with Fox, for example, we find an attempt to circumvent the problem by labelling the phenomenon a transitional form between matriliny and patriliny.[7] In Schneider we find a similar tendency: matrilocality is primary and generates matrilineal descent groups, but the matrilines can survive 'under a variety of conditions which would not suffice to create them. The *avunculocal* and duolocal systems, which exhibit the most tightly organised matrilineal descent groups, must exist under conditions quite unlike those which promote the origin of matrilineality'.[8]

There is nothing, however, which would imply that Kongo originally practiced matrilocal residence. West Central Africa displays a remarkable degree of homogeneity in both technology and basic production patterns[9] and just as striking a degree of heterogeneity in organisational forms. All of these societies practised swidden agriculture as well as hunting, gathering and fishing where possible. All had similar organisations of production. Yet, we find 'kingdoms' with provinces, districts, and villages, as well as 'stateless societies' where the village was the largest political unit. The former were located in the savanna and the latter in the tropical forest areas to the north. Within the area as a whole, we find matrilineal, patrilineal and bilineal societies.

The matrilineal regions include the Lower Congo, Kwango, Kasai and Lunda. The patrilineal forms are found among the Mongo and Fang to the north, and among the Songye and Luba on the savannah. Bolia in south-west Mongo is considered to be bilineal.

Within the matrilineal region we also find a great deal of variation. Richards, in her article on matriliny, notes that within the 'matrilineal belt' the 'remarkable degree of uniformity as to the principles governing descent and succession' cannot be extended to other domains: 'The Central African people differ in a rather striking way as to their family structure, and in particular as to the various forms of domestic and local grouping based on the family'.[10]

Among the Kongo, the matrilines are localised according to avuncular residence. Since the turn of the century, however, sons have tended to remain with their fathers, at least until the latter's death. Among the Suku, just east of Kongo, two-generation localised patrilines emerged within the pre-existent matrilineal structure in the early 1900s.[11] Teke, according to Vansina,[12] shows evidence of bilateral tendencies in matrilines of up to four generations. And among the Bushong of Kasai, the village, rather than the matriline, functions as land-holding unit and is the locus of economic co-operation and religous activity.[13] Finally, Douglas, in her comparison of Bushong and Lele, has clearly shown how significant differences in production and social organisation can be present within a single cultural, technological and ecological context.[14]

Patrilineal societies display a similar heterogeneity. In *Introduction à l'ethnographie du Congo* Vansina describes four different kinds of political organisation within a single ethnic group, the Mongo: in the south-west there are kingdoms or chiefdoms headed by *mkumu-ekapo*; in the south-east we find a 'structure politique [basée] sur une organisation de lignages segmentaires' in which the title of *nkumu* carries no more than a limited measure of prestige; in the north-east we find 'ceremonies d'initiation *lilwa*' similar to more easterly groups; in the north-west we find neither *nkumu*, developed lineage structure nor initiation ceremonies.[15]

Mongo is usually classified as patrilineal and patrilocal. We find, however, that the north-west exhibits some cognatic tendencies, that the south-west has well developed bilineal descent, and that the Ntomba Najale (also south-west) are matrilineal.[16]

These societies, however, are never unequivolcally matrilineal or patrilineal. Nor can they be simply classified as 'kingdoms' or 'stateless societies'. A gradual centralisation and hierarchisation occurred, developing up to a point at which the macro unit tended to break down. Some hierarchies (e.g. the Kongo kingdom) broke down soon after European contact (the middle of the seventeenth century) while others maintained themselves or even evolved until actual colonisation. Some of these societies appear to have oscillated between matriliny and patriliny. Ethnographic sources indicate that the Pende of Kwango changed relatively recently from a patrilineal to a matrilineal organisation[17] and that the patrilineal Ngombe and Mongo had, at an earlier stage, been matrilineal.[18] This, however, can hardly be considered decisive evidence. What we do know with some certainty is that matrilineal societies during this century have tended to become patrilocal and have lost most of their matrilineal traits.

In west central Africa, matriliny during the pre-colonial period seems to have been associated with a more highly developed political structure as well as greater economic productivity. Europeans, on first arrival, found only matrilineal 'kingdoms', patrilineal kingdoms belong to a later period. These 'kingdoms', as stated previously, were limited to the savannah region while 'stateless societies' were to be found in the forest area to the north, an area which was predominantly patrilineal. Schneider has pointed out that matrilineal societies in central Africa are restricted to the zone south of the 'tropical forest': 'South of the tropical forest is a high-grass savannah zone with few cattle and a fair number of matrilineal peoples. South of this is a scrub or dry forest area mostly occupied by matrilineal peoples.'[19]

There is, then, a clear correlation between tropical forest, patrilineality and 'stateless societies' on the one hand, and between savannah dry forest, matrilineality and 'kingdom' on the other. In those areas where the savannah penetrates the tropical forest we again find matriliny carved, as it were, out of the surrounding patrilineal woodland.[20]

One interpretation might be that the savannah/dry forest area has afforded an especially favourable setting for both matriliny and the development of 'kingdoms'. Both Vansina and Suret-Canal have adopted this kind of explanation with respect to the distribution of kingdoms: the savannah offers better possibilities of communication; cultural exchange is facilitated and the social contraditions accompanying increased social intercourse are multiplied.[21]

But we have still to deal with the relation between matrilineality and the formation of kingdoms. Contrary to conclusions based on data from other areas of the world,[22] matriliny in Central Africa seems to be associated with a more rather than a less developed form of political organisation. This political form seems to have had difficulty in penetrating the tropical forest zone, but, in some cases, judging from the available material, the greater intensity of agricultural production might be said to have caused deforestation and succession to grassland. Nicolai, for example, reports that the Lac Léopold II region, classified ecologically as dense equatorial forest, contains a large tract of unnatural savannah which has 'une estension étonnante'.[23] This savannah is located in the unquestionably matrilineal Kasai region.

Systems with prestige goods

Material from West Central Africa suggests, as Leach has maintained,[24] that matriliny and patriliny are by no means the significant categories they have been made out to be. In the following we shall attempt to show:

1. That different organisational forms are but variations of a single underlying system. This is in direct opposition to the approach

adopted by Terray. The latter seeks an explanation for the 'multiplicity of social and political relationships' encountered among 'primitive societies', but rather than adopt a structural approach in which different organisational forms are seen as variations of a single underlying structure, he attributes to each individual society a specific combination of two or more 'modes of production'. He attempts to account for the existence of a specific social phenomenon in terms of the mere co-presence of another social or technological phenomenon. By restricting himself to the specifically empirical level he places himself in the same situation as the functionalists for whom there is no possibility of dealing with inter-structural relations which are not visible phenomena.

2. That the internal rationality of the system is not defined primarily by food production but by the production of prestige articles. Sahlins in his 'The domestic mode of production'[25] has demonstrated how little 'technology' and the organisation of production can tell us about the 'superstructure' in primitive society. In Central Africa, power relationships are established, consolidated and maintained through the control of prestige articles – products which are not necessary for material subsistence, but which are absolutely indispensable for the maintenance of social relations. An individual needs prestige articles at a number of critical occasions during his life – at puberty rites, for bride-price, as payment for religious or medical services, to pay fines, etc.[26]
3. That Kongo's localised matrilines, consisting of mother's brothers and sister's sons, can only be properly understood as the result of the operation of a larger system.

Within anthropology, Kongo type societies have been regarded as matrilineal on the grounds that the macro-unit consisted of so many identical matrilineal descent groups. The macro-unit is assumed to have the same structure as each of its constituent parts. Opposed to this view students of 'alliance theory' have stressed the relations between sub-units – 'the norms of social relations and the rules governing the constitution of social groups and their interrelations'.[27] Here we must emphasise the importance of *starting* with the macro-unit as such (consisting of both specific sub-units and a structure which unites them) and with the internal dynamics of the system as a whole.

There are two structural elements common to virtually all West Central African societies; the kinship organised sub-units and the political network which binds them together. The lineage is necessarily a mere constituent part of the larger unit which is in fact neither patrilineal nor matrilineal.

Meillassoux[28] has drawn attention to the importance of prestige goods for the elaboration of power relations within kin groups. The control of such articles, which, among other things, are used for the payment of bride-price, enables the elders to establish and maintain a measure of dominance over the 'younger' members of society. Meillassoux' model locates the principal contradiction *within* the sub-unit, between 'elder' and 'younger'. The relation *between* kin groups is described as one of alliance and co-operation between 'elders'. We shall, on the contrary, suggest the existence of *two* types of contradiction: those *within* the sub-unit and those *between* different sub-units.

The very nature of prestige articles in Central Africa implies a non-egalitarian relation between local groups. The possibility of accumulation is built into the system and should one local group have at its disposal more prestige articles than its neighbours, it has the possibility of assimilating individuals from the economically weaker groups, facilitating its own expansion at the latter's expense. Prestige goods are converted into (a) wives and (b) slaves, and their increase amounts to an increase in the number of producers (of both food and prestige goods) as well as the number of 'warriors'. Economic and military superiority, thus, tends to reproduce itself on an expanded scale.

In this type of society there is a contradiction between local and regional levels. The localised segment of the matrilineage which is but part of a larger unit, has, in fact, no independent structural existence. Despite this, however, it tends to behave as an independent political unit in conflict and competition with other apparently identical groups. Thus, the successful expansion of one such unit can, as we shall see, undermine the very structural conditions for its own continued growth.

The characteristic of systems in which the accumulation of prestige articles plays a dominant role[29] is that women tend to move up the lineage hierarchy, wife-takers ranking higher than wife-givers. Those groups which control the sources, production and distribution of prestige goods have a dominant position, and the flow of these goods away from the sources of control is by far the most important mechanism of intergroup ranking. Women and slaves flow in the opposite direction:

> The superordinate chief did not keep his prestige articles; he redistributed them. But it is not simply a question of circulating prestige articles; within this process we find the important element of *converting 'money' into human beings*. The rich transferred prestige articles to subordinate groups in exchange for wives, i.e. they paid bride price, or for 'slaves'. There was political gain here, the higher chief always having the possibility of attracting more individuals from other groups than could a chief at the bottom of the hierarchy.[30]

The relation between super- and subordinate groups is expressed as one between 'men' and 'women'. In one of the Kongo origin myths we are told that Wene (the founder) came with his 'men', conquered the indigenous population and married its 'women'. In fact, most of the ideology of Central African societies is marked by a dualism in which it is imagined that the population consists of two groups, the conquerors and vanquished original inhabitants. The conquerors are 'men' and their subjects 'women'.[31] The women of (the highest) 'wife-taking' groups also had the status of 'men'. They were allowed to choose their own husbands who, while not paying any bride-price,[32] were not permitted to take additional wives.[33] Among the Yanz (*kasai*), according to Malembe, there were two categories of clans; *engom*, aristocratic and 'masculine' and *nsaan*, subordinate (commoner) and 'feminine':

> Seuls les Engom revendiquent l'attribut de virilité. Ce principe de virilité est non seulement l'apanage des hommes engom, mais même les femmes s'en réclament. C'est pourquoi les vraies cheffesses yansi choisissent elles-mêmes leur propre mari. Celui-ci doit rejoindre son épouse cheffable à Mbé et rester monogame.[34]

Apart from this, there is also evidence of a transfer of women from higher to lower groups, but this only concerns chiefs and their principal wives.[35] In several publications de Sousberghe[36] has shown that besides matrilateral cross-cousin marriage, ie. the asymmetrical flow of women from lower to higher groups, there is also patrilateral and bilateral cross-cousin marriage among the matrilineal societies of Central Africa. According to that author the Kongo practice patrilateral cross-cousin marriage, an assertion which is born out in a number of proverbs as well as by the testimony of informants who claimed to be under pressure to marry into their father's lineage.[37] There is also evidence, however, of prescriptive matrilateral marriage, (a fixed asymmetrical relation between *tata* and *muana* groups):

> Le marriage avec la fille du *Ngwa Kazi* (= MB, K.E.) pourrait théoriquement conduire à une politique dite des éxchanges généralisés. Cette politique maintiendrait les groupes alliés dans une relation continue de *Tata* à *Mwana*, de père à fils.[38]

As long as these groups remain ranked with respect to one another it does not appear likely that a *muana*-group can become wife-taker to its *tata*[39] (as this would imply a reversal of political rank). The reports of patrilateral cross-cousin marriage (presumably) date from a later period of Kongo's history when inter-group hierarchy had broken down, and where consequently it was possible for groups to be simultaneously *tata* and *muana* with respect to one another. Where hierarchy was maintained, however, marriage was matrilateral[40] –

subordinate groups gave wives to superordinate groups, and the two thereby redefined themselves respectively as *muana* and *tata*. Children belonged to their mother's lineage and were thus *muana* (= son). At a given age they moved to their mother's brother, wife-givers to their father, who was a member of their *tata* group (*tata*=father).[41]

Patrilineal societies: Mongo, Fang, Songye

In a system dominated by the production, exchange and accumulation of prestige goods patriliny would seem to be a most natural principle of descent. With patrilocal residence and patrilineality, prestige articles can be used to maximise the number of wives and therefore the number of producers and warriors. Reports from the earliest European contact with West Central Africa, however, contain no mention of patrilineal societies. All those kingdoms which Europeans first encountered were matrilineal. However, reports from the later part of the nineteenth century do reveal the existence of patrilineal societies which fall into two distinct ecological zones: (a) the tropical rain forest, and (b) the savannah to its south.

Organisational differences between the zones are immediately evident. Within the forest zone the political units are small. Mongo patrilines, for example, undergo continual fissioning, new autonomous local groups constantly emerge and relations between them are markedly weak: 'Political fragmentation seems to be a rule'.[42]

> Le besoin en terrains de culture et de chasse provoque l'éparpillement sur le territoire. Il s'ensuit le relâchement des rapports et la diminution de leur fréquence. L'arbre généalogique s'allongeant, on se sent de moins en moins apparenté . . . Chacun des segments devient un groupe autonome avec sa propre autorité et son propre chef politique . . . Cette segmentation progressive et continuelle qui forme toujours de nouvelles unités politiques, est une des principales caractéristiques de la société mongo.[43]

This is also the case for the Fang during the present century for whom the village is a 'closed' entity and where relations between them were characterised by continual feuding.[44] We find no trace of the complex alliance networks encountered in matrilineal societies.[45] The dynamic of the patrilineal system consists in the expansion and consolidation of the local group at the expense of the wider alliance network. Within a limited area, economically stronger local groups tend to assimilate their neighbours in such a way that a single large exogamous unit emerges. In the absence of increasing sources of prestige articles and possibilities of continued expansion, the resultant patrilineal unit is doomed to eventual stagnation and fragmentation, lacking the very means of its own reproduction as an exogamous group.

Mongo shows traces of a more elaborate alliance system, and Hulstaert goes so far as to assert the existence of 'indices pour une organisation ancienne plus centralisée . . .'[46] This assertion should be considered in light of reports that Mongo was matrilineal at some earlier stage. External stimulus in the form of trade serves to reinforce the centripetal tendencies which find their most extreme expression among the Songye during the era of the slave trade.

Vansina writes of the 'particular pattern of Songye settlements in the nineteenth century': 'Most Songye "tribes" occupied but one city. Exact figures are unknown but every town must have comprised thousands of inhabitants. City organisation and overall political organisation were practically synonymous.'[47]

Songye has 'une densité extraordinaire'[48] and we find reports of villages of up to 10,000 with streets of up to a kilometre in length.[49] Europeans were also impressed by their productiveness. Their fields are described as extensive and elaborately cultivated and the inhabitants as capable and industrious.[50]

Here the patrilineal form appears to have been quite successful. Through contact with slave traders, foreign prestige goods were pumped in via the central power resulting in the assimilation of individuals from peripheral areas and the establishment of dense population concentrations. By purchasing slaves from other populations (e.g. Tetela) Songye was able to obtain European goods without selling its own population. The patrilineal organisation was also particularly well adapted to the conditions of slave trade since it tended to maximise military strength. Songye was essentially a creation of the slave trade. When the latter ceased, the political unit collapsed, and by the 1940s fragmentation had gone so far that each family claimed to head its own domain.[51]

Matrilineal societies: Kongo

Let us now consider the functioning of a matrilineal system. Matrilineal societies with avunculocal residence seem at first to be a paradox since the accumulative mechanisms of the system are immediately neutralised. It is no longer possible to increase the number of one's dependents by increasing the number of one's wives. Children, rather than belonging to their father, are transferred to their mother's brother.

The system would also appear to be paradoxical from another point of view. From the perspective of the localised matriline it might seem remarkable that one group can literally give away its younger generation to another. Matrilineality, however, is but a secondary phenomenon. The patriline in Kongo-type societies is not localised but dispersed in such a way that each generation's sons in A move, at a certain age, to B (see Fig. 1).

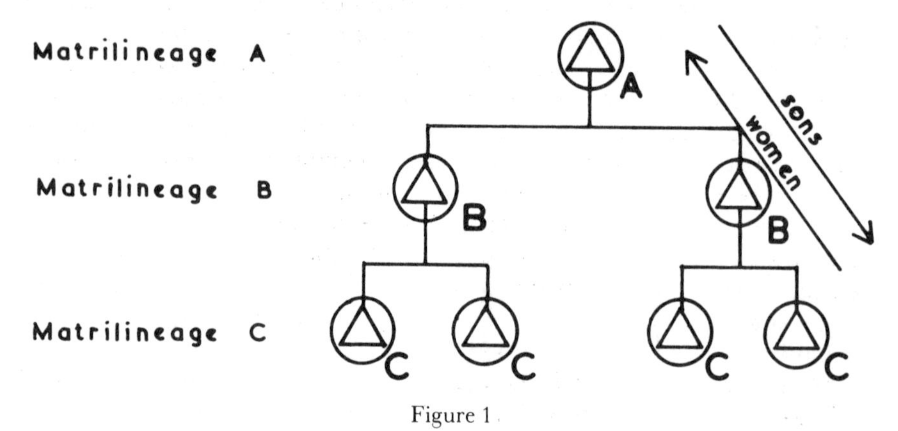

Figure 1

Women are transferred from lower to higher groups, but their sons do not remain with their fathers. They are, instead, sent off, and as a consequence, male members of any one local group are related as MB and ZS.

This combination of matri- and patrilineality implies a corresponding duality in the ideological and political structures. Each group is at once a matriline and a sub-unit in a larger patrilineal structure, and all societies in West Central Africa recognise both matrilineal and patrilineal elements. In his work on the Vili, Pechuel-Loesche distinguished 'die Familie, die Mutterreihe' and 'die Stammbaumlinie, die Ahnenkette oder Vaterreihe'.[52] This dualism is expressed ideologically as the combination of two ethnic strata, an original matrilineal population and a 'younger' patrilineal conquering group.[53] It is said, for example, that the Bolia conquered an older matrilineal population and introduced patriliny.[54] The Mongo are also said to have found an indigenous population upon arrival in their present locality. After marrying their children became patrilineally related to the immigrants and matrilineally related to the conquered group.[55]

Matrilineality is, in effect, a way of counteracting the centripetal tendencies of the political economy. As we have seen for Songye, patriliny in the presence of external stimuli leads to dense population concentrations, and this is hardly compatible with the local technology of production. With swidden agriculture and long fallow periods, increasing population density leads to a decrease in available fertile land, over-intensification, and finally soil degradation. We note here that wild game is extremely scarce in the patrilineal Songye area and that intensive techniques of cultivation such as the use of fertilisers are unique to this group.[56]

In myths concerning the rise of the Kongo Kingdom we are told how the king one day ordered his sons to leave the capital and to occupy new land. The capital area had become overpopulated and land for cultivation was scarce. The sons migrated in different directions; Mbamba to the south-west to found the province bearing his name, and Mpangu and his followers to the north-east where he settled in Mbanza Mpangu and founded the province of Mpangu.[57]

This myth depicts the migration as a historical event, but, in fact the same 'migration' is repeated in each generation. Sons leave *tata* in order to occupy their own land. The myth, thus, expresses the relationship between *tata* and *muana* and the kingdom as a whole is described as the result of demographic expansion from the centre.

More important than the regulation of demographic inequalities is the political gain to be got from the extensive alliance network which emerges in the developing matrilineal structure. This has been clearly pointed out by Mary Douglas in her work on African matriliny.[58] She writes:

> Matriliny is a form of kinship organisation which creates in itself crosscutting ties of a particularly effective kind. This is not to suggest that societies with patrilineal systems do not have such ties: they can produce them by means of cult or other associations but matrilineal descent produces them by itself. This is in its nature. If there is any advantage in a descent system which overrides exclusive, local loyalties, matriliny has it.[59]

Matriliny with avunculocal residence does not lead to the assimilation of economically weaker groups by stronger ones, but to the establishment of an alliance between the two. It is in the relations *between* local groups that the dynamic of matrilineal systems is expressed. A cannot grow numerically at B's expense, but both can win in the larger political arena and can expand at the expense of a third party. Alliance is a means to external assimilation. This is an important point: *matriliny, with its elaborate alliance network and with its relatively autonomous local groups, is an expansionist form of organisation that continually demands external areas from which to attract producers.* As long as the system continues to expand, the centripetal tendencies are directed against exterior groups. When, for one reason or another, boundaries or limits are reached, when expansion is blocked, forces are again directed inward and matriliny is weakened. This can be seen for the whole of West Central Africa. The tendency is most apparent for bilineal societies such as Bolia, but it is in evidence even in societies which are usually characterised as matrilineal. We shall return to this issue shortly.

Where the possibility of external assimilation does not exist we might expect to find a more or less even distribution of population. This, however, is not the case. The average village in the Kongo kingdom was small but Mbanza Kongo and the province capitals supported a considerable population.[60] According to Pigafetta, Mbanza Kongo, at the end of the sixteenth century, had a population of 100,000[61] – a figure which appears to be greatly exaggerated. However, after considering other estimates, Randles settles for 20,000 to 30,000 at the beginning of the sixteenth century which seems far more realistic.[62] In any event, this is a surprisingly high figure. Within these villages or towns there was a large number of slaves who were occupied in agricultural and other types of work, e.g. water transport.[63] These slaves were acquired largely through the channels of external trade. The royal guard, for example, was composed of slaves imported from Teke and other neighbouring kingdoms.[64]

The Kongo kingdom as a whole had a remarkably high population density. As Stevenson has pointed out, Kongo, with an area of 60,000 square miles and an estimated population of 2.5 million, averaged 40 persons per square mile during the seventeenth century.[65] This high demographic density can, with some certainty be seen as the result of the inflow of people from external areas. The Lower Congo area, in the early twentieth century, still had a relatively high density compared with other areas.[66] The Mbe plateau, on the other hand, had, in the middle of this century, a density of only one per 2/km^2.[67] In earlier decades this was the home of the Teke (Tio) kingdom, one which we find mentioned in the oldest historical sources as a slave exporter to the Kongo. (Slaves from Teke could be identified by their characteristic tattoo). The Ba-Teke were doubtless one of the more exploited partners in the regional competition between political units, and the depopulation it experienced can, with some certainty be explained, as Sautter suggests, by the fact that Teke's chiefs had to sell their own population in order to maintain their position in the competition for prestige.[68]

This is in accordance with Stevenson's observation that 'successful centres in the trade . . . tended to build up localised nodes of density', while less favoured areas were instead 'systematically raided and depopulated'.[69]

Marriage exchange, external trade and hierarchisation in the Kongo

With the basic properties of Kongo type structures in mind, we can now examine the way the system might react in varying political situations. But first we must consider this structure and its expansive need in more detail.

We have said that wife takers are ranked higher than wife-givers and this ought logically to coincide with matrilateral cross-cousin marriage. This accords with Mertens' observations (see Fig. 2).

Anna Mafuta and Philippe Bebi may marry because the former is the MBD of the latter, and thus 'la *kitata* de la fiancée et la *kanda* du

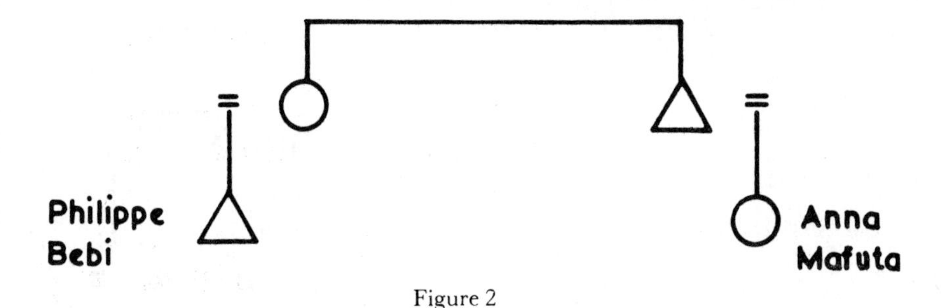

Figure 2

garçon'[70] belong to the same 'clan'.[71] We can envisage this arrangement as a transfer of women from *muana* to *tata*. But since the women remain with their fathers, and the men move to them, it is in reality a question of the transfer of men from *tata* to *muana*, from super to subordinate groups. Marriage between FF and SD which the early sources claim as an 'anomalie choquante' again implies a simple transfer of women from lower to higher groups. SD belongs to *muana*'s own *muana* and with matrilateral cross-cousin marriage she should, in principle, marry a man from her *tata* group. There was a tendency, however, for highest ranked groups to take its *muana*'s potential wives as well, ie. by taking wives from its wife-givers' wife-givers.

The lineage at the very top of the hierarchy can only be a wife-taker for there is no higher group to whom it can give women. In consequence this group retains its own women. Among the Suku these women were married with slaves 'in order that they might remain in the capital'.[72] In Loango they had very high status and, as stated previously, had the right to choose their own husbands. Aristocratic status implied that one's mother was 'eine Fürstin, durch die allein sich Blut, Rang und Besitz vererben'.[73] Royal succession in Loango was strictly matrilineal, unlike Kongo where sons as well could succeed to political office.

> Le roy doit estre pris parmi les princes du royaume. Cette qualité de prince est attaché à une famille seule, et ne se communique à la postérité que par les femmes, de sorte que pour estre prince, ou princesse, il faut estre né d'une princesse. Les enfants du roy et des princes, ne conservent pas cette qualité à moins que leur mère soit elle mesme princesse.[74]

Each unit in Fig. 3 consists of two groups, a subordinate 'feminine' group and a superordinate 'masculine' group. The dualistic ideology thus has a real foundation.

Those groups which are furthest from the centre must, in order to survive, secure wife-givers of their own, i.e. they must subordinate new groups in which they can place their sons. There is necessarily a losing party at the bottom of the hierarchy, and when it is no longer possible

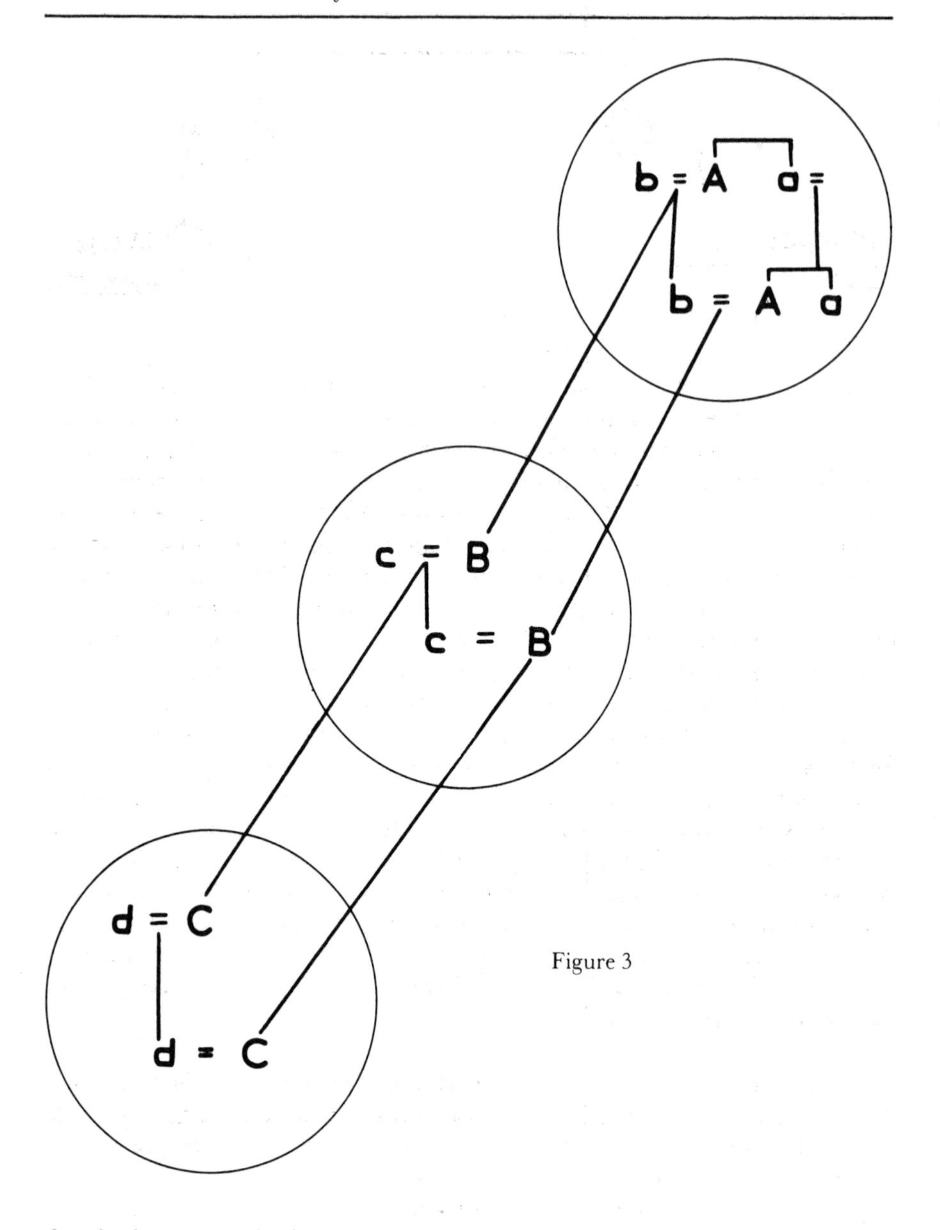

Figure 3

for the lowest ranked *muana* to acquire still lower *muana* they must lose their autonomy. The system, then, has no equilibrium state, there is either expansion or collapse.

In an earlier work[75] I discussed the relation between tribute, redistribution and the central power's monopoly over external trade. Tribute is paid, usually once a year, to *tata*. Flowing in the opposite direction is a redistribution of equivalent but different products. There is not, then, a unilateral transfer from sub- to superordinate groups, but rather exchange of products between different levels.[76]

As we can see (Fig. 4) in order for the system to function, A must have an external exchange relation with X.

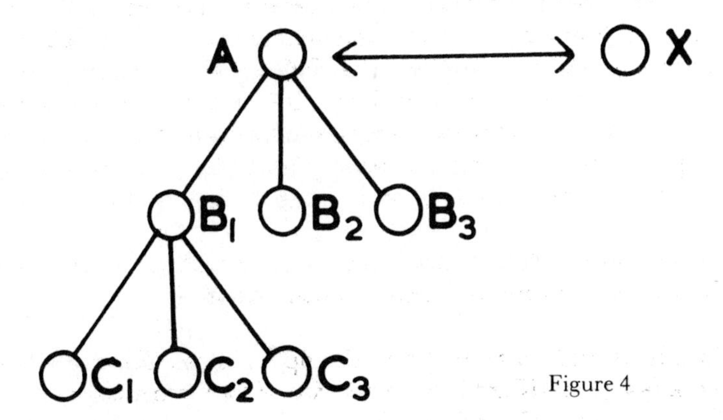

Figure 4

The relations to superiors and to inferiors are not symmetrical. There is but one group A above B while under A there are several groups (six provinces in the case of Kongo). At each level, excepting the highest and lowest, the situation is identical: one group above and several below (Fig. 5).

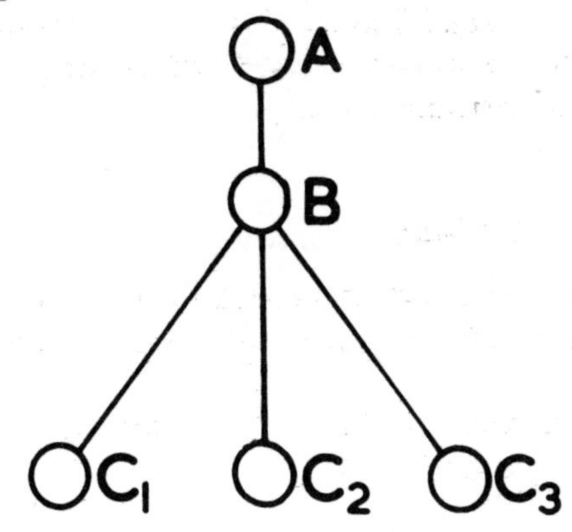

Figure 5

This implies that if B, for example, has three subordinate groups, it must distribute three times as much as each individual C. Hence A ought to produce three times as much as B, B three times as much as each C, etc. It is not likely that A could simply return its vassals' prestige articles as this would undermine its position as *tata*. The relation would then be the same as that between A and X – external trade instead of tribute-redistribution. The highest ranked groups must produce more than their subordinates, and herein lies the importance of control of natural deposits as sources of prestige goods. The centres of power in Central Africa are located in the vicinity of natural sources of prestige items, copper, salt and zimbu (shells). But these kingdoms expanded relatively rapidly and crystallised into far more hierarchical polities than warranted by the actual level of surplus production. Even if the central power in Kongo could produce more than the provincial centres (the source material describes them as being about equal in output), the difference cannot have been as great as six to one, and it is here that external trade becomes instrumental. Through its exchange relations with X, A can change internal products for foreign products and can thus appear to be economically stronger than it is in reality, i.e. in the production sphere.

Kongo type structures cannot exist in a closed space. An exterior world is a necessary prerequisite for several reasons:

1. Matrilineal relations and the development of alliance networks can only be established in the context of an ever-present exterior.
2. The character of wife-exchange implies the possibility of expansion. If new links cannot be added, they are subtracted. If the last link does not succeed in securing its own *muana*, it cannot exist as an autonomous group and is assimilated by its *tata*. The *tata* group itself is thereby put in a precarious position, having lost the group on which it depends for its own autonomy.
3. The kingdom's social hierarchy is only in part based on real surplus and is to a large extent the result of the conversion possibilities of external trade.

Changes of the system

We can now consider what happens to this structure when different forms of external influence and different political situations are encountered.

What would happen if, suddenly, a foreign agent Y began pumping in prestige articles via A (Fig. 6)?

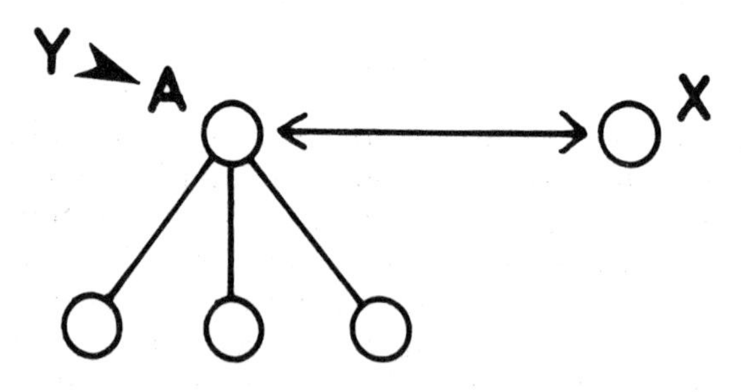

Figure 6

We might expect here that the external relation between the equals A and X would be transformed into an internal *tata-muana* relationship. A, thanks to his acquisition of foreign prestige articles, becomes economically strengthened and X would then be influenced to redirect its entire activity toward A.

This is what happened during the first stage of European-Kongolese contact. At the beginning, at least, almost all European goods were channelled through the central authority in Mbanza Kongo and the result was a considerably expanded Kongo. Upon first European contact, Kongo consisted of six provinces – Mpemba, Mbamba, Mbata, Nsundi, Mpangu and Soyo. In a letter to Lisbon, 1535, Afonso I, the reigning king of Kongo, introducted himself in the following manner: 'Dom Affonso pella graca de Deus Rey de Comgue, Jbugu et Cacomgo, Emgoyo, daque et dale nazary, Senhor dos Ambudos e Amgolla, da Quisyma e Musur, de Matamba, e Muylly, e de Musucu, e dos Amzicos.'[77] He presented himself not only as the king of Kongo, but Deus Rey of Bungu, Kakongo and Ngoy as well, and Senhor of a number of neighbouring kingdoms to the north-east, east and south. As early as the end of the sixteenth century, however, his influence had already diminished. According to Pigafetta, the king of Loango was 'traditionellement soumis au roi du Congo', but had become more independent with time and finally declared himself 'son ami et non plus son vassal'.[78] By 1607 both Kakongo and Ngoy are independent kingdoms too.[79]

If the king's monopoly over external trade is bypassed and his vassals are able to acquire European prestige articles through other channels, which is what happened after the initial phase of contact, the established hierarchy breaks down. As the prestige articles are transmitted to the local groups from outside and not via the hierarchy, the basis for this hierarchy disappears. We get secessions from the macro-unit as the local groups began competing and fighting with one another. The kingdom of Kongo collapsed in the middle of the 1600s and thereafter we observe a continuous disintegration, where the political units 'kept dividing and subdividing' until the end of the 1700s when the largest unit was a *mbanza* of only a few hundred huts and a number of even smaller villages of about fifty huts.[80]

Alliances broke down and the military strength of the local groups become the most important factor. As we have seen, the dynamics of the local groups are associated with patriliny and Kongo gives up much of its matrilineal character in this new situation. As the slave trade introduces serious conflicts between the local groups (European prestige articles were acquired in exchange for slaves, and every neighbour therefore became a potential object of slave raids and a serious threat to one's own security), they have to be strengthened militarily. During this period the chiefs do everything in their power to retain their own sons and acquire as many slaves as possible. Female slaves make patrilineal descent possible; they are stripped of their lineage membership and give birth to children who belong to their father, not to their mother's brother. These new political units are organised primarily for slave production. As Kongo increased its slave export, domestic slavery increased. Slaves were used in food production but their most important function was as soldiers or 'slave producers'. 'Wealthy persons were unable to invest their assets in anything but slaves,' writes Laman.[81] And since the increase in the number of domestic slaves in turn resulted in an increase in slave production for export, each re-inforcement of a local group resulted in a weakening of the area as a whole. The more successful the local chief, the greater the destruction and devastation.

Finally a parallel process, which takes place simultaneously and which makes up but an aspect of the collapse, is that when the possibility of external assimilation no longer exists the centrifugal tendency overcomes the centripetal tendency and economically stronger groups absorb and incorporate individuals from weaker groups.

We can clearly see this process in the descriptions of Bolia in the early twentieth-century literature. Bolia is designated as bilineal – descent is reckoned in both father's and mother's lines, and local kin groups contain individuals from both. There are two types of marriage arrangements; *esenga*, in which the children remain in the mother's 'clan', and *isongi*, in which they become members of the father's 'clan'.[82] The presence of these two principles for descent has been interpreted as the result of the combination of two different ethnic groups, one matrilineal, the other one patrilineal.[83] What it actually entails is a process in which economically strong local groups, having a matrilineal organisation, attempt to assimilate weaker groups. *Esenga* is the usual form of marriage; bride price is insignificant and the children become members of mother's descent group. But there is also the possibility of paying a high bride price and obtaining the right to one's own children. This is how *isongi* functions. Weaker groups, who have fallen into debt, can given a woman in *isongi* marriage as payment.[84]

Bolia uses the two kinds of marriages in order to maximise the size of the local group. One's own women can be married to slaves so that the marriage is *esenga* and the children belong to the mother's kin group. Men can marry female slaves so that the marriage will be *isongi*.[85] Alliances are sacrificed in favour of local group expansion. We find the same situation in the Lower Congo at the beginning of this century. Laisne writes about 'endogamous' vs. 'exogamous' marriage. The former gives 'au groupe son accroissement numerique' while the other creates 'alliances'.[86] As with Bolia, matrilines in debt were forced to pay with their own members, and in some cases, when prestige articles were lacking tribute was taken in the form of slaves.[87] The poorer groups, who could neither pay debts, fines nor tribute, simply lost their members. Mothers' brothers gave away their sisters' sons.[88]

The Bolia had no possibility of expansion in the twentieth century. There were large villages, *bompenjele* or *botanda*, and small villages, *esselo*[89] – the larger villages prospering and expanding at the expense of the smaller ones. Prestige articles were used to attract women in *isongi* marriages and put weaker groups in debt. The matrilineal organisation presupposes external areas which can function as suppliers of producers. When those external areas are lost, the society combines matrilineality with patrilineality.

Conclusion

The reason why functionalists like Radcliffe-Brown and materialists like Service have failed to come to any satisfactory understanding of matrilineality and patrilineality is that they have focussed only on the descent group in itself. The answer to why mother's brother and sister's son live together cannot be found within the matrilineage nor in the organisation of production. The problem can only be approached from the point of view of the global structure. The lineage has no structural autonomy; it is but a sub-group of the society, the structure of which can never be reduced to the structure of its component parts. The relations between the different lineages are not just 'alliances'. They belong to the fundamental structure of the larger society – and the shape and form of the lineage can only be understood within that wider framework.

Kongo with its hierarchies of matrilineages is basically a patrilineal society. The matrilineages are a secondary phenomenon, continuously reproduced by the process which separates the sons from their fathers. In the same way, the matrilateral cross-cousin marriage can be seen as the outcome of keeping daughters and giving away sons. The dividing of the matrilineage in two halves with the sisters in the superordinate and the brothers in the subordinate group will give the latter the position as wife-givers even if no women are transferred. When the perspective is shifted from the local level to that of the larger society, an entirely new set of questions emerges. What has to be explained is no longer the matrilineage but the society as a whole. As has been shown, all the different societies in West Central Africa can be seen as variations of a system where human beings are exchanged for prestige articles and where economic and political success depends on accumulation of wives and slaves. In order to explain a society, we must distinguish between its *mechanisms of functioning* and its *social form*, as the same mechanisms may manifest themselves in a number of different apparent forms due to the economic and political environment in which they operate.

Our final goal, however, is to analyse those deeper mechanisms, for in order to account for the distribution of societies in time and space we must ultimately explain the 'mechanical saw' whose camshaft generates that distribution.

NOTES

1 Radcliffe-Brown, A.R. (1968), 'Patrilineal and matrilineal succession', *in* Radcliffe-Brown, A.R., *Structure and Function in Primitive Society*, New York.

2 Radcliffe-Brown (1968), p. 48.

3 Schneider, D. and Gough K. (eds.) (1961), *Matrilineal Kinship*, Berkeley and Los Angeles, p. 656.

4 Service, E. (1962), *Primitive Social Organisation*, New York. Harris, M. (1968), *The Rise of Anthropological Theory*, New York.

5 Service (1962), p. 120.

6 Ekholm, K. (1972), *Power and Prestige: The Rise and Fall of the Kongo Kingdom*, Uppsala, p. 85.

7 Fox, R. (1967), *Kinship and Marriage*, Harmondsworth, p. 111.

8 Schneider and Gough (eds.) (1961), p. 661.

9 Vansina, J. (1966), *Kingdoms of the Savanna*, London, p. 19.

10 Richards, A. (1964), 'Some types of family structure amongst the Central Bantu', *in* Radcliffe-Brown, A.R. and Forde, D., (eds.) *African Systems of Kinship and Marriage*, London, p. 208.

11 Kopytoff, I. (1964), 'Family and marriage among the Suku of the Kongo', *in* Gray, R. and Gulliver, P. (eds.) *The Family Estate in Africa*, London.

12 Vansina, J. (1966b), *Introduction a l'ethnographie du Kongo*, Bruxelles, p. 134.

13 Vansina, J. (1964), *Le Royaume Kuba*, Musée Royale de l'Afrique Centrale, Annales Sciences Humaines, no. 49, Tervuren, p. 66.

14 Douglas, M. (1963), *The Lele of the Kasai*, London.

15 Vansina (1966b), p. 83. Vansina's typology leaves much to be desired in the way of internal coherence. Here, however, we are only concerned with the evidence for regional variation.

16 Vansina (1966b) p. 85.

17 Haveaux, G.L. (1954), *La Tradition historique des Bepende Orientaux*, Inst. Royal Colonial Belge, Section des sciences Morales et politiques, Mémoires XXXVII.

18 Colle, – (1923), 'La Gombe de l'équateur: Histoire et migrations', *Bulletin de la Société Royale Belge de Géographie*, XLVII, pp. 161-2; Van der Kerken, G. (1944), *L'ethnie Congo*, Inst. Royal Colonial Belge, Section des sciences morales et politiques, Mémoires XIII, 569 ff.

19 Schneider and Gough (eds.) (1961), p. 667.

20 Schneider and Gough (eds.) (1961), p. 668.

21 Vansina (1966a), p. 10; Suret-Canale, J. (1969), 'La société traditionelle en Afrique Noire Tropicale et le concept du mode de production asiatique', *in* Garaudy, R. (ed.), *Sur le 'mode de production asiatique'*, Paris, p. 112.

22 Murdock, G.P. (1937), 'Correlations of the matrilineal and patrilineal institutions', *in* Murdock, G.P. (ed.), *Studies in the Science of Society*, New Haven; Schneider and Gough (eds.) (1961), p. 670.

23 Nicolai, H. (1972), 'La destinée d'un pays equatorial, le lac Leopold II', *in Etudes du Géographie Tropicale offerts à Pierre Gourou*, Paris, p. 359.

24 Leach, E.R. (1961), *Rethinking Anthropology*, London.

25 Sahlins, M. (1972), *Stone Age Economics*, Chicago.

26 Ekholm (1972), p. 111.

27 Schneider, D. (1965), 'Some muddles in the models', *in* Banton, M. (ed.), *The Relevance of Models for Social Anthropology*, London, p. 26.

28 Meillassoux, C. (1960), 'Essai d'interprétation du phénomène économique dans les sociétés traditionelles d'auto-subsistance', *Cahiers d'études Africaines*, 1.

29 Before European contact, prestige goods consisted mainly of shells, metals, cloth, salt and ivory.

30 Ekholm (1972), p. 136.

31 Rombauts, H. (1945), 'Les Ekonda', *Aequatoria*; Dolisie, A. (1927), 'Notes sur

les chefs Ba-Tekes avant 1898', *Bulletin de la société des Recherches Congolaises*, 7-8, Bruxelles; Van Avermaet, M. (1954), *Dictionnaire Baluba-Français*, Tervuren, p. 168.

32 Van Wing, J. (1959), *Etudes Bakongo*, Louvain, p. 111.

33 Cuvelier, J. (1953), *Documents sur une mission française au Bakongo 1766-1776*, Institut Royal Colonial Belge, Section des sciences morales et politiques, Mémoires, XXX, p. 52; Pechuel-Loesche, E. (1954), *Volkskunde von Loango*, Stuttgart, p. 187.

34 Malembe, – (1967), 'La société politique Yanzi', *Cahiers économiques et sociaux*, p. 226. 'Only the Engom claim to possess the attribute of virility. The latter is not only characteristic for men but also for the women. This explains why female chiefs among the Yansi can choose their own husbands themselves. The latter must join their chiefly wives and remain monogamous.'

35 Doutreloux, A. (1967), *L'Ombre des fétiches: société et culture Yoruba*, Louvain, pp. 144, 192.

36 De Sousberghe, L. (1966), 'L'immutabilité des relations de parenté par alliance dans les sociétés matrilinéaires du Congo', *ARSOM, Bulletin des Séances*; de Sousberghe, L. (1967), 'Le mariage chez les Bakongo d'après leurs proverbes', *Paideuma*; de Sousberghe, L. (1968), *Les unions entre cousins croisées*, Museum Lessianum, Section missi-logique No. 50; de Sousberghe (1969), *Unions consecutives entre apparentés*, Museum Lessianum, No. 52.

37 de Sousberghe (1968), p. 86.

38 Doutreloux (1967), p. 143. 'Marriage to the daughter of Ngwa Kazi could theoretically lead to a policy of generalised exchange. Such a policy would maintain allied groups in a permanent relation of *Tata* to *Mwana*, father to son.'

39 cf. Leach, E.R. (1954), *Political Systems in Highland Burma*, London, on *mayu/dama*.

40 'In the majority of cases the husband lives in his village and the wives stay in their native villages' – Laman, K. (1957), *The Kongo II*, Uppsala, p. 58. Here 'his village' is the village of his mother's brothers and her 'native village' is the village of her father, i.e. his mother's brother.

41 Ekholm (1972), p. 63.

42 Merriam, A. (1959), 'The concept of culture clusters applied to the Belgian Congo', *S. West. J. Anthrop.*, 20, p. 376.

43 Hulstaert, G. (1961), *La Mongo: Aperçu General*, Musee Royal de l'Afrique Centrale, Archives d'Ethnographie, 5, Tervuren, p. 37. 'The need for agricultural land and hunting territory provokes the dispersal of groups within the larger area. This leads to a weakening of social relations and a reduction in their frequency. Genealogies are stretched and there is less of a feeling of kinship between groups. Each segment becomes an autonomous group with its own authority and political chief. This continual and progressive segmentation, which leads to the formation of new political units, is a principal characteristic of Mongo society.'

44 Tessman, G. (1913), *Die Pangwe*, Berlin, p. 211.

45 Balandier, G. (1963), *Sociologie actuelle de l'Afrique noire*, Paris, pp. 102, 139.

46 Hulstaert (1961), p. 36. 47 Vansina (1966b), p. 29.

48 *Congo Illustré*, 1893, p. 90.

49 Van Overbergh, C. (1908), *Les Basonge*, Collections des Monographies Ethnographiques, 3, Bruxelles, p. 196.

50 Van Overbergh (1908), pp. 211 ff.

51 Malengreau, G. (1947), *Les Droits fonciers coutumiers chez les indigènes du Congo Belge*, Inst. Royal Colonial Belge, Section des Sciences morales et politiques, Memoires.

52 Pechuel-Loesche (1954), p. 467.

53 Randles, W.G.L. (1968), *L'Ancien royaume du Congo des origines à la fin du XIXe siècle*, Paris, p. 37.

54 Philippe, R. (1954), 'Notes sur le regime foncier au Lac Leopold II', *Aequatoria*, p. 51; Van Everbroeck, N. (1961), *Mbomp-ipoku, le seigneur à l'abime*, Musée Royal de l'Afrique Centrale, Archives Ethnographiques, 3, p. 134.

55 Van der Kerken (1944), p. 532. 56 Vansina (1966a), p. 164.
57 Van Wing (1959), pp. 48-9.
58 Douglas (1963); Douglas (1964), 'Matriliny and pawnship in Central Africa', *Africa*, 34; Douglas, M. (1969), 'Is matriliny doomed in Africa?', *in* Douglas, M. and Kaberry, P. (eds.), *Man in Africa*, London.
59 Douglas (1969), p. 128.
60 Cuvelier, J. and Jadin, L. (1954), *L'Ancien Congo d'après les archives romaines (1518-1640)*, Inst. Royal Colonial Belge, Section des sciences morales et politiques, Memoires XXXVI, pp. 120-1; Cuvelier (1953), p. 24, note 1.
61 Pigafetta, F. (1951), *Relazione del Reame di Congo et delle circovicine contrade tratta dagli scritti e ragionamenti di Odoardo Lopez Portoghese*, Rome.
62 Randles, W.G.L. (1972), 'Pre-colonial urbanisation in Africa south of the Equator', *in* Ucko, P., Tringham, R. and Dimbleby, G.W. (eds.), *Man, Settlement and Urbanism*, London, p. 892.
63 Cuvelier (1953), p. 135.
64 Pigafetta (1951), Lib. II, Ch. VII; Balandier, G. (1965), *La Vie quotidienne au royaume du Kongo du XVIe au XVIIIe siècles*, Paris, p. 190.
65 Stevenson, R. (1968), *Population and Political Systems in Tropical Africa*, New York, p. 182.
66 Gourou, P. (1955), 'La densité de la population rurale en Congo Belge', Academie Royale des Sciences Coloniales, Collections science naturel et medical, *Mem. Tom* I. 1.
67 Sautter, G. (1960), 'Le plateau congolaise de Mbé', *Cahiers d'études africaines*, 1, 2, p. 5.
68 Sautter (1960), p. 39. 69 Stevenson (1968), p. 183.
70 *Kitata* is the patrilineal and *kanda* the matrilineal group.
71 Mertens, S.J. (1942), *Les Chefs couronnés chez les Bakongo orientaux,* Inst. Royal Colonial Belge, Section des sciences morales et politiques, Mémoires XI, p. 192.
72 Kopytoff, I. (1965), 'The Suku of the Southwestern Congo', *in* Gibbs (ed.), *Peoples of Africa*, p. 459.
73 Peschuel-Loesche (1954), p. 187.
74 Cuvelier (1953), p. 49. 'The king must be chosen from among the princes of the realm. The princely quality belongs to only one family, and is communicated to posterity only through women, so that in order to be a prince one must be born of a princess. Children of the king and princes only maintain their status if their mothers are also of princely blood.'
75 Ekholm (1972). 76 Ekholm (1972), pp. 22ff., 129.
77 Brasio, A.D. (ed.) (1953), *Monumenta Missionaria Africana*, Vol. II, Lisbon, p. 38.
78 Bal, W. (1963), *Le royaume du Congo aux XVe et XVIe siècles,* Leopoldville, p. 23. Pigafetta bases his evidence on information collected by Duare Lopez from the last half of the sixteenth century.
79 Brasio, A.D. (ed.) (1955), *Monumenta Missionaria Africana*, Vol. V, Lisbon, pp. 241ff.
80 Vansina (1966a), p. 190.
81 Laman, K. (1953), *The Kongo I,* Studia Ethnographica Uppsaliensis, IV, Uppsala, p. 151.
82 Van Everbroeck (1961), p. 128.
83 Philippe (1954), pp. 51ff.; Van Everbroeck (1961), p. 135.
84 Van Everbroeck (1961), p. 128. 85 Van Everbroeck (1961), p. 135.
86 Laisne, R.P. (1937), 'Chez les Dondos', *Bulletin de la société des Recherches Congolaises*, pp. 159ff.
87 Bentley, W.H. (1900), *Pioneering on the Congo*, London, p. 43.
88 Bastion, A. (1874), *Die deutsche Expedition an der Loango-küste,* Jena, Vol. I. p. 181; Dennett, R.E. (1906), *At the Back of the Black Man's Mind,* London, p. 41; Laman (1957), p. 43.
89 Van Everbroeck (1961), p. 133.

CLAUDINE FRIEDBERG

The development of traditional agricultural practices in Western Timor: from the ritual control of consumer goods production to the political control of prestige goods

The existing data on western Timor present a picture of more or less hierarchically organised communities, united within political units of varying size, some ranking higher than others, which have appeared and disappeared over time. The literature distinguishes these communities on the basis of language. In the west we have the Atoni or Dawan, Tetun, Bunaq and Ema. However, cultural limits do not always coincide with linguistic boundaries and there are considerable cultural differences within a single language group.

In the absence of local written history, there are only myths to account for the vicissitudes of Timorese communities, but these myths differ from one another in their perspective on the subject. Although we can find information on more recent history in Portuguese and Dutch colonial reports, these reports are often so foreign to the native views that they too must be treated as myths.

We do, however, find common elements in all the available data although they are differently organised depending on the community. It would appear that what we have here is a vast system of transformations in the structuralist sense of the word.

In a comparative study of Indonesian agricultural societies, L. Berthe[1] classified the societies of western Timor as 'peripheral' since they are predominantly situated on the periphery of the archipelago in contrast to the 'centrally' located societies of the inner archipelago, principally in Java. Berthe distinguished the former by a number of traits, particularly the presence of permanent groups (Houses) maintaining permanent wife-giving and wife-taking relations with one another.

However, relying on his study of the Bunaq kinship system[2] – which he emphasised was speculative – he remarked that:

> The development of the bride-price system of marriage and of an alliance system as complex as that among the Bunaq impel one to ask what factors led to such a development. In asking such a question one leaves the realm of strictly so-called structures of kinship for another more fundamental one: the level of the *production of goods necessary* to the practice of marriage by bride-price and the *distribution* of these goods.
>
> One could hypothesise that a society with an elementary kinship structure in which the economy was exclusively based on highland agriculture and totally lacking in any form of non-agricultural market, would have little chance of ever changing the fundamental principles underlying its kinship system.[3]

He put forward the hypothesis that given the absence of precious metals in the Timorese subsoil,[4] the sandalwood and wax trade, known since the twelfth century, by supplying the Timorese with gold and silver, must have provided them with 'the mechanism for unimagined qualitative transformations of their social organisation . . . especially among the groups benefitting from the trade'.

In fact, in this type of society, the acquisition of prestige goods simultaneously influences the hierarchy and the marriage alliance system. Among the Bunaq especially, one's place in the hierarchy is based upon the possession of certain objects generally made of gold: the *dato bul loro bul*, the 'foundation of power' (*bul* = foundation or basis, *dato* = the general term for nobility, *loro* = the title the Tetun give to chiefs of a fairly extensive area).

We now have information on other western Timor societies that enables us to elucidate certain characteristics reminiscent of central societies. For instance, terraces and irrigated rice cultivation among the Ema; or the central authority acting as a guarantor of fertility, receiving a portion of the harvest in exchange. We have, then, transitional elements in the process of change from 'peripheral' to 'central' type societies, a process which Louis Berthe specified as irreversible. The central type of society is distinguished by the presence of an individual sovereign, theoretically the master of the soil and the guardian of its fertility. He is surrounded by functionaries and a nobility made up of his kinsmen, and by a population lacking permanent groups but with more or less recurrent networks in which marriage alliance is not continually repeated over time.[5] At the economic level, large-scale irrigation permits increased productivity and therefore the possibility of accumulating consumer goods. The latter are siphoned off by the central authority through taxes in kind, thus enabling the nobility and functionaries to live without working the land.

To understand the dynamics of western Timorese agricultural societies we must focus both on their agriculture, i.e. the production of consumer goods, and on their opportunities for obtaining prestige

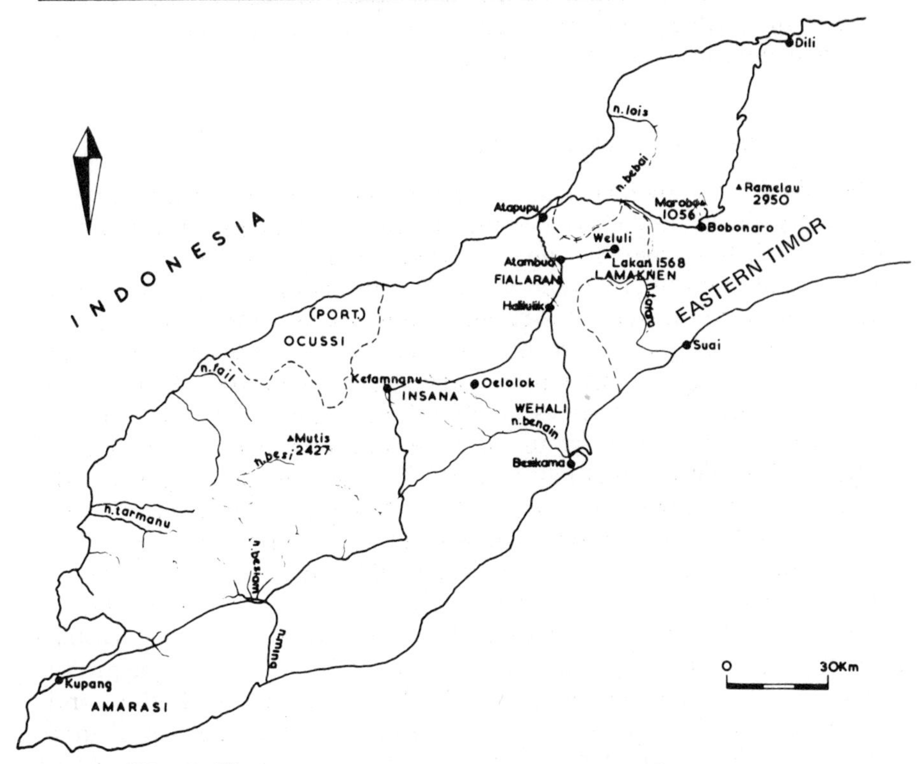

Figure 1. Western Timor

goods through the sandalwood and wax trade as suggested by Berthe. We shall first examine the way each community influences (or rather influenced, since we shall be dealing with the traditional context throughout) the productivity of its territory through both technical and ritual means. Then we shall analyse the processes of the accumulation of wealth in agricultural products on the one hand, and in those goods obtained through trade on the other. Despite the importance of marriage alliances in the network of economic exchanges and the establishment of the political hierarchy, we cannot analyse the system in detail here. Thus, we shall limit ourselves to pointing out those facts which are indispensable to understanding the data.

Furthermore, although in this article we adopt the traditional linguistic classification of groups, we shall only be giving one specific example for each linguistic group which cannot be taken as valid for the entire population speaking that language.

It should be noted that our information on each of the communities treated here is not always of the same type. Consequently, the material on each group will not always be presented in the same order. We shall begin with the Bunaq of Upper Lamaknen where we ourselves have worked and for whom we have most data. But, before proceeding with the Bunaq, we shall give an overview of the physical environment of Timor (Fig. 1).[6]

Timorese relief and climate

The island of Timor is a very broken land mass, but there are no volcanoes, in contrast to the islands of the archipelago's internal arc. The island, however, has not stabilised. Its faults are active and the entire land mass tips in such a way that the southern coast is sinking while the northern coast is rising. The island includes both ancient rock formations and sedimentary formations, the latter especially in the central depression where they were deposited during the Pleistocene prior to the elevation of the entire land mass. It seems that the latter process is still going on, since coral reefs can often be found at high altitudes (up to 1000 metres). All this contributes, along with sharply contrasting patterns of rainfall, to a high rate of erosion.

The heaviest precipitation comes when the north wind blows from continental Asia. In Timor, with its irregular land surface, rain clouds come in from the west and occasionally from the north-west or south-west. Generally the rains begin in November and end in April, with a peak in January-February, but occasionally they may begin in September or may not arrive until Christmas. In April, the wind changes and begins to blow increasingly from the south-east. Initially, this wind blowing across the body of water between Australia and Timor is still humid, carrying with it an occasional drizzle which usually falls on the southern coast and southern slopes of the mountains of the interior. Generally this light rainfall lasts from April to June. The rivers, many of which are nearly dry during the dry season, rise rapidly with every heavy rainstorm, and carry great quantities of mud which they deposit as soon as the rainfall is interrupted. Precipitation varies from one year to the next.

Methods of land use and ritual control of fertility

1. The Bunaq of Lamaknen

(a) *Overview of social organisation.* Among the Bunaq of Upper Lamaknen (the mountainous region in the south of the Portuguese* territory) the territorial unit is the village. Villages are composed of approximately 500 individuals distributed among different Houses (*deu*)[7] which form the community's basic social unit.

The status of a House is not dependent on the length of time it has been in the village or on its land, but rather on whether or not it has *dato bul loro bul*, the foundation of nobility. If it does possess these objects, then the House's rank depends on their value in the hierarchical system of valuation.

* This article was completed before the liberation of Eastern Timor.

In each village there is a superior and inactive 'feminine' chief and an active 'masculine' chief. Each usually has a 'gate' House through which one must enter. His aides are also taken from noble Houses. Furthermore, as we shall see below, there are Houses which are responsible for agricultural rituals. In Lamaknen, four villages have 'feminine' chiefs ranking higher than those of other villages and they have divided the entire territory amongst themselves. The other villages are considered as vassals to one of the four 'great ones'.

At birth, a Bunaq becomes a member of the House of which his mother is currently a member. There are two types of marriage. In the uxorilocal type, each spouse continues to belong to his or her respective House of origin and the children belong to the mother's House. In the second type, the wife and her descendants become permanent members of her husband's House, each House having several obligatory wife-giving (*malu*) and wife-taking (*ai baqa*) Houses. The first type of marriage is the most common and the choice of spouse does not conform to any apparent rule.

In contrast to what occurs elsewere in Timor, the choice between one or the other form of marriage is made at the outset. There is no transition from one form to the other and the bride-price in each circumstance is not of the same kind; for uxorilocal marriage the bride-price varies with the wife's status and must be entirely raised by the husband's kin. In the other form, the bride-price may be considerable, but it does not depend on the status of the wife's House and the wife may bring a considerable dowry with her, even including some *dato bul loro bul*. Furthermore, in order to amass the bride-price, the husband's House must rely on help from its own wife-takers who in turn appeal to their wife-takers. A good proportion of the society take part in such marriages since the wife-givers must themselves appeal to their own wife-givers in order to reciprocate some of their wife-takers' gifts. The second type of marriage is becoming less frequent and represents a 'grafting' of one House on another, as the Bunaq would say. In principle, the bride-price should be completely paid when the wife leaves her House for that of her husband. In the uxorilocal form of marriage, the couple often live together before the bride-price is paid.

Whether at marriage or on other occasions such as the rebuilding of houses or at funerals, gifts always proceed in the same direction. 'Feminine' goods – pigs and cloth – are given to one's wife-takers; 'masculine' goods – buffaloes, gold and silver – are given to one's wife-givers.

(b) *Agricultural practices and the management of cover vegetation.*[8] Village land is divided into fields for cultivation (*matas momen*) and grazing land (*bula*). The latter is held communally, while the former is distributed among the Houses which in turn distribute plots among their members. Furthermore, the *matas momen* are divided into a number of plots on which crops are rotated. In the village of Abis, where we did most of our fieldwork, there are six such plots, each is in principle used for three years. Theoretically there is a rotation period of eighteen years.

However, such a system can only function if each House (there are 24 Houses in Abis) has a piece of land in each of the six rotation fields, which is not the case. As it stands, all the most recently used land is grouped in only one of the rotating divisions. Today, the rotation period is much shorter and land is left fallow for no more than four or five years.

In the first year of cultivation, rice is grown, but only on the flattest, highest quality land. There are only limited amounts of this sort of land to be found on each domestic plot. The House members usually work together cultivating a single large field since the crop usually ends up as a communal ceremonial offering and food during marriages, funerary rights or the rebuilding of a dwelling in either their own House or that of their affines. Today, rice has remained a ceremonial food among the Bunaq, since the maize introduced by the Portuguese constitutes the staple diet. The latter cereal is planted in the second and third years. Maize is planted in the first year in fields which are too steep or rocky for rice and usually the land cannot be used for more than two consecutive years. The maize fields are generally divided up amongst members of a House who cultivate a field with two or three brothers and sisters, each assisted by their respective spouses. As most men are married uxorilocally, they end up by working their sisters' and their wives' fields.

Formerly, the people of a village lived in the 'town' (*tas*) situated on a hilltop for defence and the area between the *matas momen* and the *bula* so that pigs could be raised close to the houses. Now that war has ceased and the population is increasing and seeking more comfort, it has become more widely dispersed with people settling in areas close to sources of potable water and in choice flat and fertile locations, where a large garden can be made around the house. These gardens are usually designated by the name *kintal* – of Portuguese origin – or more rarely by the Bunaq name *leo*. Houses must be constructed on the *bula* since it is forbidden to build on the *matas momen* which is enclosed by a fence and used exclusively for cultivated fields, *mar*. Today, however, *bula* land is increasingly opened for cultivation; an act which requires, as does the building of a house on this communal land, permission from the chief and village notables. A peasant is master of his portion of *bula* as long as he cultivates it, but it can never become part of his domestic *matas momen*.

There is a great difference among fallowing methods depending on whether they are on lands used regularly by the same individuals or only occasionally cultivated. In the latter case, the land is covered by a variety of plantlife, often including a large proportion of *Lantana camara*, a thorny verbenaceous plant. Accidently imported as a decorative plant, it is considered a nuisance by the herdsmen as it has progressively invaded all the prairie and reduced the amount of possible grazing land. The agriculturalist, on the other hand, considers it beneficial because its intertwining thorny bushes provide a good form of protection for the soil. However, there is no doubt that the presence of *Lantana camara* prevents reforestation and the growth of other species, although land scarcity in Timor today is such that there is no longer time for the forest to redevelop.

On land cultivated every four or five years by the same individuals, principally on the *matas momen*, nearly all fallow vegetation consists of fast-growing arborescent leguminous plants which reconstitute nitrates absorbed by the crops (synthesising them in the nodules of their roots) and insure a sufficient amount of ash to fertilise the soil when the land is cleared. To insure the growth of this fallow vegetation, the Bunaq retain shoots and cuttings of species they consider advantageous. Some large leguminous trees are also generally allowed to remain and are pruned before the field is fired, thus ensuring the dissemination of seeds. When the land lies fallow, these species develop without any assistance and thus the cover vegetation of the *matas momen* or *zobel,* ‘the young’, is gradually completely transformed into arborescent leguminous plants which can sometimes reach a height of eight metres by the time they are recut. Thus, it could be said that the *matas momen* is a domesticated ecosystem.

If the fallow land accidentally catches fire, the result is catastrophic. In fact, fields used for cultivation are periodically weeded and all unsuitable species are removed. If the fallow cover vegetation catches fire before it has been decided that the field should be returned to cultivation, *Imperata cylindrica* will be the first species to develop, whilst the other species will only take root at a later stage. When the field is recultivated the whole job of getting rid of the *Imperata* stolons has to be begun again. Furthermore, the cover vegetation is too sparse to ensure a sufficient quantity of ash and there are fewer nitrates than with leguminous plant cover.

In the traditional social organisation, individuals known as ‘*mak*[1] *leqat*[2]’, ‘to listen[1] to see[2]’, were responsible for making sure that the rules concerning the protection of cover vegetation and the products of the land were followed. They reported to officials who then imposed variable fines depending on the infraction. One finds *mak leqat* among the Tetun and Atoni as well. The cutting of any plant, even the *Imperata cylindrica* could not be done without seeking the *mak leqat*'s permission. (Each village kept enough of this plant to ensure the re-roofing of their houses.) The vegetation around watering holes could only be cut after making offerings at the altars invariably found there and then only with prior consent of the owners of those altars. For the most important watering places, neither the cutting of bamboo or rattan, nor the taking of *sir* – the inner fibres of the *Arenga pinnata* used for covering the skylights of the houses – could take place until after the annual ceremony.

Formerly, before the cover vegetation was burnt, the plants around the plot to be cultivated had to be cut back four metres so that surrounding plots would not catch fire. On the plot itself, fruit trees and economically desirable trees (candleberry, sandalwood, etc.) had to be protected by covering the trunks with banana leaves. If this was not done, the cultivators would have been subjected to a fine. The *mak leqat*'s job was made easier by the fact that he only had to oversee the burning off of the *matas momen*. Today, when it is not uncommon to clear fields abutting directly onto grazing lands, surveillance has become more difficult. As traditional duties disappear, fines are rarely imposed when fire overruns the field being cleared and kindles all the village land, occasionally even reaching the land of neighbouring villages.

(c) *Agrarian rituals*. The Bunaq of Upper Lamaknen differ in one respect from the peoples living around them. All Bunaq consider themselves immigrants and view the right to cultivate their land as the result of a social contract. The notion of 'master of the earth' – *pan*[1] *o*[2] *muk*[3] *gomo*[4], 'master[4] of the land[3] and[2] the sky[1]' – is associated with the beings of the afterworld, the deceased original inhabitants of the earth (the *melus*) and with various local spirits inhabiting the hills, trees and rocks. These beings must be placated with offerings, but are not involved in all the actions of the living as are the Bunaqs' own ancestors. There is no gap between the first beings to have appeared on earth and the present day inhabitants of Lamaknen. The deceased share in the lives of the *roman*, 'the clear ones', i.e. those who are visible – the living.

Among the Bunaq, agricultural rituals are carried out at two principal times of the year: at planting and at harvest time. Intervening rituals preceding the ripening of the crops are mainly aimed at influencing the climate and making the rain stop. The rituals at planting times which mark the beginning of the rainy season are extremely complex. The goal of some is quite clear: for example to prevent the destruction of the seed by small predators, birds or mice. The purpose of others is less apparent and in order to understand them one must analyse the myths.

These rituals are accompanied by hunting in which the game is simultaneously: the animal that threatens to destroy the crops; the manifestation of the masters of the earth belonging to the afterworld; and a wild form of food which will be transformed symbolically into rice by the Lord of the Seed. In fact, during the period when these rituals are performed, the political hierarchy is put aside leaving the Lord of the Seed and the Masters of the rice in its place. These offices have been handed down from those who brought the first seed to the village. They in turn received the seed from their own parents who were characters in the origin myth of seeds. The episode in question is supposed to have occurred at a specific point on the journey of one of the contemporary Lamaknen lineages. In the myth, all seed – but especially rice which makes its first appearance at this point – was born from the body of a creature sacrified and then burned on the altar of the fields. It was simultaneously transformed into the bird which hails the coming of the rains.[9] The village ritually receives this seed each year before the rainy season. It must subsequently be cooled symbolically before being sown.[10]

But the sacrificed creature is only a mediator between mankind and the primordial being, the one-eared, one-eyed Lord who gave them the seed. The primordial being is not an ancestor, for not only is he cut in two, but he is unmarried and has no descendants. In the texts of the publically recited myths and rituals he appears as the creator of all things. However, in a more esoteric version which appears nevertheless in the public texts as the expression [1]*naqi* [2]*hot* [3]*gol* [4]*naqi* [5]*hul* [6]*gol*, '[3]children (of) [1]his Lordship (the) [2]Sun, [6]children of the [4]Lord [5]Moon', which is applied to all beings created including the present day Bunaq, this primordial being is presented as having been created by a couple, themselves created by a couple. It is as if the original creation blended into Infinity and only the expression 'children of the sun and the moon' remained to testify to the fact.

The time for the planting rituals comes when the group has collectively received the seed and made a request for the support and assistance of all the afterworld powers. for the coming harvest – especially from the *melus* who once lived in the village, the first ancestors who arrived in the villages, and the master of the wind and the rain, etc. The period of transition between the dry and rainy seasons, when the seedlings appear, is associated by each individual with his genealogical line of which he is merely a part. Offerings of food are brought to the tombs; the wife-givers also bring offerings and all these are taken by the wife-takers.

In Upper Lamaknen, the carrying out of rituals to ensure the ripening of the crops is the duty of the master of the seedlings and shoots. In Abis, this office is held by a man of the House, not only considered the most senior, but also heir to the 'feminine' *melus* chief's House, even though theoretically there is no link between the two. Furthermore, the *melus* are directly involved in this ritual by virtue of a discrete offering secretly carried under cover of darkness to a *melus* altar hidden in the brush near the village.

Harvest rituals vary with the plant in question. Products which might be considered luxuries: betel nuts, areca nuts, mangos or candleberries (*Aleurites moluccana*), cannot be harvested without authorisation from the guardians of the products of the earth. These products are assembled in the centre of the village and distributed in such a way that each House receives an amount proportional to its position in the political hierarchy with the 'feminine' chief receiving the largest share.

In most villages only private rituals are held for the harvesting of rice, the sacred food which was undoubtedly the staple before the introduction of maize, which is better suited to the Timorese climate and soil. As among the Atoni, the first thing done at harvest time is to call out the soul of the rice. To prevent its escape the field is surrounded with lime and crushed betel and with magical medicines. Food offerings of rice from the previous harvest and meat from a small pig are made. The offerings are made at the communal village altar to the *pan o muk*, 'the sky and the earth' (the metaphor for the primordial couple), to the village altar, to the ancestors, to the local springs, to the altar and four corners of the field, to those who died on their lands, and finally to the magical packet which contains a formula for causing the rice to come and grow abundantly and the gold disk on which the soul of the rice is supposed to rest throughout the harvest period. Those in political power receive only the baskets offered to the village altar and it is not the village chief who receives them, but any *dato*, 'noble', taking part in the harvest.

Once the harvest is over, the crop can, in principle, be eaten after the [1]*hoho*[2]*na*, '[1]to eat [2]the first', ceremony, i.e. the consuming of the first fruits during which gratitude is expressed to the ancestors for their assistance and they are asked to continue watching over their descendants.

The Bunaq carry out the same rituals for maize, both at harvest time and when offerings are made to the ancestors in each House. However, between these two rituals, a collective ceremony is held which resembles those held for the 'luxury goods' except that in this case it is purely symbolic. Only a few stalks and ears of corn are gathered and placed in the village centre and redistributed according to the political hierarchy. Furthermore, these same ears are later offered to the ancestors of each House and to the deceased on their tombs.

Thus, the Bunaq of Lamaknen only use symbolic offerings to gain favour with those who have power over crop fertility: they never repay a human being, considered to be the living guarantor of this fertility, with gifts in any quantity. Responsibility for the soil and the crops is widely dispersed: while the masters of the earth are supernatural, the masters of the rice, the Lord of the Seed, the master of the seedlings and shoots and the guardians of the products of the earth are living human beings. The territorial nature of the political chiefdom only defines the geographical limits of its power, but entails no control over the fertility of the soil. The fact that the political chief receives the greater share during the redistribution only confirms his authority. It is in no way an act of gratitude for some sort of ritual activity.

2. *The Ema of Marabo*

(a) *Altering the topography with terraces, drainage and irrigation works.*[11] The entire range of methods which the Bunaq use to be able to rotate their fields rapidly are directed solely at the cover vegetation. Such techniques never involve altering the land surface. The Bunaq cultivate sloping and flat land in the same way. If, every now and then, lines of stones seem to trace contour lines around their fields and give the impression of terraces, it is only an optical illusion. Those stones, found on the fields, have merely been piled up along the edges of the plots. Earth is never moved to make a field level, except in the case of garlic cultivation which only began about 20 years ago. As for the stones, only the large ones are removed. Small stones are thought to be good for germination because they protect the seeds from the sun and to some extent economise on their need for moisture. The only traditional alteration of the land surface occurred in the 'towns', *tas,* where the houses were often built on stone platforms. Furthermore, in myths the ancestors are always described as seeking *toiq*, 'horizontal level', or *telan*, 'flat sloping', land for their fields.

The Bunaqs' neighbours – the Ema – have constructed terraces and the contrast is especially striking if one follows the road from Maliana to Bobonaro, which winds between the Emas' cultivated terraces and the Bunaqs' unaltered fields.

The Ema are settled as far east as Atsabe, but we shall only deal with the Ema living on Marobo hill and in the valley irrigated by the river flowing down the hill. Marobo hill is a political unit with its ritual centre in the village on the top of the hill.

Part of the population is concentrated in seven villages where one finds traditional house forms. The three main villages are dominated by the three most important lineages. Each of these lineages is headed by a cold *bei* and a hot *bei*: the former being responsible for ritual and the latter for political matters. The remainder of the population is dispersed. They live in field houses, permanent dwellings established as the population expands, but which remain attached to the House of origin of their members. The House is the basic social unit among the Ema as well, but Ema Houses are composed of strictly patrilineal lineages. All daughters leave their House of origin at marriage and bride-price can be paid gradually by the husband's House, sometimes even after the couple's death.

The Ema cultivate several types of fields: sacred fields, fields 'at the foot of the enclosure', occasional clearings, irrigated rice-paddies, and orchards. The sacred fields, *asi upes* (*asi* is the term for dry field and *upes* has no meaning in Ema), are magnificent terraces – *atu*[1] *paen*[2] *ai*[3] *batan*[4], 'to pile up[2] stones[1], racks[4] for trees[3]', arranged in tiers for 300 metres beyond the warm springs of Marobo. These fields are not irrigated. Irrigation is even ritually forbidden under the threat of the fields collapsing. In fact, the source of water is a mystery since during the dry season all the springs dry up. On the other hand, during the rainy season, water pours down from the high areas and springs overflow at different spots. The water must therefore be channelled or it would accumulate along the supporting walls and the terraces would be in danger of collapsing. Consequently, Ema youth are instructed in the art of drainage as well as that of constructing terraces. The latter are not seen as a means of retaining water, but of allowing it to drain off. The ritual prohibition might thus be seen as a reflection of a lack of technical ability. Nevertheless, the Ema do have irrigated rice-paddies, but these are found on the plain.

Although they have solved the problem of protecting their soil against erosion, the problem of soil fertilisation remains. As swidden cultivators, they solve this problem by encouraging the growth of the same type of cover vegetation as the Bunaq, favouring the growth of arborescent leguminous plants and *Melochia umbellata* during fallow periods. According to their mythology, the latter species was sown by their ancestors wherever they settled.

Unfortunately, Clamagirand was unable to observe many of the techniques used in cultivating the sacred fields. The Portuguese administration had prohibited the burning off of fields in order to encourage the Ema to cultivate the irrigated rice-paddies that had been established recently in the Maliana plain by the agricultural service. Although it is still possible to burn off individual fields, it is impossible to do so on sacred fields without being seen, since the latter are worked communally after collective rituals have been performed. The sacred fields are divided into three: each third theoretically belonging to one of the three main lineages. But formerly, each of the three plots was cultivated according to a system of rotation. When one of the fields was planted, it was divided among the Houses of Marobo, all of which were attached to the three main lineages. Each of the three fields was used for four consecutive years, thus producing a fallow period of only eight years.

The Ema grow mainly maize and tubers which have a ritual role for them, unlike the Bunaq. Today, they have practically ceased to grow dry rice, (*asi*[1] *rai*[2] *teten*[3], 'field[1] of high[3] land[2]'), because some members of every House go off to cultivate the irrigated rice-paddies on the plain. Furthermore, although offerings must be of rice, maize may be offered to guests among the Ema.

The fields at the foot of the enclosure, *asi lia pun*, surrounding the village dwellings, are arranged in terraces. Generally, they are permanently under cultivation, thus marking the extreme in the tendency toward sedentism. Thus, the problem of fertilisation is even more acute here than elsewhere. Since the only known form of fertiliser is ash, all refuse that can be collected during the dry season – all sorts of leaves, corn sheathes, old roofing, etc. – is brought to these fields. Furthermore, any growing vegetation is cut down and all the roots are carefully removed. The Bunaq do the same in the gardens they are cultivating in increasing numbers around their houses.

Occasional clearings, *asi*, are fields prepared as required on land set aside for grazing near the field houses. For the first few years the fields are cultivated without even being graded, but they tend to be gradually transformed into terraces for permanent cultivation. Today, fewer fields are prepared as many Ema leave to work in the Maliana rice-paddies.

Traditionally, the Ema practise wet rice cultivation after the soil has been prepared by buffaloes trampling it into smooth mud. This technique of irrigated rice cultivation, *roe*, is known to the Bunaq who call this type of field *loeq*. Rice of several varieties grouped under the general term *ipi*[1] *zon*[2], 'wild[2] rice[1]', is broadcast and there is no transplantation.

The Bunaq distinguish two types of *loeq*: *loeq*[1] *inel*[2] *nil*[3], 'juice[3] (of) rain[2] rice-paddy[1]', and *loeq*[1] *il*[2] *pisi*[3], 'rice-paddy[1] with clean[3] water[2]', i.e. irrigated rice-paddy. It seems that the Bunaq were traditionally only aware of the former, which they organised during the rainy season into flooded beds, *liwe*, surrounded by small, evenly levelled dikes, *bataq*. Today, the Bunaq have irrigated rice-paddies on the plain of the Mali Baka and its tributaries,[12] but this practice seems to have been an innovation of the Japanese who forced the Timorese to employ this method during the last war.

The Ema, on the other hand, seem to have known irrigation techniques for a long time and have practised them both in the Be Bai valley and on strips of the plain along the upper reaches of the Marobo river. Part of the river's water is diverted into a canal, *baqo bea salan*, 'the water way', which emerges at the high point of the area to be irrigated. The latter is divided into graded compartments, separated by small dikes, *peta*, in such a way that the water can pass from one to another. Excess water returns to the river bed which thus serves as both the source of water and the drainage canal. However, special drainage canals appear to have been dug in the larger irrigated areas of the Be Bai plain.

It should be noted that differences in the levels of adjacent beds is small and never equal to that found between two terraces of the sacred fields.

The only true irrigated mountain terraces among the Ema are found in the area and coconut palm groves in areas immediately surrounding springs, *abat*, or rivers. But even here the irrigated surface is limited and permanently covered by dense vegetation, including the *Pandanus* of the *tectorius* group, and an undergrowth of ferns and selazinella. Therefore, the soil is rarely directly exposed to rainfall.

The Bunaq also have irrigated orchards, *natal*, near springs or on river banks. But, as in their other fields, no terraces are built and the canals for diverting water are the only modification of the land surface. However, as we have already noted, for about 20 years, the Bunaq have combined terracing and irrigation for growing garlic during the dry season.

(b) *Agrarian rituals*. There are certain parallels between the agrarian rituals in Marobo and those in Lamaknen. In particular, one finds the symbolic cooling of seed carried out collectively and then individually at each field altar before planting. But it seems that among the Ema emphasis is placed on water rather than the seed. The ceremonies marking the beginning of the rainy season, characterised by ritual performances at every major water source, are called 'singing the water'. The entire Marobo community carries out these rites, while the responsibility for their performance lies with the 'cold' *bei* of the three main lineages. However, there is in addition a master of the fields from one of the autochthonous Houses as well as assistants taken from other Houses.

As in Lamaknen, harvest rituals are characterised by symbolic offerings. However, the emphasis is clearly on the primordial ancestral couple who are both the Emas' ancestors and the ancestors of the basic cereals – rice and maize – upon which their descendants' prosperity depends.

During a brief investigation among the Indonesian Ema (near Atambua) we were able to find the same ritual elements, especially the importance attributed to the sources which provide the water for rice-paddy irrigation. There was also a ritual marking the flowering stage in the growth of rice; the first such ritual we had found in western Timor. Rituals accompanying the various stages in the growth of rice are very common and are more numerous among rice-growers with more evolved techniques. In Bali, for instance, one can find up to seven such rituals. This fact, in addition to what we have said about agricultural practices clearly shows that the Ema have the most evolved rice-growing techniques in western Timor.

3. *The southern Tetun*

(a) *The exploitation of the south coast alluvial plains.*[13] When the Europeans arrived, all the peoples that we have studied considered the kingdom of Wehali – known also as Malaka – as their superior within the traditional hierarchy. The inhabitants belong to the Tetun language group. Here too the House is the basic social unit, but descent is reckoned matrilineally, and men rather than women are exchanged.

In Wehali we find again the opposition between 'feminine' chief and 'masculine' chief as well as another opposition: plain and mountain. The ruler of Wehali is the 'feminine' chief of the plain, the *nai bot*. The mountain chief is the *liurai*, a 'masculine' chief. But in each village there is a 'feminine' and a 'masculine' chief.

Wehali occupies the most fertile plain in Timor. Its rich alluvial soils are all the more fertile due to the large quantities of ash washed down from swiddens of the mountain peoples. Furthermore, the area has the advantage of two rainy seasons. The vegetation is very luxuriant, but tree growth becomes sparse once one leaves the hills: here we find savannah consisting of *Borassus* and *Corypha*, typical of Timorese plains and very favourable to stock-raising. Many cattle are kept in this area. Copra plantations and irrigated rice-paddies are also found. However, these forms of cultivation were formerly unknown and the traditional method of cultivation was the dry field prepared by turning over the grass cover.

When a man marries, he calls on his kin and friends to help prepare the field. All the men are lined up with their digging sticks and turn over a strip of grass-covered earth. According to Francillon, soil prepared in this way can be used for 25 consecutive years without using any form of fertiliser. The Wehali Tetun grow maize, sorghum, rice, beans and tubers.

Formerly, they had no rice-paddies and so few fields that they were dependent on both sago products and wine gathered from wild palms. One finds such areas of wild palm groves among both the Ema and the Bunaq of Maliana plain, but the latter extract only wine from them. There may also have been two varieties of *Metroxylon* in Wehali.

It is difficult to determine the extent to which palm savannahs are natural or domesticated ecosystems. The trees are certainly not planted, but their growth is undoubtedly protected. Francillon explains how the village capital of Wehali alternated between a site at the foot of the hills and another closer to the sea, leaving one site for the other whenever the palm trees had been exhausted.

(b) *Agrarian rituals.* In Wehali, the *nai bot* is the guarantor of fertility. All agricultural tasks in the kingdoms are timed according to his work in a symbolic field of a few square metres. For example, in the past it was theoretically impossible to collect an ear of corn before the *nai bot*'s field had been harvested.

Francillon relates that Wehali considered itself the guarantor of the order of things, not only for Malaka, but for all Timor and even for all that happened beyond the seas.

However, at harvest time the people of Malaka only give the *nai bot* symbolic offerings: seven ears of corn, one of sorghum and one of rice. As we shall see below, more distant populations paid tribute.

4. The Atoni

(a) *Summary of social organisation and land use.*[14] The Atoni language speaking peoples occupy most of the zone we are concerned with here. Several political communities with common features can be found in the area, but they can in no way be treated as a homogenous unit despite the desire of an author like Schulte Nordholt to force his observations into a single framework.

Settlement and lineage affiliation seem – or at least seemed originally – to have been closely associated. In principle, a territory was occupied by the descendants of two ancestors who are said to have risen from the earth at a spot which continues to be a cult centre. While descent is patrilineal, it seems that in certain exceptional cases, when the husband is unable to pay the bride-price, the children of the union remain within the wife's House of origin. Normally, bride-price is paid in instalments by the husband's House and he lives in his wife's House as long as the payment remains incomplete. When the payment is complete, he brings his wife and children to his own House. Schulte Nordholt notes that in some poor areas at the foot of Mount Mutis, the son-in-law works for his father-in-law for a certain number of years in lieu of the bride-price payment. Two contradictory attitudes among the Atoni which sometimes co-exist in the same community are apparent in Schulte Nordholt's description. In one view, offered as the more traditional, rights over land coincide completely with lineage territory. In the lineage territory, the *pah tuaf*, 'master of the earth', is the eldest member of the eldest branch in the line of descent from the founding ancestor, supposedly 'having emerged on the spot'. In the other view the *pah tuaf* is the representative of the central authority which we shall call the kingdom. Myths tell how this authority is retained by the descendants of high-ranking persons who came from the outside, often from Wehali. For instance, Sonnebait, the chief of the greatest Atoni kingdom, is said to have been the younger brother of the *liurai* chief of Wehali.

Can we accept Schulte Nordholt's theory according to which all Atoni kingdoms or territories had the same political organisation? He proposed that the differences observable today are the results of the destruction of the traditional systems following the advent of the Europeans in the sixteenth century. These differences should rather be seen as the result of a conflict between two models. In one, the lineage settled in the area is the master of its land; in the other, the representative of an external power holds this position. But, these are models and not reality. We should not, therefore, conclude that we are dealing with a conflict between an authochthonous people and later arrivals. The situation is a manifestation of a more general problem found elsewhere in Timor. Who ranks higher: he who doesn't move, termed 'feminine', or he who does move, spoken of as 'masculine'?

(b) *Agricultural practices and shifting cultivation.* The Atoni, like other Timorese mountain people, are swidden cultivators. It appears from the accounts of Schulte Nordholt and Ormeling that they shift fields more rapidly than either the Ema or the Bunaq.

Residence is associated with lineage membership and settlement appears to be dispersed. Ormeling states that villages are only composed of 50-60 inhabitants, while Schulte Nordholt gives examples of villages with up to 360 inhabitants. No part of the territory is set aside exclusively for cultivation. Furthermore, each clearing of a new field raises a question of choice. Formerly, the forest was cleared gradually to make fields which would be abandoned after two to three years. Today, they return to fallow fields, but according to Schulte Nordholt and Ormeling a man does not necessarily return to a plot previously cultivated by him. The first cultivator of a piece of land undoubtedly retains some rights over it. If another person wishes to work it, he must ask permission of the original cultivator. However, it appears that the same field will be used by many people in succession. Proof of this is found in the customary law attributing cultivated trees, and therefore their products, to the person who planted them. In fact, the lack of association between an individual and a specific piece of land plays an important part in the attitudes toward the protection of the soil and cover vegetation. Metzner,[15] who worked among the Tetun of central Portuguese Timor, recorded the same lack of interest in these practices in a situation apparently analogous to that of the Atoni. However, Schulte Nordholt and Ormeling point out that the Atoni used to protect sandalwood groves and trees near springs where bees had established their hives, and would plant *Casuarina* and *Schleichera oleosa* on fallow fields. But these conservation practices have been neglected for several years. The above authors were disturbed about the rapid degradation of Timorese soil, an indirect consequence of the *pax Neerlandica* which led to demographic pressures accompanied by a relaxation in the observation of traditional rules. While formerly there had been enough land available for the forest to regenerate on fallow fields, the introduction by the Dutch of cattle (*Bos sundanica*) resulted in the reduction of cultivatable land. The increased population resulted in a shorter fallow period. Now, there is a decrease in reforestation. In the place of the forest, we find thickets of bushes or prairies with some trees. Insana, the only territory we visited, presented the following landscape: hills sparsely covered with deciduous trees separated by enormous flat surfaces, and coralligenous plateaus or clay depressions, some of which are extremely fertile. These vast areas of flat land are usually covered with savannah or prairie vegetation interspersed with areas of *Borassus* and *Corypha*. Formerly, the villages were located on hills for purposes of defence. It seems that the flat, fertile land was only used irregularly, during peaceful periods, whereas today most of the population has resettled along the roads cross-cutting the flat areas. Fields are prepared by turning over the soil to a depth of 30 centimetres by inserting two parallel blunt sticks into the soil simultaneously and ca. 35 cm. apart. Today, in the irrigated zones, rice-paddies are being developed due to the encouragement of the agricultural services. Formerly, they were less numerous. In the past, after the first rains, the soil was trampled by the buffaloes, then the seed was broadcast and the buffaloes were brought in again to drive in the seed.

(c) *Agrarian rituals in Insana.* Insana is one of the territories in the eastern part of Atoni land. It shares a common frontier with the Tetun and its inhabitants call themselves Dawan. We have chosen this territory for the description of agrarian rituals since it is the only one which we have studied in person[16] – this was due to the fact that Schulte Nordholt presented it as the best example of traditional Atoni organisation. The results of our research referred to here do not always agree with his data.

The kingdom of Insana consisted of four noble lineages: *us* (lord) Taoli, *us* Pupu, *us* Tombes and *us* Fal. The highest rank was conferred on the first by common agreement. The territory was divided into four parts, each headed by a *tobe naek*. (*Tobe* is the term for (1) a basket used for offerings, (2) the person responsible for local agrarian rituals, (3) the territory under his authority; *naek* means great.) The *tobe naek* are responsible for the land and its products and are in charge of collecting offerings for the noble houses, *sonaf,* from their respective territories.

The great difference between the communities described above and Insana is that in the former the nobility take part in production and work in the fields, whereas the Insana nobility may not work since *anin*[1] *kaisa*[2] *nfu*[3] *manas*[4] *kaisa*[5] *phoe*[6], '(the) wind[1] (must) not[2] blow[3] (on them), (the) sun[4] (must) not[5] dry[6] (them)'. The people are responsible for providing them with agricultural produce.

The *tobe naek* are not considered to be nobles. They belong to four lineages: Hitu, Taiboi, Banusa and Saidjae. Only the last lineage is considered native to the area; the others are considered to be immigrants, as are the four noble lineages which came from the north coast in relatively recent times. The first *us* Taoli was called Luis and his wife Maria d'Hornay, indicating that the Portuguese had already settled in Ocussi on the north coast.

In Insana, all lineages are divided into two Houses: a feminine House, *uem feto,*[17] whose members cannot move about or involve themselves in external affairs and where the sacred objects are kept; and a masculine House, *uem mone,* whose members are allowed to involve themselves in external affairs. In the noble Houses (*sonaf*) only members of the masculine House have the right to exercise political power. Thus, the political chief of Insana belongs to the masculine House, *son mone,* of the *us* Taoli. The feminine *us* Taoli house (*son feto*) is situated in what is called the root of the kingdom, *baqaf*. It is surrounded by four lineages whose duty it is to 'clean and sweep' the *sonaf* but who also share responsibility for the *baqaf*'s territory and are its *tobe naek*. They are headed by a sort of majordomo, the *kolnel bala*, who also came from Ocussi.

The *baqaf*, located more or less at the centre of the kingdom, has been moved over the ages, for security reasons, according to our informants who showed us four previous sites while taking us to the present site of Maubesi. However, given the pattern of land use, one wonders whether these successive moves might have followed the shift in the fields of the common population.

It seems that formerly the *son mone* were also located in the centre of the *baqaf*, but were subsequently placed at the outskirts – again for reasons of security. A noble lineage can settle wherever it likes in the territory where it holds power. A lord is able to move his court from one place to another, but power over local matters remains in the hands of the *tobe naek*.

In Insana, the political chiefs are said to belong to a third stratum of nobility which occupied the land abandoned by previous inhabitants. The situation is reminiscent of feudal domains in the Middle Ages in the period of population decline and uncertainty when the nobility sought peasants to work their lands and the peasants expected the nobility to give them political and military protection. However, in Insana the role of the nobility is not so restricted. The *son feto* chief of the *us* Taoli is responsible for the success of the harvest and is both master of the rain and lord of the seed, as his title *us finit* indicates. He is also called *atupas*, 'he who sleeps', since his only active work consists of guarding the sacred objects that are the basis of the kingdom's fertility. These objects are kept in the *son usapi,* a palace of *Schleichera oleosa*. There are in fact two *sonaf* in the *baqaf*: the *son usapi* and the *son kiu*. The first is located on the eastern side of a *Schleichera*. For the Dawan, this tree is the symbol of heat, light and life. Its wood is thought to produce the hottest flame and is used for the fire around which a woman stays for some days after giving birth. Its seeds were formerly used to make candles, once the only source of artificial light. The *son kiu*, the palace of the Tamarind tree, is located to the west of a *Tamarindus indicus*. (We were told that the presence of this tree was fortuitous, and no conscious symbol was associated with it.) Objects belonging to deceased *atupas* are kept in the *son kiu*.

Before the time comes to sow, the sacred objects are taken out of the *son usapi*. These gold disks and ancient glass beads – said to have come from Liurai, i.e. Wehali – are placed before representatives of the entire kingdom, known as the *saen tesan,* 'the rising and setting sun', first those from the east (Nai Hitu and Taiboi) and then those from the west (Saidjao, Banusu). After making offerings to the powers of the afterworld, pigs and buffaloes, which have been sacrificed for the occasion, are distributed among the participants.

Schulte Nordholt describes rituals in which the local *tobe* carries out sacrifices and makes food offerings before the planting of each field. The object of these rituals is to petition help from the powers of the afterworld who control the fertility of the crops: the Lord of the Earth, *us pah*, here the supernatural power (not a living official), the ancestors and the local spirits. He goes on to say that if the rains do not come, further rituals must be performed at the rocks where the ancestors are supposed to have emerged. In such cases the *tobe naek* is sometimes called upon. One would like to have more detailed information about the lineages involved and the places where these ceremonies take place in order to get a better idea of the differences in behaviour between peasants according to whether they designate themselves as autochthonous or as immigrants. We should like to have a clearer picture of the roles played by the various powers thought to have control over fertility. The only hope of obtaining such information is by studying their ritual language: the form and content of offerings, the division of the sacrificed animal, etc.

During harvest time, other rituals are carried out to give thanks to the powers of the afterworld. Then the *tobe* collect the prestations in kind that will feed the members of the *sonaf* that controls their territory. The gifts intended for the *atupas* lineage are also collected and sent directly to the *baqaf.*

The centralisation of political and ritual power, which despite the separation between two Houses remains within a single lineage, seems to be a defence mechanism against social disintegration – a possible result of the movements of the population of shifting cultivators – rather than a means of organising collective projects to increase the kingdom's production. However, it should be noted that the chiefs' power was used first by the Dutch and later the Portuguese to induce people to leave their homes in the mountains and settle on the fertile plains where permanent fields and rice-paddies were established.

Political and economic power

The political power of Timorese chiefs: an overview

The relationship between power and wealth is always a two-way affair. To what extent does power bring economic advantage and to what extent does wealth confer power? In order to analyse this relationship in the societies examined here, we must first ask ourselves the meaning of the term 'power' in the Timorese context.

It is difficult to reconstruct the traditional situation since local views have been replaced by the European model of the single, absolute, all-powerful chief, as introduced by the Dutch administration. As we have seen, throughout western Timor, the political hierarchy was headed by two figures: a 'feminine' chief and a 'masculine' chief.[18] The first of these top-ranking chiefs could neither move nor act. In Bunaq he was called the *tier mel*, the one whose duty it was to sleep, *tier*, and awake, *mel*. He was the living symbol of the established order which he guaranteed, while the mobile and active 'masculine' chief was responsible for maintaining this order.

The only assistance that either had in the maintenance of this order was the support of other members of the community. The only means available to them to arrive at concensus were discussion and persuasion. They had no army or police and were only heeded insofar as their decisions coincided with custom.

However, at least in Lamaknen, this custom, *ukon* in Bunaq, carried a major element of disuasion with it in the form of fines. Even today, all disputes in Lamaknen are settled through the imposition of fines after the problem has been discussed by the parties concerned: i.e. wife-givers and wife-takers if it is a problem between affines; the village officialdom if the matter extends beyond the private sphere; all the village chiefs if it is a quesion affecting all Lamaknen. Formerly, every offence was handled in this way, including murder and even conflicts which could lead to war if the parties did not agree on damages. Depending on the context and the offence, fines consisted of feminine goods, i.e. pigs and cloth, or masculine goods, i.e. gold, silver and buffaloes. For all violations of public order, those who settled the matter, i.e. the representatives of the noble Houses in the village, had to be compensated as well as the members of the injured House. The 'feminine' chief received the most important payments – especially the gold – although all the representatives received something.

Those unable to pay were sold as slaves and we were told that entire Houses could disappear in this way. No doubt this could only occur under exceptional circumstances. Not only would all the village nobles have to agree, but so would the affines of the House in question otherwise they themselves would be in difficulty and there would be a risk of reprisals.

Today it is very difficult to imagine what sort of power relations existed in the traditional context: whether or not there really were tyrants or whether there was a *musjawara* (the Indonesian word for concensus) rule.

What was the basis of the noble/commoner distinction and how were chiefs recruited?

Here again we find the same opposition between two views: who is superior, he who was there first, or he who arrived more recently and possesses the most prestigious insignia of power?

The first position is clearest among the northern Tetun of Fialaran. There, the chief, *loro*, is *rainaqin*, 'the Lord of the Earth', because at the beginning of time, 'when the darkness disappeared and the sun appeared, when the sea receded and the earth appeared, the *loro* was there on the mountain peak'. However, it is recognised that there are no longer any descendants, at least patrilineal descendants, of the first *loro*; the person who occupies this position today is a descendant of those who arrived by boat in more recent times. Furthermore, the *loro* who descended from the first wave of immigrants lost his position to a group of more recent arrivals who secured his wealth and power by becoming wife-givers to him.

Among the Lamaknen Bunaq, as we have seen, the nobles still retain the *dato bul loro bul*, 'the foundation of power', which theoretically descended from the sky with the first ancestors; in reality, it consists of gold disks and other objects. However, the facts are not always so clear. Among the most easterly Bunaq, the nobles came from the south with their insignia, and it is their chiefs who arrived first. In Insana, the local population asked for nobles to come to rule and protect them, but it is not said in what respect the rulers were in fact noble. Similarly, among the westernmost Bunaq of Dirun, the first arrivals went to ask one of the four great feminine chiefs of Lamaknen to furnish them with a ruler from its House.

Among other Bunaq, in the present day Portuguese territory, the lords of the Tetun kingdom are said to have brought the insignia of power. Apparently, they merely confirmed in their function those who were already local chiefs.

However, a question remains: to what extent is a gold disk simply money rather than an ornament, and in what sense is it considered to be an insignia of power? Mythical history eludes this question as well as that of the origin of these objects which are assumed to have descended directly from heaven with the first ancestors.

Before we examine the problem of the origin of gold and silver in Timor, let us look at the benefits gained by the nobility from its superior position in the hierarchy in the domain of agricultural production.

Hierarchy and agricultural production

In principle, the distribution of fields among the Bunaq does not give any House an advantage or disadvantage. We note simply that the latest arrivals, whose land is often in a single holding, risk having less varied soils and that their fields are usually the farthest from the settlement. The real imbalance in the distribution of land stems from variability in the size of Houses. For instance, in contemporary Abis, House membership ranges from 5 to 120. It is difficult to know this situation developed in the period before external intervention affected the communities' way of life. In fact, it seems that the progressive demographic inequality between Houses was a factor in Bunaq migration. However, by forbidding warfare, the Dutch administration removed the possibility of invading neighbouring lands and driving out the inhabitants. Territorial limits were thus artificially frozen at the beginning of the century. Today, if *matas momen* land is lacking, fields are cleared on the *bula*, i.e. pasture land. However, this solution is insufficient and in over-populated Houses some members go off and settle on unoccupied land around Atambua or even further away in Dawan country.

Given the system of land use, those with a great deal of land could not profit from it without the manpower needed to work it. It was quite useless having more land than one could work oneself. While a system of mutual help did exist, it was based on reciprocity. If friends helped in a specific agricultural task, one was obliged to reciprocate.

Only the feminine chief had an advantage over the others in this respect. He was entitled to the labour of the entire village – including other nobles – on a field known as the *mako-biqan*, 'cup plate', without having to reciprocate. But he had to take part in the work and supply the workers with plenty of food and drink, i.e. on each occasion he had to kill a buffalo. The resulting revelry transformed the corvée into a feast and, as the tasks were not time-consuming, the villagers owed only a few days work to their chief: one or two days for the various tasks of clearing, sowing, weeding and harvesting. Since the feminine chiefs had several villages under their authority they could repeat this operation in each village. However, they could rarely afford to do so since they had to kill an animal each time, and they and their families had to take part in the work. Thus it appears that the chiefs were not able to reap major benefits from the *mako biqan* custom since they had so many guest workers to feed.

Certainly, the Lamaknen chiefs did not take advantage of their positions of authority to organise works of public benefit. Corvée labour only came to be used for road construction and repair with colonial rule. Even in the case of *matas momen* enclosures, each House was responsible for the section built on its land.

Among the Ema, the same practice of labour service for chiefs must have existed in the past. Today, the Portuguese administration's interference with their claim to corvée labour made a detailed study of traditional forms of labour service impossible. But we can confirm that there were no large-scale works undertaken at the command of the chiefs. Mutual aid occurred amongst individuals in both agricultural activities and in the repair of terraces and drainage canals.

In Wehali, a system of mutual aid existed for agricultural work but it appears that people did not have to work in the chiefs' fields. With the exception of the symbolic offering mentioned above, they did not have to hand over any part of their crop. Francillon speaks of tribute coming from vassals outside Malaka which passed through specific channels with the authorities acting as intermediaries. Part of this tribute would have been in kind and enabled the Wehali to subsist despite their nonchalant attitude toward agriculture. Unfortunately, as Francillon points out, it is impossible to find proof for the existence of such tribute. In some places, for instance Insana, the informants we questioned even denied its existence. In Lamaknen, on the other hand, people still remember having had to make a contribution on specific occasions, e.g. for the funeral of the sovereign, the *nai bot*.

Stock-raising was an important economic resource. The widespread idea in Timor that large herds were the chief's privilege stems from the fact that the Dutch only distributed *Bos sundanica* to the chiefs, principally Atoni chiefs, when they tried to replace buffaloes with cattle. Among the Bunaq the traditional situation was not changed; the pasture land was communal and all the village members could graze their animals. There were differences between villages in the amount and quality of their pasture lands. But regardless of the grazing land available, the essential point was to have some cattle.

There were wealthy people who had many head of cattle and poor people who had none. From the present situation, we can deduce that variations in wealth did not always coincide with the existing political and ritual hierarchy, at least not in Lamaknen. In order to get a clearer picture of the situation, we shall try to analyse the causes behind a House's prosperity, relying mainly on our knowledge of the Bunaq.

The basis of a House's prosperity

In Lamaknen, the prosperity of a House depends first of all on its demographic balance. It must have enough members to provide an adequate labour force, but not too many or there will be no land for them all. What matters here, above all, is the ration of mouths to feed to the number of active workers. Productive activity includes not only work in the fields (i.e. weeding and clearing by men, sowing by women, harvesting by men and women), but also housework, performed mainly by women. This includes the feedingof pigs and the spinning, dying and wearing of cotton since it provides the basic goods which wife-givers owe to their wife-takers. Since nursing mothers are unable to do such work, not all births are regarded as a blessing.

Demographic equilibrium depends, of course, on the birth rate, but it also depends on the movements of adults by virtue of marriage and adoption – a very common institution among the Bunaq – which follows the same direction as marriage alliances.

While a House which sends out individuals receives considerable sums to compensate their loss, a House that empties too quickly is lost, even if it has accumulated much wealth in gold and silver.

In societies with a strict system of generalised exchange, the output and intake of wives is balanced, at least in theory since the number of girls and boys is not always equal. With the two forms of marriage that exist among the Bunaq, it is possible to keep both one's daughters and one's sons, as Berthe has explained.[19] This pertains especially to a noble family that receives considerable payments for marrying its daughters uxorilocally. This payment can be used again to marry its sons by the other form of marriage. In order to amass the necessary bride-price, a House will call for assistance from its own wife-takers, to whom they will give in return feminine goods obtained from their wife-givers. The latter, finally, will be compensated with part of the sum the House receives from its wife-takers.

Thus, the system is designed to keep wealth circulating and to prevent its accumulation at any point. We should not, however, get the wrong impression. Each exchange can only be accomplished in the presence of all the participants and each time the House in question must feed everyone, i.e. it must kill an animal and provide plenty of betel and alcohol. One can only acquire goods if one has them to offer in the first place. Here, as elsewhere, 'it takes money to make money'. Only those who are already well off can take the initiative in calling for others' wealth, even if most of it will be redistributed at the end of the whole cycle. One can also understand why chiefs, benefiting from fines, the hierarchical system of bride-price and the *mako biqan*, have certain advantages over the rest of the population. However, nowhere have we witnessed the possibility of accumulating a sufficient amount of goods for long distance commerce to become established (except during the final years of Dutch colonialism when the cattle they had introduced were exported). Thus, in the absence of mines, the problem of the origin of gold and silver in Timor remains unsolved.

Furthermore, it should be pointed out that we find other goods in Timor besides gold and silver which must have been imported: the famous bead necklaces made of opaque, reddish-orange glass reminiscent of coral. (The necklaces are called *muti* in Timor, from the Malay word for bead.) These necklaces move in the same direction as the women, but the Timorese are unaware of their origin. They are handed down over generations and impossible to buy on the market. They are highly valued – some at 3000-4000 francs; their value bears no relation to the material of which they are made. Identical beads found on archaeological sites on the Malay peninsula and in Sumatra have been dated to the time of Srivijaya. According to Lamb,[20] their chemical composition indicates that they were made on the spot from raw materials originating in the circum-Mediterranean area. The raw material could have come from older Mediterranean archaeological sites. Furthermore, it seems that the same process of restoring antique beads was discovered in the East Indies: van der Hoop mentioned that in Sumatra, in 1920, beads found in tombs were cleared and then sold in Timor. Therefore, it is extremely difficult to pinpoint when the first necklaces reached Timor.

Gold, silver and the Wehali hegemony

The legend of Timorese gold mines was born the moment the Europeans arrived. The first European boat to arrive in Timor was the *Victoria*, the only ship surviving from Magellan's expedition. She anchored off the north coast, no doubt on the Batu Gade side. Here is an extract from Pigafetta's account of the landing:

> There are four kings, who are brothers, from the other side of this island. Where we were, there were only towns and officials of these kings. The names of the four houses of these kings are Oibich, Lichsana, Suai and Cabanazza.
>
> Oibich is the largest town. (We were told that) in Cabanazza one finds gold in a mountain and that people buy all they need with their small pieces of gold. All the sandalwood and wax brought by the Javanese and Malaccans comes from this place. There, we

came upon a junk from Lozzon which had come to buy sandalwood.[21]

The concentration of gold and power in the south of the island corresponds to what the myths tell us of Timorese history. The term *kabanasa* – the Bunaq word for the *Planchonia* tree – is widely used in Timor as a place name. Today, there is a Kabanasa in Malaka itself and a Camenassa near Suwai. According to Francillon, the Kabanasa mentioned by Pigafetta was also near Suwai, which was under Wehali control, but nearer the mouth of the Tafara.

The mountain of gold, as we have seen, could not have been the expression for a geological formation, but was the symbol for what the peoples of northern Timor saw as inexhaustable wealth. It is difficult to imagine that these 'small pieces of gold' with which the southern people 'bought everything they needed' had originated in the tribute paid by the northern peoples. Nor is it possible that this wealth could have originated in the sale of agricultural surplus, for there was none.

On the other hand, the other remarks of Pigafetta suggest that the gold pieces may have been part of the sandalwood and wax trade. He remains ambiguous on this point since if it is evident that Kabanasa was a place where merchandise was collected, he does not say how it was exported. The problem is that the northern coast of Timor is the most accessible and is today the centre of all trade. The southern coast is far less welcoming and the sea there is more dangerous.

Nevertheless, it is difficult to see how the sandalwood and wax could have been collected in Kabanasa (could it have been tribute?) and then carried across the island again to a port on the north coast.

It is, however, possible to land ships on the south coast. During the last war K.P.M. boats anchored in the south during December and January when the west winds prevailed. It should be possible to anchor a small boat in the sheltered waters at the mouths of rivers. Kabanasa is in fact situated at the mouth of a river and must have been known as a port since Schulte Nordholt points out that in the diary of Kasteel from Batavia, between 1624 and 1636, only one arrival of a sandalwood boat is mentioned from Camenase on the south coast of Belu.[22]

Furthermore,in Bunaq mythology, the ancestors who came from the south arrived in Timor at Kabanasa where they gathered sandalwood and wax to sell in *Sina mutin Malaka*, 'White China Malaka'. Wehali myths have their first sovereign arriving from this same spot, while the Bunaq myth in which the chief of Wehali, Suri Liuri, came down to earth in a place called *Lubu dato Salaer* before he came to Timor, brings to mind the Luwu kingdom in the south of Sulawesi and the off-shore island of Salajar.

One can suggest, therefore, that sandalwood and wax were exported from a port, or even a trading post, on the south coast. By exchanging exported merchandise for prestige goods unknown in Timor, these entrepreneurs might develop political supremacy in that part of the island, either directly or indirectly through the intermediary of the oldest local noble line and thus guarantee their monopoly over the trade. Surveillance of the southern ports was facilitated by their inaccessability. This would seem all the more true since the river mouths were invaded by alluvial sands across which only a person with good knowledge of the passages could navigate. These sands are mentioned in the mythology.

The basis of Wehali supremacy in the political hierarchy is still not clear even today. It appears to have been a manifestation of the progressive control over the exploitation of sandalwood in western Timor by directing it to traders settled within the kingdom. The redistribution of Wehali wealth in the form of regalia would have been no more than payment for the sandalwood and wax delivered, perhaps in the form of tribute.

Undoubtedly, the monopoly could not have been established without a struggle. The fact that Wehali, itself pacifist and feminine, distributed magical formulas for making war (and perhaps arms in the past) and that Wehali chiefs appear as warriors in Bunaq mythology only strengthens our hypothesis. But we cannot describe in detail here these episodes in western Timor's mythical history which clearly are representations of power struggles.

The sandalwood trade was based firstly on the stability of the market and perhaps even its price stability. Secondly, one had to be sure that the merchandise would be ready when the boats arrived. It is clear that the involvement of the local chiefdoms in the trade was the best guarantee for the successful functioning of the trade. The Bunaq case corresponded to this scheme as all the sandalwood cut on a village's land was redistributed among only its noble members, and the feminine chief took a considerable proportion, thus leaving the people with nothing but the roots. This was a true privilege of the nobility.

Of course there are no longer any traces of this system since the Europeans took over the sandalwood trade at least three centuries ago. Unfortunately sandalwood is becoming increasingly rare in Timor and is now in any case the property of the Indonesian state.

The only information we have on the sandalwood trade in Timor is from the first Portuguese who accompanied local merchants. All accounts agree[23] that the boats left the Malay peninsula with the first monsoon winds in early December. They reached the island of Solor where they waited for winds which could take them down to Timor where they had to wait for the winds to change before setting sail again. There are no further details on the place at which they landed.

We are not certain as to which areas were most abundant in sandalwood. According to the experts,[24] the growth of the tree is favoured by a certain amount of humidity and rain during the dry season. Thus, its growth must have been more abundant on the south coast where, in addition to the heavy rains of the monsoon season, the south-easterly winds bring light rainfall in the dry season. The north coast is far drier. This would support our hypothesis that the sandalwood was first exploited on the south coast of Timor.

The only real evidence to support the hypothesis is the way in which the Portuguese set about securing the sandalwood trade in Timor after they had settled on the north coast and in Kupang. In 1642 they had to send an expeditionary force of 90 troops and three Dominicans against the Wehali to subdue this kingdom where the chief had converted to Islam just to spite them, 'following the example of the Bugis and Makassar people' as Schulte Nordholt says in his report of San Domingo's oral history.[25] This incident confirms the relationship between Wehali and Sulawesi merchants. However, long after 1642, the Wehali kingdom's hegemony remained alive and influential in the minds of the Timorese, at least for those at the centre of the island. If our hypothesis that this hegemony was related to the development of a monopoly over sandalwood and wax is correct, it is no less true that this hegemony survived after the Europeans had found 'valuable spokesmen', or efficient agents to put it more prosaically, in ports (particularly Kupang) more easily accessible than those on the south coast.

One wonders whether the expansion of Wehali hegemony as far as the north coast was a consequence of European intervention in the sandalwood trade and the political strategy of the mountain chiefdoms. The mountain chiefdoms, wanting their profits from the trade to continue, ensured their access to northern ports by supporting the mythical hegemony of Wehali, which was isolated on the southern plain and no longer had anything to trade. As Francillon has stated, their support was no more than an ideological justification for their trading interests.

In fact, the whole structure was based on Wehali superiority, especially on the marriage alliance system which we have not been able to describe here but which we can illustrate with a particularly important piece of Insana mythical history.

Matrilineality is the way in which Wehali confronts the problem of hierarchically organised, patrilineal societies practising generalised exchange, where wife-givers rank higher than wife-takers, as in the mountains in western Timor. Who can give wives to those at the top of the hierarchy?

No-one has to give women to Wehali since it keeps its own. On the other hand, Wehali might give wives to some of its vassals as expression of its higher rank. The origin of these women is ambigous: they are given by the Liurai of Wehali who may have been acting as a kind of relay to the mountain chiefdoms.

The history of Insana's highest ranking lineage, *us* Taoli, tells of the marriage of a masculine chief to Liurai's daughter. Even more interesting is the account of the founding of the feminine House lineage from which the *atupas*, the major figure in the kingdom is recruited. In the beginning, this feminine House was made up only of women from the lineage. To produce descendants a man had to be called in. Now, this man, Malaf Neno, who married a woman from the *us* Taoli lineage at the beginning of the kingdom's history, came from Wehali. Their son became the *atupas* and transmitted the title to his descendants. However, when the couple's first daughter was born, emmissaries from Wehali came for her. In actual fact, custom demands that one of the daughters produced in a man's marriage must be returned to his House of origin to compensate for his loss. This daughter is called the *mata musan.* In the myth, the men of Insana tried to fool the Wehali men by giving them a slave, but the Wehali men discovered the trick on their way home and returned to find the real *mata musan* who was then given to them. When she arrived in Laran, all the men of Wehali went to the palace to pay her homage. Those visiting in the morning found a child; those who arrived at midday an adult; and those who did not get there before nightfall found only an old woman. This story is the origin of the nickname *marokmak oqan,* 'child of brightness', since only a child of divine origin could transform itself in this way. But this woman aged so quickly that she could not have children and this is why, it is said in Insana, there was no longer anyone who could become the chief of Wehali.[26] Thus ended the history of this kingdom which had no wealth left and no legitimate sovereign.

Conclusion

Despite the impact which the sandalwood trade must have had on Timorese political life, it nevertheless seems that local particularities in social organisation were preserved. We might even ask whether the establishment of a market economy in Timor froze certain aspects of the agricultural system by interrupting the evolution of structures related to a purely agricultural economy. This might have been the case for practical and ritual agricultural techniques in particular, as they have remained quite similar to those existing when rice was introduced relatively recently. This is only a working hypothesis, but it should make us pay even more attention to the significance of data which could tell us more about the possibilities of an evolutionary process from 'peripheral' to 'central' societies in Timor. These data are summarised in Table I, and show that:

1. There are no parallels between the evolution of agricultural techniques toward permanent land use and better yields, and the evolution of political organisation toward centralisation. In Wehali, permanent cultivation of the same land is only possible due to the land's natural fertility. The Ema, who have more

Table 1. Agrarian practices and political organisation in Western Timor

	Insana (Dawan)	Wehali (Tetun)
Land use practices	*Slash and burn (no organisation of fallow growth); soil prepared with digging stick *Level fields, rice-paddies on soil trampled by buffalos	*Level fields, worked with digging stick *Picking and collecting of palm products (*Borassus*, Corypha and perhaps *Metroxylon*).
*Rhythm of land use**	*An individual does not necessarily cultivate the same field after it has lain fallow	*An individual cultivates the same field every year (alluvial soils are deposited during the floods of the rainy season) *The area where a village settles is dependent on the availability of palm products
Political organisation	*At the level of the kingdom, dual central power: sacred feminine chief with highest status, while masculine chief has concrete political power	*At the level of the kingdom, dual central power. The kingdom is considered hegemonic in western Timor
Who performs the agricultural rituals for the community?	*The feminine chief of the kingdom is master of the seed and the rain; he performs the pre-planting rituals of the community to ensure the success of crops	*Every agricultural task is geared to the feminine chief's work in a small symbolic sacred field
Who works the land, who controls the output?	*The nobility does not work the land; it receives prestations of maize and rice from the people living on land over which it has authority *The feminine chief of the kingdom is fed on cereals contributed by the entire population	*Everyone works the land and disposes of its output *The feminine chief has the right to have the people work a field, compensating them only with food *The feminine chief receives a symbolic offering of rice and maize.

Lamaken (Bunaq)	Marobo (Ema)	Java
*Slash and burn with domestication of the ecosystem: maintenance of a certain type of fallow vegetation; soil prepared with digging stick but without grading the slope *Rice-paddies in basin land, flooded during rainy season, soil prepared by trampling by buffalos	*Slash and burn with domestication of the ecosystem: organisation of dry terraces in the mountains *Irrigated rice-paddies on the plain using water diverted from the rivers during the rainy season; cultivation of slightly graded compartmentalised fields: soil prepared by trampling by buffalos	*Rice-paddies in irrigated terraces; organisation of water flow using lakes and springs; soil prepared with plough
*Return to the same plot after a fallow period of four-five years	*Tendency to cultivate every year those terraces near houses *Fallow period of eight years on other terraces	*Several crops a year on the same plot
*No central power for the entire territory *Village level political organisation headed by a feminine and a masculine chief	*Political organisation for a set of villages, with three high-ranking lineages at top	*Centralised power for entire kingdom with an individual as sovereign
*A lord of the seed and master of the seedlings and shoots are distinct from the feminine chief; the former is a descendant of participants in the myth of origin of seed; the latter, a descendant of the first Bunaq settlers in the village; they are responsible for village communal rituals	*Management and execution of agricultural rituals divided among different individuals within the same three chiefdoms which act in unison for all Marobo. In addition there is a master of the fields from an autochthonous House and assistants taken from other Houses	*The sovereign is responsible for fertility of the kingdom's land.
*Everyone works the land and disposes of its output *The feminine chief has the right to have the people work a field, compensating them only with food *Symbolic offerings to the Afterworld beings responsible for the crops. *Redistribution of the entire crop of luxury products: (Mango, betel, areca and candle-berry nuts) according to the political hierarchy; only a symbolic offering of maize (a few stalks and ears); rice is not redistributed	*Everyone works the land and disposes of its output *People work for the political chiefs *Symbolic offerings to the Afterworld beings responsible for the crops and to the political chiefs	*The officials and nobility drawn from the sovereign's kin do not cultivate the land; they are maintained by the people *The sovereign receives prestations which have lost their ritual value and become actual taxes

elaborate techniques, show none of the characteristics of a centralised type of society, while the Atoni of Insana, who practise a simple form of clearing without domestication of the ecosystem, have a political organisation built around a central pivot at the heart of the kingdom.

2. Despite the fact that cooperative labour existed in the traditional Timorese societies we have examined, nowhere do we find organisation of public works by those in power. However, the efforts of all the working population enabled certain individuals to work less or not to work at all. Thus in Insana we find a class which does not take part in productive labour.
3. Where there is centralisation of power, the feminine chief is responsible for fertility. He is the direct recipient of part of the crop, either in considerable quantities as in Insana, or in a symbolic form as in Wehali.

The 'central' characteristics of Insana are clearly evident, but the ruling class's power over the fertility of the kingdom's land is only apparent in ritual and does not directly influence the means of production. However, the possibility of such direct intervention exists in the system. This is clear from the manner in which the administration, relying on the chiefs' support, was able to induce people to leave their homes in the hills and settle along the roads on the rich alluvial plains, although their success was greater in Insana than among the Bunaq.

Control over fertility, however, is not exercised in the same way in all the societies we have considered. The agents held to be responsible for fertility and whose influence is sought, differ from one community to another. Generally, there is a desire to remove the ritual causes of fertility from the land and place them elsewhere. Among some Atoni, we can still witness a relationship between the descendants of distant ancestors who sprang from the soil itself and the efficacy of agrarian rituals. In Insana, rain and the power of the *atupa* over the seed is emphasised since he is the *us finit,* 'the lord of the seed'. Custom demands that the rain must begin as soon as the pre-planting rituals are terminated, during which as we have seen the sacred objects from Wehali are brought out. An equally important myth collected by Kryut and recorded by Van Wouden[27] tells how the chief of Sonnebait, the great Atoni kingdom, who was the Liurai of Wehali's younger brother, had one of his subjects killed when they brought him the fruits of the earth every year in order to 'cool' the earth. Then a neighbouring chief, native to the area, killed the Sonnebait chief, drought ensued and the rice and maize no longer grew. Later, a child whom the Liurai recognised as the reincarnation of his brother was found and just where he was the rain began to fall again. The people thus understood that they were under his authority. Here we can see how Wehali power was exercised directly over the success of the crops from a distance; locally the *nai bot*'s ritual activity continued throughout the year and applied to all agricultural tasks.

Although water is also emphasised in the Ema pre-planting rituals, the latter are directed toward both rain from heaven and the waters flowing from the springs of Marobo hill. Thus a certain ritual link is maintained with the earth, this is apparent in the presence of an autochthonous House, master of the fields. Furthermore, responsibility for ritual seems far more communal than among the Atoni. The Marobo community, constituted as other communities of Timor by a large number of local and immigrant populations of various origins, has had to reconstruct a system based on locality, in this case the hill of Marobo.

By attaching special significance to the 'Lord of the seed', the Bunaq have made their ritual control over the success of crops mobile and they can take this 'power' with them wherever they go. It should also be pointed out that this power is related to the origin myth of seeds which appears quite late in the history of the ancestors and is clearly the myth of the introduction of rice.

Timor, despite its insularity – a factor which favours the regional evolution of its communities – was not immune to external incursions. There was undoubtedly an immigration of considerable numbers of people, bringing their own customs and techniques with them. However, cultural and technical elements also reached Timor through contacts with other islands in the archipelago that did not necessarily involve population movements.

While it is not a question of reconstructing history, one can at least hope that a more thorough study, which would include an in-depth analysis of social organisation, kinship and myths, could grasp the mechanisms by which new elements were integrated into Timorese communities.

(*Translated by Anne Bailey*)

NOTES

1 Berthe, L. (1970), 'Parenté, pouvoir et mode de production. Pour une typologie des societés agricoles de l'Indonesie', *in* Pouillon, J. and Maranda, P. (eds.), *Echanges et communications, mélanges offerts à Claude Lévi-Strauss à l'occasion de son 60ème anniversaire,* Paris, pp. 703-38.

2 Berthe, L. (1961), 'Le mariage par achat et la captation des gendres dans une société semi-féodale: les 'Buna' de Timor central', *L'Homme,* I, 3, pp. 5-31. (In his later papers L. Berthe used 'q' for the glottal stop and wrote *bunaq*. In this paper all the glottal stops are indicated by 'q'.)

3 Berthe (1970).

4 The legend of the gold mines of Timor was only finally invalidated after a nineteenth-century Dutch geological expedition.

5 Berthe (1970), p. 731.

6 Some of the data presented here have already appeared in: Friedberg, C. (1974).

'Agricultures timoraises', *Etudes rurales*, vol. 53-6, Jan.-Dec., pp. 375-405.

7 The term *deu* refers to both the dwelling and the lineage group. Throughout this article we shall distinguish between the two senses by using a capital letter for the second meaning.

8 For additional information on agriculture see Friedberg, C. (1971), 'L'agriculture des Bunaq de Timor et les conditions d'un équilibre avec le milieu', *Journal d'agriculture tropicale et de botanique appliquée*, XVIII, 12, pp. 481-532.

9 An annotated text of this myth extends from line 3424 to line 4277 in Berthe, L. (1972), *Bei gua: Itinéraire des ancêtres*, Paris.

10 The role of the cold/hot opposition in the Bunaq view of germination is treated in Friedberg, C. (1972), 'Eléments de Botanique Bunaq', *in* Thomas, J.M.C. and Bernet, L., *Techniques, nature et société*, II, Paris. H.G. Schulte Nordholt (see note 14) writes of the Atoni cooling the soil and not the seed, i.e. exactly the inverse of the Bunaq operation.

11 Most of the data presented here were passed on to me by B. Clamagirand and can be found in: 'Marobo: organisation sociale et rites d'une communauté Ema de Timor', these de 3ème cycle', Université René Descartes, Paris 1975. I gathered some of the data myself when I saw Clamagirand in Marobo in 1966 and 1970 and during a visit to Be Bai valley.

12 The Mali Baka is a tributary of the Be Bai which forms the eastern border of Lamaknen with the Portuguese territory.

13 This material is taken from Francillon, G. (1967), *Some Matriarchic Aspects of the Social Structure of the Southern Tetun of Middle Timor*, Ph.D. thesis, Australian National University, Canberra.

14 The material on the Atoni presented here is taken from Ormeling, F.S. (1956), *The Timor problem; a Geographical Interpretation of an Underdeveloped Island*, Djakarta-Gröningen; Schulte Nordholt, H.G. (1971), *The Political System of the Atoni of Timor*, The Hague; and from Clark F. Cunningham's articles, particularly Cunningham, C.F. (1965), 'Order and change in an Atoni diarchy', *S.West. J. Anthrop.*, XXI, 4.

15 J.M. Metzner of the Südasien Institut der Universität Heidelberg, personal communication.

16 I spent three days in Insana where the traditional chief of Oelolok, Lorencius Arnoldus Taolin (the Dutch add an *n* to their name) received me. He sent for his elder brother, who was more versed in traditional matters. The interview got under way immediately, for as soon as they read what had been written about them, they were eager to present another version of the story, the version presented here. One might suspect that the Taolin twisted the story in their favour. However, it is difficult to believe that they would invent the complete mythical history they told me personally before witnesses. I cannot recount their version in this article. They did not try to hide the relatively recent origin of the kingdom in its present form, which does not correspond with Schulte Nordholt's assumption, although it does not preclude it since its structure corresponds to the Atoni traditional model. I should add that my informants in Insana refused to be called the *Atoni*, 'to be human', but preferred the term *Dawan* or if need be *Atoni Dawan*, 'Dawan men'. I had quite a number of informants since many peasants were arriving at the palace to have disputes settled. Thus, I was able to double-check some of the information given me.

17 *uem ume*: In Dawan, the order of letters within words is reversed to express certain offices which I was unable to discover. Thus *ume* 'house' becomes *uem*; *manas* 'sun' becomes *mansa*; *mone* 'masculine' becomes *moen*, etc. Furthermore, the *af* or *if* ending appears to denote a collective noun: one says *sonaf* 'palace', but *son feto* 'feminine palace'.

18 Cunningham (1965), note 13.

19 Berthe (1961).

20 Lamb, A. (1961), 'Some glass beads from Kakao Island, Takuapa, South Thailand', *Federations Museums Journal*, VI n.s., pp. 48-65; Lamb, A. (1965), 'Some glass beads from the Malay Peninsula', *Man*, 30, pp. 36-8.

21 Pigafetta, A. (1964), *Premier voyage autour du monde par Magellan*, translated and annotated by Leonce Paillard, Paris.

22 Schulte Nordholt (1971), p. 166.

23 See for example, Leitâo Humberto (1948), *Os portugueses em Solor e Timor de 1515 a 1702*, Lisbon, pp. 54-5; or Faria de Morais, A. (1943), *Solor e Timor,* Lisbon. Both are written using the documentation collected in the Historia de S. Domingos.

24 For information on sandalwood, see the following works: Cinatti Vaz Monteiro Gomes, R. (1950), 'Esboço historico do sandalo no Timor portugues', *Colloquio realizada na Junta de Investigaçoẽs coloniais*, pp. 1-27; Rama Rao, M. (1910), 'Germination and growth of sandal seedlings', and 'Host plants of sandal tree', *Indian Forest Records*, II, part IV; Steenis, C.G.G.J. van (1939), 'The native country of sandalwood and teak: A plant geographical study', *Hand. 8th Ned. Ind. Natuurwet. Congres Soerabaja*, 1938, pp. 408-10.

25 Schulte Nordholt (1971), p. 164.

26 Francillon says that he collected the same myth among other vassals.

27 Van Wouden, F.A.E. (1935), *Sociale Structuurtypen in de Groote Oost*, Leiden (English ed.: *Types of Social Structure in Eastern Indonesia*, translated by R. Needham, The Hague, 1968).

25 Schulte Nordholt (1971), p. 164.

P. BONTE

Non-stratified social formations among pastoral nomads

In this article I would like to put forward a few working hypotheses dealing with a subject that has received little attention from Marxist scholars. They have long continued in the tradition of the analyses developed by the nineteenth-century evolutionists which were partially taken up by Marx and Engels, i.e. the domestication of animals preceded the domestication of plants; historically pastoralism represents an earlier evolutionary stage than agriculture; pastoralist societies are characterised by their archaism.

It has now been established that nomadic pastoralist societies represent neither a very early evolutionary phenomenon nor societies which by their very nature maintain a predatory relationship with the environment. On the contrary, with few exceptions they were established well after the Neolithic,[1] and after the appearance of large scale agriculturally based State societies.[2]

Relying on the new data available, we can examine these social formations and the historical questions which they raise from a Marxist point of view (e.g. the 'great invasions' by nomads, the encounter of agricultural and urban societies with nomadic pastoralist societies). My aim is to lay the conceptual and theoretical foundations for such an analysis by bringing out the specific characteristics of these societies and by broaching the problem of their place in evolution.

This project is an integral part of a theoretical domain sketched by Marx in the *Formen*:[3] the problem of the transformation of communal forms of production and the appearance of class societies. My initial hypothesis is that this transformation occurs in a specific and original way in nomadic pastoralist societies, distinguishing their evolution from that leading to the creation of 'Asiatic' societies or that which, passing through Ancient society, ended in feudalism and capitalism. Thus my analysis is based on a fundamental recognition of *multiple forms of historical evolution*. The interpretation of these multiple forms requires the enrichment of the conceptual and theoretical tools of historical materialism.

In studying the Nilo-Hamitic pastoralists of East Africa it is possible to deal with the whole of the theoretical domain in question, the specific nature of the community and the appearance of class relations,[4] from an historical point of view. This digression through secondary sources, using the quite extensive anthropological literature, is not by chance. My own field-work was carried out among Saharan and Sahelian pastoralists (Moors and Tuareg) where there are developed class relations and where one must deal with the question of the appearance of the State. The goal of this article is to establish the logical continuity which appears to me to exist between otherwise historically distinct societies. Confirmed by initial field-work results, the hypothesis is that these Saharan societies constitute a 'developed' form of the same mode of production. The analysis of a 'simple' form i.e. of a society where class relations are not present, will give a new perspective to the analysis of later forms.

The project of the Formen

The analysis in the *Formen* centres on the problem of the transformations of the communal form of production. Marx begins with a 'primitive commune' which appears more as a working hypothesis than a truly theoretical concept. Anthropological findings, particularly among hunting societies, point to a more complex and diversified reality and suggest that this 'primitive commune' encompasses several ways in which this communal form of production may be realised. In fact, Marx's argument does not strictly depend upon the validity of this hypothesis, for he was confronting a different problem: *the transformations of this communal structure in an historical context where class relations form and develop in order to understand the conditions for the appearance of the capitalist mode of production.*[5]

Marx distinguished several modes of this transformation and defined several evolutionary lines. One of these, that which resulted in the establishment of classical slave societies, has long been given priority by the tenants of a dogmatic Marxism that developed a lineal view of evolution. Classical slave society was based on the community of free citizens of the city and the development of large-scale slave production. It allowed a considerable development of the productive forces and provided the possibility of an evolutionary path through feudalism ending in capitalism.

The establishment of *Asiatic societies* indicates another path. This concept, long condemned by one line of Marxist thinking, was revived and developed during the early sixties by several French researchers at the C.E.R.M. (Centre d'Etudes et de Recherches Marxistes) beginning with the work of Tökei. The essential characteristics of these societies have been elucidated: the combination of village communities and a despotic State intervening at some level of the process of production (e.g. carrying out large-scale irrigation works or organising trade) and their widespread historical occurence has been acknowledged.[6]

Much work remains to be done if we are to understand the forms taken by transformations of the communal structure within the Asiatic and Ancient modes of production. The existence and functioning of the community of free citizens as well as the village community can only be understood by referring to the dominant relations of production: slave relations of production and 'generalised slavery' in classical slave society.

In the *Formen*, Marx also considered a third way in which the communal structure could be transformed, setting out certain characteristics of this transformation in his study of *Germanic society*. He clearly distinguished it from the Asiatic and Ancient forms:

> Another form of the property of working individuals, self-sustaining members of the community, in the natural conditions of their labour, is the *Germanic*. Here the commune member is neither, as such, a co-possessor of the communal property, as in the specifically oriental form (wherever property exists *only* as communal property, there the individual member is as such only *possessor* of a particular part, hereditary or not, since any fraction of the property belongs to no member for himself, but to him only as immediate member of the commune, i.e. as in direct unity with it, not in distinction to it. This individual is thus only a possessor. What exists is only *communal* property, and only *private possession* . . .)[7]

There are two specific characteristics of the Germanic form: – not only does a community member have an existence distinct from the community, but the latter only exists in the actual relationships between its members. Even if the community exists in its shared history, descent, language, etc., it does not exist as a communal form of production independent of the social, economic and political relationships which join its members together and which must continuously be renewed. Marx is quite explicit on this point:

> Among the Germanic tribes, where the individual family chiefs settled in the forests, long distances apart, the commune exists, already from 'outward' observation, only in the periodic gathering-together (*Vereinigung*) of the commune members, although their unity 'in-itself' is posited in their ancestry, language, common past and history, etc. *The commune thus appears as a coming-together (Vereinigung) not as a being-together (Verein); as a unification made up of independent subjects, landed proprietors, and not as a unit.*[8]

This distinctive form taken by the community is realised at the level of the domestic group which appears as an independent production unit. A key passage from Marx sheds some light on the articulation of the domestic form and the communal form of production:

> Individual property does not appear mediated by the commune; rather, the existence of the commune and of communal property appear as mediated by, i.e. as a relation of, the independent subjects to one another. The economic totality is, at bottom, contained in each individual household, which forms an independent centre of production for itself . . .[9]

Each individual producer, as proprietor and producer belongs first of all to a domestic group. As a member of a domestic group he has access to the communal property which appears complementary to household property i.e. hunting or grazing lands, etc.:

> True, the *ager publicus*, the communal or people's land, as distinct from individual property, also occurs among the Germanic tribes. It takes the form of hunting land, grazing land, timber land etc., the part of the land which cannot be divided if it is to serve as means of production in this specific form. But this *ager publicus* does not appear, as with the Romans e.g., as the particular economic presence of the state as against the private proprietors, so that these latter are actually *private* proprietors as such, in so far as they are *excluded*, deprived, like the plebeians, from using the *ager publicus*. Among the Germanic tribes, the *ager publicus* appears merely as a complement to individual property, and figures as property only to the extent that it is defended militarily as the common property of one tribe.[10]

It is as an individual proprietor (mediated by membership in a domestic group) that a community member has access to communal property, not because his individual (or family) possession is tied to membership in the community as in Asiatic society.

Marx's analysis in the *Formen* is confined to these few general remarks. For one thing there were insufficient data available to develop a theory for these societies. On the other hand, under the influence of the evolutionist theories of the day (especially Morgan's)[11] the study of Germanic society was placed in an entirely different context, resulting in the abandonment of the concepts created to understand it in the *Formen*. It was no longer considered in terms of its specificity, but rather as a stage between the 'primitive commune' and feudalism.

The community and domestic group among Nilo-Hamitic pastoralists

The empirical data gathered by anthropologists make it possible to reintroduce and develop this concept. The wealth of material on the Nilo-Hamitic pastoralists of East Africa accumulated by English researchers gives us an opportunity to examine the relevance of this concept for the study of community structures in these societies.[12]

Among Nilo-Hamitic pastoralists, the domestic group is an independent production unit. It is also a kinship unit based on the polygynous family (2 to 3 wives on average) itself a part of a larger group, the patrilineal extended family, made up of three generations: fathers, married sons and their offspring. Within the family, most of the work is allocated according to sex and age.[13] When more extended forms of cooperation are required, especially during the dry season, roving camps of herdsmen without their families are formed. These are always unstable residential groups. The domestic group holds rights over the herd. All the various family members retain rights in the herd. The family head only has the final say in matters of management and organisation. These rights are both individual and non-specific (e.g. the cattle which a husband allots to his wife are intended for their children). As Gulliver writes: 'Property is not an individual entity residing with one person or a small group. It is a cluster of rights appertaining to some object.'[14] This form of property and generally the domestic group structure must be interpreted within the context of the *conditions of their reproduction* i.e. on the one hand, the conditions under which men and women circulate within the community; on the other hand, the conditions of the parallel circulation of livestock, the principal means of production.[15]

During this process of the reproduction of domestic units, two levels, each in turn play the primary role. These levels are respectively the patrilineal extended families and the 'houses' (*ekal*) composed of the descendants of a polygamous family head's wives.

Far from being contradictory, the fact that these two levels successively play the primary role reflects the very dynamism of the reproduction of domestic groups which requires the succession of three generations. At marriage every man allocates some livestock to his wife for her and her children's support. *Fission* in the rights over stock follows the divisions between houses in the second generation. In the alternate generation, extended families, created through the successive marriages of members of the previous generation, form new residential and economic units. Thus each polygynous family is simultaneously part of a patrilineal extended family and a point at which fission occurs. The principles of seniority establishing the order of marriages within a single generation and alternate generations operating in the reproduction of domestic groups are extended to the whole community through the age-organisation system.

The reproduction of domestic groups cannot be reduced to this process of fission or the transmission of rights over livestock. The *circulation of women* plays all the more significant role in that women represent cleavage points in the inheritance of rights over livestock. The importance of women's labour and their role as 'reproducers of producers' increases the value of their circulation.

Two requirements governing the circulation of women determine the social form which marriage takes. One is the need to establish preferential social relations with the group from which one receives a wife (alliance). The other is the necessity of retaining inherited rights over livestock within the patriline.

The result of the *clan system* is to exclude the women in Ego's own group from the set of possible wives, thereby eliminating all those in the patriline who are thought to have descended from a common ancestor and who thus have parallel rights over a herd. Marriage prohibitions extend the rule of exogamy to exclude all groups into which members of the patrilineal extended family have already married (clans of Ego's father, mother, mother's father and those clans from whom Ego's brothers have already taken wives).[16]

The clan system also serves to reinforce the unity of the domestic group threatened by the entry of an outsider who will be given substantial rights over livestock. The assimilation of a woman to her husband's clan is marked by elaborate rituals which differ from clan to clan.

The collection, payment and receipt of bride-wealth (bride-price) also express the unity of the agnatic group and promotes social control over the distribution of women. The two main factors regulating marriage age are the need to assemble a substantial number of animals in order to marry (the livestock being obtained from both agnatic kin and stock associates) and the rule ordering marriages according to seniority. Leaving aside the marriages of young men, these rules insure a certain rate of polygamy.

Without going into a detailed analysis of complex marriage systems, I shall simply draw attention to two points:

First, there is a notable correspondence between the marriage system and the transmission of wealth. Gulliver speaks of a veritable 'structural amnesia' in descent-reckoning beyond the three generations necessary to the functioning of the domestic system. Kin beyond three generations are easily transformed into possible affines since the recognition of patrilineal descent and clan affiliation is not retained. These societies are characterised by the rapid formation of new alliances and by the high degree of mobility of producers between social groups.

Secondly, and following from this coherence, we see that agnatic relationships and the social relationships which they encompass (reciprocity governing gifts of livestock, cooperation, assistance in marriage payments, co-residence) are only really established once they have become realised in stock associations. *Kinship* only exists as part of a wider system of social relations manifested in the circulation of livestock. In this case we cannot speak of descent groups. Agnatic inheritance is equally adapted to a system where rights over livestock pass through women. The transformation of kin into potential affines does not stem from actual marriage-alliance mechanisms as in societies where there is prescriptive or preferential marriage. Agnation is a purely ideological phenomenon giving a minimum of continuity (three generations) to a society where the ideal (occasionally reached, as among the Jie) is the reproduction in alternate generation of the social conditions of production within a stable community.

Thus, while kinship functions as relations of production and acts as the dominant instance in the process of reproduction in this case it does not fulfil certain functions (e.g. political) that it performs in other societies.[17] This should not obscure the fact that by manipulating kinship and alliance each domestic group can develop its social and economic relationships, increase its own productive capacities by sending out more livestock, receiving a greater number in return, acquire new avenues of cooperation and mutual assistance, gain access to numerous watering holes and grazing lands and replenish its stock more easily in case of loss.

To understand this function of kinship and alliance, they must be placed in the wider context of social relations between domestic units, the centres of production. According to Gulliver, these relations define the 'stock-associates' of a family head and the complexity of the relationship established and conceived of as a 'stock-association' – the fact that livestock circulate between production units (in marriage-alliance relationships or simply between neighbours and friends). In effect 'stock-associations' encompass preferential relationships for cooperation in work, residential associations and political and judicial support.

These relations, conceived of as reciprocal rights over livestock, are specific to each domestic production unit. Their extention throughout the society defines the form in which the community as a whole is realised in production. The limits of the social group within which these reciprocal rights operate correspond to the limits of the community within which natural resources (pastures and watering places) are exploited in common.

Within this community women and livestock circulate and disagreements must not be solved by resort to force (at least the spear is not to be used). Inversely, relations with other communities are negatively defined: disagreements are resolved by force and livestock may be stolen. By definition, members of other communities are forbidden access to pasture land. These are the terms in which Gulliver defines the tribe: 'The tribe is recognised by its communal possession of pasture lands, from which non-Jie are excluded.'[18]

The reproduction of a domestic unit ultimately appears inseparable from that of the set of domestic units constituting a community. Or rather, *the reproduction of domestic units is simultaneously the reproduction of the relations between these different units defining the form of community production.*

The role of livestock and the fetishisation of social relations

Up until now I have confined myself to the analysis of the immediately given or apparent form taken by the articulation of domestic and community structures of production. There are a number of phenomena which cannot be understood through such an analysis. In some societies, particularly those which experience a rapid rate of expansion characterised by an increase in herds and lands put under grazing there is no notion of a common territory in the social consciousness. The Turkana did not exploit a fixed territory during the period of their migration and conquests.[19]

More generally, access to a common territory, far from being a condition for domestic production is in fact a result of the circulation of livestock among domestic groups. If we are to understand this phenomenon we must examine the circulation of livestock in these societies in greater detail.[20]

In Nilo-Hamitic societies there is a custom which anthropologists have interpreted as *stock-lending*. It consists in placing animals from one's own herd in the herds of others. This involves a more or less final transfer of rights, although this transfer is always subject to the requirements of *reciprocity*. This form of circulation has an economic function. By insuring the dispersal of animals, it minimises risk in the event of plunder, disease or drought. It also promotes cooperation between herdsmen associated in this manner.

However, this is not the only function it serves. Loans of livestock are part of a network of 'stock associations' available to each herdsman as a member of a kinship group and through the marriage-alliances he has concluded. Stenning rightly remarks that through these exchanges of livestock 'a man is not exploiting his relationships for the sake of cattle, but using his cattle to form relationships'.[21] In the herdmen's minds these relationships are not seen for what they are i.e. stemming from descent and marriage rules, resulting from cooperation in work or simply a result of choices made by the producers. For the herdsmen, the circulation of cattle itself seems to determine these relationships. It conceals the actual social relations defining the community of producers formed for the exploitation of common resources and the reproduction of the social totality. We find an actual *inversion of the real conditions of social life within the social consciousness*, a case of fetishism in Marx's sense, where relations established through the mediation of commodities conceal actual social relations.

The sacrifices of livestock can be similarly analysed. These sacrifices also have an immediate economic function among Nilo-Hamitic pastoralists. The timing and spacing of sacrifices enable the Pokot to distribute meat within the ritual (also a neighbourhood) group throughout the entire year and particularly during periods of reduced milk production.[22] However, ritual and the relationship with the sacred mediated through livestock cannot be reduced to this function alone. Sacrifices of livestock which occur at all ritual occasions, permit the creation of a relationship between the human community and the divine and invoke the intercession of supernatural forces for the group's harmonious reproduction. As M. Godelier has aptly expressed it, sacrifices, an integral part of all ritual, function to establish the conditions of the community's reproduction at an 'imaginary' level.

Finally, *the Nilo-Hamitic pastoralists' immediate understanding of their society is based upon this inversion. The well-being of society and its adaptation to changing ecological conditions seem as if they were the result of the constant flow of cattle among men on the one hand and, on the other hand, between the human and supernatural worlds, the ultimate guarantor of the 'healthy reproduction' of the social system.* This manner of thinking is expressed mythically in the idea of the original unity and parallel descent of animals and men. The abilities of livestock to determine social life are completely set out in myth. Similarly we find the effects of this inversion *at the level of the individual* where the identification of an individual with a favourite animal is such that its loss can lead to suicide.

As a result the use made of livestock appears to determine the real factors of the division of labour and the means of production, the circulation of women, etc. Social and economic difficulties (disease, war and famine) are punishments for poor management, for not satisfying the human and supernatural norms governing relations between men and their livestock.

The limits of the community as a unit appear in their concealed or 'fetishised' form as the limits of reciprocal rights over cattle. Among the extremely mobile Turkana, where social organisation is highly fluid and social groups are continuously breaking up, the community seems to be realised solely in this fetishised form. Even the idea of common territory is only a blurred and unstable notion. Livestock and wealth are continually circulating among domestic groups. This constant flux is shaped and transformed by the migrations of the tribes as new pasture lands at the periphery of its territory are opened.

The unity of the community first of all exists only in the relations between domestic units which represent so many autonomous centres of production and sources of structurally equivalent rights over commonly exploited resources. Because of this the conditions of production paralleling these domestic units and the relations between them must be established at a given level of the social organisation. Livestock assumes this special function because of its central role in the reproduction of domestic units (the parallel reproduction of herds and families). This also explains why the circulation of livestock is seen as determining the entire reproduction of all the domestic units in the herdsmen's minds and actions.[23]

Thus the circulation of livestock seems divorced from other processes and appears as the precondition of reproduction. In fact, it can only be understood in the context of the conditions of production and reproduction considered in their totality i.e. in the context of the complete set of conditions of social life. Moving on from this necessary digression, I can now return to the analysis by setting out the elements of a theory of the *value of livestock*.

Community production and the community 'in-itself'

At this point a distinction should be drawn between the form in which community production is realised (division of grazing lands and other natural resources, cooperation, defence, etc.) and the community's 'existence in-itself'. This distinction has already been made by Marx in his analysis of Germanic society:

> In the Germanic form, the agriculturalist is not (a) citizen of a state, i.e. not the inhabitant of a city; (the) basis (is) rather the isolated, independent family residence, guaranteed by the bond with other such family residences of the same tribe, and by their occasional coming-together (*Zusammenkommen*) to pledge each others' allegiance in war, religion, adjudication etc. Individual landed property here appears neither as a form antithetical to the commune's landed property, nor as mediated by it, but just the contrary. The commune exists only in the interrelations among these individual landed proprietors as such. Communal property as such appears only as a communal accessory to the individual tribal seats and the land they appropriate. The commune is neither the substance of which the individual uppears as a mere accident; nor is it a generality with a *being and unity* as such (*seinde Einheit*) either in the mind and the existence of the city and of its civic needs as distinct from those of the individual, or in its civic land and soil as its particular presence as distinct from the particular economic presence of the commune member; rather, the commune on the one side, is presupposed in-itself prior to the individual proprietors as a communality of language, blood, etc., but it exists as a presence, on the other hand, only in its *real assembly* for communal purposes; and to the extent that it has a particular economic existence in the hunting and grazing lands for communal use, it is so used by each individual proprietor as such, not as a representative of the state (as in Rome).[24]

As I have already shown, in societies where descent cannot serve to define the global coherence of social groups, the community in-itself is realised at another level. Beyond the factors of common language and history, the age-organisation system takes priority over any process of immediate production in the realisation of the community. I shall return to the significant transformations in the system of age-organisation in the various Nilo-Hamitic societies later. For the moment, I shall restrict my comments to a few general observations on the functions of age-organisation.

1. Age-organisation introduces a fundamental order in the social system by extending *the principles of seniority and alternate generations* to the entire society. We have already seen the effects of these principles at the level of the domestic group. This order determines the timing of initiations and is apparent in all rituals where the participants are classified according to their place in the age-organisation system.
2. Age-organisation is *at the basis of political organisation (the gerontocratic organisation of power) and in religion*, which are themselves closely interrelated since the relationship of senior grades with the sacred forms the basis of their exercise of power. As those who intercede with the spirits and Supreme God on behalf of the community, the elders possess the formidable weapon of the *curse*, thus giving them the respect of the young men with whom they compete for livestock and women.
3. Finally, the system of age-organisation provides the setting for *resolving contradictions produced by the social system.* During periods of demographic pressure among the Karimojong, celebrations marking the succession of generations are held. Here a senior generation (encompassing several age-sets) stands down permitting the initiation of young men who are thereby able to marry. On these occasions one witnesses a veritable ritual purification of historically produced conflicts. These celebrations reforge the unity of the community by opening a new age-set which brings future producers together in a symbolic distribution of livestock among groups (in the form of clay figurines) and in the branding of cattle. At these celebrations, as on all ritual occasions, livestock are sacrificed in considerable numbers, making possible the establishment of a relationship between the human community and the supernatural world. The wealthiest men play a special role in these sacrifices which also serve to balance the distribution of livestock among groups.

The unifying function of age-organisation is expressed in functionalist terms by Gulliver: ‘insofar as the ritual and age-organisation places persistent emphasis on the essential unity and interdependence of all Jie, on internal peace and the norms of right behaviour, it powerfully reinforces mundane unity and cooperation and serves as a major integrative factor in the society.'[26]

The form taken by the community in-itself and the very conditions of its functioning are based on the inversion or fetishisation of social relations. We have described its masking effect on actual social relations above. In the final analysis, the coherence appears based in the phantasmic world of *religion* 'Sociologically, the limits of the Jie tribe can best be described in ritual terms. People of a district and of the whole tribe are kept together by indispensable ritual needs. Whilst the content of this ritual forms an autonomous system, its operation in actual life is dependent both physically and spiritually on age organisation which chiefly exists to serve it.'[27]

It is important to recognise this role of political organisation and religion if we are to understand the system's potential for further transformations, especially for the appearance of class relations at the level of the community in-itself where one social group controlling the conditions of reproduction of the social system can continually extort surplus realised at the level of the domestic group.

Basically secular and daily religious practices are related to the value of livestock and its central role in social life and the ability it has to fulfill several functions simultaneously. Livestock make communication with the supernatural possible. Communication is mediated through the most senior elders. The role of mediator is also played by prophets and 'rain-makers' whose actions are a condition for social life, good grazing lands, success in warfare and human and animal fertility.[28]

The preceding quote from Gulliver emphasises another important point. The territory exploited in common corresponds to the form of community production and is also a feature of the community in-itself. The sites of ritual activity (areas where dances and sacrifices are performed) and the territorial organisation of age-classes tend to stabilise the territory within the framework of political and religious organisation. The often apparent separation of the actually exploited territory from that serving as a ritual site reflects basic contradictions determining the dynamic of the system.

The productive forces and relations of production: the nature and development of contradictions

I shall begin with two substantive observations:

1. The various Nilo-Hamitic groups, belonging to the same linguistic and culture area and subject to the same technological

and ecological conditions present not only undeniable similarities, but also considerable variations in their social and economic organisation.

2. These variations correspond to quite radical variations in the productivity of labour and to varying degrees of specialisation in pastoralism (see Table 1).

Table 1. Comparison of specialisation in pastoralism among East African pastoralists

Groups	Agriculture		Stock unit/person[29]
Jie	Associated with herding	(considerable)	4.5
Karimojong	,, ,,	,,	4.8
Nandi	,,	,,	5.2
Kipsigis	,,	,,	3.0
Kamasya	,,	,,	3.7
Keyo	,,	,,	2.7
Marakwet	,,	,,	1.8
Total. Nandi	,,	,,	4.6
Turkana	Associated with herding	(weak)	6.5[30]
Pakot	No agriculture		17.9
Samburu	,,		14.0
Masai Tanzania	,,		17.2
Masai Kenya	,,		19.6

These variations cannot be traced to the effects of ecological factors. For instance the Masai are exclusively pastoralists in an environment where agriculture is possible, whereas the Turkana attempt cultivation in an uncomprising and arid zone. I intend to interpret these variations as transformations of the conditions of production which are linked to the relations between the productive forces and the relations of production.

I have already mentioned that *the moment of fission* during the process of reproduction is especially important. As specialisation in herding advances and the productivity of labour increases, this process of fissioning of domestic groups accelerates; production units 'nucleate'; rights over stock become individualised (see Fig. 1). The formation of small units based on the polygynous family – or even challenging the unity of this family as among the Turkana is associated with specialisation in herding and increases with it. Here again I should make myself clear; *Mobility (nomadism) and specialisation in herding are neither the cause nor the effect of the transformation of production units (the process of nucleation)*. What we have are two levels in the realisation of a single process: the *transformation of the conditions for the realisation of labour* at both the level of the productive forces and the level of the relations

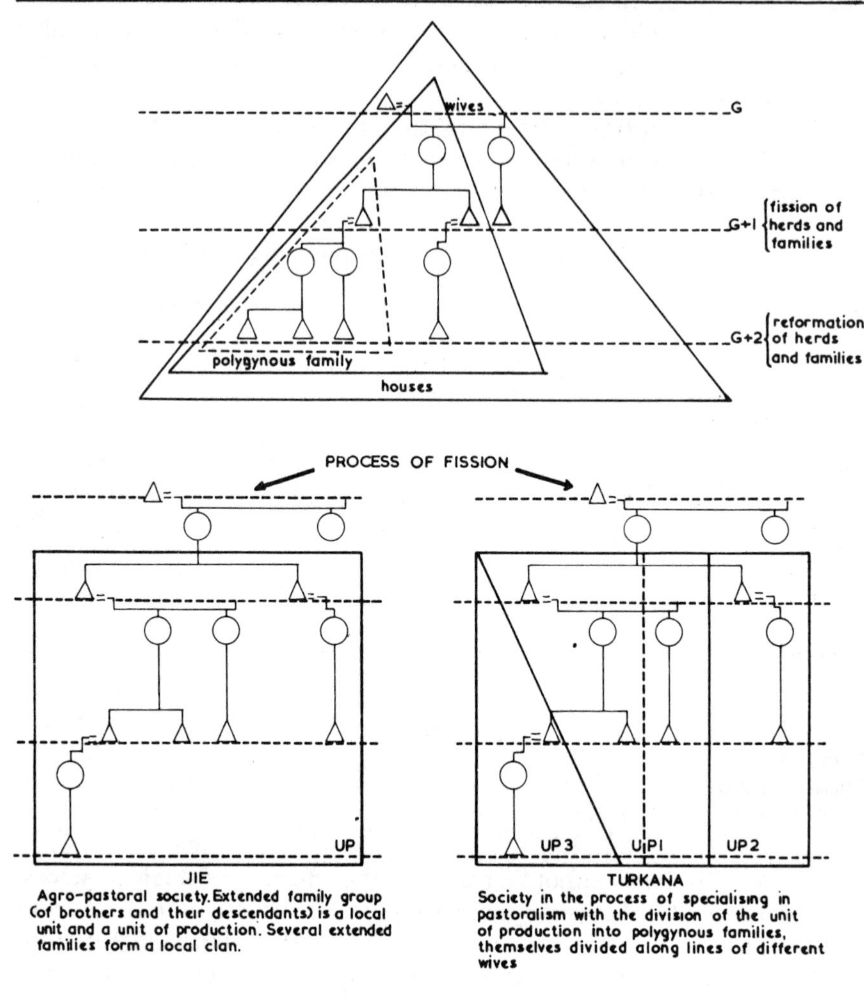

Figure 1. Transformations of domestic groups

of production. This requires some clarification.

1. At no time does the socio-economic system function at its maximum capacity. The conditions for the realisation of labour cannot be deduced from the use of a given technology in a certain environment. Variations in the productivity of labour are related to variations in the social conditions of production. However, there are limits to these variations, first and foremost those imposed by the productive forces at a given time. These appear in the over-exploitation of the environment and the over-grazing of pasture lands resulting in the greatly increased susceptibility among human and animal populations to disease and climactic change (droughts). Far from mere events, these factors are integrated within the reproductive process as *conditions of*

production. At the end of the nineteenth century, the expansion of the Masai tribes was halted at its peak (although some of these herdsmen still have very large herds) by an epidemic of cattle disease, which did not effect the more dispersed Turkana whose herds were fewer and less compact. The Turkana increased their specialisation in herding and began expanding their territory to include better grazing lands, some of which had been abandoned by the Masai.

The practice of agriculture results in an identical but less brutal readjustment of the relationship between population and resources. In the situation where agricultural output is highly problematic, agricultural products are supplementary (agricultural labour is confined to women). The less the movement of the herds, the lower the productivity. At the end of the nineteenth century one group of Masai took up agriculture and settled down. They are now considered to be one of the numerous agro-pastoralist peoples in this region.

Inversely, it could be shown that transformations of the economic system, a decline in productivity and an increase in population create the conditions for specialisation in herding. Turkana pastoralists became separated from the Karimojong agro-pastoralists in this manner.

Globally, if the level of the productive forces only sets the limits for the development of the system of production (i.e. a negative determination of the limits of possible transformations), the variations in the productivity of labour at a given level of the productive forces will correspond to the development of contradictions brought on by the conditions for the realisation of labour. This will occur at the level of the productive forces and relations of production, the dialectical interaction of which makes the transformation of these societies necessary (a positive form of determination).

It seems to me that these mechanisms help to explain the *cyclical* aspect of the region's history. The societies under consideration can be placed at different points of a cycle which can be represented as in Fig. 2.

2. We can now attempt to understand the nature of these *contradictions*. As the fissioning process develops accompanied by the nucleation of production units, social control over the circulation of livestock and women becomes more difficult and raises some acute problems for the society. Among the Jie and to a lesser extent among the Karimojong, demographic and economic stability corresponds to a 'harmonious' reproduction of the conditions of domestic and communal production through readjustments allowed by the ideology of agnation and the age-organisation system. The number of domestic units appears stable; young men's access to livestock and women is regulated

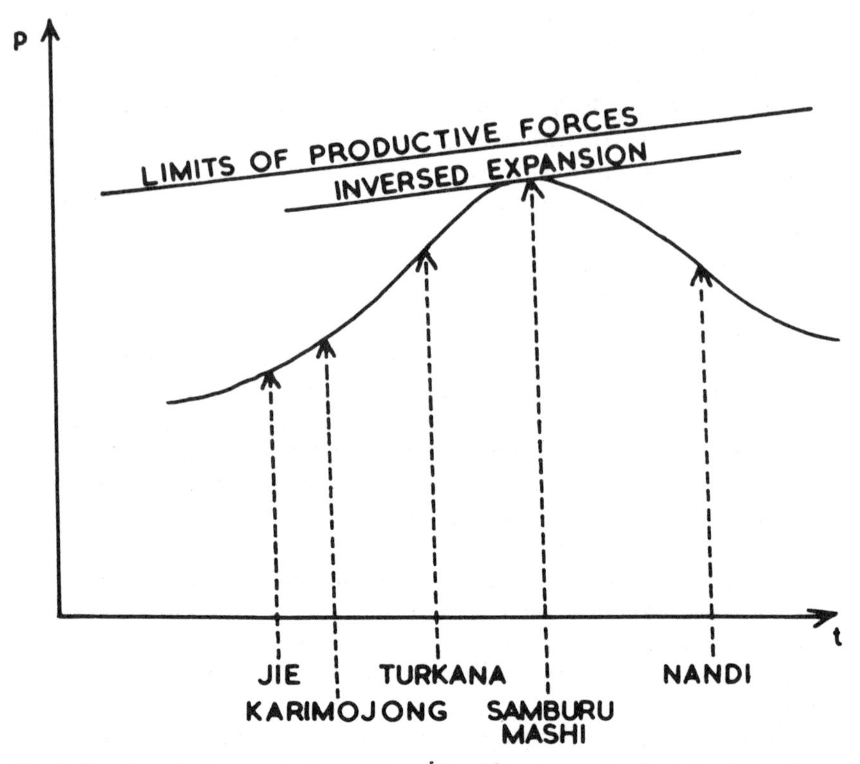

Fig 2. Synchronic representation of the cycle of development of productivity of some East African pastoralist societies.

by the clan system, the rules of seniority and the requirement of initiation before marriage which guarantee a given rate of polygamy.

Among the Turkana, the neo-local settling of married men and the opening of new pastures during the course of the 'pioneering' migrations of the generation of 'sons' helps to resolve tensions. However, tensions remain evident in the instability of social groups and between brothers in competition, leading even to fratricide in some cases. Here contradictions are resolved through the actual *expansion* of society.

This is no longer the case among the Samburu where expansion is difficult. Here the productivity of labour is high, but unlikely to develop further.[31] Tensions develop between father and son over access to livestock and women. (The father conceals livestock in order to marry again). Tension also exists between husband and wife. The resolution of these conflicts results in basic transformations of the social system especially with respect to marriage alliances. The possibilities for contracting new marriages must be more tightly controlled. Stronger ideological and political constraints are required to compel respect for the rules of clan exogamy. Relations between clans become asymmetrical. The superiority of 'wife-givers' becomes apparent in the staggering of bride-price payments: a small amount is transferred at the time of marriage and payments continue as long as relations with one's affines are kept up. Payments are continued as obligations towards matrilineal kin (one's father's affines). The ideology of agnation is strengthened and extends to the whole of society, reorganising the clan structure according to a 'segmentary' model. Local group access to communal resources also becomes more clearly defined. Individuals, however, continue to circulate easily between groups. Finally, the status of women declines and there is more conflict within marriages. Divorce is widespread among the Samburu while non-existent in the other societies. Spencer has provided an excellent description of the tension prevailing in this society and its psychopathic consequences.[32]

Thus, there is *a contradiction between the domestic form of production (the domestic appropriation of the means of production) and the social control over the circulation of the means of production (access to livestock and pastures) and women, the circulation entailing the simultaneous reproduction of the domestic units and the communal form of production.*

The development of this initial contradiction brings about the transformation of the system of production which has been outlined above i.e. an accentuation of the process of fissioning, the individualisation of rights over livestock and the nucleation of production units. The development of this contradiction furthermore entails the transformation of the whole set of social structures.

Transformations in the system of age-organisation

For reasons already mentioned, transformations are most evident at the level of the community in-itself. In the minds of the people this level appears as the ultimate locus of the conditions for reproduction. At this level we also find a great deal of activity directed toward the resolution of contraditions produced by the process of reproduction. *Transformations of the system of age-organisation* also elucidate the autonomy and special logic of the different systems making up the society (Fig. 3).

Age-organisation is based strictly on the principle of alternate generations among the Jie. There are always two generations in existence, the elders and the youths, each divided into successive age-sets which individuals enter through initiation. One generation includes all the 'fathers' (elders), the other all the 'sons' (youths). When all the men in the grade of 'fathers' have been initiated, a new age grade is opened at a feast of succession aimed at restoring harmony throughout the society. The opening of a new age-grade gives a possibility of marrying to the many men who have been waiting. Given the population stability and the unchanging rate of productivity

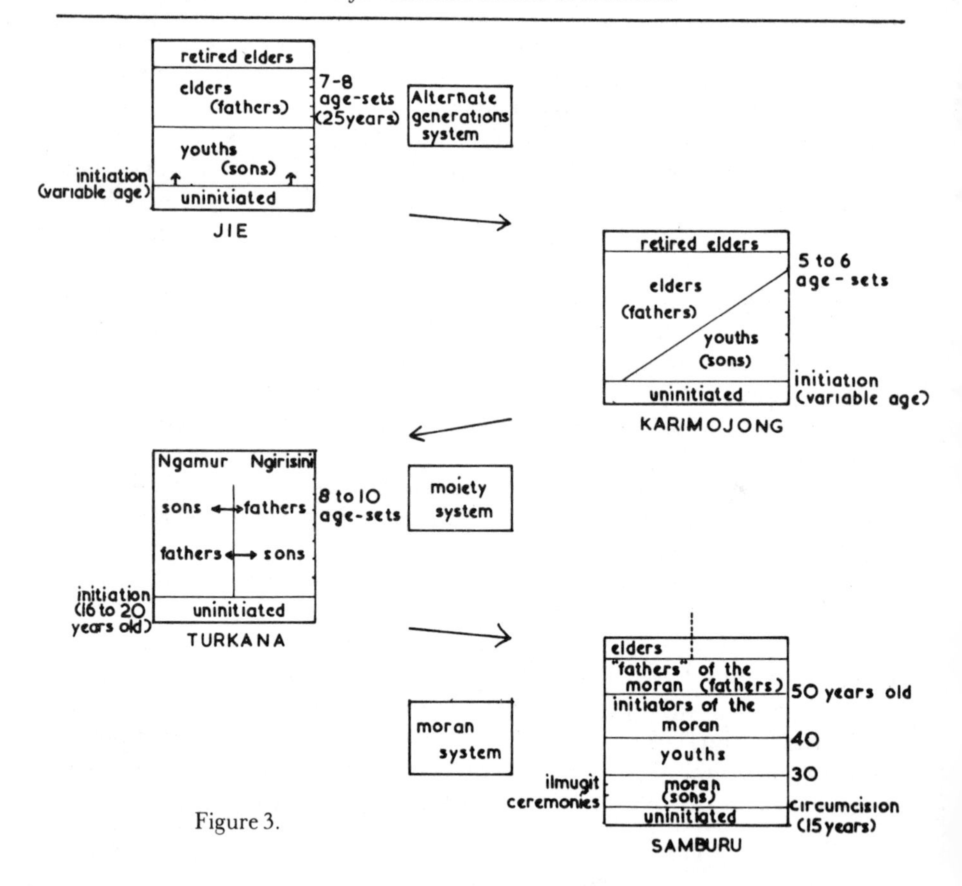

Figure 3.

in Jie society, the age-organisation system insures the 'ideal' reproduction of one generation in the alternate generation. In this way the equivalence of 'grandsons' and 'grandfathers', the control over the distribution of wealth and women and the stabilisation of concrete and symbolic forms of social life are guaranteed. In this case there is a close correspondence between the community 'in-itself' and the form of community production.

The Karimojong system of age-organisation is rather similar, but greater tensions associated with the process of expansion result in the system's 'malfunctioning'.[33] In order to overcome the problems raised by increased production and population, the Karimojong have to forfeit strict adherence to the principle of the alternation of generations and the separation of 'fathers' and 'sons' into two successive generations. At times it even becomes necessary to keep the senior generation open to recruitment after the younger generation has already been opened.[34]

Here we find the beginnings of a *moiety* system of age-organisation like that of the Turkana who moreover seem to have retained traces of the system of alternate generations.[35] The accelerated rate of expansion in this society has brought about a radical change. Individuals are divided among age-sets belonging to one of two moieties. (One becomes a member of the moiety of which one's father is not a member). In the context of unstable social forms and a mobile population, age-organisation continues to bring a minimum of order to the community in-itself and defines its form. Under conditions of expansion, a clear-cut gap emerges between the community in-itself and the form of community production, especially as regards territoriality. The functions of the community in-itself become reduced. This reduction is related to problems confronting the Turkana which they solve through continual migration and advances into frontier zones separating them from their neighbours. Age-organisation takes on considerable military importance in this situation where there is a tendency to transfer the tensions threatening social life to the peripheral areas.

This transfer of tension to the periphery is also a valuable function of the Samburu system of age-organisation which otherwise differs quite radically from the systems described above: 'The most significant function of the Samburu age-set system is, I believe, that it diverts forces which could be disruptive to the family and places them under the direct control of the elders.'[36] Here, as among the Turkana, we find moieties, but the principal division is between an age-grade encompassing all unmarried men (*moran*) and the age-grades of married men. The position of the *moran* is marked by a series of ceremonies which function mainly to delay marriage and insure the elders' social control over the circulation of livestock and women. If necessary, the elders are prepared to use their political power or their formidable sanction, the curse of God, to insure control. To avoid direct tensions between 'fathers' and 'sons', the latter are initiated into an age-set at least three sets below the 'fathers' and find themselves in a position of uneasy subordination to the 'initiators of the *moran*', the set immediately following that of the 'fathers of the *moran*'. Here the exercise of authority takes on a directly gerontocratic form (Spencer).

What is important here – and which also occurs among the Masai – is the *direct intervention of politics and religion in determining the conditions of social reproduction.* This intervention is no longer in terms of some 'imaginary' conditions of reproduction, but accomplished by delaying young men's access to women, using coercion if need be. It enables a section of the society, the 'elders', to benefit from the surplus produced within the domestic group, particularly from the labour of the *moran* warriors stationed as shepherds on the outskirts of the camps. The military organisation which develops clearly reveals this transformation. As an instrument in the accumulation of livestock and labour and as an outlet for internal tensions, military organisation takes on the almost exclusive role of social organisation among the Masai.

We are not dealing with social classes in this situation, since youths in turn will become elders and accession to this status rightfully belongs to all youths. But above all, the extortion of surplus value does not determine the dominant structure of society. To be sure, the extortion of surplus value reinforces the inequality of access to women and livestock, but it doesn't challenge the structural equivalence of the production units or the producers' access to communal resources. The ultimate function of the surplus produced, even if it can be manipulated in an inegalitarian fashion, is *the social reproduction of the community as such and not the reproduction of the difference between two social classes*.

Under certain conditions, however, this type of social differentiation can lead to the *appearance of class relations*. Transformations of the functions of politics (military organisation) and religion (the great hereditary prophets among the Masai) give us some indication of how this may come about. It presupposes a type of community where one social group is able to control the process of reproduction by controlling the ultimate conditions of reproduction.[37] This development represents another possible solution to the contradictions created in the process of reproduction. In contrast to other possible solutions mentioned above i.e. abrupt or gradual decreases in productivity, here we have new conditions for evolution. This history departs from the 'cycle' of migrations, the creation and disappearance of local sovereign groups. Only a detailed investigation of neighbouring peoples with class structures (the Galla, the interlacustrine societies) would enable us to judge the actual realisation of this historical 'possibility'.

Inter-community relations

Up until now I have been using the framework of the isolated community to interpret the functioning of Nilo-Hamitic societies. This has only been an analytical tool. *Their actual history is one of communities 'in competition'. The form of this 'competition' varies according to the level of the development of contradictions within each group.* The problem of inter-community relations is especially important since these internal contradictions may be resolved through their relationship with the exterior or periphery.

The formal relations between communities can be interpreted in the same way as internal social relations. Thus domestic groups in peripheral areas will tend to establish relations with neighbouring communities through stock associations, marriages, etc. Thus we find a whole range of relations between communities:

1. The close identification of communities within a single tribe. For instance the Karimojong are composed of groups acknowledging a

common origin and all, theoretically, maintain the same kinds of social relations. Their composite form is analogous to a single community.

2. In contrast, 'enemy' tribes are more numerous. Here relations are defined in a purely negative fashion. Killing and stealing of cattle are defined as rights. Entry into Karimojong territory is prohibited. Actual hostility depends upon the degree of competition. It appears weak among the Pokot, but intense in the case of their neighbours, the Jie.

If we are to understand this 'competition', we must go back to the kinds of *expansion processes* experienced by these societies. I have shown that expansion represents one way of solving the contradictions which develop in these societies. The tendency to expand is greatest under conditions of increasing productivity (e.g. the Turkana). War and the opening of new pastures accelerates this process of growth giving it a cumulative effect. However:

1. War is the effect rather than the cause of growth. Furthermore, military organisation as such occurs at another point of development; among the Masai, although not among the Turkana.
2. Similarly, the opening of new pastures is not an end in itself. Among the Turkana the generation of 'sons' splits off from that of the 'fathers' and settles in a new border area. This split necessitates the opening of new grazing lands and presupposes a rapid increase in productivity and population. This is not an exceptional occurrence, it reappears in the origin myths of several tribes, explaining the processes of expansion and migration.

It is clear that expansion can only provide a temporary solution. *The resolution of internal contradictions through expansion results in further contradictions between communities.* Over the past hundred years the Turkana have assimilated many foreign elements, Samburu, Pokot, Marile, Rendille, etc., mainly through marriage with peoples on their periphery. Their loose-knit and unstable social organisation has helped to integrate outside groups.

The creation of these local hegemonies has historical limits emphasised above. Turkana hegemony replaced Masai, but created the conditions for its own disappearance. Internal conflict became increasingly difficult to resolve. Collisions with peoples of bordering areas increased and the system of production became increasingly susceptible to disease and drought. New communities expand into less favourable peripheral areas. The arid and uncompromising region of Lake Rudolf, an area from which pastoralist migrations have originated, represents a kind of geographical matrix of conquest societies.

The social consequences of expansion on a smaller scale are different. The Karimojong group studied by N. Dyson-Hudson[38] experienced a series of internal divisions resulting in the formation of several tribes each following different evolutionary paths. The group continued splitting into smaller groups. The tribe was composed of sections each reproducing all the features of autonomous communities. Those furthest removed from the centre were entirely independent.

The process whereby groups split into smaller units is determined by different factors:

1. territorial size and the distance between production units
2. alterations in the structure of the community
3. divergences from the common interest.

These factors are related to aspects of actual production (productivity, size of domestic and clan units, etc.) which determine the demographic laws particular to the system. They could be quantified if more detailed information were available. These laws define a 'typical' size for community units: about 20,000 persons for the Karimojong, nearly 50,000 for the Masai.

A division gradually arises within a single system. Relations differing from those at the centre are established on the periphery. Reproduction over time results in an 'amoeboid' division ending in two identical units which may or may not remain linked with the tribal centre: 'Territorial components of the main body separate spatially and take up an independent existence as units organisationally identical with, and equivalent to, the parent group.' N. Dyson-Hudson adds that 'the pattern of development applicable to the political community may be conceived . . . as involving a single structure capable of replication by detaching spatially defined segments of common internal organisation.'[39]

Not all these societies are in the process of splitting into smaller groups, expansion or migration. The Jie tribe demonstrates considerable *stability in population and production*, which while helping to stabilise internal contradictions also reinforces external pressures on the community threatening it with extinction by conquest, assimilation or destruction.

The study of the *conditions for the reproduction of the social formation* including the examination of inter-community relations gives us a better perspective for the interpretation of historical cases. It represents a further step toward understanding the place of these social systems in history. Many questions requiring further research still remain. In conclusion, I would like to develop two points which demonstrate the fertility of this approach.

A recent book by P. Spencer raises the problem of the relationship between neighbouring societies with radically different systems of production. The camel-herding Rendille tribes are settled near the Samburu with whom they maintain close relations (marriage, circulation of livestock) despite the social and cultural differences between these two societies.

The two groups exploit distinct although adjacent environments. They do not compete for livestock and pastures. Each group sees this complementarity as a means for resolving their respective contradictions. The Rendille benefit most directly. The excess of women and male labour in Rendille society generates considerable social tension. A substantial number of Rendille move and become Samburu (one third of the Samburu acknowledge recent Rendille origin). The circulation of goods accompanies the circulation of men and women, not only making this latter circulation possible but insuring its continuity. Rendille immigrants maintain rights over livestock in their own society, in particular over camels which may be loaned out (*mal*) to enable Samburu desiring to marry Rendille women to secure the bride-price. Affinal relationships established in this way give Rendille rights over Samburu livestock and promote further migration.

The parallel circulation of goods and men and women brings about a complementarity between these two societies based on differences which thus continue to be reproduced. Similarly, the presence of an intermediary group, the Ariaal, indicates a gradual movement of a section of the Rendille population toward the Samburu. The actual direction of these movements depends on the historical period in question. At the end of the nineteenth century this complementarity resulted in a movement in the opposite direction when cattle disease led to the emigration of a section of the Samburu tribe.

We can see the relevance of this sort of analysis which has been expanded to include observations of the inter-tribal and even the inter-ethnic level. Cultural or diffusionist approaches are insufficient. Differences must be interpreted in terms of the properties of socio-economic systems. Their study reveals modes of transformation and complementarity giving us the possibility of interpreting history and the laws of historical development.

The fertility of this problematic is evident in P. Spencer's study of hunters and gatherers (Dorobo) and fishing people (Elmolo) dispersed among the pastoralists. Refusing to consider them as survivals of earlier societies, he demonstrates that the settlement of the Dorobo can only be understood in terms of two factors.[40]

First, the relations which these groups maintain with herdsmen who abandon herding in large numbers during times of drought and epidemics. As for the Dorobo side of the relationship, they are able to acquire livestock and become pastoralists through the exchange of women and goods. A section of the Samburu originated in this way.

Secondly, one must work out the specific conditions of production leading to a form of social organisation based on bands of producers where affinal relations play a determinant role and where the primacy of endogamy leads to a break-down of the clan system, to monogamy and the diminishing role of age-organisation.

Another possibility is that some groups expand their agricultural activities and follow another line of development. This occurred in the case of the Iteso who have been separated from the Karimojong branch for several centuries. They migrated westward practising both shifting agriculture and pastoralism. Urged on by the colonisers, they began raising cotton and settled down in one region. At the present time, their social and economic system is however quite distinct from the otherwise widespread village community systems in Africa.

Conclusion: structures and history

We can now conclude this study of the structural properties of the social and economic systems of the Nilo-Hamitic peoples. The analysis has gradually expanded to the point where it reaches out beyond the confines of nomadic pastoralist societies and calls for further studies of neighbouring societies.

This digression has allowed me to present some ideas on the possible transformations of these structures over time and the emergence of class relations. We have seen how some of these societies enter an apparently stable cycle of social and political transformations, how others develop systems based on hunting, fishing or intensive agriculture with a high degree of productivity, and how others eventually disappear. *The laws of structural transformations and the contradictions which they determine ultimately appear as the very laws of historical development.* In their complexity they determine the most contingent aspects of historical facts e.g. droughts and epidemics.

History is to be considered global not only because it rests on determination in the last instance by the economic, but also because it acknowledges the autonomy of the structural levels of social life and the place of kinship, religion, etc. For example, myths – myths of the common origin of men and livestock, myths of migration – are not simply reflections of the conditions of production. They play a major role in establishing the value of livestock, in regulating the relations between generations and in expanding the ability of the supernatural to intervene in social life.

In seeking this kind of understanding of history our analysis follows that of the *Formen*. There Marx discussed various forms of evolution ranging from the different modes of the dissolution of the 'primitive commune' to the appearance of capitalism. Through the exploration of one of these paths briefly outlined in Marx's writings on the 'Germanic commune', I have tried to show how it displayed original modes of organisation (the community form, the relation between this community form and the domestic organisation of production) and disclosed specific transformational possibilities (the appearance of class relations and the state).

This analysis is but a first step. It needs to be developed not only through further field research, but at the theoretical level as well. However, it seems to me that the foregoing analysis demonstrates the fertility of a non-dogmatic Marxist approach which seeks not to impose its preconceived plan on history, but on the contrary, seeks to continually create the concepts and theories necessary for the interpretation of the multiple forms taken by the process of evolution.[41]

(*Translated by Anne Bailey*)

NOTES

1 Some nomadic pastoralist societies may have been formed with an initial stage of animal domestication. This may have been the case for the Siberian reindeer herdsmen and perhaps the goat and sheep herders of the Near East at the beginning of the Neolithic.

2 Lattimore studies the way in which Chinese societies and the steppe societies starting from the same basis diverged over time: (1967), *Inner Asian Frontiers of China*, Boston.

3 References from the *Formen* are taken from the English edition of the *Grundrisse* translated by M. Nicolaus, 1973, Harmondsworth.

4. I should point out an ambiguity and a possible pitfall in the following analysis. In limiting this study to nomadic pastoralist societies alone, I do not mean to give the impression that I assign priority to ecological or technological determinism. As the article proceeds I shall show in what way the productive forces are determinant. If the constraints imposed by pastoralist production and nomadism favour the formation of a specific socio-economic system, they are by no means exclusive determinants. Other types of production may result in the formation of the same system.

5 This 'village commune', the essential production unit in 'Asiatic society', is not only an evolutionary step from the primitive commune. It was historically established as the social form taken by the exploitation of labour in the Asiatic state.

6 On this subject see *Sur le mode de production asiatique*, C.E.R.M., Editions sociales, 1969, which brings together some of the major works on the Asiatic mode.

7 *Grundrisse,* pp. 476-7.

8 *Grundrisse,* p. 483.

9 *Grundrisse,* pp. 483-4.

10 *Grundrisse,* p. 483.

11 Morgan's influence is particularly evident in Engels' *Origin of the Family, Private Property and the State* (1972), London. In fact as the publication of the *ethnological Notebooks of Karl Marx* (1973, ed. L. Krader) shows, Marx's reading of Morgan and other nineteenth-century evolutionist ethnologists was far more critical, underlining the irrelevant aspects of these analyses of evolutionary processes.

12 For a more detailed analysis of these societies see my study published at the C.E.R.M., *Sociétés pastorales 2: Organisation économique et sociales des pasteurs d'Afrique Orientale* (Cahier du C.E.R.M., No. 110, 1974). That study deals with a group of societies belonging to the Nilo-Hamitic linguistic group (Karimojong, Jie, Turkana, Samburu and Masai) who today are spread over areas of Uganda, Kenya and Tanzania. They are settled in the zone of the high plateaus separated by volcanic peaks and the Rift Valley. The fairly arid climate (due more to the irregularity of rainfall than its overall quantity which ranges between 400 and 800 mm.) makes agriculture uncertain and favours specialisation in herding which is known to have existed since the beginning of the Neolithic (first millennium A.D.). However, the allocation of labour between agriculture and herding cannot be explained by

immediate environmental determinants. Rather, this allocation is related to variations in productivity themselves linked to the conditions for the realisation of labour and the interrelationship of the productive forces and the relations of production. Where agriculture is found, it is practised by women on the banks of seasonal streams. They cultivate sorghum, gourds, etc. and recently maize on the limited areas available. On the one hand, these societies raise cattle which are left to graze throughout the year, thereby making the best use of pasture lands available. Their sheep and goats, on the other hand, provide a significant supplementary source of food. Livestock are exploited for their milk, meat and blood. Beasts of burden are rare or non-existent. The productivity of this sort of animal husbandry is low and requires quite large herds to satisfy needs (the number of stock-units per person varies between 5 and 20 depending on the social group. One stock unit = 1 head of cattle = 5 head of sheep or goats = $\frac{1}{2}$ a camel).

13 Men are responsible for most of the tasks involved in herding; women take on the domestic and possibly the agricultural chores. Young men and children act as shepherds, while adults and old men deal primarily with questions of herd management.

14 Gulliver, P.H. (1955), *The family Herds*, London, p. 264.

15 The parallels between the conditions of herd and family reproduction, between the circulation of individuals and livestock are a characteristic of nomadic pastoralist societies. The availability of labour power and livestock have to be adjusted during the formation and reproduction of domestic groups. On this point see my study published in *Sociétés pastorales 1: Sur l'Organisation technique et économique* (Cahiers du C.E.R.M., No. 109, 1973).

16 The range of clan marriage prohibitions varies directly with the coherence of the agnatic group over the three generations necessary for its reproduction. The range is more limited as the nucleation of production units increases internal fissioning of these agnatic groups.

17 There is a marked difference between this type of social organisation and a system based on descent and lineage organisation where kinship provides an *a priori* definition of statuses and roles and where the terms of marriage alliance must be firmly set out to insure not only the reproduction of domestic groups, but also that of the larger groups of which they are a part. The following quote from Gulliver brings out these differences: '. . . whatever else is presupposed by kinship,' such a bond, for both the Jie and the Turkana, establishes the right to claim animals and the obligation to give them, the right being the direct consequence of the obligation. Reciprocity comes to be a second basic support of the relationship, so that in practice each type of kinship bond operates within a wide range of expression. Further, the total field of a man's stock associates is specific to him alone, for not only is his range of kinship different from that of all other men . . . but the nature of reciprocity established is primarily a matter between himself and each of his associates individually. The total field of a man's kinship and the co-terminous field of property relations in no way attain the quality of a corporate group, either in thought or action' (Gulliver (1955), pp. 246-7). At the same time there appear to be no major obstacles to the transformation of this type of society into a segmentary lineage system. Later in the article I shall attempt to show how this transformation might occur.

18 Gulliver (1965), 'The Jie of Uganda', *in* Gibbs (ed)., *Peoples of Africa*, p. 181.

19 This is not an exceptional case. The Wodaabe Fulani began a protracted migration leading them into the grazing lands of other ethnic groups. They have no territory of their own. M. Dupire remarks that 'les fondements du *groupe migratoire nomade* ressemblent à ceux d'une bande de chasseurs mais les relations de voisinage entre ces pasteurs africains s'encastrent dans une moule patrilinéaire' (*Organisation sociale des Peuls*, Plon, 1970, p. 419). The extension of the ideology of agnation, ritual and ceremonies guarantee the reproduction of these unstable migratory groups at the political and symbolic level. Their unity as communities is realised through the

circulation of women and livestock which provides the basis of cooperation and co-residence. As we can see in the passage from Gulliver (note 17) there appear to be no major differences between these west African pastoralists and the societies under consideration here. It is a matter of the different ways in which the communities are realised. These may be interpreted as transformations if one places the factors governing these transformations on a matrix. This comparison is totally unexplored, but we might venture a few provisional hypotheses: it seems to me that an important point in this comparison is the nature of community rights over territory (their stability and the degree to which the social groups making up the communities hold exclusive rights).

20 To some extent this analysis could be generalised to cover most nomadic pastoralist societies.

21 Stenning (1963), 'Africa: the social background', in *Man and Cattle*, Royal Anthropological Institute, p. 116.

22 Schneider (1957), 'The subsistence role of cattle among the Pokot and in East Africa', *American Anthropologist*, 59.

23 For American cultural anthropologists, this sort of analysis provided the only satisfactory explanation for what they termed the 'cattle-complex'. Some anthropologists' (e.g. Harris) critique of this interpretation fails since it limits itself to the role of the economy alone.

24 *Grundrisse*, pp. 484-5.

25 N. Dyson-Hudson (1966), 'The Karimojong age-set system', *Ethnology*, 2-3, pp. 353-401.

26 Gulliver (1965), p. 191.

27 Gulliver (1953), 'The age-set organisation of the Jie tribe', *Journal of the Royal Anthropoligical Institute*, 83, pp. 147-68.

28 If we add the notion of a sole God, Akuj, who appears distant, ill-defined but all-powerful, it is interesting to note that we find elements of Ancient Judaism (one God, Prophets, sacrifices) which began in a nomadic pastoralist setting. This fact alone would justify this analysis, although it requires considerable further research.

29 See note 12.

30 Greatly underestimated according to Gulliver.

31 The differences in the number of livestock held by the Samburu and the Masai are no doubt related to ecological factors. The Samburu live in a clearly more arid zone with poorer grazing land.

32 Spencer, P. (1965), *The Samburu: A Study of Gerontocracy in a Nomadic Tribe (Masai)*, London, p. 134.

33 I am not of course reviving this typically functionalist concept which demonstrates the inability of functionalists to interpret structural transformations, despite the fact that the best of them do point to some sort of logical continuity between the different systems of age-organisation found in this culture area (e.g. Gulliver).

34 Dyson-Hudson (1966).

35 Gulliver, P.H. (1958), 'The Turkana age organisation,' *American Anthropologist*, 60, 900-22.

36 Spencer (1965), p. 134.

37 This control may be exercised over the form of community production (e.g. the Mongolian chieftain's regulation of access to pastures), the circulation of livestock (by extending and transforming loans of livestock thereby creating a network of clients) or the circulation of women. Class relations come into being through either the direct appropriation of surplus created by domestic groups in the form of labour (client relationships or corvée) or indirectly as in the case of tribute. While slavery may appear at an earlier stage, it neither challenges the existent social organisation nor plays a dominant role. For insofar as it is a form of domestic slavery, it reinforces the possibility of accumulation within the domestic group. Furthermore, slavery only really develops when the social and economic differences of class society have

increased the means of accumulation by the dominant class.

38 N. Dyson-Hudson (1966), *Karimojong Politics*, Oxford.

39 Dyson-Hudson (1966), pp. 239, 269.

40 Spencer, P. (1973), *Nomads in Alliance, Symbiosis and Growth Among the Rendille and Samburu of Kenya*, London.

41 In contrast to an empiricist approach which ultimately combines with the worst expressions of dogmatism, we might recall with M. Godelier that 'histoire n'est donc pas une catégorie qui explique mais qu'on explique. L'hypothèse générale de Marx de l'existence d'une relation d'ordre entre infrastructure et superstructure qui détermine en dernière instance le fonctionnement et l'évolution des sociétés, ne peut permettre de déterminer à l'avance les lois specifiques de fonctionnement et d'évolution des diverses formations économiques et sociales apparues ou à paraître dans l'histoire. Cela parce que d'une part, il n'existe pas d'histoire générale et que d'autre part on ne sait jamais à l'avance quelles structures fonctionnent comme infrastructure et superstructure au sein de ces diverses formations économiques et sociales.' M. Godelier (1973), Introduction to *Horizon, trajets marxistes en anthropologie*, p. viii. (Translation: History is not a category which explains but one which is to be explained. Marx's general hypothesis that an ordered relationship exists between infrastructure and superstructure, which in the last instance determines the functioning and evolution of societies over time, does not enable us to determine ahead of time the laws of functioning and evolution of societies which have appeared or are to appear in history. On the one hand, this is because there is no such thing as history in general and on the other hand, because we never know in advance what structures function as infrastructure and superstructure within these various social and economic formations.)

J. FRIEDMAN
and M.J. ROWLANDS

Notes towards an epigenetic model of the evolution of 'civilisation'

In 1949 Julian Steward published his seminal article, 'Cultural causality and law: a trial formulation of the development of early civilisations', in which an attempt was made, for the first time, to integrate archaeological data and anthropological theory into a set of general hypotheses about the evolution of early civilisations. His work has been the cornerstone of the neo-evolutionary school in American social anthropology (Service, Fried, Sahlins) as well as providing the impetus for the development of the processual school of American archaeology.

Steward's cultural ecological approach, which has greatly influenced a number of American archaeologists is based on an attempt to account for social institutions in terms of adaptation to specific techno-environments. In discussing the results of his 'Trial formulation . . .' he stresses that 'In the irrigation areas, environment, production and social patterns had similar functional and developmental interrelationships'.[1] Continuing this line of argument, he further stresses that in different environments, the same developments are unlikely to occur:

> The eras are not 'stages' which in a world evolutionary scheme would apply equally to desert, arctic, grassland, and woodland areas. In these other kinds of areas, the functional interrelationship of subsistence patterns, population, settlements, social structure, co-operative work, warfare, and religion had distinctive forms and requires special formulations.[2]

While this formulation is more subtle than that of other materialists, Steward is unable to be more systematic about the 'functional and developmental interrelationships' because he is unconcerned to determine the specific kinds of relations that link production to the other institutions of society. We find an ambiguity similar to that of White with respect to the nature of determination.

But while White stresses culture as energy capturer and transformer, Steward, emphasising the adaptation to particular techno-environments must search for more rigid correspondences. He has constructed an ordered series of economic stages which are meant to be linked to levels of socio-political development. These stages, which have served as a working model for much recent archaeology, are:

Hunting and Gathering
Incipient Agriculture
Formative (peasant community to state)
Regional Florescent States
Initial Empire
Dark Ages
Cyclical Conquests
Iron Age

As we might expect with such an unclear notion of determination, the above classification mixes technological and social features. Everything from the Formative down can be characterised as a progressive development of irrigated agriculture, the freeing of labour and its reintegration into an expanding division of labour. Crises ('dark ages') occur as the result of overexploitation of the environment, overpopulation and subsequent economic collapse and political fragmentation. They appear to alternate with periods of expanding empire until the onset of the Iron Age, or rather the incorporation of iron technology into basic processes of production. The fact that a very significant number of evolutionary stages (five out of seven) occur in the absence of direct technological determination appears to contradict the general hypothesis of techno-ecological adaptation. In fact, Steward's penetrating presentation of the material seems to indicate that the social forms themselves may have had their own internal laws of development, which, as in the case of cyclical conquests/dark ages, may have been maladaptive with respect to environmental conditions of reproduction. But this aspect of his work is never developed theoretically and has thus remained marginal to his more general formulation of the correspondence between techno-environments and social formations.

In the final analysis we are left with a series of stages which are more or less isolated from one another. For while Steward often had important insights into the structural continuity and transformational relation between stages (as in his discussion of theocratic chiefdoms and states) these were necessarily peripheral in a framework where each stage should have been, at least in principal, a specific cultural adaptation to a given techno-environment.

In subsequent years, mechanical materialism was purged of Steward's occasional insights into the processes of structural transformation, so that cultural evolutionary stages were reduced to a series of superstructural 'boxes' linked by time's technological arrow.[3]

More recently the inadequacies of this approach have come under attack even by those who have been customarily associated with the older cultural materialist tradition (Flannery, Wright).[4]

In the approach adopted here, an attempt is made to reconstruct the structures of reproduction of particular social forms. These are the social structures that dominate the processes of production and circulation and which therefore constitute the socially determined form by which populations reproduce themselves as economic entities. A system of social reproduction is characterised by a *socially determined* set of productive relations (which should not be confused, as in Steward and more recent materialists, with the organisation of work) that distribute the total labour input and output of a population and organise immediate work processes and the exploitation of the environment within limits established by a given level of technological development. The local population model[5] can be represented as in Fig. 1.

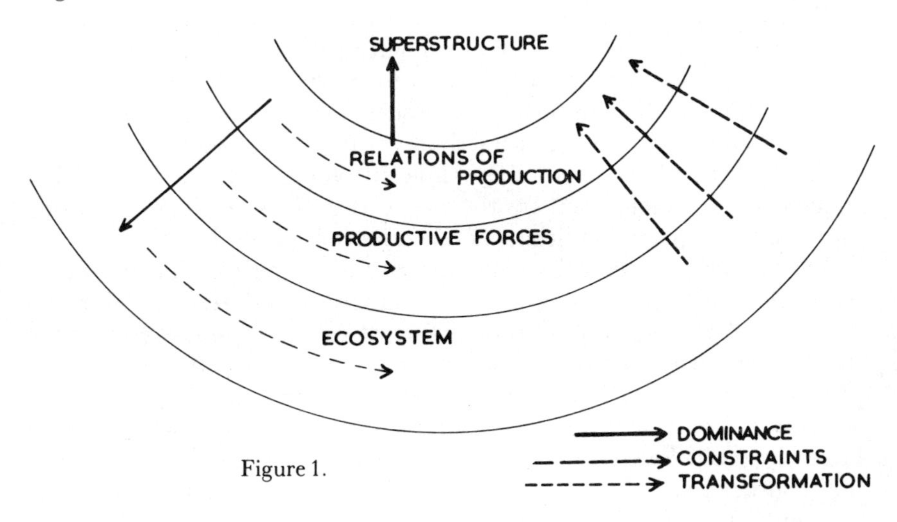

Figure 1.

Each of the levels of the social formation is structurally autonomous in such a way that the properties of one level cannot be derived from those of another level. While structurally independent, the levels are inextricably linked in the material process of reproduction by two kinds of intersystemic relation. From ecosystem up is a hierarchy of constraints which determine the limits of functional compatibility between levels – hence of their internal variation. This is essentially a negative determination since it only determines what cannot occur. Positive determination would only exist where we could find necessary and sufficient conditions for the occurrence of a given structure, i.e. where only one set of productive relations could dominate the process of reproduction. This would appear never to be the case. Working in the reverse direction, relations of production, as we have defined them above, organise and dominate the entire process of social reproduction and determine its course of development within the limits of functional compatibility between levels. When these limits are reached breakdown in the system is immanent. The limits are themselves determined by the internal properties (as a function of time) of the subsystems which make up the larger reproductive totality. It is absolutely necessary in this model to distinguish between institutional structures and the material structure of reproduction which they form in combination with one another. Thus, a kinship structure can be infrastructural if it distributes the labour input and output of society. Similarly, money may be merely superstructural if it is only used in children's games. This does not deny the fact that the internal structure of an institution determines the way it will behave in whatever functional position it occupies in material production.

As the properties of reproduction can only be defined with respect to time the model is necessarily a dynamic one. Dominant relations of production determine a given developmental pathway and functional incompatibilities in the larger totality generate divergent transformations over time. Change in cultural form as well as place in material production occur simultaneously in the process of reproduction so that evolutionary 'stages' are always generated from previous stages in such a way that we might speak of epigenesis; structural transformation over time in which the nature of the trajectories is determined by the properties of an arbitrarily chosen initial state in given conditions of reproduction.

The model as presented thus far may appear to be localised to a particular concrete society where production and reproduction are determined by a local set of productive relations. This, however, is not the case, for we must take into account that reproduction is an areal phenomenon in which a number of separate social units are linked in a larger system. As production for exchange seems to be a constant factor in evolution we must deal with a system larger than the local political unit, whether it be a tribe or a state, if we are to understand its conditions of existence and transformation. This is all the more evident when dealing with later developments in which production within the local society does not correspond to the conditions of reproduction of that society. In such cases 'external' relations must necessarily be considered. We emphasise, however, that such conditions of local insufficiency are largely created by the operation of the dominant social relations themselves. Growing interdependency is an emergent phenomenon in systems where internal specialisation and increasing demand create conditions in which the maintenance of local socio-economic activities depends upon access to a wider productive area. Thus, it is generally misleading to think of relations of production as only organising production and distribution within a single political unit since the reproduction of that unit may depend on production which occurs outside of it.

More generally, it should be evident that when discussing a stage we tend to abstract the properties of a particular social form for discussion without realising that the social form represents a local society which does not develop in a vaccuum but always in relation to a number of other societies and where the nature of the relation between the units determines some of the conditions of transformation of any one of them. Thus, the expansion of a tribe into a state occurs in the presence of other tribes connected by exchange and warfare to the evolving unit and which may be transformed into a politically acephalous periphery of the emergent state which imports a large portion of their labour force and part of their product. Similarly, long-distance trade between emergent chiefdoms and states may help stimulate local intensification of production and the political development of local centres at the expense of their immediate peripheries.

A complete evolutionary model would have to be a time/space model in which transformations over time are related to variations in space. Thus the specific evolution of social formations depends on the internal properties of local systems, upon the local constraints and upon their place in a larger system. This kind of analysis would require more space than we have here and it has not been undertaken. We stress, however, that the structures with which we are concerned should not be confused with the local societies in which they are manifested. The structures of the larger regional systems are determined by the dominant relations of production that make them up, i.e. the internal potential demands of local systems and the spatial distribution of constraints which determine the relative potential for development of the individual units with respect to one another. Thus, for example, the evolution of tribal systems into asiatic states is manifested in the actual development of concrete societies, but this evolution depends on more than the locally manifested structure of the tribal system. It depends on the existence of a larger system within which the tribal structure can expand and upon whose populations it feeds for its own growth. The structure of reproduction of a local system is ultimately the only relevant structure, but it invariably pertains to something larger than the local political unit since it includes the structural properties of the total input and output of that unit.

The specific model which follows may seem to be more or less unilineal. This is because we have chosen to analyse only one line of evolution determined by the successful expansion of a particular tribal system which we have taken as our initial state. An epigenetic model is one which appears to be unilinear only in a fixed set of initial conditions. These conditions which, at the outset, are related to the possibility of the intensification of production, will be apparent in our discussion of the actual sequences. If, however, such conditions are altered, internal functional incompatibilities must generate divergent development pathways. Where we indicate cases of devolution, or where local systems are transformed by their relations to more dominant systems, we should also expect to find different kinds of subsequent evolution. The unilineal character of the analysis, then, is due to our focus on the development of early civilisation in a few major centres without regard to later developments which were often accompanied by a spatial shift in geographical area and which began in formerly peripheral systems. Thus, our 'unilineal' development is more or less extracted from a multilineal developmental process in which the longer term structural transformations can only be understood in terms of the larger system.

Model

The aim of the present model is to account for a number of evolutionary developments in widely different geographical areas where many of the cultural traits are quite dissimilar. It might easily be objected that a single model could not possibly encompass such broad variation. It might seem more reasonable to try and construct separate models for each of the areas in turn, North China, Mesopotamia, Mesoamerica and Peru. This has not been done here because we feel, at least tentatively, that the separate culture-bound models would be no more than variants of the general model, i.e. that the underlying structures, especially those essential for generating later stages, are the same. It is from the properties of a single 'tribal' system that we shall attempt to generate the properties of later systems. Given the scope of this preliminary formulation, we shall not be able to go into a great amount of detail. Instead, we have chosen to present the main outlines of the evolutionary model in the abstract, using sequences of comparative data to exemplify particular stages and processes.

The tribal system

The tribal system's basic production and exchange units are local lineages. The latter contain no more than four or five households linked by a set of rituals to a founding ancestor. The local unit is similar in form to Sahlins' characterisation of the 'domestic mode of production'.[6] But if the unit is largely self-sufficient in the short run with respect to material reproduction it is linked to other groups by matrimonial alliances which make it *socially* dependent on a larger society for even its own *biological* reproduction (i.e. exogamy). While Sahlins is perfectly aware of this kind of relation, it is necessary here to stress that the alliance structure may be a fundamental or even dominant relation of production in these societies since it is, as we shall see, a major factor in the distribution of total social labour. We can, however, follow Sahlins' distinction between a domestic *level* of production which corresponds to the cost of social reproduction in such a society and lineage surplus production which is generated by the larger alliance structure. We assume for the purposes of the model, i.e. its generative capacity, that the local lineage is patrilineal and patrilocal so that it is groups of men who exchange women.

The structure linking production and exchange determines the specificity of the tribal system. In order to comprehend this structure we must describe the social form of production since the specificity of the latter determines the nature of the material flows in society as well as the developmental properties of the social structure. Economic activity in this system can only be understood as a relation between producers and the supernatural. This is because wealth and prosperity are seen as controlled directly by supernatural spirits. The latter, however, are not separated from the world of the living in any absolute way. On the contrary, the supernatural is no more than an extension of the lineage structure so that ancestors are spirits whose function it is to communicate with higher spirits in order to bring wealth to the group. In fact, the entire universe is usually envisaged as a single segmentary structure in which the most powerful deities are no more than more distant ancestor-founders of larger groups. The logic of this structure is one in which all local lineages are linked in a single segmentary hierarchy in which wealth produced at the lowest level appears to be the 'work of the gods'. A local lineage that produces a surplus is able to convert it into a community feast in which prestige is gained; prestige whose cultural content is very different than in our own society. The lineage that is able to produce a large enough surplus to feast the entire community can only do so because of its influence with the supernatural, and since influence is defined as genealogical proximity, the lineage in question must be nearer to such powers. This 'genealogical' differential is expressed in terms of relative social age. Within the local community, such a lineage would be an older lineage, a direct descendant of the territorial founder ancestor spirit of that larger group. Thus, status is first gained in the feast-distribution sphere. It belongs to all the members of the producing group. It is not the possession of some tangible form of wealth but rather the 'social value' attributed to the ability (which may in later stages be linked to the control of dependent labour) to produce such wealth. Women are then given to other lower status groups in exchange for a bride-price which measures the social value of the wife-giver. This relation is one where a given quantity of real wealth is exchanged for a kinship connection (matrilateral link) to the source of wealth. In such a system marriage will tend not to be reciprocal so that differences in prestige are continually converted into the relative ranking of lineages. A common form of this relation between lineages is generalised exchange or asymmetic alliance, defined here, not in terms of marriage to a specific kind of cousin (matrilateral cross-cousin), but by the combination of local exogamy plus a proscription on reciprocal marriage. The lack of reciprocity implies that bride-wealth goods must enter into the circuit, flowing in a direction opposite to that of women. The asymmetry of this form of exchange permits the differential 'social valuation' of local groups in such a way that interlineage rank is expressed by the differentials in bride-price. The existence of valuables, a category of means of circulation, is very important in the development of the tribal system, as we shall see, and its place in the processes of accumulation and hierarchisation is diagnostic of the type of system with which we are dealing. As we have defined the present tribal system such valuables have a more or less symbolic function. Their possession is an indicator rather than a source of status.

Briefly then, we might describe the system in terms of three relations of production. At the bottom is the social appropriation of nature by local lineage production. Appropriation must always be conceived as a socially and not technologically determined phenomenon since it defines the control by a local group over its immediate production process and its capacity to dispose of the output of that process. The relation between lineages is defined by matrimonial exchange which, however, involves the transfer of other products including food.[7] Along such links flow debt payments, bride-price and food at matrimonial and funeral ceremonies, and the various services and tribute that flow from lower to higher ranking lineages. Since the wife-giver/wife-taker relation is the social form of ranking we can conclude that asymmetrical marriage of some sort is the dominant exchange relation. We might also suggest that from the point of view of the process of production and circulation, the superiority of wife-givers and the patrilineal nature of the local group are aspects of a single process. Since the status of a lineage is an attribute of its members and not the result of its possession of some tangible form of wealth, the valued 'object' is the individual representative of the prestigious group. Thus people-givers rank higher than people-takers, and as the people given are women the local group is patrilocal. The third relation of production is that between the lineage and the community as a whole, the conversion of lineage surplus into distributive feasts. It is this sphere in which prestige is created in the manner discussed above.

Articulation of relations of production

The above three relations of production combine to form a single structure of social reproduction whose properties generate an evolution toward a specific type of state/class formation.

Surplus is increased along two pathways: (1) by feasting it is transformed directly into status and (2) then into relative rank via increased bride-price for lineage daughters as well as other obligatory prestations between affines. The initial outlay is thus more than compensated for by the increased control over other lineages' labour and product. Through this intensification of economic demands more surplus is produced and accrues increasingly to emerging lineages of high rank.

$$\text{surplus} \rightarrow \text{feasts} \rightarrow \text{status} \rightarrow \left\{ \begin{matrix} \text{prestations} \\ + \\ \Delta\,\text{prestations} \end{matrix} \right\} \rightarrow \left\{ \begin{matrix} \text{surplus} \\ + \\ \Delta\,\text{surplus} \end{matrix} \right\}$$

Surplus can also be converted directly into more wives and thus children, resulting in an expanded family labour force.

$$\text{surplus} \rightarrow \text{wives} \rightarrow \left\{ \begin{matrix} \text{children} \\ + \\ \Delta\,\text{children} \end{matrix} \right\} \rightarrow \left\{ \begin{matrix} \text{surplus} \\ + \\ \Delta\,\text{surplus} \end{matrix} \right\}$$

The above cycles are restricted to the growth of familial labour force and the transfer relations of goods and services between such groups. *A necessary factor in the expansion of the system, however, is the accumulation of dependent labour: internal debt 'slaves' who are unable to meet affinal obligations and external captive slaves.* The two above flows can be combined in a single system as in Fig. 2.

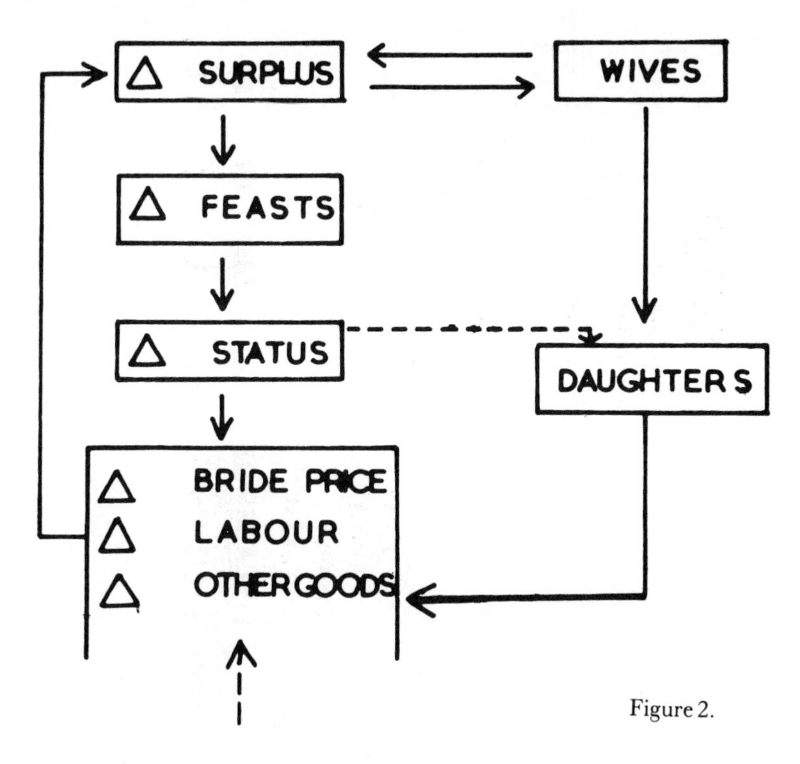

Figure 2.

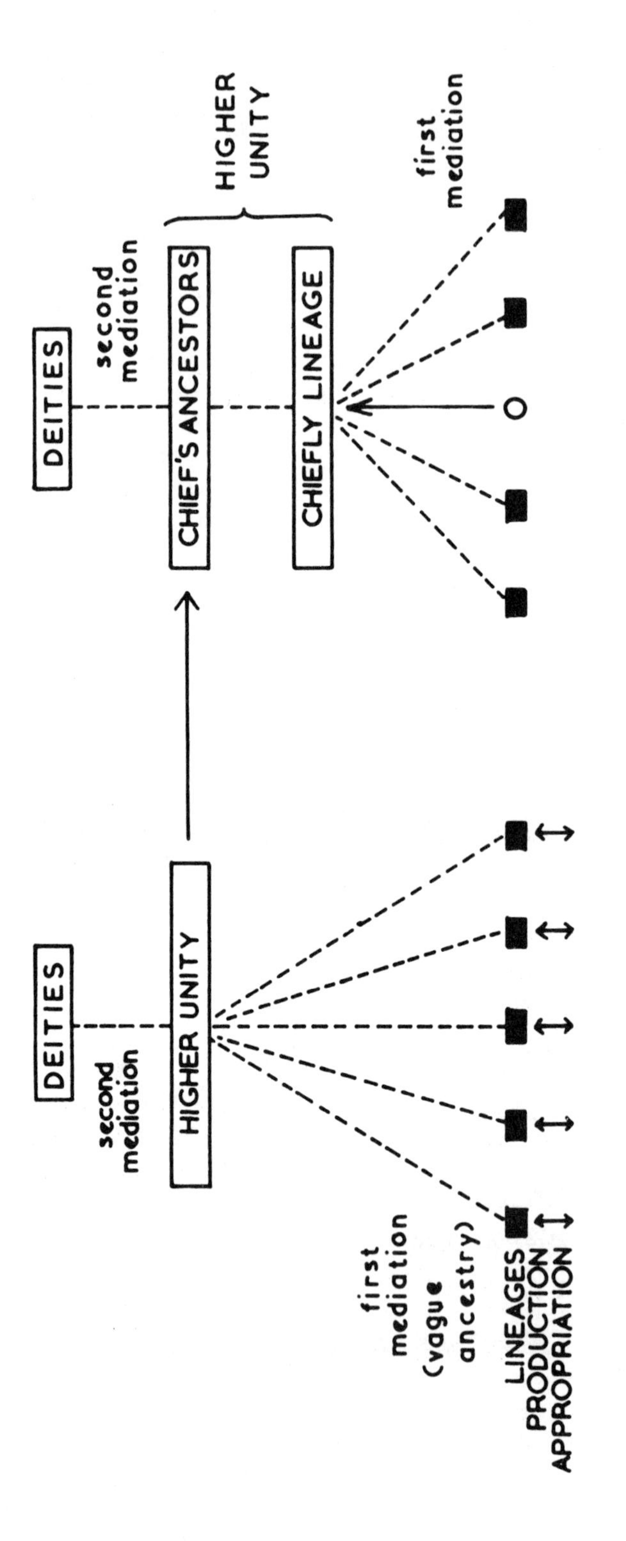
DEITIES
second mediation
HIGHER UNITY
first mediation (vague ancestry)
LINEAGES
PRODUCTION
APPROPRIATION
DEITIES
second mediation
CHIEF'S ANCESTORS
CHIEFLY LINEAGE
HIGHER UNITY
first mediation

Figure 3.

This positive feedback structure leads to increasing affinal rank differentiation. The result, however, is only a relative ranking of wife-givers and wife-takers in which formerly egalitarian marriage circles are transformed into a spiral in which rank levels are defined by the ability to meet similar obligations.

The final step and the one most crucial for further evolution, is the conversion of relative affinal rank into absolute rank. This occurs as an immediate result of the segmentary kinship structure and its place in the ritual economic system. As we saw previously, the form taken by interlineage ranking is one where affinal superiority is expressed simultaneously as 'age-rank' or a closer genealogical link to the founder ancestor of the larger group so that the wife-giver/wife-taker relation is a relation of seniority between consanguineal ancestors. This form of ranking determines the structure taken by the chiefdom where a particular line, dominant in feast giving and affinal exchange, becomes identified as the direct descendant of the territorial deity (see Fig. 3).

The emergent social form here is the conical clan headed by a chiefly lineage, nearest descendent of the local deity, where all rank relations are redefined in terms of absolute genealogical distance from that deity. We have suggested that the emergence of the chief is no more than the identification of a local lineage with the territorial ancestor-founder. This promotion, however, operates a significant change in economic relations. In the more 'egalitarian' period the community makes offerings to the local ancestor-deities who in return maintain and increase the group's wealth. As a living lineage comes to occupy the position of mediator in this activity it is entitled to tribute and corvée as the cost for performing the necessary function of seeing to the welfare of the community. Thus, through his monopolisation of the imaginary conditions of production, the chief is able to control a sizeable portion of the total labour of the community. This is a new vertical relation of production between a lineage and the community as a whole, one which emerges directly from the previous structure. The conical clan is not to be seen, then, as a particular institution, but as an emergent form of tribal society.

The tribal system is expansionist in nature. Alliance and exchange relations are continually extended into a wider region. The system is politically open at the top so that the development of chiefdoms at local levels is at the same time their alliance on a supralocal level. In effect, the range of the alliance network depends very much upon social rank so that it is only the emergent chiefs who maintain long distance exchanges (see Fig. 4).

This implies that chiefs have access to valuables from the greatest distances in a pattern of development where access to different kinds of goods depends on one's place in the social hierarchy so that only those at the top can get hold of the whole range of valuables. Thus, there is increasing internal control over both the local labour force and

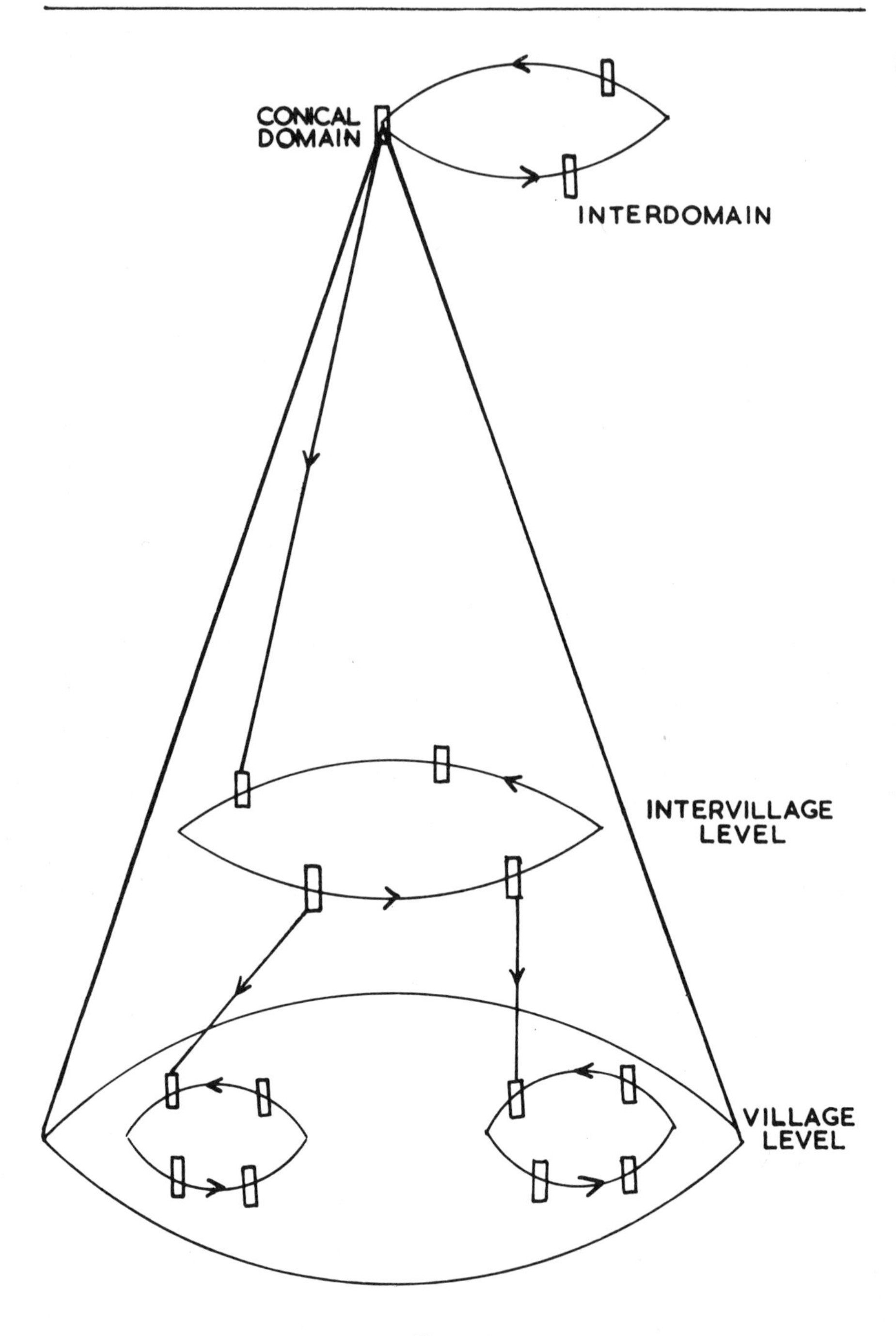
CONICAL
DOMAIN
INTERDOMAIN
INTERVILLAGE
LEVEL
VILLAGE
LEVEL

Figure 4.

its output as well as the wealth objects that normally circulate for payment of debt, marriage, price, funerals, etc. Because the nature of payments is a function of rank, the development of chiefly hierarchies is linked to an inflation that enables powerful aristocratic lineages to accumulate increasing control over the total wealth in circulation at the same time as they gain more direct control over the total labour of the community, all of which is used in the expanding external exchange network.

The growth in the demand for surplus in such systems is greater than any that could be forthcoming from a closed population. There is, therefore, a tendency to import labour in the form of captured slaves from surrounding groups. This creates a regional pattern in which centres of power expand at the expense of surrounding societies which may have had similar structures but which are reduced in the process to acephalous societies. Internal competition in the conical chiefdom diminishes as most of the potential wealth comes to be controlled, though not consumed, by the paramount chief. From this point the major stimulus to production may depend on inter-chiefdom exchange and competition. This is simply a continuation of a process that first occurs at the more local level.

The developmental situation of the chiefdom depends very much on techno-ecological conditions assuming that the degree of regional specialisation is not very marked at this stage. In montane areas, for example, where soils are shallow and runoff a major problem, chiefdoms based on swiddening technology will tend to collapse in the course of their expansion due to decreasing productivity in an economy demanding accelerating surpluses. In such areas there may be cycles of growth, expansion and collapse of conical chiefdoms, with a minimal development of class stratification in certain phases of the cycle. This should be the effect of a situation where territorial expansion is blocked, often by other expanding societies, and a consequent increase in density is incompatible with the technological conditions of production. It is important to note that the evolutionary process is not a unidirectional phenomenon. When we take a whole range of local conditions into consideration as well as the relations among a number of societies all of whom may have similar internal structures, the result is bound to be one of variation in time and space. Acephalous societies, or big-man societies in areas of dense population may be one of the devolutionary effects of the functioning of similar systems in differing conditions.[8] Societies such as the Naga of Assam and some New Guinea Highland big-man systems may be the end products of such a devolutionary pattern. We cannot in so brief a space be concerned with this kind of process, but it is of the utmost importance to take account of such phenomena in a more complete evolutionary model.

It is noteworthy that we have not taken account of specific technologies in this section. According to our general model, there is no direct causal relation between technology and social forms of appropriation of nature. Thus it is perfectly possible that the kind of tribal evolution which we have described can occur in very different technologies. If, for example, agriculture developed out of some form of intensive gathering activity under the pressure of certain ecological constraints, it might well be argued that this transition was itself selected for by the demand for increasing surplus of an expansionist tribal economy such that the latter was maintained and the technological base altered in order to preserve the social system. This might help to account for some of the proposed models of agricultural origins based on various forms of demographic and geographical expansion, but where such expansion is generated by the economy of the tribal system and not merely a natural, biologically based, phenomenon.

In this section we have considered one possible line of evolution determined by a particular, perhaps arbitrarily chosen, tribal structure. It is a system in which local production predominates in the development of differential prestige and ranking and where an independent exchange sphere of valuables or prestige goods does not exist. Such goods do, of course, circulate, and the more hierarchical the societies become the more distantly produced valuables enter into the exchange cycles. We have assumed, however, that such articles have merely sumptuary value and are not in themselves subject to independent accumulation nor a source of direct economic control. This is the kind of structure that we find in many parts of Melanesia and Polynesia as well as northern south-east Asia where prestige goods are only symbols of status and cannot be attained systematically outside of the agricultural production cycle. In Indonesia, Melanesia and Africa, however, there are also a great many societies in which the control over certain kinds of valuables is in itself a source of prestige and power.[9] In the Trobriands and Admiralties, for example, control over 'elite' goods that circulate over wide areas is the basis of political-economic power because such goods are necessary for the marriage and other obligatory payments of all groups. In this way the prestige goods accumulated through long distance contacts are converted directly into control over labour. This kind of phenomenon is widespread in Island Melanesia but also in Africa where lineage heads or elders monopolise the cloth and other goods which their dependents need to reproduce themselves as social units. The long term evolutionary potential of such systems is not clear. Meillassoux, in his well known article, 'Essai d'interprétation du phénomène économique dans les sociétés traditionnelles d'auto-subsistence,' describes a situation of control that applies only within the domestic unit. Fathers control the labour of their sons by controlling their access to bride-price goods. Now it is perfectly possible that interlineage ranking could develop in such a system as a result of differential access to external trade although this is difficult to envisage at a level lower than that of the local community.[10] Where big-men exist, i.e. a minimal social differentiation, the use of such status to control access to foreign prestige goods might be the basis for a development of increasing hierarchisation. This is undoubtedly a widespread phenomenon and may have been quite significant in early evolution.[11] This, however, would require a massive production of valuables at a very early point in the archaeological record, well before the development of state structures, and this does not seem to be the case. Nor does it seem that such development is necessary as is born out by the comparison of Polynesia with its highly developed political structures in the relative absence of elaborate prestige good systems[12] and Melanesia with precisely the inverse state of affairs. It is possible that the kinds of societies referred to above develop on the periphery of larger states where there is trade in precious raw materials or slaves and where the original source of demand is the larger state.[13] The same kind of structure, as we shall see, seems to develop out of the early 'Asiatic' state forms, but presupposes an already established state monopoly over local production and long distance exchange.

Archaeological evidence

The patterns in the archaeological data that one would expect to find for such a 'complete' model of a tribal system are, of course, difficult to investigate – especially for the earliest stages generated by the model. North China, in fact, seems to offer the only example where there is a continuous sequence from a clearly pre-state level through all the other developments that we shall discuss here. The earliest Yangshao cultures display a pattern of small hamlet settlements with little indication of social hierarchy but where a new pattern emerges in which village houses are systematically grouped around a centrally located 'long house' that appears to be a chiefly dwelling. That this is not simply a ceremonial construction on the order of a New Guinea men's house is demonstrated by the internal division of the structure into a number of small compartments which have their own hearths and seem to be living quarters for individual families. Without further evidence we might only suggest an interesting ethnographic parallel among south-east Asian chiefdoms (e.g. Kachin, Sema Naga) where the chief's house is a very long centrally located building in which live the chief's wives and dependents and a variable number of slaves and slave families. On the basis of his evidence, Chang has suggested for these early Chinese societies that there was a lineage organisation as well as some form of ancestor worship and fertility ritual.[14] These are all features which follow from the model.

A possible case of devolution also occurs in the ecologically marginal zone of Shensi. Here the settlement pattern is not concentric but diametrical. In this relatively large site we find two rows of houses which face each other across a narrow street,[15] a pattern similar to that found in parts of the Naga Hills of Assam and Burma where it has been argued[16] that in conditions of relative overpopulation, villages are characterised by an unstable reciprocity internally (including reciprocal marriage) and by a high level of intervillage warfare.

Where successful expansion of the tribal system occurs we should expect to find increasing social differentiation, economic intensification, wider and more elaborate exchange networks controlled by emergent paramount chiefs. We should also expect a certain increase in violence since the labour-hungry chiefdom must continually raid its hinterland to obtain captives. All of these charactistics seem to be present in the Lungshan period in North China. It is, as it should be, difficult to differentiate the chiefdom from the state formation since these 'stages' are but arbitrary cross-sections of a developing system. The development of class structure occurs throughout this period along with the elaboration of the theocratic institutions of the tribal system. Chang speaks of a 'theocratically vested ceremonial pattern', which, no longer the common property of the entire village, was focussed upon a selected portion of the villagers.[17] Larger amounts of luxury goods, elaborate pottery, shells, jade and some bronze are found. Along with the large ritual sacrifices of animals there is indication of differential distribution of their remains in human burials.[18] There is clear indication of ritual and some craft specialisation. All the structural elements that we find in the later state forms are already present in this period.

In all the areas considered here, this period is characterised by the development of central places in settlement patterns, ceremonial centres that are associated with ritual activities related to the fertility of Nature and economic welfare. There is evidence of increasing social differentiation and an expansion of exchange networks so that more exotic goods are found in burials of high ranking individuals. These kinds of phenomena correspond to developments in Mesopotamia from 6000 B.C. through the Ubaid period, in Peru from about 2500 B.C. to the Initial Period (2000-1800).[19] It is significant that for Peru this development was not based on agricultural technology but relied mostly on a very productive fishing economy.

'Asiatic' states

The 'asiatic' state emerges from the tribal system and develops on the basis of the same kinds of mechanisms. It is for this reason that we assume that the conditions of local production are a crucial factor permitting such a development. Thus, in fertile valleys and riverine plains the evolutionary tendencies of the tribal system are able to work themselves out to their fullest.

It is in the developing conical clan structure that rank defines the relations between lineages in terms of genealogical proximity to a single central line. In a fully formed conical structure rank is absolutely determined in a way which necessarily undermines the function of local exchange. In the previous system wife-giving was a means of establishing relative rank, but now, as social position is determined from the start, hypogamy must lose its former function. On the contrary, wives will tend to move from lower to higher ranks as a form of tribute. This is merely a generalisation of a form of exchange that already occurs in the chiefdom between the paramount and lineages of definitively lower status, especially in the case of secondary wives. The difference here is that *all* rank is definitive. Hypogamy continues to occur only where alliances to particularly powerful lineages are necessary, i.e. to the extent that the system is not entirely centralised. In any case, this occurs only at the highest levels of the hierarchy and serves as a means of political integration – some of the sacredness of the central lineage is bestowed upon another lineage in recognition of its power and importance. Hypergamy, on the other hand, is merely a recognition of the absolute superiority of the wife-taker. It is an expression of the conical structure of the state. Hypogamy is an attempt to extend that structure.

The redistributive system loses its former function as a means of converting surplus into status in an act of 'generosity'. Since status is 'given', such generosity is now reduced to an expression of segmentary position. The conical clan chief or king is entitled to tribute and corvée on the basis of his necessary function in the ritual-economic process, not because he might return all this accumulated wealth in the form of feasts. Increasing surplus is no longer redistributed in the same manner as previously. While feasts have great ritual importance and while they are often very large in scale, a major portion of that surplus is absorbed in the transformation of the old tribal aristocracy. While tribal aristocrats are economically still commoners in that they till their own fields with only a few slaves if any, the increasing surplus linked to successful intensification accentuates the verticalisation process whereby wealth appears as the result of the supernatural power of the chiefly ancestors and their descendants. In this way the status of aristocratic lines is raised and their 'economic' importance is increased. All ritual is hierarchised and all aristocratic lineage ancestors are incorporated into a single segmentary structure headed by the deified ancestors of the paramount. Necessary ritual functions logically entitle aristocrats to a share of the surplus product. We also expect to find the development of bureaucratic functions within the new upper class. The doubling of genealogical ranking by an ordered series of administrative-ritual functions reinforces status differences with a largely imaginary division of labour that tends to reduce internal competition by defining necessary activities for each segment in a larger bureaucratic entity.

The evolving structure, then, is a conical clan-state in which all noble lineages owe their position to their kinship relation to a single sacred royal line and where the new class is identical to the state in a way closely resembling Marx's notion of the 'asiatic' mode of production. We feel this a better notion than that of the 'theocratic state' or 'segmentary state' because it stresses the dominant *economic* function of the monopolisation of the supernatural. It is this control or imaginary function, religious in cultural content, which determines the nature of the class relation and is the means by which surplus is appropriated. In the 'asiatic' state, there is a crucial change in dominance, from a formation in which economic flows are organised by affinal and feasting relations to one where surplus is absorbed in the vertical tributary relations of the conical structure.

In this period there is a growth of large ceremonial centres surrounded by hinterlands of villages and smaller centres (perhaps a two tiered pattern). The tribal domain evolves into a somewhat larger political unit in which a central domain dominates several smaller domains which are themselves the product of the political and/or demographic expansion of the central unit, i.e. by sending out of non-inheriting sons to establish settlements or by the in-marriage of weaker neighbouring domains. The internal structure is one in which a main line of chiefs or kings leads a quasi-sacred aristocracy dispersed throughout the territory of the state, where the focus of control centres on a local deity at each level, and where the latter are linked to the capital by the same segmentary hierarchy that links the local chiefs to the paramount. Thus, beneath the ruler who has an absolute monopoly on the highest gods are those nobles who are sent out as sons to begin new domains or those that are linked to the centre by marriage alliance. There is a tendency for allies (affines) to become agnates since submission to the central ruler entails submission to the patrilineal gods of that ruler,[20] and in a conical clan structure such absorption is equivalent to a change of name.

The exploited class that emerges in the formation of the state contains both commoner lineages that are increasingly excluded from the ritual upon which they depend and 'slaves', produced both by debt and capture who tend to be integrated as a single category of dependents. The separation of the nobility from the peasantry is reinforced by the switch from hypogamy to hypergamy, so that high status is no longer shared with low ranking groups (high status men and women remain within their rank).[21] This is reinforced by increasing class endogamy. As such the kinship links between commoners and noble ancestors are severed so that the former are, socially, totally dependent on the latter.

The internal economic structure of the 'asiatic' state is characterised by:

(*a*) A tribute/corvée relation between local lines and local chiefs and between the former and the paramount. The rights of local chiefs to a portion of the surplus depends entirely upon their genealogical connection to the paramount.

(*b*) Chiefly estates and especially a royal estate maintained by debt slaves and captives with some contribution of corvée.

(*c*) A tribute relation between nobles and the paramount. This is a political relation within the upper class which depends upon the exploitation of the peasantry by the nobility.

The internal functioning of the state economy is in many ways a continuation of that of the tribal system. The level of intensification is very high. Ceremonial feasting takes place at all local centres, but primarily at the top where the highest deities are lodged. While competition at lower levels is largely halted due to the crystallisation of rank, it remains a principal aspect of the economy at the interstate level.

The growth in the potential agricultural surplus permits an increased division of labour. Artisans are brought into the centre to form a full time class of specialists. This is not so much a change in technology as a reorganisation of the existing one. Once accomplished, however, it fosters the elaboration of new and more productive techniques that are called forth by the increasing demand for wealth objects and massive 'public works' for the purposes of external exchange and ceremonial activities. It is in the framework of the 'asiatic' state that specialist craft production first begins to develop on a large scale (bronze, cloth, etc.) located around and controlled by the centre, and where large quantities of valuables are utilised by the elite in ritual, burials, and matrimonial and other forms of short and long distance exchange. There is an elaboration of sumptuary items which may serve to mark distinctions in rank and class as well as in function. There is a substantial increase in ritual items destined for temple ornamentation and religious activities. Interregional exchange develops markedly in this period and the quantities of exotic objects found in any one centre increases several fold. The precise nature of such exchanges is not clear, but we may assume that they are similar to the competitive exchanges of the tribal period and may be linked to marriage alliance. The regional pattern is thus one where a number of relatively small states are interconnected at the top by elite exchange, and where, since growth occurs at different rates in different areas, and if some areas are reduced to exploited suppliers of captive slaves, the larger region must be seen as the necessary field within which expansion is realised, as a larger system of combined development and underdevelopment. It would appear, however, that insofar as regional specialisation is not yet developed to any great extent, the major selective factor for growth in a situation of competitive state exchange is agricultural productivity which permits greater concentrations of labour in production for exchange, public works etc. Thus, we would expect to find the dominant 'asiatic' states in those areas of greatest potential productivity.

The centralisation of production that occurs in this period may include more than simply luxury goods. The production and distribution of certain tools may also be controlled by the state.[22] Further, the monopoly over imports may, as in the case of Mesoamerica and Mesopotamia, amount to a control over crucial raw materials such as obsidian which replace older and usually less efficient materials in tool production.

The increase in production for exchange within the theocratically oriented state gives the centre a new kind of power, a direct control over the production of wealth objects and access to foreign trade. This structural development is, as we shall see, crucial in the transformation of the 'asiatic' political structure.

The 'asiatic' state is a relatively small affair and should not be confused with the great 'oriental despotic' empires which are often grouped under the heading 'asiatic mode of production'. The latter are based on a developed division of labour, a private commercialised economy as well as a state sector, and the existence of several conflicting forms of property in the means of production. The apparent sacredness of the ruler seems to be more of an ideological reinforcement of direct political control than the immediate basis of the class structure. The notion of 'asiatic state' is restricted here to the earliest state formations, the size of which may not exceed the area of a twenty to thirty kilometre radius with a population numbering perhaps in the ten thousand range. The size of the political unit depends largely on the ability to centralise the economy and to prevent accumulation of labour and surplus in peripheral areas. As this is usually difficult in a system based on ritual hierarchy, there is a high probability of fission as the size of the local domain grows. There is, thus, a tendency for a number of similar units to be generated in the normal process of territorial growth. Any expansion beyond a given limit would presumably require some stronger politico-economic link. A territorial extension of this sort might necessitate a distribution of centrally controlled luxury items to peripheral chiefs in order to maintain their loyalty. This new kind of relation, unlike that occurring in the centre, appears to become a dominant form in the next stage of development. In fact, the use of luxury goods as a reward to subordinate lineages in return for tribute is clearly a mark of the weakness of the 'asiatic' state, either as the result of economic crisis or internal competition.

The problem of succession within the royal lineage proves to be a major area of conflict as the 'asiatic' state develops. We stated earlier that bureaucratisation may effectively neutralise the claims of lower ranking lineages by associating them with subordinate functions in the bureaucratic hierarchy. But there will undoubtedly be a growing conflict among closely related sibling lineages. This results from the combination of patrilineal succession and the fact that a king tends to have a great many wives, producing a situation in which the relative rank of sons may be extremely difficult to determine. A great many claims tend to be made not on the basis of patrilineal descent but through the matrilines established by royal marriage. The problem is all the more acute where there is royal endogamy or marriage between lineages of the same name. This and other forms of rank endogamy produce an effective cognatic structure within the conical patriline so that matrilineal and patrilineal ties become equivalent means for making claims.[23] Such conditions necessitate new means for making rank distinctions among the aristocracy. Upper class kinship would appear to become more bilineal in this situation, both in terms of claims and ranking. As rank, from the start, was linked to affinal relations, the emergence of matrilineality is really no more than a reification or institutionalisation of previous relations. It is also likely that lower-ranking, non-inheriting, males will become more matrilocal so that the difference between high and low ranks will coincide with the distinction between patri and matrilocality. We might suggest that the access to prestige goods may itself be a basis for internal competition. For while the king nominally controls such goods, there are probably lower ranking lines involved in the actual exchange activities, giving them possibilities of accumulation and, in certain cases, a degree of executive control (i.e. where they are officially in charge of trade relations).

As with the previous system, there is a potential contradiction between the economic relations that generate increasing population density, especially in the vicinity of the capital, and the capacity of the techno-environment. In areas where agricultural intensification is difficult, for example, the development of the 'asiatic' state is strictly limited. Where, as in Mesopotamia, intensification is relatively easy, it might still be argued the the variation over time in the costs of maintenance of local populations will determine the location and geographical shifts of dominant centres. Where food cannot be imported, this intersystemic relation is extremely important in determining where and when the large states develop and the length of their duration. Where there is a decline in productivity, the resultant pressure on the economy may induce various forms of specialisation as well as a transformation in the socio-economic structure. Where specialisation occurs, the selective factors involved in political development might include geographical proximity to communications networks or to sources of raw materials. In a system with a high demand reinforced by increasing taxation, the ability of the society to survive depends on successful intensification and/or 'profitable' specialisation in conditions of increasing density.

As we saw above, the development of prestige good production is at first compatible with the 'asiatic' structure as such goods only serve as luxury and ceremonial items which reinforce ritual superiority since the enormous royal accumulation of wealth is proof of the supernatural effectiveness of the ruler. With the increase in competition, however, prestige goods can begin to represent an entirely new form of control. Where such goods serve as a general exchange good for bridewealth, funeral payments, and other payments, the control over their production or importation can become a direct means of economic control, and one different from the situation with respect to brideprice goods in the tribal system. In that system, the accumulation of prestige goods is a function of agricultural output and its conversion into feasts. Here prestige good production is independent of agricultural production, and represents an autonomous economic sector. The control over such goods depends, of course, on a pre-existent hierarchy, but once the latter is established it permits a new kind of domination, one which depends not on segmentary position (i.e. genealogical proximity to the gods), but on the monopolisation of valuables that are necessary for the social reproduction of all local groups.

Archaeological and textual evidence

The pattern in this period is characterised by a substantial elaboration of ceremonial centres, large scale politico-religious constructions, an increase in local population, developed craft specialisation around the centre, and a settlement organisation in which large centres are surrounded by a number of small villages or hamlets (two tiered). Three and four tiered settlement hierarchies are more characteristic of the next period in which the territorial control of the ceremonial centre would seem to be greatly expanded. We have stressed that these early states are rather small in size and that they retain many of the principal traits of the former chiefdom economy.

In Shang China, late Ubaid and early Uruk in southern Mesopotamia, and at sites such as La Florida in Peru, we find fairly large agglomerations, perhaps towns, centred about a number of ceremonial buildings. These centres are in turn surrounded by a hinterland in which population is more dispersed in villages many of which have small ceremonial complexes. The Shang states show evidence of very large scale feasting activity.

> D'énormes richesses sont consacrées au culte (animaux d'élévage, métaux, produits de l'agriculture, gibier, prisonniers de guerre) et presque tous les biens que possède cette société font l'object de dépenses somptuaires lors des funerailles des rois et des grands nobles ... Des offrandes de 30 ou 40 boeufs à un seul ancêtre ne sont pas exceptionnelles et il existe des caractères speciaux d'écriture pour désigner les sacrifices de 100 boeufs, 100 porcs, 10 porcs, blancs, 10 boeufs, 10 moutons.[24]

The areas of political control, however, do not appear to be of very great extent. The regional pattern in this period is an extension of the chiefdom regional exchange network where long distance trade takes on a more important role. We would also expect to find that large ceremonial centre states can only develop at the expense of surrounding populations so that from a situation in the early tribal period where there may have been a large number of competing groups we arrived at one in which there are a smaller number of states surrounded by dominated 'underdeveloped' tribes that are a major source of captive labour for the centres. This relation between local centre and periphery is developed to a much greater degree in the next period.

Exchange between the centres consists primarily in luxury goods whose production is increased throughout this period. These goods are apparently destined only for use by the highest levels of the aristocracy, in ritual, in temple construction and in elite burials. There is no evidence that the valuables produced for exchange circulate anywhere but within the highest levels of the social hierarchy.

There is evidence from China of some form of conical clan organisation in both Shang and Chou periods. There is similar evidence from Mesopotamia, but as it is much weaker we shall not discuss it here.[25] Most of the Chinese data are difficult to classify with regard to the period of reference, but there are a number of social structures that are common to both the 'asiatic' and subsequent periods. There is evidence that religion and ritual power have a fundamental role in the conical structure.[26] Aristocratic lineages are associated to locally ranked deities in such a way that the gods are ranked in terms of the same genealogical structure that unites all noble lineages with the royal line. Lower ranking nobles that marry into the kingdom may attach their genealogies to that of the ruler as a sign of their subordinate position within the larger domain. This act is equivalent to the acceptance of the ancestor spirits of the local ruler as providers for the newcomer's wealth and prosperity. Among the highest ranks there is evidence that wife giving could still be used as a form of subordination of competing lineages.

> Il arrivait qu'un chêf dont le nom 'grandissait' imposait à un de ses proches de même 'nom', de le reconnaître pour son seigneur, non pas seulement à titre de chêf d'un groupe domestique, mais à titre de chêf d'un clientèle. Comme marque d'alliance et de subordination, l'agnat vassalisé reçevait alors de l'agnat reconnu seigneur, une fille en marriage. Il devenait (par violation de la règle exogamique et substitution d'une consubstantialité inféodante à une consubstantialité communautaire) un gendre, et même un gendre annex; un mari-gendre.[27]

This pattern is in contrast but not contradictory to the usual pattern in which lower ranking nobles will give wives 'up' as a form of tribute. The latter situation is, however, one in which the difference in rank is pre-established in a rather absolute way unlike the case reported above in which an equal is converted into a subordinate.

The evidence for crisis is difficult to establish. In China this seems to have occurred towards the end of the Shang period, and it is not unreasonable to postulate that the society dominated by Anyang is transitional to another kind of system.[28] Evidence that central authority declines is linked to an apparent increase in the use of 'benefices' in exchange for political and economic loyalty. This kind of relation also occurs where the kingdom expands beyond its normal 'patrimonial' borders. If such 'benefices' are similar to later Chou practice they probably include various sorts of valuables as well as titles.[29] It is likely that a number of changing conditions would favour the shift to a more direct form of exchange relation between central areas that become increasingly able to control the production of highly valued craft goods and external trade, and subordinate but potentially powerful nobles, especially those on the periphery who may have the means to create their own autonomous centres.

The next period thus begins with an expansion of the old domain to new territories and a creation of a new kind of political hierarchy.

Prestige good systems: dualistic states[30]

Centrifugalism

The emergence of an economy based on prestige good production is related to the expanded use of such goods in the political alliance structure. This is a phenomenon which already begins to appear in the former period as a result either of the attempt to expand territorial control or to maintain the loyalty of subordinate lineages. Such a transformation would seem to be associated with a greatly expanded regional trade network where the monopoly over certain kinds of production or trade enables a central group to maintain an advantage in the larger region. In such a system we would expect to find an increase in the production (mass production) of specific types of goods at the centres and their distribution over wider areas. As the goods are passed down to lower ranks they enter into the local exchange networks where they are necessary for bride-price, funerals and many other ritual transactions. The structure of such a system is one where there are centres of control over specific kinds of luxury goods and where access by local populations to these 'necessary' goods depends on the establishment of alliances to the centre, either directly or through subordinate local centres (see Fig. 5).

In this way the former tribute relation becomes a somewhat more reciprocal relation between the central royalty and more peripheral

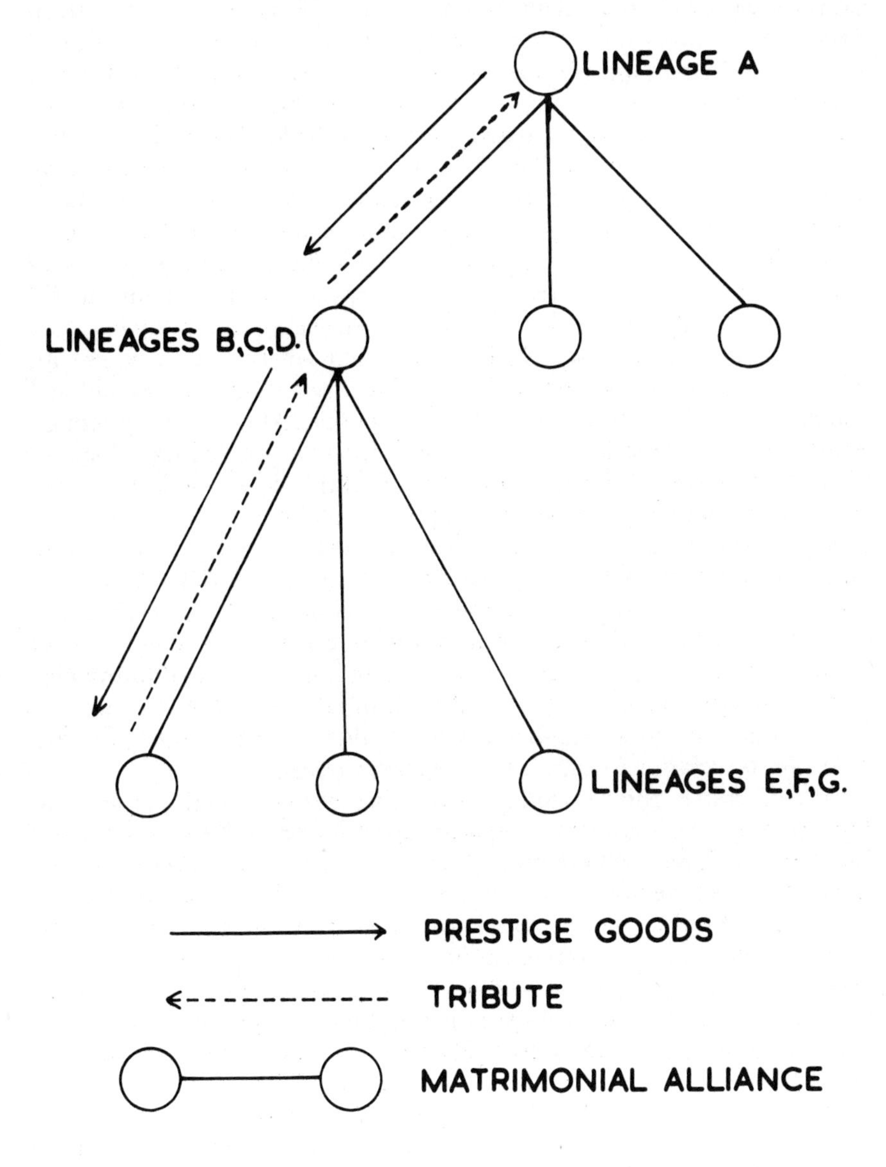

Figure 5.

aristocrats who in exchange for goods from the centre maintain a supply of local products to that centre. In this period we should expect to find a clearer settlement hierarchy in an area larger than that for the 'asiatic' state. This in turn should be associated with a quantum jump in the level of trade and especially in the quantity of prestige goods produced.

The form of expansion of such systems depends on a major structural change in the aristocracy. Territorial growth may result from the outward movement of lower ranking aristocrats in a pattern which is reminiscent of that described for certain 'matrilineal' kingdoms where expansion is not so much a question of moving into formerly unoccupied land as a political subordination of a large area to a single centre. Here, local groups may be ranked according to their distance from the centre. The alliance network connecting the royal patriline to numerous external aristocrats establishes matrilineal links between royal 'sons' and their maternal homelands in such a way that royal offspring can be ranked within a single patriline in terms of matrilineal origin. This structure may provide a mechanism for the 'sending off' of sons to rule in the provinces. It is also likely that conquest may play a role in this period but where following this an alliance is established between incoming aristocrats and their local counterparts. The kind of model proposed by Ekholm for the Kongo kingdom[31] may be relevant to this period. In her model, uxorilocality is dominant at all levels but the top, and it is combined with asymmetrical marriage so that higher ranking men move into the groups of lower ranking women. Thus the local group will contain the men of one lineage who are outsiders and related as MB and ZS and their wives who represent the local matrilineage. Such a situation reflects a social and ideological dualism opposing higher ranking men/lower ranking women, patriliny/matriliny, nobility/commoner, outside people (invaders)/original inhabitants. It is further expressed in a spatial concentric dualism which opposes centre to periphery in terms of the relation father/son = royalty/vassals.

In the centre, the previous competitive situation within the royal lineage may break down into a pattern of rotation between matrilineal heirs to the throne. Where matrilineal links are stressed there will be a dualism at the very top of the state structure in which the highest ranking wife-taker of the royal line also provides the heirs to the throne. There are, of course, innumerable variations on this theme. What is crucial, however, is that the bilineal determination of rank provides a finer means of distinguishing between potential heirs than the former unilineal succession. Where a particular wife-taker provides the future king, all other 'sons' are excluded by definition.

The development of the prestige good economy and its use in maintaining political-economic relations undermines the former source of control based on genealogical proximity to the deities. Monopoly over the sources of prestige items is a new form of control which becomes differentiated from the older ritual-economic form. Within the royalty this would correspond to the development of dual power. The theocratic state apparatus which monopolises trade as a single entity is at the same time functionally split into two halves, one of which would appear to represent ultimate religious power and another which is increasingly occupied with external politico-economic relations. This dualism of function might be compared to the development of bilineality which we described above since both correspond to the prevalent dualism in the ideology. It might easily be argued that the emergence of this new form of control can be contained within the former theocratic structure, and it appears that the degree of dualism is indeed quite variable. We might suggest that the stress on bilineality is a necessary condition for the clear emergence of dualism in the political and ideological structures. The importance of matrilineal linkages in the determination of rank is that at least two lineages are recognised in the definition of royal status. If the determination of the king's status depends as much upon his mother as his father, then we are clearly faced with the existence of two very high ranking lineages whose respective statuses may be equivalent in some way. The common division, in such a situation, between political versus ritual position expresses a functional differentiation within the elite that institutionally polarises the bilineal status ambiguity within the royalty.

In any case, this dualism is not at first expressed by a distinction between religious and secular. Rather it may begin as a split within the theocratic structure itself, as a dual specialisation in respectively ritual and political activities (king/prime minister, head of temple hierarchy vs. political chief etc.). There is a marked dualistic development in the structure of the supernatural. In the 'asiatic' religion, sky and earth, male and female are all combined in a single supreme deity. There are from the very start, of course, many lesser spirits including local territorial agricultural gods, but all are linked in a single segmentary hierarchy. In the 'asiatic' period matrilineal links are ideologically incorporated within the patrilineal-conical structure. Patriliny is the 'encompassing structure'.[32] In the prestige good system, on the contrary, there is a separation of sky and earth gods just as there is a separation of male and female principles in the ideology. In effect, what is occurring is the emergence within the sacred nobility of a new economic form made possible by the previously established conical structure.

Throughout this period there is, as we have seen, a truly massive increase in production for exchange. This implies a high demand for labour which is obtained by the importation of slaves who are employed directly at the centre. We might suggest that a slave trade develops in this period between political centres and more distant peripheral areas (e.g. Mesopotamian plain – Zagros Mountains, Chou – northern and western barbarians) so that areas often referred to as those of the 'barbarian' tribes in the texts[33] are incorporated into the larger regional exchange system. Valuable items produced in the centre are traded for slaves, raw materials and other products of the local areas. This kind of relation, which also characterises the connection between the Mediterranean states and their northern European neighbours in the bronze and iron ages, might help account for the sudden population explosion in the developing political centres during this period as well as the one following.

As this period is characterised by a political hierarchy linking a number of centres and sub-centres, while we would expect population to increase in all centres there is bound to be a greater increase in those dominant centres that have the most wealth and power. The hierarchy of centres tends to extend itself so that larger areas are brought into a single political domain. Thus, at this stage, expansion is geo-political as well as demographic, and while centres may all increase in size there is a tendency for new centres to form which are directly linked to politically dominant larger centres according to the pattern described at the start of this section.

The general increase in production in this period may be linked to the beginnings of product differentiation especially within the elite good sphere. There is evidence of a large increase in the production of specific kinds of goods, often in standardised form (cloth, bronzes), and there would appear to be a whole range of items that are socially ranked, from the highest elite goods to those, such as certain kinds of cloth, for example, that circulate as a kind of money, accessible to the whole population.[33]

The instability of the prestige good system is due to the difficulty of maintaining a clear regional monopoly over long distance exchange contacts. In the next section we shall see how the same basic structure in conditions of internal competition leads to a breakdown, in the regional hierarchy, a contraction of population into a number of competing urban centres and the beginnings of a commercial city state economy.

Archaeological and textual evidence

Various sources of evidence indicate a clear reorganisation in the political structure during this period. The Western Chou period is spoken of as feudal as opposed to the former 'patrimonial' Shang era.[35] Investiture was a matter of exchange in which valuables; bronze vessels, cloth and clothing, weapons, chariots, were distributed by the capital in exchange for a steady flow of tribute and, it is assumed, a pledge of loyalty. To the extent that production of the most important valuables, or their importation, was monopolised at the centre it served as a means of control. Not enough is known about cloth production in China, but from at least the Western Chou period it appears to have been necessary for bride-price and other payments. Granet claims that it was an early form of money.[36] It is also quite probable that from this time on (although we have only later Eastern Chou sources) relations between lower and higher ranks were characterised by a reciprocal exchange in which tribute went up in return for different kinds of products.[37]

The Inca use of cloth may give us some insight into the functioning of prestige-good systems. The production and distribution of massive quantities of cloth of different types is a well known feature of that society,[38] and the royal control over the most highly valued *cumbi* cloth seems to have been a significant form of political-economic power. 'The simple fact that a fine cloth like *cumbi* had come to be defined as a royal privilege made it possible for grants of it to be highly appreciated by the deserving.'[39] Cloth in the Inca empire was a primary means of exchange in which socially necessary payments such as marriage prices were made. High quality cloth, produced under royal control, was distributed to local nobles in return for various local products which were paid as tribute.

This period is characterised by a politico-territorial expansion of significant proportions – not the formation of new settlements so much as the unification of formerly independent centres. There is a quantum jump in trade activity and a concomitant growth of specialised production. Dominant centres increase in size, but there is also a general population increase, most likely an increase of imported slaves. Population triples on the Susiana plain in the early Uruk period with the development of what we define as a prestige-good system, and there is evidence that 'there was a greater concentration in the larger, centrally located area'.[40] In the Ubaid to middle Uruk periods there is a transition from a pattern of single large centres of 'capitals' surrounded by small villages and hamlets (two-tiered) to a larger regional settlement hierarchy in which there is a transitive dependence of smaller centres on larger centres and where the entire region is linked to other more distant areas through the capital.[41] In Chou China, this kind of expansion is apparently linked to the sending out of nobles to rule in the hinterland or at secondary centres.[42] Similar connections of members of the royalty or lower ranking nobles to specific geographic areas outside the capital is also found among the Inca.[43]

The bilineal character of the kinship structure is documented for the Inca. Zuidema describes a situation in which the political hierarchy might be depicted as a dispersed patriline and where residence is, except at the top, more or less matrilocal: 'In the capital the succession of kings was patrilineal, but we may assume, from the data on the North Coast, that the local connections of the twelve sons of the second king were due to matrilocal influence.'[44] This is because sons were sent out from the capital to rule in subordinate centres, perhaps their matrilineal places of origin. The *ayllu* seem to have been patrilineal conical clans divided internally into ranked matrilocal groups, rank which was expressed in generation terminology (F/S/SS). In his major work on the organisation of Cuzco, Zuidema argues for the prevalence of asymmetrical marriage.[45] This would seem to correspond quite well to the form of ranking of matrilocal groups sketched above, especially if sons did, in fact, move out every generation to their mothers' groups. This might account for the evidence that lower rank coincides with greater distance from the capital. As Ekholm has shown, if sons move out every generation and marriage is asymmetrical, the patriline is dispersed over a wide area consisting of local matrilines, and the generational ranking of groups will be expressed in terms of spatial distances.[46]

In Western Chou there is similarly an indication that matrilocality or avunculocality played an important role. The ideology seems to have been one which opposed a matrilineal commoner population to a patrilineal nobility,[47] a common representational form in this kind of system.[48] Granet speaks of the 'separation des garçons de leurs soeurs et pères'[49] and their life 'auprès de leurs oncles (maternels)'.[50] The pattern, however, is not clearly established and the most we can do is to stress the apparent importance of relations in the matriline as well as the patriline.

The structural significance of this kind of phenomenon finds expression in the ethnographic material from Polynesia. Here, a transformation from 'asiatic' to prestige-good systems might be demonstrated in a comparison between Hawaii and Tonga. Hawaii is a comparatively late development relative to Tonga, yet it is taken as a classic example of the Polynesian state at its height. The Hawaiian aristocratic hierarchy combined political and ritual power in which those of highest rank were thought to be sacred. High 'priests' were 'members of the royal line,'[51] and there is no clear distinction between secular and ritual power. Descent ideology tended to be patrilineal, especially in the highest ranks, but affinal, i.e. matrilateral, and matrilineal connections were of utmost importance in making claims to rank positions. The political structure was represented as a segmentary organisation in which patrilineal seniority was the sole determinant of relative rank, or at least where relative social age was the only means of expressing such rank. The situation, however, may have been undergoing significant change, for while 'specific historical evidence for Hawaii points to the characteristic Polynesian pro-patriliny as the older tradition',[52] it appears that matrilineal relations began to take on increasing importance – so much so that some authors 'believed that the inheritance of rank – the real issue in linearity – had become pro-matrilineal'.[53] The suggestion that acute conflict in the area of rank succession and competition between local potentially paramount lines generates a series of variant strategies of heirship finds some support in the evolving Hawaiian state[54] where there is evidence of a pattern, 'according to which upper pro-patrilocality is matched by lower rank pro-matrilocality. In Hawaii, status bilaterality had in fact upset the sheer patrilocality of the upper ranks. Thus the pronounced matrilocality of low rank families in Kaiu may be represented as a response to a pattern of status differentation.'[55]

Tonga by contrast provides us with an institutionalised form of bilaterality in rank determination: 'Tonga combined traditional grading of ranks by relative seniority with a pattern of bilateral ranking based upon the constant superiority of a sisters' to a brothers' line.'[56] Goldman tends to see this in terms of the opposition between eastern and western Polynesian society, but the contrast is quite significant in terms of the structural model under consideration here:

> In eastern Polynesia, families stood to one another as senior-junior, regardless of their public rank but simply by virtue of relative seniority of brothers. In Tonga, relative seniority was joined by the constant hierarchy of the sexes. Eastern Polynesia followed through the implications of seniority consistently; Tonga juxtaposed the seniority principle with one of an entirely different character.[57]

There is, however, some indication that the difference between Hawaii and Tonga might be accounted for in terms of a more historical structural approach. Goldman speaks of an early period when the paramount ruler *Tui Tonga* 'may be presumed to have been more completely religious'.[58] The next period, beginning ca. 1200,[59] in which secular power seems to have become more prominant, is marked by an apparent dual division between sacred and secular authority. This is also the period of political expansion into Samoa and Fiji. Ritual authority remains in the *Tui Tonga* line while secular authority is 'delegated' to junior lines such as *Kanotoplu*, wife-givers to *Tui Tonga*, who became the politically dominant line in the kingdom.

We might suggest that the Tongan type structure evolved from a previous structure which was closer in form to that found in Hawaii. Tonga appears to have become engaged in a much larger exchange network than that of Hawaii. There is evidence of a large scale craft organisation controlled by the paramount and involved very heavily in production for exchange. Goldman stresses the 'focus on exchange and on the circulation of goods rather than on display.'[60]

An important aspect of the development occurring in this period, in virtually all the cases where there is information, is the division within the ceremonial centre between sacred and more secular elements. The Inca capital of Cuzco, for example, was divided into two 'moieties'. The palace of the upper moiety, associated with political power, external relations and with invading conquerors of the original population, was 'situated beyond the true centre of the town'[61] while the lower moiety, associated with sacred authority, with the interior, and with the original inhabitants had its official buildings in 'the centre proper'.[62] In southern Mesopotamia, in the middle to late Uruk period at Uruk proper and in the early Uruk period at Susa, a dual division of function appears within the theocratic complex. A structure separate from the temple appears to be increasingly associated with external trade and internal administration, the gradual development of a more secular form of political authority. The archaeological data are not clear for China, but there is some basis for claiming that from western Chou times there exist 'double cities',[63] and in later material it appears that the outer enceintes are associated with commercial or trade functions. While the king resides in the centre, the 'prime minister' lives in the outer city, and it is interesting in this respect that this personage is often a close affinal relative of the king. A similar pattern of development occurs among the Maya where, towards the middle to late classic period, a palace is constructed along side of the temple, in a period when external trade seems to be greatly expanded and where ritual goods seem to be replaced by more secular luxury items.[64]

Territorial and city states

Centripetalism

It is the very expansion of the prestige-good system which encourages the development of new centres capable of their own autonomous production. This should be especially marked where centres can specialise in local products of high value which are controlled directly at the local level. This situation is generated by the high demand for different kinds of special products in the increasingly larger trade system. Thus, the very existence of a prestige-good system undermines the centralised control which is its foundation by increasing the regional division of labour and the ability of sub-centres to become independent in a region larger than that of the politically dominated area. Where this occurs, the political hierarchy breaks down into a number of centres which compete over labour and perhaps land. This competition is likely to begin between older centres and those that grow up on the peripheries of their former domains. The general intensification of production which occurred previous to this creates a situation where specialisation in craft production becomes increasingly dependent on (1) labour to produce artisan goods, and (2) agricultural land and labour to support the increasing non-agricultural work force. This double demand for labour and the related demand for agricultural land causes conflict over both territory and population and leads to a state of warfare in which large nucleated and fortified cities appear.

Where the portion of the population engaged in craft production is greater than that which could be supported by local agricultural output, the importation of food becomes an absolute necessity, i.e. the conversion of a portion of the craft goods into subsistence imports. This can only occur, however, where there exist larger trade systems within which some societies specialise in the production of agricultural surpluses for foreign exchange. In any case, the level of interdependency that develops in such urban forms greatly increases the risk factor. Purely commercial city states become totally dependent on their trade networks in order to survive. Irrigation based city and territorial states must maintain a constantly high level of labour input in order to prevent disastrous breakdowns in what becomes a very complex technology.

The emergence of the commercial economy

With an increasing shift towards the maintenance of the local political system through participation in external trade, the emergence of important administrative institutions at the centre focusses on the articulation of long distance trade with the production of craft items and the elaboration of a local exchange network to ensure increased food supplies and local raw materials to the centre. The ceremonial centre therefore now takes on the function of a central place[65] and the growing external sector will foster new divisions of labour. Hence the conditions for intensifying external exchange lie in the capacity of the system to maintain an increasing number of non-food producing specialists from the surplus of a more intensive subsistence production or the importation of food which presupposes a more specialised regional system. This is regulated by the development, begun in the previous period, of institutions that directly control flows of manufactured products from the centre to the countryside, the organisation and storage of surplus foodstuffs and other goods and their redistribution to nonfood producing specialists, the organisation of craft production at the centre through the control of raw material supplies, and the administration of external exchange.

The scale and complexity of decision-making at the centre therefore increases in proportion to the degree to which the maintenance of the local political unit depends upon control over external exchange. There is a clear tendency for the previously dispersed segmentary hierarchy to be drawn into the centre. All the heads of subordinate conical clans will be drawn in as a kind of topological transformation of a dispersed structure. This implies that the population that does remain in the more distant hinterland of the centre loses its semi-autonomous political status and is directly dependent on the subordinate chiefs now resident in the capital. As a result, there will be a second tendency; for dependent clan members to move into the centre, within the constraints of the subsistence economy. This will be particularly so where competition exists between centres for control of population. The abandonment of dispersed settlement and an increasing nucleation of population around an urban centre is therefore a rapid or even sudden development. Since the conditions for intensifying external exchange lie in the capacity of the system to maintain an increasingly nucleated population within a tightly circumscribed area, the limits of the process are dependent, in the first instance, upon the degree to which agricultural intensification is possible. Where such possibilities are not severely limited, e.g. irrigation agriculture, population will rapidly become fully nucleated. Intensification is a self-reinforcing process whereby division of labour is increased, amplifying in turn the range and scale of external trade.

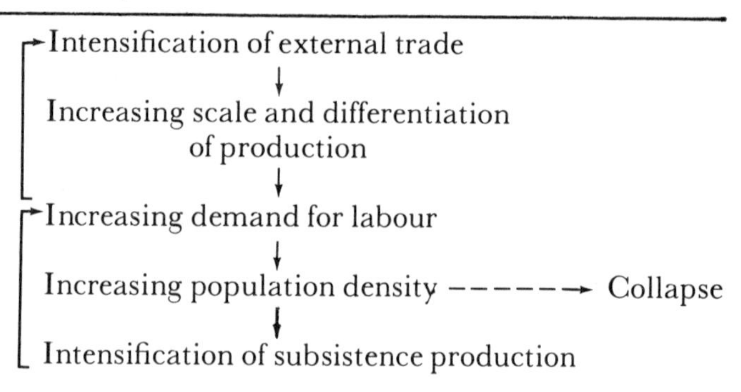

We suggest that the emergence of urban territorial states will occur in techno-economic conditions where there is a combination of effective land scarcity plus the possibility of extreme agricultural intensification. Effective land scarcity should not be confused with real overpopulation in a homogeneous region. Rather it is linked to the competition for labour, land and external trade resulting from the expansionist nature of the state economies. The same kind of nucleation process occurs where there is an intensification of the production of high value craft, industrial or luxury goods, whose value makes it possible for them to be exchanged for large quantities of lower value agricultural goods. This creates a pattern of autonomous urban centres each specialising in the production of certain craft goods and/or foodstuffs for which they may have a comparative advantage in external exchange. Pure specialisation in commodity production or middle-man activity depends on a previous development of highly productive agricultural areas. Thus, these kinds of states are, logically speaking, a secondary development (see below).

Thus both intensive irrigation and the production of high value exchange goods can serve as the basis for the development of compact urban forms. Over time it is likely that the former will appear first and be transformed in part into the latter since irrigation city states may be faced with an increasingly costly subsistence base, and the possibility of disastrous breakdowns. With dangers of inefficient drainage, soil deterioration and declining yields, there will be a constant tendency for trade in foodstuffs to become increasingly important in the external exchange relations of city/territorial states.

Although we have been discussing trade states along with the irrigation based states in order to stress the various conditions for the formation of compact settlement, it must not be forgotten that pure trade states are not a primary form in the epigenetic model we are using here. The agriculturally based urban state is the only structure logically implied in our model while the trade state is by definition a secondary development which depends on already elaborated state exchange networks in which the division of labour on a regional scale is quite advanced.

The emerging urban state will at first be organised into wards or sectors belonging to each of the conical clans now resident at the centre. Each ward will contain the residences of the clan chief and other aristocrats and clan members together with the temples or shrines to the clan deities and ancestors. The wards and temples may be ranked in terms of the respective positions of the chiefs in the political hierarchy. The centripetal movement of the aristocracy creates the conditions for a more 'egalitarian' form of government, especially since the central lineages gradually lose their absolute control over the economy. As the royal line is now surrounded by the chiefs of formerly dispersed clans, its power, based on its previous nodal position in the distribution of foreign goods within the local region, can no longer be maintained. Decision making will often rest with a council of chiefs or 'clan elders' each of whom is responsible for the internal affairs of his ward. Control over land will be increasingly emphasised given the importance of subsistence production for maintaining the system as a whole. This will be particularly so with the increasing weight attached to rights in land in an intensive system of agriculture.[66]

The growing trade sector in the economy will foster new divisions of labour especially in the production of craft and luxury items. Some of the former prestige items will tend to become increasingly generalised and take on the functions of commercial money to facilitate the growing number of exchanges. With growing economic specialisation the possibility occurs of individual accumulation of money and other forms of wealth. A class of wealthy individuals emerges, mainly from the old aristocracy, since it is they that had access to wealth at the start. Aristocratic control over external trade tends to increase but will suffer from the inroads made by middle-men, who are involved in various areas of the rapidly growing complex exchange network, and by lower ranking officials to whom a good deal of the administration of trade must be delegated. These categories of individuals will continually have opportunities for personal profits through entrepreneurial gain. Land, as a scarce and increasingly valuable commodity becomes alienable and a new emerging class converts wealth gained through exchange into land and labour which represent an independent source of wealth and status. Growing commercialisation tends to encourage the emergence of local markets. The ceremonial centre of previous periods remains, but outside of this circle we are likely to find a number of industrial and craft areas as well as an urban market.

The class structure goes through a major transformation throughout this period. The nobolity, up, until this point, had depended first upon genealogical access to the sacred royal lineage, and then upon access to centrally controlled prestige goods, i.e. through matrilineal links which were themselves ordered by the previous rank structure. The collapse inward of the prestige good economy and the emergence of new points of accumulation of such goods, the generalisation of these goods as a commercial currency, permit the accumulation of other factors of production as well as slave labour. The new wealth based class which emerges primarily out of the former aristocracy comes to dominate. Throughout this period there is competition between the new oligarchic class and the 'natural' nobility of past periods. The conical clan structure must inevitably be destroyed as clan lands are now alienable. Private estates emerge alongside the clan and state land. Commoners are transformed increasingly into landless labourers. With the emergence of landed property, degrees of freedom and unfreedom develop which did not previously exist. The former slave category, i.e. those who were outside kinship, tends to be merged with the new category of landless labour to form a single class of expropriated producers.

Within the oligarchy there are those who control the means of production of the artisan industries or who are directly involved in trade, and those who own land. To the extent that agriculture remains the dominant sector, the majority of the oligarchy will also form a landed aristocracy. This is the state of affairs in all areas where the low productivity of labour (i.e. relative and not absolute surplus) prevents the freeing of a large portion of the work force for increasing industrial specialisation. Those communities which concentrate more on production for trade, even for basic food stuffs, may tend to develop purely commercial oligarchies. Where this is not the case, however, there will be a tendency for accumulated commercial wealth to be invested in land and dependent labour.

The most important feature of this latest transformation is the separation of the relations of production from the state structure. This implies a further differentiation of 'economics' from 'politics' so to speak, which corresponds to a shift of the state into a more superstructural position (a change in function which is not, of course, meant to imply a diminished importance). As economic control no longer depends on position within a hierarchy, that hierarchy loses a great deal of its stability. The state structure is now an arena for political manipulation, where decisions with respect to economic relations do occur but where the economic relations themselves are predefined. Where bureaucratic structures existed based on kinship rank, these positions become increasingly filled by a wealthy landowning aristocracy. Administrative and governmental processes may become formally instituted at this stage. Assemblies, councils and the like will appear, peopled by the members of a *de facto* obligarchy where ranking is no longer significant. In more compact urban forms 'democratic' institutions may emerge as an extreme form of this kind of political (superstructural) development.

The religious dualism of the earlier period is elaborated into a more complex structure. The mythical landscape contains a great number of characters who were formerly spirits in a single segmentary hierarchy. The separation of religion from the relations of production may lead to a depersonalisation of the former principals embodied in the deities, so that natural forces become separated from the figures that once represented them. This occurs with the destruction of the segmentary structure of the supernatural. The former hierarchy of spirits beneath a paramount becomes a pantheon of gods and goddesses which may tend to be increasingly anthropomorphic.

The three relations of production which we have discussed, 'asiatic', prestige good, and monetary/property, are all present in this stage, in terms of cultural content but not in terms of material function. Strict monopolisation of the supernatural as in the 'asiatic' state no longer implies direct control over labour but only a share in the surplus product distributed by the royalty. The dualism that develops in the prestige-good period between secular and religious control becomes completely asymmetrical. The royalty now owes its power to its ability to maintain control over a substantial sector of the labour, land and currency of the society. Its legitimation may still depend on sacredness or even descent from the highest gods, and the religion may still be an expensive affair linked directly to the maintenance of the wellbeing and prosperity of the larger community. These institutions, however, are now ideological, and if they serve to consolidate state power, they are not in themselves a form of economic control. The latter depends on the ownership of land and the direct control of labour. Where the royalty loses such control, a phenomenon which can easily occur where the money economy becomes strong enough to alienate the majority of clan and state (another form of clan) land, the kingship becomes a purely political position with no effective dominance over the labour process, replaced entirely by the emergent oligarchy. The ruler may often be no more than the strongest member of such an oligarchy, and the strength of the royalty will ultimately depend on its ability to assume control over means of production and labour directly, in opposition to the oligarchy. There will be a tendency in this kind of system for an oscillation between periods of political fission in which local accumulation destroys centralised power, and recentralisation where an element of the wealthy aristocracy takes control of the larger economy by expanding the direct economic prerogatives of the state. In the city state this is expressed in the opposition between 'democratic' and 'autocratic' phases. In the more dispersed territorial state it is an opposition between 'feudal' and 'despotic' phases. The disappearance of the royalty only appears to occur in such secondary formations as the trade states of the Mediterranean where land ceases to be technologically crucial for the local population even if it is politically necessary in defining social position. In those states where irrigated land is still the basis of other forms of production it might well be argued that the ideological function of the fertility-prosperity centred religion remains in full force so that the state's control over the land represents a political element of utmost importance and will be in opposition to any economic fragmentation resulting from private accumulation of wealth. In a more obvious way, the fact that the land remains a major source of wealth implies that the state-class structure of previous periods never disappears entirely although its function is changed. Thus, the alienation of state lands in any but a purely commercial based system is likely to have strict political limits.

As spatial systems, city and territorial states are quantitative variations on the same theme. The difference between the city state and the more or less compact urban-dominated territorial state is a difference in degree and not in kind. The underlying condition permitting the formation of compact urban forms is the high productivity of a given territory, either through trade or the intensification of the subsistence base, which reduces the amount of surface area necessary to support a given population. Thus the whole political system is reduced in spatial scale and the formerly dispersed segmentary political structure is collapsed into a small urban area. This phenomenon will be most marked where subsistence depends entirely upon imports.

The larger region containing competing city/territorial states is not politically stable, but rather an arena within which trade alternates with warfare. An important characteristic of this period is the cyclical formation of empires by conquest, a pattern described by Steward and others.[67] The formation of such empires is linked to the attempt by individual states to establish a more secure basis for their own reproduction by converting trade relations into tribute relations. This need is itself a product of the increasing material dependence of individual political units on wider productive regions for their very survival. Empires in this period tend to be short lived insofar as they are not accompanied by radical reorganisation of the regional political and economic structure. So long as the basis for the existence of politically autonomous urban states is not destroyed the ability to maintain hegemony over a number of similar politico-economic units is severely limited.

It is only in the next period, which we shall not discuss here, that more stable empires and larger national states are formed. It is noteworthy that this period is marked by the earliest conscious attempts to eliminate local autonomy, to reorganise entirely the regional economy – often by acts of extreme violence – in such a way that a given centre becomes a necessary administrative instrument for the maintenance of a vast territory.

Archaeological and textual evidence

Most evidence for this period indicates the emergence of a fully commercialised economy in which the previous ceremonial centre becomes a market centre as well as a unit of commercial production in a larger trade network where dependence upon external exchange, in order to maintain a given complex of social and economic activities, becomes almost absolute. In the transition from the prestige good economy, the reorganisation of the larger economic region is of utmost importance. New centres of accumulation of wealth and power develop on the periphery of the prestige good centred systems. This is clear in the Mesopotamian material where, just before the centripetal movement that gives rise to city states, we find that formerly peripheral centres at the bottom of the settlement hierarchy grow much larger than they should if still under the dominance of a single capital. These peripheral settlements become the new cities of the following phase of contraction and competition. Territorial and city states develop out of a more dispersed organisation by a rapid process of concentration which takes place at a number of points of attraction. This is not, therefore, an isolated affair, but would appear to occur simultaneously throughout a region formerly connected by a redistributive network. The pattern occurs in Mesopotamia throughout the Jemdet Nasr and Early Dynastic (ED) periods, in Peru at the end of the Chavin period and the beginning of the early Intermediate period,[68] and in China in the Eastern Chou period. As indicated above, the actual formation of a group of urban based states occurs in an area formerly integrated by a more centralised exchange network. The connections between such networks (long distance), and their rate of expansion and development, both affect the moment of their transformation so that urban development occurs at varying times in the larger region. Thus, urban centres emerge at different times in different parts of Mesopotamia. The highland development of city states in the early Classic of Mesoamerica is much earlier than the recently documented process of urbanisation in late Classic Maya. This latter case is, in fact, one of our best examples of the transformation of a larger regional hierarchy of centres into a situation of competing autonomous centres – where former peripheral centres on the coast and inland break away from Peten control and begin to enter long distance trade independently of Tikal, a development which is itself linked to changes in the highlands.

The formation of the city state is accompanied by a quantum leap in intensification. In areas where local agricultural production provides the basis of increasing specialisation and division of labour; in Mesopotamia, Peru, Mesoamerica, and China, there is a marked intensification of technique, especially in the form of large scale irrigation works. In more specialised trade networks, subsistence surpluses from more distant regions becomes the basis of local intensification of manufacturing and commerce in the absence of large scale local agricultural development. This seems to have been the case in much of the Mediterranean and Athens is its classic example where in the fourth century 'perhaps two thirds of its wheat'[69] was imported as well as the great majority of its raw materials. In all cases there is a development of specialised craft production and, usually after some time, a market area within the city. In Peru there is evidence in Moche, for example, of a 'textile factory, with several weavers working under the supervision of a foreman'.[70] A similar development of large workshops occurs in all the major urban areas.

There is evidence of private property in land and other means of production in Mesopotamia, Eastern Chou China and Greece. For the more purely commercial city states such as those of Greece, more democratic forms of political control emerge, with councils of 'citizens' replacing the older aristocracy. Such democracy which exists primarily for the new oligarchy, usually alternates with periods of despotism in which a particular faction of the wealthy class assumes more direct control. This is especially prevalent with the formation of empires. In the agricultural based city states oligarchic councils exist along side of the royalty which never disappears and tends, with increasing warfare and the development of empires to become a dominant despotic institution. In the more dispersed territorial states like that of Chou China, the emergent power of the oligarchy which replaces the older nobility is documented by Hsu. In this period when 'land becomes a purchaseable commodity',[71] the new wealthy 'great families' tend to replace those with kinship ties to the royalty and to exercise an increased authority over the affairs of state. Here, however, the oligarchy has the appearance of a more rural gentry rather than a commercial elite.

The emergence of city and territorial states is characterised by the formation of a fully developed areal economy in which the local centres become increasingly dependent upon the production of a wider area. The formation of empires often seems to be an attempt to ensure control over the circulation of goods outside the local territory. The Aztec method of transforming trade into tribute by military force is an excellent example of this phenomenon, and it appears that in earlier Teotihuacan the same kind of extension of control was attempted.

The formation of stable empires in the next period is related to the tendency described above, but where there is a conscious attempt to destroy all forms of local autonomy. This is clearly the case in Akkadian Mesopotamia and in Ch'in and Han China, where local aristocrats are usually replaced by appointed officials and where former states are reduced to administrative provinces of the larger state. Thus in China, 'des circonscriptions administratives sont peu à peu substituées aux anciens fiefs'.[72] And in Mesopotamia, 'The "nomes" ceased being traditional self-governing states and became administrative districts headed by royal officials whose title "ensi" was now a mere sound'.[73]

The regional economy is completely reorganised as well as the political structure in such a way that local units become more completely interdependent on one another and on the directive control of a central authority. It is this last period which is properly characterised by the term 'oriental despotism' in which a powerful state dominates a very complex commercially oriented economy, and it should not be confused with what we have referred to as 'asiatic' states.

Regional sequences

It is emphasised that the general model outlined above forms an abstract delineation of certain developmental processes that in this form do not apply directly to any particular empirical sequence. Instead, these processes will combine with particular regional conditions to predict a range of variants within the limits necessary for the sequence to develop to its fullest. It is maintained that the different developments found for each of the four areas examined can best be viewed as regionally specific configurations of the general processes found in the model. Where appropriate, attention will also be drawn to variants where the conditions are such that various devolutionary or truncated evolutionary lines are encountered. Hence the general model predicts a multi-linear evolutionary trajectory in which variant pathways are generated by the constraints imposed by particular local conditions.

Indicators

The particular form of tribal system isolated in the model implies certain essential characteristics that can be used to organise the available archaeological data. Throughout this period settlements should be small, of roughly uniform size, and evenly distributed, without evidence of a settlement hierarchy. Each settlement should be roughly concentric in form with house units of roughly equivalent size, but including a larger, primarily secular structure with stronger ritual associations. Minor ritual remains would be expected from all house units (clay figurines, ritual hearths, pottery, etc.). Evidence for ritual activity focusing on fertility, prosperity and ancestor worship is likely to be variable and exhibit an order of importance equivalent to the position of the occupants in a segmentary hierarchy. During this phase, there should be increasing evidence of control over religion and involvement in ritual affairs for the community as a whole. This would be confirmed by associated evidence for ritual feasting and redistribution and exclusive access by elites to high status goods produced by craft specialists or gained through external exchange. Evidence for the latter, in particular, would indicate the development of competitive exchange between elites for valuables that have primarily sumptary value. These valuables would be consumed in burials and ritual and votive offerings. The art forms are likely to be abstract, geometric and/or depicting animals, birds, plants and non-naturalistic human figures, as representations of the various spirits or deities related to fertility and economic welfare. However, it is unlikely that a significant amount of labour would be mobilised for the construction of monumental architecture.

The appearance of ceremonial centres and the construction of monumental architecture are taken to indicate the achievement of absolute ranking and an emerging class structure characteristic of the 'Asiatic' State phase. This would coincide with the appearance of a two-tiered settlement hierarchy in which a ceremonial centre is surrounded by dispersed rural settlements. We should emphasise at this point that such States are relatively small affairs and a number of centres are likely to be found in any particular region. This would produce a pattern of regionally localised styles. We can anticipate an increase in rural population and in the number of specialists resident in the centre. The rural settlements would be characterised by their relative self-sufficiency in subsistence and the craft production of utilitarian items. Long distance exchange in scarce resources would be administered by centres, possibly in the guise of ritual exchange organised by the nobility. By the end of this phase, the consumption of sumptuary valuables in the paramount centres could assume significant proportions. Hence there would be an enormous increase in the consumption of high status objects in burials and votive offerings. Since access to such items is the absolute prerogative of the royal lineage, we would expect few high status items to be found on rural sites.

Increasing internal competition leads to direct control by the religious-political hierarchy of specialist craft production and the circulation of certain high status commodities (for example cloth, metalwork, status insignia) and sophisticated utilitarian objects down to all levels within a rapidly expanding political domain. Thus the previous pattern of localised regional styles characteristic of the asiatic state will be replaced by a more uniform style in craft products and status items. We can expect high status items with symbolic ritual-political associations to be found widely distributed throughout the political hierarchy (particularly in burials). Ranking within the system could in fact be estimated by the quantity and quality of such goods found at different status levels.

The fact that control over the supply of prestige items is an important aspect of political expansion in this phase stimulates craft production and increases dependence on long distance trade. We can expect, therefore, an increase in population at the centre and heightened importance attached to the construction of religious-ceremonial architecture, both at centres and sub-centres, since it is access to supernatural as well as secular authority that is being 'shared out'. There should also be evidence of a reorganisation of functions at the centre associated with an emerging dualism in the religion and a distinction between secular and political functions in the political system. A dichotomy in religious architecture between male/female, sky/earth type deities would be expected, associated with the construction of storage, administrative and other secular public buildings within the ritual precinct.

The complexity of such an expanding system is likely to be reflected in a more intricate three to four tiered settlement hierarchy. Links between the different levels will be indicated by downward flows of specialist craft goods and upward flows of tribute (mainly foodstuffs and raw materials), and a hierarchy of ritual and administrative buildings and artefacts diminishing in importance with the scale of the settlement. It is also predicted, although the archaeological evidence may be scanty, that links between centres and sub-centres will be established through matrimonial alliances through which will be transmitted rights to perform ritual duties characteristic of the elite, honorific titles and insignia of status expressing the dominance of the paramount centre. Towards the end of this phase, we can expect increasing competition between secondary centres on the margins and the paramount centre of the domain, which in turn will be linked with a contraction of population into an increasingly reduced hinterland around each major centre or emerging centre.

Such a rapid nucleation of population will appear as a kind of topological transformation as communities previously dispersed in a segmentary hierarchy will be drawn into their respective dominant centres. The residential areas of the city will be divided up into wards or quarters which in turn may be separated into compounds or multi-roomed complexes. We are likely to find numerous smaller temples and public buildings for each ward or part of a ward and these are likely to form the most important local administrative units within the city. In the initial phases we can expect a strong emphasis on kinship and descent as the principal mode of urban organisation. As the process of agricultural intensification and the acquisition of wealth through commerce favours the emergence of an aristocratic oligarchy, the alienation of land and a different form of economic dependence will encourage a new form of stratification to emerge. Evidence of commerce, markets, mediums of exchange, administrative complexity, secular kingship and oligarchic control over large landed estates and dependent labourer/slave classes will emerge. A chronic emphasis on warfare and conquest will develop coinciding with the expansion of autonomous city states into territorial states. The general trend towards despotic divine kingship and centralised bureaucraticisation will be reflected in the construction of elaborate secular palace/administrative complexes separate from the ritual complex and a symbolic reorganisation of the state-empire to emphasise dependence on the centre. The evolution of spatial organisation corresponding to our epigenetic model can be represented as in Fig. 6.

Figure 6. 1. Tribal system.

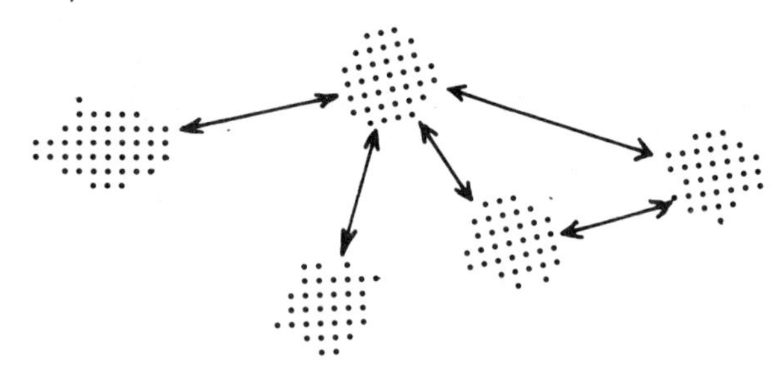

Figure 6. 1a. Hierarchy.

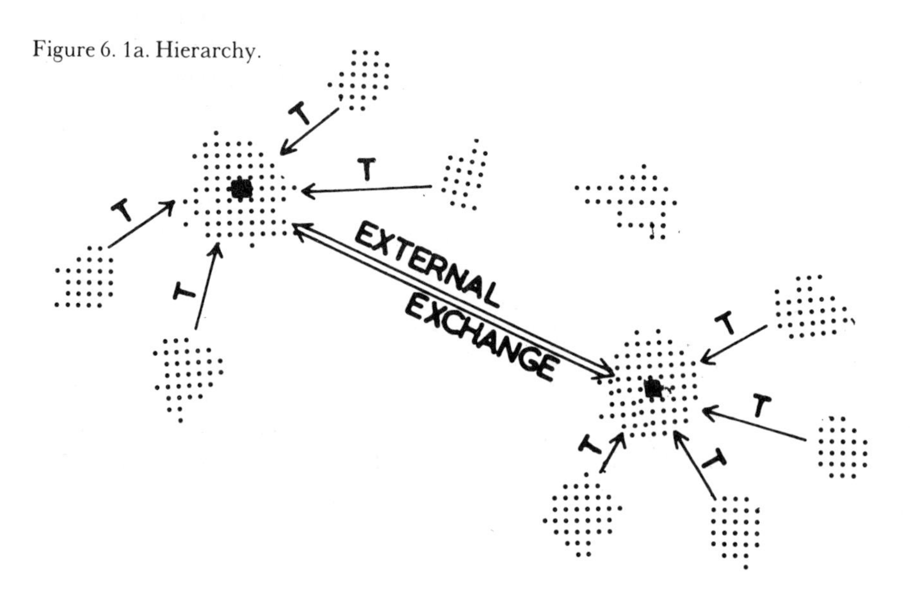

Figure 6. 1b. Dualism (devolution).

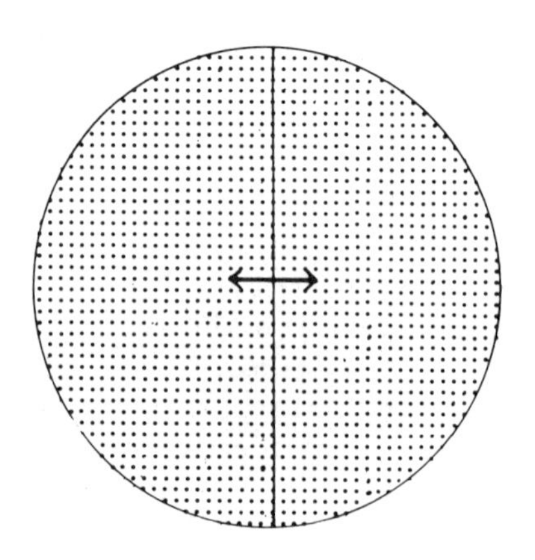

Figure 6. 2. Asiatic state.

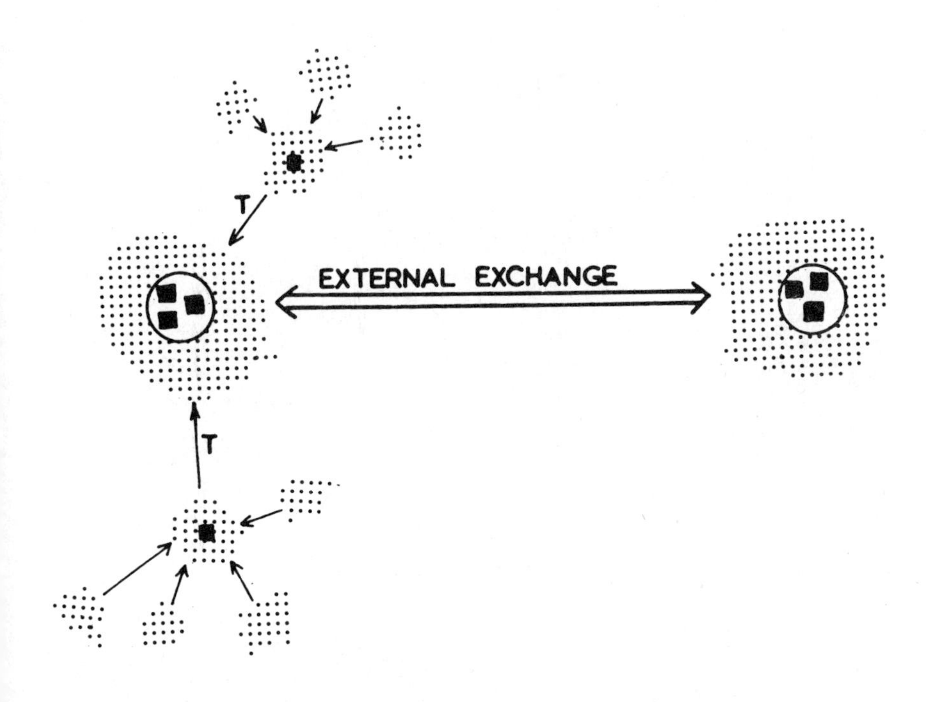

Figure 6. 3. Prestige good system.

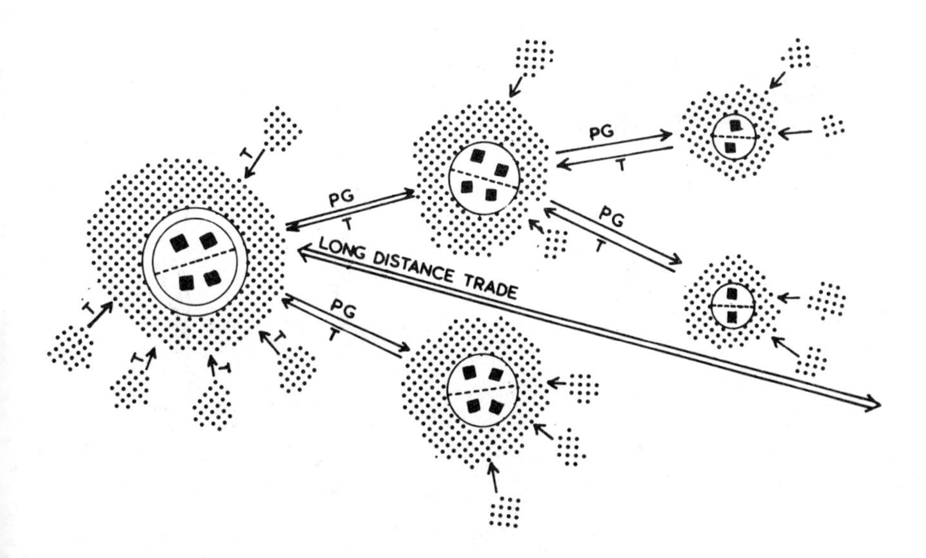

Figure 6. 3a. Evolution of centrifugal to centripetal.

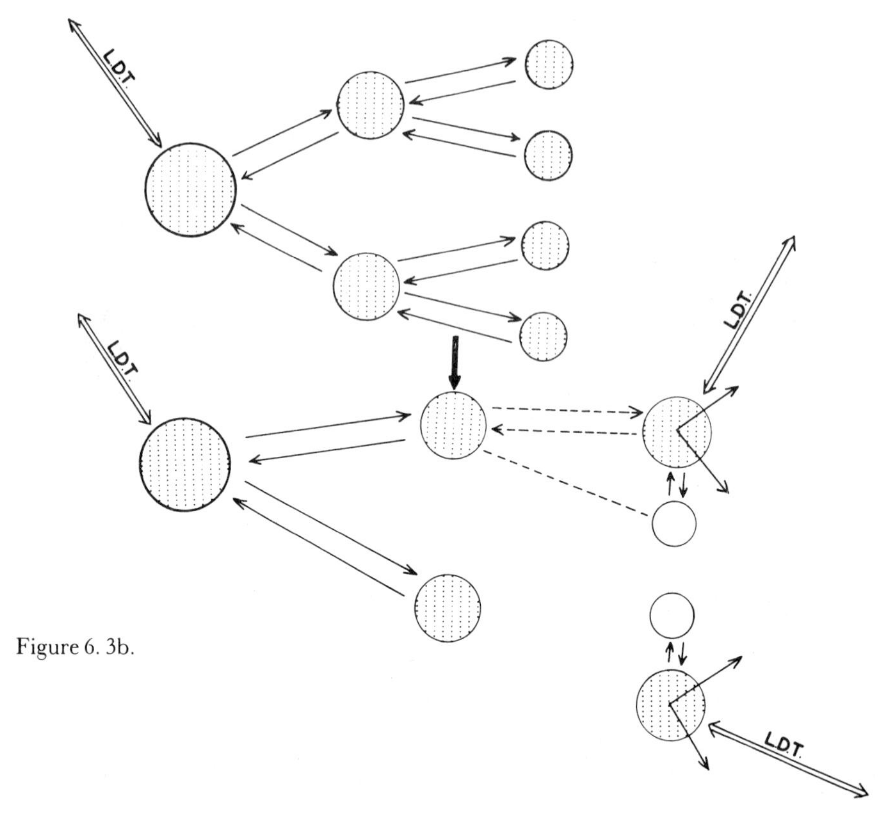

Figure 6. 3b.

Figure 6. 4. Urban-commercial states.

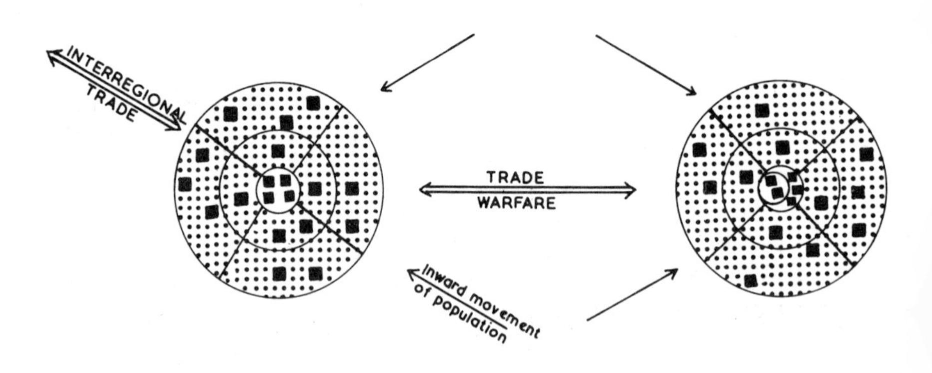

PG - PRESTIGE GOODS
T - TRIBUTE
LDT - LONG DISTANCE TRADE

North China

The early Neolithic Yangshao culture is concentrated along the Huangho, Fenho and Weis-hui river systems which was to form the core area for the later Shang civilisation. Early sites are often in pairs at the confluence of two streams. In late Yangshao, Watson says that there is evidence of agglomeration of several sites into single larger sites, whilst both Chang and Wheatley argue that settlements fission and form clusters, often using common fixed facilities such as cemeteries.[74] There is some evidence to suggest a descent ideology which linked together members of different settlements. Chang has suggested that 'the planned and segmented village layouts indicate lineage or clan localisation'. He also identifies limited evidence for ancestor worship, from the burial custom, and the practice of fertility rites to ensure growth of crops and success in hunting and fishing.[75]

The early settlements in the main Huangho valley are composed of a central cluster of semi-subterranean rectangular houses and storage pits surrounded by a ditch. In later phases, the houses are rearranged to cluster with their doors pointing towards a larger long house situated in a central area. The central long house is best interpreted as a chief's house since it is divided into compartments, each compartment has a hearth and thick occupation deposits.

Towards the end of the Yangshao and in early Lungshan, a general expansion of settlement occurs eastwards to the edge of the coastal alluvial plain and northwards and westwards into Shensi, Kansu and Shansi. Lungshan settlements are larger and more permanent than those of Yangshao, indicative of a shift to a more intensive short fallowing system. A similar pattern to Yangshao settlements continues, with houses arranged around a central long house. However, there is evidence for increasing status differentiation in house types (depending on whether they are semi-subterranean, built at ground level, or on stamped earth platforms); in burial practice, ranging from internment in wells or rubbish pits to single supine burials with or without rich grave goods; and in access to high status goods, including elaborate ceremonial pottery, imported shells and jade and occasional bronze metalwork. Chang suggests there is evidence for craft and ritual specialisation in the service of or as part of the functions of political elites. A developed ancestor cult focussed on the welfare of a royal lineage is indicated by late Lungshan with evidence of special altars attached to the central long house, ritual vessels, scapulamancy, figurines and burial practice. Chang concludes that in Lungshan 'there were specialist craftsmen, administrators, priest-shamans, theocratic art and a theocraticly vested ceremonial pattern focussed upon a selected portion of the village'.[76]

The sequence from Yangshao to late Lungshan seems to conform quite well to the development from tribal system to the emergence of the 'asiatic' state as postulated in the model. In the early Shang, there is considerable evidence for strong continuity from Lungshan with an increased level of stratification. At Ehr-li-tou (said to be the T'ang capital of Po) there is a large T-shaped building set on a stamped earth platform in the centre of the settlement. To the south of this there are three clusters of rectangular buildings of varying size set on stamped earth platforms, and there are numerous storage pits and pottery kilns in the area. There is evidence for absolute ranking not only in burial practice but also in the rich deposits of high status goods made from imported stone, jade, turquoise, bronze and shell that are found in the graves. By this phase, we would appear to have evidence for the full development of the 'asiatic' state and it is possible to speculate that there were a large number of similar centres to be found within the main Shang area. At the later sites of Cheng-chou and Anyang, a semi-urban pattern is established for the Shang capital, with a royal palace-temple complex and royal cemetery at the centre to house the members of the royal lineage, the ancestral shrines and servants and retainers. Radiating out from the centre were nucleated settlements of specialist craftsmen and finally farming villages, all of which were linked as a network to the centre. Secondary centres with a similar semi-urban structure were probably scattered over the North China plain and linked to the Shang capital through matrimonial alliance and ritual political dependence. A late Shang domain therefore could be viewed as a series of concentric circles centred on the Shang capital and, at the periphery, expanding against the outer 'barbarian' fringes. Chang has interpreted the late Shang royal Tzu clan as a conical clan structure with evidence of dualism at the top and acting as wife-taker to other clans that were the rulers of domains within the state which were not directly under the control of the Tzu royal lineage.[77] Whilst much of the evidence for this comes from Western Chou texts, there is increasing evidence for continuity of structure from late Shang to early Chou. The probability exists that a transition to a prestige good system occurred in late Shang (Yin phase). This is supported by evidence for the very substantial increase in the production of prestige goods at this time, many of which were used in the greatly inflated rituals of the capital but which were also channelled increasingly into long distance trade. Shang elite goods are now widely distributed over the North China plain and penetrate beyond into South China. At this time, there is evidence of rapid territorial expansion to the east and west and there are a number of conquest myths associated with this period, none of which can be demonstrated archaeologically. The later historical evidence for the Chou invasion may in the future be found to be exaggerated, and the archaeological evidence may show that there was no significant alteration in the structure of Chinese society from late Shang into the Western Chou period.

In the texts usually associated with the Western Chou, but which may also refer to late Shang, there appears to be a radical change showing a number of similarities to our centrifugal phase prestige good system. There is some evidence of a matrilineal inflection in the kinship system (or at least bilineal). It was apparently a rule that sons should be separated from their fathers and in one of the few texts describing royal succession, the title passes from mother's brother to sister's son, while the sons are sent off to rule distant provinces. There is a great deal of evidence indicating dualism both at the political and ideological levels. The relations between the king and his prime minister are often described as that between man and wife. This also applies more generally to the relations between king and vassal and between nobility and people. At the top of the hierarchy we find that the prime minister is often the wife-giver to the king and they are usually described as an inseparable pair. In the religion, there appears to be a marked division between sky and earth deities, the latter being vaguely associated with the common people, while the former is associated with the ruling Chou clan. Bodde suggests that the sky deity T'ien was a Chou and not a Shang divinity.[78] It is interesting in this respect that the older glyph for this god contained the sign for both earth and sky while the later form does not contain the sign for earth.

The Eastern Chou period seems to be marked by the beginning of a centripetal tendency. The previous Western Chou hegemony breaks down into a large number of territorial states that successively compete with each other for dominance during this period. The older ceremonial centres now become enclosed within a larger perimeter that includes artisan workshops, a market, and merchant quarters. Wheatley stresses the erosion of the sacred character of the royal Chou by the eighth century and the emergence of secular rulers that adopted the Chou royal style which previously had been the prerogative of the ruler and the expression of his divine status.[79] Granet provides us with a number of interesting texts which portray the competitive nature of the relations between 'warring princes', which he interprets as a form of potlatch. The formation of city states and their expansion into territorial states coincides with evidence of intensive commercial activity. Bronze prestige goods of the former period appear to become standardised as a form of currency. The concentration of an increasing number of specialists within the city walls occurs at the same time as evidence for a great deal of competition for control over labour and commerce. The period is also characterised by increasing intensification of agriculture and possibly the first development of irrigation technology. The increasing value placed on land is shown by the fact that land now becomes alienable and is accumulated in large quantities by the emergent oligarchy.

Hsu has demonstrated that throughout this period, there is a growing conflict between a new wealth-based aristocracy and the old 'natural aristocracy'.[80] He provides a picture of an aristocratic oligarchy emerging during the spring/autumn period that owed its position to private ownership of land and commercial wealth rather than to nearness of descent or kinship to the ruler. The picture of chronic inter-state conflict is matched by the internal organisation of all these states being characterised by struggles between noble families, and noble families and rulers. The emergence of unified territorial states in the contending states period also marked a transition to a political structure in which the ruler exercised despotic power over a bureaucracy largely appointed by merit rather than by wealth or kinship. The reunification of China under the Ch'in dynasty in the late third century B.C. therefore marks a transition to empire organised on formal bureaucratic procedures characteristic of the Oriental despotic state.

Mesopotamia

The Near Eastern evidence probably best supports the supposition that the emergence of a tribal system is intrinsically related to and a social determinant of the transition to food production. The pre-agricultural Natufian settlement of Ain Mallaha contained c. 50 huts concentrated around a cleared central area and intramural burials provide clear evidence of relative ranking. Habitation I has been variously interpreted as belonging to a compound head or a Natufian chieftain[81] and the practice of intramural burial and dismemberment of leg bones and skulls after burial are clear antecedents of the 'skull cult' indicative of ancestor worship found in the PPN period at Jericho. Imported elite goods such as dentalia shell and obsidian can be taken to indicate ranking in burial and also exchange relations between elites at different Natufian settlements.

Ain Mallaha is the only excavated Natufian open site known in any detail, with an economy based on intensive gathering and hunting. If it is at all typical, it would suggest the emergence of a form of tribal system in the late Mesolithic (about 10,000 B.C.) of the coastal Levant. But, in more marginal ecological zones, where the intensification of hunting and gathering economies was more limited, there would have been a much greater incentive for a shift to a food produciton technology in order to supply the increasing demands for surplus generated by the developing tribal system. If correct, the development of complex stratified society found for example at PPN Jericho and a millennium later at Catal Hüyük would represent the logical development of tendencies already found in the Natufian to a more asiatic state type structure.

The ecological factors that curtailed such early developments in the Levant and Anatolia would appear not to have operated at a later period in the southern alluvial plains of Mesopotamia. Here the possibilities of agricultural intensification with the development of irrigation raised the limitations on the fuller development of the evolutionary sequence outlined in the model. Unfortunately, information on the pre-Ubaid in the south is totally lacking, although a close relationship between Ubaid 1 and 2 (Eridu and Hajji Muhammed phases) and the Samarran/Choga Mami transitional phase in the north is well established.[82] However, the internal organisation of all these sites indicates a degree of stratification, wealth, ritual and economic specialisation, that would not concur with that postulated for the tribal stage.

Only Eridu has a sequence going back to Ubaid 1 and 2 and provides the earliest evidence for ritual architecture in Mesopotamia. Al Ubaid, Tel Uquair, Ur, Eridu, Uruk and Kish had developed into major ceremonial centres by the Late Ubaid (late fifth millennium B.C.) and each appear to be a focus of a number of dispersed settlements within enclaves along the stream courses of the Euphrates. Adams and Nissen describe the Warka region as occupied by a small number of dispersed settlements and small towns of which Uruk is probably a centre of some prominence.[83] The initial construction of the Anu ziggurat and the expansion of the temple platforms in the Eanna precinct at Uruk occur in the early Uruk period, corresponding with evidence for an increasing tendency for smaller settlements to be clustered around the enlarged ceremonial centre. Both Adams and Gibson have suggested that similar processes occur at different times in southern Mesopotamia, possibly earlier in the Nippur and Kish areas.[84] Wright and Johnson's work on the Susiana plain would indicate a much earlier sequence there since a three-tiered settlement hierarchy and a centralisation of craft production are established patterns by the early Uruk period.[85] In the Susiana D and the Susa A periods (equivalent to late Ubaid), an earlier site and then Susa formed ceremonial centres with elaborate buildings and storerooms which dominated a number of small, uniformly sized settlements dispersed around them.

The indicators for the late Ubaid would seem to conform quite well with those predicted for the developed 'asiatic' State stage. On the Susiana plain, a major change occurs in the Early Uruk period, indicated by the development of a three to four tier settlement hierarchy. Evidence such as wall cones and stamp seals have been used to recognise differentiated administrative/political functions in sub-centres dependent on Susa. A significant increase occurs in the amount of the imported goods found on secondary and tertiary centres, particularly in Middle to Late Uruk, and the finds of seals and bullae on these sites suggests that these goods were obtained from Susa in exchange for local resources such as bitumen and possibly foodstuffs. To support this, there is clear evidence of a sudden shift in craft production from local levels to centralised mass production in the early Uruk period. The sophisticated products of pottery workshops, centralised at Susa, are found on all settlements at this time and the spacing of settlements is altered to adapt to increased local exchange functions. During the Middle Uruk, Susa becomes differentiated into an older upper town which had a variety of special purpose buildings besides the temple complex, including storage and scribal areas, and the new lower town which is likely to have contained the residences and workshops of craftsmen and specialist administrators. The bulk of the farming population was almost certainly rural and dispersed about a number of secondary centres.

The early Uruk period witnesses the rapid political expansion of Susa to include a number of smaller centres that were politically autonomous in the terminal Ubaid. At slight later dates (Middle to Late Uruk) a similar process seems to occur widely on the Mesopotamian plain, at centres such as Nippur, Kish, Uruk and Ur/Eridu. It is also quite clear that the development of these expanded polities did not occur in isolation: e.g. it is highly likely that the expansion at Uruk inhibited similar developments and possibly robbed population from the Ur/Eridu region. That these expansionist tendencies resulted in hostilities between different states is indicated in the reliefs from Uruk showing bound prisoners depicted in a Susa art style. Johnson had also produced evidence to show a collapse and depopulation of the Susiana plain during the same period.[86] By the Middle to Late Uruk, therefore, we see a picture of a number of competing and expanding states in southern Mesopotamia, accompanied by a massive increase in external trade, increased production of status items and craft goods, increased warfare between centres for control over communication routes and probably to obtain prisoners or slaves.

The more detailed evidence from Uruk for the late Uruk and Jemdet Nasr periods gives strong indications of secular administrative functions developing in the temple hierarchy. During this period, the Eanna precinct is expanded and rebuilt to incorporate a range of public buildings that have been said to include a 'treasury', a 'palace', administrative and storage rooms. It is also interesting to note that by late Uruk, at the latest, there are two separate precincts at Uruk, one dedicated to Anu – the male sky god – and the other to Inanna – a female deity of fertility, the date harvest and the storehouse (viz. earth associations). In later Sumerian religious tradition, Anu is said to have been the earlier deity and there is good reason to believe that at one time was conceived to be the supreme ruler of the Sumerian religious pantheon.[87]

This evidence for an emerging dualism and secularisation of religious authority in Mesopotamian society is also supported by the reference, probably at the latest by the Jemdet Nasr period, to the titles of *en*, apparently associated with ritual activity referred to as either male or female, and *sanga,* translated as high priest, but with primarily administrative functions within the temple hierarchy.

In the Jemdet Nasr–Early Dynastic 1 period, there is evidence of increasing hostilities between centres over much of the Southern Mesopotamian plain. That warfare was primarily over trade is indicated in one of the Sumarian epic poems referring to the exploits of Enmerkar, a predecessor of Gilgamesh on the 'throne' of Uruk.[88] The conflict between Uruk and Aratta, a land to the east in the highland of Persia, revolves around a quarrel over the barter of corn from Uruk for precious metals and stone from Aratta and ends in the subjugation of the latter by the former. More important for understanding the process involved is the evidence for the emergence of autonomous centres on the periphery of areas controlled by primary centres. On the Susiana plain, for example, the role of Choga Mish changes from that of a secondary centre of Susa to one of autonomy and competes with Susa for control over trade routes from the Zagros to the southern Mesopotamian plain. In the Warka region, dominant sites in settlement clusters on the margins of the Uruk hinterland develop into secondary centres, some of which by ED 2-3 emerge as autonomous city states (e.g. Umma, Shuruppak and Zabulam).

Throughout this period increasing competition between centres for control over land and population serves to attract the inhabitants of rural dispersed settlements into nucleated centres. The resulting reduction in hinterland (estimated about 12 km. radius for Uruk) and increasing pressure on land results in intensification of irrigation agriculture, greater risk of soil deterioration and greater dependence on trade as an alternative economic strategy.

From ED 1-3 various forms of complex city states are found widely distributed within Southern Mesopotamia. The Sumerian city was divided into a number of wards each of which had a temple. The temple of each ward was known by its respective deity and it seems likely members were bound together by ties of kinship and descent. Each ward was broadly responsible for administrative, fiscal, notarial, judicial and police functions and appointed their own 'functionaries' to carry out these tasks. The Council of Elders seems to have been composed of representatives of these wards on some kind of rotating basis, whilst the city assembly (the *unken*) was made up of 'freemen', i.e. representatives of land-holding corporate kin groups. Members of the Council of Elders also appear to have had functions in the temple hierarchy. Whilst we do not support the extreme views of Falkenstein, the unity of the ward temples and the temple of the city deity and the hierarchy of freemen, elders and rulers could be conceived as a single unitary structure in which the ranking of descent groups and the temple hierarchy were closely interconnected, if not the same structure.[89]

An older land-based aristocracy and an emerging oligarchy, who gained new access to wealth through commerce and could convert this wealth into land holdings, were responsible for the erosion of the older clan structure and the appearance of a new form of stratification. As the economy of Sumerian city states became increasingly dependent on commerce, conducted by specialist traders at least notionally attached to the temple, clan land became alienable and was appropriated by the ruler and 'big families' to form large estates worked intensively by dependent labourer and slave classes.[90]

From ED 2, a reorganisation of functions occurred in the politico-economic structure which ultimately led to what Diakanoff calls a division between State and Community. The title 'en' was replaced by that of either 'ensi' or 'lugal'. Although initially in the service of the temple and elected by the Public Assembly, these titles appear to achieve a high degree of autonomy very quickly. The city ruler lived in a palace outside the temple complex (formerly the 'en' had special quarters – the *giparu* – within the main temple precinct) and was one of those most actively involved in the acquisition of clan land. Priestly functions were to devolve more and more on the 'sanga' who came to head the temple hierarchy. Members of the noble families were able to build up estates in the same way, worked by dependents (probably dispossessed clansmen) who had put themselves under the protection of palace, noble or temple. Temple land could not be alienated and the ruler and noble families competed with each other over its control. There are frequent references in the texts to power conflicts among noble families and between rulers and emerging wealthy oligarchies. The public assembly and the Council of Elders acted initially as a check on the power of the ruler since his accession was not hereditary and any decisions affecting the city had to be confirmed by them. The example of Gilgamesh bypassing the Council of Elders and appealing directly to the Public Assembly implies that this was never a secure check on power conflicts between the ruler and the noble families. By ED 3 the apparent separation of the ruler from the temple hierarchy, the increasing opportunities to control economic resources directly and the curtailment of the power of the aristocracy, resulted in the separation of political control from the community structure (the Council and the Public Assembly). By the end of the third millenium these bodies had few functions beyond the regulation of local community affairs.

The foundation of royal dynasties is witnessed for the first time at Ur in ED 3 where the ruler was elected by divine wish of the city deity rather than through confirmation by the public bodies. Whereas formerly the 'ensi' or 'lugal' held a position within the temple hierarchy, his power by this phase was absolute and he controlled the religion. Texts refer to the ruler appointing his own relatives as chief priest or priestess of all the temples in the city and appropriating the use of temple land and labour for his own uses (abuses, amongst others, which the reforms of Urukagina of Lagash attempted to correct). There are references by the late ED of city rulers being deified posthumously and by Akkadian times, the king was divine in his own lifetime (e.g. Naramsin).

Whilst the logic of centripetalism entails concentration of

population into urban centres, it is unlikely that single autonomous city states was ever the political pattern in Mesopotamia. The logic of the formation of city states is in itself expansionist, with centres attempting to take over other centres to exploit the productivity of their labour. Sumerian city states are, as a result, always territorial states with a major city usually dominating several smaller city states and attempting to expand against other major city/territorial states. The political pattern of the early Dynastic, therefore, is one of conflict between compact city states to achieve higher degrees of unification, a pattern that never seems to have been successful in southern Mesopotamia and was only achieved further north in Akkadian times. Sargon of Akkad was not only able to unify Mesopotamia but also to begin the institution of various reforms which served to undermine the autonomy of the Sumerian cities and thus change irreversibly the conditions of their political autonomy. With the development of the higher level of political integration characteristic of empire, the evolutionary precondition for the development of Mesopotamian society was changed irreversibly such that later history would always be a pattern of unification and dislocation of cycles of empire formation.

Mesoamerica

Mesoamerica provides a striking variant of the general model in the sense that we seem to be dealing with a highly segregated spatial system in which regional shifts of dominance occur over time as differing ecological and geographical factors favour certain locations for the development of different stages. By the early Classic, we encounter a regional system of enormous complexity and we can only point to some of the major developmental trends in this summary.

By the early Formative, settled communities were established in the southern and central Highlands and along the Pacific coast of Guatemala/Chiapas and the gulf coast of Vera Cruz and Tabasco. During the early and middle Formative, Mesoamerica is characterised by a Lowland dominance of centres along the Pacific coast and particularly the Gulf coast (Olmec) enclosing and interacting with at least two autonomous Highland complexes (Tlatilco style, and West Mexico). Recent work has tended to undermine the traditional picture of Olmec dominance (colonisation, trade imperialism, etc.) in the Highland in the early Formative.[91] There are now sufficient indications that pre-Olmec societies of some complexity existed in the area including the Basin of Mexico, much of Morelos, and Western Puebla. The earliest Tlatilco graves, Grove's La Juana and early San Pablo A phases in Morelos and Grennes' La Manuela phase material from Iglesia Vieja all predate Olmec influenced phases in the Highlands and in particular would indicate that a number of Olmec features, such as the bottle complex, roller stamps, hollow figurines and metallic mirrors, were of independent Highland origin.

This has stimulated increasing interest in Flannery's model of Olmec-Oaxaca interaction based on alliance and exchange between elites of systems only differing slightly in complexity. This results in a charismatic absorption of a number of the status symbols and beliefs of the more complex by the less complex society.[92]

However, it is unlikely that these Highland societies can be viewed as miniature copies of the Olmec centres. Although the published information available is extremely difficult to interpret, the differences between the Highland and Lowland centres of the early and middle Formative periods are quite striking.

The construction of a ceremonial centre at San Lorenzo Tenochtitlan in the Olmec heartland begins in the Bajio phase (about 1400 B.C.), possibly associated with the construction of temple mounds by this time. The figurine material also suggests that the were-jaguar motif appears by then. The Chicarras phase provides the first evidence of monumental sculptures – probably of colossal heads – being erected on the long ridges. Coe has interpreted these sculptures in later phases as memorials to members of royal lineages that ruled at San Lorenzo.[93] Many of the elements characteristic of the developed Olmec culture had therefore appeared by about 1200 B.C. In the following San Lorenzo phase most of the colossal monuments were carved, large engineering works were carried out, and population around San Lorenzo reached a maximum.

San Lorenzo was probably one of several major ceremonial centres to be built on the Lowland Gulf coast in the early Formative. The low density of population at San Lorenzo itself (estimated at 1,000-1,200 people) suggests this work was carried out by tribute corvée labour for the support of a ritual/political elite that administered a religion in which the were-jaguar and the crying child were dominant themes. The complex cosmology of this religion focused on agriculture, fertility and rain.

Prior to the development of irrigation in the Highlands, tropical swiddening in the Lowlands was the most productive agricultural system in Mesoamerica. It continued to support population densities high enough to maintain chiefdoms and non-urban states in the Lowlands until the post-Classic period.

There is considerable evidence to suggest that a major change occurred in the structure of Olmec society (strictly speaking only San Lorenzo at present) in the San Lorenzo phase. The San Lorenzo B phase, in particular, witnesses a major expansion of links between the Olmec heartland and the rest of Mesoamerica. There is a marked increase in the range and quantity of resources coming down to the Gulf area from Highland centres. San Lorenzo at this stage is importing obsidian from at least eleven different Highland sources.

Other materials, such as ilmenite, magnetite, haematite, mica and serpentine, many probably in the form of finished artefacts, were also imported from the Highlands. Extensive workshops for obsidian and brown flint, lapidary work for the producton of earspools and beads, and probably for pottery and figurines, have been excavated at San Lorenzo. There is strong evidence, therefore, for a major concentration of craft specialisation and workshops at the centre.

We seem to be witnessing the development of an autonomous economic sector based on control over craft goods, external trade and the internal redistribution of products. This process of centralisation is linked to a major expansion of the political influence of San Lorenzo. It is also striking that this expansion occurred prior to the sudden collapse of San Lorenzo and the emergence of new centres, particularly La Venta, with which it would appear to have been in competition. Since all these features are characteristic of the development of a prestige good system out of an 'asiatic' state structure in our model, it seems reasonable to suggest that other aspects of this system are likely to have been present. In particular, evidence for the major expansion of San Lorenzo and La Venta, increasing competition and hostilities between centres both for control of products and to gain slaves, and the emergence of competing centres on the margins of older political domains.

As stated, contemporary with the development of the Olmec centres, an autonomous complex of regional cultures sharing many similarities in material culture is to be found in the central and southern Highlands. However, there are striking differences in the development of these centres in comparison to the Olmec. Grove's La Juana phase in Morelos indicates that small regional centres had been established in the central Highlands prior to any evidence of Olmec 'influence'.[94] The pottery and figurine complexes and status insignia such as the small haematite mirrors would also indicate that these were ranked societies although the form this ranking took cannot be determined. Certainly, fairly large settlements of perhaps 30-40 acres and large cemeteries (e.g. Group I at Tlatilco?) with rich grave goods would not appear to be untypical. Olmec influence, particularly in the introduction of kaolin ceramics, pottery motifs and some of the figurines, appear in Oaxaca in the San Jose phase, in Morelos in San Pablo A and B, and in the Valley of Mexico in the Ixtapaluca phase, i.e. roughly contemporary with San Lorenzo A and B on the Gulf coast and with the development of the prestige good sector in the economy there.

None of the Highland sites have significant evidence of ceremonial/public architecture nor can they be interpreted at this stage as forming ceremonial centres. If Flannery's excavations at San Jose Mogote are at all typical, it is striking how secular these Highland centres appear to be. At San Jose, for example, Flannery found house mounds and patios of elite residences aligned like those found at San Lorenzo. These were surrounded by the workshops and houses of craft specialists with evidence of intensive production of magnetite mirrors, shell, mica and shale ornaments and pottery. That access to such resources was controlled seems to be indicated by evidence from a nearby site, Barrio del Rosaria – which should have had equal access to these raw materials – where only a few pieces of shell and magnetite were found. The presence of shell, pearl oyster and richly decorated pottery also indicates that the products were not all being sent to Olmec centres, since the shell and pearl oyster were almost certainly derived from the Gulf coast. In other words, a site such as San Jose appears to have been a supplier of prestige goods/status items to other dependent sites in the Etla valley at this time.

If this is a general phenomenon, then the political advantage of controlling resources, craft production and exchange acts as a basis for increasing hierarchisation in the Highlands. This is particularly the case once these centres become integrated with the more dominant Olmec centres. This case would appear to be a variant of a wider principle in which the emerging prestige good sector of an 'asiatic state' economy tends to stimulate the growth of peripheral prestige good systems in those areas on which it is dependent for resources to maintain itself. In consequence, the Highland centres move from a ranked tribal system to a prestige good system without going through the 'asiatic' state phase.

We can expect therefore that the erection of monumental architecture will be a later phenomenon in the Highlands than in the Lowlands. The ranked society is, of course, already theocratically organised so that the religious element is still present in subsequent developments. It is likely, however, that it becomes secondary or rather more ideological in function at a much earlier point, so that control over the production of luxury goods may be dominant although 'encompassed' by the tribal religious ideology. Later monumental constructions are an indication that this is indeed the case. Such architecture is not an indicator of theocratic control over the economy but of the central place of religion in the cultural identification of the elite. While control over fertility and monopolisation of the supernatural may be an attribute of this system, it is not a direct form of control of labour and its output. Political domination is effectively 'economic' in the sense that the logic of the system depends on control over resources, agriculture and the administration of long distance trade.

This would seem to be confirmed by the fact that in the Highlands, sites with what might be called monumental art – in an almost pure Olmec style – all date to the middle Formative and are contemporary with La Venta on the Gulf coast (e.g. Las Bocas, Chalcatzingo, Juxtlahuaca, Oxtotitlan, San Miguel Omoco etc). The fact that this coincides with the widespread distribution of Olmec portable artefacts (jades, figurines etc.), and with the appearance of regional Highland complexes of utilitarian material culture without any evidence of Olmec influence in the Middle Formative, is significant (i.e. Zacatenco, El Zarco and Guadaloupe phases). Thus, in contrast to the early Formative, Olmec prestige items tend to be more securely associated with an elite, indicating the greater absolute status emerging in Highland political hierarchies.

The shift in dominance from early Formative San Lorenzo to middle Formative La Venta therefore represents the period of widest Olmec influence in Mesoamerica. The logic of the prestige good system implies expansion and La Venta almost certainly had a number of sub-centres dependent upon it in the Lowlands. In the same way, a number of Highland centres, such as Las Bocas and Chalcatzingo, may have been directly dependent and incorporated within the Olmec sphere through matrimonial alliance and dependence on Olmec prestige goods. This would appear to be particularly true of sites with the Olmec monumental art style and in those areas with the highest density of portable Olmec artefacts. The Highland centres would also tend to be expansionist. Initially this would be on a smaller scale than that found on the Gulf coast and we should expect to find a number of dominant centres emerging. Grove's recent excavations at Chalcatzingo, where he has discovered a Middle Formative centre with ceremonial architecture including a long platform mound, ceremonial rooms and a possible ball-court, are likely to be replicated elsewhere in the Highlands.

Thus, by the end of the middle Formative, we can distinguish a larger regional system in Mesoamerica in which the Lowland Gulf centres still hold a dominant position. Other Lowland centres have emerged, particularly on the Pacific coast of Chiapas and Guatemala. It also seems likely that the Olmec centres had established alliances with and stimulated the growth of the Lowland Mayan centres in the Peten (Mamom-Chicanel complexes). However, there are good reasons why a shift in dominance to the Highland centres should occur. Unlike other areas of early civilisation, e.g. Mesopotamia, the Highlands of Mesoamerica contained both the conditions for intensification of agriculture beyond swiddening (i.e. irrigation) and direct access to the raw materials needed for specialist craft production. In the competition between centres, the Highlands would have a decided advantage in the nucleation of population and the intensification of food production for the maintenance of large numbers of non food-producing specialists. The influence of these factors is found already in the middle Formative with the formation of larger nucleated settlements in the Highlands in contrast to the more dispersed rural pattern found in the Lowlands. The conditions necessary for urbanisation existed initially in the Highlands and only with considerable limitations – if at all – in the Lowlands, (c.f. later evidence of semi-urban developments and intensification at late Classic Mayan centres).[95]

These factors are of particular significance in the centripetal phase that characterises the early centuries of the late Formative. La Venta is destroyed and largely abandoned and the Olmec sphere collapses into a number of smaller centres on the Gulf coast, of which the only ones known in any detail are Tres Zapotes and Cerro de las Mesas. This coincides with the autonomy of the Lowland Mayan centres and the development of Izapa on the Pacific coast. However, it is in the Highlands that the full development of the centripetal phase occurs by the terminal Formative period. In the late Formative, a number of centres in the Highlands appear to expand in importance and influence after the Olmec collapse (Monte Alban and Mitla in Oaxaca, Cuicuilco in the Teotihuacan valley, and Kaminaljuyu in Highland Guatamala). Although it is difficult to tell, in some cases they may have been peripheral centres to the Olmec and their increasing dominance may have been largely responsible for the truncation of Olmec trade routes into the Highlands.

Cuicuilco, for example, was first settled in the Middle Formative and initiated the first religious architecture in the Valley of Mexico. It also developed a distinctively non-Olmecoid material culture, which by the end of the middle Formative had replaced the typical Olmec were-jaguar/baby face motifs on other sites in the valley. In the late Formative, it develops into a major ceremonial centre and dominates a number of smaller sub-centres in the Valley of Mexico (e.g. Ticoman, Zacatenco, Tlapacoya and Copilco). If this kind of pattern is found repeated elsewhere, then it constitutes a typical centripetal response in which marginal centres gain autonomy and expand at the expense of primary centres. In the case of Cuicuilco, its dominance seems to have been undermined by the same process during the Late Formative. This results in the creation of other competing centres in the Valley of Mexico by the terminal Formative. Of these, Teotihuacan was the most important.

Both Cuicuilco and Teotihuacan shared exceptionally good conditions for urban growth, since they were sited on good water sources for irrigation and near obsidian deposits. Just after the volcanic destruction of Cuicuilco (about 150 B.C.), Teotihuacan undergoes a rapid expansion and concentration of population. By the end of the Patlacique phase (150 B.C.-B.C./A.D.) a nucleated population of 20,000 plus has been estimated for Teotihuacan.[96] The rapid urban growth of Teotihuacan seems to be supported by Millon's suggestion that quarters for obsidian and other craft specialists were of major importance in this phase. The effects of Teotihuacan as a market centre were already being felt, and its shrines were renowned throughout Mesoamerica. It seems highly likely that a similar centripetal process and growth of urbanism occurred elsewhere in Highland Mesoamerica. However, the capacity for intensive food production at Teotihuacan was critical for the achievement of the degree of urban growth found nowhere else in Mesoamerica. Having achieved this dominance, Teotihuacan was subsequently able to reorganise settlement and productive activity within the Valley of Mexico and beyond (particularly encouraging economic specialisation and market exchange).

By the fourth century A.D. Teotihuacan is the major territorial state in Mesoamerica. Associated with its growth, the Highlands gain a dominant position in Mesoamerica which it retains until the Spanish Conquest and beyond. Urban growth in the Highlands effectively reorganises trade and economic activity resulting in a dependence of the Lowland centres on the Highlands. It is a striking feature, for example, that the temporary collapse of Highland dominance tends to be associated with major developments in the Lowlands, as if Highland unification acts as an inhibitor of Lowland growth. The Lowland Mayan centres of the late Formative early Classic share all the features characteristic of an asiatic state/prestige good system transition. During the early Classic they are linked economically and – in the case of Tikal – possibly politically (through matrimonial alliance) to Teotihuacan and Kaminaljuyu. Centres in the buffer zone are in turn dependent upon core area centres.

Rathje has shown that the core centres controlled complex skills associated with Mayan astrology, ceremonial, stelae construction, calendrics and hieroglyphics.[97] During the early classic, these skills were 'exported' to centres in the buffer zone. He also suggests that at some point in the Classic sequence at least one important commodity – cloth – was produced in large quantities at centres in the core area and sent out to dependent centres. Dualism in the core area is attested by the appearance of palace complexes in the temple complexes during the early and late Classic. Stelae and memorials of the late Classic also refer to the formation of matrimonial alliances between core and buffer zone centres in a period when the latter were expanding and competing with the former. Rathje's interpretation of the form this matrimonial alliance took (reciprocal exchange of women between centres) is however sufficiently ambiguous to be open to alternative interpretations. The evidence available could just as well support an argument for a bilineal type of structure with strong matrilocality. This would produce a pattern either of sons from core centes (acting as wife-takers) becoming resident in buffer zone cetres at marriage, or sons of a sky dynasty woman marrying into a Buffer Zone elite, inheriting titles through the mother's as well as the father's line. Daughters in turn would be married into sub-centre elites, thus effectively creating a widespread alliance linking centres. The evidence is sufficient to suggest that the dominance of centres over sub-centres in the Mayan realm was expressed and articulated through prescribed marriage rules. It also seems likely that this was an established practice in the early Classic and had to be re-established in the late Classic after the Mayan hiatus.

The hiatus and the later growth of the late Classic Mayan centres, particularly in the so-called Buffer Zone, occurs with the collapse of the influence of Teotihuacan in the Mayan region. In this situation it can be predicted that the early Classic Mayan Lowland centres would be at greatest risk and the Buffer Zone centres would have greatest advantage in capturing the trade with the Highlands. This pattern of temporary collapse at the centre and the expansion of the marginal centres fits the evidence for the differential construction of stelae during the hiatus. A number of authors have pointed to this correlation and there seems little doubt that the late Classic Mayan centres develop into full prestige good systems during this period.[98] By taking advantage of political disunity in the Highlands and controlling the trade routes in to the Highlands, the centres in the Buffer Zone are at a particular advantage over the older centres in the Mayan Lowlands. Increasing competition between the Buffer Zone and the core area of the Mayan Lowlands occurs throughout the Late Classic with evidence of hostilities and complex alliances being established between different centres. At the same time, as Haviland and Puleston have shown at Tikal, this is associated with an increasing tendency towards urban growth in the major Mayan centres. The Classic Mayan collapse, therefore, would appear to be the result of a combination of internal competition between centres consistent with the centripetal phase of a prestige good system, the problems of intensifying agricultural systems in tropical lowland conditions, and the reunification and return to dominance of the Highlands under the Toltecs. The expansion of the Toltecs to regain control over Highland/Lowland trade and the realignment of trade routes to the Gulf Coast – thus avoiding the Lowland Mayan centres – results in the formation of urban centres on the Gulf Coast and Yucatan peninsula in the post-Classic and the final collapse of Mayan centres in the core and buffer zones.

Hence the Post-Classic presents a complex regional pattern of differential urban growth and political unification in Mesoamerica. The problems of maintaining control over widely dispersed and ecologically distinct areas, in order to support a regional economy based on a high degree of specialisation and market exchange, appear to have been more formidable in Mesoamerica than in other areas of empire formation. It may well be that the attempt by the Aztecs to create a centralised, bureaucratised empire would have failed for the same reasons as found for Teotihuacan and Tula.

Peru

A more limited discussion of the Peruvian data is presented here in order to suggest that another variant of the general model exists in this sequence.

Permanent settlements emerge on the northern and central

Peruvian coast in the late Preceramic (i.e. Pampa, Playa Hermosa, Conchas and Gaviota phases). Coastal settlements were based largely on the extensive exploitation of marine and littoral resources, whilst agriculture (probably flood-farming) was a more important strategy in settlements situated at the alluvial mouth of rivers and on upper river valleys. In the Gaviota phase, a number of large settlements with public architecture including temples, pyramids and alters is found on the coast (e.g. Rio Seco, Ancon Tank site and Culabras I). Similar sites exist in the river valleys, away from the coast, and if the evidence of Chuquicanta is representative, each of these river valley centres had a number of smaller dependent farming settlements.

The same pattern of settlement continues into the Initial Period and extends down the south coast, and is now associated with evidence for increasing dependence on agriculture. Corvée labour employed in the construction of large public/ceremonial buildings, such as the pyramid/temple at Las Haldas, is well attested by this phase, as is evidence of intense stratification and craft specialisation in the service of an elite. The shift of focus to settlement in the alluvial river valleys during this phase indicates that the spread of agriculture in coastal Peru has to be seen very much as a technological change selected for by the set of political relations characteristic of an 'asiatic state' type structure. Agriculture did not allow the growth of sedentary village life and the construction of ceremonial centres in Peru, instead it is clear that the evolution of the political structure manifested in the latter selected for the increased productive capacity of agriculture.

The size of territory unified around each of these ceremonial centres appears to be relatively small in the Initial period. Around each of the major centres, such as Las Haldas, La Florida and Ancon Tank site, there were a number of smaller settlements with local shrines. A state probably did not enclose more than part or at most the whole of a river valley and its adjacent coast. Certainly the material culture pattern is one of localised, regional styles with limited exchange between centres. The coastal centres were heavily dependent upon marine resources throughout the Initial period. Elites at these centres controlled the exchange of food stuffs within each domain, particularly between inland, valley sites and the coastal sites. They probably had exchange relationships with centres in the Highlands, (e.g. Kotosh), dealing in small quantities of elite goods – with cloth already an important elite item in the late Preceramic/Initial periods. The carvings of Cerro Sechín also indicate that relations between centres were highly competitive, and towards the end of the Initial period, warfare seems to have been the usual form that these relationships took.

The rapid spread of the Chavin cult would therefore be consistent with a centrifugal phase in a prestige good system developing out of an 'asiatic' state type structure. Prestige goods associated with a complex of ritual and cosmological beliefs rapidly come to dominate a wide region. In contrast to the absence of significant exchange between regions in the Initial period, most sites now show high densities of pottery, textiles, bone, wood and stone artefacts decorated in the Chavin style. Copper and gold work were introduced for the first time: they were restricted to elite goods decorated with Chavin symbolic motifs. This territorial expansion is accompanied by supposed religious innovations, dualism in the religion, and a division between male and female deities. The primary expansion of the Chavin cult served first to unify central and northern Peru, which in the Initial period had been divided into a number of smaller states. In the same way as these now seemed to become dependent on a single centre, areas that were previously marginal were now incorporated as vassals within a Chavin sphere of influence. This created a spatial pattern of all ceremonial centres and dependent settlements being incorporated into a single domain constituted by a paramount centre and dependent vassals and surrounded by a nucleated, non-stratified population. We can only surmise that these areas would have been continuously expanded against as outlets for trade and for population.

In the south, the Chavin period is followed by a rapid contraction into a large number of urban dominated territorial states (Early Intermediate period). This is consistent with the centripetal phase of a prestige good system. Population becomes concentrated into fortified urban centres, associated with a major increase in organised warfare. The introduction of intensive irrigation systems served to increase agricultural productivity and maintain high densities of population in river valleys with limited amounts of well-watered fertile soil. It is also apparent that these large urban political units reorganised economic activities, encouraging specialisation and exchange. The period as a whole is noted for major innovations in craft technology and a massive increase in the production of sophisticated craft goods, both utilitarian and luxury. Coastal settlements were incorporated into these larger political units. The possibility of exchanging fish for agricultural produce and craft products at markets in urban centres stimulated technological innovations in fishing and in the storage of the increased catch.

The early Intermediate period in the south is characterised by the formation of territorial states that expand against each other and quickly collapse when they extend beyond their productive capacity to maintain continued expansion. In the north on the other hand, the preceding pattern of dispersed population and ceremonial centres continues, although now broken up into a number of distinct regional units. It would seem, therefore, that whilst urban centres emerge in the south (particularly the southern Highlands), in the north a more confused pattern emerges. This might constitute a case in which contraction into fully urbanised centres occurs later in the north (the dominant area in the Chavin period) than in the south (scene of emerging peripheral centres). Full urbanism may also have been limited to a semi-urban pattern due to ecological factors (particularly narrow river valleys and high erosion risks) in the north. It is significant that the importing of foodstuffs, which was a vital necessity for northern cities in the late Intermediate, was not a viable strategy in the early Intermediate. The fact that cities develop in the north in the late Intermediate may be due more to the changed economic conditions introduced with the expansion of Huari, and the development, for the first time, of a pan-Peruvian trade network.

The Middle Horizon is dominated by the expansion of two of the southern Highland urban states: Huari and Tiahuanaco. In both cases, continuity with the Chavin cult has been noted. However, there is good reason to see this phase corresponding to the transition from territorial state to empire. The possibility that this resulted in the transformation of the northern states into a number of urban centres dominated economically and probably politically by Huari, would seem to be indicated by the revival of Moche pottery and art forms in the succeeding Chimu empire.

Whilst the late Intermediate is characterised, therefore, by the emergence of urban dominated territorial states in the north, in the south, after the collapse of Huari and Tiahuanaco, population is redispersed into rural settlements and small non-urban ceremonial centres. The development of the Chimu empire might therefore be interpreted as a repetition at a later period in northern Peru of the same evolutionary tendency that resulted in Huari and Tiahuanaco in the south. Further evolution of urban territorial state into full empire in Peru appears, therefore, to have been limited repeatedly by environmental constraints and probably by the difficulties of politically administering a large and ecologically diverse area. The emphasis on road-building from early Intermediate times would indicate that difficulties in transport and communication were significant problems for any centralised political authority.

In the development of the Inca 'empire', we find an excellent example of the structure predicted for the expansionist tendencies of a prestige good system embedded in the spatial framework of a territorial state. Murra has demonstrated the extreme importance of cloth in the Inca economy, both in ritual and various crucial exchange relations, especially marriage payments. The production of cloth and especially the finer varieties of cumbicloth was controlled from Cuzco. There is strong evidence of matrilateral marriage and perhaps the sending off of sons to rule in the provinces. Subsidiary sons of the ruling class may have been sent off with cloth to marry into subordinary groups. The *allyu* appears to be a kind of patrilineal conical clan which is, however, divided into matrilineal marriage classes which are ranked as F/S/SS. There is ample evidence of dualism at all levels. The myth of Inca conquest is very much developed although the archaeological evidence for this is unclear. The capital itself is divided into two moieties: Hurin Cuzco, associated with the original population, with the temple of Viracocha the creator god, and with priestly functions; and Hanan Cuzco, the superior half, associated with the conquerors, with the temple of the Sun and with political functions. The same kind of dualism appears to exist at all political and territorial levels. The same kind of structure permeates the kinship institutions: Collana/Payan/Cayao, which represent ideologically the major groups of society (*allyu* groupings, marriage classes, and personal kinship terms for ego/S/SS) are also associated with the division Inca conquerors – political rulers/original population, lords of the land; priests/commoners. Needless to say the 'church' plays a very important role in the Inca system. The priests are very close kin of the ruler, but it is the latter position which is dominant. The control over cloth and other prestige good production is instrumental in political domination and is closely linked with Inca expansion.

Thus, we seem to be dealing fairly consistently with a kind of oscillation between the centrifugal-centripetal territorial state phases of prestige good systems which in Peru never develop fully into empire. In addition to this oscillation over time, we also encounter a spatial oscillation of dominance between north and south, as summarised in Table 1.

Table 1. Comparison of cultural sequences in northern and southern Peru

Period	*N. and central Peru*	*South Peru*
	Asiatic state	Tribal
Early Horizon	Centrifugal phase (Chavin)	Centrifugal phase (Chavin)
Early Intermediate	Centrifugal/centripetal phase (Moche, Nasca)	Centripetal phase/ Territorial state (Huari, Tiahuanaco)
Middle Horizon	Centripetal phase (Huari 'influenced')	Territorial state/ Empire (Huari/ Tiahuanaco)
Late Intermediate	Territorial state/Empire (Chimu)	Break down into prestige good system (Rural dispersed)
Late Horizon	Territorial state with centrifugal characteristics of prestige good system (Inca)	Territorial state with centrifugal characteristics of prestige good system (Inca)

We do not imply that these sequences represent a single evolutionary trajectory, as is frequently represented in the literature. Rather, the table shows an alternation in dominance of the southern and northern centres. Also, we would maintain that the developments in each area are directly linked with each other: such that conditions in the dominant centre of one period provides the structural prerequisites for future developments in the other.

Conclusion: on epigenetic models

It is usual, as we have said, in evolutionary theory to treat stages as if they were objects, abstractions from particular types of institutions. We have suggested that an ordered juxtaposition of types such as band, tribe, chiefdom, state, is in itself inadequate to the problem at hand. This is not to deny that social institutions can be classified in such categories. Rather it is a question of the kind of theorising that results from such preliminary categorisations. Most attempts at explanation have singled out factors such as technological improvement or population growth as causes of evolution; factors which can be shown to be variables whose values can not be independently determined. We know that technology can develop and that population can grow. We also know that technology does not develop itself and that the birth rate, which appears increasingly to be the dominant factor in systematic population growth, is socially and not biologically determined. Such factors must be accounted for in terms of dominant social relations and cannot be treated as independent variables. Multivariate models constructed along systems theoretic lines may avoid some of the above problems, but since they are normally restricted to such abstract categories as population size and density, technological organisation, trade, warfare, they are not specific enough to account for the actual transition from one social form to another. This must necessarily be the case where the models in question contain no social properties. It is the integration of the above categories in a social formation which determines their specific effectivity.

In this very tentative paper we have attempted to overcome the above mentioned problems by defining, at the outset, specific social forms of the reproduction of populations. A form of reproduction is one in which social institutional properties are imprinted upon the production-distribution cycle in a way that necessarily defines a dynamic system, i.e. one whose properties can only be expressed as a function of time. In this way what we have chosen to call stages or periods are not discrete entities. Rather, they are those sections of a continuous developmental and transformational process in which it can be said that a particular social form dominates material reproduction. We use the notion of epigenesis to indicate the specific quality of this kind of model. That is, since the structures with which we are concerned are the structures of processes and not of institutions, we must deal with systems of trajectories in which elements are internally transformed as they take on new roles in the larger system of material reproduction. In this way we expect to be able to predict the dominant forms of social reproduction in the next stage in terms of the properties of the current stage. This is possible because the reproductive process is itself directional and transformational.

The properties of the 'asiatic' state, the definition of politico-economic control in terms of monopoly over the supernatural as an 'economic' necessity, depend upon the tribal structure, in which production and the supernatural are already linked in a way that determines the 'asiatic' character of the hierarchisation process. The emergence of the prestige good system is more difficult to demonstrate structurally, but the elements which we suggested are all contained within the former system. Thus, the control over production for exchange is established on the basis of the former theocratic control. The progressive centralisation of craft production is linked to the specific form of inter-state competitive exchange, and the increase in the production of elite goods, linked both to temple and exchange activities, are the foundation for the expansion that occurs in the next period. This development is in turn linked to the necessary internal conflicts over succession in a highly polygamous royalty, the difficulty in maintaining a monopoly over the increasing quantity of wealth items, and the ensuing re-emergence of exchange as a means of political domination. It is clear that the early 'asiatic' states are extremely limited in size and power, and the prestige good system may itself be an early form of politico-economic expansion, as well as a new means of internal control. The dualism that develops in the former theocracy – documented for almost all areas – indicates again a differentiation within the pre-existent state in which a new form of politico-economic control emerges from the transformation of the older system. The formation of political hierarchies in larger regions, on the basis of the monopolisation of the production and import of prestige goods, generates, in a relatively short time, a subsequent transformation into city or territorial states. This form of control is not politically strong enough to prevent the development of new political units capable of entering the larger interregional exchange system independently of the former monopolist. The interregional network is greatly expanded throughout this period as prestige goods and more useful craft items circulate in great quantities between redistributive centres. The intensification in craft production creates demands for specialities from different areas, and goods controlled by the dominant centre are usually exchanged for a tribute of local goods and food from the subordinate centres. The very expansion of such systems will enable certain secondary centres, which are in a potentially advantageous position, both with respect to local production and exchange (geographically), to compete with the original centre. The ensuing breakdown is accompanied by the formation of compact urban forms that compete for land and labour. The emergence of monetary wealth begins in this period. The monetary form itself is a development of the former prestige good which is generalised in conditions of competition following the breakdown of monopoly. This is at first a question of extension and not a change of form. The earlier prestige goods were themselves ordered in different 'denominations' with measurable relative values, and it appears, as in ethnographic and historic examples of such systems, that they were already not so restricted a form of money. The centripetal movement of the period destroys the geographic basis of the former centralised power, and the existence of a number of points of accumulation of wealth becomes the basis for a process of commercialisation. Land, which as a result of the same contraction of population becomes a scarce and valuable commodity (especially where it is irrigated), is subject to sale. There develops a final form of politico-economic control based on property in the means of production and labour (slaves).

We have suggested that evolution might be conceived as a single set of homeorhetic[99] processes in which there is a certain structurally determined order. As such, our 'stages' are always described in a terminology of becoming, i.e. they are time periods within which the process of change is dominated by a particular structure and where that structure emerges and is transformed throughout the stage. Thus it would be difficult indeed to find a fixed set of institutions for any one 'stage' because they are no more than cross-sections of a complex of processes. For example, when we discuss the emergence of the city state we describe a number of developments which do not occur simultaneously but which are connected over time. The emergence of a commercial economy and the development of property in the means of production and labour are much more gradual than the actual formation of urban states. On the contrary, this change in relations of production develops fully only after the formation of compact cities. Thus what we mark off as a new stage is the beginning of a period in which new dominant structures evolve. It is not simply a question of describing a stage by a list of static traits. Furthermore, it should be evident that dominant structures are not simple transformations of such former structures, since change in material function is just as characteristic as change in form.

By considering societies in terms of forms of reproduction we are brought to a re-evaluation of space as well as of time. Just as stage theory in evolutionary anthropology abstracts institutions from the larger processes of which they are a part, so it abstracts social entities from the spatial systems to which they belong. Thus, it must be recognised from the start that evolution is not stable in space. It is usually characterised by a spatial shift in centres, very often one that is, more specifically, a shift from centre to periphery. Such would appear to be the case in the sequence leading from western Chou to eastern Chou, from Chavin to Nazca and Ica valley cities, and from single-centre dominated Uruk to multicentred systems where formerly peripheral settlements such as Umma and Lagash become major centres. These cases, which belong to the transition from prestige good systems to urban states, are perhaps the most obvious examples of a systematically produced shift in dominance, since it is the prestige good system itself that encourages the development of powerful subsidiary centres.

Tribal and 'asiatic' systems have different modes of areal integration, usually of a more limited kind. In the tribal system, areal integration is part of the expansion process itself. Exchange networks expand at the same time as hierarchy increases. The accumulation of captive labour also increases and is linked directly to the competitive nature of intertribal exchange relations which themselves may be transformed into political relations of dominance/subordination. The same kind of regional integration characterises the 'asiatic' state in its early stages, but there is increasing intensification as production of craft goods is more centralised. A tribal periphery tends to develop which specialises in supplying local products to the dominant centre in exchange for titles and goods from that centre. This may be an area where prestige good systems develop such as western Chou on the periphery of Shang development or the highland suppliers of goods to the Olmec. Where these peripheral societies are already emergent 'asiatic' states they may become the dominant centres of the next period.

The 'competitive' exchange of elite goods continues into later periods as well as the massive expenditure on ritual institutions. Granet's description of the prestige contests of the 'warring states' period is similar to the types of exchange that we presume to have existed in the earlier 'asiatic' period. In the later urban states, however, it represents only a fractional part of a much larger economy which is dominated by strictly commercial transactions.

All this external exchange, which tempts us to signal the importance of the larger regional system, is not simply a fortuitous juxtaposition of local societies. From the point of view of reproduction, the local society only rarely has at its disposal all the means necessary for the maintenance of a given social form of existence. While earlier tribal societies may have been more locally autonomous, this certainly did not remain the case for very long. This is not essentially a question of ecology nor of basic resources, though it is surely the case that relative access to certain kinds of goods may provide the basis for a necessary exchange relation. The kind of phenomenon which concerns us here is a social one. The development of states, the absolute increase in production and its growing differentiation, imply, from a very early period, the necessity of exchange over wider areas in order to maintain social systems. The precise kinds of needs, the use to be made of imports etc., are of course dependent on the structures that develop within societies, but the larger network is the condition of reproduction of that local system and can have a strong selective effect on internal structures.

The development of the early central civilisations clearly depended on the productive activity of very large areas, and in order to fully understand the evolutionary process it is necessary to take account of these larger systems of reproduction. The transformation of societies does not occur in a vacuum and the relation between units in a larger system may determine the conditions of evolution of any one of them. The type of development that occurs in the city states of classical Greece depends on their place in a larger areal system which enabled them to obtain food and other necessary items to maintain their economy at a given level. Generally, the development of complex trade systems tends to increase the internal dependency of the political units involved. Mesopotamian societies could and did use tools made of locally produced clay in early periods, but the more complex stone and metal technology, which depended entirely on importation and which determined the level of development of productivity as well as ensuring centralised control over the production of factors of production, demonstrates the extent to which the maintenance of a given level of development depends on a wider regional system. It is, of course, this same phenomenon that accounts for the complementary development of large-scale manufacture for exchange in the evolving centres.

If the pattern we have presented here appears to be unilineal, it is because we have dealt with the properties of only one system of trajectories where we believe that a single set of structural properties dominates the developmental process. But this evolution, if it occurs in a number of places, only occurs in a given 'structural' time period, in specific local and regional conditions, and does not apply to the evolution of later centres of civilisation. Social forms which developed on the periphery of the early 'civilisations' discussed here may well have different structural properties so that when the centres of development shift to these areas (or at least when they begin to develop on a large scale) we have to deal with a new set of developmental pathways. It is clearly this kind of process that Childe was alluding to in his discussion of the emergence of secular urban centres on the periphery of the major centres of Near Eastern civilisation.[100] This process in turn may have seriously affected northern European tribal systems that were incorporated into the extensive trade networks as suppliers of local products, especially raw materials. Whilst Childe's excessive diffusionism has recently been criticised[101] on the basis of revisions in dating and specific items of cultural content (megaliths, burial practices, etc.) it would be unacceptable to ignore the relations between these tribes and Mediterranean societies as of decisive importance in later European prehistory. The early commercialisation of this area, for example in late La Tène, before the emergence of any centralised state control, may be significant for understanding later feudal developments and the particular decentralised feudal/mercantile formations that led to

European capitalism.[102] The mercantilism that developed in Mesopotamia may also be the economic basis for the later growth of a great number of commercial city states and trade empires of varying sizes that dominate the subsequent history of the Indian Ocean and the Middle East.

This admittedly superficial examination of some consequences of the model is only meant to suggest some possibilities for further, more intensive research. In effect we have ourselves restricted our analysis to only one aspect of the larger framework with which we should like to work, concentrating specifically on a single set of evolutionary processes. What is required in the way of an abstract model would best be represented by some kind of topological space in which social forms of different types were integrated into larger structures and where the structure of the space changed over time in such a way that the evolution of local forms could be comprehended within a transformation of the total space. This is not to imply that the larger structure is dominant but only that it comprises the total relevant universe for the analysis of evolution, where both internal dynamics of local societies and local and regional conditions of reproduction are clearly articulated in a larger system. It is by attempting to construct such larger models that we will come to a clearer understanding of the necessary and sufficient determinants of social evolution.

NOTES

1 Steward, J. (1955), 'Cultural causality and law: A trial formulation of the development of early civilisations', in *Theory of Culture Change*, Illinois, p. 199.

2 Steward (1955), p. 208.

3 Harris, M. (1968), *The Rise of Anthropological Theory*, New York; Fried, M. (1967), *The Evolution of Political Society*, New York; Binford, L. (1962), 'Archaeology as anthropology', *American Antiquity*, 28, No. 2, pp. 217-25.

4 Flannery, K. (1972), 'The cultural evolution of civilisations', *Annual Review of Ecology and Systematics*, 9, pp. 399-426; Wright, H. (1970), 'Toward an explanation of the origin of the State', ms.

5 Friedman, J. (1975), 'Tribes, states and transformations', *in* Bloch, M. (ed.), *Marxist Analyses and Social Anthropology*, London, pp. 161-5.

6 Sahlins, M. (1972), 'The domestic mode of production', *in* Sahlins, M., *Stone Age Economics*, London.

7 Bride-service is also a possibility and many societies combine the two. The transfer of valuables however is subject to a wide range of variation which would be rather limited if there were only bride-service (i.e. without profoundly altering the residence structures). Lineages in such cases would become husband givers to some extent, and with matrilateral marriage this would imply matri-uxorilocal residence and perhaps a matrilineal inflection.

8 Friedman, J. (1972), *System, Structure and Contradiction in the Evolution of 'Asiatic' Social Formations*, Ph.D., Columbia University; Friedman (1975), pp. 186-93.

9 Meillassoux, C. (1960), 'Essai d'interpretation du phénomène économique dans les sociétés traditionelles d'autosubsistence', *Cahiers d'études africaines*, 4; Ekholm, K., in this volume; Berthe, L. (1961), 'Le mariage par achat et la

captation dans une société semi-féodiale: les Buna de Timor Central', *L'Homme*, I, 3; Schulte Nordholt, H.G. (1971), *The Political System of the Atoni of Timor*, The Hague.

10 Dupré, G. (1973), 'Le commerce entre sociétés lignagères: les Nzabi dans la traité à la fin du XIXe siècle', *Cahiers d'études africaines*, 12.

11 The Trobriands, as well as number of societies of this type in Indonesia and Africa, combine a stress on rituals of agricultural productivity with a stress on external trade in a distinct fashion, which we shall discuss later in this paper.

12 The case of Tonga contradicts this but in no way makes good theoretical sense, as we shall see.

13 Such developments may have occurred in the European late Bronze and early Iron Ages; see Frankenstein, S. and Rowlands, M.J. (in press), 'The evolution of political structures in the European Iron Age'. It might also be the kind of phenomenon that occurred in pre-colonial West Africa as well as in parts of Melanesia where external trade stimulus seems to have played a fundamental rôle.

14 Chang, K.C. (1968), *The Archaeology of Ancient China*, Yale, p. 103.

15 Chang (1968), p. 97.

16 Friedman (1972).

17 Chang, K.C. (1962), 'China', *in* Braidwood, R. and Willey, G. (eds.), *Courses towards Urban Life*, Chicago, p. 184.

18 Chang (1968), p. 172.

19 For the particular conditions of irrigation in southern Mesopotamia, see Adams, R.McC. (1965), *The Evolution of Urban Society*, London, pp. 38-78.

20 Granet describes a situation where 'lignées mineurs disposées hierarchiquement autour d'une lignée majeure, ce groupe comprend des non-agnats qui sont des vassaux, nobles où non ...' and when these nobles may keep their ancestors only 'qu'en raison de leur participation au culte des ancêtres seigneuraux'. Granet, M. (1939), 'Catégories matrimoniales et relations de proximité dans la Chine ancienne', *Ann. Sociol.*, Ser. B. Fasc. 1-3, p. 122.

21 This is in contrast with the tribal system where hypogamy is a way of establishing relative rank for a wife-taker and is a way of converting status into real social superiority for a wife-giver, since the wife-giver represents the social value of her group to the husband's group.

22 See, for example, Wheatley, P. (1971), *The Pivot of the Four Quarters*, Edinburgh, p. 76.

23 For examples of this kind of conflict in state structures of this type, see Valeri, V. (1972), 'Le système des rangs á Hawaii', *L'Homme*, 12, 1; Kuper, A. (1975), 'The social structure of the Sotho-speaking peoples of Southern Africa', Part 1, *Africa*, XLV, 1.

24 Gernet, J. (1970), *La Chine ancienne*, Paris, p. 52. 'Enormous amounts of wealth are consecrated to cult activities (herd animals, metals, agricultural products, game, prisoners of war), and almost all goods possessed by this society are the object of sumptuous expenses at the funerals of kings and nobles ... Offerings of 30 or 40 cattle to a single ancestor are not unusual, and there are special written characters to designate sacrifices of 100 cattle, 100 pigs, 10 white pigs, 10 cattle, 10 sheep.'

25 See Adams (1965), pp. 85, 88. He deals with a somewhat later period but there is a strong probability that this form of organisation predates the period from which his evidence comes.

26 Maspero, H. and Balazs, E. (1967). *Histoire et institutions de la Chine ancienne*, Paris.

27 Granet (1939), p. 122-3. 'It often occured that a chief whose name was "becoming great" forced one of his close kin to recognise him as his sovereign, not only as a domestic chief, but as chief of a clientele. As a symbol of alliance and subordination, the vassalised agnate received a wife from his superior. He became (by violation of the rule of exogamy and the substitution of a feudal for a communal consubstantiality) a son-in-law, and even an annexed son-in-law: a "married-in-husband".'

28 See Chang (1968), pp. 243-4.
29 Wheatley (1971), p. 61.
30 The present discussion of prestige good systems is derived largely from the theoretical analysis of Central African societies by K. Ekholm (1972, *Power and Prestige: The Rise and Fall of the Kongo Kingdom,* Uppsala, and the article in this volume). Other areas where aspects of her model have been recognised include large parts of Indonesia (Friedberg in the present volume), the Inca (Zuidema, R., 1964, *The Ceque System of Cuzco,* Leiden) and parts of Melanesia and Polynesia. While Ekholm's model is somewhat modified here, its general outlines correspond to an apparently widespread and general structural phenomenon.
31 Ekholm, K. (1972), *Power and Prestige,* Uppsala. See also her paper in this volume. The evidence of dualism (to be discussed shortly) is quite variable and much clearer in the material from China and Peru than from Mesopotamia.
32 For the notion of 'encompassing' see Dumont, L. (1970), *Homo Hierarchicus*, London.
33 The word for slave in Sumer meant 'hillman' or derived from the word for a foreign country (Adams 1965, p. 96). By the later Early Dynastic, however, slaves were obtained from neighbouring city states and from impoverished freemen (c.f. reforms of Urukagina of Lagash).
34 See Murra on the ranking of Inca cloth: Murra, J. (1957), *The Economic Organisation of the Inca State*, Ph.D., University of Chicago, Ch. IV.
35 Wheatley (1971), p. 118; Bodde, D. (1956), 'Feudalism in China', *in* Coulborn, R. (ed.), *Feudalism in History*, New Jersey.
36 Granet, M. (1959), *Danses et legendes de la Chine Ancienne*, Paris, Vol. I, p. 93.
37 Granet (1959), pp. 92-3.
38 Murra, J. (1962), 'Cloth and its functions in the Inca State', *American Anthropologist*, 64, pp. 710-23; Murra (1957).
39 Murra (1957), p. 135.
40 Wright, H. and Johnson, G. (1975), 'Population, exchange and early state formation in Southwestern Iran', *American Anthropologist*, 77, pp. 275-6.
41 Johnson, G. (1973), 'Local exchange and early state development in Southwestern Iran', Anthrop. papers No. 51, Museum of Anthropology, Michigan.
42 Maspero and Balazs (1967), p. 7.
43 Zuidema, R. (n.d.), 'Hierarchy and space in Inca social organisation', ms., p. 5.
44 Zuidema (n.d.), p. 12.
45 Zuidema, R. (1964), *The Ceque system of Cuzco*, Leiden, Ch. III.
46 See Ekholm's paper in this volume.
47 Gernet (1970), p. 42; also Granet (1939).
48 For an African example, see Bonafé, P. (1973), 'Une grande fête de la vie et la mort, le miyali cérémonie funeraille d'un seigneur du ciel guya (Congo-Brazzaville)', *L'Homme*, XIII, 1-2.
49 Granet (1939), p. 173.
50 *ibid.*
51 Goldman, I. (1970), *Ancient Polynesian Society*, Chicago.
52 Goldman (1970), p. 215.
53 *ibid.*
54 Valeri (1972).
55 Goldman (1970), p. 216.
56 Goldman (1970), p. 290.
57 *ibid.*
58 Goldman (1970), p. 287.
59 *ibid.*
60 Goldman (1970), p. 301. Also Kaeppler, A. (1971), 'Eighteenth century Tonga: New interpretations of Tongan society and material culture at the time of Captain Cook', *Man*, (n.s.) 6 (2), pp. 206-10.

61 Zuidema (1964), p. 243.
62 *ibid.*
63 Eberhard, W. (1957) 'Data on the structure of the Chinese city in the pre-industrial period', *Economic Development and Cultural Change*, 3.
64 Webb, M. (1973), 'The Maya Peten decline viewed in the perspective of state formation', *in* Culbert, T.P. (ed.), *The Classic Maya Collapse*, Santa Fe, p. 392.
65 In the sense of market centre.
66 It is important to stress at this point that we do not envisage any separation of the aristocratic hierarchy from the temple in Mesopotamia. Diakanoff's interpretation that the segregation of temple from community did not occur until ED 3 reinforces this claim. See J. Oates' paper in this volume. To argue for the separation of religious and secular institutions in Sumerian society (temple, community, councils, etc.) prior to the emergence of secular political bodies to dominate the economy in ED 2-3 seems to be to ignore the evidence that, at least as late as the Jemdet Nasr period, the temple and chiefly hierarchies were closely interconnected: Diakanoff, I.M. (1969), 'The rise of the despotic state in Ancient Mesopotamia', *in* Diakanoff, I.M. (ed.), *Ancient Mesopotamia – socio-economic history*, Moscow.
67 Steward (1955), p. 204.
68 Using Lanning's terminology: Lanning, E.P. (1967), *Peru before the Incas*, New Jersey, P. 25.
69 Finley, M.I. (1973), *The Ancient Economy*, London, p. 133.
70 Lanning (1967), p. 125.
71 Hsu (1965), *Ancient China in transition: An analysis of social mobility*, Stanford.
72 Gernet (1970), p. 82.
73 Diakanoff (1969), p. 195.
74 Watson, W. (1972), 'Neolithic settlement in East Asia', *in* Ucko, P.J., Tringham, R. and Dimbleby, G.W. (eds.), *Man Settlement and Urbanism,* London, pp. 336-7; Chang (1968), pp. 94-7; Wheatley (1971), pp. 24-5.
65 Chang (1968), pp. 102-3.
76 Chang (1962), p. 184.
77 Chang (1968), pp. 240-5.
78 Bodde, (1956), p. 62.
79 Wheatley (1971), pp. 116-17.
80 Hsu (1965), Ch. 4.
81 Mellaart, J. (1965), *Early civilisation of the Near East,* London, pp. 24-7; Flannery, K. (1972), 'The origins of the village as a settlement type in Mesoamerica and the Near East', *in* Ucko, Tringham and Dimbleby (eds.) (1972), p. 73.
82 Oates, J. (1973), 'Early farming communities in Mesopotamia', *Proc. Prehist. Soc.*, 39, pp. 172-5.
83 Adams, R.McC. and Nissen, H.J. (1972), *The Uruk Countryside*, Chicago, p. 86.
84 Adams, R.McC. (1972), 'Patterns of urbanisation in early Southern Mesopotamia', *in* Ucko, Tringham and Dimbleby (eds.) (1972), pp. 738-40; Gibson, McG. (1973), 'Population shift and the rise of Mesopotamian civilisation', *in* Renfrew, C. (ed.), *The Explanation of Culture Change,* London, p. 454.
85 Wright, H. (1972), 'a consideration of interregional exchange in Greater Mesopotamia, 4,000-3,000 B.C.', *in* Wilmsen, E. (ed.), *Social Exchange and Interaction,* Anthrop. papers, Museum of Anthropology, Michigan, no. 46; Johnson (1973), pp. 90-2; Wright and Johnson (1975), pp. 267-89.
86 Johnson (1973), p. 156.
87 Kramer, S.H. (1963), *The Sumerians*, Chicago, p. 118.
88 Sandars, N.K. (1972), *The Epic of Gilgamesh*, Harmondsworth, pp. 18-19.
89 Falkenstein, A. (1954), 'La cité-temple sumérienne', *Journal of World History*, 1, pp. 784-814.
90 Diakanoff (1969), pp. 173-203; Diakanoff, I.M. (1959), *Structure of Society and State in Early Dynastic Sumer*, English resumé of *Sumer: Society and State in Ancient Mesopotamia*, Moscow.

91 Flannery, K. (1968), 'The Olmec and the valley of Oaxaca: a model for inter-regional interaction in Formative times', *in* Benson, E.P. (ed.), *Dumbarton Oaks Conference on the Olmec*, pp. 79-110. Tolstoy, P. and Paradis, L. (1970), 'Early and Middle Preclassic Cultures in the Basin of Mexico', in *Science*, 167, pp. 344-51; Grove, D.C. (1974), 'The Highland Olmec manifestation: a consideration of what is and isn't', *in* Hammond, N. (ed.), *Mesoamerican Archaeology: New approaches,* London, pp. 124-6.

92 Flannery (1968), pp. 105-8.

93 Coe, M.D. (1968), *America's First Civilisation: Discovering the Olmec*, New York; Coe, M.D. (1970), 'The archaeological sequence at San Lorenzo Tenochtitlan, Veracruz', *Contributions of the University of California Arch. research Facility*, No. 8, pp. 21-34.

94 Grove (1970), pp. 110-11.

95 Sandars, W.T. amd Price, B. (1968), *Mesoamerica: The evolution of a civilisation*, New York; Haviland, W.A. (1970), 'Tikal, Guatemala and Mesoamerican urbanism', *World Archaeology*, 2, no. 2, pp. 186-98.

96 Cowgill, G. (1974), 'Quantitative studies of urbanisation at Teotihuacan', in Hammond (1974), pp. 381-5.

97 Rathje, W.L. (1973), 'Classic Maya development and denouement: a research design', *in* Culbert, T.P. (ed.), *The Classic Maya Collapse*, Santa Fe; Molloy, J.P. and Rathje, W.L. (1974), 'Sexploitation among the Late Classic Maya', *in* Hammond (ed.) (1974), pp. 431-44.

98 For example: Willey, G.R. (1974), 'The Classic Maya hiatus: a "rehearsal" for the collapse?', *in* Hammond (1974), pp. 417-30.

99 *Homeorhesis*: for definition see Waddington, C.H. (1968), *Towards a Theoretical Biology*, Edinburgh, Vol. I, pp. 12-13. In homeorhetic processes what is constant or stable is a structure defined with respect to time and not a specific systemic state.

100 Childe, V.G. (1954), *New Light on the Most Ancient East,* London.

101 For example: Renfrew, C. (1973), *Before Civilisation*, London.

102 Frankenstein and Rowlands (in press).

SECTION III

Evolution and political differentiation

E. TERRAY

Event, structure and history: the formation of the Abron kingdom of Gyaman (1700-1780)

At the beginning of the eighteenth century, a small band of Akwamu immigrants entered the Bondoukou region, an area north-east of present-day Ivory Coast, north-west of present-day Ghana. In sixty or seventy years a kingdom strong enough to be considered a serious threat by the Ashanti had grown up around these immigrants and this kingdom had a political structure radically distinct from those of neighbouring countries and related peoples. In the following pages I shall try to understand how and why this structure was created. In so far as its appearance in the area in question represents a considerable transformation, this study may be a useful contribution to the debate on the evolution of social systems.

The political organisation of the Kingdom

Most of the traits common to the Akan States of the eighteenth and nineteenth centuries appear in the political organisation of the Abron kingdom. These traits have been repeatedly described and analysed in the works of Ellis, Rattray, Busia and Wilks.[1] We shall limit ourselves to a brief review.

1. Power is exercised by a sovereign selected from a royal matrilineage. Certain genealogical rules influence this selection; when the pretenders to the throne belong to different segments, the order of seniority of the female founders of these segments is taken into consideration. But these rules do not operate automatically; they only come into play at the initial selection, after which there are always several remaining candidates: at this point there is the possibility of an actual choice, a choice subject to extremely varied considerations and in which the *ahemma*, the oldest descendant in the female line of the founding ancestress, always plays a very important part.

2. The sovereign is both assisted and controlled by a council composed of high officials holding specific posts at court. Each of these high officials is himself the head of a lineage which is the real holder of the post in question; the selection of lineage head is governed by the same rules which govern the selection of the sovereign form within the royal matrilineage.
3. The sovereign's powers are military (he decides questions of peace and war); diplomatic (he makes alliances); judicial (all sentences delivered in the kingdom may be appealed against before him and only he can punish certain crimes and inflict certain punishments, particularly the death penalty); economic (he organises the levying of tribute and duties and under certain circumstances can determine the amount levied, finally he manages the State treasury); and religious (he carries out the rites and ceremonies necessary for the prosperity and greatness of the kingdom).
4. There is a close correspondence between the political and military organisation of the kingdom: each high official also holds a specific strategic post when the army is in the field.

However, the political organisation of the Abron kingdom reveals a number of specific characteristics which distinguish it from its Akan counterparts. Firstly, Gyaman is divided into five provinces, the territories of which are discontinuous and cross-cut one another. But the actual royal domain, the largest of these provinces, has the form of a star the points of which enclose the disjointed parts of the other provinces.

Secondly, the sovereign of Gyaman is selected from within the royal matrilineage according to a rule of several degrees of alternation: the alternation between two maximal segments, known respectively as *Yakase* and *Zanzan*, and the alternation between local minimal segments within each of these two maximal segments. Every sovereign of Yakase origin must be succeeded by a sovereign of Zanzan origin. Succession rotates between the *Tangamuru* and *Adania* branches within the Yakase and between the *Herebo* and *Tabagne* branches within the Zanzan. During the course of the kingdom's history, one can see that only the first of these rules of alternation was strictly followed. In the sixteen royal successions since the Abron arrived in their present territory, i.e. from the end of the seventeenth century to the present time, there has only been one infraction of this rule: Kofi Fofie of the Zanzan segment, who died during a disastrous war against the Ano around 1820, was succeeded by Kwasi Yeboa of the same segment for reasons that we shall return to. At the second level of alternation, that of the minimal local segments, Tangamuru, Adania, Herebo and Tabagne, rotation is far more irregular, and what is taken as a rule is perhaps more a wish than an actual norm.

But the important point here is that this duality between the maximal segments of the royal matrilineage is apparent throughout the whole of the kingdom's political organisation. First of all, both maximal segments have their own *ahemma* or queen. At the level of the whole kingdom, the queen 'in office' is from the segment holding power at the time. When the sovereign dies she stands aside as her opposite number in the other segment takes her place. Furthermore, there is a division between the provinces on the basis of their loyalty to either the Yakase or the Zanzan segment.

The four provinces which together with the royal domain make up the Abron kingdom enjoy a considerable measure of autonomy. In the areas under their jurisdiction, the chiefs exercise most of the prerogatives exercised by the king in his domain. Of course their judicial decisions are liable to be appealed against before the king, but he almost always upholds their decisions. The political decisions of consequence, such as entering into war or concluding an alliance, must always be decided unanimously. Furthermore, province chiefs are excluded from succeeding to the throne. However, there is a network of close ties between these chiefs and the sovereign which can be summed up in the following outline:

– Ankobia province (Siengi) is governed by the agnatic descendants of various sovereigns from the Yakase segment. The *Ankobiahene* is regarded as the 'son' of the king. When a king from the Yakase segment is to be elected, the Ankobiahene and the Yakase *ahemma* choose the candidate whose name is placed before the entire segment and all the chiefs for ratification. Finally, at the enthronement ceremony, the Ankobiahene holds the left arm of the future king as the latter places his hand on the stool.[2]

– Fumasa province is governed by the agnatic descendants of the *Diabe* chief who joined the Abron migration. At the ceremony enthroning a sovereign from the Yakase segment, he holds the right arm of the future king.[3]

– Akyidom province is governed by the agnatic descendants of the *Gyamanhene* Kofi Sono and his brother Bini Yao, both members of the Zanzan segment. The *Akyidomhene* is also considered to be the king's 'son'. At the election and enthronement of a king of Zanzan origin, he plays a role exactly analogous to that of the *Ankobiahene* toward a king of Yakase origin.[4]

– Finally, Penango province is governed by the agnatic descendants of a *safohene* (captain, military commander in war time) of King Kofi Sono. At the enthronement of a sovereign of Zanzan origin, the *Penangohene* plays a role analogous to that of the *Fumasahene* at the enthronement of a sovereign of Yakase origin.[5]

Thus, for each of the two segments of the royal matrilineage, there are two provinces, one governed by a 'son', the other by a *safohene* of the rulers chosen from that segment.

Within each province, succession is governed by a rule of alternation between two (in the case of Ankobia, Fumasa and

Penango) or four (in Akyidom) local segments. Here again the rule is sufficiently flexible to give way to an actual election. The identity of the electors participating in the different provincial elections presents another indication of the same cleavage:

– When a new Ankobiahene is to be selected, the Yakase *ahemma,* the Ankobia *ahemma* (or rather the *ahemma* of the specific Ankobia local segment in question), the sovereign, if he is of Yakase origin, and the Fumasahene all participate in the selection.[6]

– When a new Fumasahene is selected, the Ankobiahene, the *ahemma* and those Fumasa segment elders whose turn it is, participate in choosing the successor. The Ankobiahene is the person who enthrones the final choice.[7]

– When a new Akyidomhene is to be selected, the Zanzan *ahemma*, the *ahemma* of the Akyidom segment in question, the sovereign, if he is of the Zanzan segment, and the Penangohene participate in the selection.[8]

– Finally, when a new Penangohene is selected, the Akyidomhene plays a role analogous to that of the Ankobiahene in the selection of a new Fumasahene.[9]

Thus, two subsets can be distinguished within the Abron totality: one formed by the Yakase segment, the provinces of Ankobia and Fumasa, the other made up of the Zanzan segment and the provinces of Akyidom and Penango. Within these subsets, the three constituent elements are united through specific and preferential ties, particularly apparent in the role played by the ruler of any one (of these three domains) in the selection and enthronement of the two others.

Nevertheless, two factors moderate this clear-cut cleavage. We have already mentioned one of these: the manner in which the territories of the different provinces cross-cut one another, preventing the transformation of either subset into an independent entity. The second factor is a result of marriage alliances between the segments of the royal matrilineage and the patrilineages of province chiefs. Princesses of royal blood can marry not only Fumasa and Penango chiefs, but also Ankobia and Akyidom chiefs, since cross-cousin marriage is permitted. Of course the children of these unions could theoretically succeed to both the royal throne and their father's position, but in such a situation the principle of incompatibility is strictly upheld by the Abron. Royal blood is crucial: only the son of a province chief and a princess (of royal blood) can claim the right to the highest office. Thus the distinction between the royal and provincial thrones is safeguarded. They cannot be occupied by the same individual either simultaneously or even successively. There were a number of kings – Kofi Sono, Kwaku Agyeman and Tan Date II among others – who were sons of province chiefs and one should not underestimate the importance of the 'personal' ties created in this way. For – and this is what interests us here – these ties extended beyond the boundaries separating the two subsets mentioned. To give but one example, King Tan Date II, who reigned from 1904 to 1922, was the son of Kusia Dubia, a Zanzan princess, and the fourteenth Ankobiahene, Apo Siakwan.[10]

The effects of the structure

A structure of this type has several aspects each entailing specific political consequences. First of all, a system of succession by rotation is established. The effects of this system have been extremely well analysed by Jack Goody.[11] In enlarging the foundation of the dynasty by giving each of its members the theoretical possibility of acceding to the throne, this system promoted the interest of many people in the kingdom's destiny, thus reinforcing its cohesion. Furthermore, through the operation of this system, conflicts over succession are localised and both their intensity and scope are limited. Once rotation becomes institutionalised, these conflicts break out, not *between* the segments among which the royal stool circulates, but *within* each of these. Indeed, at the time of any succession, only one of these segments can have a legitimate claim to supreme power. No doubt those segments which are excluded from succession on that occasion may enter the debate, siding with a particular pretender, but their own interests are not being challenged directly, since it is not their turn. In other words, the conflicts over succession do not set the elements constituting the dynasty against one another. Thus the gravity of threats to the unity of the kingdom is lessened.

However, there are other effects produced by the system of succession by rotation: in particular, its ability to counter effectively the arbitrary exercise of royal power. When a new ruler is enthroned, he vows to forget his own family's interests and grudges and to dedicate himself to the well-being and glory of the entire Abron people. The alternation between the Yakase and Zanzan segments no doubt contributes to his keeping his word. A ruler who abused his position for the benefit of his friends and relatives would be leaving them open to reprisals by his successor upon his death, since the latter is necessarily a member of the opposite segment. Generally, given the system of alternation, no sovereign can be sure that his projects or policies will be continued after his death: this situation discourages him from embarking on excessively 'personal' or original policies in comparison to those followed by his predecessors. Thus, the system of alternation contributes to continuity in State policy.

As for the permeation of the entire Abron political organisation by the duality characteristic of the royal matrilineage, we would suggest that it ensures respect for the system of alternation, thus serving to consolidate the benefits which the system accrues to the entire State. Indeed, owing to the extension of this duality, the maintenance of the system of alternation is no longer merely the business of the royal matrilineage; the whole kingdom has an interest in its continuity. If either of the segments, the Yakase or Zanzan, attempted to keep the throne beyond its turn, it would be opposed by members of the other segment and its provinces: in all, half the country.

Finally, within the two subsets, we have seen how each of the three parties concerned – the ruler and the two provincial chiefs – in some way owes his election to the intervention of both other members. None of them, therefore, can shelter behind the question 'Who made you king?'. This is one of the surest guarantees against despotism.

We shall not be able to discover these effects of the structure through an abstract analysis alone. Only by examining the kingdom's history shall we find empirical confirmation of these effects.

First of all, as we have already said, the 'law' of alternation has been followed faithfully; the only infraction in over two centuries has been mentioned, i.e. the replacement of Kofi Fofie by Kwasi Yeboa – another member of the Zanzan segment – which took place around 1820. How can this anomaly be explained? Fofie succeeded to the throne after the Ashanti defeat of the Abron on the banks of the river Tain in 1818 and after the death of Adingra. Against the advice of two of the four provincial chiefs and several high officials, he had no sooner taken office than he embarked on a war against the Ano which ended in another disaster during which he lost his life. According to the elders and the *cheneba*, Nana Atta Kwadio of Tabagne, his reign could have only lasted a year. Thus, the immediate return of the Yakase segment to the throne would have upset the equilibrium which the system of alternation was meant to insure. This is why his 'little brother', in fact his parallel cousin, Kwasi Yeboa, was chosen as his successor.[12] According to the Gyamanhene Kofi Yeboa, the only available heir in the Yakase line was too young to assume the throne at the time; he was referring to the future King Kwaku Agyeman, who was probably no more than ten years old at the time.[13] It would be wrong to dismiss this explanation off-hand: the Tain disaster had just occurred and one can imagine that the Yakase segment had sustained especially heavy losses. Its members would have been killed or captured as was the son of Adingra's sister (Ama Tamia), a boy called Kofi Adjei, who was taken to Kumasi and kept at the Asantehene's court for over fifteen years.[14] Finally it is very likely that when Fofie died, the Ashanti opposed the return to power of the segment, represented by Adingra, that had just risen against them. Their recent victory and the harshness of the war which it ended would explain this unusual case of Ashanti interference. In any event this was the version given to Tauxier by the Akyidomhene, Kwan Kosonu.[15] In fact, the three accounts just cited do not appear incompatible to us. The various alleged reasons could each simultaneously point about this infraction of the law of alternation is that it occurred at a decidedly exceptional point in the kingdom's history: it had just sustained two defeats – one immediately after the other – which rank among the most tragic episodes in its history.

Given the length of time between alternating rulers, quarrels over succession arise within the two segments, Yakase and Zanzan. For example, when Kwasi Yeboa died three candidates clashed: Kwadio Apia of Adania, Osei Yao and Kwaku Agyeman of Tangamuru. Their quarrel was resolved (in Kwaku Agyeman's favour) through negotiation and no trouble ensued.[16] Thus, Gyaman did not suffer from the sort of rivalry among pretenders which led to civil war on several occasions among the Ashanti. Only at the end of the nineteenth century would Gyaman be torn apart by crises provoked by the problems of succession; these problems arose not in connection with the royal stools, but over the Ankobia and Fumasa provincial stools. It would take too long to go into all these conflicts here; we can simply say that the first occurred when the previously observed rule was broken, and Kwaku Diawusi, who could have equally aspired to the throne, acceded to the Ankobia stool. The second crisis occurred when Yao Adjei, the legitimate heir to the Fumasa seat, was accused of shortening his predecessor's reign by means of poison. He was stripped of his rights despite the support of several high officials in the kingdom. In both these cases, however, conflicts of a purely political nature – due to the king's refusal to share in decision-making with the chiefs and due to his pro-European foreign policy – were added to and aggravated these succession crises.

Finally, there is no doubt as to the continuity of Abron policy in the area which we have been able to observe. For example, in the case of foreign policy before European interference had sown discord, the actions of Abo Miri (Yakase), Kofi Sono (Zanzan), Kwadio Adingra (Yakase) and Kwasi Yeboa (Zanzan) were inspired by the same principles: the struggle against Ashanti tutelage, hostility toward Buna and desire for an alliance with the Kong. E.A. Agyeman is struck by this continuity which he sees as occurring despite the alternation of segments.[17] In our view, alternation, far from being an obstacle to continuity should be seen rather as one of its principal causes. Similarly, we do not agree with Jack Goody when he presents the Yakase and Zanzan segments as two political factions taking opposing stands and periodically confronting each other.[18] There can be no doubt that the kingdom has been fraught with factional conflicts on several occasions. However, with the exception of the final years of Abron independence during which the successive Samouy, English and French interventions distorted the political picture, we do not believe that factional cleavages coincided with either the division between the Yakase and Zanzan or that between their related provinces. In 1879, King Kwaku Agyeman (Yakase) ran up against a coalition of his half-brother, Kofi Kokobu – both were sons of the eleventh Ankobiahene Kwasi Date – and the Akyidomhene Kwaku Kosonu, the famous Pampe, of the Zanzan segment.[19] In 1889, at the time of the Lethbridge mission's visit to Bondoukou, an incident occurred between Pampe and Major Ewart. The latter claimed the right to impose a fine on his adversary and the Abron were unsure of the proper procedure in this case. Freeman gives us the details:

> According to the report that reached us, Papi, Boitin and Kokobu were in favour of repudiating the fine and allowing us to exact it by force if we could; but the King and Edu Kudju thought it best to pay and avoid further unpleasantness.[20]

We can identify these individuals. We already know King Kwaku Agyeman and his brother Kokobu, who by then was the Ankobiahene, and the Akyidomhene, Pampe ('Papi'). 'Boitin' is the fifteenth Fumasahene Kwadio Buatini, of the Yakase segment. Finally, 'Edu Kudju' was the heir apparent to the throne, Adu Kwadio, of Zanzan origin, who was to die at the end of 1893 before acceding to the throne. Here again we find Yakase and Zanzan on both sides of the issue.

The advantages for the Abron kingdom presented by its form of political organisation are evident: the limits placed on the king's power to rule in an arbitrary fashion, the toning down of conflicts over succession, and political stability and continuity. One can also well understand why these, rather than other advantages were sought. The Gyaman state was established by conquest; it is inhabited by people of very different ethnic origin, language and culture amongst whom the invaders constitute only a small minority. It took them nearly a century (c.1690-c.1780) finally to eliminate the last pockets of resistence and pacify their territory. Thus, the Gyaman profited from none of the linguistic, social, cultural or religious factors uniting a State and its people found elsewhere, e.g. among the Ashanti. In Gyaman, the only guarantee of the unity and even the existence of the kingdom was, in the last resort, the cohesiveness of the conquering class. We have only to recall that the Abron, who fell under Ashanti domination in or around 1740, never abandoned the struggle to liberate themselves. Hence we can understand better the value they assigned to this cohesiveness, without which they had no hope of success against such powerful masters.

Genesis of the structure

We have rapidly outlined the political organisation of the Abron kingdom and then tried to describe its main effects. The problem now is to understand the precise implications of this description. In presenting these effects, have we also explained the organisation that produced them and at the same time have we explained the reasons for the development of this organisation? The available material on its genesis will enable us to answer this question to a certain extent, but, as we shall see, the answer is not a simple one.

The alternation between two 'families' holding the throne is one of the earliest and best known traits of the Abron political system. While it escaped the attention of Smith, Lonsdale, Treich-Laplène, Binger and Freeman, it was first noted by Braulot in 1893. From then on it was noted by most of the observers of the Abron Kingdom: Clozel, Villamur, Nebout, Benquey, Delafosse, Tauxier and, more recently, Ward and E.A. Agyeman. However, there are two opposing schools of thought on the date and circumstances of its introduction. One school believes that it was instituted upon the arrival of the Abron in the Bondoukou area. For example, Captain Benquey writes:

> The Abron tribe, of Ashanti origin, is not very homogeneous. It is divided into two distinct and rather hostile groups: the Zanzan and the Yakase. Each of these groups takes turns in providing the king. The date of this division cannot be fixed exactly, but it goes back several generations to when the Abron came to the territory. At that time, only one chief governed the tribe. But one of this chief's brothers, who wielded an enormous amount of influence because of his great wealth, gathered a number of supporters and their families to his side. As time went on, their number grew rapidly and he soon came to offset the king's authority, so much so that in the end his family came to take turns in providing the king. The Zanzan are the usurping group.[21]

Tauxier seems to be in agreement with this version and believes that the duality between the Yakase and the Zanzan dates from the settlement of the Abron in the territory they occupy today. This is also E.A. Agyeman's opinion. He states that 'The dynasties originate from the time of Brong rule in Gyaman'.[22] He explains the Abrons' adoption of this system in terms of their desire to avoid future arguments over succession such as those which had led to their leaving Akwamu and migrating to Gyaman. He relates a piece of Dwenem tradition according to which the founders of the two dynasties were:

> . . . cousins from the same stock in a matrilineal descent group who, in order to bring peace during the succession, agreed to share the stool alternatively between them.[23]

As we can see, the members of this first school are agreed upon two facts: the two 'families' are in fact two branches of a common original unit and the principle of alternation was adopted upon their arrival in the territory they occupy today. As for the reasons behind their adopting this principle, Benquey and Agyeman offer differing views. But in both cases they concern problems internal to the kingdom.

For Braulot, Clozel and Delafosse, on the other hand, the two families have completely different origins, even distinct ethnic origins. According to Braulot:

> In Gaman, supreme power (the stool) is rotated between two different families. The Ardjimani family (Yakase, E.T.) are originally from Siangui and bear a strong resemblance to the Pakhallas; the Adou Kouadio family (Zanzan, E.T.) on the other hand, is composed of racially pure Tons.[24]

According to Clozel and Villamur, the Yakase family descended from the Agni of Bona. According to Delafosse on the other hand, the Zanzan family was 'Agni by origin, but Abron by choice'. The rotation of power between the two families is seen as having been introduced after Abo Miri's defeat by Asantehene Opoku Ware in 1740 as a direct consequence of this defeat. Clozel writes:

> (Opoku Ware) had Abo killed and an Achanti named Kofi Sono Akpin put in his place as king of Bondoukou. Upon the death of the latter (c. 1770 or 1780) the Gaman, afraid of antagonising the Achanti by placing one of Abo's descendants on the throne, but not wanting another Achanti sovereign, chose a Bonda called Adingra as their king.[25]

Delafosse likewise has Kofi Sono as an Ashanti ruler who was imposed on the Abron by Opoku Ware and states that upon his death:

> The country's notables, afraid of antagonising the king of Kouman by elevating an heir of Abo to the stool and furthermore not wanting to be subject to an Assanti, chose as their king a notable named Agyumani, a member of a section of the Agni tribe of the Bonna, a section which was established in the Zanzan mountains, south of Bondoukou, where the kings' tombs are found. From this time on, Abron kings were chosen alternatively, although without absolute regularity, from the Yakase family of Abron origin and then from the so-called Zanzan family, Agni by origin but Abron by choice.[26]

Despite their differences on certain points, notably on the identity of Kofi Sono's successor, Delafosse and Clozel agree that the principle of alternation is related to Ashanti intervention. Ward takes up this hypothesis, formulating it in a different manner:

> Opuku Ware tried to weaken the power of Gyaman by killing Abo the Gyamanhene and placing on the stool a certain Kofi Sono from a rival family. No doubt he hoped that the Gyaman would waste their strength in civil war; but as a matter of fact, the Gyaman soon made an agreement to take their chiefs alternately from the two rival families, so that Opuku Ware's plan failed.[27]

How can this debate be settled? The assertion that the Yakase and the Zanzan constitute two completely distinct families can be set aside immediately. In fact, the statements of those concerned in either segment and their genealogies testify against this assertion. For the same reason, we can reject the thesis according to which King Kofi Sono is seen as an Ashanti – this is not to say, as we shall see, that the Ashanti played no part in his accession to the throne. It should be noted that these claims rely on the data gathered by Braulot on the eve of a period of confrontation between members of the two segments, and by Clozel and Villamur or Delafosse in the wake of this conflict. No doubt the data gathered are scarcely more than a reflection of this confrontation. In actual fact when the Abron arrived in the Bondoukou region, the royal matrilineage was an undivided unit. Some of its members had stayed behind and set up the Dormaa kingdom, but those who continued constituted a single unit. In the course of their journey, they were joined by the Asantehene's old servant Usua's men, who were to form the population of Fumasa, the first of the four great chiefdoms. This was the situation as it existed when the Abron settled in Gyaman territory.

How was this situation transformed into that described at the beginning of the article? First of all, let us remember that any matrilineage, by its very nature, is capable of dividing into several segments. Thus the problem here is not the origin of the two dynastic lines – this is something previously given in the lineage structure itself – but to know when the alternation between the two segments becomes a rule, a formally recognised institution. Now this transformation is not something which occurs over night; it is the result of a process within which several states can be delineated.

During the initial stage, the two segments separated physically. The Zanzan King Kofi Yeboa and the prince (*oheneba*) of Tabagne depict this separation in the following manner: when the Abron, having left Dwenem under the leadership of King Tan Date, arrived in Bondoukou, Akomi, the Nafana chief of Bondoukou and master of the surrounding region, granted them the site of the present-day village of Zanzan. He had no desire to have them living too close to him. From a chronological perspective then, Zanzan was the first Abron settlement in the region. King Tan Date ended his days and is buried there. But prior to his death, his uterine brother or his nephew, Adingra – the future Gyamanhene Adingra Panyin – had left Zanzan in search of gold. At one point in his prospecting, he set up camp on the site of what is today Yakase village, and decided to settle there with his relatives. When it came time for him to assume the throne, he refused to return to Zanzan and remained in Yakase, so that from that time onward the members of the royal matrilineage were divided between the two villages. One of the reasons for the royal family's dispersion could have been a precaution against all its members being killed or captured in a single battle if war broke out. In any case we find no reference to conflict for the origin of this division.[28]

Chief Kofi Kereme and the Adania chief Tan Kwaku, both of the Yakase segment, offer a somewhat different version. After leaving Dormaa, king Tan Date first settled in Yakase and then left Yakase making his way to Bondoukou.[29] After this, Adingra retraced his steps and settled with his dependents in Yakase. There is a rivalry between the two accounts: depending on the order in which the two villages of Zanzan and Yakase were established, one of the two segments could claim some priority over the other. I would tend to believe the Zanzan version as it best accounts for the choice of Zanzan for a royal cemetary which includes the tombs of Yakase kings as well. But what remains evident from these accounts is that the physical separation of these segments was an accomplished fact by the time of the death of King Tan Date: a section of the royal matrilineage stayed with Tan Date in Zanzan and remained there after his death; the other section followed Adingra to Yakase, and the two villages which gave their names to the two segments, as is the custom among the Abron, date from this time.

At the death of Tan Date, Adingra succeeded him and the seat of royal power was transferred to Yakase. According to the Adania chief Tan Kwaku, at Adingra's death a conflict over succession broke out between his nephews Bina Kombi and Abo Miri, who are presented as sons of Adingra's sisters, therefore matrilateral parallel cousins. The rule of alternation was adopted at this time to put an end to this quarrel.[30] In fact, Bina Kombi succeeded Adingra; at first he lived in Zanzan, but then he founded the village of Nasan where he ended his days. The stool was then given to Abo Miri, who settled initially in Yakase, but shortly afterwards founded the village of Asuefri where he lived until the war of 1740.

King Kofi Yeboa and the prince of Tabagne maintain a different version. When Adingra died, Bina Kombi succeeded him, and it was at this point that the principle of alternation was established under the following circumstances: Adingra's sister, Asumia, had two daughters; one of them, Anima, lived in Zanzan, the other, Kalia, lived in Yakase. Both of them had married and become pregnant at the same time. Anima was the first to give birth to a son; since the birth took place on a Friday, the child was given the forename Kofi. Anima immediately sent a man to Yakase to inform her sister. But her messenger was a hunter and whilst on his way to Yakase he happened upon an elephant and could not resist the temptation to follow it. The hunt lasted three days and the elephant was finally killed in a place which was later called Nasan, meaning 'three days' (*nna (e) san*). But the hunter had strayed a good distance from his path and only reached Yakase on the following Friday. On that very day Kalia gave birth to a son, whom she also named Kofi. The Yakase notables refused to consider the hunter's excuses and admit that Anima had given birth before Kalia. It was possible to predict that upon the deaths of Bina Kombi and Abo Miri and in the absence of an older heir, the conflicting claims to succession by the two princes would be insoluble. In order to avert such a conflict, the two groups agreed to adopt the principle of alternating succession: thus, Anima's son, Kofi Sono, would rule first and be succeeded by Kalia's son, Kofi Agyeman.[31] As it turned out, this situation occurred around 1740 when Abo committed suicide after a disastrous war against the Ashanti: Bini Yao, the heir apparent, had died prior to this time under circumstances which will be described later. Kofi Sono and Kofi Agyeman succeeded to the throne.

Let us emphasise a feature common to both versions: they both see the adoption of the principle of alternation as a measure to prevent a quarrel between two matrilateral parallel cousins, i.e. between two lines descendant from sisters. Furthermore, we should note that the two lines are not inherently incompatible; in fact in the genealogical tree of the Abron dynasty one finds that the lines of Bina Kombi (Panyin) and Abo Miri were sterile: they provided no other kings until colonisation. Whatever the causes of this sterility – we have no way of knowing in the case of Bina Komba's line, although we can guess at the reasons behind that of Abo Miri's line, as we shall see later – even if the principle of alternation had been adopted when Adingra died, this decision could not have settled the matter once and for all. It had to be reaffirmed at a later date for the benefit of other lines than those of Bina Kombi (Panyin) and Abo Miri. In fact, at least one episode in King Kofi Yeboa's account appears to be firmly established: that in which Anima and Kalia are depicted as the founders of the two lines between which the throne alternates. Chief Kofi Kereme of the Yakase branch[32] confirms this point as do our data on genealogies: all the kings who reigned from 1740 to the colonial conquest were descendants of one or the other line.

Also prior to the 1740 war, we find that a new element had appeared in the Abron political structure: the Ankobia (Siengi) stool It had been created by the Gyamanhene Adingra Panyin who entrusted it to his nephew, Tan Kokobo, King Tan Date's son.[33] It would later be occupied by the sons of King Adingra Panyin and King Kofi Agyeman (Yakase) and their patrilineal descendants. What prompted its creation? I believe that its origin is related to the initial phases of Abron expansion and the organisational and administrative problems which this expansion raised for the kingdom's rulers. Around 1720, during Tan Date's reign, the Abron coming from the east encountered other immigrants coming from the south: the Anyi from Bona. War broke out and ended in the Abron's favour. The Bona-Asuadie chief, Angwa Bile, was killed and the Bona became the vassals of the Abron.[34] In my opinion, Adingra Panyin created the stool of Ankobia to oversee these vassals. In fact, Tiedio, the capital of the new province, and the majority of its villages are located in the south of Gyaman. Furthermore, from that time on the Ankobiahene would 'lead the Bona in the name of the king'; he is the officially constituted intermediary between the Bona and the royal court. The Bona must go through him in order to address the king; moreover his tribunal is the court of appeal for judicial decisions handed down by Bona chiefs. Finally, he commands the Bona troops in times of war.

With the defeat of 1740, we find the final elements of the kingdom's political structure introduced with the enthronement and reign of Kofi Sono. First of all, as we have seen, Kofi Sono's enthronement marks the formal recognition and institutionalisation of the alternation between the Yakase and Zanzan segments. Furthermore, Kofi Sono created the stools and provinces of Penango and Akyidom. We do not know whether this was done simultaneously or successively and, if the latter, which was first established. Their creation occurred under the following circumstances:

(*a*) *Penango:* The Penango stool was created by King Kofi Sono and entrusted to his *safohene*, Adu Tile, as a reward for the latter's military achievements. Afterwards, the agnatic descendants of Adu Tile occupied this position.[35] In my opinion, the creation of this stool was in response to the same concerns which had led to the creation of the Ankobia seat 20 years earlier. Kofi Sono, who had taken his position as king following the 1740 disaster, tried to reconquer his kingdom seven years later in 1748-9. In the course of his military reconquest, he was able to recover not only all of Gyaman, but he also placed the Anyi of Bini and the Kulango of Nasian and Barabo under his authority. These new vassals were placed under the care and surveillance of the Penangohene, whose relationship to them was analogous to that between the Ankobiahene and the Bona.

(*b*) *Akyidom*: In order to explain the creation of the Akyidom stool we must go back to the origins of the 1740 war. First of all, we must remember that in the armies of the Akan kingdoms, the Kyidomhene led the rear guard and the reserves. Prior to 1740, the Abron army undoubtedly had a Kyidomhene, but we know neither who he was nor what became of him during the war; in any case, he was not a province chief. As for the events leading to the war, Nana Kobenan Gboko, *okyeame* of the king, gives the following account: An Ashanti and his son had come and settled in Kinkwa in search of gold. To have the Abron accept his presence, he presented himself as a chicken farmer. Every evening he would go out looking for termites to feed his chickens and would return with the gold he had found hidden in bits of the termite-hill. When found out, he was executed by order of the Gyamanhene Abo Miri. His son was sent to Kong to be sold as a captive. Shortly afterwards, another Ashanti arrived in Kong to buy captives and found the child. He then made his way to Gyaman and demanded an explanation from the Abron chiefs. Faced with their denials of guilt, he suggested that they should all swear to their innocence. Everyone, including the heir to the throne, Bini Yao, took the oath. The Ashanti was convinced and left for Kumasi, but en route he learned that Bini Yao had died, so he returned to Gyaman and declared: 'You have sworn an oath and now Bini Yao is dead, therefore you have lied and you were the ones who sold the child'. He returned to Kumasi and reported the whole affair to the Asantehene, who vowed to take vengence on the Abron: this was the origin of the war.[36]

Bini Yao knew that his false oath would cost him his life, but he sacrificed himself in order to spare his people from Ashanti reprisals. A few years later his younger brother Kofi Sono, who had succeeded him as Gyamanhene, wanted to pay homage to his memory and demonstrate his gratitude. He created therefore the seat of Akyidom and entrusted it to Bini Yao's eldest son, Kofi Ngetia. Thereafter the seat would be held by the younger sons of Bini Yao, the sons of Kofi Sono and by the agnatic descendants of both.[37]

Nevertheless, the province of Akyidom only took its final form during the reign of Kofi Sono's successor, Kofi Agyeman. Having conquered and killed the Kulango king of Wolobidi, Uludabia, Kofi Agyeman prepared to have his subjects massacred when Adu Yao Panvin, the third Akyidomhene, asked him to spare them and sell them to him for sixty measures of gold. Wolobidi and its neighbouring villages became part of Akyidom province and were to form its most important centre until the advent of colonialism.[38]

Was the structure derived from outside?

The main stages in the genesis of the Abron political system have been briefly outlined. A final point should be emphasised: in contrast to Delafosse and Ward, the oral traditions we have drawn upon say nothing about direct intervention by the Ashanti during the course of this genesis. To be sure, one has to make allowances for a kind of national chauvinism: the traditional historians tend to minimise the effects of the defeats suffered at the hands of the Ashanti on the political institutions and life of the kingdom. In this case, however, I would willingly give credit to the oral tradition. In the first place, as I have tried to show, alternation, at least the possibility of alternation, is inherent in the very structure of the matrilineage and in the principle of the lateral succession of uterine brothers. Thus, internal factors are sufficient to explain its introduction without having to look for an explanation in the assimilation of foreign elements. In any event, prior to 1740, the throne had begun circulating between the Yakase and the

Zanzan. Furthermore, the attribution of such a profound transformation of Abron institutions to Ashanti initiative is scarcely in line with what we know of Ashanti imperialism in 1740. At that time, it was still based on the principle of 'indirect rule': 'It was no part of the Ashantee policy . . . to alter the government of the conquered country'.[39]

Ashanti interference only became more direct and brutal during the 'Kwadwoan revolution' of the 1760s, described by Wilks. But even when this interference affected the autochthonous political system, it tended to introduce Ashanti-type institutions rather than make any original changes:

> It is in their relations with the provinces that Ashanti policy becomes crystallised. The category of provinces included the Akan states . . . These states were distinguished broadly . . . by the introduction there of the institutions by which the Ashanti had forged their own centralised state.[40]

No doubt the principle of alternation between several dynastic segments was found in the Ashanti state of Mampong, but according to Rattray 'All Ashanti at any rate appear to recognise some irregularity in the Mampon stool succession'.[41]

This, therefore, is a case of an institution decidedly foreign to the Ashanti political system, at least at the level of the confederation. In my opinion it would be difficult to argue that its introduction among the Abron was due to the Ashanti. This is not to say that the Ashanti played no part in this matter, but I would say that their influence worked at a different level. As we have seen, from 1740 until today there have been no kings from Abo Miri's line. Now the genealogies prove that this line had not died out. Therefore I would willingly go along with Delafosse in thinking that the exclusion of this line from the throne was the effect of Ashanti pressure. Furthermore, Ashanti and Abron oral tradition agree that Kofi Sono was only allowed to assume the throne with the consent of the Asantehene Opuku Ware, who presided personally over the ceremony.[42] In other words, Ashanti intervention focussed on individuals and did not affect the political system.

Thus, the original structure which we have described was not imposed on the Abron from the outside, nor was it borrowed from a neighbouring state. Contrary to Tauxier, Claude-Hélène Perrot believes that there never has been an alternation between two opposing lines inheriting the throne among the Ndenye.[43] In the Gonja system, described by Jack Goody,[44] there are undoubtedly a number of features analogous to its Abron counterpart. The principle of succession by rotation is applied in both cases. Furthermore, at the selection of a new king, the intervention of the Ankobiahene and the Kyidomhene, who are both related to the royal matrilineage and excluded from succession, is reminiscent of the rôle of chiefs of terminal divisions in the Gonja system. But there is no Abron equivalent of the Gonja system of 'gates': among the Gonja, the immediate heirs to the throne are the chiefs of the five main divisions of the kingdom, called 'gates'. They have acquired this position after having passed through a series of promotions within each division, and even before acceding to the throne they are powerful and respected chiefs. Nothing of the kind occurs in Gyaman. There, within each of the two dynastic lines there is an individual known as the *Abakomahene*, who is the ruling king's heir and who governs a few villages in the name of the latter. But the villages he governs are few in number – from six to eight – and do not constitute an autonomous unit; they are part of the royal domain. The Abakomahene is simply the sovereign's representative and possesses no more power than any royal *safohene*: 'He only boasts', as the Abron say. Finally, the Abakomahene's accession to the throne is in no way guaranteed: if he is a member of the same lineage as the king he must wait until the next turn of the lineage. In all cases, he must submit to a selection process in which other candidates may be preferred when none holds a special position within the royal matrilineage. In addition to the royal domain, the kingdom of Gyaman also includes four important divisions, but these are governed by individuals – 'sons' of the king or *safohene* – who are permanently excluded from succeeding to the throne. Given these considerable differences, it is highly improbable that the Gonja system could have served as a model for the Abron.

Event, structure and history

We have described a structure generated entirely within the kingdom over a period of approximately 60 years. Within its genesis, two distinct processes can be seen, corresponding to the appearance of the two main elements of the structure: the first led to the adoption of the principle of alternation; the second led to the creation of the chiefdoms and their distribution along the line of cleavage separating the two dynastic lineages.

Now, at least during the initial period, i.e. preceding the 1740 war, these two processes appear to be completely independent. The first concerned the 'internal affairs' of the kingdom; it occurred entirely within the royal matrilineage where a rule of alternation – aimed at preventing conflicts over succession – was introduced. On the other hand, the second process concerned 'foreign affairs' since it arose in response to problems raised by the growth of the kingdom. As we have seen, the chiefdom of Ankobia had been created in order to 'administer' the new Bona vassals. It was during the reign of Kofi Sono that these two previously completely separate sequences came together. While alternation became a fundamental law of the state, the chiefdoms created by Kofi Sono – who was of Zanzan origin – became attached to his lineage and were symmetrical to the pre-existing chiefdoms. Among the latter, Fumasa had existed even before the arrival of the Abron in Gyaman; Ankobia had been founded by a Yakase sovereign, but prior to 1740 neither of them had been 'branded' in terms of royal lineage affiliation. With the formation of the 'Zanzan' chiefdoms, the two pre-existing chiefdoms went to the Yakase side, becoming 'Yakase' chiefdoms.

If we now examine these two processes separately, we arrive at similar conclusions. We have seen that each of these processes was comprised of several stages. Within the process which produced the principle of alternation three stages can be distinguished: the physical separation of the Yakase and Zanzan lineages during the reigns of Tan Date and Adingra Panyin; the *de facto* alternation during the reigns of Bina Kombi Panyin and Abo Miri; and the transformation of this *de facto* alternation into an institution with the accession of Kofi Sono. Similarly, at least two stages in the process which produced the chiefdoms can be detected: the pre-1740 creation of the Ankobia seat, and the creation of the Penango and Akyidom seats after 1740. In both cases, the stages are largely independent of one another. Each is initiated under the stimulus of a cause specific to it. Each stage makes the following possible, but does not foreshadow or predetermine it.

Let us first of all consider the genesis of the system of alternation from this point of view. At the origin of the separation of the two lineages we have Adingra Panyin's gold prospecting and his refusal to return to the village from which his predecessor ruled. Following this incident, alternation appears, initially as an immediate solution to a specific problem. This problem must recur if it is to acquire the status of a general norm. As for chiefdoms, their appearance was initially related to the kingdom's successful conquests between 1700 and ca. 1770. Necessities of a different sort – notably internal in nature – could have played a rôle in their formation, particularly in the case of Akyidom and Penango, but the conquest of new territories (which we will come back to) remained the necessary precondition for the creation of a chiefdom. These conquests were the results of wars, each of which had a specific cause. Around 1720, the Abron and the Bona were in competition for control of the same territory, the conflict over sovereignty raised by this competition had to be settled. In 1748-9, Kofi Sono, on his return from Kong to Gyaman, conquered and subjugated the peoples he found along his path, some of whom had attempted to prevent his passage. Around 1760 or 1770, Kofi Agyeman took revenge on Uludabia, the Kulango king of Wolobidi who had taken advantage of the Abrons' defeat in 1740 to pillage their goods and reduce some of them to the state of captives. Thus it is evident that none of these wars was initiated with a view to establishing a new chiefdom. In each case, the creation of a new chiefdom was the effect, not the goal, of the war.

On the basis of these remarks we can draw an initial conclusion. There is no way in which the genesis of the kingdom's political structure can be regarded as the progressive realisation of a pre-established plan. Moreover, one would be hard pressed to identify the author of such a plan. What in fact occurred was quite different: events – such as a conflict or war – took place which elicited certain responses and produced certain effects. During the initial period, these effects, like the events which produced them, remained isolated and independent of one another. Then, at some time, they coalesced and became articulated with one another: it was then that the structure took shape. In other words, the processes generating the various elements of the structure are separate and autonomous. The structure is constituted by elements already there, already given, which have not been produced for the structure. To describe this development, one is tempted to draw upon Claude Lévi-Strauss's image of *bricolage* which he uses to illustrate the workings of the 'savage mind'. In his depiction of the *bricoleur*, Lévi-Strauss writes:

> His universe of instruments is closed and the rules of his game are always to make do with 'whatever is at hand', that is to say with a set of tools and materials which is always finite and is also heterogeneous because what it contains bears no relations to the current project, or indeed to any particular project, but is the contingent result of all the occasions there have been to renew or enrich the stock or to maintain it with the remains of previous constructions or destruction.[45]

Similarly, here the various processes in which the elements of the structure are formed are distinct from the process in which the structure is formed. The former necessarily preceded the latter, but beyond this 'topological' link there is no clear relationship between the two. Again, using Lévi-Strauss's expression, the structure makes do with whatever is at hand.

Let us say that we are agreed on this point. But if it can effectively be conceded that the formation of the elements of the structure is not carried out according to a plan, does not the formation of the structure itself – using the materials with which it has been provided – presuppose the intervention of an organising agent? In the Gyaman case, this role might have been played by King Kofi Sono. In my opinion, intervention of that type cannot be excluded, but was in no way necessary for the formation of the structure. It may be postulated and confirmed by the written or oral documents available; in any case it is not necessary. The building up of a structure is most frequently a case of *bricolage* without a *bricoleur*.

To return to the example of the Abron. It is the apparent perfection of the structure, its symmetrical regularity and its realisation of perfect equilibrium that lead us to seek the action of an organising agent in the origin of the kingdom's political system. And this impression of perfection finds confirmation in the fact that after 1740 the structure was not to be significantly modified, remaining unchanged until colonial conquest. There are certain indications that this completed form is itself undoubtedly the result of a kind of historical accident, and that the Abron did not regard their political organisation, as established during the reign of Kofi Sono, as a closed and intangible system. Thus King Bina Kombi Kuma (c. 1790) of the Zanzan lineage wanted to make his son Adu Kononie, chief of Merezõ, a province chief equal in standing to the four 'great ones'. His attempt failed, for in the absence of further expansion of the kingdom, he would have had to remove villages from the authority of existing chiefdoms to create a new province, and this step would have brought about unyielding opposition from the existing province chiefs. In the end Adu Kononie was given the command of a few villages in the royal domain, some of which were taken back from his successors. His rank was scarcely above that of the king's other *safohene*.[46] We are similarly told that King Kwasi Yeboa (c. 1820-c. 1850) did not give any villages to his son Kwadio Tawa, the first prince of Tabagne, because no war had broken out after the latter had reached governing age. Thus it was impossible to set up a new domain for him.[47] In other words, the cessation of the kingdom's territorial expansion was the factor which gave its political structure the characteristic of a finished product and which hindered any further development or modification. Following the period when the whole region between the Volta and the Comoe was under its control, around 1770, Gyaman could hardly have expanded further. It was bounded by the Ashanti Empire to the east and south; by Buna under Ashanti protection to the north; and by Kong to the west, with whom an alliance was necessary if they were to withstand their threat. At the same time, the Abron, enclosed by what had become unalterable frontiers, could no longer go on forming new chiefdoms, although such expansion was in no way inconceivable in their eyes and was certainly envisaged by some of Kofi Sono's successors.

All in all, the Abron example offers, in my opinion, an excellent illustration of this dialectic of event and structure in the movement of history. Certain events call for determinate responses – the adoption of a certain principle, the creation of a certain institution – on the part of a social group, a society or class. These are conscious responses: at first fragmentary and isolated, they later become organised into a structure owing to the mere fact that their coexistence in the same social field compels their collocation and their definition through their relationship to one another. This crystallisation of the structure can also be the product of a conscious act, but most often it is entirely or to a large extent unconscious and consequently its result – the structure – is equally unconscious. This structure will in turn determine not only the responses of the social group to future events, but more importantly, which facts will constitute events for it in the future. Depending on the social structure in question, a particular technical innovation will be a mere novelty in one period but constitute an upheaval in another; an invasion might simply have superficial effects in one case and cataclysmic results in another. This is how Mao Tse-Tung could write:

> The fundamental cause of the development of a thing is not external but internal.[48]

Given both the unconscious and determining nature of the structure, history is opaque to the men who make it. Too often we present our arguments as if a given society or class had a collective brain and behaved as a subject capable of setting out its objectives and working toward their realisation. In reality, even the classes who, given their place in the structure, are in a position to view the structure in its totality and are thus able to work for its total transformation, are producers of new unconscious structures, even when they are in the process of carrying out this transformation. These new structures, coming 'from behind' and hidden from their sight, will determine their subsequent evolution and trajectory. Thus, the idea of the transparency of history stems from either religious belief or ideological mystification: whatever their society or class of origin, political and social theoreticians and practitioners have always known the deceptiveness of history at some point, even though they have not always admitted it.

To confine my remarks to our discipline and its problems, I shall conclude with a comment on method. I have described above the effects produced by the political structure of the Abron kingdom: the localisation of conflicts over succession, the stabilisation of state policy, etc. There are real effects. We have seen that they were actually produced by the structure. To be exact, they are a translation of the structure's historical efficacy, its ability to shape and direct the course of events and the responses which they elicit. An analysis must locate and reveal these effects. On the other hand, they can in no way be used to explain the origin of the structure. These effects are consequences: they could only become causes if a subject capable of presenting them as the goals of his action existed. There is no such subject. This is the principal difficulty in functionalist types of explanation. When it claims not only to describe the effects of a structure but to account for its very existence, it necessarily presupposes the intelligent intervention of a mysterious demiurge who, as the case may be, will be called God, Society or History. Once these myths have been eliminated, we can begin to make our discipline a science.

(*Translated from the French by Anne Bailey*)

NOTES

1 Ellis, A.B. (1887), *The Tshi-speaking Peoples of the Gold Coast of West Africa*, London; Rattray, R.S. (1929), *Ashanti Law and Constitution*, Oxford; Busia, K.A. (1951), *The Position of the Chief in the Modern Political System of Ashanti*, Oxford, Wilks, Ivor (1967), 'Ashanti government', *in* Forde, D. and Kaberry, P. (eds.), *West African Kingdoms in the Nineteenth Century*, Oxford.

2 Tiedio: Nana Yao Agyeman, Ankobiahene, and elders, 17 January 1968; Kikereni: Nana Kobenã Gboko, 22 March 1967; Bini Kobenã; Nana Bini Kwadio, 13 April 1967.

3 Bondoukou: Nana Dua Kobena, Fumasahene, and elders, 5 May 1967.

4 Gumere: Nana Kofi Kosonu, Akyidomhene, and elders, 8 July 1967; Herebo: Nana Kofi Yeboa, Gyamanhene, and elders, 16 March 1967; Kikereni: *idem*, 22 March 1967; Bini Kobenã: *idem*, 13 April 1967; Welekei: Nana Kobenã Tah, Penangohene, and elders including Nana Papa Sian, 11 May 1967.

5 Welekei: *idem*, 11 May 1967.

6 Kikereni: *idem*, 22 March 1967; Tiedio: *idem*, 18 January 1968.

7 Kikereni: *idem*, 22 March 1967; Tiedio: *idem*, 9 August 1970.

8 Kikereni: *idem*, 22 March 1967; Welekei: *idem*, 11 May 1967; Gumere: *idem*, 10 July 1967.

9 Kikereni: *idem*, 22 March 1967; Welekei: *idem*, 11 May 1967.

10 Tabagne: Nana Ata Kwadio, *oheneba*, Nana Kwadio Dongo, *safohene*, 15 March 1968.

11 Goody, J. (1966), 'Introduction' and 'Circulating succession among the Gonja', *in* Goody, J. (ed.), *Succession to High Office*, Cambridge.

12 Tabagne: *idem*, 14 May 1968.

13 Bini Kobenã: *idem*, 12 April 1967.

14 Gumere: *idem*, 11 July 1967; Tangamuru: Nana Kofi Kereme, 21 January 1968; Claridge, Walton (1915), *A History of the Gold Coast and Ashanti*, London, II, p. 219; Fuller, Sir Francis (1921), *A Vanished Dynasty: Ashanti*, London, pp. 54 and 85.

15 Tauxier, Louis (1921), *Le Noir de Bondoukou*, Paris, p. 107 note.

16 Amanvi: Nana Kwame Yeboa, *safohene*, 10 August 1970; Ahuitieso: Prince Kobenã Nketia, 16 August 1970.

17 Agyeman, E.A. (1964), *Gyaman, Its Relation to Ashanti*, M.A. thesis, Legon, p. 16.

18 Goody, J. (1965), 'Introduction', *Ashanti and the North West*, Research Review, Institute of African Studies, Legon, Supplement, no. 1, pp. 30 and 33.

19 Ellis, A.B. (1883), *The Land of Fetish*, London, pp. 195-202.

20 Freeman, R.A. (1898), *Travels and Life in Ashanti and Gaman*, London, p. 305.

21 Benquey, in Clozel, F.J. and Villamur, Roger (1902), *Les Coutoumes indigènes de la Côte d'Ivoire*, Paris, p. 192.

22 Agyeman (1964), p. 15.

23 *ibid.*

24 Braulot's report on his mission of 1893; *Archives F.O.M. Côte d'Ivoire*, III, 3.

25 Clozel, in Clozel and Villamur (1902), p. 17.

26 Delafosse, Maurice (1904), *Vocabulaire comparatif de plus de soixante langues ou dialectes parlés à la Côte d'Ivoire*, Paris, p. 103.

27 Ward, W.E.F. (1948), *A History of the Gold Coast* (2nd ed. 1966), London, p. 142.

28 Herebo: *idem*, 16 March 1967; Bini Kobenã, *idem*, 12 April 1967; Tabagne: *idem*, 14 May 1968.

29 Tangamuru: *idem*, 21 January 1968; Adania: Nana Tan Kwaku, *Adaniahene*, and elders, 14 February 1968.

30 Adania: *idem*, 14 February 1968.

31 Herebo: *idem*, 15 March 1968; Tabagne: *idem*, 14 May 1968.

32 Tangamuru: *idem*, 21 January 1968.

33 Tiedio: *idem*, 17 January 1968.
34 Kikereni: *idem*, 21 March 1967; Tiedio: *idem*, 19 January 1968; Atuna: Nana Kwame Doh, *safohene*, 26 August 1970.
35 Bini Kobenã: *idem*, 12 April 1967; Welekei: *idem*, 11 May 1967; Herebo: *idem*, 16 March 1968; Tabagne: *idem*, 14 May 1968.
36 Kikereni: *idem*, 21 March 1967; Herebo: *idem*, 16 March 1968.
37 Gumere: *idem*, 8 July 1967; Herebo: *idem*, 16 March 1968.
38 Gumere: *idem*, 8 July 1967.
39 Cruickshank, Brodie (1853), *Eighteen Years on the Gold Coast of Africa*, London, I, p. 340.
40 Arhin, Kwame (1967), 'The structure of the greater Ashanti, 1700-1824', *Journal of African History*, VIII, 1, p. 78.
41 Rattray (1929), p. 235 note.
42 Kikereni: *idem*, 21 March 1967; Bini Kobenã: *idem*, 12 April 1967; Tauxier (1921), p. 91; G. Niangoran, 28 September 1973.
43 Personal communication.
44 Goody (1966), *op. cit.*
45 Lévi-Strauss, C. (1968), *The Savage Mind*, London, p. 17.
46 Herebo: *idem*, 17 March 1968; Siedia: Nana Kuru Kwam and elders, 15 August 1970.
47 Tabagne: *idem*, 17 May 1968.
48 Mao Tse-Tung (1968), *Essays on Philosophy*.

MAURICE BLOCH

The disconnection between power and rank as a process: an outline of the development of kingdoms in Central Madagascar

Introduction

The complex ranking systems of south Asia and Polynesia offer a special challenge and a special trap to the anthropologist or historian attempting to explain their development. He will inevitably trace the political and economic development of the state and link those to the appearance of new types of power groups and new structures of stratification. The trap lies in identifying and correlating directly the actors' concept of these groups, the distinctions and associations made in the emic system, with interest groups identified by analyses of the political or economic structures. This may be done consciously or by implication by translating actors' category terms by words such as 'nobility', 'ruling class', 'bourgeoisie'. This is likely to lead to gross ethnocentric assumptions and obscure the specific nature of the ethnographic example. The danger of such an approach has been explained well by Dumont and Pocock for the most complex and the most famous of such hierarchical systems. They point out how the Indian caste system does not fit either in structural form or in ideological content models borrowed from feudal or class systems. Indeed such comparisons obscure the essentially religious aspect of Hindu ideology contained in the scheme.[1] Similar criticisms would also be pertinent to the way the hierarchical systems of Central Madagascar have been analysed, and for very similar reasons.

If the trap offered by the study of such systems has been brilliantly identified by Pocock and Dumont, the challenge on the other hand has been refused. The study of caste produced by these writers, however illuminating it is of the Indian case in separating power and religion, and in pointing out that the latter cannot be reduced to the former, goes no further. However much the religious principle of purity is in practice reinterpreted in particular situations, it remains for them unaltered. Immaculately conceived in Indian theology, it has survived equally unsullied. There is, however, another legitimate and more ambitious way of handling such systems. It is the way suggested in part by Leach.[2] While Dumont sees the economic and political base as affected by the ideology of caste, the ideology itself is for them unaffected by the transformations in the base. By contrast with this approach, the case of central Madagascar will be examined here as a two-way relation where the economic base is not just being affected by the ideology but the ideology is being indirectly created by the base. Neither is reduced to the other since both transform themselves within their own logic, which because of their different nature is a different logic. The disconnection between rank or status and power is seen as a result of the evolution of states in central Madagascar, not as a reason to give ideology an existence and an origin of its own, or, in other words, to put it beyond explanation in material terms.

In order, however, not to fall into the reductionist trap outlined above, we shall proceed by identifying separately the two systems of power and rank within their own logic before attempting to reveal the dialectic which controls them.

The area under consideration in this paper is that inhabited by the Merina and Betsileo peoples of Madagascar. It is, therefore, an area inhabited today by over two million people and we are concerned with a time span of two centuries. During that period and in that area in spite of striking uniformities of culture a bewildering number of states existed and disappeared. As a result the historical study which follows must remain very general and tentative and for the sake of the argument much detail has been omitted. At the present state of our knowledge what is needed is an overall perspective and this is what is attempted here.

The history of power in central Madagascar in the eighteenth and nineteenth centuries

Our first task in understanding the evolution of states in central Madagascar is to carry out what might be called a class analysis of central Madagascar; an analysis of the domination of one group over another and the mechanisms by which the superior groups extracted a surplus from their inferiors. To do this we must gain an understanding both of this area and the nature of domination. At this stage I shall consider this history not in terms of the ideological categories of the Merina or the Betsileo but in terms of the process of social production and reproduction; only later shall I move to an examination of how such a history and such a historical system produce the concepts and the evaluations by which the actors organised their lives and reproduced their society.

There are two difficulties in the way for such a task. The first is the backward state of our knowledge of Merina and Betsileo history. This is not for lack of material, whether it be in the form of documents produced by outsiders, or oral history recorded from the early nineteenth century from Merina and Betsileo informants, or even for lack of an archaeological record which, although largely unanalysed, is abundant. This backwardness comes from the absence of historical work focussing on economic and social history. There is much about the origins of kingdoms and of royal families, there are analyses of genealogies, of battles, and of the succession of kingdoms and even more on the relations between the Merina and Betsileo on the one hand, and the European powers on the other, but there is little analysis of the nature of the economic and political control exercised at different stages. This paucity means that our analysis must be still largely tentative and not supported in the detailed way which only a modern historical approach would make possible. There is, however, one previous attempt at synthesis which renders the task much easier, this is the study of the geographical basis of Merina monarchy by H. Isnard.[3] This taken together with the complementary work of J.P. Raison[4] and J. Dez[5] gives us the framework for the following.

All these three works, however, in spite of their value, suffer from a defect which they have inherited from their sources whether Malagasy or European. This is the distorting effect of looking at the area only from a point of view centred on Tananarive and the Merina Kingdom as it developed in the nineteenth century.

One of the most extraordinary aspects of the history of Madagascar is the sudden growth, starting at the beginning of the nineteenth century or perhaps a littler earlier, of the development of a state (the future Merina state) from an area which had been little more than 10 km. in radius from a central capital to, by the end of the nineteenth century, a size practically equal to the whole of Madagascar (i.e. the size of France, Holland and Belgium put together). Any study of the history of Madagascar must consider how this happened. This does not mean, however, that right from its earliest beginnings there was something exceptional about this kingdom. Isnard rightly stresses as the basis of the development of the Merina kingdom the involvement of the royal administration in the agricultural and especially the hydraulic system of the peasantry, an involvement initiated by, among others, the great Merina king Andrianampoinimerina. This is admirably demonstrated but it was not a unique event. As we shall see there are many known instances of other rulers of other kingdoms doing precisely the same and developing a stronger state as a result. The archaeological record of other states and especially the siting of capitals and their movement[6] suggests the probability that this was an even commoner process. The subsequent expansion of the Merina kingdom in the nineteenth century under Radama seems to be due, as we shall see, to other factors than the hydraulic initiative of Andrianampoinimerina. This expansion has meant, however, that the other kingdoms swallowed up by the Merina kingdom have been largely forgotten. The oral histories gathered at the turn of the nineteenth century necessarily stress only the antecedents of the Merina kingdom and minimise its earlier defeated rivals operating another example of 'ascending anachronism'.[7] It is for this reason that we shall take as our focus at first, not the Merina kingdom, but the area in which the Merina kingdom as well as others existed, since the period which concerns us is largely pre-nineteenth century.

Isnard's study suggests the existence of two types of early Merina states, one in which the rulers were uninvolved in irrigation and agriculture, and the other where the rulers took on the task of organising some sectors of agriculture. This implied contrast will be retained here but it will be expanded to refer to classes of state rather than to a single example. The first type of state where the rulers take no part in agriculture will be called 'pre-take-off states' and the others, where the rulers do take part in agriculture, will be referred to as 'take-off states'.

Geographical and sociological bases

Before starting an examination of the nature of both take-off and pre-take-off states certain aspects of central Madagascar must be described.

Central Madagascar is a fairly clearly delineated geographical area normally referred to as the plateau area. It is in fact a mountainous area of a certain altitude which occupies almost a quarter of the total island. It is the traditional homeland of the people now referred to as the Merina and the Betsileo. Overall the land is characterised by the contrast between hills and mountains on the one hand, and the much less extensive lowland areas. The hilly land referred to as *tanety* is formed by tropical lateritic soil covered with thin grass which allows occasional cultivation and poor grazing. Much more important for the period under consideration is the richer land of the lowlands. This however is very restricted by contrast with the vast expanses of hillside. The lowlands are of two kinds: on the one hand, there are the valley bottoms which divide the hills and, on the other, there are marshlands. The valleys contain rich soils which are usually well watered for at least six months of the year by the streams and rivers which flow in them as well as by rainfall. The other type of lowlands are permanent marshlands. The lowlands are of crucial importance for the economy of central Madagascar because it is there that the staple of the inhabitants is grown: rice. Although rice was perhaps once grown in non-irrigated fields, for the whole period we are dealing with irrigation was the only significant way of obtaining this essential and central crop. The great importance of irrigated rice throughout the whole area does not, however, mean that in a fuller study the importance of other crops, other techniques, and regional variation could be ignored. The techniques of irrigated rice cultivation are different in the smaller valleys and the marshes and these will be considered in another section. The irrigation of the valleys presents few hydraulic problems. The rivers need to be diverted to the terraces and water-works need to be undertaken but the abundance of water means that no massive works such as are needed in more arid parts of the world are involved. Terracing is the main work required for this type of agriculture and was more elaborately developed in the Betsileo area than the Merina area. The basis of valley rice irrigation is therefore small areas where the land has been transformed and the water controlled, surrounded by large expanses of semi-barren hillside.

The second preliminary to understanding the nature of central Malagasy states is grasping another near constant element: the human groups associated with these irrigated rice valleys. This element consisted of discrete groups of cultivators living around one or several linked rice valleys. They would probably live in several small villages. These people would be both co-owners and cultivators of the valley and they would also form a descent group (*deme*).[8] These descent groups had and still have a strong sense of their permanance and their attachment to the rice valley. This is marked by the central symbol of the Merina: their tombs, which seals this attachment of people to land.[9] Their exclusivity was achieved by high inmarriage which insured the non-dispersal of their rights to land as well as their distinctness from other similar groups. These groups (*demes*) governed themselves for day to day matters in assemblies led by elders whose status was based on acknowledged wisdom and acknowledged age rather than any other overt form of power.[10] These acted in village assemblies as orators and were the agents of consensus decisions. These assemblies were, therefore, the descent group acting as a whole and no aspects of their political organisation could be described as bureaucratic. Two of the main concerns of these assemblies were the regulation of the irrigation system (the organising of communal work involved with this, especially the clearing of irrigation ditches of weeds and the maintenance of the channels) and the settlement of disputes within the *demes*. This organisation was sufficient to carry on the day-to-day affairs of the *deme* and indeed seems to have been sufficient for all aspects of political organisation when these *demes* were left alone by the military rulers, as was, for example, the case in the area north-east of Ambohitrolomahitsy for about fifty years. One of the results of endogamy meant that all their kinship ties bound every member of the *deme* to every other. There were no kinship ties between *demes* and so they formed small isolated units. This isolation was reinforced by the nature of the territory, in which valleys suitable for irrigated rice agriculture are separated from one another by large expanses of mountain and savannah land unsuitable for settlement. The reason why these *demes* can be considered as semi-permanent elements in

Merina and Betsileo history is that it is well attested in all our sources that these groups continue much beyond the duration of the wider political units which may incorporate them. They are affected by the wider political units, but they survive them, and – equally significant – the *deme* organisation can exist for long periods completely independently of any kingdom organising their own affairs and their agriculture.

Pre-take-off states

It is because of the self-sufficiency of the *demes* that it seems justified to talk of the simplest Merina and Betsileo states as forming a *double* type of society. On the one hand there are the *demes* forming a civil society and over them, forming a military society, there were the kingdoms. These kingdoms were very literally over the *deme* peasants since they really existed only at the top of mountains where the king and his followers encamped themselves behind elaborate fortifications.[11] The Merina word for this type of village and the word for mountain is the same, and there is hardly any mountain-top in cental Madagascar which does not show evidence of having been made into a fortified camp – the capital of a small kingdom. The only principle behind the siting of these royal villages seems to have been military and they therefore were as high up as possible so long as they could maintain a water supply which would enable them to resist sieges for any length of time. The rulers and the other members of the royal villages lived most of the time in virtual isolation from the villages. They obtained a living from the peasants by an informal kind of taxation requiring continual gifts from the peasants who considered themselves under their authority (especially regular gifts consisting of the rump of any animal killed in the area as well as other gifts of rice and product). These gifts were for the most part slightly disguised exactions obtained by what were really gangs of brigands terrorising a given area. At harvest time these 'rulers' descended and took their cut and withdrew again to their fortifications. The size of the area over which these rulers governed was indeterminate but on the whole they must have been small, little more than 15 km. from the mountain tops. Indeed the multiplicity of these kingdoms is quite extraordinary and it is only matched by their impermanence. Dubois, talking of this period for the Betsileo area, says 'the inhabited areas are divided by a collection of tiny kingdoms ruled over by people of a quarrelsome and unsteady disposition' (quoted by Edholm).[12] It seems that the kings and their followers usually originated from one of the *demes*, from what must have been something like a local gang. They then left the agricultural villages and set themselves up on any suitable mountain-top dominating several valleys. To do this, of course, created the emnity of other similar and longer established groups of rulers who would try to fight them off, but, if the new kingdom was successful, they would establish themselves until they were removed by other similar adventurers. The relationship between different kingdoms was therefore one of continual hostility and warfare – warfare over the right of 'protection' over peasants, who most of the time were left to their own devices to produce a sufficient amount for their own needs and a surplus which would be taken away from them by one or other of these rulers. It is clear that these kings in no way involved themselves with irrigated rice agriculture and left well alone, only interesting themselves closely with what was happening when the harvest was safely taken in and they could exact varying amounts. This type of state is best described as a pre-take-off state. In spite of their multiplicity vouched for by the archaeological record we have little detailed records of their organisation. This is because the oral histories collected deal almost exclusively with the large states and especially the Merina state. They are however mentioned in passing in all the traditions. A clearer picture of their organisation will only emerge with better archaeological fieldwork. In spite of this impermanence we know that much of the ideology of Merina and Betsileo states were present. The ranking of *demes* in these tiny impermanent units is recorded throughout the Tantaran'ny Andriano and the semi-divine character of their rulers is clear however impermanent and irregular their rule.[13]

Take-off states

The other type of state found in this area is a development of the pre-take-off states; it implies a stabilisation of it and above all a transformation in the relations of production. I shall call this type take-off states. The most famous example of a take-off state is the Merina state of Andrianampoinimerina and the politico-economic transformation implied in the passage from pre-take-off to take-off state is admirably outlined by Isnard[14] for this case. It is, however, important to stress again that this transformation is not unique to the Kingdom of Andrianampoinimerina. It took place in several other cases as, for example, of Alasora, Arivonimamo, Ambohitsakady, in the Merina area and best documented of all Lalangina in the Betsileo area in the eighteenth century.[15]

The passage from pre-take-off state to take-off state is based on the fact that the state becomes, to a certain extent, involved in the agricultural process. This occurs when a pre-take-off state is militarily successful against its rival long enough to establish it on a more secure base. Although take-off states are identified by the introduction of royal agriculture it does not mean as we would expect from the theses of Wittfogel or Steward that this new type of agriculture replaces the old. On the contrary the *demes* and their irrigated valley continue to operate largely independently although controlled and exploited more closely by the rulers. What appears is, side by side with the old agriculture, a new type of irrigated rice agriculture: marsh irrigation. As we saw, the plateau contains two sorts of land which can be used for irrigated rice agriculture. First of all, there are the valleys, which require terracing and irrigation channels, and these have always been under cultivation by the *demes*. They form the basis of the pre-take-off states. There are also marshlands, usually fairly extensive, which can also be used for irrigated rice. These potentially produce far more than is possible in the narrow valleys since all the marsh area can be transformed into a vast uninterrupted rice field. However, the transformation of marshes into rice-producing land requires much more important earthworks than is the case for the valleys. Basically, the marshes require the building of large dykes which divert the surplus water and thereby drain the marsh which can then be planted with rice. The geography of central Madagascar therefore opens the possibility for gearing up to a much more productive type of agriculture so long as a large labour force can be gathered to build drainage dykes. This is the possibility which was taken up at regular intervals by the few take-off states in the Merina and Betsileo areas. The pre-take-off states which were most stable and most successful after a while took the decision of changing their policy of living off an agricultural system with which they were unconcerned and instead began actually to take a hand in agriculture by building a large dyke and draining a marsh. Not only does the use of marsh lands mean the possibility of far more extensive rice fields, it also means the possibility of planting and harvesting at another time. This is the *vary aloha* (early rice) technique which gives a higher yield at the cost of high labour inputs. Raison sums up its advantages and disadvantages in the following way:

> Le *vary aloha* semble un médiocre pis-aller, une culture contre nature. Semés très serrés dès avril-mai, avant les grands froids, les plants restent au moins cinq mois en pépinière; un assèchement brutal les met en repos vegetatif: jaunis, âgés, ils semblent peu aptes à taller. L'irrigation des pépinières et des rizières contraignait à d'importants aménagements: grands réservoirs, canaux d'irrigation supposaient une belle maîtrise de l'hydraulique et un entretien régulier. Comme déjà le *vary sia*, le *vary aloha* imposait le repiquage, qui n'était pas encore une règle générale dans l'Imerina des années 1820, et qui doit s'étendre plus largement quand la crise de l'artisanat textile reduisit beaucoup de femmes au sous-emploi.
>
> Pourtant, cette culture n'était pas un simple pis-aller, couteux en travail, adopté faute de grands riz flottants qui supportent l'inondation. Ses rendements furent, jusqu'à date très récente, sensiblement supéreurs à ceux du riz de deuxième saison, parce que, le plus souvent, elle beneficiait, grâce à l'irrigation, d'un meilleur contrôle de l'eau. Le riz de première saison avait d'autres avantages aux yeux des Merina: ses éspèces donnaient des grains

> plus lourds, perdant moins au décortiquage, gonflant plus à la cuisson; récolte tôt, il se vendait a des prix élevés, et donnait un regain. En 1906, G. Carle estimait le rapport d'un hectare de *vary aloha* entre 300 et 380 francs, contre 150 à 375 francs pour le riz de deuxième saison, et notait que beaucoup de paysans du Betsimitatatra creusaient leurs rizières pour pouvoir cultiver du *vary aloha*.[16]

The main cause for the necessity for higher labour input for cultivation of *vary aloha* comes from the necessity of building immense dykes which partially drain the marshes by raising the level of the river bed. It is not surprising therefore that the traditional histories relating to take-off monarchs such as Andriamamelo at Alasora, Andrianampoinimerina at Tananarive and Andrianonindranarivo in Lalangina talk as much of their dyke building as of their military exploits.

The rice fields produced by the draining of marshes were administered completely differently from the *deme* territory. In large parts their product went directly to the king or if attributed to individuals they were heavily taxable both in kind and in labour.[17]

Three facts seem to be results of the involvement on the part of the state in marsh irrigation: (1) a change in the place and the nature of capitals (2) the development of a bureaucracy (3) a need for increased labour inputs. The change in the nature of the capital, as kingdoms pass from pre-take-off states to take-off states, is very simple. The capitals move away from their remote mountain tops to sites nearer the royal marshes. This move was operated, for example, by Andrianampoinimerina as he took his capital from Ambohimanga to Tananarive. At the same time as this change takes place the capital changes from an armed camp to a genuine capital designed to house the court, administrators, and the army. As the state controlled the irrigated marshes so it had to organise the work done on the dykes and this necessitated officers. The creation of officers to look after dykes is well attested in all cases of pre-take-off states.[18] The third result of marsh irrigation is, as noted by Raison, the sudden demand for labour. There were two ways whereby the rulers could obtain this, one was by an increase in corvée labour, the other was by importing slaves. In all the cases of take-off states of which we know, both solutions were used. The passage from pre-take-off state to take-off state meant for the subject a change from taxation in kind to principally taxation in labour (under Radama, Copalle notes, corvée meant four days of every week).[19] This solution, however, was clearly unpopular and therefore politically dangerous. Thus Dubois talking of Andrianonindranarivo of Lalangina, a typical take-off monarch, says: 'Il fit creuser des canaux, le peuple n'y vit d'abord qu'un acroissement des corvées, il murmura et le roi se vit contraints de se servir de ses esclaves'.[20] So the take-off state rapidly has to move to an expansionist stage in order to capture slaves.

In order to do this it needs an army. The feeding of the army can be in part supplied by the produce of the irrigated marshes and in part by the fact that military service becomes an alternative to corvée labour. Similarly, the labour dramatically taken out of the *deme* by the need for soldiers is also in part made up by slaves supplied by conquest.

The sequence of development of the take-off state can be represented as: Corvee Labour → Marsh Irrigation → Army → Slaves → (Marsh Irrigation and Valley Irrigation). At this stage, however, the sequence becomes a closed one feeding on itself and requiring continual expansion to reproduce itself.

Irrigation
↗ ↘
Slaves ← Soldiers

Two features follow from this. The direct exploitation of ruled by rulers of the pre-take-off state is replaced by an indirect exploitation in that the ruled are no longer suppliers of goods or labour for the rulers but become principally suppliers of slaves to work for the rulers. Secondly, the system to survive requires in the take-off state the ability on the part of the ruler to conquer his neighbours ever faster. This requirement was the cause of the break up of all central Madagascar take-off states, except for one, leading both to their political disappearance and the abandonment of their always fragile marsh irrigation and dykes.[21] The traditional histories of these states usually give as the reason for the collapse of the take-off states domestic succession disputes. The rules of succession of the states were totally unclear and legitimacy was established normally *post hoc facto*.[22] When a ruler, through success over his rivals, had established himself as a successor, he would then invent a rule of succession which explained and justified his position. However, very frequently no single successor managed to establish himself and the warring factions divided the kingdom, usually allowing the big drainage dykes to decay, and each kingdom would soon revert to a pre-take-off state, and the capital would be rebuilt on a fortified hill top. The other reason for failure has already been mentioned. The take-off states seem to have required continual expansion in order to maintain the supremacy of the ruler inside his own realm. However, until the beginning of the nineteenth century none of these kingdoms possessed a decisively superior military technology over any other; the expanding kingdom would therefore most likely be checked sooner or later, especially since its rapid expansion united its neighbours against it. With the kind of system described above, the fact that the kingdom was checked seems to have been sufficient to destroy it, since the necessary supply of slaves stopped coming in and the internal disputes became all the more intense as no one group controlled the army.

The Merina state

The one exception in the sequence of events which led to the ultimate collapse of take-off states is, of course, the Merina Kingdom of Andrianampoinimerina. The reason for this exception can, however, be understood in terms of the internal logic of all pre-take-off states as outlined above.

The history of the kingdom of Andrianampoinimerina seems to have followed exactly the normal pattern for take-off states. Having established a really powerful pre-take-off state at Ambohimanga he moved the capital to Tananarive (the present-day capital of Madagascar), a site already used by other take-off states, on the edge of the Betsimitatra marsh and began massive drainage works which have been well described and analysed in the literature.[23] From the rice land thus obtained he fed a large army and began a relatively successful campaign against his neighbours whose lands he absorbed. This was continued by his son Radama.[24] However, unlike other rulers of take-off states Radama was not checked in his expansion and was able to keep off rivals to the throne. The reason for this is to be found in a development which was taking place outside Madagascar itself. The beginning of the eighteenth century saw a sudden increase in interest in Madagascar on the part of various European governments, especially the French who had held footholds on the island since the seventeenth century, and from the British from their base in Mauritius. Before that time the main contacts with the outside world were on the west and northern coast of Madagascar and were very largely in the lands of Sakalava rulers. From these contact they obtained guns of varying manufacture.[25] As a result, they then dominated the island, and at various points obtained tribute from the central Malagasy states. Right up to the period of Andrianampoinimerina tribute was sent to the Sakalava.[26] The people of central Madagascar by contrast only obtained a trickle of firearms from the time of Andriamjaka from the European pirates of the east coast[27] and perhaps from the extraordinary adventurer Count Benyoski.[28]

The Europeans, on the other hand, were able to offer rifles, and as they began to trade and interfere on the east coast, European weapons – rifles and cannons – became available in very limited supply and infiltrated towards the centre. The Europeans in return for this seem to have obtained slaves and the hope of trading rights. The combination of the availability of efficient weapons and the fact that the time when they were beginning to circulate the Merina kingdoms was in its expansionist take-off stage, meant that trade in weapons, like other trade, was inevitably channelled towards Tananarive. Its king was able, therefore, to obtain a fair number of these. Ellis writes in the first part of the nineteenth century:

During the reign of Impoina (Andrianampoinimerina), Imerina

> and the interior of the country generally became an extensive market for slaves. These consisted principally of the prisoners taken in war, who were exchanged to the slave-dealers for arms and ammunition, by which farther conquests might be made, and additional supplies for the slave-market procured. The exportations were principally to Bourbon and the Isle of France. Amongst the largest slave-dealers at that time visiting Tannanarive were Jean René and Fisatra.[29]

The sequence Marsh Irrigation → Army → Slaves of any take-off state therefore became complicated in the case of the kingdom of Andrianampoirimerina and Radama to:

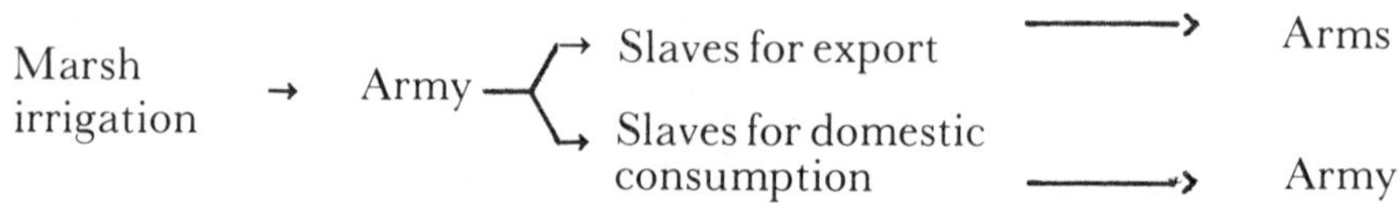

Later still, when the British missionaries convinced Radama for short periods to abolish the slave trade, Radama insisted that this would be done only on condition that he was indemnified with arms and ammunition, the original purpose of the slave trade anyway.[30]

It is interesting to note what are the accidental aspects of the growth of the Merina kingdom as well as what general principles are involved. The fact that the Merina state had reached take-off point was in no way exceptional and was one of the possibilities in the overall system of production of central Madagascar, a possibility which had been taken up again and again. The fact that the Merina state during its expansion period canalised trade and weapons towards itself is also a general feature which one could have expected on general principles. What is accidental is that it should have been this particular Merina kingdom which was in its expansion phase at the very moment when European weapons were available. The Merina therefore were available to arm their army with more efficient weapons than were available to their enemies and indeed to make use of other European techniques which became available to them as Europeans trying to gain influence in central Madagascar and vied with each other in giving technological assistance to the nascent kingdom.[31] This meant two things. First, the process of territorial expansion was neither reversed nor checked and so the Merina were able to continue and indeed accelerate the rate of conquest, thereby producing more slaves, freeing more Merina to become soldiers, producing more conquests, more slaves, and so on. Second, it meant that dynastic struggles no longer meant the end of the kingdom, as the Merina state could not be replaced by others since they did not have the weapons to defeat the Merina even in times of weakness. Rather the struggles became internal between different factions in the Merina state trying to seize control of its inner mechanisms. This process is what explains the amazing growth of the Merina Kingdom between 1810 and 1890 when it expanded from a tiny area to the whole of Madagascar. It is also worth noticing that this meant the inevitable mortgaging of Merina power for future dependence on outside colonial powers.

The actors' representation of rank and of the state

The analysis of the evolutionary process which has been outlined in the previous section has been carried out within terms defined externally to the concepts of the Merina and Betsileo. The next step required is to see which notions held by the actors correspond to our analytical concepts; in other words to find out if Malagasy words can suitably translate our terms 'rulers' and 'ruled'. Thus, we find that historians and anthropologists have translated words such as *Andriana* for the Merina as 'noble' or 'aristocrat' or 'rulers' and have tried to trace the history of such groups to understand the development of domination in Central Madagascar. The passage from an observer perspective to an actors' perspective has, in these cases, been made by an unexamined linguistic equation. This procedure is common enough in the work of such writers as Wittfogel, Seward, or Linton.[32] They have tried to interpret the social characteristics of hydraulic civilisation in ways which although different, are of similar kind to the analysis in the previous section, but they have then gone on, mistakenly to my mind, to take the next step of identifying their analytical categories with recognised social categories present in the social discourse of those people whose societies they had studied. Certain attempts at understanding the political significance of the economic base in Madagascar seem to have equally shared its failing.[33] By contrast in this section it will be shown that the representation by the actors of social hierarchy corresponds neither in form nor in nature with the way we have analysed it so far.

Two features in particular stand out. While, in the history given above, the discontinuity in class interests between a small group of rulers and the large body of the population is clear, we find that rank is represented in the categorical system of the actors as a regularly graded hierarchy evaluating a multitude of small groups in a fastidiously minute order of precedence. Secondly, while the unstability and brutal history of replacement of power holders, whether between kingdoms or within kingdoms, is obvious to any historian of Central Madagascar[34] we find that by contrast in Malagasy ideology power is *represented* an an unchanging essence closely linked to nature and only transmitted to legitimate holders.

Rank

As we have seen, Merina or Betsileo kingdoms are made up of several *demes*, some members of one of which form the ruling class in the pre-take-off and take-off states.[35] This is where the division in terms of power exists; between some members of a *deme* and the rest, consisting of other members of their *deme* together with the members of all other *demes*. The representation of differential rank between *deme* works, however, on a totally different principle. First all members of a *deme* irrespective of their political power have the same rank. Secondly, all the *demes* are in a ranking hierarchy with no very sharp difference between them except their precedence in a graduated scale of hierarchic positions. The *deme* from which the rulers come is likely to be at or near the top but the various other *demes* whose members in class terms are all equal are represented as unequal with differential rank in a continuous scale. This means that all the *demes* are either higher or lower one to another. The representation of society is permeated by a principle of hierarchy which is formally very much like the Indian caste system. Another similarity with the caste system is that although the ranking forms a gradual hierarchy there are certain steps in the ladder which are particularly stressed. There are several, but the main ones are in the Merina case that between the higher group of demes which are called *andriana* and those which are called *hova*. About the top half of *demes* in the kingdom of Andrianampoinimerina fell in the *andriana* category, although, as one might expect, where exactly the dividing line fell was a matter of disagreement,[36] and it was not fully accepted which *demes* belonged to which side of the division. Nonetheless this division between *andriana* and *hova* was the stressed division in the hierarchy. In terms of power, however, this stressed division is totally irrelevant. The proportions of *andriana* to non-*andriana* for the Merina shows how completely misleading it would be to assume that this division corresponds to a distinction between ruled and rulers; there are far too many *andrianas* for them to represent a ruling class and we know well that they did not. The ruling group in all these kingdoms is tiny yet the rank of *andriana* for the Merina extends to the total free population of wide areas of the kingdom.[37] In all cases several whole *demes* belong to the higher category. The division, therefore, in no way corresponds to a real political division. The real political division is between a few people in the higher category and the great majority of the others in that higher category together with those in the lower categories. This problem of non-correspondence between two systems has caused much difficulty for European historians and anthropologists who have translated the word *andriana* as 'noble' and tried to attribute political functions to the people so designated. This has proved as totally misleading to them as this misrepresentation of power is misleading to the actors. Other steps in the ladder both within the *andriana* group and within the *hova* group also existed and were variously stressed in varying circumstances. None corresponded in any way with the division of ruler and ruled. The hierarchy is well documented although often with significant inconsistencies in such works as the *Tantara'ny Andriana*.[38] The Betsileo hierarchies are equally complex and varied although there the stressed divisions are between the higher groups called rather confusingly *hova* and the lower group called *olompotsy*. There again this distinction is only one such in a ranked hierarchy of much greater complexity[39] and there again the hierarchy does not correspond to political or economic divisions. Kottak writing on the Betsileo in 1970 states: 'suffice it to say that in terms of access to strategic resources and to real power there is not now, nor does it appear likely that there has ever been a significant contrast between senior commoners (*olompotsy*) and nobles (*hova*)'.[40] We can therefore represent the difference between the power or class situation and the representation of rank in terms of hierarchy as in Fig. 1.

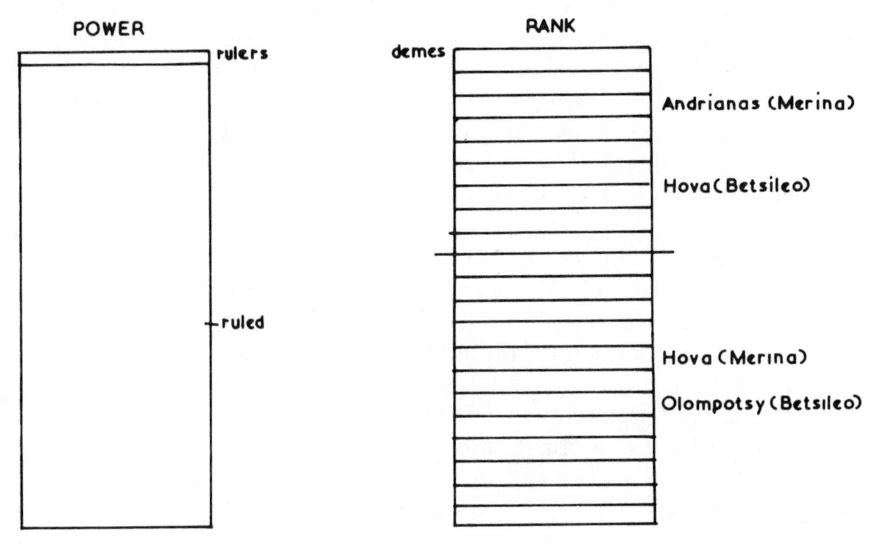

Figure 1

There is yet a further way in which the rank representation hides the power representation, and again one which is reminiscent of the caste system. As was noted the actual power holders normally only form a part of one *deme* (sometimes of several). Yet the rank they have is shared by all their kinsmen within their *deme*. In other words the existence of the rulers is merged with that of a wide group in which they, so to speak, hide. The very vocabulary itself reflects this ambiguity in that the word *andriana* is not only a word which describes several *demes* but also is a word for ruler. Similarly, the Betsileo word *hova* means both the ruler, the ruling clique and a large section of the population. This makes historical texts and traditions extremely difficult to interpret[41] since it is not clear whether the ruler or the wider category of people is being referred to. This difficulty is of more than historiographical significance; its means that in Betsileo or Merina discourse this ambiguity was always present. The interest of the *andriana* in the Merina case (*hova* in the Betsileo case) as ruler were inextricably confused with those of almost half the population. The possibility of class consciousness of the ruled would be reduced as terminologically a high proportion of them would be identified with the rulers. This confusion, however, goes beyond a simple terminological association, but implied also the belief in a shared essence and shared privileges of an illusory kind. To understand this, however, we must turn to the believed content of the hierarchical rank system of the Merina and the Betsileo.

Hasina

If we can see that the differences in ranks of *demes*, and the distinctions between *andrianas* and *hovas* or between *hovas* and *olompotsy*, are not based on observable control of resources or people, it is not surprising to find that what the higher *demes* and rulers are believed to have more of, is an intangible and mystical essence like the 'purity' of the higher castes in the Hindu system.

Underlying both the notion of hierarchy and rank, as well as the notion of continuity and of the 'natural' quality of power, is the concept of *hasina*. The best discussions of this for the Merina are to be found in the work of A. Delivré,[42] and for the Betsileo in the unpublished thesis by F. Edholm already referred to. The word has proved to be one of the most difficult to translate from Malagasy. The first translation of *hasina* and of its adjectival form *masina* was 'holy'; thus the earlier missionaries translated 'Holy Spirit' by *fanahy* (spirit) *masina*. All notions of spirituality, of superiority as of essence, are describable as *masina*. However, the word also has a political aspect where it means legitimate or traditional authority. Thus, the hero kings of Madagascar are thought to be the epitomy of the quality of *hasina*. The sites of their tombs and of their capitals are themselves *masina*. In this sense the word means power, vigour, fertility, efficacy or even sainthood. It is the essence of royalty and the essence of superiority of one person over another through 'virtue' in the old sense. It is closely associated with the notion of power and virility, *mahery*, which is in fact the fetishised virility created by the circumcision ceremony and which is associated with descent and repetition of life channelled through the tombs.[43]

Hasina is linked with the mystical power of nature especially the power of reproduction, both in its human aspect and its aspect in relation to crops. In its human aspect the possession of *hasina* by the rulers and the *demes* is what ensures the passing on of life from generation to generation and the transcendence of death which can be seen as the kernel of Malagasy thought.[44] In its agricultural aspect it is the presence of *hasina* which ensures fertility and climate; thus we see that those with *hasina* are able to bless crops in times of drought.[45] The same can be said of the Betsileo notion of *hasina*. Dubois defines it as a 'vertue inhérente à un être' and Edholm goes on to say that it is 'given at birth – not acquired by political leadership. *Hasina* is quite widely possessed, although carefully maintained within the same group as a result of stringent rules of exogamy . . .'.[46] Dubois says that a man possessing *hasina* had a 'nature supérieure et une authorité sacrée'.[47] Here again, therefore, *hasina* is inherent to certain people and its presence assures fertility. The pre-eminence of the ruler comes from his supreme possession of *hasina*: 'He stands for the permanence and rightness of justice and authority and spiritual superiority.'[48] *Hasina* is a supra-human quality and therefore although contained by certain demes in differing degrees it is not the result of their achievement but is given in their nature. The concern of the *hasina* holders should be to preserve it; creating *hasina* is out of the question. The concern of those who hold less or no *hasina* should be to preserve it in those who have it because they too benefit from it.

Thus the authority of the ruler is seen as a manifestation of something which has always existed, which is given in nature by the order of the world. The ideological picture could not be further removed from the short-lived, brutishly extortionate reality of traditional Merina and Betsileo power. This sort of notion is found associated with traditional authority in many parts of the world.[49] We find the same concepts again and again: thus Southall referring to *Ker* among the Alur sees this notion as denoting power, beneficial domination and, in Balandier's words, an 'organising and fertilising force'.[50] Balandier, following Mauss, also points out another essential aspect of such concepts which is particularly relevant here: how the concepts of innate authority transcend and are a way of vanquishing the instability of real power. These concepts can, therefore, become agents of transformation in a conceptual alchemy where the achieved and therefore unstable turns into the permanent and therefore cosmic.[57]

J. Pitt-Rivers goes further in associating such concepts especially in bringing together the notion of *mana*, which in its political manifestation for the Maori is similar to that of *hasina* for the Merina and Betsileo,[52] and the European concept of honour; in doing so he shows up the essential and necessary ambiguity of such notions. On the one hand honour and authority is unchallenged, given and religious, on the other, it is dependent on the actions of others since they must show their acceptance of the superiors' honour or *mana*. Thus the abstract word honour is dependent on the verb 'to honour' – the actions of inferiors.[53] In the same way we find that there is another side to the word *hasina* than the one of innate religious superiority with which we have been concerned so far. This side of *hasina* turns out not to be a *state* of superiors but an *action* of inferiors. For the sake of clarity I shall call that part of the semantic field which corresponds to the former idea *hasina* mark I, while that part of the semantic field which corresponds to the latter *hasina* mark II.

Hasina mark II manifests itself in the rendering of homage by somebody with lesser *hasina*. He gives *hasina* to the superior in the same way as the inferior renders honour to the honourable. This recognition on the part of somebody with lesser rank takes the form of the giving of gifts of respect and honour of a special kind, the use of certain greetings and the giving of precedence at such times as formal assemblies. Of particular relevance is the fact that the most significant gift which marks differential rank is the gift of an uncut silver coin; the coin is itself called *hasina*.[54] This coin is the Maria-Theresa Thaler which was in circulation throughout Madagascar for the period during which we are concerned. Its symbolical significance comes in part from the fact that it was '*tsy vaky*', unbroken, while most thalers in circulation were cut to obtain smaller denomination. The coin therefore was the suitable gift to give to a superior to recognise his authority. At the important state rituals the differences in rank were marked by the giving of *hasina* mark II by subjects of differing *demes* to the ruler and by inferiors to superiors of any kind right down to fathers and sons.[55]

The apparent contradiction between *hasina* in its mark I aspects and its mark II aspects is, however, not clear to the actors working within their own cultural system and mystified by its representation of power. To the analyst of the system the contradiction turns out to be of crucial significance for linking up the system of power described in the earlier section and the system of rank described in this one. What the ambiguity of the term *hasina* produces is the possibility of the representation of *hasina* as an innate quality possessed by superiors, which is a benefit and a blessing, to inferiors, while in fact this illusion is created by an act which is its opposite; the giving of a benefit, *hasina* mark II, by the inferior to the superior. *Hasina* mark II is thus doubly the opposite of *hasina* mark I; while the latter is natural the former is supernatural, while the latter flows downwards, the former flows upwards. The difference can be represented in the following diagram which shows a ranked hierarchy of *demes* in the light of *hasina* mark I and mark II. In the light of the former *hasina* is an essence which flows in the form of fertility from the superior to the inferiors; in the light of the second *hasina* is gifts going the other way (Fig. 2).

Thus, by the ambiguity of the term *hasina*, the supernatural gift of the superiors turns out to rest, as we know it must (hence the generality of this ambiguity) on the natural act of the inferior who instead of receiving the blessing of *hasina* creates it. Indeed, this reversal is still to be seen in family relations among the Merina and Betsileo to this day in the institution of the *tsodrano*.[56] This word means the blowing of water and it is performed by elders for their juniors as a kind of blessing for fertility and success. The elder stands those he wants to bless in front of him and sprays them with water from a saucer he holds before his lips. Here we have the notion of *hasina* mark I transferring a blessing of fertility on the juniors because of the power of the holiness of the elders. However, in order that the elder may be able

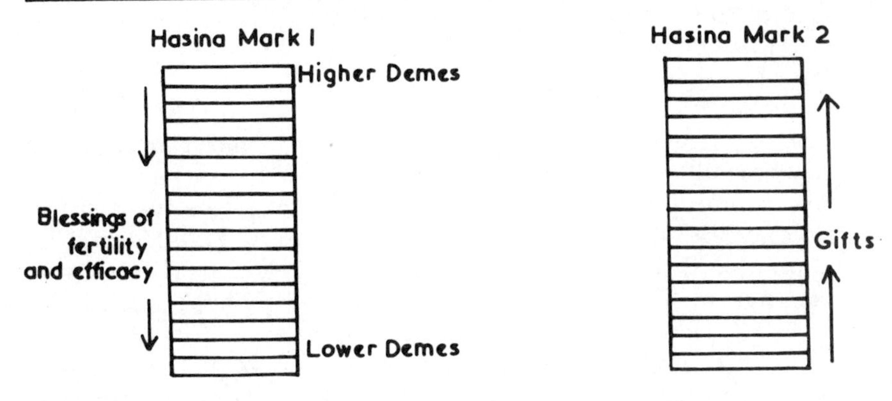

Figure 2

to do this he must be given coins, preferably the same coins as those used in the royal *hasina* giving. The coin is placed in the water that is sprayed on those receiving the blessing, but it is pocketed by the elder as is the case for *hasina* mark II.

When hasina is manifest

So far I have stressed the disconnection between power and rank and how a turbulent state based on unscrupulous exploitation by a small minority of rulers of a large majority of ruled is misrepresented as an orderly harmonious system of fine gradation of rank which contains no sharp social breaks. We have seen how the representation of differential rank is seen in terms of a supernaturally given essence held in greater degree by those with high rank but which benefits all, an essence which not only comes from beyond men but has effect beyond men, since it accords with and stimulates the natural processes of reproduction. This cultural mystification is, however, more than just a veil over the eyes of the actors; by hiding the reality of exploitation and transforming it into an ideology which stresses the beneficent effect of the presence of the ruler it serves to preserve the power of the rule, to facilitate its acceptance and thereby to maintain it. By drawing the line between rulers and ruled in the way that is done by the ranking system, the possibility of class consciousness on the part of the ruled is made much less likely and so here too the ideology preserves and indeed is an essential element of exploitation. The non-correspondence we have noted is, therefore, more than an ethnographic or a historical puzzle: it is one of the innermost mechanisms of the reproduction of the political system. This view of ideology is of course familiar in the social sciences through the insight of Marx as well as several preceding and subsequent writers. Most recently one of its most elegant formulations has come in M. Godelier's analysis of the Inca state where he shows how the transfer of surplus from inferior classes to superior classes is represented as a small return for the divine gift of fertility from the gods mediated by the Inca Shinti and his collaborators.[57]

If our task could be limited simply to demonstrating the function of ideology as a mechanism for the reproduction of social formations, this paper could end here. However, the perspective of social evolution of this volume pushes us to a further question. If the ideology of Merina and Betsileo states obscures reality so as to reproduce it, the question of how this representation can have come about becomes of prime interest. The simplest answer, and one perhaps implied in Godelier's article, is that the false representation is a device on the part of the ruling class to maintain that which is plainly to their advantage. This, however, conjures up a totally unreal situation and is incompatible with the fact that all the evidence suggests that rulers were as mystified as ruled.[58] The anthropologists must therefore do more and produce theories which account for the rise of ideologies maintaining certain social systems, without falling into the trap of thinking that these ideologies are either, on the one hand, actual reflections of reality, or on the other, conscious Machiavellian devices thought up by rulers to fool their subjects. The second half of this paper is an attempt to outline tentatively how a theory which avoids both these pitfalls can be constructed.

The first step in this case is to ask a question which should follow from the preceding section. If *hasina* is primarily a false mystical essence, what are the observable manifestations of this illusion and, secondly, when do they occur?

These manifestations are of two kinds, first, minor and frequent manifestations and, secondly, major infrequent manifestations. Of the minor manifestations the most important ones are greetings. People of differing rank should be greeted by different types of greeting, so *andrianas*, in the wide sense, in Imerina and to this day should be greeted by the phrase *Tsara va Tompoko* while other phrases should be used for non-*andrianas*. In a sense, *andrianas* have their rank at least at the beginning of conversations. Apart from this, in the past in both Betsileo and Merina kingdoms different ranks had rights to wear certain types of clothing, to speak at public assemblies in a certain order, and to be exempt from a few laws, none of great significance. For example, high *demes* in Imerina had the privilege of not having their blood spilt. So when they were condemned to death, instead of being killed in the usual ways they were either strangled or drowned. Also of significance were rights relating to tombs. Higher *demes* could have their tombs within the village walls, while lower *demes* could not, and the very highest *demes* had special shaped tombs the topmost part of which were called *trano masina*: holy houses. (*Masina* in this case is the adjectival form of *hasina*.)[59]

Apart from these minor manifestations of differential *hasina* the demonstration of royal *hasina* from which all others sprang was focussed on four major national rituals of outstanding importance: the circumcision ritual, the coronation ceremony, the ceremony of the royal bath, and royal funerals. Only a very brief outline of these can be given here.[60]

The circumcision ceremony of the Merina and Betsileo is similar and it is the only one of the four which is still practised today, though in a changed form. Every seven years or so, the ruler would declare the time for the circumcision come and for the following week or perhaps longer a series of rituals are performed. First, the whole kingdom is cleaned, both literally, and mystically in the case of witches, who are killed if they are discovered through the administering of a poison oracle to the whole population. Then *hasina* (mark II) is offered by all groups in ranking order to the ruler and also probably within the *demes* and between *demes* equally in order of rank. Then to mark the ritual state of the population all plaited their hair in a characteristic and complex way. The king as well as all the heads of *demes* go to the tombs of their predecessors and ancestors (assumed to be the same) and make offerings and prayers which in the case of the ruler are climaxed by the phrase 'Ho masina anie', 'Let me be *masina*'. Then follows the ceremony of the fetching of the *rano masina* holy water.[61]

This water is fetched from several fixed places and its significance is that it increases the fertility of humans; thus through the agency of these with *hasina* the forces of nature are harnessed to be passed on in the increased fertility of the next generation which is the principal aim of the ceremony. Then the *hasina* giving is repeated and all take part in a complex dance called *soratra* which is said to '*hampandroso hasina*', to 'force *hasina* to enter', but which at the same time acts out the differential *hasina* of the various *demes* of the kingdom.[62]

The circumcision ceremony stresses very explicitly certain themes which we shall find again in the other ceremonies. (1) The king is associated by the ceremony with his royal predecessors and through contact with them he indirectly passes on fertility to the whole population. (2) The king is associated by the ceremony with the reproductive force of nature and because of his *hasina* he can canalise this to the rest of the population. (3) The king's and the *demes' hasina* is created by the giving of *hasina* mark II as well as by the dance; at the same time the relative amount of *hasina* is defined.

The second ceremony where the *hasina* of the ruler is stressed is the accession ceremony. This takes place at a spot called Mahamasina (the place which renders *masina*) (the present-day football stadium of Tananarive), where apart from receiving the *hasina* from his subjects in ranked order the king absorbed the *hasina* from his predecessors by drinking water containing earth drawn from the tombs of the previous kings which he claimed to be descended from.[63] This ritual clearly demonstrates the incorporation by the present king of the *hasina* of his predecessors, which is seen as reproducing itself again and again from generation to generation channelled in one unchanging line. Of course, this type of material descent, contact with the corpses of predecessors, which is typical of central Madagascar,[64] is also highly manipulable, since it is not descent through any notion of filiation but descent through incorporation of predessors which can be done by anybody irrespective of who his parents were.[65]

The same elements are again stressed in the famous elaborate royal funerals of the Betsileo but there evident above all is the concern of conserving *hasina* and passing it on to the next generation. These ceremonies have been described often[66] and their strangeness has made them a common example in nineteenth-century anthropological treatises.

The rituals involved first encouraging the decay of the body of those of high *deme* rank, usually kings, then gathering the putrefying liquids in a barrel until maggots manifested themselves in it. One of these maggots was then selected and believed to grow into a snake whose close association with the king's successor was essential. The whole ritual lasted several weeks and was accompanied by what has been described as 'sexual orgies' when aggressive sexual intercourse and aggression was permitted between any members of the opposite sex irrespective of the usual social rules. This type of ritual activity was associated with all royal rituals and was in part linked with the maintenance of the fertility giving power of *hasina*. F. Edholm has shown how the central concern of these funerals is the handling of the body of the dead ruler so as to canalise his *hasina,* very literally canalise the bodily fluids which flow from his decomposing corpse, so that it is retained for the future reproduction of *hasina* and flowing from it the future reproduction of material resources of the subjects.[67] Secondly, we have the emphasis on the continuity of the rulers by a kind of descent which is natural and not dependent simply on filiation, an essential for an ideology of rule which represents power as innate and permanent while it really rests on uncertain competitive succession. Thus Dubois, talking of the *fanono*, the maggot transformed into a snake, says 'le nouveau souverain . . . commençait pour ainsi dire un nouveau règne, faisant comme un trait d'union entre la royauté passée et la présente car on assurait que le *fanono*, remis en liberté, se plaisait à faire le va-et-vient entre son ancienne résidence royale et *l'antera* (l'eau sacrée tout proche)'. Not only does the snake therefore link the different generation of rulers, it also links all rulers to that ultimate source of natural power and fertility, nature which is symbolised as it was in the circumcision ceremony (and, as we shall see again, for the royal bath) by water.

Finally, and perhaps most interestingly, we have the yearly ceremony of the royal bath, the *fandroana*, probably a ceremony of Islamic origin.[68] A large literature on the *fandroana* is available, especially the full-length study by L. Molet called *Le Bain Royal à Madagascar,*[69] which explains the ceremony, on rather little evidence, as a survival of a form of cannibalism, when people ate their ancestors so as to reincorporate their *hasina*. The best study available, however, is to be found in A. Delivré's *Interpretation d'une Tradition Orale.*[70] Delivré stresses how the royal ceremony, involving much singing and dancing and other ritual activity and lasting for anything up to a month, shows a clear pattern emerging, on the one hand the passage of the old year and the coming of the new and on the other the repetition of kingship, not only within a reign, but beyond it from reign to reign.

The main rituals of the Fandroana are in order:

1. A moratorium on funerals;
2. Opening up of the tombs followed by a tidying up of the tomb of his predecessors by the king echoed in all *demes* by similar tidying up in *deme* tombs;
3. The ritual of the royal bath which gives the ceremony its name. The ruler, after receiving *hasina* in the form of the coin from his subjects in order of rank, takes a bath with much ritual. He then blesses the subjects by spraying them with the water of the bath. This increases their fertility and that of the crops. On stepping out of the bath the ruler says: 'Ho masina anie', 'May I be *masina*'. He then receives the gift of *hasina* again. This is echoed by gift giving throughout the whole kingdom as inferiors give to superiors.[71] The night preceding the actual bath is marked by the whole population taking part in a torchlight procession and in the past by a period of sexual licence. The cause of both these is as much the royal bath as the fact that the royal bath coincides with the new year, the passage from the month of Alahotsy associated with death to the month of Alahamady associated with fertility. This is also the mid-point between harvest and the beginning of sowing the new crop of rice.
4. Forward looking ceremonies at the royal tombs and closing of the tombs (echoed at *deme* tombs).

The combination of the passage of time of rituals symbolising rebirth and of the power of the ruler are elegantly summarised in the diagram from Delivré which is reproduced as Fig. 3.[72]

First, the cycle of the year is linked with the actions of kinship. Then and by inevitable extension the fertility of the crops is linked with the *hasina* of the king and made dependent upon it. The giving of rank by the subjects to the king is linked to the giving of rank by all inferiors to all superiors, whether superior and inferior *demes,* or fathers and sons, or elder brothers and younger brothers, etc. In other words, the receiving of *hasina* by the king is seen as the final result of a wave of *hasina* giving throughout the society.

The recognition of rank by all is merged with the continuation of all, symbolised by the conquest over death, of which tombs are the symbol, as well as the fertility-giving blessing of the bath-water. This conquest over death for each *deme* and each family is seen as

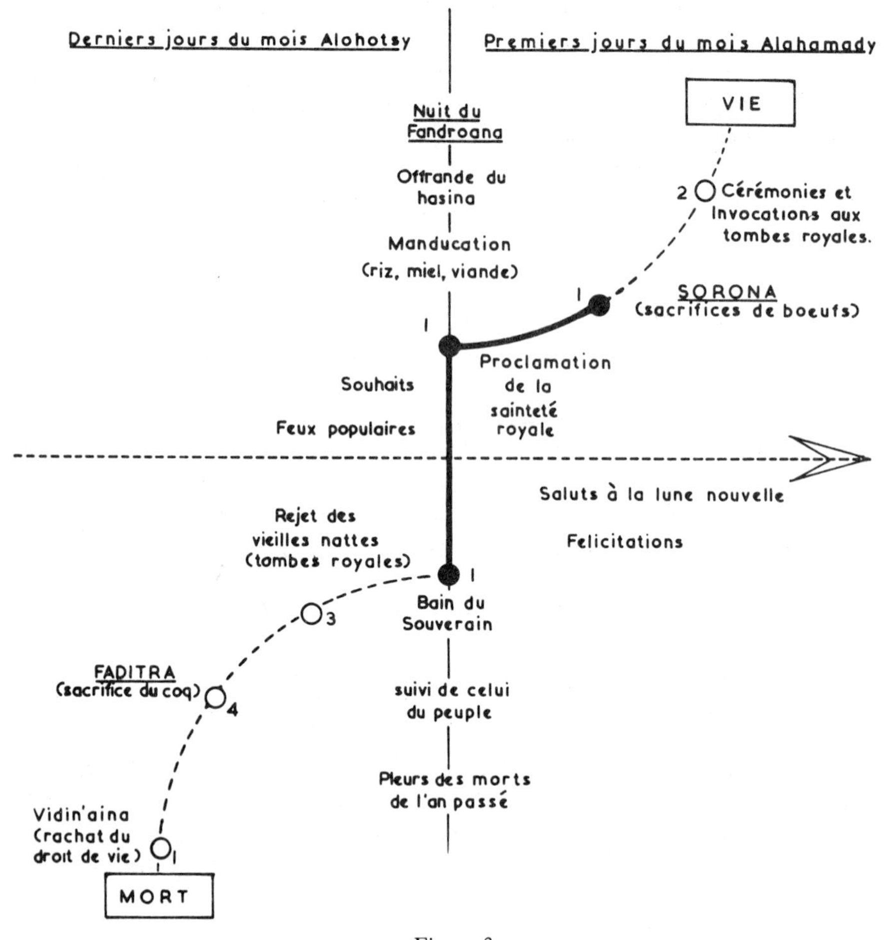

Figure 3

1. Eléments de la fête, sous Ralambo, d'après les Manuscrits Mering.
2. Adjonction d'Andrianjaka, fils de Ralambo (institution d'un sacrifice au tombeau de Ralambo).
3. Sous Andriantsitakatrandriana, fils d'Andrianjaka.
4. Sous Andriamasiravalona.

From: Delivré (1967 p. 203) Fig. 12

dependent on the conquest over death of the kingship. For this the present incumbent must be the rightful successor of other kings whose tombs are his tombs. Thus, the theme we already saw in the royal Betsileo funerals is here again repeated. Material and essential succession is merged with a process which is in fact manipulable but which, when looked back upon, has all the appearance of biological descent, since it involves the transfer of material substance between generations of rulers.

The actual bathing also re-echoes central themes of both the circumcision ceremony and the royal funerals. The water for the bath should be obtained from the same places as the water for the *rano masina,* the holy water of the circumcision ceremony; by contact with the body of those with *hasina* it transforms natural fertility into social fertility, which is then used to bless the assembled multitude in the same way that the *rano masina* is poured by the elders on the penis of the child. This use of water also re-echoes the *tsodnano* discussed above. In all these ceremonies then we see the association of the power of nature and the power of men inextricably linked to become *hasina.* The substance which gives rank its legitimacy is as much of nature as of men; it is, therefore, beyond question and infinitely desirable since on it relies the life of all.

The passage from one year to the next and the promise of the future rice harvest is associated with the passage of kings from year to year through time, a passage which is continuous since the present king is the representative of the corpses inside the tombs where his predecessors have been buried which will contain him and his successors. The ritual associates the king and his bath with the renewal of human fertility through the water of the bath which, as in other ceremonies, symbolises the continuity of human life. The whole ceremony is focussed on the ritual at the Palace but is re-echoed by many observances inside every Merina home. Its centre is marked by the bath, preceded by a night of unbridled sexual licence which has won it much fame among European writers but which often marks the turning-point in ceremonies of continuing fertility in Madagascar. The whole ceremony establishes, recognises and differentiates between degrees of *hasina.* As the king comes out of his bath he utters the phrase: 'Ho masina anie', 'that I may be *masina*', and accompanying this both immediately preceding and following the bath he is given *hasina* mark II by the other high ranking members of his entourage; a gesture repeated throughout the kingdom by those of lesser rank giving to those of higher rank, repeated inside every family by sons giving *hasina* to their fathers, younger brothers giving *hasina* to their older brothers, etc. At the very moment when the king manifests his supreme *hasina*, associating it with the recurring cycles of nature and reproduction, the whole hierarchical rank system of the kingdom is, so to speak, activated in order to mask the actual power situation. The masking process takes place in the transposition of political power, achieved by force against subjects and predecessors, to an aspect of the natural life-giving processes of nature and human sexuality; in other words power is represented as beneficient nature – it is the transposition of unique achievement into repetitive and therefore infinite events and the transposition of a sharp break between rulers and ruled into a continuum of differential *hasina.*

The four royal rituals we have looked at so far carry the same message, an amazing message in the light of the reality of Merina and Betsileo history. The message is that political power is an aspect of a mystical power distributed throughout the population in differing degrees. This power is not primarily political but is an aspect of nature.

Like nature it is repetitive but unending. Like nature it is life-giving. Like nature (by definition) it is not created by man but exists independently of man. The present ruler if he has *hasina* is, therefore, nothing but the continuation of his predecessors, the vessel of the *hasina* which they had. The life of the subjects and the produce of the earth is dependent on the communion with the religious forces of the universe which is achieved through him.

The analysis of the four royal rituals which has been outlined above show when it is that the illusion of *hasina* and rank are created. Apart from the minor manifestation of *hasina* and rank discussed above it is during rituals that power is transformed into sainthood that *hasina* mark II takes on the illusory appearance of *hasina* mark I. For periods of varying length, normal activity is suspended by rituals where the experience of exploitation and intimidation, implied by political rule most of the time, is transformed into a totally different picture, depersonalising the relationships of oppression to relationships of protection by rulers who are vessels of universal beneficence in the form of fertility.

The fact that *hasina* and rank are illusions of certain times but not all times is what I believe can furnish us with an answer to the question posed above: how can a misrepresentation of political and economic reality come about without anybody working the system consciously so as to mislead others? The answer will come by looking at what is special about those times when *hasina* and rank appear to have reality in other words by utilising a theory of ritual.

The reason why a theory of ritual is relevant to the understanding of the relation between rank and power comes from the fact that when we are looking at power we are looking at unformalised (unritualised) action using ordinary language and physical force for its communication. We are looking at activities for which the manner in which things are done is secondary to what is done. When we are looking at rank, by constrast, we turn to rituals, whether religious or secular, whether large-scale extended affairs like the Ceremony of the Bath or very small-scale affairs like greetings.

These rituals use a type of communication different from other communication: formalised language, song, formalised bodily gestures, dance and communication by material symbols. When we are looking at power and rank we are therefore looking at *different* activities and *different* types of communication involving the *same* actors. From time to time life is 'lifted up', so to speak, to another plane and we must understand the significance of this 'lifting'. It is important to stress that the difference between power and rank refers to different types of activities in which the actor is involved and not a move from the observer's to the actor's category (I believe this is a fairly common mistake in anthropology). Indeed, the perception of exaction in its unadorned form is just as much part of the experience of the actors as the experience of rank in rituals, but it occurs at different times and in a different mode of communication. The Merina peasant is sometimes faced by armed superiors who take away part of his crops but a few months later he is a singer and a dancer in the ceremonies of the bath.

Communication in ritual

Only a very brief outline of a theory of ritual can be given here. The argument is presented in an article entitled 'Symbols, song, dance and features of articulation: Is religion an extreme form of traditional authority?' published in the *European Journal of Sociology*.[73] The starting-point of the argument is the observation that ritual, whether religious or not is characterised by certain special (extraordinary) types of communication. These are mainly formalised speech and song, formalised bodily movement and dance and material symbols which replace words. All these media of communication share features in common in contra-distinction to more ordinary communication especially ordinary language. The first and most fundamental aspect of ritual communication is that although it appears richer in aesthetic and emotional values it is poorer as to its semantic potential and its ability to carry a logical argument. This is because, as has been shown by generative semantics, the logical potential of communication is dependent on aspects of syntax, and these are weakened or destroyed in these media. Ordinary language depends for its ability to say new things within a given mould on the articulations which unite a continuous unit of communication. In ordinary language one bit of communication can be followed by any other bit. This is because syntax is a system which can link meaningfully practically any two propositions. In ordinary language one bit can be followed by a near infinity of other bits within a framework which gives this sequence meaning.

In the case of formalised language, and especially song and such non-linguistic communication as dance, this high flexibility in the articulation of communication is either greatly reduced or almost absent, and so the potential for saying new things within a given structure is equally reduced or absent. The articulation of communication becomes, so to speak, arthritic. While in ordinary language the suppleness of communication means that unit A can within the rule be followed by an infinity of units B, in ritual language or song A can, within the rule, be followed by very few or even only one B. Thus, while for ordinary language the only reason which links A and B is the nature and force of the argument, in ritual the link between A and B is partly given by the nature of the communication. Two points follow from this: (1) Communication is not easily or at all adjustable to the reality of a particular place or time because of its arthritic nature. (2) Reasoned contradiction or argument, which implies a supple form of link-up with previous utterances, is equally reduced or ruled out. As a result the communication of ritual is protected by its form from challenge, rapid modification, or evaluation against other statements or empirical data. Secondly, not only does ritual communication restrict the articulations between parts of the message, it also dramatically limits the range of words of larger units of communication which are appropriate. Particularly it reduces the range of possible illustrations which are thought suitable parallels to matter at hand. Often it specifies that any illustration must be drawn from a scriptual corpus or from a single historical tradition. The effect of this restriction on communication is particularly interesting; it means that any single ritual event is, in the perspective of ritual communication, going to be seen simply as a manifestation of an event which recurs or which is cyclic. Ritual communication makes the social world appear organised in a fixed order which recurs without beginning and without end. As a result the social is like the natural, even a part of nature, and so ritual communication projects the political, the social, the discontinuous, the cultural and the arbitrary into the image and the realm of repetitive nature. Since ritual cannot 'come to grips' with reality this is transformed to something quite different.

The theory is relevant to what we have been looking at so far in the following way: it explains why the ritual representation of rank is apparently unchallenged by very different experiences of power. It also explains why rank and *hasina* are represented as cyclic and therefore permanent. It also makes clear why statements of power which are 'given' in the universe (since they cannot be challenged), and repetitive, inevitably link up with the processes of nature and especially its beneficial cyclical aspects, fertility and reproduction. Putting statements into ritual language puts them outside society and into nature since the statements appear to have transcended the actions of men and are experienced as though from outside the individual (*pace* Durkheim).

The theory of ritual under discussion however, has some more directly evolutionary implications. We should think of rituals less as a given, more as part of the process of leadership. Political leaders have been divided between those with traditional authority and those with charismatic authority. It is clear that it is those with traditional authority who use rituals.

This was brilliantly analysed by Weber who stressed the processual side of this. Those who acquire power institutionalise it to make it less vulnerable from the attacks of rivals, they put this power 'in the bank of ritual'. They do this by creating an office of which they are the legitimate holders, but which has reality beyond them. This is done by gradual ritualisation of the power holder's communication with the rest of the world, especially his inferiors. As this ritualisation process proceeds, communication loses the appearance of a creation on the part of the speaker, and appears like repeats of set roles specified by the office which appears to hold him. Reality is thus reversed and the creation of the power holder appears to create him. This process means two things; power having become authority appears less and less challengeable, but at the same time it becomes less the power holder's own. This results in the fact, also emphasised by Weber, that traditional authority is eminently transferable.

This is because as the leader puts his control 'in the bank' he removes it from his own achievements by making it unrelated to history and part of nature (see above). Ritualising power means that the achieved power is transformed into ritual rank by rituals, but it also means that in the process rank becomes separated from its origin, i.e. the acts of power, and any direct feedback is ruled out by the very process of rituals. In this way rank will inevitably become disconnected from power. Power produces rank through ritual but this gives rank independence, a 'realism' which results in greater time persistence. Then power will change but the rank it has produced will stay.

The fact that ritualisation removes authority from the person of power holders has another evolutionary implication which we must touch on briefly, to return to it below. This removal is a problem for the ruler himself, in that it not only removes events from place and time and compels others by placing them in a repetitive and apparently external system, but it also depersonalises him, removing from him the possibility of manipulation. If a ruler totally adopts the mode of communication of ritual for carrying out his will he at the same time loses his ability to affect events for his own *personal* ends as opposed to the ends of his office. He must therefore continually switch from the mode of communication of ritual to a secular mode of communication using the former for statements concerning his unchallenged role as 'father of his people', the latter in order that he may play the astute politician.[74] In evolutionary terms one can see this whole process as one whereby rulers as they become accepted ritualise their communication with their subjects to protect themselves from short-term challenges, but as they do this they begin to need two alternative codes, playing one after the other which correspond to two roles which they may well alternate, that of priest and politician, that of orator and patron. The superior who tries to avoid separating the contradictory roles of father of his people and politician is a successful ruler, but he is at all times facing the danger of being kicked upstairs as a priest or kicked aside by a successful rival who takes over the role he has created.

Evolutionary processes bringing about the disconnection

I believe that the theory of ritual briefly outlined above gives us a possible answer to the question of how the misrepresentation of power into the language of rank comes about without having to assume that anybody at any time deliberately sets about to mystify the actors. How this comes about has been hinted at above but we can go a little further on two specific points which have emerged as being of crucial importance for our understanding of the disconnection between power and rank. The first and most important point concerns the representation of rank as a gently graded hierarchy encompassing everybody while in reality there is a sharp break between a small group of rulers and the mass of the ruled.

In order to understand the evolution of the continuity of hierarchy, we should imagine the situation of a ruler who has just taken over power in a state, or who has created a new kingdom. We can assume that he is not arriving in a vacuum but is replacing another already existing group of rulers. The already existing group of rulers through the fact of having achieved a certain degree of permanence will already have to some extent mystified and transformed this power from initimidation to *hasina*. The problem of the new ruler is therefore to remove the old one yet achieve *hasina* for himself. We have seen that it is the nature of the products of ritual to be projected away from any particular individual onto the processes of nature. This is how the *hasina* of the ruler gains a pseudo-realism which appears undeniable. This fact presents a special kind of problem for the new ruler. The earlier ruler has not just legitimised himself through ritual but had created an entity and an order which organises perception of the whole world and which therefore appears to have reality beyond him. This is so because it is one of the central features of the communication of ritual that it separates its creation from its creator and places his message outside the realm of any social action. The new ruler is thus in a position where be cannot deny the existence of *hasina*. In any case, he is not likely to want to since he is aiming to prove his own possession of *hasina*, not to disprove its existence. The problem would be irresolvable if it were not for the already noted fact that the ideological system and the definition of *hasina* contains within itself the possibility of creating a new *hasina* holding group. This possibility is a direct result of the ambiguity of *hasina*. On the one hand, *hasina* is mark I (rank given to individuals in nature) and on the other it is mark II (something which is created by inferiors by their giving *hasina*, a gift of respect such as suitable greetings or symbolical gifts, especially the uncut silver coin). Furthermore we saw that in reality since *hasina* mark I was an illusion it is totally dependent on the real practice of inferiors giving to their superiors (*hasina* mark II). So the solution is to force the newly created subjects to give to the new ruler. In particular it is essential to insist on the central giving of *hasina* (mark II) by the group of the previous rulers. By forcing the old group of rulers to do this, their *hasina* is recognised to be inferior to that of the new ruler. This gift, however, implies a recognition of the reality of the *hasina* previously held by the old rulers, it therefore appears not to deny the innateness of *hasina* mark I. Indeed, the significance of the giving of *hasina* mark II by the previous rulers is dependent on their *hasina* mark I, since it is because of *its* legitimacy that the recognition of the differential *hasina* between new and old rulers is legitimate. In other words new rulers can transfer *hasina* (mark I) to themselves only by the recognition of the *hasina* (mark I) of the old rulers. This process is much less problematic than it might seem at first since it does not require that the old ruler himself gives *hasina* (mark II) to the new ruler. This would be a problem indeed since in most cases the old ruler has been killed. It is sufficient that members of the old ruler's *deme* give *hasina*, since *hasina* is thought to be equally distributed throughout the *deme* (see above).

The solution for the usurper who needs to obtain *hasina* (mark I) is, therefore, to receive *hasina* (mark II) from the *deme* members of the old ruler, but this is also dependent of the *hasina* (mark I) of the old ruler. Now, the only way that the old ruler's *deme's hasina* (mark I) can exist is by a *third* group giving *hasina* (mark II). This third group will be the old ruler's (now the new ruler's) subjects. The coming of a new ruler implies, therefore, at least three ranks. In descending order of *hasina* mark I there are: (1) The rank of the *deme* of the new ruler (2) the rank of the *deme* of the old ruler (3) the rank of an inferior *deme* to that of the old ruler. These three ranks are necessary if the new order is to be within the logic of *hasina*.

Now if we imagine the process of replacement of old rulers by new rulers occuring again and again, as we know it did, the system of rank complicates itself. Each new ruler creates a new rank by placing himself at the top of the hierarchy requiring *hasina* (mark II) from the member of the *demes* of the ruler he supplanted. This, to be valuable, is dependent on their *hasina* mark I which is dependent on their receiving *hasina* mark II from the *deme* they supplanted and so on . . .

In this way we can see how the turbulent history of central Madagascar produced the complex rank system we have here. Furthermore, this process explains another apparent disconnection between power and rank in central Madagascar. That is the fact we already noted that the stressed breaks in the system of rank (the break between *andriana* and *hovas* among the Merina and between *hovas* and *olompotsy* for the Betsileo) occur much further below any real break between rulers and ruled. The hierarchy is really only of importance for the top *demes* for the justification of the position of the ruler. The sharp break between *andriana* and non-*andriana* for the Merina, and *hova* and non-*hova* for the Betsileo, does not occur between the rulers and the ruled, but where it occurs is between those whose relationships of hierarchy are essential for the *justification* of the position of the ruler and those whose relationships of hierarchy are not so necessary. This is probably also the reason why the ranking of the lower *demes* tends to be imprecise.[75] Direct historical evidence for the process of the reorganisation of ranking is not easily available and would no doubt require more extensive historical research. In any case such reorganisation would be most likely passed over in the oral traditions on which we would have to rely. However, the strongest evidence is the actual ranking order itself which by contrast is very well documented. A constant there in the speeches of Merina monarchs at their accession is their statement or restatement of the order of *demes* in terms of rank, as least in so far as it concerns the higher *demes*.[76] Each of these re-statements follows roughly the pattern to be expected. The theory outlined above would lead us to expect the *deme* of the ruler on top immediately followed by the *deme* of the previous ruler just below and so on. The list of ranking order of the *demes*, for the higher ones at least, turns out to be a kind of encapsulated history of previous ruling groups who have sequentially pushed each other out. The process is somewhat complicated by the fact that because of the nature of political conflicts in central Madagascar we are not simply dealing with one group replacing another in the same area, but one group or ruler may take over the territory of several previous rulers or only part of the territory of a previous ruler. This means that sometimes elements of several hierarchies have to be joined together. This is the case with the Merina hierarchy in the time of the latter part of the reign of Andriampoinimerina which combines the hierarchies of Imerina proper and Imamo.[77] Nonetheless, we are still dealing with the same principle. The evidence from the various Betsileo kingdoms, although less full, seems also to accord well with this theory (e.g. the ranking order of Isandra given by Dubois.[78])

Cases when the ruler's demes *are not at the top of the hierarchy*

Although what has gone before can account for nearly all features of the ranking hierarchies of central Madagascar there is one significant exception. In one case at least and perhaps for others we do not find the *deme* of the ruler at the top of the hierarchy, but in fact one down. The case in question is that of the Andriantompokoindrindra (Zano Tompo) who were higher in terms of rank than the ruling *deme* of the Andriamasinavalona.[79] My field notes of the oral history of the old kingdoms of Manohilahy suggest a similar situation. What makes these exceptions particularly interesting is that they push the parallel of the Malagasy case with the Hindu caste hierarchy further since we find that those right at the top in both systems of the ranking hierarchy are not always the power holders (the Brahmins in the Indian case) but that the power holders are second down. We have here yet another disconnection between the system of rank and the system of power, a disconnection which for the case of the caste system Dumont emphasises,[80] in order to conclude that the status hierarchy is not basically a political phenomena; or rather that there are two separate phenomena in India, one political, the other religious.

The first point to notice about the Malagasy anomaly is that the events leading up to the establishing of differing rank between the top and the second *deme* is rather different from the events which lead to the establishment of other hierarchical relations. The ancestors of the two *demes*, Andriantompokoindra and Andriamasinavalona, were two brothers and Andriantompokoindrindra was probably the rightful heir.[81] (His name means literally 'The lord who is the absolute superior'.) Basically the story is that the dynastic struggle between the two brothers which took the form of a game of *fanorana*, a chess-like game, was resolved by the victory of Andriamasinavalona in political terms while Andriantompokoindrindra retained the superior rank. It is interesting in this respect that Andriantompokoindrindra is associated by tradition with the most arcane and abstract aspects of *hasina*. For example he is credited with the invention of the *hasina* enhancing dance which was mentioned above in connection with the circumcision ceremony, and he initiated the building of the *trano masina*, the 'holy houses' which mark out the tombs of the very highest *demes*. Similarly to this day members of this *deme* claim precedence over all others although this is not, nor ever was, associated with any political power. The position of the Andriantompokoindrindra is anomalous in yet a further way in that although they are not the power holding *deme* they are the *deme* with the most *hasina* (mark I) yet they still give *hasina* (mark II) to the power holders. In spite of this double anomaly, however, the situation can still be accounted for in terms of the logic of *hasina* and the theory of ritual outlined above.

The point to notice is the *deme* identity of the two brothers and the fact that Andriantompokoindrindra was the senior brother in the story given above. This means that Andriamasinavalona's could not be inferior in terms of *hasina* to his older brother. There was, however, another possibility and this was given by the way ritual tends to separate out the person of the power holder into the roles of priest and of politician. We noted how this separation is often pushed further with the two roles being carried by different people who act in theory for each other.[82] This seems to be the solution reached here. The ritual aspects of power are given to the Andriantompoloindrindra and the political aspects are taken by the Andriamasinavalona. As in Hindu theory the two act for each other, though it is clear in this case who is most powerful: the Andriamasinavalona, in spite of the apparent ritual superiority of the Andriantompoloindrindra. Furthermore, this apparent superiority is itself turned to the advantage of the Andriamasinavalona. This is because although they are the carriers of supreme *hasina* (mark I), the Andriantompokoindrindra render *hasina* (mark II) to the Andriamasinavalona, and in the end, who is superior to those worshipped by the holiest?

In this way this final disconnection too can be seen as the product of a historical process working within the framework of a cultural system. In this case too the ideology thus produced also serves to reproduce the system by further legitimising the power holders.

Conclusion

Dumont's characterisation of the Indian caste system and his insistence in the disconnection between status and power gave us our starting point. While fully accepting the strictures on the danger of reducing one of these systems to the other I have tried to show that in an analogous case it is still possible to see the ideology of hierarchy as a product of political economic history. Of course, Malagasy history does not explain the specific form of the Indian system. To use it in this way would be to fall again into the reductionism and ethnocentricism Dumont criticises. What the study presented here does show is a system with striking similarities with the Indian caste system which can be accounted for. This is especially so since the similarities between the two systems, the gradual and all-encompassing nature of the hierarchy, the disconnection between religious and secular power, the continuity in the religious interpretation of human society and of nature are precisely those features of the Indian system particularly stressed by Dumont.

The method here has been to outline the existence of two systems. The first is the system of political economy evolving according to its own logic and affected by such things as the ecology of central Madagascar and the technology of what Goody has called the 'means of destruction'.[83]

Then I have considered another system, the system of ideas held by the Merina and the Betsileo, and I have outlined the system as having two different kinds of relations to the first system. The system of ideas must, on the one hand, be in part congruent with the economic and political system, since it must offer a practical system of communication to operate it, in the same way as it must offer a practical system of communication to exploit nature and obtain a living from it. On the other hand, the system of ideas is in certain domains separated from the reality of life and feeds on itself to create another pseudo reality. This is possible only because of the semantic implications of ritual communication which protect ideas from challenge by empirically generated knowledge, and which links up ideas in a way which is sub-logical. The system of ideas is therefore made up of two kinds of systems of communication which can never interact since they use different media. It is because of the existence of this second system of ideas that a disconnection occurs between ideas and reality, rank and power. Once this disconnection has occurred and the system of ideas in some matters gains a life of its own, its relation to such events as the growth and death of kingdoms becomes indirect, evolving within its own mystical rationality and creating further disconnections with the base.

It is because of this disconnection that most evolutionary theories, whether past or present, appear simple-minded or simply wrong. They all try to establish a direct and unique relation between the economico-political base and ideology while any study of a particular case shows this not to be valid. On the other hand, if we have to use much more complex theories in the future I hope I have shown, whatever the value of this particular case, that we need not give up.[84]

NOTES

1 Dumont, L. and Pocock, D. (1958), 'A.M. Hocart on caste: religion and power', *Contributions to Indian Sociology* II; Dumont, L. (1966), *Homo Hierarchicus*, Paris.

2 Leach, E.R. (1954), *Political Systems of Highland Burma*, London; Leach, E.R. (1960), 'The frontiers of Burma', *Comparative Studies in Society and History*, 3; Leach, E.R. (1968), 'Introduction', *in* Leach, E.R. (ed.), *Dialectic in Practical Religion.*

3 Isnard, H. (1953), 'Les bases géographiques de la Monarchie Hova', *Eventail de l'histoire vivante: Hommage à Lucien Fèbvre*, Paris.

4 Raison, J.P. (1971), 'Utilisation du sol et organisation de l'espace', *Tany Malagasy*, 13.

5 Dez, J. (1970), 'Eléments pour une étude de l'économie agrosylvo-pastorale de l'Imerina Ancienne', *Tany Malagasy*, 8.

6 Mille, A. (1970), *Contribution à l'étude des villages fortifiés de l'Imerina Ancienne*, Travaux et Documents, Musée d'art et d'archéologie de l'Université de Madagascar, II.

7 Delivré, A. (1967), *Interprétation d'une tradition orale*, Unpublished thesis, Paris.

8 Bloch, M. (1971a), *Placing the Dead*, London and New York, pp. 33ff; Bloch, M. (1975a), 'Property and the end of affinity', *in* Bloch, M. (ed.), *Marxist Analyses and Social Anthropology*, A.S.A. Studies 1, London.

9 Bloch (1971a).

10 Bloch, M. (1968), 'Astrology and writing in Madagascar', *in* Goody, J. (ed.), *Literacy and Traditional Society*, Cambridge; Bloch, M. (1971b), 'Decision making in councils among the Merina of Madagascar', *in* Richards, A.I. and Kuper, A. (eds.), *Councils in Action*, Cambridge Papers in Social Anthropology, No. 6.

11 Mille (1970).

12 Dubois, H.M. (1938), *Monographie des Betsileo*, Travaux et Memoires de l'Institut d'Ethnologie, XXXIV, Paris. Quoted by Edholm, F. (1971), *Royal Funerary Rituals among the Betsileo*, unpublished thesis, London.

13 Copalle, A. (1970), *Voyage à la capitale du roi Radama 1825-1826*, Documents anciens sur Madagascar I, Association Malgache d'Archéologie, p. 40 on Ambohibeloma; Callet, R.P. (1908), *Tantaran'ny Andriana*, Tananarive, pp. 68ff, pp. 303-6; Dubois (1938), Book 2; Sibree, J. (1870), *Madagascar and its Peoples*, London, p. 279.

14 Isnard (1953).

15 Dubois (1938), p. 199; Edholm (1971), p. 48.

16 Raison (1971), p. 111. 'The *vary aloha* seems a poor make-shift, an unnatural agriculture. Sown very densely from April and May, before the coldest period, the seedlings remain in the nursery for at least five months; severe drainage leaves them in a state of dormancy; yellowed and aged, they seem incapable of suckering. The irrigation of the nurseries and paddies implies significant inputs of construction work: large reservoirs and canals presuppose a well developed hydraulic science as well as regular maintenance work. As with *vary sia, vary aloha* requires replanting, which was not yet the general rule among the Imerina of the 1820's, but which must have developed when the crisis in textile production reduced many women to a state of unemployment.

'This form of agriculture, however, was not simply a make-shift, costly in labour time, employed where large-scale floating paddies based on flooding were lacking. Output was, until very recently, significantly higher than late rice because it usually benefited, thanks to irrigation, from a better control of water. Early rice also had other advantages in the eyes of the Merina: this species was characterised by heavier grains that lost less weight in shelling and expanded more in cooking; as an early harvest it could be sold at higher prices, assuring a substantial profit. In 1906, G. Carle estimated the value of a hectare of *vary aloha* at between 300 and 380 francs as against 150 to 375 francs for late rice, and noted that many peasants among the Betsimitatatra constructed their paddy fields in order to be able to cultivate *vary aloha.*'

17 Dez (1970), p. 29.

18 Julien, G. (1908-1909), *Institutions politiques et sociales de Madagascar*, Paris; Dubois (1938), p. 199.

19 Copalle (1970), p. 54; Dubois (1938), p. 892.

20 Dubois (1938), p. 189.

21 Raison (1971).

22 Delivré (1967), p. 310.

23 Isnard (1953); Dez (1970); Raison (1971); Delivré (1967).

24 It seems very likely that the whole process is much more the work of Radama than of Andrianampoinimerina, but tradition seems to have projected back in time the achievements of Radama on to his father so as to increase their legitimacy by the process of 'ascending anachronism' brilliantly isolated by A. Delivré (1967).

25 Kent, R.K. (1970), *Early Kingdoms in Madagascar 1500-1700*, New York.

26 Ellis, W. (1838), *History of Madagascar*, London, Vol. II, p. 123.

27 Deshamps, H. (1972), *Les Pirates à Madagascar,* Paris; Ellis (1838), p. 137.

28 Kent, R. personal communication; Callet (1908), p. 140; Cheffaud, M. (1936), 'Note sur la chronologie des rois d'Imerina', *Bulletin de l'académie malgache,* n.s. XIX, p. 46.

29 Ellis (1838), p. 127.

30 Ellis (1838), p. 196.

31 Ellis (1838), *passim.*

32 Wittfogel, K. (1958), *Oriental Despotism*, Chicago; Steward, J. (1957), *Irrigation Civilizations, a Comparative Study*, Pan American Union of Social Science Monograph no. 11; Linton, R. (1939), 'The Tanala of Madagascar', *in* Kardiner, A. (ed.), *The Individual and his Society*, New York.

33 Boiteau, P. (1958), *Contribution à l'histoire de la nation malgache*, Paris, p. 77; Orlova, A.S. (1958), 'The village community of feudal Madagascar', *Kratkiye Soobshcheniya*, 29.

34 Delivré (1967), p. 303.

35 In the Merina Kingdom after Radama this ruling class consisted of members of several *demes*.

36 Bloch, M. (1967), 'Notes sur l'organisation sociale de l'Imerina avant le règne de Radama I', *Annales de l'université de Madagascar,* no. 7.

37 Bloch (1971a), p. 48.

38 Callet (1908), pp. 149. 303ff., *passim*; Ramilison, E. (1951-1952), *Ny Loharanon'ny Andriana nanjaka teto Imerina. Andriatomara, Andriamamilaza*, Tananarive; Ratimanana, J. and Razafindrazaka, L. (1909), *Ny Andriantompokoindrindra*, Ambohimalaza.

39 Dubois (1938), pp. 127. 128. 189.

40 Kottak, C. (1971), 'Social groups and kinship calculation among the Southern Betsileo', *Am. Anthrop.* 73, no. 1; my parentheses.

41 Edholm (1971), p. 129.

42 Delivré (1967), pp. 177-88.

43 Delivré (1967), p. 188.

44 Bloch (1971a), p. 222.

45 Copalle (1970), p. 52; Delivré (1967), p. 182.

46 Edholm (1971), p. 144.
47 Dubois (1938), p. 99.
48 Edholm (1971), p. 153.
49 Bloch, M. (1961), *Les Rois thaumaturges: étude sur le charactère surnaturel attribué à la puissance royale particulièrement en France et en Angleterre,* Paris; Chaney, W.A. (1970), *The cult of kingship in Anglo-Saxon England,* Manchester; de Heush, L. (1966), 'Pour une dialectique de la sacralité du pouvoir', *Le Pouvoir et le sacré,* Annales du Centre d'Etudes des Religions, Brussels; Balandier, G. (1970), *Political Anthropology* (translated from the French), London; see Ch. 5 for the clearest exposition of such notions.
50 Balandier (1970), p. 104; Southall, A. (1956), *Alur society*, Cambridge.
51 Balandier (1970), pp. 110-13.
52 Salmond, A. (1975), 'Manners maketh man', *in* Bloch, M. (ed.), *Political Language, Oratory, and Traditional Society,* London and New York.
53 Pitt-Rivers, J. (1974), *Mana,* The London School of Economics and Political Science.
54 Callet (1908), p. 291; Delivré (1967), p. 186.
55 Ellis (1838), p. 427.
56 Bloch (1971a), p. 163.
57 Godelier, M. (1973), *Horizon, trajets marxistes en anthropologie,* Paris, p. 83.
58 Radama actually seems to have exercised a high degree of cynicism about the divine character of his rule, but this in no way affects the question since he was not the creator of the ideological system within which he worked (Copalle (1970), *passim*).
59 Callet (1908), pp. 301-74.
60 The ceremony of the bath has already been much studied by Razafimino, C. (1924), *La Signification du Fandroana,* Tananarive; Molet, L. (1956), *Le Bain royal à Madagascar,* Tananarive; Delivré (1967); and others. The circumcision ceremonies will form the subject of a forthcoming book by M. Bloch. The Betsileo royal funerals have been analysed by F. Edholm (1971).
61 This water is nowadays more commonly called *rano mahery*, 'powerful water'.
62 Callet (1908), pp. 73-82.
63 Ellis (1838), Vol. 1, p. 420.
64 Bloch (1971a).
65 The officers in Betsileo royal installations and funerals were called *mahamasinandriana*, 'those who render the ruler *masina*'.
66 Sibree, J. (1898), 'Remarkable ceremonial at the decease and burial of a Betsileo prince', *Antananarivo Annual,* IV; Dubois (1948), pp. 700-19; Richardson, J. (1875), 'Remarkable burial customs among the Betsileo', *Antananarivo Annual*; Grandidier, G. (1920), 'Ethnographie', *in* Grandidier, G., *Histoire physique, naturelle et politique de Madagascar,* Paris, Vol. 4, Book 3; Edholm (1971), chapter 5.
67 Edholm (1971).
68 Kent (1970), p. 239.
69 Molet (1956).
70 Delivré (1967).
71 It should be noted that gift giving in Madagascar is always a sign of inequality, while demands are a sign of equality.
72 Delivré (1967), p. 203, fig. 12.
73 Bloch, M. (1974), 'Symbols, song, dance and features of articulation: Is religion an extreme form of traditional authority?', *European Journal of Sociology*, XV.
74 Bloch, M. (1975b), 'Introduction', *in* Bloch, M., *Political Language, Oratory, and Traditional Society*, London and New York.
75 Delivré (1967), pp. 132-5.
76 Callet (1908), pp. 149-53, 713-14, 1211-17; Ramilison (1951-1952); Rabeson, E. (1950), *Tantaran'ny Tsimianboláhy*, Tananarive; Ratsimanana and Razafindrazaka (1909).
77 Delivré (1967), p. 349.

78 Dubois (1938), p. 127.

79 Delivré (1967), p. 413.

80 Dumont (1966).

81 Delivré (1967), p. 317. Oral traditions disagree on several points relating to this story: Callet (1908), p. 303; Ratsimanana and Razafindrazaka (1909).

82 Bloch (1975b).

83 Goody, J.R. (1971), *Technology, Tradition and the State in Africa*, London.

84 This paper relies heavily on the unpublished thesis by F. Edholm, *Royal Funerary Rituals among the Betsileo of Madagascar*, London School of Economics, 1971. I have at several points merely paraphrased this work.

I am also especially grateful for valuable comments and suggestions on earlier drafts of this paper from Professor G. Aijmer, Miss F. Edholm, Dr. J. LaFontaine, Dr. J. Parry and Professor J. Shapiro. I also wish to thank Professor R. Kent and G. Berg for valuable historical information. Since this paper was written, the work of A. Delivré has been published as *L'Histoire des Rois d'Imerina*, Paris, 1974.

S.C. HUMPHREYS

Evolution and history: approaches to the study of structural differentiation

Social change, evolution and history

The proportion of historical studies among the contributions to this seminar raised implicitly the question of the relation between historical studies of social change and a theory of evolution. It is of course true that nineteenth-century evolutionary theory was a way of seeing the world in historical terms: but surely no one proposes to revive evolutionism as a way of classifying societies on a historical scale running from the Lower Savagery of the Palaeolithic to the Higher Civilisation of the industrialised West. Nineteenth-century evolutionists put forward linear models of a unified world history; what implications have the change from unilinear to multilinear concepts of evolution and the sophistication in the use of non-historical comparative typologies developed during the functionalist period, for the relation between evolutionary anthropology and history?

The historian may well feel tempted to start by remarking that social change can be studied in the field, while evolution cannot. Some anthropologists may disagree. Yet the term 'evolution' has traditionally implied concern with long-term processes and it also, I would suggest, implies a significant distribution in time of processes of social change: the processes which originally produced the incest taboo, the city, writing or the State cannot be observed today.

No doubt it is possible to devise formal analytical categories which can handle both the emergence of culture and the modernisation of the Third World, but analogy with the development of synchronic structural theory suggests that the study of processes of change occurring in relatively simple societies may have a useful contribution to make. I am not personally much convinced that the comparative study of processes of social change – the comparison of structures seen dynamically and not statically – will produce results which could appropriately be called a theory of evolution, but this is perhaps not very important at present: we can surely agree that such a study is worthwhile in any case.

Of the two case studies incorporated in this paper, the first deals with structural differentiation and the conceptual articulation of functionally differentiated sub-sections of the social system (politics, religion, the economy); the second with the relation between structural differentiation and thought during the period when the early Greek thinkers transformed a religious cosmology into a scientific and philosophical account of the world. The ancient world offers abundant material on structural differentiation as well as evidence for processes of historical 'breakthrough' which offer a challenge to comparative theory.

Studies of social change in the modern world deal with the impact of highly complex societies upon simpler ones and consequently provide only a limited range of evidence for the study of structural differentiation. As Gershenkron[1] has conclusively demonstrated, processes of development and modernisation in the modern world take place in a constantly developing environment, and changes in this environment modify the form of the process. The sequences of the process of economic development in a country industrialising with the help of foreign capital today are not the same as those of the Industrial Revolution in England. Similarly, the process of structural differentiation in a primitive society undergoing modernisation in a world which already has banks, factories, newspapers, universities, political parties and trade unions bears little resemblance to processes of structural differentiation in pre-industrial societies. In the latter the units created or modified by differentiation were simpler and in general changed more slowly, and combined in more varied ways. One of the questions most relevant to the problem of evolution, perhaps, is whether we can say that some of the structural configurations found in archaic societies had greater evolutionary potential, were more adaptable and more favourable to further differentiation, than others.

Study of the variety of structures exhibited by archaic societies and of the slow differentiation of new roles and organisations in them prompted the considerations of the concepts 'articulation' and 'setting' which form the second section of this paper. Particularly in using the concept of the social setting as a framework for interaction, I have tried to work with a conception of social structure which combines the on-the-ground reality of concrete social organisations with the models of appropriate behaviour which actors carry in their heads. For me, as a historian, the analysis of social change is not completed until its meaning to actors has been analysed. History is not merely a source of new specimens to be added to the anthropologist's repertoire of societies used in synchronic (or timeless) comparative studies; it is about processes of change and how people live in changing structures with models which accommodate and legitimate change. One of my main reservations about the concept of evolution in social anthropology is that it leaves aside this question of meaning in human action. To insist on the consideration of meaning does not imply that change is always intended, or even always perceived; what has to be shown is how objective changes in behaviour, perceived or not, are meaningfully related to previous patterns. The breakthrough in the biological theory of evolution came with the explanation of the mechanism underlying the process; so far no comparable development has occurred in social anthropology. Functionalism has signally failed to explain *how* societies adapt. Since in the history of social anthropology evolutionism and functionalism have appeared – however paradoxically – as opposed tendencies, I hope that the return to an evolutionary point of view implies an attempt to solve this problem. It may well imply also a divergence between studies focussing on processes of change triggered by alterations in a society's environment (physical or social) and those concerned with endogenous processes of elaboration and drift. An adequate theory of social change must however account for both.

The third section of the paper contains an analysis of the process of structural differentiation in ancient Athens seen from the point of view of the resulting articulation of functionally differentiated institutions and conceptualisation of their reciprocal relations. Athenian society provides an example of a loosely-articulated social structure in which different social settings were free to develop their own norms and conventions. The dominant status of political values did not prevent the relatively autonomous elaboration of other values in non-political contexts. This loose articulation of the social structure permitted both the development of new roles and interaction-settings and the relatively free passage of actors from one setting to another which formed the preconditions for the development discussed in the fourth section of my paper: the new cosmologies replacing the implicit logic of myth with explicit reasoning put forward by Greek intellectuals in the sixth and fifth centuries. It might be possible to develop this line of research further to study the function of intellectuals in Athens as a source of explicit models of the integration of an increasingly complex society and culture. For the present, however, I have confined myself in the concluding section of the paper to more formal and methodological questions concerning the relation between evolution towards more complex social structures and the degree of choice available to actors.

Articulation and setting; tools for the analysis of structural differentiation

Structural differentiation has been a central theme in studies of social evolution since the time of Spencer, and structural-functionalism equally recognised the utility of classifying societies as simpler or more complex according to the diversity of their component units – roles and corporations, the latter being defined as presumptively permanent regulatory units, i.e. units which outlive their members or incumbents and submit them to rules: lineages, formally constituted associations, estates and corporate status categories in general (e.g. slaves), offices, colleges, councils, *etc.*[2] The assessment of complexity should include consideration of the way in which these units are articulated as well as their variety; the mode of articulation may be especially important in influencing the way in which further differentiation takes place in the structure, and for this reason is considered at some length here.

All societies must organise the flow of their personnel into roles and groupings in such a way that individuals are not normally required to perform incompatible roles simultaneously. Although most societies use a number of modes of articulation in combination, different modes predominate in different structures and contribute to their characteristic configurations. The following list of examples is not intended to be exhaustive, and concentrates mainly on articulation in relatively simple social structures.[3]

Segmentary articulation, that is, replication of units of similar form and functions arranged in a pyramid of increasingly inclusive units, occurs over the greater part of the scale of societal complexity, being exemplified by the relation between central and local government in modern states as well as in the segmentary lineage systems of acephalous tribes. As these examples indicate, segmentation may or may not be accompanied by organisational hierarchy. Hierarchically ordered segmentary systems are more complex than those which rely solely on differences of situational relevance to decide which unit shall act in a given case.

One of the simplest modes of articulation in societies which have more than one type of corporate group has been well described by F. Gearing[4] as the 'structural pose': the whole society changes formation simultaneously as it moves from peace to war, from ritual to political debate, or from one tye of economic activity to another.

For functionally differentiated organisations to operate simultaneously and continuously, other modes of articulation must be found. All (male) members of the society may serve in each organisation for a limited period, either based on an age-grade system or some other form of rota allocation; in either case the selection of those due to serve may be made individually or by groups. (The rota principle is also used, as an alternative to simultaneous change of structural pose, to allocate leisure periods within a serving or occupationally specialised group). In relatively undifferentiated societies individuals may also be left to divide their own time between spatially segregated organisational settings requiring different roles and behaviour-patterns: farm, village centre, hunting country, town market.

Different roles, statuses and contexts may or may not be differentially ranked in the value-system of the society. Age, sex, jural or ritual statuses may so far outweigh any others that there is no context in which they are not relevant; and the ideologies supporting such ranking may vary considerably in their degree of elaboration. In the Indian caste system strong emphasis seems to be laid on the relevance of the rules of ritual purity to personal interaction in all contexts, although this does not imply that caste hierarchy is preserved in power relations outside the ritual sphere. Helot status is likely to have been much more pervasively relevant in ancient Sparta than slave status in Athens. The ranking of roles and statuses may be closely linked with the ranking of types of activity. In a militaristic society it may be impossible to argue publicly that public finances are insufficient for war. Late Antique holy men could cow even emperors; but such a concentration of value in a single charismatic role could hardly have been tolerated if the role had not also been firmly associated in most cases with a peripheral position in society. Beyond village level, the Holy Man operated as an outsider.[5]

The question of the range of relevance and the ranking of religious, political and economic values and statuses is problematic in many societies: I return to this point below in the discussion of structural differentiation in ancient Athens.[6] Value-ranking may, further, assign alternative patterns of behaviour and types of relationship to different stages of the individual's life cycle, as in the case of alternative mating patterns in some West Indian societies,[7] or homosexuality in classical Athens.

A fuller study of the relations between modes of articulation and value-systems cannot be attempted here. All that has been done is to point to a few cases where values appear to play a crucial role in articulation. The extent to which principles of articulation are explicitly asserted and elaborated ideologically seems to be very variable.

The examples so far given illustrate alternatives to articulation through full-time occupational specialisation. As occupational specialisation develops it seems to be accompanied by the development of an increasing number of what one might call 'service' institutions, specialising in exchange, communication and arbitration. Even in simple forms occupational specialisation requires some system of redistribution or mechanism of exchange: palace 'rationing', market-place, or the formal redistribution of the village harvest in the Indian *jajmani* system.

Such service institutions may have either a central or peripheral place in the social structure; they may be a part of the apparatus of the state (lawcourts, planning ministries), or their efficacy may depend on segregation from the everyday context of social relationships. Appeal to oracles takes disputes into the realm of the sacred; market-places provide a detached social setting, with its own rules of interaction, for 'disembedded' economic transactions.[8]

The concept of social structure as an articulated set of roles and corporations used above to define complexity might serve for the study of the process of differentiation in modern developing societies where new roles can be rapidly instutionalised on the basis of pre-existing models and new corporations set up by well-established mechanisms. In archaic societies, however, the process of institutionalisation could be very slow. In a sense the differentiation of the role of philosopher in ancient Greece can be said to begin with Hesiod in the eighth century B.C.; the process was fully concluded only with the establishment of fully organised philosophical schools four centuries later. Thus, although much structural differentiation does take the form of fission of existing corporations or creation of new, functionally specialised corporations of existing types (as in e.g. the proliferation of collegiate commissions in classical Athens as functionally specialised committees of the Council), there are other forms of differentiation which can only be studied by looking behind roles and corporations to find the matrix in which they develop.

Linguists working on phonetic change have found that the structuralist concept of language as a homogeneous system governed by unambiguous rules has to be replaced by a more flexible notion which takes account of variation in speech norms between one social context and another, in relation to the character of the social setting and the status of the speakers. Language is seen as containing 'variable structures ... determined by social functions'.[9] The emphasis in recent work has been mainly on the marked differences between formal and informal speech, and on the influence of speakers' models of correct or modern pronunciation on their performance, especially in formal test situations. Speakers are aware of differences in speech between classes and age-groups. Their model of linguistic rules is stratified, takes account of change over time and allows for situational variation.[10]

Social stratification and social mobility naturally occupy a large place in sociolinguistic studies in modern societies. In an early study on semantic change using a similar approach, Meillet[11] had already observed that 'seule, la considération des faits sociaux permettra de substituer en linguistique à l'examen des faits bruts la détermination des procès', and had emphasised that every social grouping has its own shared culture which includes particular turns of speech. Every occupation, recreation, deviant group has its own vocabulary created partly by assigning special meanings to words with a wider connotation in the language at large, and partly by borrowing or inventing new terms. Common interests and frequent communication provide the optimum conditions for the elaboration of this common culture and the acceptance of innovations. At the same time communication between members of different interest-groups makes it possible for such innovations to be spread beyond the setting in which they were originally introduced, often losing specificity in the process.

Let me give an example from anthropology. The term 'sibling', an Anglo-Saxon word which seems to have gone out of use in the early Middle Ages, was reintroduced with the meaning 'brother or sister' by physical anthropologists working on the characteristics of twins; they had learnt the word from Karl Pearson, who besides his statistical work in the Galton laboratory at U.C.L. had made a study of the early kin terms of the Germanic languages in which he asserted that 'sib' and 'sibling' came from a root meaning 'to suckle'.[12] Social anthropologists borrowed the word from the physical anthropologists some time later.[13] Lowie, who introduced it, was of course German; Pearson had studied in Germany in his youth and retained throughout his life a strong interest in German history and culture. Thus this innovation which has such obvious functional utility is the result of a complex chain of interactions across ethnic and disciplinary boundaries.

It is surely clear that this conception of rules of behaviour as linked to specific social settings, associated with differentially valued reference-groups, and evolving because people accept innovation from those whom they regard as associates in a common enterprise or as prestigious, has wide applications outside the sphere of language. It provides an approach to the study of processes of social change which can accommodate both the cases where change results from a conflict of interests, stressed by transactionalists, and the equally important cases where groups innovate, consciously or unconsciously, without conflict, because their shared values and aims lead them to do so. Even traditionalistic societies may develop an involuted elaboration of their norms[14] through a series of innovations which are accepted as being entirely in accordance with tradition.

An institutional setting, as understood here, is a concrete interaction-context defined for actors by spatio-temporal segregation and/or symbolic scene-marking devices, and associated with a particular set of roles and behavioural norms. Such settings vary in their degree of closure and in the specificity of their norms. Sacred places, 'total institutions',[15] convivial gatherings of various kinds, theatrical performances, military settings and the meeting-places of secret societies and deviant groups all exhibit relaxation or reversal of some of the norms of everyday public life with varying degrees of closure and tendencies to involution in their behavioural norms. In the ancient world the stylised conventions of the Athenian gymnasium and symposium are cases in point. Similar elaboration of rules and conventions however may also be found in political assemblies, lawcourts, market-places, places of work, *etc.*

Structural differentiation in ancient Athens

As the above examples show, some institutional settings are dominated by and identified with corporate groups, while others are not.[16] Freedom to elaborate and innovate in different settings may be controlled by the mode of articulation of the institutions concerned, the proportion of corporation-dominated settings and the corporate structure of the society.[17] Ancient Greece provides valuable material for the study of such differences, because different Greek city-states articulated very similar sets of institutions in different ways. The reorganisation of Spartan society in the sixth century B.C. placed the greater part of all social settings under the control of one or another of a set of interlocking corporate groups (men's houses, military units, age-sets) with explicit and well-integrated norms which left little place for innovation.[18] Athens had a much less rigid social structure in which a considerable number of social settings with well-defined norms of behaviour were neither regulated by the State, corporation-based, or explicitly integrated into a comprehensive scheme of values: the market-place, the gymnasium, the symposium, the philosophical discussion, the workshop, the bank. The corresponding occupational roles – trader and shopkeeper, athletics trainer, philosopher, entertainer, pimp, courtesan and parasite, craftsman, banker – were not linked to any organised corporate units. Roles and settings developed together. In the theatre, tragic poets at first took major parts in their own plays, and the idea of acting as a special skill, deserving public recognition in the form of prizes as much as the gifts of the poet, was slow to develop; actors' awards began only about 440 B.C. Jokes based on parody, reversal and inappropriate application of contextual norms are frequent in the fifth-century comedy of Aristophanes: assembly debates conducted by women (*Ecclesiazusai*), demagogic speeches in the idiom of the market (*Knights*), mock trial (*Wasps*), sale of children disguised as pigs (*Acharnians*), discussion of treaties in terms appropriate for food (*ibid.*). In the late fifth century upper-class young men at symposia parodied the Eleusinian mysteries and the conventions of the assembly and the philosophical discussion.

Symbols were used to mark the transition from one setting to another. Gluckman[19] has suggested that such ritualistic definition of social settings is likely to be found in comparatively simple, small-scale societies where the same persons circulate through all settings.[20] By the use of role-defining oaths as *rites de passage* the Athenians both marked the assumption of political roles and reiterated the norms governing behaviour in political contexts, particularly the obligation to leave aside all personal interests. Oaths of this kind were taken not only to mark the acquisition of citizenship and the beginning of military service at eighteen, but also whenever a citizen took office as magistrate, councillor or juror. Role-defining oaths were also quite frequently taken in the Greek world by mercenary soldiers entering service, and by armies before a particularly critical campaign or battle. Military organisation would seem to be altogether a fruitful field for the study of symbolic role- and context-marking; it is a question how far this is a case of emphasising group identification rather than avoiding potential role-conflicts. There is really no reason to suppose that there is only one reason for the accumulation of ritual around social settings. Where the setting is one in which opposed interests conflict, the ritualisation of procedural conventions helps to limit conflict and tensions and to provide common ground on which opposed parties can agree (or about which they can disagree as a way of evading more serious issues). Furthermore, elaboration of these symbols of agreement may occur either because the parties involved legitimately wish to present themselves as the representatives of the community as a whole or because they wish to disguise non-democratic processes of decision-making behind democratic forms.

In archaic and classical Athens we can observe the process of elaboration of political procedure and norms governing interaction in a variety of settings. Some norms, like the rules of political procedure, are formally enacted; others are based on tacit understanding and enforced only by informal sanctions. It is with the latter, and especially with the conventions concerning the articulation of political, religious and economic activities, and of the corresponding categories in Athenian thought, that the following discussion is mainly concerned. Athens, as has been said, seems to provide an example of a loosely-articulated social structure in which heterogeneous social norms applicable in different settings were integrated only by the segregation of the settings and the conventions – few of them enforceable by law – which associated different values and behaviour-patterns with different contexts.

Occupational specialisation developed only slowly: it is not until the late fifth and the fourth century that Greek thinkers begin to show concern over the question of the division of labour, and occupational roles become a target for ridicule in comedy. Antiochos of Syracuse (Jacoby, *F.G.H.* 577 F. 13), Herodotos, Hippodamos of Miletos and Plato were fascinated by the idea of occupational castes; and we shall presently return to the debate over the fitness of urban workers for political responsibility. It seems that it was only in the later fifth century that specialisation developed in Athens to a point where different occupations began to be perceived as blocs in the society and not merely as isolated or part-time skills. The earlier assumption – which remained influential – had been that all citizens performed all roles in turn, moving from one context to another. Roles based on charismatic inspiration (poet, seer) or skilled crafts (potter, shipwright, smith) were not sufficiently numerous in the archaic period to affect the predominantly agricultural character of the society. This free circulation of persons through the roles belonging to different interaction contexts, on the implicit assumption that the appropriate norms and values would be respected in each case, prevented the development of an explicit, institutionalised hierarchy of roles and functions, and left the question of their ranking to subsist unresolved.

I believe that the analysis of this form of role-specialisation, associated with social settings rather than with particular performers or with organisations, and of its effects on the process of social differentiation in Athens, can throw some light on Athenian thought about the articulation of social functions and the relation between the individual and the State. Greek influence on our own categories of thought makes it sometimes easy to overlook peculiarities in the structure of Athenian society and social thought which are worth singling out for discussion.[21]

The main point to note is the progressive exclusion from Athenian political contexts of appeals to divine authority or to economic discontents. Assembly and Council were the dominant social settings of the city, and the fact that their activity was thus limited to merely administrative regulation in matters of religion and to public finance and taxation in the economic sphere tended to lead Athenians to overlook the central role played by the State both in the relations between men and gods and in the economy. (Aristotle – not an Athenian, but resident in Athens – is even weaker on religion than on economics.) Context influenced classification: the fact that public finance was discussed in assembly and council while other economic matters, with the exception of the corn supply, were not, prevented the development of a unified conception of the economy, and a parallel selectivity in the handling of religious matters in the same context tended to encourage a separation in thought between public cult and private devotions.

No attack on the primacy of political life was mounted from the side of religion before the rise of Christianity, though earlier developments in religion and philosophy prepared the ground. Revolts motivated by economic distress, though rare in Athens, were common elsewhere in Greece; but they aimed only to redistribute wealth and power within the existing institutional framework, and drew their justification from the dominant value of the political sphere, justice. The only attempt to create an alternative base of authority from which to criticise the values, norms and operation of the political sphere came from the intellectuals – poets, philosophers and historians.

The relation of the intellectuals to political authority is relevant in this connection because we find here what is lacking in the relation between politics, religion and economics: the monopolisation of specialist roles by a limited number of individuals who thereby relinquish their opportunities of holding oher roles and circulating freely through all social settings. Greek philosophers, like medieval holy men or 19th-century nonconformist industrialists, lost on the swings what they gained on the roundabouts. The way in which they developed their alternative basis of authority (which involves notions as fundamental to us as science, liberty and conscience) was conditioned by the norms of the political settings from which they excluded themselves; in the first place by their acceptance of an association between secularisation and rational argument which was already well developed in political contexts by the late sixth century B.C., and in the second place by the need to find a different perspective and idiom from that of political debates.

Let us now look more closely at these two aspects of differentiation in Athens – the purely contextual differentiation of politics, religion and economics, and the role-specialisation of the intellectuals.

(*a*) *Politics and religion.* It is clear that the gradual elaboration of rules of procedure and criteria of relevance in the context of political assemblies and councils in Athens, between c. 600 and c. 350 B.C., meant a progressive elimination of appeals to divine authority and religious feeling from the political sphere; and it is noteworthy that the process of secularisation here seems to have been carried out with far less polemic than in the intellectual transition from myth to philosophy. The relation between religion and politics is worth examining in more detail: it illustrates very well the peculiar characteristics of the process of functional differentiation in ancient Greece which were outlined above.

Leading roles in the religious sphere in ancient Athens can be divided into six classes. (1) The annually elected magistrates of the State (whose offices went back at least to the seventh century B.C.) each performed certain sacrifices and rituals; one of them, the *archon basileus*, had a special responsibility for supervising the organisation of religious festivals and presiding over the judgment of cases concerning religious matters. The 'kings' of the four tribes Geleontes, Hopletes, Argadeis and Aigikoreis supported him in these functions. (2) A certain number of priests were also appointed annually in the democratic State, beginning with the priests of the eponymous heroes of the ten new tribes created by Cleisthenes in 507 B.C. (3) Other priesthoods created in the period of democracy were held for life by women appointed by the State. (4) But the life priesthoods which already existed in the seventh and sixth centuries were owned by descent groups (*genē, sg. genos*); these had their own complex norms of appointment, which tended to work in favour of hereditary succession. (5) Experts on religious law (*exēgētai*) were also appointed by the *genē*; from the time of Solon, however (early sixth century) the State had a second board of *exēgētai* selected by the Delphic oracle from candidates elected by the whole *dēmos*. (6) Finally, a charismatic commission as mantis, seer and expert in matters of religion, could be held by anyone who could command sufficient credence.

Instead of a gradual separation of religious and politico-military offices and bases of power, we find that both were gradually thrown open to a wider range of candidates. Although by the later fifth century appeals to religious feeling in political debates were exceptional, it was never considered inappropriate for a politician to take a leading part in ritual or for a priest to hold political office. (The evidence on this last point has not been systematically collected, but it is a presupposition of the *genos* system that priesthoods and political office may be combined. Hipponicus son of Callias of Alopekê was both Torchbearer of the Mysteries of Eleusis and general in 426/5; Lycurgus of Boutadai was priest of Poseidon Erechtheus and director of Athens' finances in the 330s. Only in the case of the Hierophant of the Mysteries is it possible that taboos may have prevented the combination of religious and political office.)

If Homer is a reliable witness, at an early stage in Greek history the political authority of kings *was* sometimes challenged by seers. The model of the absolute, divinely inspired certainty of the prophet had its place in Greek culture; it is enough to refer to the figure of Tiresias in Sophocles' *Oedipus Rex*. But prophets were rare in the aristocratic *polis*. The appeal to oracles in the Archaic period was characteristically an appeal to a divine authority located outside the boundaries of the State. We hear more of seers in the later sixth and the fifth century, but their claims to influence rest on learning and mastery of the technical aspects of ritual rather than on inspiration (they are the democratic counterpart of the aristocratic *exēgētai*), and their position is ambiguous: the *mantis* is a stock subject for jokes in Old Comedy, and Plato's religious expert Euthyphro complains (*Euthyphro* 3c), 'When I say anything about sacred matters in the Assembly, foretelling the future, they laugh at me as though I were a madman'. After the rules of rational discourse in political meetings have been fully established, we find attacks on the introduction of religious values into political contexts as a manifestation of superstition, lower-class ignorance and lack of emotional control.[22] But during the process of elaboration of the rules there is no sign of a split in the upper class between religious and rationalist factions. There seems to have been a mutual agreement progressively to limit the use of the long-range weapon of appeals to divine power. Even the intellectuals, for whom the secularisation of the cosmos and of the past involved a serious struggle with traditional beliefs, seldom found themselves radically at odds with society and traditional institutions on the issue of the relation between religion and politics; their criticisms of the irrationality of the political sphere were directed at the purely secular failings of tyrants in the sixth century and of the Athenian democracy in the fifth.

The combination of minimal specialisation in the religious sphere with the progressive exclusion of religion from political contexts may well have been one of the major preconditions for the development of something approaching a personal religion, alongside the public rituals of the city, in Greece. The growth of mystery cults in the sixth century might well be studied in relation to the elaboration of political institutions at the same period: the chronological relation between the increased popularity of cults which denied the relevance of social stratification and changes in the bases and political correlates of stratification is obscure. In classical times, it is clear that the segregation of religion from politics – which *de facto* implied subordination – meant that religion was increasingly regarded as a part of private life.[23] Furthermore, every level of organisation and every type of social grouping had always been represented in cult and had its own appropriate rituals: household, village, phratry, tribe, age and sex categories, occupations. A man's cult allegiances therefore expressed his identity and interests; as Athenian society, from the time of the Peloponnesian war onwards, became more urbanised, mobile and differentiated, many new voluntary associations with their own cults were formed; the range of choice increased, and this may have further encouraged the feeling that religion was a matter of personal idiosyncrasy rather than ascribed group-affiliation.

Public cult meanwhile became increasingly a matter of spectacle and the financial administration required to provide it. The tyrants in the sixth century and the democracy which followed the reforms of Kleisthenes in 507 B.C. had a common interest in bringing cult finances more firmly under State control and limiting the use of personal wealth in this context by rich men hoping for electoral favour. Competitions between tribal teams or choruses, a large number of which were instituted under the tyrants and during the first half of the fifth century, divided the cost of the performance between four or, after Kleisthenes, ten backers and the credit of victory between the backer and the actual performers. The liturgy system, instituted probably in 502/1, regulated the distribution of these financial burdens and the corresponding political advantages and laid down minimum rates of contribution. But in addition to regulating the use of private wealth in public cults, the fifth-century State, with its huge revenue from empire, could make private contributions appear insignificant by its own level of spending. A rich man could still win popularity by his generosity, and might sooner win an opportunity to show his capacities in office, but the city did not depend on his wealth. There is a marked distinction here between the city as a whole and its constituent communities, the demes, which did rely very largely on the wealth of their richer members and consequently tended to be dominated politically by them.

(*b*) *Politics and economics.* Research on kinship in ancient Greece suggested to me the importance of the increasing separation of public and private life in classical Athens. Political life, normally, belonged entirely to the public sphere; privacy tended to be equated with secrecy. Political manoeuvring carried on in private, 'behind the scenes', features in the fifth-century sources only when revolution is being planned. Religious life, as we have just seen, tended to be split into a public and a private aspect, but this separation was not problematic. (It was Socrates' critical examination of traditional values rather than his personal *daimōn* which disturbed the Athenians). In the case of economic affairs, however, the boundary between public and private life did create tensions and value-conflicts.

In public life formal rationality in economic matters was fully accepted. Private contributions to the State's expenditure were, as we have seen, regulated through the liturgy scheme. Public accounting had begun in the temple treasury, where the need to keep the property of the god separate from that of his servants could not be questioned. (On the Acropolis, the property of Athena Polias had been supervised by a board of periodically elected treasurers, and not by the priestess, at least since the sixth century. In small country shrines where priests had more financial responsibilities the situation was sometimes different.) Pericles built up Athens' reserve fund in the fifth century by giving money to Athena: a purely secular reserve would have been too easily dissipated. There was no feeling of conflict between economic rationality – as being 'materialistic' – and religion. It is quite characteristic that the reform programme of Lycurgus in the 330s comprised both the reorganisation of Athens' public finances and a revival of traditional religion.

Our sources convey, however, a strong feeling of opposition between the economic and political spheres, in the form of anxiety over the intrusion of economic motives classed as private into public political decision-making. Although the economic consequences of alternative courses of action for public finances were carefully considered, it was a principle of the articulate Athenian Right that the economic consequences for individuals were a matter of purely private concern and should not be taken into account. Whereas economic calculation in the public sphere was associated with the ceremonial dignity of temple inspections and the formal presentation of accounts to Council and Assembly by outgoing magistrates, in the private sphere it was associated with the haggling, jostling and trickery of the market-place. In economic transactions between the State and individuals, the progress made in regularising the State's receipts and expenditure did not lead to any corresponding increase in predictability for the individual. The demands of the liturgy system on the estates of the rich continued to be irregular in both cost and timing. Similarly, it was difficult for soldiers and rowers to know in advance when they would be called for service and how long the campaign would last. The surviving public financial records from the fifth century show clearly enough the very considerable difference in State expenditure between years of peace, in which tribute money accumulated in the Acropolis reserves, and the years of heavy fighting in which these reserves were depleted. The effects of war service on labour supply and of wage payments to troops on consumer demand were felt throughout the economy. It is scarcely surprising therefore that the *demos* did not disregard their economic interests when war policy was discussed.

The Athenian elite's refusal or inability to recognise that the State was a large-scale economic enterprise exerting a dominant influence over the whole economy has parallels in later history. Their emphatic separation of public finance and private economic interests is reflected on the Janus-head faces of mercantilism and classical economic theory: the one centred on the financial well-being of the State, the other on the behaviour of individuals in a market, while both equally distinguish the economic transactions of individuals from the legislative intervention of the State. There is therefore considerable historical interest in tracing the history of the boundary between economy and polity in ancient Greece.

In the Solonian crisis of the early sixth century B.C. in Athens, political and economic issues were closely related to each other. Checks on the economic exploitation of the poor by the rich went hand in hand with the extension of a minimum of political rights to all citizens; civic status and rights were correlated with different forms of military service and therefore (since the soldier provided his own equipment) with wealth. The further stages in the democratisation of the Athenian constitution were however, achieved without any threat of revolution from below, by action initiated from within the upper stratum of Attic society. Economic issues played no part in the reforms of Kleisthenes and Ephialtes; and Pericles' economic interests were focussed almost entirely on tribute, democratic political institutions, and the fleet. In the fifth century the State dominated the economy by participation, but this domination was largely unrecognised and did not lead to any attempt at regulation by law. Economic inequalities were allowed to subsist while the process of democratisation in politics continued, with the sole exception of the introduction of pay for political service to ensure that economic stratification did not completely nullify the attempt to achieve political equality.

The growing use of slave labour and, in the fifth century, the increasingly important role of the State as an employer of labour, were crucial factors here. Rich and poor rarely confronted each other in the fifth century as employers and employed. Those employed by the State were regarded either as self-employed contractors (working on public building projects) or as citizens performing their political duties (as soldiers, rowers, jurors, *etc.*). Competition for economic resources was deflected away from the private sphere into competition for control over the economic activities and policy of the State. This competition took, of course, a political form, and was staged in the assembly; its economic component was subordinate and, in the opinion of the literate upper class, illegitimate – an intrusion of mere irrational individual appetites into the rational dialectic of public decision-making.[24]

Further work is required to determine the extent to which this model of the relations between polity and economy in Athens is applicable to other Greek city-states, where the State's participation in the economy was in general far less significant. The subordination of economy to polity was of course equally definite, though differently articulated, in Sparta; and the subordination of private to public life was far more rigorous. It was Sparta which inspired Plato entirely to eliminate private life as the Athenians knew it from the social organisation of the Guardian class in his *Republic*; by eliminating property, the family and the differences in education and way of life between men and women, he hoped to eradicate inequality and irrationality.

Most other cities were less successful than Athens and Sparta in freeing the State from dependence on the economic resources of wealthy individuals, and consequently tended to be both more oligarchic in government and more liable to experience revolutions and counter-revolutions motivated by clearly economic aims. However, even here Athens and Sparta provided institutional models and ideologies and, in the classical period, dominated the political and economic environment of their neithbours. The articulation of polity and economy in Athens and Sparta was not typical, but it was decisive.

The idea that citizens should be equal and similar in the political contexts of the city as they were on the battlefield in the hoplite phalanx thus led to a progressive hardening of the boundary between public and private life. This distinction between the public and the private, primarily concentrated in the political sphere, cut across the economy and men's relations with the gods. The consequence was that the economic and even to some extent the religious activities of the State came to be seen as subsections of the polity, while the economic and religious activities of the individual citizen were not considered to be the concern of the State, provided that they did not clash with the requirements of the public sphere. This proviso was, as we have seen, problematic already in the fifth century in the case of the citizen's private economic interests. In the case of religion it was perhaps inevitable, given the increased size, urbanisation, mobility and heterogeneity of classical Athenian society, that the distance between primary-group rituals and public ceremonies should widen. In a secular State, this could easily bring a shift of focus, for the devout, from public safety to personal protection or salvation.[25] It furthermore enabled the intellectuals to accept traditional religious forms in the public sphere while developing new beliefs – rationalistic, metaphysical or mystical – in private. The dichotomy between public and private religion helped to prepare the ground for martyrdom.

(*c*) *Individualism and intellectuals.* These conclusions perhaps suggest a new approach to the relation between the State and the individual in ancient Greece. Except in Sparta, the individual was only required to subordinate his own interests to those of the community in specifically political contexts. The dichotomy between public and private life, though it admitted little questioning of the primacy of the former (while the *polis* maintained its independence), left considerable freedom in the private sphere. The attempt to maintain a clear-cut distinction between political and non-political activity carried with it a laissez-faire attitude to the latter and so set up the balance which would later tip to support the individual's claim to non-interference as a right. Although there is confusion and exaggeration in the claims for a 'discovery of the individual' in ancient Greece, some of the preconditions for the later development of individualism were created in classical Athens.

The freedoms of the non-political domain included freedom of thought and speech – at least within limits. This leads directly to the question of the position of the intellectual in Greek society. It is only in the case of the intellectuals that we have to deal with an influential category of *persons* standing outside the political sphere, rather than a class of *arguments* excluded from political debates. There were three bases of the intellectual's claim to a transcendental authority independent of the political sphere: art, reason and revelation. The first is by its nature removed from possible conflict with political authority, and seems to have been stressed particularly by poets who stood in a somewhat dependent relation to their patrons (Homer, Pindar). But the primacy of reason over revelation in Greek intellectual history demands a closer consideration of the relation of the intellectual to the political sphere, and of the articulation of politics and religion.

As has been said, politically oriented prophecy of the Jewish type was very rare in Greece. Poets and philosophers who claimed special knowledge of theology described an eternal, ordered pattern in the universe; they did not transmit messages from supernatural beings. Even in the *Iliad* and *Odyssey* the interventions of the minor gods in human affairs are limited by the power of Zeus, who does not intervene in person; and the idea that even Zeus is powerless against fate is already present. Hesiod goes further, associating Zeus with an abstract principle of justice in the cosmos. Men and gods are irretrievably separated and estranged – the sacrifices men offer to the gods re-enact the deceit which caused the estrangement; the justice in the world of the gods is contrasted with the injustice in the world of men.

To some extent Hesiod appears to be reacting against the conventions of heroic epic. Homer presented his noble *basileis* as intimately associated with the gods, and often of divine parentage or ancestry; the association, by implication, emphasised the close ties between the gods and Homer's noble audience. Hesiod would not concede this to the *basileis* of eighth-century Boeotia. Yet even Homer does not take his gods very seriously. If the eighth-century peasant could feel alienated from a religion dominated by the aristocracy, the *basileis* themselves were little inclined to let the gods get the upper hand. In a situation where each leading family had its own priesthoods and responsibility for a different element in the cult and festivals of city or countryside, a balance of power on earth required a balance of power in heaven – a balance guaranteed by the sovereignty of Zeus, who is bound by fixed principles and decisions taken in the past, whether his own or fate's. To claim a special relationship to a god implied involvement with the power-struggles of the upper class. There is some evidence that families of ritual specialists and seers were in fact absorbed into, or were accomponent in, the aristocracy, at least in Attica and Elis.

If the field of communications between gods and men was problematic, the business of communication between human groups was, on the contrary, full of opportunities. Poets were in demand, in the archiac age, both as bearers and creators of a shared culture which reached as far as the Greek language, and as privileged intermediaries between nobles and people in their own communities. Because poetry was not the language of political debate, poets could make comments excluded by the rules of the political arena. The ritualisation of poetry in classical Athens only increased this trend, restricting personal attacks to comedy, while tragedy raised the fundamental questions about the nature of Athenian society for which there was no place in the debates of the assembly.

In the seventh and early sixth century it was perhaps still possible that the intellectuals might have been, like the religious specialists, absorbed into the ruling elite. The legend of the Seven Sages, though it clearly reflects the unity of archaic Greek culture and the focal role of Delphi, also implied that there was a place of honour open to the intellectual in his own city. Power-struggles within the aristocracy had brought many cities to the point of exhaustion and breakdown; they were prepared to accept tyranny, the dictatorship either of the victor in the conflict or of a compromise candidate. Two of the Sages, Thrasybulus and Periander, were tyrants. Solon could have been tyrant in Athens and accepted the position of lawgiver instead.

It was commoner, however, for intellectuals to find themselves subordinated to the tyranny of others, and to react either by emigrating or by turning their attention away from Greek society to wider horizons, to geography and cosmology. The Ionian natural philosophers found in the structure of the universe and the arguments of the lecture-room the principle of equality and procedures of debate which had disappeared from the city. Those who travelled to escape tyranny found themselves still cut off from politics by the fact of being strangers. Notions of citizenship were being formalised; the cities were beginning to turn in upon themselves.

The change in Greek politics brought about first by tyranny, and then by the increased formalisation of political procedures which followed it, was decisive for the independent stance of the intellectual. From the late sixth century onwards the ambiguities surrounding the position of the charismatic sage and of the poet – mediators between nobles and demos, between past and future – begin to dissolve. One might almost say that the intellectuals, from being middlemen, move into the position of outsiders. They are outside city politics and comment on them from every point of view which an outsider can take: comparing Greek institutions with those of barbarians, propounding theories of the effects of climate on national character, setting the city-state in a wider context by writing histories of wars, satirising, asking fundamental questions in philosophical debate and in tragedy about the meaning of conventional values. Even though in Athens most intellectuals are citizens and not foreigners, they exert their influence through non-political media.[26]

This detached stance, though related to growing formalisation in the political sphere, was also encouraged by differentiaiton among the intellectuals themselves. Philosophers, doctors and historians distinguished themselves from poets by their use of prose; their polemic against traditional myths provoked poets into finding new insights in the old stories. Conventions of genre divided up the intellectual's field of action. The large city audiences of the fifth century could be reached only through a formalisation and ritualisation of the context and techniques of communication.

Eventually, after the magnificent balance between formal discipline and profound, radical reflection achieved in classical Athens, the intellectuals of the late fourth century B.C. began to turn in upon themselves, to address themselves to a small band of disciples and fellow professionals rather than to society as a whole. They drew apart from the city, justifying themselves with the idea of the *bios theōrētikos*, the contemplative life, as the highest type of occupation. But the true turning-point, as we have said, came earlier: at the point when – approximately in the sixth century – philosophers and poets were offered a choice between a political role as sages and avoidance of politics. The majority chose to make their comment on society outside the political arena, and by this choice acquired the freedom to say what they liked – at the price of having their remarks considered irrelevant to political decision-making. Of course the fifth-century sophists did, indirectly, influence the character of Greek politics very considerably. There was even a somewhat abortive attempt to develop a literature of political pamphlets. But the boundaries of the different contexts of theatre, assembly and lecture-room, and the conventions of genre associated with each, created a *prima facie* presupposition of non-interference. Just as the Athenian was expected to forget his private interests in the assembly, he was also expected to forget Aristophanes' jokes at the expense of prominent politicians. The sophists' criticisms of traditional religion and values were difficult to accommodate because they claimed to be telling a truth valid everywhere, in the temple as much as in the lecture-room; but even here the impression of intolerance produced by the prosecution of philosophers in fifth-century Athens does not imply any general restraint on free intellectual discussion. Parody of sacred rites or mutiliation of sacred objects was of course another matter: this was considered a direct attack on the gods and the reaction was correspondingly sharp.

By choosing to speak outside the political context, Greek intellectuals set themselves free to travel – as some poets had done from earliest times. In the period of the sages, some (Pythagoras, Epimenides) appealed to religion as the source of a wisdom which did not require knowledge of local conditions. But the majority worked to develop a new style of context-free communication, truth proved by argument instead of authority, general theories which encompassed the whole Greek world. The philosophical discussion and sophistic demonstration had, of course, their own conventions; but there was a new effort to make discourse status-free, to state explicitly, or question, hitherto unstated assumptions: to cut out the multiple channels through which an act of communication can be socially coloured, and let the words speak for themselves. This was the invention of formally rational discourse. The new idea of truth, the new role of the full-time intellectual, who lived by writing and lecturing, and the general increase in social and geographical mobility in the classical period, led to a new search for more abstract, situation-free definitions of values and norms and for a personal integration able to unify the manifold contexts of experience. The impact of Socrates on his contemporaries was surely due above all to their recognition that his disregard for conventions was inspired by a profound search for personal integrity and coherent values.

Differentiation and communication: the evolution of thought

I should like to pursue further the suggestion of a connection between structural differentiation, together with increasing mobility, and the development of individualism (or at least some of its preconditions) and of formally rational discourse, by connecting it up with the work of Basil Bernstein on the relation between communication and social context. I have analysed more fully elsewhere[27] the process of differentiation of intellectual roles in Greece, stressing the mobility of intellectuals from the sixth century onwards and the spiritual and/or physical withdrawal from involvement in city politics of the early Ionian philosophers, which may well have been connected with the rise of tyranny. Intellectuals were expected to innovate continuously; their writings travelled even when they did not, and many of the early philosophers in any case lived the life of wandering gurus on lecture-tour; they faced a variety of audiences of whose local affairs they had limited knowledge, and who had not much idea what the new speaker would have to say. Certainly the fact that the early philosophers became dissatisfied with the mythical and religious tradition which did form a common culture for all Greeks, and began to seek for a new kind of cosmology, cannot be explained by looking solely at the conditions in which they communicated their ideas. But the emphasis on formal rationality in argument, and on a relational cosmology which made explicit statements about the processes connecting one type of phenomenon with another, brings Bernstein's work readily to mind.

Some preliminary remarks on the aspects of Bernstein's works which are most relevant to the present theme seem to be required. If I understand him correctly, the essential difference between restricted and elaborated codes lies in the degree to which the message communicated is made verbally explicit (elaborated code) or left implicit and inferred from the hearer's understanding of a culture shared with the speaker and of information conveyed by the speaker's social status, tone of voice, body movements, etc., and by the context of communication (restricted code). The elaborated code is thus – in the extreme, ideal-type case – a single-channel, context-free mode of communication, the restricted code multi-channel and embedded in its context. Consequently, elaborated codes require a more highly differentiated lexicon (see further below) and syntax than restricted codes. Restricted codes will be used in small-scale, homogeneous societies or groups, elaborated codes between members of complex societies who occupy different social positions and consequently differ in social and cultural experience.[28] In addition, elaborated codes are found especially where the boundaries between functionally differentiated groups are weak and communication across boundaries relatively frequent: this was the case, I have argued above, in Athens, and the same is true of the Ionian cities.

It seems legitimate to see an analogy between the difference, on Bernstein's definition, between restricted and elaborated codes, and the differences of form between the mythology and religious cosmology of archaic Greek culture and the formally articulated arguments of Greek philosophy and science; and consequently legitimate to postulate a connection between the 'elaborated code' of this formally rational discourse and the increasing differentiation and mobility within Greek society in the period when it was developed, i.e. the sixth and fifth centuries B.C.

The central importance of the relation between speech and context is well illustrated by an example of restricted-code use given long ago by Malinowski,[29] in a case where social class is irrelevant. Men cooperating in a familiar technique have no need of an elaborate syntax but use a restricted number of stereotyped, laconic phrases – even if the operation is one where new decisions have to be made quickly in response to a changing situation, as for example in small boat sailing. Understanding of the context makes verbal explanations redundant.

Malinowski went on to contrast such situations with the context-free discourse of modern science – but later corrected himself, saying that the difference was 'only a matter of degree'.[30] Even the language of modern science cannot be separated from its social context. Nevertheless, the relative distinction may be an important one. As Bernstein has recently stressed in making a distinction between speech code and speech variant,[31] the basis of the classification of restricted and elaborated codes is the way in which information is transmitted (how much by speech and how much by context); the form of articulation of speech is only an indicator of coding, and may also have other significations. The formal characteristics used in some of the earlier test work as indices of the use of an elaborated code (complex sentence structure, etc.), may carry their own social significance as status markers, may be part of the accepted style expected of all speakers in certain formal contexts (seminars, lectures). (They may also, perhaps, be required to handle a subject-matter which itself consists of verbal constructs – definitions, theories, *etc*. The relations between the concepts of science, whether made explicit in a particular discourse or not, can only be learned from scientific texts and not directly from experience. Most communication on such topics is likely to require an elaborately organised form of speech, however, small and intimate the group concerned.) Consequently the formal features which distinguish the explicit, exploratory use of speech from the repetition of acceptable formulae are not the same in all contexts.

These difficulties, however, concern the recognition of elaborated rather than restricted codes. There seems to be good evidence on the relation of speech to context in simple societies illustrating the formal characteristics used by Bernstein as indices of restricted-code use in small, homogeneous groups. Take Malinowski's observations on Kiriwinian: 'The relation of the words, as well as the relation of the sentences, has mainly to be derived from the context. In many cases the subject remains unmentioned, is represented merely by a verbal pronoun and has to be gathered from the situation'.[32] He also comments on the lack of terms for general concepts, as opposed to the proliferation of particular terms in areas significant to the islanders (e.g. agriculture).[33] This perhaps suggests that in lexicon and taxonomy, as in syntax, it is differentiation into hierarchically organised structures and not the mere multiplication of options which marks the elaborated code, if one compares simple and complex societies; the difference probably would not be perceptible in comparing elaborated and restricted codes within a complex society, where the multiplicity of different activities makes general terms necessary for reference to occupational fields other than the speaker's own.

The essential point, however, is the use of implicit rather than explicit relations between words and sentences singled out by Malinowski. Labov's attack on Bernstein for failing to recognise the 'logic of non-standard English'[34] in fact demonstrates that this logic, though perfectly adequate for vigorous expression of a simple argument, *is* implicit. Steps in the argument omitted by the speaker are supplied by Labov. The example (a New York negro boy's statement of his reasons for not believing in Heaven) is too simple and brief to prove much; it does show that lower-class speakers in complex societies can produce effective context-free discourse (which should not in my opinion have been doubted), but it is not an example of fully explicit reasoning.

The distinction between implicit and explicit logic is related to Max Weber's distinction between substantive and formal rationality. (In both cases we are dealing with ideal types, and in concrete instances the distinction will be merely relative). Take law as an example. A substantively but not formally rational system of law, based on equity – on the court's feeling for the just solution in each particular case – can only work smoothly and acceptably where norms are homogeneous and the circumstances surrounding each case are widely known. The decision is rational because it is an acceptable expression of shared norms in a particular contect. More complex societies, however, require a formally rational legal system in which a common set of principles, from which applications to particular cases can be deduced, must be explicitly stated. The rationality in this system lies in the explicitly specified relation of law-court decisions to each other rather than in their relation to the circumstances of each individual case.

Most of the experiments of the Bernstein group have been concerned with specifically linguistic phenomena; but one, carried out by Dorothy Henderson, deals with the implicit logic of conceptual categories in a way which is very relevant to the present discussion. Henderson[35] asked mothers to select the definitions they would use in explaining the meanings of words to their seven-year-old children. In each case they were offered a choice of four explanations: a) a general definition, b) an antonym, c) a 'concrete explicit' example and d) a 'concrete implicit' example.

Cool
(*a*) It's a little bit warmer than cold.
(*b*) It's the opposite of warm.
(*c*) It's when something is no longer hot to touch.
(*d*) It's what you feel when the sun goes in.

Mix
(*a*) To put things together.
(*b*) It's the opposite of separate.

(*c*) It's what you do when you put different paints together to make different colours.
(*d*) When I make a stew the food is all mixed up.

The important point here for us is the difference between the two types of example. (Working-class mothers chose more concrete examples and, within these, more of the 'concrete implicit' type). In the 'concrete explicit' type the relevant feature of the experience offered as an example is explicitly pointed out. In the 'concrete implicit' type the child is left to infer it; the speaker assumes that the mixed-ness of stew and the coolness of the sun going in are equally obvious to everyone.

Henderson's 'concrete implicit' examples show the sort of implicit logic pointed out by Lévi-Strauss in the classifications underlying totemism and myth. (Note also the deliberate play on such implicit classifications in riddles, well developed in many primitive and folk cultures.)[36] Mythical thought, in contrast to scientific thought, is characterised by the use of concrete entities (*zoèmes*) rather than abstractions, and by the fact that their relationships are inherent in them and not separable from them, are left implicit and not explicitly stated. Anthropologists found myths, judged by nineteenth-century standards of formal rationality, illogical, until Malinowski pointed out the substantive rationality in the relation of each myth to its institutional context; Lévi-Strauss's treatment of myth can be seen as an attempt to provide a general structural-functional theory in which the *ad hoc* adjustments by which myths are adapted to different cultural contexts can be seen as manifestations of underlying laws of human behaviour.

Despite the revolution in the study of myth achieved by Lévi-Strauss through looking away from the relation of each myth to its context, to focus on the relation of myths to each other, his work demands a return to the study of myths in context. He has himself stressed the importance of this task.[37] Because the symbols of myth are *zoèmes* and not arbitrary signs, and because their relationships are left implicit and not explained in the myth, the structural analysis of a myth can only be validated by showing its continuity with its cultural context. Furthermore, it is surely *because* myths are embedded in their cultural context that they are transformed when they cross cultural boundaries. The process of transformation can only be understood by studying it in context.

The evidence available for this task is at present lamentably inadequate. Most myths have been published only in translated plot summaries, stripped of all their contextual and auditory dimensions, supplemented to make explicit what was not stated in words by the narrator;[38] most were recorded in artificial conditions, many from informants speaking the recorder's language and not their own. Lévi-Strauss's definition of myth as sense divorced from sound[39] certainly fits most of the data he was using. Even those anthropologists who took care to collect verbatim texts were unable to publish more than a handful of them, and it is only very recently that attention has been paid to the context and mode of narration.[40]

Nevertheless, the limited evidence available suggests that myth resembles Bernstein's definition of a restricted code in three ways. In the first place, narrators of myth make extensive use of paralinguistic and kinesic channels of communication. Change of voice, sometimes accompanied by movement and/or music, or even developing into dramatic representation, gives colour to the personalities of the characters in the story (which are also coloured by the audience's knowledge of their exploits in other tales, as pointed out by Jacobs[41]), and vividly conveys their emotions. (Contrast the quantity of words expended on these two functions in any modern novel). The audience may be drawn into the narration by joining in the songs which punctuate it. (*Cf.* Bernstein's concept of 'sympathetic circularity' in restricted codes? The frequent use of repetitions in myth-telling might also be considered here). Context radically influences the mode of narration: the same incidents may be classed as sacred lore, clan history or children's story, according to the context of narration and the status of the speaker[42] – a phenomenon which has surprised Western observer who expected to find differences of content between the three 'genres'.

Secondly, besides being a multi-channel mode of communication in which context and paralinguistic and kinesic signals play a part as well as words, myth is also as Lévi-Strauss has shown, characterised by superimposition of codes within its purely verbal level. Different sets of categories – for example, modes of cooking, animals, meteorological phenomena – play out, in the same story, their own relations of contrast and association, without being explicitly harmonised with each other. The structural parallels between them detected by the analyst are only unconsciously apprehended by narrator and audience. Here again, where an elaborated code transmits an integrated message through a single channel, the restricted code juxtaposes several channels and leave their relations implicit.

Finally, myth overtly displays at the verbal level a simple linear structure. It takes the form of a narrative: a string of incidents happening one after the other, the causal relations between them seldom explicitly stated. (It is probably this lack of causal connections in the narrative which, more than any other feature, led modern students to characterise myth as 'illogical'; lack of causal connections is also one of the traits by which nonsense verse is characterised). Similarly, Bernstein's restricted-code speakers prefer parallel to subordinate clauses and use 'and', 'then' and 'but' rather than less common conjunctions, whereas elaborated-code speakers use a wide range of subordinating devices to build up complex sentence structures.

Geoffrey Lloyd[43] has analysed in detail the development, in the early stages of Greek philosophy, of concepts and modes of argument which made explicit the relationships of contrast and homology implicit in earlier cosmologies.[44] Much recent work on the history of science in the sixteenth to seventeenth centuries has likewise shown how modern sicence emerged through the process of making explicit, systematising and testing patterns of thought inherited from magic and from pre-scientific visions of the world. I have myself tried to show, for ancient Greece, how the development of philosophy corresponded to changes in the place of the intellectual in Greek society and the introduction of new forms of communication in which the assumptions shared by speaker and audience were fewer and new ideas had to be presented in more explicitly structured arguments.[27] During the time of transition between the first adumbration of the philosopher's role in the sixth century B.C. and the permanent establishment of philosophical schools in the fourth century, the basis of shared assumptions underlying communication between the philosopher and his audience was very limited; and these two centuries were a period of remarkable concentration on the formal properties of argument and classification, culminating in Aristotelian logic and taxonomy. It was also in the same period that the range of the philosopher's knowledge was greatest, and its subdivisions least marked. Plato represents the high-water mark of the 'integrated code' here; with Aristotle we are already moving from 'integrated code' to 'collection code',[45] different topics being treated in different books and the integration of the whole teaching into a single cosmology receiving less emphasis. Aristotle in the 'esoteric' works we have is already addressing himself to students in his own philosophical school, who may already have some grounding in philosophy, rather than to a general public (almost nothing of his 'exoteric' writing for a wider audience has survived).

This last point indicated that if the distinction between restricted and elaborated codes can be applied to the evolution from mythical to scientific thought, the development traced will not be wholly rectilinear. Although some steps in the evolutionary process have irreversible effects – the introduction of writing is the most obvious example – trends towards restriction and towards elaboration may well succeed each other in an evolutionary spiral (I am assuming for the sake of the argument a society which is growing steadily more complex), as new social boundaries are drawn, harden, and later are again called into question. Kuhn's concept of paradigm-development and paradigm-change[46] seems to fit in here. As a paradigm becomes established, the boundaries between the relevant and the irrelevant harden, and they are reinforced by parallel divisions in the structure of groups and organisations. Within each division the shared culture acquires greater density: communication becomes easier, more can be taken for granted. To some extent rivalry between or within groups may take over the function of ensuring explicitness of argument, when it is no longer necessitated by the novelty of a new paradigm and lack of a shared culture in the public to which it is addressed. Indeed explicitness of argument may become a general norm of scientific roles and contexts. As I suggested earlier, the abstract and verbal nature of the subject-matter of a developed science may make this inevitable. Nevertheless, explicitness is never complete and the inclination not to state explicitly, and not to question, what everyone in the group knows, is strong.

'Strong framing' of knowledge, with well-institutionalised boundaries between subjects – which may be backed by educational specialisation from an early age – increases the need for elaboration and explicitness in any communication across boundaries. The effort has to be made, if shared culture is not to turn into shared illusion; and the reason why we may hope, in a complex society, that we are sharing belief in truth along with our errors, is that the complexity of the society does make full cultural homogeneity impossible and elaborated-code communication necessary.

Differentiation, choice and change

The preceding discussions of the articulation of functionally differentiated institutions in Athens and of communication-codes both imply a concern with the difference between restrictive and flexible social forms at approximately the same level of structural complexity as well as with the process of evolution from simpler to more complex structures. The difference between Athens and Sparta in the classical period lay in the articulation of the different elements in the social structure rather than in the variety of units involved. And groups may surround their area of discourse with 'strong framing' and accept statements on the basis of the status of the speaker and the context of speech, rather than explicit argument, in the most complex societies.

The same preoccupation with questions of choice and flexibility can be seen in Rappaport's paper. This convergence is scarcely surprising, but does indicate some of the difficulties of reviving the concept of social evolution in the present day. In the nineteenth century theories of social evolution combined three elements: the assumption of development towards increasing complexity, the search for laws determining a unilinear sequence of stages in this development, and belief in progress. The position now seems to be that studies of the correlates of increasing complexity do not imply any faith in progress, that the search for regularities in processes of social change is not associated with the assumption of a unilinear sequence and need not be associated with the idea of evolution at all,[47] and that studies of the pre-conditions and genesis of developments which contributors to the seminar appeared to value as progressive (the incest taboo, sedentarisation, the city, the state, philosophy and science) coincide only partially with studies of social evolution in the formal sense of increasing complexity.

The axis of our comparisons thus seems to be shifting from the contrast between simple and complex societies to the contrast between adaptable and inflexible ones.[48] But how do societies adapt? To answer this question, we need further research on two topics in particular: forms of social integration or institutional articulation, and the ways in which change is legitimised. Human societies both utilise institutionalised mechanisms of adaptation and are composed of thinking individuals whose actions are influenced by their perception and interpretations of what goes on around them.

The study of communication obviously provides a link between the two problems. Bernstein's work on communication as a mechanism of social integration – and of social control – continues the work on exchange in homogeneous and in differentiated structures begun by Mauss.[49] Communication in a restricted code, like gift-exchange, is part of a 'fait social total' in which medium of exchange, social context and status of actors are linked together. Elaborated-code communication, like 'general-purpose' money[50] or complex forms of marriage[51] enables actors to handle a much wider range of situations with an instrument which they perceive as differentiated, not attached to particular settings and statuses. Such mechanisms of exchange and communication facilitate adaptation not only because they are relatively (not absolutely) context-free, but because they are thought of as being context-free and available for use in new circumstances. 'Elaborated codes . . . contain the potentiality of change in principles'.[52]

Thus the institutional study of adaptive mechanisms in society leads back inevitably to the question of the actors' perceptions and experience. We cannot compare the capacity of different societies to change, and the amount of choice allowed to their members, without asking how change and choice are perceived.

As well as developing more dynamic and variable models of social structure in their own work, anthropologists need to recognise that actors too have dynamic and variable models of the structure of their society. The ideal-type traditional society whose members believe that nothing ever changes would be extinct by now, if it had ever existed. Actors' models are not synchronic maps of a total social structure of the type produced by structural-functionalist ethnographers, but diachronic in scope and uneven in coverage. They are based on concrete experience of social settings and the norms of behaviour attached to them, and at the same time they shape the actor's perceptions of his experience. The study of processes of structural differentiation raises particularly interesting questions about the perception of changes in social structure. Sometimes the introduction of a new institutional setting creates the conditions for the rapid development of new clusters of norms – as in the case of the introduction of dramatic competitions in classical Athens; sometimes it is a new role which develops and only slowly becomes attached to particular settings (the Greek philosophers).[33] The study of the process of differentiation of political, economic and religious functional spheres (which of course have different boundaries in different societies) prompts questions about the conceptualisation of these functions and their articulation. Here, if anywhere, it should be possible to demonstrate the relation and interaction between the boundaries of institutional groupings and of conceptual categories. If the study of social evolution is no longer an end in itself, it is still an important approach to the understanding of societies in time and in change.[54]

NOTES

1 Gershenkron, A. (1972), *Economic Backwardness in Historical Perspective*, Cambridge, Mass.

2 See Smith, M.G. (1974), *Corporations and Society*, London.

3 For a different treatment, focussed on the control of potential conflicts between group interests rather than the individual's role-management, see Smith (1974), pp. 191-2, 260-2.

4 Gearing, F. (1958), 'The structural poses of 18th-century Cherokee villages', *American Anthropologist*, 60.

5 Brown, P. (1971), 'The rise and function of the Holy Man in late antiquity', *Journal of Roman Studies*, 61.

6 See also the discussion of religion and law in the twelfth century A.D. in Brown, P. (1975), 'Society and the supernatural: a medieval change', *Daedalus*, 104, 2.

7 Smith, M.G. (1962), *West Indian Family Structure*, Seattle.

8 See for example Benet, F. (1957), 'Explosive markets: the Berber highlands', *in* Polanyi, K., Arensberg, C., and Pearson, H. (eds.), *Trade and Market in the Early Empires*, Glencoe, Ill.

9 Weinreich, U., Labov, W., and Herzog, M.I. (1968), 'Empirical foundations for a theory of language change', *in* Lehmann, W.P. and Malkiel, Y. (eds.), *Directions for Historical Linguistics*, Austin and London, p. 188.

10 Labov, W. (1972), 'The internal evolution of linguistic rules', *in* Stockwell, R.P. and Macaulay, R.K.S. (eds.), *Linguistic Change and Generative Theory, Essays from the U.C.L.A. Conference on Historical Linguistics*, Bloomington. *cf.* also Bailey, C.J.N. (1972), 'The integration of linguistic theory: internal reconstruction and the comparative method in descriptive analysis', *ibid.*

11 Meillet, A. (1906), 'Comment les mots changent de sens', *L'Année Sociologique*, 9.

12 Thorndike, E.L. (1905), 'Measurement of twins', *Journal of Philosophy, Psychology and Scientific Methods*, 2; Pearson, K. (1897), 'Kindred group-marriage', *in* Pearson, K., *Chances of Death and Other Studies in Evolution*, London.

13 Lowie, R. (1920), *Primitive Society*, London, p. 26.

14 Cf. Goldenweiser, A. (1936), 'Loose ends of theory on the individual, pattern and involution in primitive society', *Essays in Anthropology presented to A.L. Kroeber*, Berkeley; and Geertz, C. (1963), *Agricultural Involution*, Berkeley.

15 Goffman, E. (1961), *Asylums*, Garden City, N.Y.

16 In complex modern societies most interaction settings are supported in one way or another by a complex infrastructure of corporate units even if these units exercise only marginal control over some settings. But this is much less true of archaic societies.

17 Cf. Smith (1974), p. 261.

18 See Finley, M.I. (1968), 'Sparta', *in* Vernant, J.-P. (ed.), *Problèmes de la guerre en Grèce ancienne*, Paris/Hague.

19 Gluckman, M. (1962), 'Les rites de passage', *in* Gluckman (ed.), *Essays on the Ritual of Social Relations*, Manchester; cf. Kuper, A. (1971), 'Council structure and decision-making', *in* Richards, A.I. and Kuper, A. (eds.), *Councils in Action*, Cambridge.

20 See however, Goffman, E. (1956), *The Presentation of Self in Everyday Life*, Edinburgh, for examples, on a more limited scale, from complex societies.

21 I have to thank Professor Louis Dumont for stimulating me to look at Athenian institutions from this point of view.

22 Momigliano, A. (1973), 'Freedom of speech in antiquity' and 'Impiety in the classical world', *Dictionary of the History of Ideas*, New York.

23 Theophrastus' Superstitious Man, *Characters* 16, attests this view clearly for the late fourth century. In the fifth century Thucydides (7.69.2.) emphasises religion in a speech made to a demoralised army and consisting entirely of appeals to personal attachments: family pride, safety of wives and children – old fashioned feelings, he says, such as men are not ashamed to call on in emergencies. I do not think it is entirely Thucydides' practice of using speeches to convey interpretation and analysis which leads him to present speeches before battle delivered in more hopeful circumstances as concerned largely with strategic and tactical matters (e.g. 2.89). But the subject needs further investigation.

24 This analysis owes much to Vernant, J.-P. (1965), 'La lutte des classes', *Eirene*, 4, reprinted in Vernant, J.-P. (1974), *Mythe et société en Grèce ancienne*, Paris. Following a recent discussion with Joel Kahn, I would stress that the Athenian classification of roles and activities as 'economic' or 'political' was based on their experience of society as made up of a variety of social settings with markedly different norms, which obscured for them the connections between those settings. The relationship between political decisions and the level of activity in the market was only partially perceived, and understanding of the interrelations of tribute, military activity, the movements of money and labour, trade and production was hampered by the fact that the most important part of the discussion was carried on the idiom of politics. It was the concrete social experience which gave the ideology its change of success.

25 Mystery cults were spreading rapidly already in the sixth century. Both the generally anomic state of Greek society in this period of transition between traditional aristocratic control and the development of formal political organisation, and the tendency of tyrants to favour a somewhat impersonal, spectacular type of religious festival may have had an influence here.

26 Sophocles, the least political of the dramatic poets in his plays, is the only one known to have held a major political office; his contemporary Ion of Chios tells a story implying that neither he nor Pericles took his election as general very seriously (*F.G.H* 392 F.6.).

27 Humphreys, S.C. (1975), ' "Transcendence" and intellectual roles; the ancient Greek case', *Daedalus*, 104, 2.

28 Bernstein's work is explicitly based on Durkheim's contrast between the mechanical solidarity of simple societies and the organic solidarity of complex ones. It is also principally concerned with the functioning of speech codes as mechanisms of social control. This aspect of Bernstein's work is not my concern here, but is developed in this volume by Maurice Bloch.

29 Malinowski, B. (1923), 'Meaning in primitive languages', *in* Ogden, C.K. and Richard, I.A. (eds.), *The Meaning of Meaning*, London, pp. 310-12.

30 Malinowski, B. (1935), *Coral Gardens and their Magic*, London, Vol. II, p. 58.

31 Bernstein, B. (1974), *Class, Codes and Control*, Vol. I, 2nd ed., London, pp. 11ff.

32 Malinowski (1935), II, p. 36; cf. also Lee, D. (1959), 'Codifications of reality; lineal and non-lineal', *in* Lee, D., *Freedom and Culture*, Englewood Cliffs, N.J.; Finnegan, R. (1967), *Limba Stories and Story-Telling*, Oxford, pp. 75ff.

33 Malinowski (1935), II, p. 66.

34 Labov, W. (1969), 'The logic of non-standard English', *Georgetown Monographs on Language and Linguistics,* 22. (Reprinted in Giglioli, P.P. (ed.) (1972), *Language and Social Context,* Harmondsworth.)

35 Henderson, D. (1970), 'Contextual specificity, discretion and cognitive socialisation: with special reference to language', *Sociology,* 4.

36 Cf. Finnegan, R. (1970), *African Oral Literature,* Oxford.

37 Lévi-Strauss, C. (1960), 'La structure et la forme: Réflexions sur un ouvrage de Vladimir Propps', *in* Lévi-Strauss, C. (1973), *Anthropologie Structurale Deux,* Paris.

38 Compare the literal and free translations in Malinowski (1935) and Finnegan (1967).

39 Lévi-Strauss, C. (1971), *Mythologiques IV: L'Homme Nu,* Paris.

40 Cf. especially Finnegan (1967), (1970).

41 Jacobs, M. (1960), 'Thoughts on methodology for comprehension of an oral literature', in Wallace, A.F.C. (ed.), *Man and Cultures, Selected Papers of the Fifth International Congress of Anthropological and Ethnological Sciences (1956),* Philadelphia.

42 Firth, R. (1961), *History and Tradition in Tikopia,* Wellington; Finnegan (1970).

43 Lloyd, G. (1966), *Polarity and Analogy,* Cambridge.

44 cf. also Parry, A. (1970), 'Thucydides' use of abstract language', *Yale French Studies,* 45.

45 Bernstein, B. (1971), 'On the classification and framing of educational knowledge', *in* Bernstein (1974).

46 Kuhn, T.S. (1962), *The Structure of Scientific Revolutions, Chicago.*

47 Smith, M.G. (1960), *Government in Zazzau,* London; also Smith (1974).

48 For parallel developments in evolutionary biology see Huxley, J. (1954), 'The evolutionary process', *in* Huxley, J. *et al.* (eds.), *Evolution as a Process,* London.

49 Mauss, M. (1925), 'Essai sur le don', *L'Année Sociologique,* N.S.I., 1923-1924. (*The Gift,* London, 1954.)

50 Bohannan, P. (1959), 'The impact of money on an African subsistence economy', *Journal of Economic History,* 19.

51 Lévi-Strauss, C. (1966), 'The future of kinship studies', *Proceedings of the Royal Anthropological Institute 1965.*

52 Bernstein (1974), p. 200.

53 See Gernet, L. (1945), 'Les origines de la philosophie', *in* Gernet, L. (1968), *Anthropologie de la Grèce antique,* Paris.

54 This paper presents some of the results of a research project on 'transformations in ancient political and religious concepts, organisation and values' carried out in association with Professor A. Momigliano, with support from the Social Science Research Council. I should like to express here my gratitude to both.

WARWICK BRAY

Civilising the Aztecs

The title of this paper is borrowed from a short article, written as long ago as 1948, in which Paul Kirchhoff drew attention to the wealth of documentation existing for the later centuries of native Mexican history.[1] Although most of these chronicles were first written down after the Spanish conquest, many of the authors were Indian noblemen or first generation mestizos who were familiar with prehispanic culture from the inside, and who supplemented their personal experience with information from both oral tradition and native pictographic records.

One of the central themes of the chronicles is the interplay, political and cultural, between Mesoamericans and Chichimecs. The former represent 'civilisation', the sophisticated urban life of Mesoamerica proper, identified in prehispanic Mexican mythology with the Toltecs and their descendants;[2] the Chichimecs, by contrast, represent 'savagery', the life of the nomadic and semi-nomadic tribes who lived beyond the northern frontier in the desert zone where settled life was impossible.

The history of Mexico from the tenth century A.D. is a story of successive Chichimec incursions into civilised Mesoamerica, and of the cultural assimilation of these invaders by the old-established peoples.[3] As Kirchhoff noted, such authors as Ixtlilxochitl,[4] Chimalpahin,[5] Tezozómoc[6] and others, were – and were proud to be – the descendants of Chichimecs who had become Mesoamericans. Kirchhoff also emphasised the wider usefulness of these chronicles:

> The data contained in these sources may be used statically for the purpose of reconstructing the culture of both Mesoamericans and Chichimecs as it was at the time when they first met, but it seems to us that their principal value lies in the light they shed on certain historical *processes*, both indirectly on those which, on either side, paved the way for the interplay between peoples of high and low culture, and directly on those that grew out of their association.[7]

The present paper follows up this suggestion by examining the history of a single Chichimec tribe, the one which we know as the Aztecs.

Most of the current models of social evolution[8] are based on cross-cultural comparisons between existing, or archaeologically reconstructed, societies widely separated in space and time. The technique consists of clumping these communities into 'bands', 'tribes', 'chiefdoms' or whatever, and then listing the features which such communities have in common, thus creating an *ideal type* of society which represents a particular *stage of development*. The process of social evolution can then be studied by comparing the qualities of each type of society with those of the types of society which come before and after it in the evolutionary scale. This method has yielded stimulating results, especially at a descriptive level, but it has one major disadvantage: the processes of transition from one idealised stage of development to another are inferred, not directly observed. Inevitably, therefore, the theoretical model reflects the individual analyst's personal philosophy of how society *ought to have developed*.

The Aztec case can be used as a control on this kind of approach by showing the way in which one particular non-European community made the transition from tribe to state, and even to empire. This change was self-generated. From the time when they gained their independence, the Aztecs were never conquered by outsiders until the European invasions of 1519-21, by which time the development was largely complete. Although change was never *imposed* upon the Aztecs, it was (as Kirchhoff observed) stimulated in the early stages by contact with more civilised peoples.

Before examining the processes of social change it is necessary to give a brief outline of Aztec political history. The following account suffers from over-compression and simplification, but can be amplified by reference to the recent books of Davies[9] and Brundage.[10]

Aztec political history

Aztec history can be divided into three phases: (1) a period of wandering, which ended with the foundation of Tenochtitlan in 1345,[11] (2) a period during which the Aztecs consolidated their position in the Basin of Mexico under foreign control, and (3) a period of independence, expansion and conquest during which the Aztecs and their allies brought most of Mexico under their sway. This came to an end when the Aztecs themselves were conquered by the Spaniards in 1521.

The period of wandering, twelfth century A.D. until 1345

The only documentation for this period is in the form of legends, often contradictory and invariably written down long after the events they purport to describe. The impression left by these legends, though untrustworthy in detail and lacking all archaeological proof, is probably not far from the truth.

In their own historical records the Aztecs claimed, with some pride, that they were of Chichimec stock. They figure in the documentary sources as a migratory tribe, perhaps a composite group of a few thousand people,[12] just one of the several Chichimec bands which made their way into central Mexico after the collapse of the Toltec empire in the late twelfth century.

In Mexico the word 'Chichimec' was used as a general term which could mean anything from 'immigrant' to 'barbarian'. As Martínez Marín has already pointed out, Aztec culture during the migration period already included many Mesoamerican traits.[13] According to Durán[14] and Tezozómoc[15] the Aztecs spoke Nahuatl, cultivated a few crops and understood the techniques of irrigation, constructed stone buildings whenever they halted for long enough, wore garments of woven cactus fibre, had a social organisation based on *calpullis* (see below), and were familiar with the 52-year sacred calendar and the ritual ball game. This considerable list suggests that the Aztecs were marginal representatives of the Mesoamerican tradition, one of the relatively unsophisticated tribes from the northern marches of the old Toltec empire. In this connection, Nahuatl sources make a distinction between two kinds of Chichimecs: the semi-civilised *tamime,* and the *teochichimeca*, the 'extreme' or 'true' Chichimecs who remained hunters and gatherers, lived in caves, wore skin clothing, and were ignorant of the rituals and religious ceremonies which were common to all the civilised Mesoamerican peoples.[16]

Armillas has put forward impressive evidence for a period of reduced rainfall on the northern frontiers in the late twelfth and early thirteenth centuries. Increasing drought, in a zone where agriculture was already precarious, would quickly render the settled Mesoamerican pattern of life impossible, leading to a retraction of the frontier, abandonment of the marches, and a southward migration of the frontier farmers.[17] As these tribes fell back on the old civilised core territory, the lands which they had abandoned were occupied by nomadic Chichimec bands, some of which made deep inroads into the settled regions, causing further confusion and breakdown.

If this interpretation is correct, both *tamime* and *teochichimec* groups were involved in the disturbances which accompanied the collapse of the Toltec empire. In these terms the Aztecs are best considered as *tamimes*, while the *teochichimec* element is represented by the followers of Xolotl who established their rule over several towns in the northern and eastern sectors of the Valley of Mexico.[18] The native histories of Texcoco, a city whose royal dynasty was directly descended from Xolotl, give a detailed description of the life-style of these Chichimecs and of the processes of acculturation by which they gradually became civilised.[3]

Aztec history begins with a period of wandering during which (according to one version of the migration legend) the priests discovered a cave containing a miraculous speaking idol of the god Huitzilopochtli, which guided the tribe during its travels. The early parts of the story belong rather to myth than to history, but the picture becomes clearer in the late thirteenth century, when the Aztecs entered the Valley of Mexico to find the land already divided up among some 60 city states, many of which were ruled by other Chichimec dynasties of fairly recent arrival. The stronger powers had by that time reduced the weaker states to subjection, and had carved out miniature 'empires' in which the conquered cities paid tribute to their overlords but retained a good deal of internal independence.

In this setting the Aztecs gained a precarious living, squatting on the land of other people and being continually moved on. From about 1250 to 1298 they were the vassals of Azcapotzalco, capital of the Tepanec 'empire' which dominated the western part of the Basin. They next lived under the overlordship of the city of Culhuacan, until driven out into the swamps of lake Texcoco. Here in 1345 they founded a settlement, which they called Tenochtitlan, on an uninhabited island surrounded by marshes, left in peace only because they were not worth the trouble of destroying and because the territory they had chosen was an inhospitable no-man's-land which was coveted by none of the surrounding powers. From Tenochtitlan a splinter group of the tribe moved to a nearby island in about 1358 to found the second Aztec settlement at Tlatelolco.

Consolidation in the Valley of Mexico, 1345-1428

The new settlements came once again under the yoke of the Tepanec kingdom, and the Mexica-Aztecs were forced to pay tribute and to fight as mercenaries in the wars of their overlord. By the late fourteenth century Tenochtitlan felt powerful enough to petition the mainland states for a king of its own, and the city got its first real monarch in the person of Acamapichtli (1372-91), a prince of the Culhua dynasty. Under their next two rulers, Huitzilíhuitl (1391-1415) and Chimalpopoca (1415-26), the Aztecs remained under Tepanec control. The fourth ruler, Itzcóatl (1426-40), organised an alliance with the other lakeside towns of Texcoco and Tlacopan in an attempt to break the grip of Azcapotzalco, and in 1428 this alliance defeated the Tepanecs in battle. With this victory, the Aztecs gained their independence.[19]

The victory was the turning point in Aztec history. The allied cities found themselves the heirs of the Tepanec empire, and the gains were shared out between them. The victors were now powerful enough to dictate terms to the other Valley states, and the situation was formalised in the 'Triple Alliance', a treaty between Tenochtitlan, Texcoco and Tlacopan which provided for mutual defence and a sharing of the spoils of future conquests. Within the framework of the

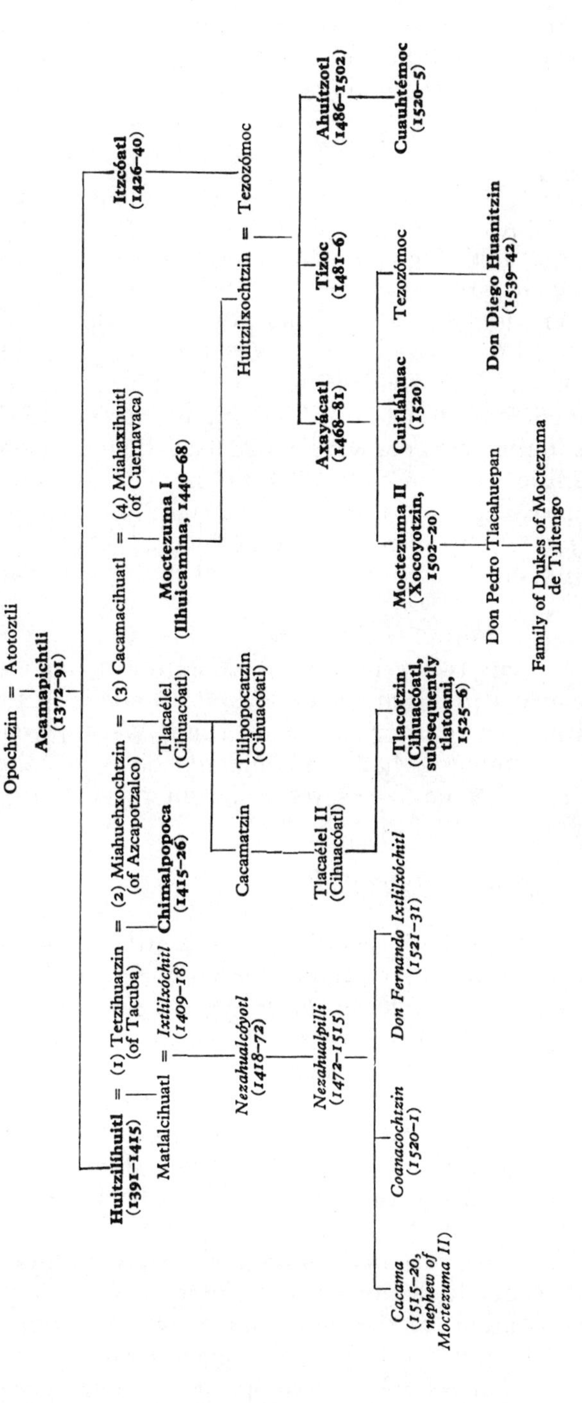

Rulers of Tenochtitlan are set in bold type, rulers of Texcoco in italic.

Figure 1

alliance each city remained sovereign and independent. This Triple Alliance was the major force in Mexican politics for the next century, and what is loosely called the 'Aztec Empire' was in fact under the joint control of the rulers of the three allied cities, though as time went on Tenochtitlan became the dominant partner.

Expansion and conquest, 1428-1519

During the reign of Itzcóatl the remaining Valley states were overrun by the Alliance armies. Successive rulers carried conquests further afield, outside the high plateau country and into the lowlands, allowing the allied cities to exact tribute from a new range of environments. The full story of conquest and expansion need not be detailed here. By 1519, when the Spaniards landed on the Gulf Coast, some 489 towns and cities paid tribute to the allies, and the 'Aztec Empire' straddled the isthmus from the Atlantic to the Pacific. The subject peoples in this vast area were not Aztecs, though participating in a common Mesoamerican cultural tradition. Tenochtitlan, which began its existence as a cluster of reed huts, had by 1519 grown into an imperial metropolis. In political terms it had become a superpower, with all the rewards and problems which that status implies.[20]

The development from Chichimec tribe to city state and imperial power took less than two centuries. Such rapid change required constant adjustments in social, political and economic institutions, with the result that Aztec society was never static. What it would have become, if the Spaniards had not intervened, is a matter for speculation, but in 1519 the Aztecs were still riding high.

Alternative models of social change

Broadly speaking, models of socio-cultural evolution can be divided into two categories. In the first group come those explanations which select changes in one variable as the 'prime mover', the principal impetus for change, and which trace its effect on all the other variables which make up the socio-political system. These explanations have been characterised as *linear models*[21] or *cause-and-effect* models.[22] In the second group are *systemic models*[21] or *equilibrium models*,[22] which start from the assumption that social change comes about through the mutual interaction of many variables, each of which affects, and is affected by, all of the others.

The theoretical issues have been argued elsewhere,[23] and it should no longer be necessary to demonstrate the inadequacy of any simple monocausal explanation for the development of civilisation. In the present paper the equilibrium-systemic explanation is taken for granted, and the changes which took place in Aztec society are analysed in terms of such a model.

I owe a special debt to a recent paper by Don E. Dumond, which discusses the relationship between population growth, the adoption of intensive means of production, and the centralisation of political control.[24] Although Dumond makes no reference to the Aztec case, all three phenomena are clearly recognisable and are, in fact, unusually well documented.

Dumond argues that when a population increases, and when this growth is not checked by birth control, infanticide or out-migration, the natural strategy is to expand subsistence resources. Once this decision has been taken, 'the expansion of subsistence . . . initiates a positive feedback measure, resulting in a self-intensifying spiral as population increase and subsistence expansion reinforce each other, constituting what Maruyama (1963) has called a deviation amplifying process. It seems clear that the adoption of a decision leading to this spiral portends other cultural adjustments.'[25]

The overall direction of these changes, Dumond suggests, will be towards increased centralisation. The general development will be from an *egalitarian* society (with 'as many positions of valued status as there are individuals capable of filling them') to a *ranked* society ('fewer positions of valued status than persons capable of filling them') to a *stratified* society (in which 'adult members . . . enjoy differential rights of access to basic resources', and an upper social class emerges). The *state* is considered to be 'the inevitable result of the achievement of stratified society'.[26]

Besides this general proposition, Dumond makes a number of specific predictions about what may be expected to happen in the course of such changes. Having complained that the study of evolution in terms of ideal types of society is founded on intuition rather than observation, I must acknowledge that in the case of the Aztecs nearly all Dumond's predictions come true. In the following pages, some of these are examined in more detail within the context of a systemic analysis of Aztec history.

Evolution of the Aztec socio-political system

In this section the various factors which influenced change are examined separately as subsystems of the total socio-political system, with special emphasis on the ways in which they interacted with each other.

Population

There is abundant evidence for rapid and continuous population growth (not just in Aztec territory, but throughout the Basin of Mexico as a whole) throughout the Chichimec and Aztec periods, from the thirteenth century until the Spanish Conquest. The data are summarised by Sanders,[27] and derive from archaeological field surveys which show that sites became larger and more numerous as the Aztec state developed.[28]

The documentary sources also make it clear that the size of the Aztec community underwent rapid growth. At the time when the Aztecs were still a small and semi-nomadic tribe they were divided into only 7 *calpullis* (roughly translatable as 'clans', see below).[29] By 1345, when Tenochtitlan was founded, the number of *calpullis* had risen to 15 or 20,[30] and reached 80-90 in urban Tenochtitlan at the time of the Conquest, when some 150,000-200,000 people were resident in the capital alone.[31]

Dumond's model is couched in terms of natural increase, without considering immigration. In Aztec Mexico both factors were present. Tezozómoc records that while the Aztecs were temporarily settled at Chapultepec in the closing years of the thirteenth century,

> they did not cease to multiply and increase in number, after the fashion of the Sons of Israel in Egypt under King Pharaoh. And their neighbours, when they saw the growth in their numbers, began to be troubled and to make war upon them, with the intention of destroying them, that their name might be no longer known upon the face of the earth, and that their kind might not establish itself there.[32]

It is impossible to give precise statistics, but it seems that the unusually rapid growth was due more to large-scale immigration than to natural increase on the part of the original Aztec community. The chronicle evidence shows that the growing wealth and power of Tenochtitlan and Texcoco attracted immigrant groups from all over Mexico,[33] and the high rate of population growth induced by this immigration must in part account for the speed of social change in the emerging Aztec state. At very least, the influx of new people rendered more acute and pressing the problems of adaptation which the Aztecs had to solve.

Agricultural expansion

In Dumond's model, expansion of the subsistence base may take two forms: the intensification of local productivity and/or the 'capturing' of resources from somebody else. The first alternative includes both agricultural improvement and an increase in commercial and industrial activities.

Crafts and commerce are examined in a later section, but agricultural intensification is abundantly attested for Aztec times. In the Teotihuacan Valley,[34] in the Texcoco area,[35] and in the southern part of the Basin of Mexico[36] this period saw the first occupation of the marginal lands on the upper slopes, with the construction of agricultural terraces. The canal system which irrigates the hillsides of Texcotzinco, near Texcoco, is of similar date, though Parsons emphasises that many of the canals in the east-central sector carried water for luxury purposes (royal gardens and baths etc.) rather than for farming needs.[37] This was also the period when the swampy lands in the bottom of the Valley were reclaimed for agriculture. The lakeshore plain on the eastern side of the Valley was turned into prime farmland by means of large drainage works,[35] and in the Chalco-Xochimilco lake basin more than 120 km^2 of freshwater swamp were converted into enormously fertile *chinampa* gardens. Other *chinampa* plots were created around Tenochtitlan, Tlatelolco and Azcapotzalco. Archaeological survey and excavations by Armillas[38] and Parsons[39] demonstrate that *chinampa* construction began no earlier than A.D. 1200 and reached its peak after 1400. This is corroborated by the evidence from documentary sources (see 'land ownership' below).

Land ownership

Dumond maintains that, in a ranked society, land and resources will be controlled by localised, kin-orientated, self-sufficient social units with rights of access distributed more or less equally among members. As a ranked society evolves into a stratified society, private ownership (with the right of transfer from person to person) will become more widespread. By clever manipulation, particularly in the redistribution of vacant land, a minority of governing officials can become large landowners, forming the nucleus of an upper class with the right to levy taxes on the populace. If 'improved' land (e.g. irrigated land, which represents an investment of labour) is involved, the emergent aristocracy is likely to control most of this.[40]

All these predictions fit the Aztec case. The terminology of Aztec landholding is complicated and there are certain ambiguities,[41] but property ownership falls into three basic categories:

(*a*) land owned in common by the *calpullis*, to one of which every Aztec belonged by right of birth. This land was not worked in common, but was parcelled out among the families which made up the *calpulli*. Nevertheless, ownership remained vested in the *calpulli*, to which the land reverted when it was no longer needed by the individual family.

(*b*) private estates owned by the ruler or given by him to noblemen, successful warriors and to members of the merchant class. Certain of these estates were owned outright and could be inherited. Others were given 'for life', reverting to the ruler on the owner's death. In practice, however, these estates tended to be given to another member of the family if a suitable candidate was available. The owners of private estates did not work the land in person but rented it out in return for a percentage of the yield.

(*c*) office lands set aside for the upkeep of the temples, the palace, civil service, judiciary etc., and to finance wars. These lands pertained to the office rather than to the office-holder, and were transferred when the office changed hands.

There is good evidence that private ownership was increasing at the expense of *calpulli* ownership as the Aztec state developed. Data on the very early period are scanty, but property rights of any sort cannot have been very important to a mobile tribe. The real shift of power can be traced back at least to 1428, the year of the victory over Azcapotzalco.

According to official Aztec history, represented by the works of Tezozómoc and Diego Durán, the common people had been afraid to go to war, though the warriors under the ruler Itzcóatl and his chief advisor, a man called Tlacaelel,[42] were anxious for a trial of strength. The debate went in favour of the warriors, but in the process a curious compact was struck between the parties:

> The king and his men replied, 'If we do not achieve what we intend, we will place ourselves in your hands, so that our flesh becomes your nourishment. In this way you will have your vengeance . . .'. 'Let it be as you have said', answered the people. 'You yourselves have delivered your sentence. We answer: if you are victorious, we will serve you and work your lands for you. We will pay tribute to you, we will build your houses and be your servants . . . In short, we will sell and subject our persons and goods to your service forever.'[43]

This singular event is recorded only in post-Conquest sources, but it represents official Aztec doctrine. Given the general Mexican custom of falsifying history for propaganda purposes, the incident itself may never actually have taken place. What is more important is that the Aztecs themselves appreciated that the victory of 1428 had initiated a new social order, and felt the need to justify or rationalise this in terms of a voluntary compact made after full consultation and debate.

Whatever the historical validity of this compact, the result of the victory confirmed its terms. When the lands of Azcapotzalco were expropriated, Itzcóatl and Tlacaelel received 10 units each, the warrior nobles received 2 units apiece, and the common people nothing at all (except for small grants to a few outstanding fighters). Only a small proportion of the land was handed over to the *calpullis* to be used for the maintenance of their temples.[44] Proof that these events are not historical fiction comes from Calnek's studies of land archives in Mexico City.[45] A similar unequal shareout was made after the conquest of Coyoacan.[46]

At the same time, the ruler gave out titles and offices to the members of the nobility. Tlacaelel was able to tell the recipients,

> Friends and brothers, your sovereign, King Itzcóatl, my close relative and yours, greets you and wishes to honour you according to your merit. He wishes to give you titles of preeminence over others, as well as lands which will support you and your families.[47]

As Davies has already pointed out, land-holding provides the key to the social order.[48] By taking the greater share for themselves, the ruler and his nobles assured themselves of a basis of economic power independent of the communal (*calpulli*) organisations.

The distinctions between the classes were reinforced in various ways. Estates granted to noblemen could only be sold to other nobles or to merchants. These private estates were in the hands of absentee landlords who paid no taxes but claimed up to 50% of the harvest for their personal use. The owner took no active part in cultivation, which was controlled by the state through its appointed officials. These men administered estates on behalf of the owners, but had no obligation to consult them. Like everything else, agriculture was organised in the service of the state.[49] By contrast, an individual commoner who received a grant of land could either work it himself or sell it to another commoner, but he could not employ others to labour in his fields. In other words, the ordinary man was not allowed to own more land than he could cultivate in person. Entrepreneurial activities were thus limited to noblemen and merchants who enjoyed usufruct rather than working the land themselves. As Calnek has demonstrated from his study of land tenure documents, the private *chinampa* estates of the noblemen were geographically separate from those owned by the *calpullis*, and were many times larger than those worked by individual peasants.[50] Since rents were based on a percentage of production, there is every reason to believe that the big landowners were concerned to promote agricultural efficiency.

Although precise statistics are unobtainable, the processes outlined above seem to have gained momentum as the Aztecs transformed themselves from a tribe to a state. Chinampa construction is recorded at Tenochtitlan in the reign of Acamapichtli (1372-91) and under the first ruler of Tlatelolco at about the same time.[51] Calnek has shown that the first attempts at land reclamation after the founding of Tenochtitlan and Tlatelolco were carried out on a massive scale, but did not lead to the emergence of a centralised state system. In 1382-85 these *chinampas* were destroyed by flood, and it seems that by 1415 they had still not been reconstructed. It was during this period, when the most fertile plots were out of action, that the system of markets was organised in Tenochtitlan and Tlatelolco, and the merchant class (the *pochteca*) emerged as an important entity in the latter city. As Calnek emphasises, this short period of just over 30 years seems to mark the transition from a rural to a predominantly urban, market economy.

The situation changed dramatically with the victory over

Azcapotzalco. By expropriating the lands of the Tepanec cities the Aztecs acquired a new agricultural support area, but (as we have seen) these new lands were not given to the *calpullis* but to the elite class estimated at 10% of the total population. The planned layout of these new *chinampas* argues for state enterprise rather than individual initiative. This is even more true of the aqueducts and protective dikes constructed by royal decree, and using corvée labour, in the reign of Itzcóatl, culminating in 1450 with the building of a dike nine miles long by the joint efforts of Moctezuma I and the ruler of Texcoco. By this time we can undoubtedly talk of a hydraulic system under state control.

At this point it becomes essential to distinguish between land as a source of food and land as a source of wealth and status. Calnek has conclusively shown that, in spite of state control and large-scale reclamation, the *chinampa* plots could satisfy only a small part of the city's food needs.[52] Not only that, but after 1415 most of the city's inhabitants were not engaged in food production at all. In this situation, agricultural intensification is unlikely to be the sole – or even the main – agency of social change.

Consideration of land as a source of status and political power shows that changes in the pattern of land-ownership were linked in a feedback way with other factors of social change. Since merchants and nobles did not till their lands in person, they were free to hold state office and to fill the positions of leadership. Thus a strong connection grew up between social class (noble status, often deriving from blood relationship with the ruler), hereditary wealth, and a monopoly of the important jobs in administration, the state religion, the army and foreign trade. By a process of mutual reinforcement, changes in each of these sub-systems initiated a period of rapid social evolution, resulting in the emergence of an aristocratic, elitist and highly stratified society.

Class structure: the rise of the aristocracy

The previous section has shown one of the ways in which the nobility consolidated its power, but we have not yet considered how or why an aristocracy emerged in the first place. For this, we can refer back to Dumond's model, and in particular to three of his predictions:

1. *That in simple societies there is rank but not social class* (i.e. that most people live at a similar level of subsistence, even if some hold office and others do not).
2. *That, as society becomes more complex, certain executive offices emerge, and may be filled by ranked members of a particular class.*
3. *That, once society reaches a certain size, the ranked members become numerous enough to constitute a class apart: they begin to identify with each other rather than with unranked members of their own kin group.*

Aztec social organisation during the period of wandering is difficult to reconstruct, but the chronicles (though differing on points of detail) give a reasonably consistent impression. The Aztecs began as a tribal society which had no single leader. As Davies puts it: 'Their leadership at this stage was of a somewhat theocratic nature, with religious, political and military functions closely linked.'[53] The hierarchy, insofar as there was one, was based on the ritual number four. The main documentary sources (Tezozómoc, Chimalpahin and Torquemada) speak of four *teomamas*, 'bearers of the god', who interpret his instructions and pass them on to the people. The same sources mention military leaders or war chiefs from three to twenty in number, though never a single ruler. Since many of the names mentioned in the *teomama* lists also recur as military leaders, there seems to have been a good deal of interlocking. In addition, the heads of the 7 *calpullis*, into which the tribe was at that time divided, had a say in the decision-making process. Although there was no chief, let alone anything which could be called a king, the office of *tlatoani* (ruler) may have existed in embryo, for Tezozómoc's *Crónica Mexicáyotl* speaks of a 'Rey' during the period of migration.[54]

During the early years of settlement in the Basin of Mexico, changes are apparent. In the course of their short stay at Chapultepec early in the 14th century, the Aztecs experimented with one-man government by appointing a supreme chief, but soon returned to collective leadership.[55] At a later date, Tenoch, the founder of Tenochtitlan, occupied a similar position of leadership. In the Codex Mendoza he is portrayed with the blue speech scroll of the *tlatoani* (the title means 'he who speaks'), but he does not wear the diadem of later rulers. He appears as the principal leader among many (the number varies from four to twenty in different chronicle sources).

Kingship was not formalised until 1372 when Acamapichtli became *tlatoani* of Tenochtitlan at the request of the city's inhabitants. Clavijero, writing in about 1780, contrasts the early and later styles of government and suggests reasons for the change:

> [at first] the government of the Mexicans was aristocratic, and the nation was controlled by a body made up of the most noble and distinguished persons. According to their pictorial records, those who commanded at the time when the city was founded numbered 20, among whom the one with the most authority was Tenoch. The low state in which the nation found itself, the troubles it suffered from its neighbours, and the example of the Chichimecs, Tepanecs and Culhua obliged them to establish monarchical government, believing that royal authority would give some lustre to the entire nation and that in the new chief they would have a father who would watch over the state and also a general who would confront these dangers and defend the people against the insults of their enemies.[56]

Acamapichtli was the son of a Culhua prince and a Mexican woman. Since Culhuacan was a refugee Toltec city, he could claim Toltec blood on his father's side, thus allowing the Aztec royal house to claim descent from the dynasty of Tula, the source of all legitimate political power. In the male line Acamapichtli was not decended from the indigenous Aztec chiefs, and it was a *new* class of nobles which he founded through his progeny. According to the Codex Ramírez, each of the *calpullis* (which now numbered twenty) provided a wife for Acamapichtli. From these political marriages sprang the class of *pipiltin* (hereditary nobles by birth) but – since at that time the Aztecs owned little territory in their own right – we should not yet think in terms of a landed nobility. The emergence of a land-holding aristocracy seems not to have come about until the defeat of Azcapotzalco in 1428, which gave the Aztecs access to lands expropriated from the Tepanec cities.

The later history of the monarchy shows a growth in the power of the ruler and his lineage, with a corresponding reduction in the power of the *calpulli* heads and the common people. In part these changes may have been a function of the size of the community. Popular consultation is feasible in a tribe of a few thousand, impossible in a state with tens of thousands of subjects. For the same reason, as the political unit grows larger and more complex, the ordinary man sees only a fraction of what is going on in the community. The main work of any administration is to obtain and collate the information which is the key to decision-making at state level – and this process was kept firmly in the hands of government officials who were drawn from the noble classes. Only the upper classes attended the *calmecac* schools where future leaders were trained. Here they learned the arts of administration, reading and writing, the finer points of history, law and religion. The common people, in contrast, attended a lower category of school where they learned to be good citizens and soldiers, and to know their place.[57] Access to state archives was therefore reserved to a single class (cf. prediction (2) above) and it was made very difficult for the ordinary citizen to participate in government at national level.

This whittling down of civil rights can be seen in the changing composition of the body which elected successive rulers. The first two monarchs, Acamapichtli and Huitzilíhuitl, are said to have been chosen by a broadly-based electoral college which included priests, old people and *calpulli* officials – not a democracy, but at least a sort of oligarchy.[58] The elective element remained, but from the time of Itzcóatl the *tlatoani* was chosen by, and from, the members of an inner council consisting of the chief minister and the four great war chiefs. All members of this council were close kin, usually cousins or brothers, and were of the lineage of Acamapichtli.[59] All important decisions were taken by this council. The *calpulli* heads no longer had a say in affairs of state, and were reduced to the status of 'parish councillors' responsible for the local schools, temples, land registers and taxes within the clan territory.

Dumond's third prediction was also fulfilled. The *calpullis* themselves were ranked, both internally and relative to each other. The social position of an individual depended on the relative rank of his *calpulli* and on the position of his lineage within the *calpulli*.[60] Within the *calpulli*, offices were monopolised by the preeminent lineage, and at supra-*calpulli* level all the important posts were held by members of the elite lineages of the highest ranking *calpullis* – i.e. by the nobility.

These distinctions were reinforced by marriage patterns and the practice of polygamy among the aristocracy. The ruler of any city was normally related by marriage to many of his neighbours, and his pedigree read like a page from the Almanach de Gotha. The rulers of Mexican states, like the monarchs of nineteenth-century Europe, can in many respects be considered as members of a single class or lineage which cross-cut national boundaries.

At the level of anecdote, this feeling for class rather than nationality is expressed in the words of an Aztec messenger attempting to persuade an enemy ruler to come to Ahuitzotl's coronation: 'O powerful monarch, there are times when one must be an enemy, but there are others when one must heed the natural obligations which exist between us.'[61] Equally revealing is Durán's comment on the secrecy which attended the visit of enemy rulers to witness the dedication of the great temple in 1487:

> . . . they did not wish the common people – soldiers and captains – to suspect that kings and rulers made alliances, came to agreements and found friendships at the cost of the life of the common man, and the shedding of his blood.[62]

The chronicles also suggest that the nobility had built up a similar network of alliances from which commoners were largely excluded. In life-style and in attitudes, the Aztec aristocracy at the time of the Conquest was almost completely divorced from the rest of the population.

Commerce, trade and tribute

In Dumond's model, expansion of resources can be achieved in two ways: by increasing local productivity and by 'capturing' resources elsewhere. The first of these alternatives has already been touched upon in the section dealing with agricultural expansion. Analysis of tribute lists and land tenure documents confirms that population increased faster than the food supply, with the result that, from quite an early stage in its development, Tenochtitlan was not self-sufficient in foodstuffs.[63] As Calnek has noted, the Aztec state of the fifteenth century was no longer an agricultural society, and the lack of an adequate agricultural basis implies 'a nearly total dependence of the urban population of Tenochtitlan on external support areas for subsistence. It is consistent with the great emphasis placed on military, administrative, commercial and craft specialisation in the standard histories and chronicles.'[64]

Increased craft production, even if not on an industrial scale, represents an expansion of local production, but when the surplus is used for foreign trade it also plays a part in the 'capturing' of resources from elsewhere.

The existence of large numbers of specialised craftsmen in all the major cities is attested by documentary and archaeological evidence, though most of the high prestige craftsmen (featherworkers, jewellers, lapidaries etc.) who worked for the luxury end of the market, were probably immigrants or descendants of the pre-Aztec peoples of the Valley. It is recorded, for instance, that whole groups of craftsmen moved en bloc to Texcoco during the reign of Nezahualcoyotl, and that they constituted an entire barrio of the city.

Foreign trade was in the hands of a class of specialised merchants, the *pochteca*, whose growth in numbers, wealth and political importance is a striking feature of Aztec history. The nature of *pochteca* activity has been often described.[65] According to chronicle sources, long-distance trade became important in Tlatelolco in the days of its first ruler, Cuacuahtzin (1372-1418), and thereafter increased steadily in scale. Under later Aztec rulers, the *pochteca* were granted privileges which put them almost on a par with the nobility, and raised them well above the rest of the craftsmen, farmers and workers. Private estates owned by *pochteca* were interdigitated with those of the nobles, and the two classes could sell land to each other.[66] The merchants had their own courts, were granted insignia of rank, and (like the warriors) had the right to dedicate human sacrifices at some of the main religious festivals.

The rising status of the merchants is a function of both their economic and political importance. In the absence of trade figures their contribution to the economy cannot be measured, but of their political significance there is no doubt. The *pochteca* corporations (like the East India Company in British history) were used by the ruler as an instrument of foreign policy – forcing trade on (often reluctant) partners, spying out the land, acting as agents provocateurs to cause incidents which could serve as an excuse for conquest and annexation. At this point, legitimate trade begins to merge with extortion.

Trade and tribute-extortion can therefore be regarded as two faces of the same coin: in Dumond's phrase, they are both means of capturing resources from someone else. The *Codex Mendoza* and other documents show that enormous quantities of basic materials and luxury goods came to the cities of the Triple Alliance in the form of tribute from conquered provinces, and quickly became indispensible to the economy.[67] Much of this tribute consisted of staple foods to make good the shortfall in local agricultural production, but there was also a considerable flow of luxury goods (cacao, quetzal plumage, jade, gold, turquoise, rubber, jaguar skins and cotton clothing) from distant tropical provinces. The *pochteca*, too, imported primarily prestige goods and slaves, rather than the bulky but mundane products of the highlands.

With these points in mind, we can now show how trade and tribute interacted with each other, and how the commercial subsystem was related to the other subsystems under discussion. The situation has been excellently summed up by Davies:

> the Aztec ruler, not content with the avalanche of tribute which flowed into Tenochtitlan, would use his merchants to sell the tribute of one subject province for the free produce of another. And, quite apart from the ruler's own property, the goods which the merchants themselves traded must also have been partly manufactured from raw materials obtained as tribute. Thus, by monopolistic commerce, the ruler multiplied his tribute, sometimes even imposing unfair terms of trade on conquered provinces and selling them goods which they did not value.[68]

In short, a mercantile economy backed up by military force.

At this stage of discussion, two more of Dumond's predictions fall into place:

1. *That in a stratified society the elite will increasingly want to acquire luxuries too expensive for poorer members.*

The documentary sources suggest that, as more and more exotic products reached the allied cities, these luxury goods altered the habits of the aristocracy and created new needs which could be satisfied only by further conquests and still more loot – a classic instance of the 'revolution of rising expectations' and of the 'multiplier effect' between the commercial and social subsystems.

This process was not only recognised by the Aztecs themselves, but was used quite consciously and deliberately as a means of creating social distance between the commoners and the governing class. This can be seen most clearly in the sumptuary laws of the native rulers. The law code promulgated by Moctezuma I included the following clauses:

> Only the king may wear a golden diadem in the city, though in war all the great lords and captains may wear such. It is considered that all those who go to war represent the royal person . . .
>
> Only the king is to wear fine mantles of cotton embroidered with designs of different colours and featherwork. He is to decide which

> type of cloak may be used by the royal person to distinguish him from the rest. The great lords, who are twelve, may wear certain mantles and the minor lords wear others. The common soldier may wear only the simplest type of mantle and is prohibited from using any special designs or fine embroidery that might set him off from the rest. The common people will not be allowed to wear cotton clothing under pain of death, but only garments of maguey fibre.[69]

Other laws indicate which categories of people may wear gold ornaments, jade and feathers, and at the same time men were forbidden to buy jewels and insignia in the marketplace.

These prestige materials were given out by the ruler as a reward for service:

> From now on the sovereign will deliver them as payment for memorable deeds . . . He who does not dare to go to war, even though he be a king's son, from now on will be deprived of these things.[70]

Death was the penalty for anyone caught wearing ornaments to which he was not entitled. In this way a man's rank was instantly recognisable from his appearance and dress. The segregating effect of wealth and status was thus backed by the whole force of the state system, and the nobles were singled out at the expense of the commoners.

This leads on to another of Dumond's predictions:

2. *That, as society becomes more stratified, gift-giving, becomes more formalised. Goods produced by the people as a whole are channelled through the leader, who gives to other leaders who in turn redistribute to their people. This will tend to reinforce the official status of the upper class.*

In this context one must remember that, in later times at least, there was no distinction between the state treasury and the ruler's private wealth. Tribute from vassals, presents from foreign rulers and the taxes levied on his own subjects all entered the storehouse of the *tlatoani*. So, too, did the voluntary gifts made to the ruler by the merchants and nobles in connection with some of the festivals.[71]

A good deal of this material was redistributed on certain formal occasions. The main religious festivals were occasions when the ruler gave out insignia to successful warriors, acknowledging their help, confirming their high place in society, cementing personal loyalties, and putting the recipients still further into the ruler's debt. Similarly when a warrior dedicated a captive he gave a feast at which gifts were given to the guests, who included officials and members of the warrior's *calpulli*. In this way the warrior was able to demonstrate both his generosity and superiority, and the chain of redistribution reached down to barrio level.[72] Even a quick glance through the ethnohistorical literature shows that occasions for formal gift-giving were numerous and not exclusively religious, and also that the custom was used to reinforce social stratification.

Religion

Since religion played a part in every aspect of Mexican life it can legitimately be considered as a sub-system within the overall socio-political system. The ruler and his chief assistants had religious as well as secular responsibilities; the principal religious officials were drawn from the nobility; priests went to war and took captives. Church and State usually spoke with one voice, though the ritualised battles which took place between priests and warriors at certain festivals hint at some tensions between the groups.[73]

The development of the state religion parallels and reinforces the social changes already discussed. During the migration period, government was in the hands of the *teomamas*, the bearers of the god Huitzilopochtli, and there seems to have been some overlap between political and ecclesiastical government. The major trends in development can be briefly summarised: (1) changes in the cult of Huitzilopochtli, bringing the god into ever closer association with warfare, conquest and the warrior aristocracy, (2) increased importance of human sacrifice, and (3) increasing elaboration of rituals and ceremonies, with growing differentiation between the religious practices of the nobles and the commoners. These three phenomena are different facets of a single process.

Unlike the pan-Mexican gods, Huitzilopochtli was a specifically Aztec deity, with little following outside Tenochtitlan and Tlatelolco during the pre-imperial era. The early history of this god is obscure,[74] but he may have begun as a deified tribal leader. With success in war, his preeminence was assured. Warfare and religion became so inextricably involved with each other that they were rationalised into a single spiritual unity. Huitzilopochtli became a warrior god, the ideal Aztec hero, identified with the sun which itself gave life to the universe.

By this process of rationalisation, political and religious needs were made to coincide. War provided tribute and material benefits; it also provided captives for sacrifice. War thus became a holy act. The blood of the prisoners nourished and strengthened the gods, ensuring the stability of the universe – and in gratitude the gods favoured the Aztecs with further conquests which provided yet more captives. The propaganda value of this system of beliefs was appreciated, and was consciously manipulated for political ends from the time of Itzcóatl onwards, encouraging the Aztecs to think of themselves as a 'chosen people' whose role was to conquer and rule in the name of Huitzilopochtli.

It is in this context that we must consider the increasing importance of human sacrifice. The custom was widespread throughout Mexico and has a long history among Chichimecs and settled communities alike. There are references to occasional sacrifices during the early stages of Aztec history,[75] but the full ritual of mass sacrifice did not come into operation until about the mid fifteenth century, when the Aztecs were rapidly becoming an imperial power.

This is not a coincidence. Men like Tlacaelel (and the successive rulers he served) deliberately fostered the cult of human sacrifice for social and political ends. Sacrifice reinforced the 'chosen people' myth, and at the same time was used to inspire terror in conquered peoples and potential enemies.[76] In the reign of Moctezuma I the custom grew up of inviting foreign rulers and nobles from enemy territory to witness the *tlacaxipeualiztli* ceremonies in Tenochtitlan. This festival was one of the most important in the calendar, and war captives were sacrificed in large numbers. The political intimidation was carefully calculated. The visitors were loaded with rich gifts, but left in a chastened frame of mind:

> The lords from the provinces who had come to observe the sacrifice were shocked and bewildered by what they had seen, and they returned to their homes filled with astonishment and fright . . . Having sacrificed the Huaxtecs in this way, the Aztecs believed that they had intimidated the whole world.[77]

At the same time, the cult of sacrifice encouraged the formation and maintenance of class barriers at home. In her analysis of the calendar festivals, Broda has demonstrated the ways in which the official state religion was calculated to legitimise the highly stratified social system.[78] Rank, which depended on a combination of high birth and military valour, was reflected in the right to perform certain ceremonies. Since the provision of victims was of prime religious importance, these ceremonies were also an expression of social prestige. Only warriors could acquire captives, and it was their privilege to dedicate victims for sacrifice. When, in special circumstances, this right was extended to members of the *pochteca* and artisan classes, for war-captives they were forced to substitute (less prestigious) slaves bought in the market.

The status of the warrior, who was able to offer his captive to the gods, was confirmed by the ruler's gift of clothing, arms and insignia. The distribution of these luxury goods, which was made by the ruler in a context of religious ceremony, seems to have coincided rather closely with the main dates on which tribute was delivered to Tenochtitlan, and it is reasonable to assume that some of this material was redistributed at once as part of the festival. In this way, the economic and political strength of the ruler found direct expression in ritual.[79]

The various segments of the population participated in different aspects of the state religion. The priests, *calpulli* officials and common people were the main participants in festivals connected with fertility and agriculture (rain, crops, pulque etc.), while the nobles and warriors were preeminent in those ceremonies with political overtones (dedicated to such gods as Huitzilopochtli, Xipe Totec, Mixcoatl etc).

Many ceremonies dealing with fertility or rain took place at the local level (in the houses of the common people, at *calpulli* temples, in fields or on mountains) or else at specific temples within the main precinct. It seems that offerings were made on behalf of the group as a whole, rather than under the sponsorship of any single individual. By contrast, the festivals patronised by the warriors and nobles usually took place at the main temple. With the ruler's permission, captives were offered by the individual warriors who had taken them prisoner, and the members of the warrior orders thus gained personal, not merely group, prestige by this act.

The duality between aristocratic and popular religion may directly reflect the political history of the Basin of Mexico. The cult practices of the original settled population (or at least the farmers among them) seem to have centred on agriculture, fertility and the worship of the old gods, chief among whom was Tlaloc, the Rain God, recognisable in the archaeological record during the early centuries A.D. and, more controversially, as early as the first millennium B.C.[80] Superimposed on these rituals, and continuously increasing in importance, were the practices of the nomadic (and often non-agricultural) Chichimecs who preferred the astral and solar deities and their own tribal patrons, such as the upstart Huitzilopochtli. According to the *Historia Tolteca-Chichimeca*, certain forms of sacrifice (by shooting to death with arrows, and by gladiatorial combat) were the customary ways by which the Chichimecs dealt with war captives as early as the twelfth century,[81] and from the Chichimecs seem eventually to have passed into the Aztec repertoire.

In the *Relación de Texcoco* the chronicler Pomar obs[illegible] that 'the idol known as Tlaloc is the most ancient in this land, [illegible] say that the Culhuas [themselves of Chichimec descent] found [illegible] already established here. Since the Chichimecs did not know of him, they began to worship him as the god of the waters.'[82] This duality between the native and the intrusive Chichimec segments of the population, and between the warrior nobles and the commoners, was formalised in the architecture of the main temple of Tenochtitlan with its twin shrines, one dedicated to Huitzilopochtli, the other to Tlaloc.

War

It will now be clear how warfare interacted with the other subsystems discussed above. War provided foodstuffs and raw materials (in the form of tribute) for the Aztec cities whose growing populations could not be sustained from local resources: it was simultaneously a religious duty, an instrument of foreign policy, the means by which a man gained wealth, and a stimulus which helped to change Aztec class structure.

More than that, it was an essential factor in the national psychology. The Aztecs had learned that aggression pays. Special paradises were reserved for warriors who died in battle or on the altar; physical bravery was taken for granted, and a glorious death was something to be welcomed. This attitude is expressed in innumerable Nahuatl songs and poems, of which the following is a fairly typical sample:

> O my heart, you are not afraid.
> Here on the battlefield,
> My heart yearns for the obsidian death.
> All my heart desires is death in war.[83]

Conclusions

The Aztec situation offers an unusually good opportunity to study social evolution and change in a native American community uninfluenced by European contact. The changes discussed in this paper were already complete in 1519, and owe nothing to European example or to the arrival of European trade goods and technology. Nor, for that matter, was the period marked by any fundamental innovation in indigenous technology or subsistence patterns. The existence of native documentary sources, as well as Spanish accounts, allows an insight into the motives underlying this rapid socio-political change *as perceived by the Aztecs themselves.*

Several points of a more general interest emerge from this case study.

1. It proved impossible to single out any one factor as the prime mover in the process of social transformation. The systemic model incorporates just about all the factors which have been put forward by those who believe in monocausal explanations for the development of states (population growth, agricultural intensification, war, hydraulic works, trade, ecological symbiosis etc.), but none of these has primacy over the others.
2. Studies of social evolution have tended to concentrate on the emergence of the 'pristine state', ignoring the fact that most of the states which have existed in human history are no such thing. The Aztec case illustrates the role played by emulation. The civilising of the Aztecs, like that of many Chichimec groups before them, was a deliberate and conscious attempt to emulate the existing pattern in the Valley of Mexico. As Carrasco has

already pointed out; 'In this perspective [the context of Mesoamerican society as a whole] the Aztec transformation, more than an evolution from tribe to state, represents the change of a marginal subject group to a politically dominant position at the expense of the previously dominant group. But Mesoamerican society did not change; all we have is a shift of power from one group and from one city to another.'[84]

3. Looked at another way, the transformation from marginal tribe to imperial power is just one instance of a general adaptive process analagous to that which takes place between an organism and its environment.[85] The social institutions (and also the political and cultural aspirations) appropriate for tribal life on the frontier were poorly adapted to the civilised conditions of central Mexico. Since the Aztecs at the time of their arrival in the Valley were not strong enough to change the existing political environment, their only hope of competing with the established states was to modify their own culture and institutions – thus conforming with that time-honoured principle 'if you can't beat 'em, join 'em'.
4. There has been a tendency among certain anthropologists to assume that only the outside observer is capable of appreciating what is really taking place in the society under study. In extreme instances one is left with the impression that the system changes its state without any human intervention at all. In the case of the Aztecs, there is abundant evidence that the overall direction of social change was recognised and approved, was encouraged by deliberate intervention, and that certain individuals (such as Tlacaelel and Itzcóatl) had a disproportionate influence on the course of events.
5. Like the Madagascan kingdoms described by Bloch (this volume), the Aztec system could only be maintained by continuous territorial expansion, coupled with an accelerating rate of social change. Once checked (by the Spanish invasion), the system immediately collapsed. Faced with the challenge of a completely unfamiliar problem, the strain on its powers of adaptation proved too great.[86]

NOTES

1 Kirchhoff, P. (1966), 'Civilizing the Chichimecs: A chapter in the culture history of ancient Mexico', *in* Graham, J.A. (ed.), *Ancient Mesoamerica: Selected Readings*, Palo Alto, pp. 273-8.

2 The Toltec state, and its capital at Tula, are the subject of continuing archaeological and historical investigation. For a review of the latest work, v. Diehl, R.A. (ed.) (1974), 'Studies of ancient Tollan: A report of the University of Missouri Tula Archaeological Project', *University of Missouri Monographs in Anthropology* I. Although there was an original Chichimec component in the population of Tula (v.

papers by Feldman in Diehl 1974), by the time of the city's decline, in the twelfth century, the Toltecs had become archetypal Mesoamericans.

3 León-Portilla, M. (1967), 'Los Chichimecas de Xolotl y su proceso de aculturación', *Historia Prehispanica*, 6, Mexico.

4 Ixtlilxochitl, Fernando de Alva (1952), *Obras Históricas* (ed. A. Chavez), Mexico.

5 Chimalpahin, Domingo Francisco de San Anton Muñon Cuauhtlehuantzin (1958), *Das Memorial Breve acerca de la Fundación de la Ciudad de Culhuacan* (eds. W. Lehman and G. Kutscher), Stuttgart.

6 Tezozómoc, Hernando Alvarado (1944), *Crónica Mexicana* (ed. M. Orozco y Berra), Mexico; Tezozómoc, Hernando Alvarado (1949), *Crónica Mexicáyotl*, Mexico.

7 Kirchhoff (1966), p. 273.

8 For instance, Service, E.R. (1962), *Primitive Social Organization: An Evolutionary Perspective*, New York.

9 Davies, C.N.B. (1970), *The Mexica: First Steps to Power*, Ph.D. thesis, London University: translated as *Los Mexicas: Primeros Pasos Hacia el Imperio*, Mexico (1973); Davies, N. (1973), *The Aztecs*, London.

10 Brundage, B.C. (1972), *A Rain of Darts: The Mexica Aztecs*, Austin and London. For general surveys of Aztec culture, v. Soustelle, J. (1964), *The Daily Life of the Aztecs*, Harmondsworth; and Bray, W. (1968), *Everyday Life of the Aztecs*, London.

11 Chronicle sources place the date of the foundation of Tenochtitlan anywhere between 1300 and 1369, with 1325 as the favourite. I have followed Jiménez Moreno and Davies in preferring the figure 1345 (Davies, C.N.B., 1970 Appendix A).

12 Davies, N. (1973), p. 7.

13 Martínez Marín, C. (1964), 'La cultura de los mexicas durante la migración: nuevas ideas', *Actas y Memorias del XXXV Congreso Internacional de Americanistas, 1962*, Mexico, vol. 2, pp. 113-23. See also Bernal, I. (1967), 'Los Mexicas: De la Peregrinación al Imperio', *Historia Prehispanica*, 8; and Carrasco, P. (1971), 'The peoples of central Mexico and their historical traditions', *in* Wauchope, R. (gen. ed.), *Handbook of Middle American Indians*, Vol. 11, 2, Austin and London, pp. 459-73.

14 Durán, D. (1964), *The Aztecs: The History of the Indians of New Spain*, D. Heyden and F. Horcasitas (eds.), New York, p. 9.

15 Tezozómoc (1944), and (1949), p. 26.

16 Sahagún, B. de (1961), *Florentine Codex: General History of the Things of New Spain* (eds. C.E. Dibble and A.J.O. Anderson), Book 10, *Monogr. Sch. Am. Res., Santa Fe*, 14, XI.

17 Armillas, P. (1964), 'Condiciones ambientales y movimientos de pueblos en la frontera septentrional de Mesoamerica', *Homenaje a Fernando Marquez Miranda*, Madrid, pp. 62-82. Armillas, P. (1969), 'The arid frontier of Mexican civilization', *Trans. N.Y. Acad. Sci.*, Ser. II, 31, 6, pp. 697-704.

18 Calnek, E. (1973), 'The historical validity of the Codex Xolotl', *Am. Antiq.*, 38, 4, pp. 423-7.

19 Chapman, A. (1959), 'La Guerra de los Aztecas contra los Tepanecas: raices y consecuencias', *Acta anthrop. Méx.*, Epoca 2, Vol. 1, 4.

20 Bray, W. (1972a), 'Land-use, settlement patterns and politics in prehispanic Middle America: a review', *in* Ucko, P.J., Tringham, R. and Dimbleby, G.W. (eds.), *Man, Settlement and Urbanism*, London, p. 920.

21 Hill, J. (1971), 'Report on a seminar on the explanation of prehistoric organization change', *Curr. Anthrop.* 12, 3, pp. 406-8.

22 Bray, W. (1976), 'From predation to production: the nature of agricultural evolution in Mexico and Peru', *in* Sieveking G. de G. et al. (eds.), *Problems in Economic and Social Archaeology*, London, pp. 73-95.

23 Renfrew, A.C. (1972), *The Emergence of Civilization: The Cyclades and the Aegean in the Third Millennium B.C.*, London. Flannery, K.V. (1972), 'The cultural evolution of civilizations', *Annual Review of Ecology and Systematics*, 3, pp. 399-426.

24 Dumond, D.E. (1972), 'Population growth and political centralisation', *in* Spooner, B. (ed.), *Population Growth: Anthropological Implications*, Cambridge, Mass., pp. 286-310.

25 Dumond (1972), p. 291.

26 Dumond (1972), p. 295.

27 Sanders, W.T. (1972), 'Population, agricultural history and societal evolution in Mesoamerica', *in* Spooner, B. (ed.), *Population Growth: Anthropological Implications*, Cambridge, Mass., pp. 101-53.

28 Parsons, J.R. (1971), 'Prehistoric settlement patterns in the Texcoco region, Mexico', *Memoir No. 3, Museum of Anthropology, University of Michigan*; Parsons, J.R. (1971), *Prehispanic Settlement Patterns in the Chalco Region, Mexico*, m.s., Museum of Anthropology, Univ. of Michigan; Parsons, J.R. (1973), *Reconocimiento superficial en el Sur del Valle de Mexico*, ms., Museum of Anthropology, Univ. of Michigan; Parsons, J.R. (1974), *Patrones de asentamiento prehispánicos en el noroeste del Valle de Mexico, region de Zumpango*, ms., Museum of Anthropology, Univ. of Michigan; Blanton, R.E. (1972), 'Prehispanic adaptation in the Ixtapalapa region, Mexico', *Science, N.Y.*, 175, pp. 1317-26; Sanders, W.T. (1965), *The Cultural Ecology of the Teotihuacan Valley*, Pennsylvania State University.

29 Tezozómoc (1944), p. 8.

30 Davies, N. (1973), p. 26.

31 Calnek, E.E. (1973), 'The localization of the sixteenth-century map called the Maguey Plan', *Am. Antiq.*, 38, 2, pp. 190-95; Bray, W. (1972b), 'The city state in central Mexico at the time of the Spanish conquest', *Journal of Latin American Studies*, 4, 2, p. 174.

32 trans. Davies, N. (1973), p. 27.

33 Brundage (1972), p. 49.

34 Sanders (1965), pp. 60-4, 145-53.

35 Parsons (1971), p. 221.

36 Parsons (1973).

37 Parsons (1971), pp. 146-50.

38 Armillas, P. (1971), 'Gardens on swamps', *Science, N.Y.*, 174, pp. 653-61.

39 Parsons (1973).

40 For an early sixteenth-century colonial example of this situation v. Sanders (1965), p. 63.

41 For fuller discussion v. Kirchhoff, P. (1954-5), 'Land tenure in ancient Mexico', *Revta. mex. Estud. antrop.*, 14, pp. 351-61; Zorita, A. de (1965), *The Lords of New Spain*, (ed. B. Keen), London; Katz, F. (1966), 'Situación social y económica de los Aztecas durante los siglos XV and XVI', *Monograph No. 8, Série de Cultura Nahuatl*, Mexico.

42 Lawrence Feldman (in Diehl, p. 156) has questioned the key role of Tlacaelel in transforming Aztec society. He points out that the sources attributing great importance to Tlacaelel can be traced back to the same informant, while those deriving from other informants rarely, if ever, mention him.

43 Durán (1964), p. 57.

44 Durán (1964), p. 59.

45 Calnek (1973), p. 194; Calnek (n.d.), 'The organization of urban food supply systems: the case of Tenochtitlan', to appear in *Actas, XL International Congress of Americanists, Rome 1972* (in press).

46 Durán (1964), p. 72.

47 Durán (1964), p. 70.

48 Davies, N. (1973), p. 79.

49 Calnek (n.d.)

50 Calnek, E.E. (1972), 'Settlement pattern and Chinampa agriculture at Tenochtitlan', *Am. Antiq.* 38, 2, pp. 190-5.

51 Davies (1973), p. 44; Brundage (1972), p. 51.

52 Calnek (1972), and (n.d.).

53 Davies, C.N.B. (1970), p. 35.

54 Davies, C.N.B. (1970).

55 Davies, N. (1973), p. 26.

56 Clavijero, F.J. (1971), *Historia antigua de Mexico*, Mexico, p. 74.

57 Bray (1968), pp. 58-64.

58 Durán (1964), pp. 39, 44, 50. 59 Brundage (1972), pp. 115-16.

60 Monzón, A. (1949), *El calpulli en la organización social de los tenochca*, Mexico. Elsewhere Monzón has suggested that there were six high lineage *calpullis*, one of which was the ruler's ('La organización de los Aztecs', in *Mexico Prehispánica*, Mexico, p. 793). The nature of *calpulli* organisation is still a matter of debate and controversy. For a recent summary, with discussion of earlier studies, v. Carrasco, P. (1971), 'Social organization of ancient Mexico', *in* Wauchope R. (gen. ed.), *Handbook of Middle American Indians*, Austin and London, vol. 10, pp. 349-75.

61 Durán (1964), p. 189. 62 Durán (1964), p. 193.

63 Calnek (1972) and (n.d.); Bray (1972a), (1972b).

64 Calnek (1972), p. 114.

65 Sahagún, B. de (1959), *Florentine Codex: General History of the Things of New Spain* (eds. C.E. Dibble and A.J.O. Anderson), book 9, *Monogr. Sch. Am. Res., Santa Fe*, 14, X; Acosta Saignes, M. (1945), 'Los Pochteca', *Acta anthrop., Méx.*, 1, 1. Garibay, A.M. (1961), *Vida económica de Tenochtitlan 1: Pochtecayotl (arte de traficar)*, Mexico; Chapman, A. (1957), 'Port of trade enclaves in Aztec and Maya civilizations', *in* Polanyi, K., Arensberg, C.M. and Pearson, H.W. (eds.), *Trade and Market in Early Empires*, Glencoe, Ill., pp. 114-53.

66 Calnek (n.d.).

67 Molíns Fábrega, M. (1954-5), 'El Códice Mendocino y la economía de Tenochtitlán', *Revta. mex. Estud. antrop.*, 14, pp. 303-35; Borah, W. and Cook, S.F. (1963), 'The aboriginal population of Central Mexico on the eve of the Spanish Conquest', *Ibero-Am.*, 45; Parsons (1971) pp. 214-16.

68 Davies, N. (1973), p. 137. 69 Durán (1964), p. 131.

70 Durán (1964), p. 142. 71 Zorita (1965), p. 188.

72 Broda de Casas, J. (1972), 'Estratificación social y ritual Mexica', *Religión en Mesoamérica: XII Mesa Redonda,* Mexico, pp. 179-92.

73 Broda de Casas, J. (1970), 'Tlacaxipeualiztli: a reconstruction of an Aztec calendar festival from sixteenth-century sources', *Revista Española de Antropología Americana*, 5, pp. 197-274; Broda de Cases (1972).

74 Brotherston, G. (1974), 'Huitzilopochtli and what was made of him', *in* Hammond, N. (ed.), *Mesoamerican Archaeology: New Approaches,* London, pp. 155-66; Bernal (1967); Davies, C.N.B. (1970), pp. 30-4; Davies, N. (1973), pp. 14-18.

75 e.g. Durán (1964), p. 26.

76 Broda de Casas (1970), pp. 235-7. 77 Durán (1964), pp. 112-13.

78 Broda de Casas, J. (1971). 'Las fiestas de los Dioses de la Lluvia (una reconstrucción según las fuentes del siglo XVI)', *Revista Española de Antropología Americana*, 6, pp. 245-327; Broda de Casas (1970) and (1972).

79 Broda de Casas (1970), and personal communication.

80 Coe, M.D. (1968), *America's First Civilisation: Discovering the Olmec*, New York, p. 111.

81 Preuss, K. Th. and Mengin, E. (eds.) (1937), 'Historia Tolteca Chichimeca', *Baessler-Arch.*, Beiheft 9, pp. 16, 28, 29, 62-5.

82 Pomar, J. (1941), 'Relación de Tezcoco', *in* Garcia Icazbalceta, J. (ed.), *Nueva Colección de Documentos para la Historia de México,* Mexico, pp. 14-15.

83 Translated from Garibay, A.M. (1953), *Historia de la Literatura Náhuatl,* Mexico, vol. I, p. 217.

84 Carrasco (1971), p. 372.

85 Bray, W. (1973), 'The biological basis of culture', *in* Renfrew, C. (ed.), *The Explanation of Culture Change: Models in Prehistory*, London, pp. 73-92.

86 Johanna Broda, Edward Calnek and Nigel Davies suggested several improvements to the first draft of this paper, but – to avoid guilt by association – it must be emphasised that they do not necessarily approve of the final version. The figure is reproduced, by permission of the author and publishers, from N. Davies, *The Aztecs* (Macmillan, London, 1973).

SECTION IV

Demography, trade and technology in evolution

DAVID R. HARRIS

Settling down: an evolutionary model for the transformation of mobile bands into sedentary communities

It is a truism that the evolution of complex societies depends on the interaction of many variables. Students of the emergence of 'civilisation' have, however, generally failed to confront this fact and to attempt to specify the variables and to investigate their relationships. Most hypotheses have proposed causal mechanisms whereby one variable is selected as the most plausible factor inducing change. The search for such 'prime movers' and the discussion of their relative importance has dominated thinking about the emergence of agriculture, urbanism, civilisation, and the state for many decades, during which time numerous factors have been proposed to explain the evolution of these complex phenomena. Conspicuous among these factors are changes in the physical environment; competition for scarce resources; and the effects of population growth, warfare, irrigation, trade, and religion. Recently, several authors have published critiques of these factors as they relate to their own universes of study; for example, Flannery,[1] Dumond,[2] and Carneiro[3] in relation to the state, Renfrew[4] in relation to Aegean civilisation, Adams[5] and Wheatley[6] in relation to urbanism, and Harris[7] in relation to agriculture. These authors emphasise the inadequacy of single-factor hypotheses and attempt to delineate and to assess relationships between those variables that they regard as relevant.

Therein lies the crux of the problem of explanation. At one extreme it is easy – but unprofitable – to take refuge in the truism that 'everything affects everything else'. At the other it is tempting to adopt a reductionist approach in order to demonstrate a direct relationship between two variables, although this is done at the risk of ignoring other variables of equal or greater relevance. Between the Scylla of self-evident generality and the Charybdis of blinkered 'proof' lie the turbulent waters where the most satisfactory explanations of cultural evolution are likely to be found. There, testable hypotheses that postulate processual relationships between numerous variables can be generated. Rigorous 'scientific' proof of these hypotheses cannot be expected, because the dependence and independence of variables in a cultural system can seldom be precisely determined, but the relative explanatory power of competing hypotheses can be tested with reference to ethnographic, historical, archaeological, and other categories of evidence. If synchronic evidence alone is used it may not be possible to do more than establish the general plausibility of an evolutionary hypothesis, but, if the hypothesis can be related to diachronic evidence too, then its validity as an explanation can be evaluated more effectively.

Although the main focus of this book is on the evolution of complex societies, it is appropriate that some participants concern themselves with changes towards greater complexity among simpler, more egalitarian bands and 'tribes'. The aspect of such change most commonly considered is the transition in subsistence from predominant dependence on wild plant and animal resources to predominant dependence on domesticated plants and animals. Interest in the shift from foraging to food production has tended to inhibit consideration of the more general process of cultural change of which it is a part. Preoccupation with the search for 'the origins of agriculture' has diverted attention from the broader question of how mobile 'hunter-gatherer' bands gave way, as a dominant mode of human organisation, to permanently settled, complex communities. I have recently argued that developmental pathways towards agriculture should be examined in the same intellectual framework as those pathways that led to other patterns of resource specialisation,[7] and my aim in this paper is to take this approach further by examining the relationships between changes in population, mobility, and socioeconomic organisation that may underlie the early stages in the transformation of simple into complex communities.

Demographic change

In the last few years demographic change, particularly population increase leading to intensified pressure on resources, has come to be viewed as an independent variable capable of inducing other changes in cultural systems.[8] The general relevance of demographic to cultural change is not in doubt, but most formulations that incorporate population pressure as an explanatory variable avoid the question of how population increases in the first place. It is often assumed that population increase is the 'normal' condition of mankind.[9] In the biological sense that, as in other animals, the reproductive cycle is shorter than the life cycle, and because man's reproductive capacity greatly exceeds the capacity of the sociophysical environment to support human life, this assumption is true. But in the sense that increasing rather than stable populations have been the normal condition of mankind through historic and prehistoric times it appears improbable.

The most naive objection to the assumption that population increase was normal in the past is the enormous time interval that separates the emergence of the hominids from the earliest settled communities with substantial populations of which we have evidence. It is sometimes suggested that, prior to that time, cumulative increases in the human population were accommodated by dispersal to, and the 'filling in' of, continental and island landmasses. However, it is difficult to believe that, if population growth were cumulative from the start, it did not lead to local population pressure and the development of substantial sedentary settlements in some parts of the world prior to the post-Pleistocene appearance of village communities in the Near East, Mesoamerica, and elsewhere.

More compelling evidence against the assumption that population increase has been the normal condition of mankind comes from the study of surviving hunter-gatherer groups. Recent studies of such groups in tropical desert, semidesert, and rainforest environments have demonstrated that they live at population densities well below the capacity of the physical environment to support them.[10] Such groups as the !Kung Bushmen,[11] the Hadza,[12] and the Mbuti[13] in Africa, and various Aboriginal groups in Australia,[14] live at population levels below the carrying capacity of the physical environment as determined by their techniques of exploitation. That their populations do not approach carrying capacity is confirmed by the limited time – on average 2-5 hours per adult per day – that they devote to the food quest. We do not know whether hunter-gatherer groups in temperate and polar environments also lived at population levels below carrying capacity, nor whether the predecessors of twentieth-century tropical hunter-gatherers did so, but in the absence of evidence to the contrary we may assume that they did. Certainly malnutrition and starvation sufficient to reduce a population appears to be most unusual among hunter-gatherers in all but arctic and subarctic environments.[15]

The assumption that past and present hunter-gatherer populations have normally stabilised at levels below the carrying capacity of the environment, exploited at a given level of technology, is further strengthened if evidence for the cultural regulation of births and deaths is considered. Such controls on fertility and mortality as sexual abstinence, contraception, abortion, infanticide, and senilicide are widely reported among hunter-gatherer bands,[16] and, as is suggested later, their use may relate in particular to band mobility.

If population increase is to be used as an explanatory variable in hypotheses dealing with the transition from simple to complex communities, and if it is correct to assume that hunter-gatherers have normally limited their populations at levels below carrying capacity, then it is necessary to postulate some process whereby the cultural regulation of births and deaths is relaxed sufficiently to allow population to increase. It could simply be argued that population control is not always effective and that certain hunter-gatherer groups experience sufficient population growth to be transformed into larger communities with more complex socioeconomic institutions. This is possible, but it is too general and undemonstrable a proposition to be useful in framing testable hypotheses. It is only when we relate demographic change to the other variables assumed to be significant – changes in the physical environment, in resource use, and in mobility – that it is possible to build an empirically useful model.

The regulation of hunter-gatherer band size

Figure 1 indicates the principal variables that appear to affect the population size of hunter-gatherer bands and it suggests the pattern of interactions that links these variables together. The effects of some of the variables upon population size are obvious and require little elaboration. Changes in the physical environment of sufficient magnitude to be regarded as natural disasters – events such as hurricanes, tidal waves, and severe droughts – clearly affect population size, both directly and by drastically reducing local carrying capacity. Similarly both immigration and emigration can directly alter the size of the band; indeed recent studies have shown that group size is in constant 'flux' seasonally and as individuals move between bands. As Fig. 1 suggests, these and other variables also affect population size indirectly through changes in the availability of food resources, in the size of the subsistence territory, and in patterns of mobility, which in turn have feedback effects on the cultural regulation of births and deaths.

The pattern of interaction among the variables portrayed in Fig. 1 represents a largely closed equilibrium system that is capable of maintaining band size at levels below the carrying capacity of the physical environment. In the absence of major externally generated disruptions, such as natural disasters or human invasions, the system can, by encompassing minor, short-term fluctuations in population size, maintain demographic equilibrium over long periods of time. it thus helps us to understand why human population groups appear to have remained so small throughout the Pleistocene. The parts of the system that concern us most directly are the feedback effects that link mobility, size of territory, and the cultural regulations of births and deaths. I will therefore examine this nexus of relationships more closely, before considering ways in which demographic equilibrium may be upset and greater complexity of socioeconomic organisation begin to emerge.

Recent studies of contemporary hunter-gatherers have shown that

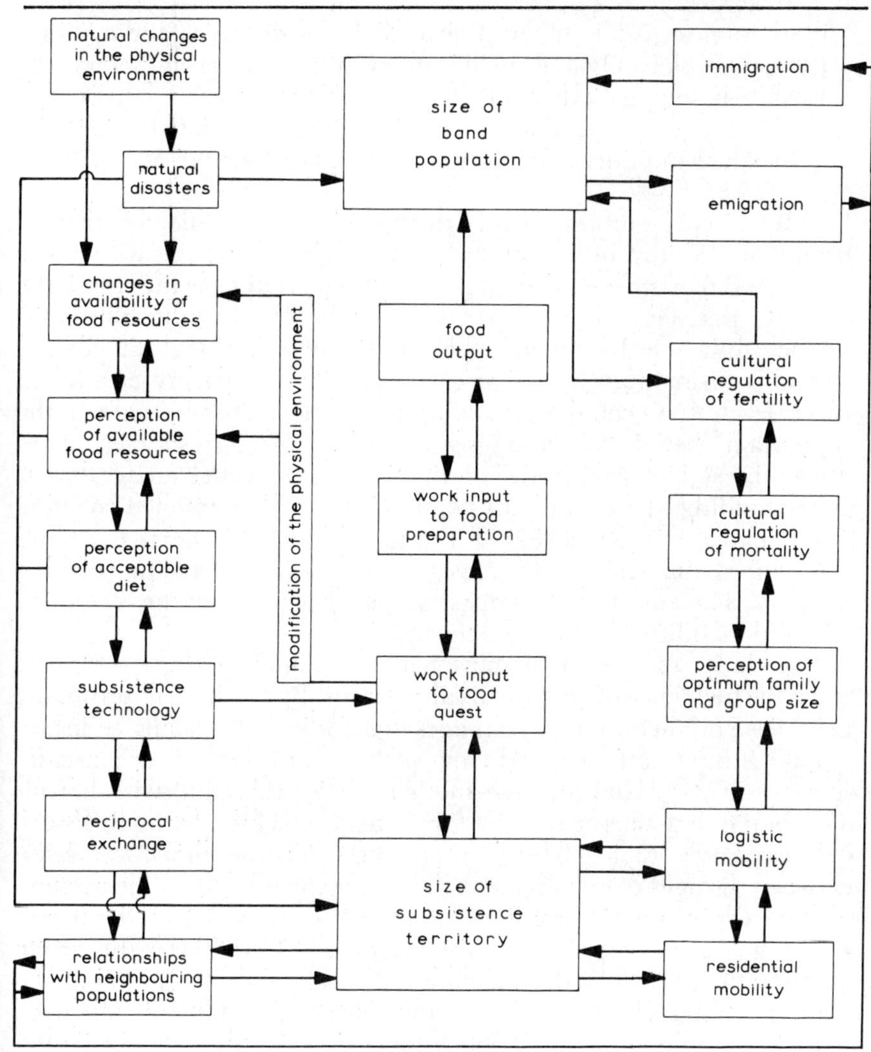

Figure 1. The interaction of variables affecting the population size of hunter-gatherer bands.

band size, composition, and territory are highly variable over time and in space.[17] Seasonal variation in the size, composition, and territorial spread of band populations is usual. Periods of clustering into relatively large aggregates of 100 or more people commonly alternate with periods of dispersal into small family groups. Lee[18] points out that the attractions of living in a larger group in one place, particularly the intensification of social life that it allows, are counterbalanced by an increased incidence of conflict and by the need to work harder to obtain sufficient food as local resources are progressively used up. For the Bushmen

living in large groups was a mixed blessing. It offered the people a

> more intense social life but it also meant harder work and a higher frequency of conflict. But, like many other hunter-gatherers, the Bushmen sought both kinds of social existence, the intensity and excitement of a larger grouping and its attendant risks, and the domestic tranquility and leisure time of smaller groups.[19]

The Bushman solution to this dilemma was to come together in groups of 100 and over around water points during the winter dry season and to disperse in small family-based groups for the rest of the year. As Lee suggests, this pattern of mobility not only minimises conflict, but the Bushmen's 'perception of the threat of conflict functions to maintain group size and population density at a much lower level than could be supported by the food resources if the population could be organised to use those resources more efficiently'.[20] This perspective on band size contributes further to our understanding of why human population groups remained so small throughout the Pleistocene, but it does not in itself indicate *how* band populations may have been regulated at levels well below carrying capacity. The answer to this question may be sought in the reciprocal effects of mobility, fertility, and mortality.

The daily and seasonal movements of hunter-gatherers directly affect the incidence of both births and deaths. Birdsell,[21] Binford,[22] and Lee[23] have pointed to the advantages that wide birth spacing confer on mobile hunter-gatherers. Among such groups infants are usually suckled for 3-4 years and the mother carries the child with her for most of the time during the first three years of its life. !Kung Bushmen mothers carry their children everywhere for the first two years; between the ages of two and four the infant spends some time in camp in the care of others; and it is not until the age of six or seven that carrying ceases entirely and the child walks wherever the group goes.[24] The average birth interval is four years and this is maintained without contraceptive measures and with a post-partum taboo on sexual intercourse that is effective for one year only after the child's birth.[25] Wide birth spacing is not alone sufficient to regulate the population, but such excess fertility as there is is counteracted by infant mortality (including infanticide) and by some emigration.[26]

Lee suggests that the principal mechanism by which a 4-year birth interval is maintained among the !Kung Bushmen is the suppressant effect on ovulation of prolonged lactation as the mothers suckle each child for 2½-3½ years.[27] There is uncertainty as to how generally effective this suppressant effect is among mobile populations. Most studies of it relate to settled populations where mobile work demands are lower. Among Australian Aboriginal populations studied in 1948 at four locations in Arnhem Land lactation was reported as going on 'unabated until the next pregnancy supervenes' although 'without a subsequent pregnancy, lactation usually lasts from two to three and a half years'.[28] In this case lactation was not apparently suppressing ovulation effectively, but the populations had been at least partially settled for some time around missions where daily movements were reduced and where soft foods suitable for weaning were more readily available. Whether prolonged lactation was as generally effective in regulating birth interval and hence fertility among mobile hunter-gatherers as Lee implies remains uncertain, but it is likely to have been one of the principal regulatory mechanisms in pre-contact situations, and, perhaps, in Pleistocene times also.

Birdsell[29] lays great stress on infanticide as a means of maintaining a minimum 3-year birth interval among unacculturated Australian Aborigines, and, by extension, among all human groups in the Pleistocene. Yengoyan[30] also regards infanticide as the primary means of population control among pre-contact Aborigines and suggests that it may have extended to 15-30% of all births. The widespread incidence among hunter-gatherers not only of infanticide but also of other direct controls on mortality and fertility, such as senilicide, abortion, contraception, and sexual abstinence, has already been mentioned. Evidence is too scanty for general estimates of the relative importance of these various controls to be made, but it is clear that they represent alternative or additional means by which hunter-gatherers could adjust their populations to the demands of group mobility.

The ways in which variations in mobility influence the dynamics of band populations are less obvious but no less significant. Binford[31] distinguishes residential mobility, which takes place when the entire group moves from camp to camp, from logistic mobility, which refers to the movements of members of the group engaged in the food quest. Social visits between bands may fall into either category, according to whether the entire group moves or only certain members of it. The two types of mobility are distinguished in Fig. 1 because they have significantly different demographic and socioeconomic implications; in particular their relative importance within a band has feedback effects on fertility.

If the group is one in which adult males devote much of their time to hunting migratory herd ungulates, then male absence on hunting trips may be sufficiently prolonged to reduce the frequency of conception and thus to restrict the birth rate. Binford[31] suggests that the prolonged absence from camp of caribou hunters was a principal means whereby wide birth spacing was maintained in the Nunamiut Eskimo group that he is studying; although the work demands that the more local food quest made on the women reinforced this effect. If, on the other hand, the food quest does not involve the prolonged separation of adult men and women, as is characteristic of many tropical hunter-gatherers who exploit a broader spectrum of resources within smaller subsistence territories, then male logistic mobility will have little or no negative feedback effect on fertility. The !Kung Bushmen, whose foraging activities seldom involve overnight absence,[32] illustrate this situation in a tropical desert environment, as does the daily food quest of Australian Aboriginal groups in the more humid tropical environments of Arnhem Land,[33] and Cape York Peninsula.[34]

The breakdown of demographic equilibrium

The argument thus far has sought to establish that the regulation of hunter-gatherer populations at levels well below carrying capacity is likely to have been the demographic norm in pre-contact situations and that its 'explanation' lies in demonstrable feedback effects that link group mobility, size of subsistence territory, work input to the food quest, and the cultural regulation of fertility and mortality (Fig. 1). We can now return to the central question posed earlier, namely in what circumstances may demographic equilibrium have broken down sufficiently to initiate evolutionary trends towards greater complexity of socioeconomic organisation?

Re-examination of Fig. 1 suggests five logical possibilities. I have already commented briefly on three of them. Two, namely natural disasters and immigration on such a scale as to amount to invasion, represent externally generated disruptions capable of upsetting demographic equilibrium. It is difficult to propose plausible hypotheses that might account for the emergence of greater socioeconomic complexity in bands afflicted by natural disasters, beyond the naive proposition that reduction of subsistence territory and/or of available food resources might lead to population pressure on resources and to radical changes in economic and social organisation. Given the mobility of hunter-gatherers and the flexibility of their foraging procedures, it seems more likely that, where feasible, emigration would be the usual short-term response to a natural disaster. However, as is suggested below with reference to the Nunamiut, a severe reduction in a staple resource might trigger compensating adjustments in mobility which could in turn upset demographic equilibrium and lead to changes in socioeconomic organisation.

Invasion can also be envisaged as a process by which demographic equilibrium could be disturbed and socioeconomic change precipitated. However, ethnographic evidence suggests that spatial relationships between hunter-gatherer bands are flexible and socially regulated in such a way as to minimise conflict. Furthermore, if we postulate invasion by a more 'advanced' or complex group then we beg the question of how greater complexity develops in the first place. I do not minimise the significance of contact with more advanced groups as an agent of change among hunter-gatherers, but this is a secondary process which is not directly relevant to the central question of evolutionary change under 'pristine' conditions.

The third logical possibility previously mentioned is that the regulation of births and deaths might over long periods of time be ineffective in maintaining demographic equilibrium and that resulting population growth might transform bands into larger, more complex communities. As a proposition this is undeniable, but it is inherently unsatisfactory because it does not specify how the regulatory mechanisms fail to keep population growth in check. We may accept that such failure is a necessary condition for the transformation of bands into larger communities, but it is not a sufficient explanation of the process. To devise a more satisfactory hypothesis we must consider the two remaining possibilities: change in the availability of food resources and reduction of mobility.

As is indicated in Fig. 1, change in the availability of food resources may result from natural changes in the physical environment, from human modification of the environment as a result of the food quest, for example by persistent burning of vegetation, or from innovations in subsistence technology and in the perception of acceptable diet and available food resources. If the changes apply only to minor food resources and are of short-term duration they are unlikely to affect the socioeconomic system as a whole, but if the availability of staple food resources changes, in either a positive or a negative direction, then major readjustments in the system may follow.

Binford's study of the Nunamiut provides us with an example of the consequences that can flow from a reduction in one staple food resource.[31] After 1898 the caribou on which the Nunamiut primarily depended were drastically reduced in number. As a result the long-distance hunting of caribou, which had involved the younger adult males in prolonged absence from camp, gave way to the more local exploitation of a wider variety of game and fish. Logistic mobility thus decreased, and, because nuclear families now remained together for longer periods, the average interval between births was reduced and the population increased. At the same time the shift to a more localised but broader-spectrum pattern of resource exploitation demanded more frequent residential moves and a greater work input to the food quest, which was provided for by the larger population.

This example neatly demonstrates how the effects of an initial change in one variable can be amplified through the socioeconomic system and result in a larger population which may establish a new equilibrium based on a broader-spectrum pattern of resource exploitation while remaining residentially mobile. As I have suggested elsewhere,[35] such a self-amplifying process of subsistence and demographic change may be discernible in the late-Pleistocene and early post-Pleistocene archaeological record of Europe north of the Alps, of eastern North America, and of parts of the Near East. If a shift towards dependence on a broad spectrum of relatively localised food resources accompanied by increases in population proves to be a widespread early post-Pleistocene phenomenon, then we may be witnessing in it the initial breakdown of a long sustained pattern of Pleistocene mobility and population regulation and the first emergence of larger, less mobile, and more complex communities.

This process suggests one possible evolutionary pathway from small, mobile hunter-gatherer bands towards larger, more territorially localised, but still residentially mobile communities. Examination of this pathway has already introduced the last factor to be discussed – reduction in mobility – and we can now take the last step in the argument by considering the effects of a shift from residential mobility to sedentism.

From residential mobility to sedentism

Many different circumstances can be envisaged in which a hunter-gatherer band accustomed to moving from camp to camp might shift to a more sedentary existence based on the year-round occupation of one site. Territorial confinement – whether as a result of natural environmental limits as, for example, when a band occupies a small island, or owing to inter-group hostility – is one obvious possibility. Another is the adoption of technological innovations, such as seed grinding and storage, that allow more intensive exploitation of locally available resources such as the seeds of grasses and forbs. A third is the occupation of sites which give access to sufficiently rich and diverse resources within a small area to allow or encourage year-round settlement. As I have previously argued, sites within transitional zones or ecotones between major ecosystems, such as forest-grassland boundaries, upland-lowland margins, and the conjunction of terrestrial and aquatic ecosystems along rivers, swamps, lakes, and coasts, offer optimum access to assured and variable supplies of wild plants and animals and are likely to have been associated with the development of sedentism.[36]

However my purpose here is less to speculate about the varied circumstances in which sedentism may have developed than to examine the effects of a shift to sedentism on the socioeconomic organisation of a hunter-gatherer band. In doing so we must draw on data obtained from the study of contemporary hunter-gatherers undergoing sedentisation as a result of contact with modern, complex societies. Such data must be used with caution, in particular because the transition from mobility to sedentism is likely to have taken place more gradually in the past than in the present when modern governments encourage or enforce it, but in seeking to understand the process we cannot afford to ignore the insights the ethnographic data afford. The most relevant data available to me come from Binford's and Lee's work among the Nunamiut and the !Kung Bushmen, and from several demographic studies of northern Australian Aboriginal populations.

The Nunamiut Eskimo studied by Binford became sedentary at a government settlement at Anaktuvu between 1950 and 1964, during which time the population increased from 76 to 128.[31] We have already seen that the population had increased earlier this century as a result of a reduction in logistic mobility following decline of the caribou herds. This led temporarily to increased residential mobility as the population shifted to a more localised but broader-spectrum pattern of resource exploitation. When this shift in turn gave way to sedentary life, residential mobility was eliminated and logistic mobility was again reduced. As a result the population increased rapidly, particularly because reduced female mobility led to still closer spacing of live births, which may have been partly a function of a decreased incidence of miscarriage. Perhaps of greatest interest is the way in which the Nunamiut adjusted socially to this rapid increase in populaton. Binford reports that, faced with the problem of numerous unruly youngsters in the settlement, the adults formed a 'council of elders' to discuss problems generated by the changed population structure and to attempt to adjudicate in disputes.[31] This suggests that one way in which social differentiation might arise and become institutionalised, and the egalitarian life-style of hunter-gatherers break down, is as a response to population increase following a shift to sedentism.

A somewhat similar conclusion may be drawn from Lee's study of the !Kung Bushmen who became sedentary and began to cultivate crops and raise goats during the 1950s and 1960s. Lee does not differentiate sharply between logistic and residential mobility, but he does point out that 'with reduced mobility a woman may shorten the interval between successive births and continue to give each child adequate care while keeping her work effort a constant'.[37] He demonstrates that 'settling down removes the adverse effects of high fertility on individual women' so that 'three-year birth spacing becomes no more strenuous to the mother than was four-year birth spacing to mothers under nomadic conditions'.[38] In fact a birth interval of 33 to 36 months occurs among the more sedentary Bushmen and it is suggested that the availability of soft food alternatives to human milk – goat's milk and grain mush from maize and sorghum – shortens the period of lactation and permits an earlier resumption of ovulation, thus leading to earlier conception and a reduced birth interval.[39] Other factors, such as changes in infant mortality (which Lee explicitly excludes from his discussion), affect positively or negatively the observed increase of population that follows the adoption of sedentary life. But it is the socioeconomic adjustment to this increase that is of particular interest here.

In discussing the intensification of social life among the !Kung, Lee[40] explains that their shift towards sedentism was stimulated by contact with Bantu-speaking immigrant Herero pastoralists around whose newly established cattle posts the Bushmen began to cluster.

There the !Kung maintained groups of 100-200 people for most of the year. These aggregations proved more durable than the traditional winter dry-season camps which normally broke up after about three months when spring rains allowed dispersal and by which time there was a strong desire to avoid the further escalation of conflicts that arose in the larger winter camps. The Bushmen solved the problem of living in larger semipermanent – and eventually permanent – groups only by their attachment to the Herero pastoralists and, indirectly, to governmental authority. The Herero provided the Bushmen with milk, meat and agricultural produce in return for labour and they fulfilled the vital role of mediators in disputes between Bushmen.

In this example, therefore, the socioeconomic adjustment to sedentisation and population increase was not internally generated to the same extent as it was by the Nunamiut, but was more directly a function of the contact situation that initiated sedentisation. Such processes whereby hunter-gatherer socioeconomic organisation is transformed through cultural contact with pastoralists and agriculturalists have no doubt operated widely in the past, but they contribute only indirectly to the explanation of how bands evolve *independently* under 'pristine' conditions towards higher levels of cultural complexity.

Data on Australian Aboriginal populations throw little direct light on the question of socioeconomic adjustment to sedentisation and population increase, but they do support the view that there is a positive relationship between the latter variables. In a study of the Aboriginal population of the Northern Territory as a whole Jones[41] shows that, after an initial post-contact decline which lasted until about 1930, the total population has begun to increase rapidly. This increase relates to the progressive sedentisation of the Aboriginal population at missions and government stations, but the data do not allow clear discrimination between the effects of different demographic factors such as reductions in infant mortality and in average birth interval. Yengoyan[42] reports a comparable increase since the 1930s of Aboriginal populations settling at missions and government stations in central Australia and he shows that, for the Pitjandjara at least, sedentisation has led to an intensification of ritual life.[43]

The Tiwi population of Bathurst Island off the north-west Australian coast became effectively sedentary at a mission by the late 1940s. It was studied in detail by Jones who found that it increased by 44% in just over ten years, from 657 in 1951 to 948 in 1961, although the latter figure may be somewhat inflated.[44] From 1952 to 1961 the rate of natural increase of the population at the mission averaged 2.3% per annum, and after 1957 it rose to 2.5% per annum. This latter rate represents a doubling of the population every 28 years, and it is equalled and even surpassed by the rates of natural increase of other mission-based Aboriginal populations in the Northern

Territory, such as those at Roper River, Yirrkalla, and Groote Eylandt.[45] Jones[46] notes that in 1961 the Bathurst Island population was characterised by high fertility and high mortality, which suggests that a reduction in average birth interval following sedentisation is contributing more to population increase than any decline in infant mortality associated with the suppression of infanticide or improved medical care. Indeed, in relation to the latter, Jones suggests[47] that the 'rapid increase, due to an excess of births over deaths, tends to produce overcrowding and a temporary deterioration in standards of sanitation and hygiene, and that this in turn leads to higher mortality among the young'.

From the point of view of the argument developed in this paper the principal shortcoming of the Australian Aboriginal data is the lack of precise demographic information on populations before and after sedentisation. In an effort to overcome this deficiency I have made use of Tindale's compilation of genealogies for the Kaiadilt population of Bentinck Island in the Gulf of Carpentaria.[48] He recorded them in 1960 at the mission on nearby Mornington Island where the Kaiadilt were resettled in 1947-48 after the Bentinck Island population had suffered a series of dry years in the early 1940s which led to conflict and attempts to leave the island, and which culminated in a tidal wave in 1948.[49] The example is not ideal, partly because data for the period from 1900 to 1948 suffer from uncertainties relating to age estimates and other genealogical details, and partly because of the limited mobility of the pre-contact island population. However, it does suggest that a near-equilibrium situation prevailed prior to the stresses of 1942-48 which reduced the population severely, and that since 1948 the population at the mission has increased substantially. Between 1910 and 1940 the total population increased from 105 to 123, or at about 5% per decade, whereas under the mission regime, after an initial decline, it has increased at a rate of nearly 10% per decade.[50]

If the number of years between births is computed from the genealogies for all mothers born after 1892 and for all children born before 1942 the average birth interval for this pre-contact period is found to be 4.5 years. This compares with an average birth interval of 3.3 years for the population living at the mission. This contrast is reflected in a corresponding increase in average family size (omitting wives dying without children) from a pre-contact figure of 2.56 to 2.80 at the mission. Tindale could not obtain precise information on infant mortality but he does comment that after the population was settled at the mission 'births of children were numerous . . . (although there were) . . . some losses due to a high infantile mortality, some possibly owing to exposure to new diseases in the changed environment'.[51] It appears therefore that the pattern of demographic change among the Kaiadilt following settlement parallels that among the Tiwi and other northern Australian Aboriginal groups settled at missions. It also resembles the situation among the !Kung Bushmen in the close correspondence shown between the birth intervals recorded before and after sedentisation.

Examination of the data on changes in mobility and in population among the Nunamiut, the !Kung Bushmen, and two Australian Aboriginal hunter-gatherer groups confirms the positive relationship between the adoption of sedentary life and population growth that is taken as the starting point for the self-amplifying, evolutionary system shown in Fig. 2. The processual sequence, which leads from population increase via resource specialisation to food-production and the specialised exploitation of wild resources, has previously been proposed,[52] although the elaboration of social organisation was not

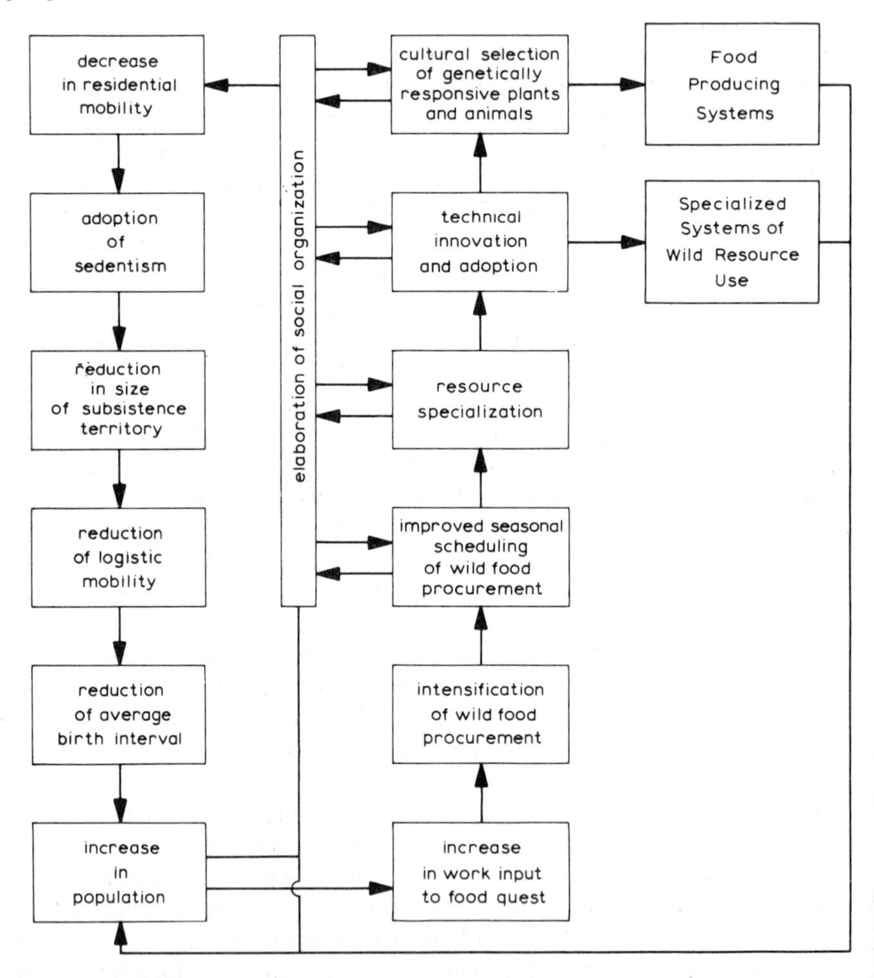

Figure 2. A self-amplifying, evolutionary system showing the effects of a shift from residential mobility to sedentism. The diagram indicates a possible processual sequence from the adoption of sedentism to the emergence of complex communities based either on food production or on the specialised exploitation of wild resources.

included in that formulation. The sequence as such will not be discussed, nor will the particular pathways leading to five sub-systems of specialised resource use (grass- and forb-seed harvesting, root and tuber harvesting, herd-ungulate exploitation, wild tree-nut harvesting, and fishing and aquatic mammal hunting) that are suggested in that paper. No attempt can be made here to test the validity of the sequence diachronically by detailed reference to archaeological data. But I suggest that the early post-Pleistocene archaeological record of Eurasia and North America contains much evidence that accords with the self-amplifying system outlined in Fig. 2, and I propose it as a tentative and partial 'explanation' of the transformation of hunter-gatherer bands into larger and more complex communities based on food production or on the specialised exploitation of wild resources.

NOTES

1 Flannery, K.V. (1972), 'The cultural evolution of civilizations', *Annual Review of Ecology and Systematics*, 3, pp. 399-426.

2 Dumond, D.E. (1972), 'Population growth and political centralization', *in* Spooner, B. (ed.), *Population Growth: Anthropological Implications*, Boston, pp. 286-310.

3 Carneiro, R.L. (1970), 'A theory of the origin of the state', *Science*, 169, pp. 733-8.

4 Renfrew, C. (1972), *The Emergence of Civilisation: The Cyclades and the Aegean in the Third Millennium B.C.*, London.

5 Adams, R.Mc. (1966), *The Evolution of Urban Society*, Chicago.

6 Wheatley, P. (1971), *The Pivot of the Four Quarters: A Preliminary Enquiry into the Origins and Character of the Ancient Chinese City*, Edinburgh, pp. 223-369.

7 Harris, D.R. (1973), 'Alternative pathways towards agriculture', Paper prepared for International Congress of Anthropological and Ethnological Sciences, Chicago, to be published in 1977 *in* Reed, C.A. (ed.), *The Origins of Agriculture*, The Hague.

8 Smith, P.E.L. (1972), 'Changes in population pressure in archaeological explanation', *World Archaeology*, 4, pp. 5-18; Spooner (ed.) (1972).

9 Kunstadter, P. (1972), 'Demography, ecology, social structure, and settlement patterns', *in* Harrison, G.A. and Boyce, A.J. (eds.), *The Structure of Human Populations*, Oxford, pp. 315-51, ref. on p. 348.

10 Lee, R.B. and DeVore, I. (eds.) (1968), *Man the Hunter*, Chicago; Sahlins, M.D. (1972), *Stone Age Economics*, Chicago and New York, pp. 1-39.

11 Lee, R.B. (1968), 'What hunters do for a living, or, how to make out on scarce resources', *in* Lee and DeVore (eds.) (1968), pp. 30-48; Lee, R.B. (1969), '!Kung Bushman subsistence: an input-output analysis', *in* Vayda, A.P. (ed.), *Environment and Cultural Behaviour*, Garden City, New York, pp. 47-79; Lee, R.B. (1972a), 'Work effort, group structure and land-use in contemporary hunter-gatherers', *in* Ucko, P.J., Tringham, R. and Dimbleby, G.W. (eds.), *Man, Settlement and Urbanism*, London, pp. 177-85; Lee, R.B. (1972b), 'Population growth and the beginnings of sedentary life among the !Kung Bushmen', *in* Spooner (ed.) (1972), pp. 329-42; Lee, R.B. (1972c), 'The intensification of social life among the !Kung Bushmen', *in* Spooner (ed.) (1972), pp. 343-50.

12 Woodburn, J. (1968a), 'An introduction to Hadza ecology', *in* Lee and DeVore (eds.) (1968), pp. 49-55; Woodburn, J. (1968b), 'Stability and flexibility in Hadza residential groupings', *in* Lee and DeVore (eds.) (1968), pp. 103-10; Woodburn, J. (1972), 'Ecology, nomadic movement and the composition of the local group among

hunters and gatherers: an East African example and its implications', *in* Ucko, Tringham and Dimbleby (eds.) (1972), pp. 193-206.

13 Turnbull, C.M. (1968), 'The importance of flux in two hunting societies', *in* Lee and Devore (eds.) (1968), pp. 132-7; Turnbull, C.M. (1972), 'Demography of small-scale societies', *in* Harrison and Boyce (eds.) (1972), pp. 283312.

14 Gould, R.A. (1969), *Yiwara: Foragers of the Australian Desert*, New York; McArthur, M. (1960), 'Food consumption and dietary levels of groups of Aborigines living on naturally occurring foods', *in* Mountford, C.P. (ed.), *Records of the American-Australian Scientific Expedition to Arnhem Land, 2, Anthropology and Nutrition*, Melbourne, pp. 90-8; McCarthy, F.D. and McArthur, M. (1960), 'The food quest and the time factor in Aboriginal economic life', *in* Mountford (ed.) (1960), pp. 145-94; Sharp, R.L. (1940), 'An Australian Aboriginal population', *Human Biology*, 12, pp. 481-507; Thomson, D.F. (1939), 'The seasonal factor in human culture illustrated from the life of a contemporary nomadic group', *Proceedings of the Prehistoric Society*, 10, pp. 209-21.

15 Dunn, F.L. (1968), 'Epidemiological factors: health and disease in hunter-gatherers', *in* Lee and DeVore (eds.) (1968), pp. 221-8, ref. on p. 223.

16 Benedict, B. (1972), 'Social regulation of fertility', *in* Harrison and Boyce (eds.) (1972), pp. 73-89; Birdsell, J.B. (1968), 'Some predictions for the Pleistocene based on equilibrium systems among recent hunter-gatherers', *in* Lee and DeVore (eds.) (1968), pp. 229-40; Divale, W.T. (1972), 'Systemic population control in the Middle and Upper Palaeolithic: inferences based on contemporary hunter-gatherers', *World Archaeology*, 4, pp. 222-43; Hayden, B. (1972), 'Population control among hunter/gatherers', *World Archaeology*, 4, pp. 205-21; Turnbull (1972).

17 Helm, J. (1968), 'The nature of Dogrib socioterritorial groups', *in* Lee and DeVore (eds.) (1968), pp. 118-25; Lee (1972a, b, c); Turnbull (1968); Woodburn (1968b), (1972); Yengoyan, A.A. (1968), 'Demographic and ecological influences on Aboriginal Australian marriage sections', *in* Lee and DeVore (eds.) (1968), pp. 185-99.

18 Lee (1972a).

19 Lee (1972a), p. 182.

20 Lee (1972a), p. 183.

21 Birdsell (1968), pp. 236-7.

22 Binford, L.R., quoted in Pfeiffer, J.E. (1969), *The Emergence of Man*, New York, Evanston, and London, p. 218.

23 Lee (1972b).

24 Lee (1972b), p. 331.

25 Lee (1972b), p. 337.

26 Lee (1972b), p. 337.

27 Lee (1972b), p. 340.

28 Billington, B.P. (1960), 'The health and nutritional status of the Aborigines', *in* Mountford (ed.) (1960), pp. 27-59, ref. on p. 34.

29 Birdsell (1968).

30 Yengoyan, A.A. (1972), 'Biological and demographic components in Aboriginal Australian socio-economic organization', *Oceania*, 43, pp. 85-95, ref. on pp. 88-9.

31 Binford, L.R. (1972), personal communication.

32 Lee (1969), pp. 58-61.

33 McArthur (1960); McCarthy and McArthur, (1960).

34 Sharp (1940); Thomson (1939).

35 Harris (1973).

36 Harris, D.R. (1969), 'Agricultural systems, ecosystems and the origins of agriculture', *in* Ucko, P.J. and Dimbleby, G.W. (eds.), *The Domestication and Exploitation of Plants and Animals*, London, pp. 3-15.

37 Lee (1972b), p. 338.

38 Lee (1972b), p. 339.

39 Lee (1972b), p. 341.

40 Lee (1972c).

41 Jones, F.L. (1963), 'A demographic survey of the Aboriginal population of the Northern Territory, with special reference to Bathurst Island Mission', *Occasional Papers in Aboriginal Studies Number One*, Canberra, Australian Institute of Aboriginal Studies.

42 Yengoyan (1972).

43 Yengoyan (1972), p. 91.

44 Jones (1963), pp. 25-8.

45 Jones (1963), pp. 53-4.

46 Jones (1963), p. 54.

47 Jones (1963), pp. 54-5.

48 Tindale, N.B. (1962), 'Some population changes among the Kaiadilt people of Bentinck Island, Queensland', *Records of the South Australian Museum*, 14, pp. 297-336.

49 Tindale (1962).

50 Tindale (1962), p. 311.

51 Tindale (1962), p. 316.

52 Harris (1974).

JIM ALLEN

Fishing for wallabies: trade as a mechanism for social interaction, integration and elaboration on the central Papuan coast

> By no conquest do the Motuans live here, but simply because the Koitapuans allow them, saying, 'Yours is the sea, the canoes, and the nets; ours the land and the wallaby. Give us fish for our flesh, and pottery for our yams and bananas'.[1]

The post-Darwinian occupation of New Guinea by Europeans created the almost unique situation of completely traditional Stone Age societies being recorded by men at least acquainted with modern anthropological theory. While today the inhabitants of the Port Moresby region are largely urban dwellers, it was here that scores of missionaries, administrators and anthropologists first met the people they had come to conquer or to save, and their impressions and observations of the inhabitants of this area allow good reconstructions of traditional life: good but not perfect, for the data are often sketchy and uneven.

This paper offers a reconstruction of the social and economic life of the Motu, coastal dwellers along 125 kilometres of this coast, of which Port Moresby is both the approximate geographical centre, and in recent prehistoric times the apparent socioeconomic centre of Motuan activities, based on these written sources. It attempts to indicate the articulation of Motuan social and economic ties with their coastal neighbours both east and west, and with inland groups. It attempts to demonstrate Motuan interaction with the local environment, and is thus perhaps too naively environmentally deterministic. It hypothesises that the intensification of the social organisation of the groups individually and collectively has led to an increased population capacity under existing subsistence regimes, and offers trade as the explanatory mechanism for the intensification. Existing archaeological evidence is invoked to support the argument drawn primarily from the ethnography, but is in no way offered as 'proof' of the model, which has developed from both lines of enquiry.

Environment

Climate in the Port Moresby region is controlled primarily by the wind systems which alternate seasonally (Fig. 1). From April/May to November/December the southeast trade winds bring dry and cooler conditions, particularly in June-September, the period of greatest intensity. From December to April the rain-bearing north-west monsoon winds predominate. As elsewhere the two wind systems are normally separated by transitional 'doldrums'. Rainfall, temperature and humidity are all controlled in a general sense by these wind systems. Both the coast and ranges in the area are aligned parallel to the prevailing winds, which results in abnormally low rainfall compared to other areas in New Guinea.[2]

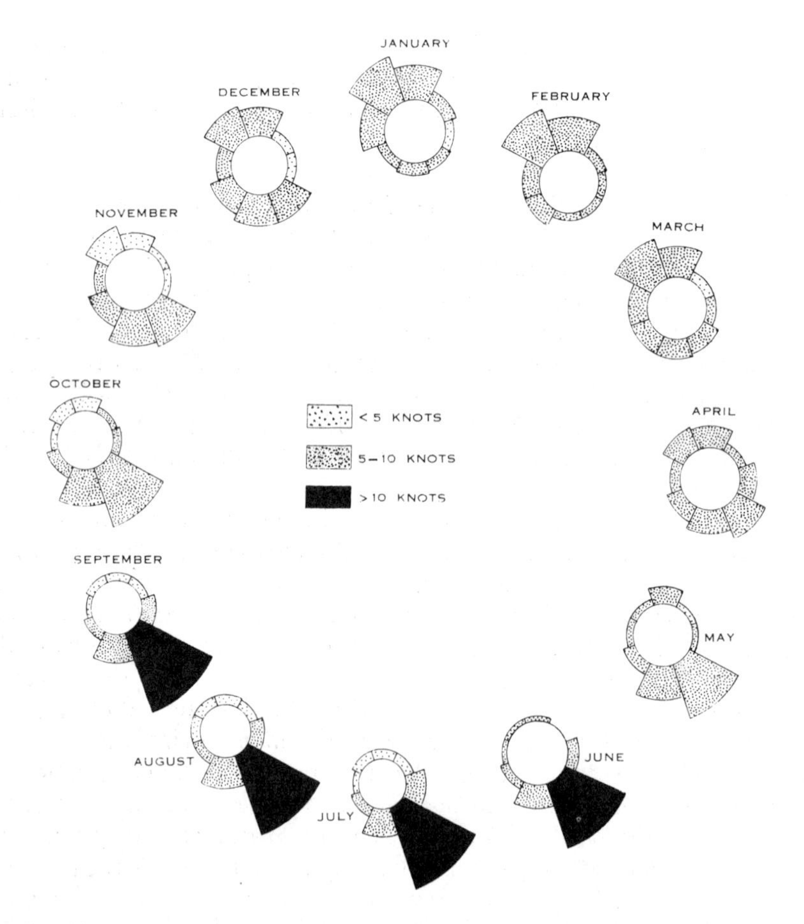

Figure 1. Monthly wind roses from Port Moresby, showing percentage frequencies of wind from eight compass point intervals with their associated mean velocities and the frequency of calm conditions (represented as the area of each central circle).

Isohyets also run parallel to the coast, with rainfall increasing from the coast inland. Thus in a distance of some 45 kilometres, mean average rainfall increases from less than 100 cm. p.a. on the coast to approaching 350 cm. p.a. inland (Fig. 2), with strong seasonality in all zones being more accentuated nearer the coast. Evaporation is high and the flora of the region, unlike the lowland tropical rainforests elsewhere along this coast, range from sub-tropical to temperate in their make-up, with large areas of savannah grassland. There is no clear consensus of opinion as to whether these grasslands are the result of low rainfall or burning by man, but certainly today both factors combine to maintain, and in some cases intensify, this vegetational pattern.

Annual temperature variation is relatively small, maxima ranging from 28°C to 32°C (August and December respectively) and minima 23°C to 24.5°C for the same months. Similarly mean relative humidity remains high and ranges only narrowly throughout the year, between 74% and 82%.[3]

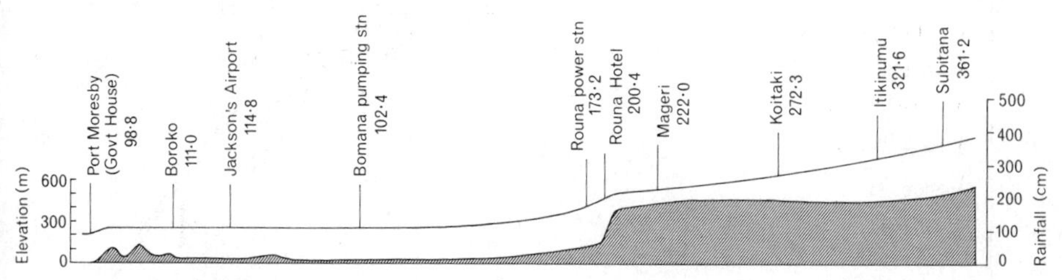

Figure 2. Relationship between mean annual rainfall and altitude along a profile inland from Port Moresby.

Detailed geological, geomorphological and pedological data are available for the region,[4] from which several aspects are germane to this paper. Fringing and barrier reefs protect the shoreline from Hall Sound, north-east of Motu territory, to beyond Gabagaba, the south-eastern-most Motu village. All along Motu territory the barrier reef stands 4-5 kilometres offshore, but beyond Gabagaba this distance is widened. North of Hall Sound the reef is submerged. Within the region chert outcrops of varying quality are common, and a variety of clay soils is widely distributed throughout.

On the basis of these data Mabbutt and his colleagues[5] have delineated six clearly different environmental zones, running inland from the coast and parallel to it and contained within a distance of 35 kilometres (Fig. 3). It is this diverse ecological region which is occupied by the Motu and their inland neighbours, the Koita and the Koiari (Fig. 4). The majority of Motu coast is hilly and covered with savannah, and although there would be no shortage of water throughout the year, true estuarine conditions are absent except for Galley Reach, on the mouth of which the village of Manumanu is the extreme north-western Motu village. It is here that the two major

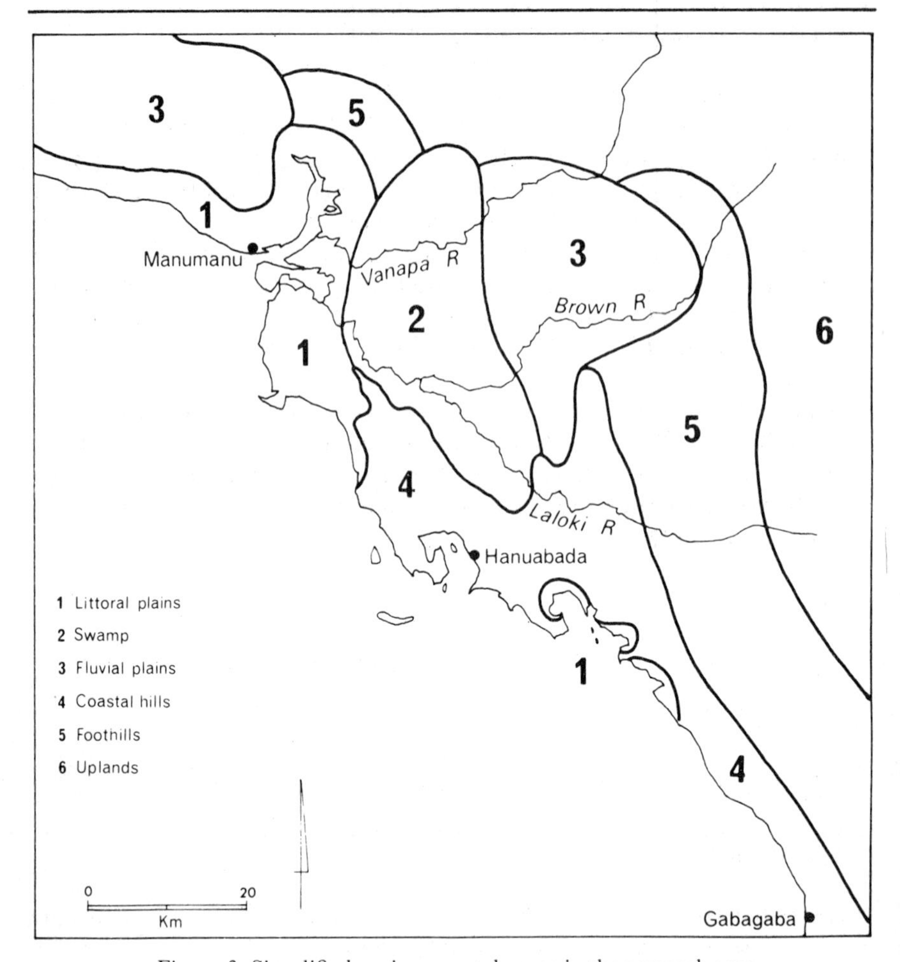

Figure 3. Simplified environmental zones in the research area.

rivers of the area, the Brown and the Laloki, meandering westwards from the uplands, meet the sea.

The Motu

The Motu speak an Austronesian language (AN) which contrasts with the non-Austronesian languages (NAN) in the region (particularly those of the Koiaric family, to which the Koita and Koiari belong), but which shows a close relationship to the surrounding AN languages, all belonging to the central Papuan family. It is generally agreed that the NAN speakers represent the original settlers in the region, and that the AN speakers are descended from later arrivals on the coast. Linguists disagree, however, as to how or when these later 'immigrant' languages arrived. Capell[6] postulated three waves arriving variously from Borneo, central Celebes, and Java,

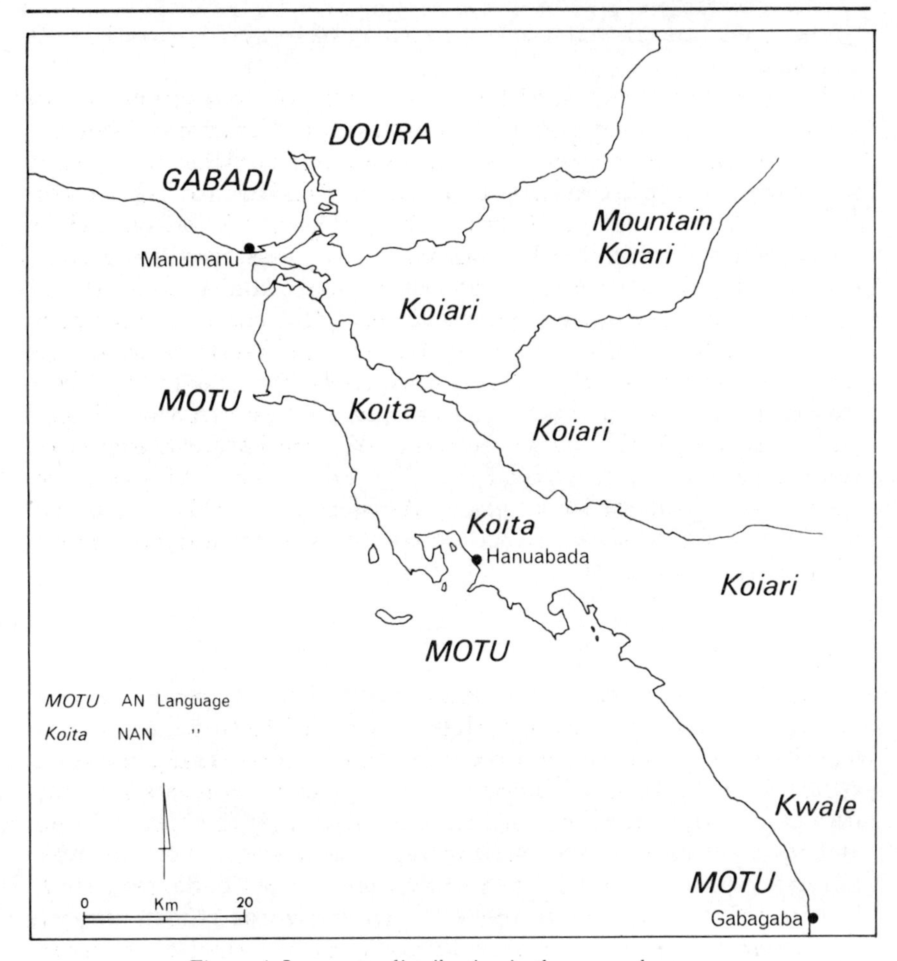

Figure 4. Language distribution in the research area.

Sumatra, and the Malay peninsula. He suggested that the present AN languages in the region of Port Moresby belonged to the third wave, represented 'wandering adventurers', and that an upward limit of around 1200 A.D. was warranted for the formation of these languages,[7] i.e. Motu speakers 'have come in later and superimposed their language and certain aspects of their culture'.[8] Chretian, using statistical techniques on Capell's data, arrived at similar conclusions on most points, but rejected the hypothesis of more than one movement, favouring instead as a better explanation the idea of this area of the coast acting as a central exchange point in the coast-wise trading networks.[9] Dyen[10] on the other hand considered that the diversity of AN languages could have been the result of long settlement in the islands off south-east Papua with differentiation occurring and spreading from this region. More recently, Pawley has suggested that all these AN languages may be derived from a single ancestral language from outside Central Papua, but within

Melanesia[11], and that the divergence may have started around 3,000 years ago.[12]

The Motu further divided themselves into two major groups, the Western Motu, comprising the villages of Manumanu, Rearea, Porebada, Hanuabada and Pari, and the Eastern Motu, comprising the villages of Tubusereia, Barakai, Gaire and Gabagaba. Three other Motu-speaking villages, Boera, Tatana and Vabukori, while geographically within the Western Motu, are considered in this local classification to be different from either group and to some degree dissimilar from each other.[13] Several cultural differences do exist apart from minor dialectal ones between Eastern and Western Motu: the former are not known historically to have directly sponsored the *hiri* trading expeditions (see below), and at contact Eastern Motu villages were built completely in the sea, while Western Motu villages were constructed on the intertidal zone or on beaches. As the three ungrouped villages are more like the Western Motu in these respects, they are included with this group for the present purpose, except where specifically stated.

Population

Among the gaps in the ethnographic data, there is a general lack of distinction between Motu and Koita living in Motu villages, and a lack of precise distinction between Koita and Koiari. Thus population estimates lack precision. As well, although such estimates are met with frequently in the literature, they are mainly for the Motu villages, and even here extreme variation is enountered. For example, estimates for the largest of the Motu villages, Hanuabada, range from 700 in 1875[14] to 1,310 in 1888-9[15]. These figures reflect not only human error, but also population fluctuations caused by loss of canoes on trading expeditions or epidemics of measles or smallpox. Stone[16]

Table 1

Western Motu		*Eastern Motu*	
Manumanu †	300	Tubusereia*	476
Rearea*	209	Barakau?[17]	200
Boera*	315	Gaire*	263
Porebada*	349	Gabagaba †	450
Tatana*	205		
Hanuabada*	1,310		
Vabukori*	184		
Pari*	306		
Total	3,178	Total	1,389
Total Motu	4,567		

† Estimated by Chalmers:[18] For Manumanu, August 1880; for Gabagaba July 1884.
* L.M.S. Census 1888-9. Taken from L.M.S. Annual Report 1890.[19] ? Estimate.

alludes to such an epidemic in Hanuabada a decade before his visit, and notes that the village may have been double his 700 estimate before that time. Table 1 is offered essentially as a guide, with Koita components of these Motu villages still included.

According to Rosenstiel's figures, which include numbers of houses and a breakdown into male, female and child categories, male and female distribution is roughly equal, and children constitute exactly 50% of the population. A household contained 5.5 people of whom 2.7 were children.[20] These figures are apparently calculated from the gross totals of her table, but additional calculations for individual villages show no great variations:

1. Percentage ratios for children to total population range between 40% (Tubusereia and Rearea) and 57% (Hanuabada).
2. Total household size ranges between 4.6 per house (Boera) and 6.1 per house (Gaire and Vabukori).
3. Children per house range between 2.0 (Boera and Rearea) and 3.1 (Gaire).

No differences are to be seen between Eastern and Western Motu groups in respect of these figures.

In terms of coastal distribution of people these figures indicate 36.5 people per kilometre, a figure which increases to beyond 40 per km. when the populations of the five known Koita coastal villages are included. Possible smaller hamlets on the coast which may have been unrecorded might increase this density. These figures appear the most reliable so far located, but other figures indicate household populations as high as 11.3.[21]

Social organisation

The social organisation of Motu villages has been well reviewed in the literature.[22] Specific aspects only will be mentioned here. The important social unit is the *iduhu*, which is 'primarily a residence unit based upon one or more separate lineages of patrilineal emphasis'. In this way it is strictly not a clan, which consists of people claiming common descent.[23] At the time of contact, most Western Motu villages contained one or more *iduhu* of Koita people. Chalmers, in one population estimate for Hanuabada, put the population at 1000 of which 300 were Koita.[24] There are numerous references to Motu-Koita intermarriage in the literature, and a major difficulty is separating Motu and Koita in any particular village:

> Normally after marriage both Motu and Koita live in the village and village section of the husband; all sons throughout their lives, and all daughters until they are married, live in their father's village and village section. (Residence is viripatrilocal). In mixed villages

> people call themselves Koita if they live in a village section that was originally constituted by immigrant Koita, even though their culture is now entirely Motu; otherwise descendents of immigrant Koita call themselves Motu. In recent generations, however, there has been so much intermarriage between Koita minority sections and Motu majority sections in mixed villages that people calling themselves Koita because they live in a Koita section by virtue of their agnatic descent from an original Koita immigrant, may in fact be as much as seven parts Motu to one part Koita; their fathers, grandfathers and greatgrandfathers may all have married women from Motu sections of the villages.[25]

This factor in Motu village composition indicates the difficulty of isolating clearly those aspects of Motuan culture which might be considered typically Motuan as opposed to those that have been influenced by the Koita. (The converse, Motu influence on the Koita, may not be so difficult to analyse, as references to both coastal and inland 'pure' Koita settlements do exist.) Although the north-westernmost Motu village, Manumanu, probably did not ever contain Koita *iduhu*,[26] its immediate environment and the subsistence patterning based on it seem sufficiently different from other Western Motu villages for it to be of little comparative value. On the other hand, Eastern Motu villages apart from Tubusereia have had less Koita influence.[27] Given the differences between Eastern and Western Motu already alluded to above, specific points can be checked with these villages as a control.

One is struck by the amount of ceremonial life in the Motu villages, with taboos, feasts and rituals intimately connected with the social and economic aspects of life. While men aspiring to power might attain it by war, trading, gardening, marriage or sorcery, sponsoring a dance provided the only means of displaying and commemorating a person's ascendancy over his rivals.[28] Only 'strong' men, men with social prestige and economic standing, were able to sponsor a dance, since it involved not only the individual's personal wealth and initiative, but also the number and power of kinsmen and allies owing him allegiance, and thus the power of his *iduhu*. Groves notes two major feast-and-dance cycles; the *hekara*, which provided the machinery for the prosecution of a quarrel, where, by the distribution of food one of the parties had to be defeated by bankruptcy, and the *turia*, a ceremonial held to honour a deceased kinsman, which might also be occasioned by a quarrel and which also might enhance the sponsor's status, but which would not be pursued until a competitor was forced to retire. In addition dances were sponsored at the time of harvesting the yams. As Groves points out however, dancing and gardening activity lack any precise causal connection. While the traditional dance was not necessary to the harvest, it might be more plausible to suggest that the harvest was necessary to the dance.[29] From an archaeological point of view such feasts and dances are important because they required the acquisition and display of decoration and ornaments, and as will be seen below often the erection of specific structures.

Houses

Houses were located along the beach and intertidal zones in the case of Western Motu, and completely in the sea in the case of Eastern Motu according to the ethnographic literature. Seligman[30] indicates that some village activities of this latter group involved constructions on shore, but in general the distinction does stand. The actual construction of houses does not appear to be significantly different in any of these villages. Houses were erected in lines according to *iduhu* groupings, all on piles at an approximate height of 3 metres above the ground for the shoreward houses. As the tidal variation along the coast is in excess of two metres the seabound houses required at least a similar height above the seabed. As far as can be judged from the numerous photographs, piling was of relatively thin, and seldom straight mangrove trunks, with as many as forty piles closely spaced being employed for a single house. Each house was rectangular, with an open platform verandah at the 'front' or shoreward end. Constructed of grass thatch[31] or pandanus,[32] they consisted of a single room without partitions with a simple pitched roof. Floorboards were normally the sides of old canoes being reused. A hearth on a bed of clay existed in the centre of each house.

The leader of each *iduhu* in Western Motu villages lived in the front house of that *iduhu*, and his *dehe* or verandah provided the *iduhu*'s ceremonial focus. On it were placed the foodstuffs during a feast and dancing took place in front of it, on the ground.[33] In this sense it is related to a more precisely ceremonial structure, the *dubu*, noted in a number of Motu villages, but considered by Belshaw[34] to be a predominantly Koita structure. The *dubu* consisted of four main posts, elaborately carved, and supporting usually a two-storey platform used for the display of food and for dancing. According to Belshaw 'the same purpose was served in Motu culture by a line of posts known as *eva* to which people tied their feast foods'. Belshaw does note that the Motu might participate in the erection of such a platform and that at least one Motuan man was responsible for the erection of a *dubu* in Poreporana (Hanuabada).[35] Barton photographed a *dubu* and plotted the groundplans of three such structures in the Eastern Motu village of Gaire, well outside Koita territory,[36] a fact which supports Seligman's assertion that the origin of the *dubu* should be sought in the region of the Sinaugolo inland from Gabagaba to the east.[37] Williams, discussing the *dubu* in a Koiari village, noted it as a cultural item which had been borrowed from the 'coastal people' but it is unclear whether he meant the Motu, Koita or another group.[38] Regardless of who introduced the *dubu* it would seem likely that its use by Motu as well as Koita can be accepted, and that its wider distribution outside of the Motu and Koita domains is certain. What is of interest is that unlike the majority of houseposts, suggested here to be probably of mangrove timber, *dubu* posts in all illustrations so far seen have a far bigger circumference, and the timber is clearly derived from a different source. Further comment on this structure is included in the section on Koita, below.

Subsistence

The universal distinction drawn between the Motu and the Koita in the literature is that the Motu were principally fishermen and traders, and the Koita gardeners and hunters. While on close examination these absolutes start to blur, probably as the result of intermarriage and occupation of the same villages by both groups, nevertheless the distinction holds and cannot be doubted. The degree to which the Motu components of the mixed villages gardened, as opposed to the Koita components, is a problem which seems unlikely to be solved. What can be said is that apart from Badihagua village, which was established several hundred metres from the beach near Hanuabada,[39] no known Motu village was built higher than the beachline. Motu owned land which was restricted almost entirely to the tops of the first range of hills backing the coast,[40] hills which for the most part have little soil and are exposed to the sea winds for most of the year. Notwithstanding this, Stone noted some 350 acres under cultivation in the immediate vicinity of Hanuabada.[41]

The most commonly noted crops directly related to the Motu were yams, and bananas. Coconuts, although growing in profusion on other parts of the coast do not flourish around Port Moresby, except in very limited localities where sufficient water exists. The yam crop, and to some extent bananas, were seasonal, with new gardens being made in August-September, planted in October-November before the rains, and harvested afterwards in April-May. Given a normal or good year of rains, garden produce directly from Motu gardens would support the population only until August. Given drought during the wet season, the period would be one of famine. Gardening was a family affair with the men clearing and building fences to protect the plots against pigs and wallabies, and the women planting, harvesting, carrying and cooking. Domestic pigs and chickens were noted by the early ethnographers in both Western and Eastern Motu villages. In the latter pigs were maintained in pens over water.[42] Mentions of domestic pig are, however, not common, and possibly this lack reflects the true situation in regard to the density of these animals, because feeding them in an area with little vegetable surplus would be a difficult and expensive task.

Fishing is an occupation on which the ethnography places much emphasis in regard to the Motu, and one which, given the Motuan settlement pattern, must have been important as a year-round occupation. It is strange then that no detailed discussion of it has been located in the ethnography. The most peculiar aspect of Motu fishing is that the line and hook were not employed, although they existed to the south-east of Motu territory at Hula.[43] As well, Turner recorded an unbarbed tortoiseshell hook from Elema to the north-west.[44] Instead a variety of nets appears to have been the chief means of procuring fish and dugong and possibly turtle, although the latter seems more likely to have been taken while nesting or by spear.[45] The use of poison, such as derris root, is still well known today, and although not mentioned in the literature may certainly be included in the techniques used. Turner notes the Hanuabada fishing ground as 'near the reef opposite the harbour', possibly in the vicinity of Daugo Island.[46] Modern techniques of net fishing have probably not changed radically from traditional ones. Today several canoes will unite with their nets to close off a bay or indentation at the mouth. No attempt will be made to drag the net to the shore, because of net damage from coral and stones. Instead the fishermen wait for the falling tide and either land their fish in this manner or with the spear. Nets in excess of three hundred metres have been noted in use, and may have exceeded this length in former times.

Hunting and gathering activities of the Motu are not well documented. In the case of mixed villages, Motu men seem likely to have engaged in wallaby hunting during the large Koita hunts (see below) but most ethnographers see hunting as the speciality of this latter group. Wild yams can be gathered in the area, but they are not mentioned in the literature. Shellfish gathering on the coast is still engaged in today by Motu women, and while no mention of this activity has been noticed in the literature, shell middens are a common archaeological manifestation on this coast.

Manufactures

Pottery manufacture is an industry for which the Motu villages were renowned, and which is mentioned in almost every ethnographic account. While in some instances specific clay sources are mentioned,[47] the wide variety of clay deposits in the region suggests that little difficulty was experienced in gathering the raw material for this occupation. The technique employed for potting appears to have been a standard one throughout the Motu domain, and consisted of breaking up the clay in old canoe hulls, tempering it with sand, mixing it with salt water, hand moulding the preliminary shape in a broken pot (which possibly gave rise to the misconception that pots were formed in two halves[48]) and completing the pot with paddle and anvil. Bulmer[49] has reviewed the ethnographically recorded pottery types, which range from ten[50] to three[51] and which functionally consist of cooking, storage and water pots of a globular shape, serving bowls and cups.

Motuan pottery formed the basis of the extensive trading network which these people operated, both along the coast and inland and which is treated more fully below. Shell ornaments also played a large part in this trade, but information on this industry is less clear. Motuans certainly traded armshells from the east to the west, but possibly made few themselves. Seligman[52] noted the manufacture of the small shell discs called *ageva* in the Port Moresby area but restricted their manufacture to Tatana and Vabukori, which interestingly are two of the three villages within the domain of the Western Motu, but not classified as such (above).

In addition to the variety of fishing nets already alluded to, the Motu manufactured net bags[53] for use and trade, and *pani*, a specially woven rope for carrying firewood.[54] While canoe hulls were purchased in the Gulf on trading voyages, they were fashioned by the Motu themselves, who employed rattan cane gathered from the vicinity of the Laloki River for lashing for canoes, as well as hafting axes, roofing houses, and presumably other activities.[55] Salt, made from sea water also formed an important trade item.

The Koita

An analysis of the ethnographic literature pertaining to the Koita and the Koiari is not yet complete. This and the following section will be used to point up the essential differences and similarities between these two groups and also the Motu.

As already stated the Koita spoke a NAN language closely related to the Koiari and belonging to the Koiaric Family. No date has been given for the splitting of the Koita and Koiari, but on the basis of Dutton's work we can say with some certainty that at some time in the past, and possibly due to population pressure, the Koita were forced from the inland down to the coast and coastal plains.[56]

At the time of European contact the majority of the Koita population was sharing Motuan village sites. It seems clear that in almost all cases it was the Koita who merged with existing Motu villages and not the reverse.[57] In addition however five entirely Koita coastal villages also existed, together with a number of inland villages and hamlets. Population estimates for the Koita are not as readily available as for the Motu. For the two Koita *iduhu* in Hanuabada Seligman lists one with 20 houses and 129 people and the other with 22 houses and 93 people,[58] a figure which accords reasonably well with Chalmers' estimate of 300 Koita in Hanuabada.[59] For the coastal hill village of Barune, Chalmers noted the population at 300, but also noted that the village in fact consisted of four or five distinct hamlets.[60] While at the time of contact the inland settlements were fewer in number than the archaeological evidence suggests for the preceding centuries, these do appear mainly to have been hamlets rather than villages, usually built along ridge tops for defence. The numbers of houses in these hamlets were usually in the range of 5-10, and if the household size suggested by Seligman is any indication, the population of a hamlet would range from around 30 to 60 individuals. Despite the general lack of settlement inland, at contact all the land on the seaward side of the Laloki River, between Bootless Bay and Galley Reach was clearly considered to be owned by the Koita, and the area may have been greater in prehistoric times.[61]

In terms of social organisation the Koita practised an almost precisely similar system to that described for the Motu, above. Seligman claimed that throughout their territory the Koita were divided into 'sections', an undefined unit, and could be further divided into eastern and western 'moieties', but that every Koita village was divided on the basis of *iduhu*.[62] On this point, Dutton notes that he was unable to collect any Koita term for either 'section' or *iduhu*.[63] If, as is suggested by the linguistic and oral traditional evidence, the Koita were offshoots from original Koiari stock, the similarity of social organisation between the Koita and Motu points strongly to the adoption of it by the former from the latter. Otherwise one would expect both Koita and Motu patterns to share Koiari aspects, which is not the case. This suggests a long and close contact between the two coastal groups.

The ceremonial life of the Koita as described by Seligman also points strongly to the similarities between themselves and the Motu. Seligman lists six major feasts, of which three are mourning feasts.[64] Of the remainder, *koriko*, the most common, was a food distribution ceremony, or in other words a stylised exchange ceremony wherein vegetable surplus was distributed to neighbours with the understanding of a reciprocal distribution to take place later. The *hekarai* is clearly identical to Groves' *hekara* (above) and was a feast or series of feasts which were used to prosecute a quarrel. The final feast, the *tabu* feast, was a large-scale ceremony involving all friendly groups from the surrounding countryside, and one practised by coastal groups to the east, outside the Koita-Motu domain, as well as by the Koita themselves. The specific function of this feast is not stated by Seligman, but it appears to have been organised at the *iduhu* level and involved large-scale distribution of food, mainly at the principal feast, but also during preliminary and terminal feasts associated with the *tabu* itself. It would appear to be definitely involved with status. As well Seligman wrote: 'Most *dubu* – I believe I am justified in saying all *dubu* – are built in preparation for a *tabu* feast, and each is built in that part of the village in which the houses of the *iduhu* to which it belongs are situated and often on the site of a previous *dubu*.'[65]

As well as the *dubu*, Koita houses within Motu villages, and also at least in Barune,[66] appear to have been built totally within the Motu tradition, that is on stilt piles. Inland, however, houses, while still on piles, were much lower to the ground. In addition each village or hamlet appears to have had one or more houses constructed for defence in the branches of tall trees, sometimes 15 metres or more above the ground.

Seligman relates that Koita sections each owned tracts of land, divided amongst the *iduhu* in that section. Each man would have a share in his *iduhu* land which would descend to his children. Hunting, grass-burning or gardening on another's land would frequently lead to fighting or demands for compensation.[67] While much of the stated Koita domain would be infertile hills, certain edaphically determined localities such as the fringes of the Waigani swamp and the stream and river banks would have provided areas of relatively good gardening land. To the principal crops of the Motu, yam and banana, one might add for the Koita sugar cane, sweet potato and taro, all crops mentioned in the literature, as well as mango, pandanus, wild yam and cycad nuts, to mention only a few of the number of uncultivated edible plants available in the area.[68] Cooking techniques vary from those of the Motu, and although both pottery making and use is recorded for this group,[69] both are regarded as having been learnt from their Motuan neighbours. Instead the use of heated cooking stones appears to have been the original fashion.

Direct evidence of Koita burial practices is poor, and this probably means that the Koita sharing Motu villages followed the Motu custom of interment in shallow graves within the village, with either a small grave house above, or a stake on which the weapons or utensils of the deceased might be placed. The grave would be filled with beach sand, and might be disturbed at a later date to recover various bones to be worn by relatives.[70] Inland Koita practices may have been more like Koiari, where primary interment seems to have been less favoured than exposure in houses, on platforms, and bundle burials in trees.[71] Secondary burial took place, and in one account a pit grave is described as circular, lined with stones and having a small wooden conical frame above on which was suspended the valuables of the deceased.[72] Archaeological evidence would add cave and rock fissure interment to these practices.

The greatest distinction between Koita and Motu can be summed up by quoting Lawes: 'The Koitapu are hunters, not fishermen. They possess no canoes and have nothing to do with the sea; but they excel in hunting the kangaroo and wild pig, and are superior to the Motu in the chase. They barter large quantities of kangaroo meat to them for fish, etc.'[73] Lawes, while probably overstating the case, is supported in general by Seligman, amongst many others: '[The Koita] take part freely in the *hiri* . . . and may even captain the composite craft (*lakatoi*) in which these voyages are made. But in spite of this few Koita take part in turtle and dugong fishing; and even in the immediate vicinity of Port Moresby, where perhaps fusion has been most complete, no

Koita possess the strong large meshed net with which these animals are caught.'[74]

Wallaby hunting, as an organised activity, appears to have been largely seasonal, beginning towards the end of the dry season and continuing to the beginning of the rains. It occasioned the amalgamation of hunters from various villages and even sometimes hunters from both the Koita and Koiari villages. At the end of a valley a wall of nets would be erected and guarded by men with spears. Perhaps 8 km. away a second group similarly armed would fire the long dry grass, which, fanned by the prevailing south-easterly wind, would drive the game towards the nets, where they would be dispatched. Anything between 500 and 1000 wallabies might be taken in a single hunt in this fashion; the meat would be smoked and distributed and taken back to the hunters' respective villages to be eaten or traded. Feral pig and other game caught in the drive would also be taken.[75]

Apart from such food items the Koita contributed other articles to the inland trade. These included cassowary and parrot feathers, matting, netting fibre and bark cloth.[76] Rattan cane, used for canoe lashing, house building and so on, grew in Koita territory along the Laloki River, and while it is not mentioned as a trade item of the Koita it is recorded as growing in this location and being used for these purposes. 'Betel-pepper' was also procured here.[77] The Koita also probably acted as middlemen in the inland trade between the coastal Motuans and the Koiari, and Seligman notes the existence of a market in the vicinity of the junction of the Laloki and Goldie Rivers for this purpose.[78]

The Koiari

The Koiari, occupying the plain and backing mountains north of the Laloki River, divided themselves according to their environment into 'Grasslanders', 'Forest-men' or 'Mountaineers'.[79] Williams considered the population to be meagre in terms of what the countryside might support, but this statement appears to have been made in terms of the subsistence patterns which he observed and which he imagined might be intensified. From Chalmers' accounts of his inland excursions, villages appear to have been relatively close together.[80] Unlike the drier coastal regions, the soils of the forest and mountain components of the Koiari, given the heavier and more constant rainfall, were particularly fertile. 'Game is plentiful enough, especially in the grasslands, but the Koiari are very definitely gardeners and quite dependent on the soil.'[81] Williams clearly recorded swidden systems in operation in the forest, clearing and burning off garden patches and abandoning garden sites after each harvest, and recorded yam as the staple diet, which conflicts to some degree with the observations of Chalmers, who on one inland journey between 15 July 1879 and 26 September of the same year noted taro 14 times, but yam only twice and sweet potato not at all.[82] This trip was also of interest in that prior to 18 August no mention of wallaby hunting was made, but on four separate occasions after this date Chalmers noted that a hunt was in progress, or that men were away from villages hunting wallaby. The seasonal aspect of this occupation appears quite clear.

If the linguistic picture is to be believed and the Koita did in fact break away from the Koiari, two interesting differences may be remarked. Whereas it has been noted above that the social organisation of the Koita was similar to that of the Motu, Koiari social organisation was quite different, with male children being classed with the father's group, and female children with the mother's, a bilateral system called sex affiliation by Williams.[83] While there is no clearly defined unit such as the Motu and Koita *iduhu*, Williams did note an approximate term for group amongst the Koiari, and it may well be that this term has some connection with the Koita 'section' used by Seligman (above). In addition Williams noted an institution which he termed 'plant emblem' which, while differing from true totemism, bore some relationship to it.[84]

The second difference is in the land systems of the Koita and Koiari. This can in part at least be explained in terms of environment, but the land was owned by the local group, and not individually by its members. It was not therefore individually inherited but was 'inherited' only in the sense that a child remained a member of a land-owning group.[85]

House location on hilltops and spurs, construction on shorter piling, and the use of tree houses were used by the Koiari in the same manner as described for the Koita. Again the Koiari lived in hamlets rather than villages, with the average size being around 8 houses, containing 40-50 people.

The cooking techniques of the Koiari were also similar to those described for the Koita, although numerous references exist to Motu pottery being seen in Koiari villages. In essence the subsistence patterns for both groups seem to have been quite similar, with perhaps a greater emphasis being placed on vegetable foods amongst the uplanders.

While the Koiari appear to have been more self-contained economically, still the trade from the coast was important to them. Pottery has already been mentioned, and salt, but ornaments, both teeth necklaces and particularly armshells, which played an important role as bride-price,[86] were clearly of economic importance. Koiari items of exchange included food, stone axes, bark cloth, tobacco, betel nut, ginger and lime (for eating with the betel).[87] As Dutton points out, the lime trade, wherein the lime was manufactured from burnt marine shells, might logically have been thought to go the other way, but Turner is quite specific on this point. The Koiari visited the coast to collect shell, carried it inland up to 35 kilometres, manufactured the lime, then carried it back to the coast to trade. The Motu did not make it because their forefathers had not done so, and it had always been made by the Koiari.[88] While some of the trade to the coast may have passed through the Koita-Koiari market mentioned above, this statement suggests that the Koiari also traded directly with the Motu, a situation corroborated by Chalmers, who, visiting a 'chief' in a Koiari village, noted 'His wives and children have gone with great burdens of betel-nuts and taro to trade at the sea-side'.[89]

Exchange systems

The various exchange systems of the Motu can be divided into three hierarchical levels which correspond with those proposed for the Maya by Hammond[90] and which are here termed internal, local and external.

Internal exchange amongst Motu villages seems likely to have been a year round activity arising from minor differences in local resources, and which may have been related to village level specialisation or separate from it. In certain instances ceremony obviously facilitated and proved the mechanism of exchange, but in other instances such exchange was of a clearer commercial nature. The spatial distribution of Motu villages along a single line (the coast) appears to have produced a tendency for the centre to manipulate the wings as goods passed to and fro along it, with a concomitant concentration of population at the centre.

At the extreme north-west of Motu territory Manumanu was situated on a river which provided easy access to inland groups outside the Koita-Koiari domain, and this village thus articulated a separate inland trading system, and provided vegetable foods, crabs, canoes and sago petticoats for the villages further east.[91] The village of Rearea, situated adjacent to mangrove swamps, provided timber for house construction,[92] while Eastern Motu villages exchanged banana and yam for pig, boars' tusks and shell beads,[93] the latter, as noted earlier, being the specialisation of two villages close to Port Moresby.

Local exchange, between the Motu and their inland neighbours, indicates some intensification of the trading pattern. Goods were exchanged across the environmental zones which produced them either on an informal basis between individuals or as organised trading expeditions,[94] and in the case of foodstuffs also sometimes ceremonially. Seligman noted the existence of a Koita-Koiari market on their border,[95] but as already noted above, this was obviously by-passed on occasions. Indications of barter for this trade are contained in the literature[96] with prices either conditioned by supply and demand or set by custom. The important exports of the three groups were as in Table 2.

Table 2

Motu	*Koita*	*Koiari*
pottery	vegetables	vegetables
net bags	wallaby meat (and pig?)	stone axes
coconuts	cassowary and parrot feathers	bird of paradise and other plumes
fish	matting	bark cloth
salt	netting fibre	tobacco
armshells	bark cloth	betel nut
dogs' teeth necklaces	rattan cane	ginger
other shell and coral ornaments	betel pepper	lime
woven rope		

External exchange of the Motu, unlike its internal and local counterparts, appears always to have involved deliberately planned and highly organised expeditions. Of these the most important was the *hiri* expedition, which journeyed annually to the Papuan Gulf, some 350 kilometres to the north-east. To partake in the *hiri* was an exploit deeply involved with status acquisition and the expedition was thus intimately connected with ceremony and taboo. According to Barton's account of the voyage[97] the decision to fit out a trading canoe or *lagatoi* would be made by leading men in various villages as early as April or May for a voyage beginning in the following September or October. From this time onwards the man and his chief associate in the venture would not cohabit with their wives until they had returned from the west. In traditional form the crew of a *lagatoi* would be organised months before any actual preparation for the voyage began. In August the entire crew would begin fitting out a *lagatoi* which comprised perhaps 4 dug out canoes known as *asi* and which were of larger size than the normal Motuan canoe. From this time on there would be a general increase in taboos, particularly food taboos, washing and associating with wives. The *lagatoi* was both ceremonially charmed and decorated with special ornaments, and when everything was in readiness, the *lagatoi* were subjected to trials on the harbour in which the leading men did not take part.

The *hiri* was primarily a pottery trading expedition, with each man taking care of a specific batch of pots. Barton calculated that the average number of men in a *lagatoi* was 29, and that one specific *lagatoi* in 1903, consisting of 4 *asi*, carried 1294 pots, so that allowing for 20 *lagatoi* in a *hiri* fleet, the total number of pots taken west were 25,920 (although 1294 x 20 = 25,880) so that each man would be responsible for around 45 pots. However, Barton also quotes figures supplied to him by Lawes for 1885, where four *lagatoi* from Port Moresby averaged 1628 pots each,[98] so that 20 *lagatoi* so loaded would have shipped 32,560 pots at approximately 56 per man, an average figure which accords well with Chalmers' account of one man with 70 pots to dispose of.[99] In summary an annual figure of 30,000 pots exported on this one expedition appears a reasonable estimate, particularly in view of Groves' observation that in 1957, at a time when the traditional economy of the Motu had been largely disrupted by the European presence, ten vessels, none of them true *lagatoi*, from 4 Motuan and 1 Koita village, sent almost 10,000 pots westwards to the Gulf villages.[100] However, Groves[101] stresses that several of these were motor-powered scows, and feels that estimates in the literature for totally traditional *hiri* might be exaggerated.

In addition to pottery, the *hiri* fleet carried with them a variety of shell ornaments, both locally made and imported from further east, together with stone axes traded to them by the Koiari,[102] and boars' tusks.[103] These goods would be used initially as 'gifts' from each crew member to his own particular trading partner, and some of them, particularly armshells, would be used to purchase logs for new canoe hulls. These 'gifts' however had specific value and goods would eventually be given in exchange. After an initial feast the early part of the visit was spent in bartering the pots and ordering trees for canoe hulls. Once the trees had been procured, the Motu began shaping them themselves. The Gulf villagers then went into the sago swamps and manufactured the sago they required to pay for the pots. Strict accounting and rates of exchange were applied.[104]

In the west the *lagatoi* were dismantled and the newly made *asi* added, so that a returning vessel might have as many as 14 *asi* making it almost a square raft. Again using Barton's figures, each *lagatoi* would return with between 25 and 34 tons of sago, giving an approximate figure for the *hiri* fleet of 600 tons of sago per annum.

In all, the *hiri* fleet would remain in the west up to 5 months, returning normally in January.[105] The product of the voyage would provide the staple diet of the Motuans during the wet season and until the harvest, with the excess being distributed both inland and to the Eastern Motu villages who sponsored no *hiri*, and the Hula people visiting Port Moresby at that time.

Two reciprocal trading visits to the Motu were of importance, both again dependent on the south-east north-west wind patterns. At the end of the monsoonal season several months after the return of the *hiri*, a trading fleet from the east of the Gulf District would arrive to trade more sago with the Motu, possibly exchanging it this time for shell valuables.[106] Williams also indicates that trading canoes from the western end of the Gulf sometimes reached as far as the Motu, although in the main usually only visited their eastern neighbours, with the trade being bows and arrows and tobacco for shell valuables.[107]

The second trading fleet came from the east. From Keapara an annual visit of short duration was made to exchange armshells for sago. The armshells they had themselves received from further east. This visit would take place at the same time as their Hula neighbours were at Port Moresby. The Hula annually arrived while the *hiri* fleet was absent, bringing coconuts and remaining to fish on the Motu fishing grounds, supplying the Motu who were not on the *hiri* with fish. In exchange the Hula received pottery, and on the successful return of the *hiri* fleet, they would share in the sago, and sometimes the new canoe hulls. It was through this trade that fictive kinship relationships between the Hula and Motu developed, and although the Hula were known raiders along the coast and enemies of the Koita, trade ties were sufficiently strong for the Motu to remain on friendly terms with the Hula, and also to prevent bloodshed between the Hula and Koita.[108]

Two important points emerge from this review of the literature. First, the three exchange systems delineated here are interlocking and interdependent, as food items, utilitarian goods and valuables all pass through the Motu central exchange. Secondly there is clearly no hierarchical 'value' system operating whereby valuables are only exchanged for valuables, food for food and so on. To the examples of this already cited can be added Chalmers' observation:[109]

> An article of very great value to the native is the ornamental toea or arm-shell. A few small ones are made on this part of the coast (Motu territory), but the best come from the east, as far away as the D'Entrecasteaux Group. They trade them for pottery etc, to the Dauni natives, whilst the Dauni natives sell them again to Mailuikolu for sago, dogs, etc, and these to the Aroma natives for pigs, dogs, and canoes. The Aroma natives trade them to the Hood Bay, Kerepunu, Kalo, Hula, Papaka, and Kamari natives for birds' plumes of various kinds, and these again to the Motu natives for sago, and the Motuan to the Eelemaites for sago in bulk . . .[110]

What is also apparent from the latter part of this statement is the profit motive on which Motu exchange was based.

Archaeological evidence

Apart from a minor wartime excavation[111] and some work on rock art[112] the first professional archaeology of the region began with Sue Bulmer's survey and excavation in the immediate vicinity of Port Moresby in 1967.[113] Since that time approximately 70 prehistoric sites have been located in the research area, of which five have been excavated. In addition, Vanderwal's excavations in the Yule Island area to the north-west, and more recently Irwin's work to the south-east in the region of Mailu, allow for the following tentative cultural sequence to be proposed.

Vanderwal's site of Kukuba Cave yielded two C14 dates of almost 4,000 years ago for aceramic (and almost certainly preceramic) occupation of the cave, which almost 3,000 years later also housed pottery-using people.[114] These earlier dates are by far the oldest yet for the region, and despite the few sites for which dates are available, the lack of preceramic sites does at least open speculation on the possibilities of only shifting occupation prior to about the birth of Christ.

At this point in time the archaeological evidence can only be interpreted as a widespread migration into the southern Papuan coast of pottery manufacturing people. From Amazon Bay in the east, moving through Marshall Lagoon,[115] the Port Moresby region,[116] the Yule Island area[117] and the Papuan Gulf,[118] sites which are consistently dated in their lower levels to around 2,000 years ago are producing distinctive and highly similar ceramic material, and one suspects that the boundaries of this ceramic distribution have not yet been located. Sites are found on offshore islands, coastal beaches and hilltops and inland both on hills and in valleys. In addition to pottery, the newcomers had the pig and dog, exploited marine and terrestrial food sources and despite the lack of direct evidence can be suspected of having been horticulturists. Trade was clearly in use along the coast, best exemplified by obsidian derived from Fergusson Island to the east, and probably armshells and other shell ornaments.[119] In addition the highly similar sequence of ceramic styles between Port Moresby and Yule Island, which ensued for perhaps 1,000 years is strong evidence of close contact between at least these two areas, although further to the east, the sites located by Irwin may prove to have a different subsequent development. While on the basis of his extensive data from Yule Island Vanderwal has been able to postulate Initial and Developmental Phases for the first ceramic people on the coast,[120] the evidence from the smaller excavation at Nebira 4 near Port Moresby[121] and Irwin's initial impression of the Amazon Bay sites[122] indicate that this division in the pattern of development between 2,000 and 1,000 years ago may not be as clear cut elsewhere as on Yule Island. While terminal C14 dates for this manifestation of ceramic using and manufacturing people are as yet only available in the Port Moresby and Yule Island areas, and these not completely satisfactory, a round figure date of approximately A.D. 1000 is agreed upon. In overall terms, therefore we can look to the occupation of the south Papuan coast by closely related people practising a mixed gardening, hunting, and maritime economy, who appear to infiltrate the coast and hinterland and maintain good communications throughout the first millennium A.D. For want of a better name this manifestation is here designated the Early Ceramic Horizon.

Why these people disappear at about the same time in both the Port Moresby and Yule Island areas is a question not yet answered. However the occupation of Kukuba Cave at a late point in the sequence, the possible removal of the people from the valley floor site of Nebira 4 to the adjacent hilltop site of Nebira 2 and the occupation of the offshore island site of Daugo near Port Moresby, where ceramics are almost all of the most recent phase of the Early Ceramic Horizon, all point to these occupants being under pressure, probably, at least in the case of Port Moresby, from inland groups. Nebira 2 for example, with a thin bottom stratum of these earlier ceramics, is later occupied by a different group who in terms of the material remains can reasonably be identified as Koita people, an interpretation which fits well with oral tradition, for the Nebira 2 site is known as Koma, the original settlement of the eastern Koita.[123]

The remainder of the prehistoric sequence in the Port Moresby area as posited by Sue Bulmer[124] included a middle period dated A.D. 1000-1400 when two different pottery components may have been introduced in the region and a late period equated with the introduction of the modern Motu ceramic industry.

Of the middle period, one ceramic component is seen by Bulmer to be closely related to both the prehistoric and historic industries from a number of areas in the Milne Bay district and is termed Massim. Pottery of this type is found in the Nebira 2 site, but apart from this, its presence around Port Moresby is limited to surface collections. Nowhere, with the single exception of a small site near present day Boera village, is this pottery found discrete from other types, nor is it particularly plentiful on any site. For this reason its cultural status (whether trade pottery, the reflection of transient fishermen/trader visits, or settlement) is far from unequivocal, nor yet has it been demonstrated to cover the time span suggested by Bulmer. The second pottery component by which the middle period is defined is called Boera/Taurama after the two sites where it had been most heavily collected, and is defined in terms of its decoration (painted or incised/impressed). Comment on this component will be made after the discussion of the Motupore site below, except to note here that Bulmer does acknowledge the possibility of the Boera/Taurama component being ancestral to modern Motu pottery.[125] Bulmer's final period is isolated by only those ceramic types which can be directly related to ethnographically recorded Motu pottery.

Perhaps the most interesting fact resulting from Bulmer's work in the Port Moresby area so far is the prehistoric settlement pattern which has emerged from the site survey.[126] Her table reproduced here (Table 3) demonstrates the geographic locations so far found.[127]

Table 3

	Prehistoric Sites	*Historic Sites*
Offshore Island	4	0
Beachfront	16	21
Beach Hill	11	5
Inland Hill	32	0
Inland Lowland	5	3
	68	29

Of the prehistoric sites only eleven relate to the earliest tradition discussed above, and these are distributed through all locations. Given then that the remaining 57 sites date to later than A.D. 1000 two points emerge:

1. That unless the few earlier period sites were of an immense size in comparison to those which followed (and the surface evidence does not suggest it) then during the last 1,000 years there was a significant population build-up on the inland plains. While a number of the inland sites (if not all) were hamlets rather than villages during this time, the implications at present seem at least to suggest that the idea of a population expansion in the inland plains does hold.
2. That despite this build up, by the time of European contact the inland between the coast and the Laloki River was almost entirely depopulated.

Motupore Island

Apart from Sue Bulmer's 1972 excavation at Taurama Beach, for which no details are to hand, the only recent period site in the Port Moresby area so far excavated is the offshore island site of Motupore. For the present purpose only a general summary of the archaeological evidence will be attempted here.

Motupore is a submerged hilltop in Bootless Bay some 16

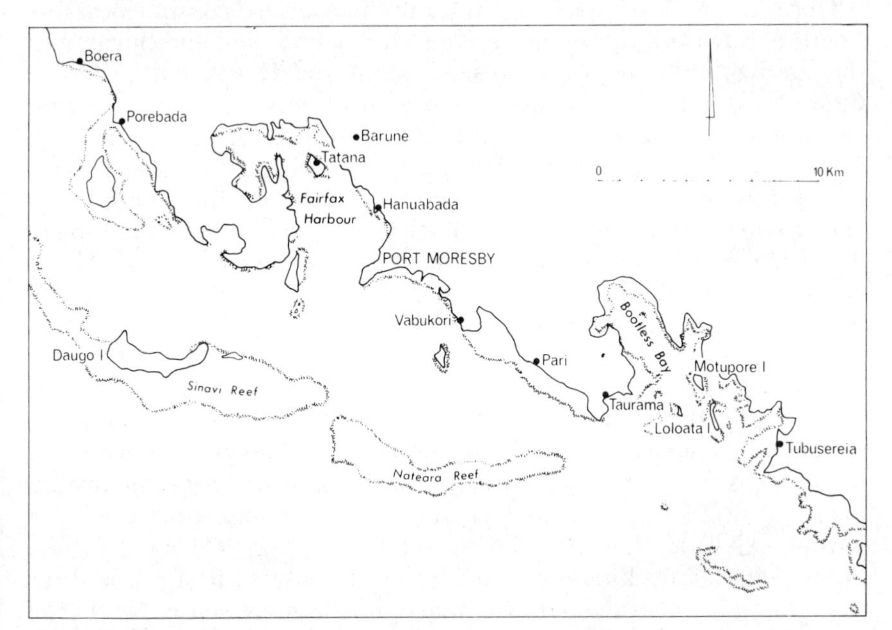

Figure 5. Location map of the Port Moresby area, showing Motupore Island and related locations mentioned in the text.

kilometres to the east of Port Moresby and 650 metres offshore, within the barrier reef and surrounded by fringing reef (Fig. 5). It is a narrow and steep island approximately 800 metres long, 200 metres high and less than 200 metres wide at its widest point. At the northern end a cuspate sand spit has been formed and consolidated, fronted by a sand beach and tidal spit from whence it derives its name (Motu = island; pore = gravel bank, sand bank).

Surface pottery can be recovered over the entire area of the flat land, and extending into the intertidal zone along the sand spit, when it is exposed at low tide. However, no trace of any occupation has been located on the hill-slopes or top ridge of the island. The site was certainly not occupied when the Europeans first settled Port Moresby, nor is there any significant claim of ownership of the island, in a region where extensive land claims are now being brought before the courts. Nor does the site draw mention in the oral traditions of the Motu, with one exception:

> The Motu trace their origin from the island of Motu Hanua (Motupore) in Bootless Inlet, where they say they lived at a time when the present inhabitants of Tupuseleia dwelt on a neighbouring island of Loloata . . . Constant feuds raged between the Motu and the inhabitants of Loloata, with the result that the Motu, both from Motu Hanua and Gwamo, joined together and founded a village on Taurama or Pyramid Point.

Here, the account goes on, intermittent warfare continued across Bootless Bay until the village at Taurama was sacked and burnt, and the survivors moved to the present location of Hanuabada.[128] Nigel Oram, working on Western Motu traditions and genealogies, encountered numerous informants who traced their descent back to Taurama, but so far has found only one man who claims descent back to Motupore.[129] On the evidence available to him Oram has constructed a genealogical chronology which places the foundation of Taurama in the second half of the sixteenth century.[130] Given the admitted difficulties of this sort of research, nevertheless it seemed likely that the Motupore site might have been abandoned about this time, so that it was surprising that three dates submitted to Gakashuin Laboratory, all in stratigraphic succession and the stratigraphically earliest of them well over one metre below the surface all returned modern dates of less than 200 years. Given that the site was truly as young as this, the fact that it was not remembered posed a problem. Two further preliminary dates from the 1973 season, ANU-1177, 330±55 B.P. and ANU-1212, 390±65 B.P., the latter being a check date on the stratigraphially earliest of the three modern dates mentioned above, make a little more sense. Neither of these dates however relates to the most recent occupation. There will be more dates forthcoming to assist in solving this problem, but at present we might expect the abandonment of the site between two and three hundred years ago. The initial occupation, on the other hand, is more secure. Two dates, ANU-1211, 810±80 B.P., and I-5903, 740±105 B.P. are both stratigraphically, and in terms of C14 determinations, the oldest on the site, and a number of younger dates later in the sequence both fit well and argue against any major break in the occupation of the site from perhaps somewhere before A.D. 1200 to around A.D. 1700.

The site has yielded very large amounts of pottery and flaked stone, and in addition it contains a large volume of bone and shell faunal remains and exotic articles such as shell jewellery. In all, 188 square metres of the site have been opened up, and although this represents well under one percent of the total site on dry land, test squares suggest no earlier occupation. A wide range of occupational evidence, including 40 burials, has been recovered.

No attempt will be made here to describe the ceramics except to note that the major change in the ceramics was in terms of decoration. This was a replacement of shell impressed and combed decoration by incised or stick impressed decoration. Painting, particularly of the globular pot forms, was present throughout almost the entire sequence and only in the latest levels had it disappeared completely. Basic shapes appear not to have altered throughout. Although the earliest and latest ceramics look remarkably different, present opinions are that changes were gradual and evolutionary and that the ceramics on the site reflect a single cultural continuum from beginning to end.

A similar impression is gained from the burials, where, although in two major burial areas the bodies were oriented in different directions, the distinctive burial practice of filling the shallow graves with beach sand remains the same in both early and late periods. In the largest area of graves uncovered the graves were clearly associated with post holes which may represent houses, or smaller grave houses, or stakes as recorded ethnographically for the Motu and other coastal people.[131]

The excavated stone material from Motupore consisted in the most part of flaked chert found in a number of places around Port Moresby, including the island itself. The industry has been described previously[132] and the interesting point about it is that of secondarily worked flaked stone perhaps as much as 50% is of a single type, the drillpoint used to tip drills, presumably similar to the pump drill described for Tatana by Stone.[133] Hundreds of shell disc beads in all stages of manufacture from roughouts to the finished product have been recovered from the excavations, and this manufacture, recorded ethnographically only for Tatana and Vabukori, was undoubtedly being practised on Motupore. In addition, evidence of other forms of shell jewellery manufacture was recovered. Polished axes and axe flakes were recovered throughout the site, made from a non-local green diorite, similar to that described several times in the ethnography as coming from the Koiari.[134] The faunal remains from the midden 2m. x 2m. test square have received a preliminary analysis.[135] The points which emerge from this analysis are:

1. The relatively narrow range of food animals present in the site. Of the marine animals present, which are the principal finds, the fish are almost entirely confined to shallow reef and harbour species, which could be captured by netting, spearing or poisoning. Thousands of shell net sinkers were recovered throughout the site, but nothing which could be interpreted as a hook, so that these results are consistent with Motu ethnography for fishing techniques.
2. The relatively small amount of pig bone in the site, which is in keeping with the ethnographic indications that pig raising might of necessity have been a minor resource; and the absence of dog which reflects a number of ethnographic observations that the Motu did not eat dog, although it was eaten on other parts of the coast.
3. That with the exception of one rodent and one lizard vertebra, the only wild terrestial animal represented is the agile wallaby. Not only is it represented, however, but there are 158 individuals present in the sample. While it is by far the most common animal found on the inland savannah hills and valleys, it would seem likely that if the inhabitants of Motupore were hunting themselves, the various phalangers, cuscus and cassowary would be represented, if only in small amounts. The wide age range of the wallabies present does indicate their indiscriminate exploitation in just the way the Koita hunts are described, and given the ethnographic picture, it appears entirely reasonable to view the archaeological evidence as evidence for the sort of food exchange described for the Motu and their inland neighbours in the ethnography.
4. The final point to make is that these patterns appear to be consistent throughout the site from the beginning to the end.

Detailed examination of the shell remains from Motupore is only just beginning. Pamela Swadling[136] who is conducting the analysis comments that at this very preliminary stage the shell evidence does not suggest the abandonment of the site for any long period throughout its history, although there may be some indication of a lessening in the exploitation of this resource through time. Given the better development of other food resources and a growing population on the site the value of this resource might have lessened except in periods of stress.

While Motupore has yielded a lot of evidence in regard to structures on the site, no clear pattern was observable in the field and the data is yet to be analysed. Given the ethnographic photographs of Motuan houses, with their numerous house piles going in many directions, the field evidence is at least consistent with the lack of patterns one might predict from piled houses using thin and irregular piles. In one area of the excavation however, dated to around 600 years ago, the post hole patterns differed quite considerably. They were much larger and deeper, and the stratigraphic evidence suggests rapid rebuilding. The possibility that this is an area of *dubu* construction is being further investigated.

One final point of sociological importance is that of the burials, 39 were shallow graves with each body extended and on its back. In some instances at least the grave had been disturbed in antiquity and often the mandible, or the entire skull, had been removed. Again this is consistent with various descriptions of burial practice amongst the Motu and their neighbours, where after burial various bones would be removed and worn by relatives. Of greatest surprise however was that one grave consisted of a pit which had been dug and filled with loose bones. Presumably not all the bones fitted, so a second adjacent hole was dug for the remainder. Lying over these pits was a necklace of approximately 60 dog's canines. Given that this is the only example in 40 graves of a secondary burial, together with its apparent similarity to Koita and Koiari burial practices (notably Stone's account quoted above[137]), it is well within the range of archaeological interpretation to view this as evidence of Koita influence or settlement within the village at Motupore. The grave has not yet been precisely dated but appears to be in the vicinity of 400 years old on stratigraphic evidence.

In terms of the site itself, the overwhelming feeling on the basis of the social, economic and industrial activity pursued there, the burials and other structural evidence noted, the stone industry and the bone and shell tools, is that they are too similar to the ethnographically described Motu for the likeness to be fortuituous. The pottery, while different in terms of decoration to ethnographic Motu pottery, also illustrates a close similarity in terms of shapes and manufacture. The decoration of the prehistoric pottery indicates a devolution in complexity, and in this sense at least, the absence or simplicity of decoration on ethnographically recorded Motu pottery appears simply to be in keeping with this trend. While at present there seems little way of proving it, one might postulate the case that as the ceramic industry grew, i.e. as new markets were exploited, simplification of decoration increased as a response to mass production. Groves noted in Manumanu in 1958 that the *hiri* preparations were running late, and that the women were trying to finish pots at break-neck speed, one reason perhaps for the large proportion of breakages in firing that year.[138] The decline in decoration of pots under these conditions would be understandable.

Motupore is seen as having been continuously occupied by the same group of people for around 500 years from c. A.D. 1200 and that these people were ancestral to the present day Motu. For this reason a certain adjustment needs to be made to Sue Bulmer's proposed culture sequence. The ceramics which comprise her Taurama/Boera component are largely identical to those excavated from Motupore, at least in the decorative aspects by which they are defined, and at Motupore they are seen to evolve through a simple incised/impressed phase which can be merged with the ethnographically recorded Motu pottery. On this basis one can point to only two major ceramic occupations of the coast, the first occupying the first millennium A.D., and the second, at least at Motupore, beginning somewhere before A.D. 1200 and continuing to the present. The hiatus between the two is therefore reduced, and it is into this hiatus the Massim industry described by Bulmer must be fitted. The status of the people represented by this pottery still requires elaboration through excavation, but it seems that if they were settlers they were in Bulmer's own terms 'less successful maritime traders'.[139] On the present evidence it may well be that there was no hiatus at all, and that the Massim component infiltrated during the brief period of disequilibrium following the disappearance of the earlier inhabitants and during the establishment of ancestral Motuan groups.

Discussion

Binford has argued that if equilibrium systems do regulate population density below the carrying capacity of an environment, apart from a change in the physical environment itself the only other conditions which could provoke disequilibrium would be change in the demographic structure of a region in which one group impinges in the territory of another.[140] Binford's argument continues that if such a change occurred amongst hunter-gatherer groups so that population density increased beyond the carrying capacity of the natural environment, increased manipulation of the environment might be anticipated, leading subsequently to agricultural subsistence patterns.

It appears probable that the central argument might be extended to agricultural groups: that if population density is raised above the carrying capacity of any existing subsistence pattern, intensification of that pattern, either by the introduction of new techniques, skills or ranges of domesticates, or alternatively by the more 'economic' manipulation of previously discrete subsistence units into a larger single economic unit, will serve to increase that unit's productivity, and hence its carrying capacity in terms of human population.

Present archaeological evidence points strongly to the Motu having impinged upon the existing central Papuan coastal population from outside the research area some 800 years ago. It is proposed here that while they were able to intensify the exploitation of one zone, the marine environment, this was insufficient for their needs. They found it necessary to manipulate food resources outside the immediate area they occupied.

The mechanism of manipulation was exchange; not merely simple exchange, but rather a highly articulated and complex series of systems related to the environment and based on an annual cycle. This trade brought into the Motu 'catchment' not only the goods of these neighbours, but possibly inland goods from other inland trading systems. Many of these goods were not retained by the Motu themselves but were passed on eastwards, westwards and inland. This middleman activity was clearly conducted on a profit basis and it is in this respect that the entrepreneurial abilities of the Motu appear to have been, together with their sailing abilities, the decisive factors in intensifying the exploitation of available resources.

Although the exchange systems of the Motu have here been classified into three groups on the bases of distance, organisation and intensity, it is at the same time apparent that these were interdependent. All Motu exchange would appear to fulfil 'a latent socio-cultural function for levelling cultural differences and acting as a mechanism for wider socio-cultural integration'.[141] Implied social differences between food distribution with obligations of reciprocity and long distance trading on a profit basis appear therefore in the case of the Motu to require cautious application: certainly whatever the manner of exchange (ritual or otherwise) the ethnographic evidence points clearly to the fact that valuables were exchanged directly for food or to facilitate food exchange in many different exchange situations. Motu exchange thus fits more comfortably into Sahlins' model of a single spatial continuum ranging from distinctly positive to distinctly negative reciprocity[142] in which the successful acquisition of food meant also the acquisition of status for individual traders, itself perhaps the simple explanation for the exchange of valuables for food.

As already stated, the Motu required the integration of their exchange systems because their own ecological niche was not self-sufficient in terms of food production. Sago provided the staple in the early wet months of the year before the harvest. Their own garden produce was exhausted at least by August and their principal dependence turned to inland meat and vegetables. While a large proportion of the able manpower was away trading in the west, eastern neighbours supplied coconuts and worked the fishing grounds, which at all other times were exploited by the Motu themselves. In short it is a simple matter to see how the system worked to the advantage of the Motu but less clear to see why it should work. How were the Motu able to impose these trading systems on groups which appear to have been previously economically self-sufficient?

When one attempts the culture-historical reconstruction of the Port Moresby region, the existing archaeological evidence suggests the rapid occupation of both the coast and hinterland by pottery manufacturing people around 2,000 years ago, whose economy, while in principal similar to the later exploitation patterns described above, appears to be more extensive than intensive. The factor of trade in this economy is difficult to quantify on present evidence. Long-distance coastal trading is evident in such things as obsidian, but local exchange with inland groups seems harder to pinpoint.

The demise of this Early Ceramic Horizon is sudden all along the coast. It has been suggested that in the hinterland of Port Moresby pressure from inland groups may have been responsible, and on this point the evidence of both linguistics and oral tradition appears quite convincing.[143] Not only were the Koita driven towards the coast, but some Koiari groups appear to have been continually pushed 'off the edge' of the high country. In this light it is tempting to see the Koita gaining control of the Port Moresby coast and inland plains at the expense of the Early Ceramic Horizon people. Having done so, of course, their strategic position was not good, with inland aggression at the rear and perhaps the need to defend a long coast against sea raiders. On the basis of the archaeological evidence the coast was not long underpopulated, and if this argument is correct, apart from any economic benefits which might accrue, the strategic value for the Koita to have one entire 'border' occupied by a friendly group is obvious. Such a defensive pact between the two groups seems certainly to have been in operation in later times. Chalmers noted 'I have never heard of the two tribes fighting, but often the Motu tribe have helped the Koitapu against their enemies; especially have they prevented the Hulans making raids on them'.[144]

In return, benefits from such a symbiotic arrangement for the Motu are equally obvious. The validity of the security argument stands equally for the Motu, although given their flanking location they might be considered to have held the strategically better position, particularly if they held alliances with their neighbours, as they seem certainly to have done through trade at least. A stronger value for the Motu was in the economic necessity of maintaining access to the inland meat, vegetables and other raw material resources. To solidify the arrangement, however, the strength of Koita sorcery over the Motu is frequently alluded to in the ethnographic accounts, and it seems significant that by these means the Koita were considered able not only to inflict illness and death on the Motu but also to control the weather upon which the Motuan economic system depended.[145]

While the strategic imperative for Koita participation appears strong, a similar explanation cannot be posited for the Koiari. In the absence of strong data to the contrary it can be hypothesised that one value of entering the trading system was that it provided the means for converting perishable food items into ritual or wealth objects, as has been suggested elsewhere in New Guinea,[146] which in turn could well open up the possibility of the alteration of Koiari social organisation and values in imitation of their coastal neighbours. Such a self-reinforcing process of purchasing status paraphernalia can at least be suggested on the ethnographic evidence, which emphasises the value placed on bride-price armshells and dogs'-teeth necklaces by the Koiari, and evidence from elsewhere in the world where similar processes have been documented, for example Olmec influence in the Valley of Oaxaca, and two supporting examples for the Oaxacan case.[147] One of these in particular, McClellan's study of the Tlingit speakers on the southeastern Alaskan coast, indicates a number of parallels to the Motu relationships with their inland neighbours, not the least important being the manner in which the inland Tagish and their neighbours became gradually 'Tlingitised'.[148]

In the case of the Koiari, however, it must be observed that to date there is no evidence that a similar trading relationship did not exist with the earlier pottery people of this coast, so that it is unknown whether the Motu merely supplied an existing market or whether they initiated the trade between the Koiari and the coast. Either way, it appears to have been to the advantage of the Motu to exploit this source at an early stage.

While it is perhaps unwise to generalise too far on the basis of a single excavation, the evidence from Motupore does suggest that the Motu-Koita relationship was also entered into very quickly. Almost all those aspects of the archaeological evidence which might be taken as reflecting the symbiosis described in the ethnography, appear to occur early in the Motupore sequence and continue with little change until the end. If this claim is substantiated in other sites, the proliferation of inland Koita hamlet sites at this time makes more sense, not only in terms of the defensive value of the Motu on the coast, but also in terms of more intensive Koita exploitation of the inland plains and their possible role as middlemen in the inland trade – both activities needed for them to stay in the system and for the system to operate successfully. However, the ethnographic literature, linguistic evidence, oral tradition and the little archaeological evidence available all point to continuous inland pressure on the Koita, the end result of which appears to be the increasing merger between Koita and Motu until both groups were largely sharing the same villages, while still maintaining to a large extent their own traditional economic roles. If the model has validity, this condition was still economically necessary even at the point of European contact and may have been an important factor in the maintenance of Koita language and culture even when sharing the same village.

Two important implications stem from this argument. The first is that the Motu arrived as developed pottery makers and marine traders along this coast, and represent a sufficiently different population to argue against them being merely a local group developing internally towards a higher level of adaptation and specialisation. The archaeological evidence at least would support such a contention. At the most basic level, there appears no way one could derive the earliest ceramic styles from anything which had gone before in the immediate region. This is also the case in the Yule Island region, where the Urourina site exhibits a range of ceramics almost identical to the earlier levels of Motupore and is dated there at 720±105 (ANU-730).[149] Also from the outset the Motu economy is more specifically based on shallow reef and immediately coastal exploitation than has been observed for earlier periods. The high specificity of site location also indicates the imposition of a specialised group. Motupore Island for example, protected both from natural problems such as big seas and winds, and from human foes on the mainland, is an ideal site for the sort of economy practised by the Motu, but the absence of earlier occupation on the island may well reflect the restrictiveness of such a location for the sort of more general economy postulated both for the earlier pottery users and for inlanders forced down onto the coast.

The second implication is that the ancestral Motu arrived in sufficient numbers to create the initial disequilibrium posited above, and to implement at least in embryonic form the exchange systems documented ethnographically. In the absence of 'hard' archaeological data considerations stemming from this viewpoint perhaps enter too far into speculation. Nevertheless, the model would appear to require a migration of people in spearhead fashion along the coast, and with open lines of communication behind them, and thus all available evidence would suggest that we must look to the east for these. Some support for this view might be found in the only other long sequence so far excavated in this direction on the coast: at Mailu, some 300 kilometres east, Irwin[150] has suggested some general similarities between the ceramics which immediately overlie the early pottery horizon and those found in the lower deposits of Motupore, although he can perceive fewer similarities in aspects such as site location, and perhaps the subsistence base.

Equally speculative at this stage of research is the question of the development of the exchange systems themselves. While the archaeology at Motupore has been interpreted to suggest rapid inland interaction, something as specifically elaborate as the *hiri* may have had a slower evolution, and so far one can only isolate general indications such as the reduction and simplification of ceramic decoration which may correlate with increased mass production. Nor can we assume that Motu social values have remained static – indeed this would seem unlikely; thus the element of cultural choice, for example exchange as a method of personal status acquisition as opposed solely to economic necessity, remains at present impossible to qualify.

It remains probable however that the ancestral Motuans arrived by sea, which raises an important further point. Almost universally in the literature one implication has been that the Motu were forced to trade for sago in the west to supplement the poor food-producing potential of a region with low rainfall and infertile soils. In view of the foregoing argument that the Motu arrived as fully developed marine exploiters, sailors and traders, it would seem more sensible to examine their location in terms of the sea rather than the land. When this is done, several points of interest emerge:

1. The Motu occupy that area of the Papuan coast where the barrier reef runs consistently along it, and 4-5 kilometres offshore, which is as close as it comes to the shore anywhere along this coast. While this reef can be considered a resource in terms of fishing, a far more important function that it serves is to break down the ocean swell, enabling canoe transport to utilise the corridor at most times of the year. This is obviously an extremely valuable 'resource' for any group dependent upon sea travel for trading.
2. While the distribution of Motu villages and population at the point of European contact was relatively unevenly distributed (with the average distance between villages being 16.7 km. with a standard deviation of 8 km.), the heaviest clustering of population was towards the centre and particularly around Fairfax Harbour on which Port Moresby now stands. This reflects the value of the sheltered harbour on what is otherwise a relatively open stretch of coast, and also, perhaps, the proximity of the two largest reefs on the coast, Nateavi and Sinara, the latter of which surrounds Daugo Island. Fishing in this area was certainly of importance.
3. The other major indentation along this coast is Bootless Bay in which both Motupore and Loloata Islands supported prehistoric Motu villages and for which there is evidence of fierce fighting amongst the Motu themselves. At the time of European contact this area was a no-man's-land, but originally it must have possessed many of the same locational qualities as Fairfax Harbour, and it may be no coincidence that Motupore Island, on which ancestral Motuan occupation is as old as we might expect to find on present evidence, marks the geographical boundary between Eastern and Western Motu.

Motupore Island also marks the eastern end of the Koita domain. If the symbiosis between the groups was an early development, the subsequent western occupation by the Motu locating their houses on the intertidal zone as opposed to the eastern villages in the sea might find its explanation in the lack of a buffer relationship to the east.

What can be said is that if the model offered here is at all correct, the view of the Motu occupying a marginal ecological niche must be reconsidered. Allowing that they arrived with specialist coastal exploitation skills, as well as being experienced canoe builders and traders, then the local marine environment and the central position in relationship to the wider coast, coupled with the diversity of inland resources and the existing position and skills of the owners of the land at that time, would have made the ecological niche an ideal rather than marginal one.[151]

NOTES

1 Chalmers, James (1887), *Pioneering in New Guinea*, Religious Tract Society, London, p. 2.

2 Fitzpatrick, E.A. (1965), *Climate of the Port Moresby-Kairuku Area*, part 4 of Mabbutt, J.A. *et al.*, *Lands of the Port Moresby-Kairuku Area, Papua-New Guinea*, Land Research Series No. 14, C.S.I.R.O. Canberra, pp. 84-90. Figs. 1 and 2 are adapted from pp. 84 and 89.

3 Fitzpatrick (1965), pp. 91-3.

4 Glaessner, M.F. (1952), 'Geology of Port Moresby, Papua', *in* Sir Douglas Mawson Anniversary Volume, Adelaide, pp. 63-86; Speight, J.G. (1965), *Geology of the Port Moresby-Kairuku Area*, part 5 of Mabbutt *et al.* (1965).

5 Mabbutt *et al.* (1965).

6 Capell, Arthur (1943), *The Linguistic Position of Southeastern Papua*, Sydney.

7 Capell (1943), pp. 274-6.

8 Capell (1943), p. 20; but see: Dutton, T.E. (1969), *The Peopling of Central Papua*, unpublished mimeographed paper, Dept. of Anthropology, R.S. Pac.S., Australian National University, Canberra, p. 4 note 1, for a contradiction within Capell's argument. Fig. 4 is adapted from Dutton.

9 Chretian, C.D. (1956), 'Word distributions in southeastern Papua', *Language*, 32, p. 108.

10 Dyen, I. (1965), *A Lexicostatistical Classification of Austronesian Languages*, Supplement to *I.J.A.L.*, 31 (no. 1).

11 Pawley, A. (1969a), *On the Internal Relationships of Eastern Oceanic Languages*, unpublished mimeographed paper, Dept. of Anthropology and Sociology, University of Papua New Guinea; Pawley, A. (1969b), *Notes on the Austronesian Languages of Central Papua*, unpublished mimeographed paper, Dept. of Anthropology and Sociology, University of Papua New Guinea.

12 See Bulmer, Susan (1971), 'Prehistoric settlement patterns and pottery in the Port Moresby area', *Journal of the Papua and New Guinea Society*, 5 (2), pp. 30-7, for a general discussion of these data in archaeological terms.

13 Groves, M.C. *et al* (1958), 'Blood groups of the Motu and Koita peoples', *Oceania*, 28, p. 224.

14 Stone, Octavius C. (1880), *A Few Months in New Guinea*, London, p. 38.

15 London Missionary Society census figures in Rosenstiel, Annette (1953), *The Motu of Papua-New Guinea: a study of successful acculturation*, unpublished Ph.D. Thesis, Columbia University, p. 145.

16 Stone (1880), pp. 47-8.

17 Barakau is not referred to in ethnographic literature so far seen and Nigel Oram (pers. comm.) suggests that it is a post-contact village. If so, it should be deleted from this table.

18 Chalmers, James and Gill, W. Wyatt (1885), *Work and Adventure in New Guinea*, Religious Tract Society, London, pp. 155, 283.

19 Rosenstiel (1953), p. 145.

20 Rosenstiel (1953), p. 144.

21 Chalmers and Gill (1885), pp. 281, 283.

22 e.g. Seligman, C.G. (1910), *The Melanesians of British New Guinea*, Cambridge, pp. 41-193; more specifically on Koita components of Motu villages, see below; Belshaw, C.S. (1957), *The Great Village*, London, *passim*.

23 Belshaw (1957), p. 13.

24 Chalmers, James (1887), *Pioneering in New Guinea*, Religious Tract Society, London, p. 1.
25 Groves *et al.* (1958), p. 229.
26 Groves *et al.* (1958), p. 229.
27 Renagi Lohia, personal communication.
28 Groves, M.C. (1954), 'Dancing in Poreporana', *J.R. anthrop. Inst., 84,* p. 81, and *passim.*
29 Groves (1954), p. 87.
30 Seligman (1910), Plate VIII.
31 Stone (1880), p. 51.
32 Turner, W. (1878), 'The Ethnology of the Motu', *J.R. anthrop. Inst.*, p. 486.
33 Groves (1954), pp. 80-1.
34 Belshaw (1957), p. 12.
35 Belshaw (1957), p. 16.
36 Seligman (1910), p. 64 and Plate VIII.
37 Seligman, C.G. (1927), 'The *dubu* and steeple-houses of the central district of British New Guinea', *Ipek, Jahrbuch für prähistorische und ethnographische Kunst,* 1927, p. 178.
38 Williams, F.E. (1932a). 'Sex affiliation and its implications', *J.R. anthrop. Inst. 62,* p. 52.
39 Belshaw (1957), p. 11.
40 Dutton (1969), p. 36.
41 Stone, Octavius C. (1876), 'Description of the country and natives of Port Moresby and neighbourhood New Guinea', *Journal of the Royal Geographical Society,* 46, p. 38.
42 Chalmers and Gill (1885), pp. 282-3.
43 Chalmers and Gill (1885), p. 285.
44 Turner (1878), p. 487.
45 Stone (1876), p. 47.
46 Turner (1878), pp. 487-8.
47 e.g. Groves, M.C. (1960), 'Motu pottery', *Journal of the Polynesian Society*, 69, p. 11.
48 Turner (1878), p. 489.
49 Bulmer (1971), p. 63.
50 Lindt, J.W. (1887), *Picturesque New Guinea*, London, p. 122.
51 Stone (1876), p. 489.
52 Seligman (1910), p. 93.
53 Lawes, W.G. (1878), 'Ethnological notes on the Motu, Koitapu and Koiari tribes of New Guinea', *J.R. anthrop. Inst.*, 8, p. 373.
54 Dutton (1969), p. 35.
55 Chalmers and Gill (1885), p. 315.
56 Dutton (1969).
57 Seligman (1910), p. 47; Dutton (1969), p. 34.
58 Seligman (1910), p. 66.
59 Chalmers (1887), p. 1.
60 Chalmers and Gill (1885), p. 319.
61 Seligman (1910), p. 41.
62 Seligman (1910), p. 49.
63 Dutton (1969), p. 27, note 2.
64 Seligman (1910), pp. 141-50.
65 Seligman (1910), p. 63.
66 Stone (1880), p. 87.
67 Seligman (1910), p. 87.
68 Bulmer (1971), p. 39.
69 e.g. Lawes (1878), pp. 372-3.
70 Turner (1878), p. 485; Chalmers and Gill (1885), pp. 150, 255-6, 306.

71 Chalmers and Gill (1885), p. 103; Lindt (1887), p. 45.
72 Stone (1880), p. 118.
73 Lawes (1878), p. 373.
74 Seligman (1910), p. 45.
75 Romilly, H.H. (1893), *Letters from the Western Pacific and Mashonaland 1878-1891* (edited by S.H. Romilly), London, p. 327.
76 Dutton (1969), p. 35.
77 Chalmers and Gill (1885), pp. 315-16.
78 Seligman (1910), p. 94.
79 Williams (1932a), pp. 51-2.
80 Chalmers and Gill (1885), *passim*.
81 Williams (1932a), p. 52.
82 Chalmers and Gill (1885), pp. 87-132.
83 Williams (1932a), p. 53 and *passim*.
84 Williams (1932a), pp. 55-6.
85 Williams (1932a), p. 73; the point has been made previously by Dutton (1969), p. 27 note 2.
86 Williams (1932a), pp. 69 ff.
87 Dutton (1969), p. 35.
88 Turner (1878), p. 493.
89 Chalmers and Gill (1885), p. 95.
90 Hammond, Norman (1973), 'Models for Maya trade', *in* Renfrew, C. (ed.), *The Explanation of Culture Change*, London, p. 601.
91 Seligman (1910), pp. 93-4.
92 Chalmers and Gill (1885), p. 269.
93 Seligman (1910), pp. 93-94.
94 Groves (1960), p. 8.
95 Seligman (1910), p. 94.
96 Chalmers (1887), p. 11; Oram, Nigel D. (1968), 'Culture change, economic development and migration among the Hula', *Oceania*, 38, 4, p. 250, for the adjacent Hula people.
97 In Seligman (1910), pp. 96-102.
98 Seligman (1910), p. 114.
99 Chalmers (1887), p. 33.
100 Groves (1960), p. 9.
101 Personal communication.
102 Seligman (1910), p. 115.
103 Williams (1932a), p. 126.
104 See for example Seligman (1910), p. 115; Williams (1932a), pp. 126-7.
105 Williams (1932a), p. 127; Groves (1954), p. 83.
106 Romilly (1893), pp. 214, 258; Holmes, J. (1902), 'Notes on the religious ideas of the Elema tribes of the Papuan gulf', *J.R. anthrop. Inst.* 32, p. 431.
107 Williams, F.E. (1932b), 'Trading voyages from the Gulf of Papua', *Oceania*, 3, 2, p. 140.
108 Oram (1968), p. 249; Chalmers (1887), p. 3.
109 In Lindt (1887), pp. 124-5.
110 The special nature of food exchange noted widely in anthropological literature is not in question here: as Sahlins has noted, 'the immorality of food-wealth conversions has a sectoral dimension' (Sahlins, M. (1972), *Stone Age Economics*, Chicago, p. 219), and it would seem that the socially peripheral point at which such conversions take place amongst the Motu is confined perhaps to village or *iduhu* level. Certainly food-wealth conversions took place between Eastern and Western Motu villages, and perhaps between villages within these divisions.
111 Leask, M.F. (1943), 'A kitchen midden in Papua', *Oceania*, 13, pp. 235-42.
112 Williams, F.E. (1931), 'Papuan petroglyphs', *J.R. anthrop. Inst.*, 61, pp. 121-55.
113 Bulmer, Susan (1969), *Archaeological field survey and excavations in Central Papua,*

1968, unpublished mimeographed paper, Dept. of Anthropology and Sociology, University of Papua New Guinea.

114 Vanderwal, R. (1973), *Prehistoric Studies in Central Coastal Papua*, unpublished Ph.D. Thesis, Australian National University, Canberra, pp. 51-2.

115 Irwin, personal communication.

116 Allen, Jim (1972), 'Nebira 4: an early Austronesian site in Central Papua', *Archaeology and Physical Anthropology in Oceania*, 7, pp. 92-123.

117 Vanderwal (1973).

118 Bowdler, personal communication.

119 Vanderwal (1973), p. 152.

120 Vanderwal (1973), pp. 204-9.

121 Allen (1972).

122 Personal communication.

123 Seligman (1910), p. 43.

124 Bulmer (1971), pp. 84-5.

125 Bulmer (1971), p. 77.

126 Bulmer (1971), pp. 42-51.

127 Bulmer (1971), Table 1, p. 50.

128 Murray, J.H.P. (1912), *Papua or British New Guinea,* London, pp. 153-4.

129 Oram, personal communication.

130 Oram (1969), 'Sources of Motuan Prehistory, *Journal of the Papua and New Guinea Society*, 2, 2, p. 86.

131 Turner (1878), p. 485; Chalmers and Gill (1885), p. 150.

132 Allen, Jim (1971), *Recent Lithic Assemblages from the Papuan Coast*, unpublished paper delivered to the 8th Congress of the Far Eastern Prehistory Association, Canberra.

133 Stone (1880), p. 72.

134 e.g. Seligman (1910), p. 115.

135 By Dr. Jenny Hope of the Dept. of Prehistory, A.N.U., to whom I am most grateful.

136 Personal communication, Pamela Swadling, Department of Anthropology, University of Papua New Guinea.

137 Stone (1880), p. 118.

138 Groves (1960), p. 18.

139 Bulmer (1971), p. 85.

140 Binford, L.R. (1968), 'Post-Pleistocene adaptations', *in* Binford, S.R. and Binford, L.R. (eds.), *New Perspectives in Archaeology*, Chicago, p. 328.

141 Rowlands, M.J. (1973), 'Modes of exchange and the incentives for trade, with reference to later European prehistory', *in* Renfrew, C. (ed.), *The Explanation of Culture Change*, London, p. 589.

142 Sahlins (1972), pp. 196-204.

143 Dutton (1969), *passim.*

144 Chalmers (1887), p. 3.

145 Chalmers (1887), p. 2.

146 Lees, Susan H. (1967), *Regional Integration of Pig Husbandry in the New Guinea Highlands*, unpublished paper read at the 1967 meeting of the Michigan Academy of Sciences.

147 Flannery, K.V. (1968), 'The Olmec and the valley of Oaxaca: a model for inter-regional interaction in Formative times', *in* Benson, Elizabeth P. (ed.), *Dumbarton Oaks Conference on the Olmec*, Harvard University, Washington D.C.

148 McClellan, Catharine (1953), 'The inland Tlingit', *in* 'Asia and North America: Transpacific Contacts', *Memoirs of the Society for American Archaeology*, no. 9, pp. 47-52.

149 Vanderwal (1973), p. 52.

150 Personal communication.

151 I wish to thank Geoff Irwin, Jim O'Connell and J. Peter White for comments and advice on this paper. Win Mumford drew the figures.

JOAN OATES

Mesopotamian social organisation: archaeological and philological evidence

> Social structure is not susceptible to direct archaeological influence and we should not try to persuade ourselves that it is, just because we would like it to be.[1]

Many factors have been discussed in relation to the evolution of social structure, among them environment and man's choice of adaptation to it, level of technology, size of population, concepts of property, a society's ideology. I began putting together this paper with the excessively optimistic intention of assembling the Mesopotamian data, such as they are, for family structure and status distinctions in relation to such factors. Time and lack of space have forced me to reduce these data to an unsatisfactory series of vignettes, though as such I hope they may prove useful contributions, and caveats, to more general and theoretical topics.[2]

Consecutive, or 'diachronic', evidence for social evolution is comparatively rare. That from Mesopotamia offers two advantages: ancient Sumer is one of only two, at most three, areas in the world where 'pristine' urban development and its accompanying social complexity can be traced. Moreover, there exists a body of contemporary and at least indirectly relevant textual material. The greatest obstacle to constructive interpretation is simple lack of evidence, due more to the nature of the subject than to any excavator's negligence. In addition, single period sites are almost non-existent, and rarely has more than one per cent of any prehistoric site been excavated. Thus for a given period we cannot predict with any degree of accuracy total site sizes or the distribution of settlement, and hence population, within them. Moreover, the association of artefacts with structures cannot be studied in societies that kept their floors tidy, an all too common Mesopotamian habit. Nor can such associations have meaning without the complete recovery of house plans, an unlikely product of currently fashionable soundings.

Inability to deduce social structure from existing evidence has led many archaeologists to interpret their data in terms of ethnographic parallels which reflect, inevitably, societies that have not progressed beyond 'primitive' levels. Such interpretations may well overlook the very factors that were crucial to the development of 'civilised' society and should thus be of prime relevance to any study of social evolution. If ethnographic parallels must be sought, it would seem reasonable to expect those in the archaeologist's immediate area to be more relevant than material derived from general cross-cultural surveys. Nevertheless, a recent study of the evolution of culture in Mesopotamia has drawn on agricultural parallels with New Guinea and North America with no mention of local practices nor, perhaps more surprisingly, of a well-known Sumerian text known as the 'Farmer's Almanac',[3] which describes in detail agricultural practices in the late third millennium.

I. Archaeological evidence

A. Upper Palaeolithic

Evidence for Upper Palaeolithic occupation in lowland Mesopotamia is lacking, although Mousterian industries are found scattered throughout the southern countryside. The few cave sites that have been excavated in the Zagros provide an incomplete picture of small groups of nomadic hunter-gatherers, but such remains are far from well-documented. Recent work suggests a broader exploitation both of resources and habitat than hitherto envisaged and the likelihood of seasonally occupied, open-air settlements.[4] We can say with certainty that the Zagros type site, Zarzi, was not, as conventionally represented, a 'base-camp', but we remain ignorant of the true pattern of settlement of the 'Zarzian' people. In evolutionary terms one would like an answer to the question whether the general similarities among the blade-tool industries and apparent level of subsistence in the Levant, the Caucasus and even as far afield as Soviet Turkmenistan are to be considered parallel or in some way related developments.

B. Intensified food collection (10,000-8,000 B.C.)

Climate: changing from cool steppe to warmer oak-pistachio savannah; not unlike modern climate, probably cooler and drier

Settlement type: open-air camps, some perhaps semi-permanent, together with some seasonal cave occupation

Economy: intensive hunting and gathering; increasing reliance on a variety of collected foods; increasing facilities for storage

Archaeological sites:

1. *Karim Shahir*[5]

location: Iraqi Kurdistan, intermontane valley

elevation: c. 800 m.
size: 0.4 ha.
% excavated: 18%
settlement type: thin deposit representing temporary encampments; no architecture; 30,000 artifacts recovered
date: c. 9000 B.C.

2. *Zawi Chemi Shanidar*[6]
location: Iraqi Kurdistan, intermontane valley
elevation: c. 425 m.
size: debris scattered over 5 ha.
% excavated: 0.2%
settlement type: 1-2 m. deposit suggests continuing though probably seasonal occupation; traces of a circular structure perhaps 12.5 m.^{2} in area, rebuilt three times
economy: as above; possible domesticated sheep 'by end of deposit'
date: W-681, 8900 ± 300 B.C.

3. *M'lefaat*[5]
location: piedmont, on Erbil road east of Mosul, N. Iraq
elevation: 300 m.
size: 1 ha.
% excavated: 0.6%
settlement type: 1.5 m. deposit comprising 5 occupation levels; possible oval pit house, c. 9 m.^{2} in area; traces of 'enigmatic' stone wall, curved
date: 9000-8000 B.C.

Settled life introduces a new dimension into the investigation of social systems, leaving as its artefactual remains new types of evidence from which inferences concerning at least rank and wealth differentials, and in certain very limited cases even residence and descent, can be made. But can we identifiy any of the factors that led some but, significantly, not all societies in the Middle East to opt for settled life? An honest answer would be 'no', although we can be certain that agriculture *per se* played no part. The shift that can be seen towards the end of the Pleistocene to the exploitation of a wide variety of foods provided a background for the ultimate selection of certain cereals and ungulates as the first domesticates, while semi-settled life led to a reduction in the number of environmental niches exploited by any given community. Climatic change is now recognised as one factor in the cultural changes that took place at the end of the Pleistocene[7] but it alone cannot adequately explain why the shift from an apparently efficient hunting and gathering economy to one based ultimately on settled agriculture. took place. A knowledge of the vagaries of human nature might even suggest that the aesthetic attractions of a particular camp-site may have weighed as heavily as any archaeologically demonstrable factor in man's decision to spend longer and longer periods 'at home'. Of course, intangible and possibly even from our point of view illogical factors of this sort must forever elude us in attempts to analyse how any prehistoric society regulated its behaviour.

Sites 1-3 represent the total excavated evidence for the crucial 'pre-village' stage in Mesopotamia. At Karim Shahir there is a greater emphasis on chipped flint tools and at Zawi Chemi on pecked and ground stone, the manufacture of which must have required an inordinate amount of time and the use of which an increasing dependence on plant food. Differences can be noted also in the tool kit at M'lefaat and one must ask whether these differences reflect a chronological progression or seasonal and functional variations. The evidence is inconclusive though the differences in elevation of these three sites might favour the latter as at least a possibility. Hunting is still of major importance at Zawi Chemi, however, judging from the enormous numbers of animal bones, and it seems likely that this site at least was a 'multipurpose' habitation. There is no evidence for territoriality, residence, group size, nor for differentiation of settlement types as has been suggested by Hole and Flannery for Iran.[8] One can see many ways in which the existing archaeological evidence can be amplified, but political difficulties in recent years have impeded work in the area.

C. Early village settlement

At a slightly later date a much more complex picture can be observed in the Levant, for example at Ain Mallaha and Jericho, for which there would appear to be no Mesopotamian parallel. Much of the relevant data has been admirably summarised by Flannery in the context of settlement patterns.[9] Only three points need be made here, two concerning the general aspect of settlement, the third relating to the change from curvilinear to rectangular house types that can be observed over much of the Middle East, and the possible social implications, if any.

4. *Ain Mallaha*[10]
location: near Lake Huleh, Israel
elevation: c. 70 m.
size: 0.2 ha.
% excavated: 12%
settlement type: semi-subterranean circular huts, permanent or semi-permanent
economy: hunting and collecting; grindstones, pestles, mortars, sickle blades and storage pits but no traces of domesticated plants or animals (cf. Zawi Chemi)
date: 9000-8000 B.C.

5. *Mureybet*[11]
Location: left bank of Euphrates, nr. Meskene, N. Syria
elevation: 300 m.
size: c. 3 ha. (later material on site)
% excavated: 1%
settlement type: early levels, apparently contiguous circular structures with stone foundations, area 5-12 m.^{2}; later levels, multi-roomed rectilinear houses, 12-25 m.^{2}
economy: · probable cultivation of einkorn and barley (still morphologically wild); hunting and collecting
date: 8000-7500 B.C. and earlier 'Mesolithic' village

6. *Beidha*[12]
location: southern Jordan, nr. Petra
elevation: 1000 m.
size: 0.4 ha.
% excavated: c. 50% of extant site
settlement type: permanent village
economy: hunting, collecting, cultivation of emmer and wild barley; possible goat-herding; ? trading station
date: 7000-6200 B.C. (Pre-pottery Neolithic)

Ain Mallaha represents a very early pre-agricultural village type, while Mureybet and nearby Abu Hureyra can almost certainly be identified as the earliest known villages of 'cultivators'. There is little comparable evidence in Mesopotamia, though so far as we can tell environmental conditions in the upper Tigris valley and the northern Jazirah would not have been unlike those in northern Syria. At Ain Mallaha Perrot estimates that there may have been as many as 50 huts in use at one time; one unusually large example (shelter 51, 50 m.^{2}) is compared by Flannery to Tiv huts for receiving visitors, while he suggests that one atypically well-made structure may belong to the 'compound head'.[13] Burial practices confirm the possibility of status distinctions,[14] while the well-known plastered skulls, which are found at Ramad and Beisamun as well as Jericho,[15] suggest a preoccupation with lineage that we shall see is entirely lacking in Mesopotamia.

At Mureybet the early evidence for differentiated structures is more equivocal owing in part to the small area excavated. Nevertheless, one oval structure, if completed at its apparent rate of curvature, would have provided 112 m.^{2} of floor space, again suggesting some form of 'public' building. By 7500 B.C. multi-roomed houses are found which could have housed nuclear families. Some of the individual rooms, as at perhaps contemporary Ganj Dareh in Iran (see below), are exceedingly small (less than 3m.^{2}), but it can be seen from later Mesopotamian sites (p. 468) that these are not abnormally small room sizes in what at a later period are clearly nuclear family residences.[16]

In Palestine it is clear that by the eighth millennium B.C. there is evidence for a complexity of society unknown elsewhere. Ain Mallaha must represent an early stage in this development but its apogee is undoubtedly to be seen in PPNA Jericho, for which radio-carbon dates give a possible range of 8300-6700 B.C. There is no need to elaborate on the well-known evidence for this massively-walled and so far unique settlement (area c. 4 ha.), and there can be no argument with the assertion that community public works on this scale must have required both central authority and wealth. Unless Jericho represents the ultimate Neolithic 'folly', however, its social and cultural development cannot be viewed in isolation. It is necessary to ask why and against what or whom such defenses were constructed, and the only reasonable answer inevitably implies a general level of social, economic and political development in the Levant for which archaeological evidence is at present otherwise lacking. We must recognise, of course, that human behaviour is only 'reasonable' in the context of a society's own ideology, but even a 'bettering the Joneses' mentality or conspicuous display requires the existence of other groups worthy of being so impressed. A millennium later in Turkey a society of undoubtedly greater complexity created the town that is now Çatal Hüyük, some 15 ha. in area, three or four times the size of PPNA Jericho. The site is particularly striking in its evidence for highly developed and organised ritual activity, and for specialised craftsmanship at a high level of competence. Like Jericho, however, although it represents a level of cultural attainment apparently unique for its time, it represents too a highly developed society that came to nothing in the broader sense of cultural evolution. Perhaps one of the most illuminating questions we can ask ourselves is whether it is possible to isolate particular factors relevant to the development of urban society in Mesopotamia that were absent or failed to operate in the Levant and Anatolia, areas climatically comparable at least in part with Mesopotamia and which appear to have followed very similar patterns of economic and technological development. It has been suggested that Çatal be seen as the result of an efficient exploitation which had reached an optimum, or possibly even a maximum, and that more and similar sites were not viable because greater exploitation was not feasible within the limits of existing resources and technology.[17] But this does not explain the failure to improve existing technology or to develop techniques, political or economic, for exploiting greater resource areas, factors which can be seen in operation in proto-urban Mesopotamia.

We turn to Beidha to make a third point about early village society in the Levant. A popular model for reconstituting Palaeolithic hunting groups in the Near East postulates bands consisting of 6-8 males each associated with 1-3 adult females and their children; such bands are characterised as having weakly developed concepts of descent and territoriality, their size fluctuating with the availability of resources; division of labour is along sex lines.[18] Flannery has noted the widespread occurrence in the Near East of curvilinear house structures as the earliest form of dwelling and their close resemblance to African hut compounds where a generally comparable social structure obtains.[9] In the Near East these circular structures were commonly replaced by rectangular units often associated with nuclear or extended families. We may reasonably ask whether such a social development can be inferred from the Near Eastern evidence. Beidha is cited as the finest example of this phenomenon, and the excavator has suggested that the rectangular houses that appear in the upper levels perhaps represent 'newcomers'.[19] But Beidha provides a striking case where a close examination of the archaeological evidence, especially in it local context, leads to conclusions radically different from those that might reasonably be inferred from more superficial cross-cultural comparisons. The earliest level (VI) reveals a classic example of a honeycomb network of circular dwellings (Fig. 1a) that can be closely paralleled among virtually identical hut compounds in Rhodesia.[20] In level II is found the best preserved example of the later house type, a large unit (area c. 30 $m.^2$) to which are attached groups of very regular rectangular buildings of identical size and construction (Fig. 1b). An analysis of the artefacts found in both types of house group shows that in both cases there is a living unit accompanied by what can only be interpreted as 'workshops'. In level VI three separate groups of circular rooms/houses have been excavated. The larger rooms are intercommunicating through anterooms and short corridors; smaller storage units are built into the interstices. Each separate cluster is surrounded by its own encircling wall with a courtyard beyond; the only extant hearths were in these courtyards. The best-preserved cluster contained at least nine rooms, of which four were living or working quarters some 4 m. in diameter (area c. 12.5 m^2). Room XLVIII can be interpreted as a possible living room; it contained querns and a variety of heavy stone implements. Two doors away, XLIX contained a preponderance of bone tools *and their raw material*, and XVIII contained 114 flint arrowheads and points in mint condition, ready for retouching. These two rooms are unlikely to have been 'female' working quarters, although this assumes a division of labour for which there can be no *direct* proof. Evidence for family structure must remain inconclusive but it is clear that the 'compound' could have housed a single family with living and work rooms plus storage.

The later rectangular house units are perhaps more easily interpreted as a living unit plus workshops, among which are those of specialists in horn, bone tools and beads, and a single butcher. The excavator herself notes that these later houses represent 'the cluster principle in a different guise',[21] and it must be obvious that there is no basic change in the structure of Beidha society as represented in its house plans. Moreover, Mortensen's analysis of the chipped stone material has shown conclusively a strong traditional development

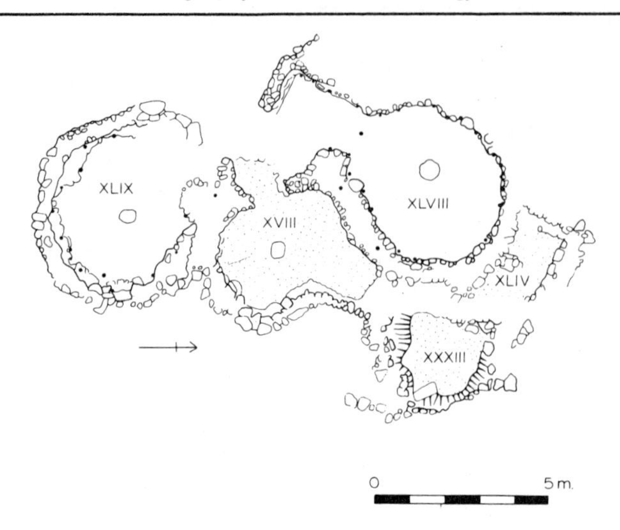

Figure 1 Beidha (*a*). Level VI house, after Kirkbride, *P.E.Q.*, 99, 1967, Fig. 1.

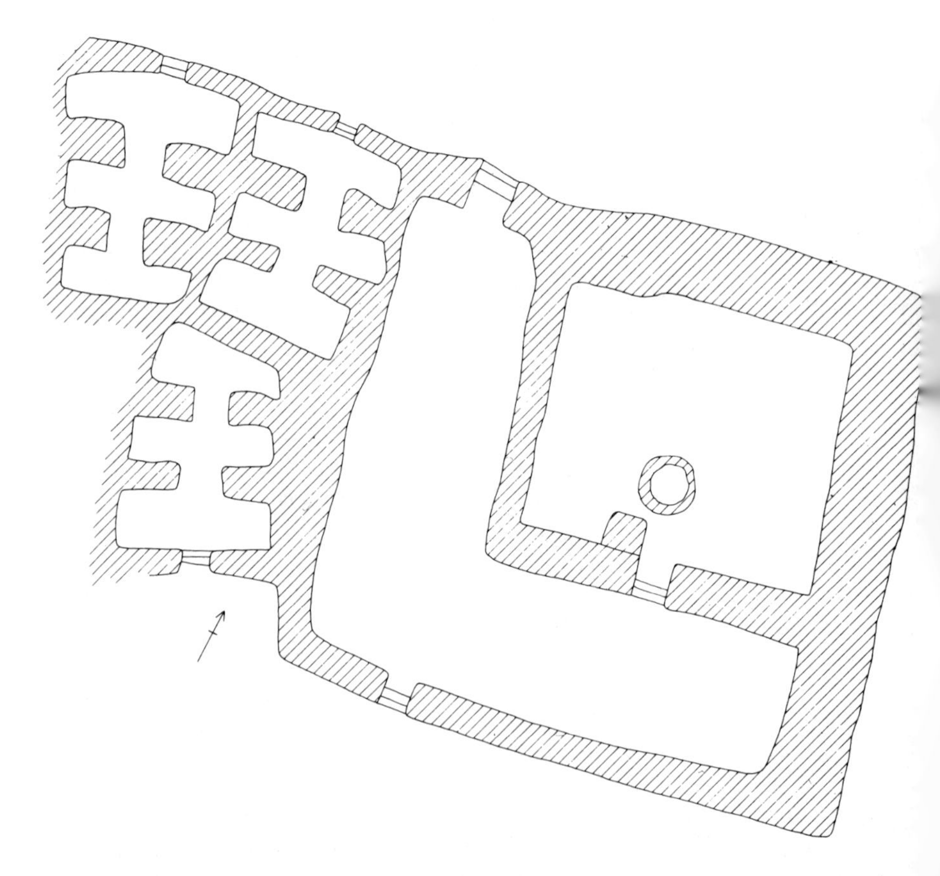

Figure 1. Beidha (*b*). Level II house and 'workshops', after Kirkbridge, *P.E.Q.*, 98, 1966, Fig. 2.

from generation to generation within the same group of people with 'no reflection of new population elements'.[22] Perhaps most convincing of all is the fact that the apparently culturally significant change from circular to rectangular houses can be explained in straightforward structural terms.

Curvilinear structures, at least in some areas of the Near East, represent a form of probably portable dwelling unit widely employed by nomadic and semi-nomadic peoples; thus their occurrence in the earliest levels of many settled sites undoubtedly indicates an early state in the settlement of such peoples. In itself a curvilinear plan is no indication of either social structure or economy. Moreover, the sequence at Beidha illustrates clearly the care that must be used in making inferences about social structure based solely on ethnographic data. Another plausible explanation of the architectural changes seen at Beidha must immediately occur to anyone who has observed the sequence of settlement on a small Near Eastern army post. The process of transformation from a very temporary to a permanent establishment is:

1. The pitching of tents on ground that has, at most, been cleared of stones and roughly levelled; this leaves only post or peg-holes to mark the site.
2. Reinforcement of the sides of the tents with piled stones, which serve both as anchors and draught-proofing ('enigmatic stone structures' or 'foundations'); a more effective, and more labourious, way of providing this protection is
3. The excavation of the floors of individual tents to a depth corresponding with the height of the walls, leaving only roofs above ground level. This represents the most luxurious stage of the temporary post (in archaeological terminology, 'semi-subterranean' or 'pit' houses), which is then followed if necessary by
4. The erection of permanent buildings. A tent or hut may be round or rectangular depending on the number of poles employed, but when a permanent structure has to be roofed, the simplest technique is a system of parallel roof-beams that are most easily supported on a rectilinear wall plan. A careful examination of the archaeological evidence from Beidha shows precisely this sequence. We need not, in fact, postulate changes in social structure or people when the architectural development can be explained more simply.

D. Early village sites, Zagros Mountains

7. Ganj Dareh Tepe[23]
location: plain nr. Kermanshah, Iran
elevation: 1300 m.

size: 0.13 ha.
% excavated: 14%
settlement type: apparently permanent village, 8 m. Neolithic deposits; rectangular cubicle-like rooms, probably supporting an upper storey
economy: domestic goat; equipment for processing and storing plant foods
date: before 7000 B.C.

8. *Jarmo*[5]
location: Chemchemal valley, Iraqi Kurdistan
elevation: c. 750 m.
size: originally c. 2 ha.; 1.3 ha. extant
% excavated: 1%
settlement type: permanent village, 7 m. deposits; multi-roomed rectilinear houses
economy: cultivation and animal husbandry; collecting and hunting still important
date: 6750- 5900 B.C., or slightly later

9. *Tepe Guran*[24]
location: northern Luristan
elevation: 950 m.
size: 0.9 ha.
% excavated: 0.5%
settlement type: early levels, seasonal occupation, wooden huts with two or three small rooms, rectilinear or slightly curved walls; later levels, permanent village, rectangular multi-roomed houses
economy: early levels, transhumant goatherds, little evidence for hunting; late levels, cultivators of barley, increased emphasis on hunting
date: 6500-5500 B.C.

There is no evidence for status distinctions; the earliest structures are multi-roomed and rectilinear, ? nuclear families. A typical Jarmo house size is 30 $m.^2$ (living area perhaps 14 $m.^2$) plus 3-4 $m.^2$ walled courtyard.[25] The Jarmo village contained perhaps 20-25 houses, population ? 150-200, i.e. approaching or above Forge's figure of 150, comprising 35 adult males, proposed as a critical size above which integrative bonds other than basic relationships of kinship and affinity are necessary.[26] The wide distribution of 'tadpole' pottery (Kermanshah and Luristan to Chemchemal and Mandali) could imply either deliberate exchange or, if it is assumed that pottery was at this stage made by women – and it must be recognised that there is no direct evidence for such an assumption – exogamous virilocal marriage. There is 'bulk-carrying trade' in obsidian (45% of chipped stone in upper ceramic levels at Jarmo).

E. Early village sites, Mesopotamia

10. *Umm Dabaghiyah*[27]
location: steppe nr. Hatra, southeast of Mosul, N. Iraq
elevation: c. 200 m.
size: 0.85 ha.
% excavated: perhaps 40%
settlement type: permanent village, multi-roomed rectilinear houses (40-50 m^2) with barracks-like communal 'storerooms' around a central enclosure 200 m^2 (Fig. 2).
economy: some agriculture (rainfed); heavy emphasis on hunting, especially onager
date: sixth millennium B.C.

11. *Yarim Tepe (I)*[28]
location: plain south of Jebel Sinjar, N. Iraq
elevation: c. 370 m.
size: mound of 0.8 ha.; the earliest settlement is said to approach 2 ha. in area
% excavated: 18% of visible mound
settlement type: permanent village; earliest levels (13-8), small and simple rectangular (25 m^2) and round (5 m^2) 'houses'; level 7 upwards, larger houses predominantly rectangular; typical nuclear house 6 rooms, 40 m^2
economy: agriculture (rainfed) and animal husbandry; full domestication
date: sixth millennium B.C.

12. *Hassuna*[29]
location: just west of Tigris valley, south of Mosul, N. Iraq
elevation: c. 200 m.
size: mound of 3 ha. but size of smaller Hassuna settlement uncertain
% excavated: 1%
settlement type: multi-roomed rectangular houses, 1 circular structure (area 28 m^2); house sizes 20-25 m^2 up to 45-70 m^2 in later levels, plus courtyards; room sizes 2-12 m^2
economy: as Yarim Tepe I
date: sixth millennium B.C.

Mention should be made of two contemporary non-agricultural sites, one, Sarab (nr. Kermanshah) apparently without architecture but according to faunal studies occupied year-round;[30] the other, Bouqras, on the Euphrates in Syria, with substantial architecture, 5 m. of deposit and an economy based on hunting and collecting,[31] confirmation, if such were needed, that settled villagers even in the Near East need not pursue an agricultural economy.

13. *Tell es-Sawwan*[32]
location: on bluff overlooking Tigris, south of Samarra, central Iraq
elevation: 65 m.
size: 2.5 ha.
% excavated: perhaps 20%
settlement type: permanent, rectangular multi-roomed houses up to 285 m^2 in area
economy: probably irrigated agriculture
date: 5500-5000 B.C.

14. *Choga Mami*[33]
location: central Iraq, east of Baghdad at edge of alluvium
elevation: 137 m.
size: maximum 5-6 ha.; earliest settlement c. 3.5 ha.
settlement type: permanent village, multi-roomed rectangular houses of very regular plan (32-54 m^2) with very small rooms (2.2-3.6 m^2) (Fig. 3b)
economy: irrigation agriculture, animal husbandry
date: c. 5500-5000 B.C.
excavated evidence for small irrigation channels c. 2 m. wide throughout Samarran phase at Choga Mami; by end of period (before 5000 B.C.) canal 6 m. or more in width, requiring *minimum* 5000 man-hours construction.[34]

It is at this time, during the sixth millennium B.C. in Mesopotamia, that the first archaeological evidence is found that can be interpreted as indicating organised communal activity, hence the probability of some authoritarian structure. Both at Yarim Tepe and at the earlier nearby site of Tell es-Sotto (as yet unpublished), as at Umm Dabaghiyah, are found large well-planned complexes of rooms that can only have served for storage purposes for groups of families or even the whole community. At Umm Dabaghiyah their communal nature is especially clear, situated on three sides of a large central court with residential houses to the west (Fig. 2). One is tempted to suggest the division of the community into two clans or lineages, although the two buildings are far from identical and other explanations are certainly possible. Whatever its purpose, the layout of the settlement at Umm Dabaghiyah clearly shows deliberate and conscious planning.

At the perhaps marginally later Samarran settlements in north central Mesopotamia (nos. 13-14) are found the first indications of rigidly observed property rights, the recognition of private ownership (stamp seals) and a more conscious specialisation of labour in the use of potters' marks.[35] The extent of the ground stone industry at Tell es-Sawwan implies an extraordinary concentration of specialised craftsmen, to say nothing of surplus wealth. In addition the peculiar nature of the graves and associated buildings (180-280 $m.^2$) must indicate some form of religious centre. The graves have been described

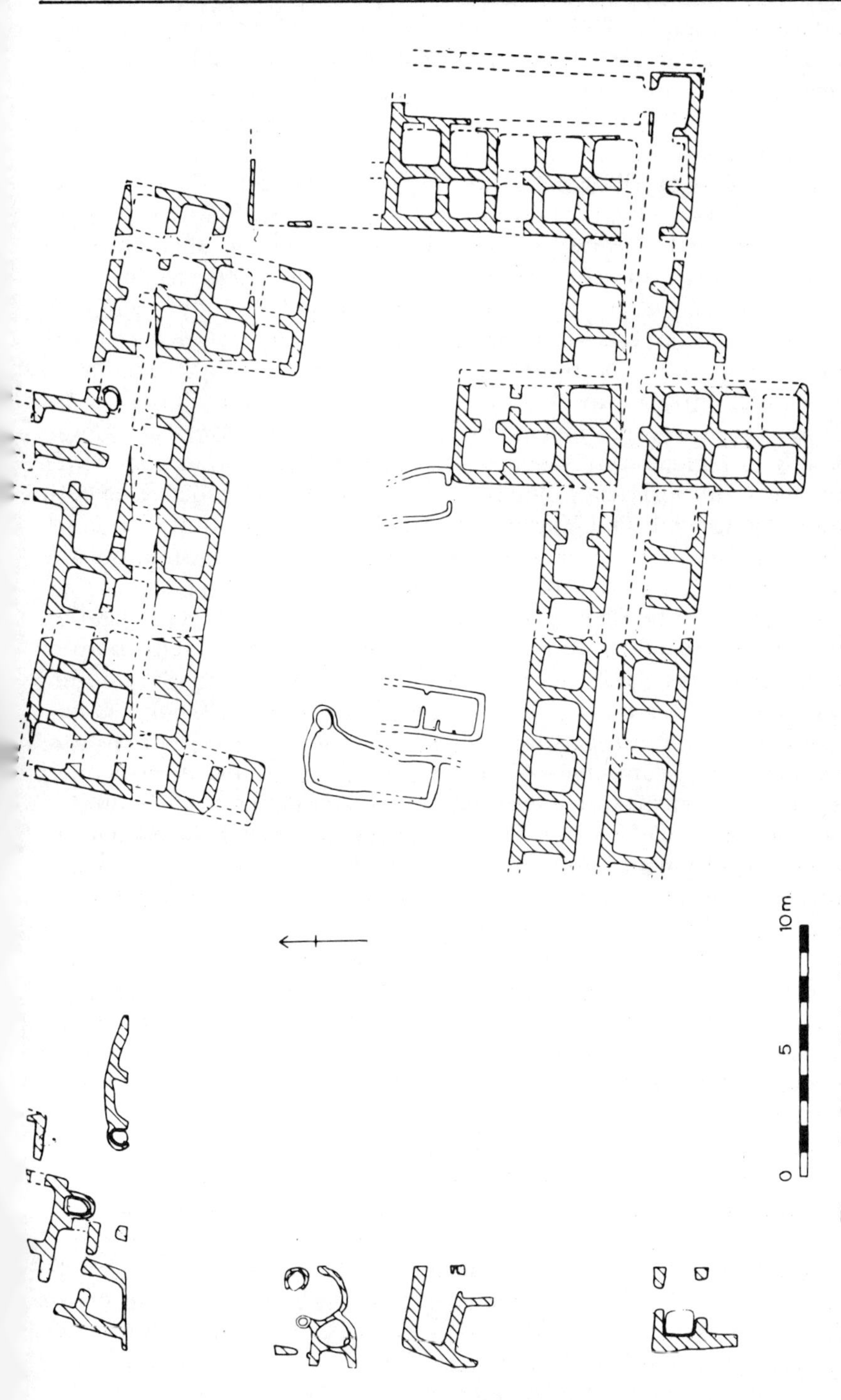

Figure 2. Umm Dabaghiyah, level 3. After Kirkbridge, *Iraq*, XXXV, 1973, Pl. LXXVII.

as those of 'infants of high status'[36] but it must be emphasised that virtually all of the very large number of graves contained comparable grave goods[37] which can only be interpreted as having some cultic significance and indicating widespread wealth, but need not imply status distinctions.

House plans at all of these sites suggest essentially nuclear family accommodation which is altered and added to in such a way as to imply extended family occupation. The size of the Hassuna settlements with an economy based on rainfed agriculture is in the order of 1 ha., with larger sites like Yarim Tepe approaching a maximum of 2 ha. On Mesopotamian sites it is impossible to tell how many houses were occupied at any one time, but a conservative estimate for early Yarim Tepe I would be at least 50 and possibly 80-100 houses, with a minimum population of 250-300 and a maximum possibly as high as 750. Naroll's data suggest that a population of over 500 needs 'authoritarian officials'.[38] Archaeological evidence at both Umm Dabaghiyah and Yarim Tepe indicates a community structure more complex than, for example, at Jarmo or even Hassuna, but the data from the latter two sites are far less complete.

Samarran settlements, with an economy based on irrigation agriculture, are substantially larger in size, perhaps a factor both of increased yields and the necessity for community effort in maintaining irrigation schemes on the scale that we have found at Choga Mami. Increasing trade contacts are shown by the presence not only of obsidian but at a number of sites of marine shells and at Sawwan of turquoise and carnelian whose sources lie far to the east. The earliest Mespotamian evidence for the use of copper comes from Sawwan (level I) and Yarim Tepe (level 13). At Yarim Tepe an 'industrial quarter' is suggested by the presence of a number of surprisingly sophisticated two-stage kilns, arranged in groups, sometimes marked off by boundary walls; one group was associated with an unusual large circular building, 78 m.^{2} in area. At Sawwan one group of buildings is interpreted as 'granaries' but the evidence is obscure (Fig. 3a). Hassunan sites are unfortified but at Sawwan part of the site was surrounded by a wall and ditch (level III) and at Choga Mami a tower guarded one of the town entrances.[39]

Halaf settlements are less well-documented than the Samarran, but there is increasing evidence for craft specialisation[40] and apparently organised trade. Large quantities of obsidian are utilised and recent evidence indicates that pottery from a single manufacturing source, as yet unidentified, reached both Mersin and Choga Mami, over 1000 km. apart.[41] The excavated sites are no larger than those of the Hassuna phase (Yarim Tepe II was originally some 1.4 ha. and Arpachiyah is smaller than Yarim Tepe I), but it is likely that the major sites lie buried under later mounds. Arpachiyah may well be merely an outlying industrial complex associated with a major settlement at Nineveh.

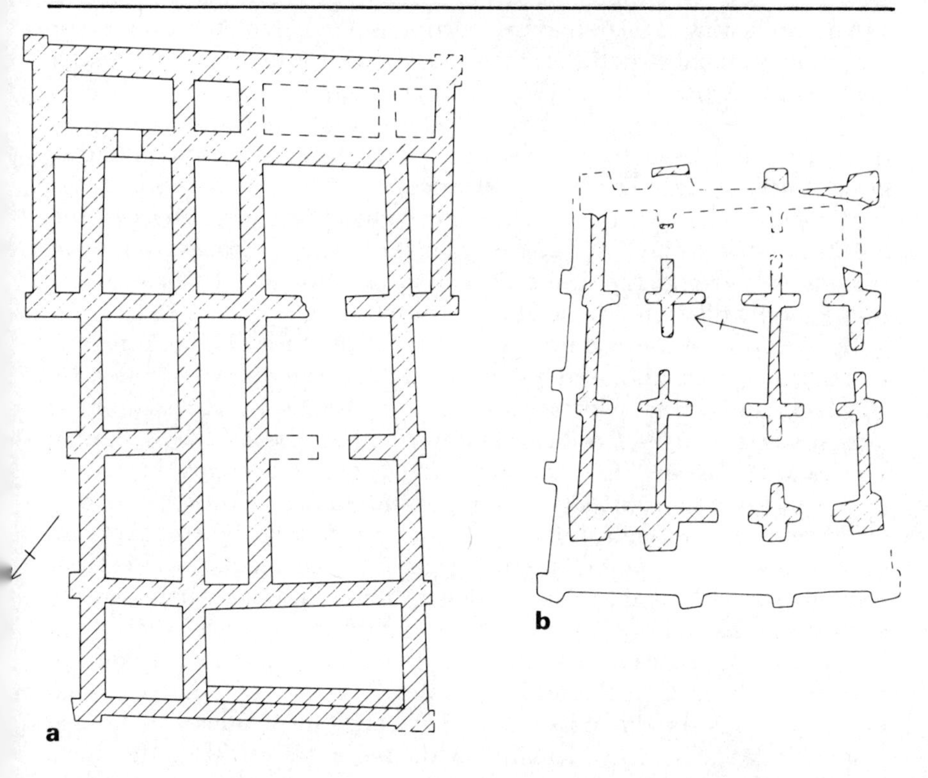

Figure 3 (*a*). Tell es-Sawwan, level IV, T-shaped Samarran building, after Al-A'dami, *Sumer*, XXIV, 1968, plan 1.

Figure 3 (*b*). Choga Mami, level 2 Samarran house overlying earlier house walls, after Oates, *Iraq*, XXXI, 1969, Pl. XXIV.

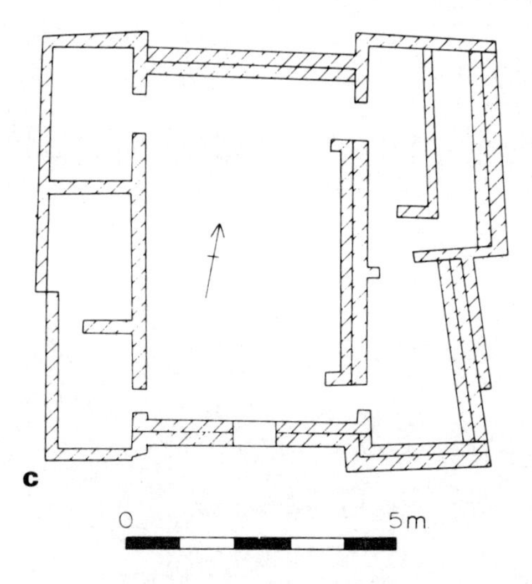

Figure 3 (*c*). Qalinj Agha, Uruk house, after Hijara, *Sumer*, XXIX, 1973, Pl. 3 (Arabic section).

An interesting Halaf feature pertinent to arguments about the evolution of social structure is the return of the round house. Although the tholoi at Arpachiyah and Gawra are thought to have some religious significance,[42] it is clear at Yarim Tepe II that the round structures there are purely domestic in character, 7-12.5 m.^{2} in area with one as large as 19 m.^{2} The very great differences between Hassuna and Halaf settlements considered with Halafian connections with areas to the north in Turkey and Syria and even as far as the Caucasus, that is, in regions far beyond the limits of 'Hassuna', indicate the probability that a totally different ethnic group is represented.

By the time of the 'Ubaid settlements of the fifth millennium B.C. social structure is undoubtedly becoming more complex, although we still lack convincing evidence for status distinctions. The size of the largest settlements is significantly greater than those of the Samarran phase, with 'Uqair, for example, approaching perhaps 11 ha. in area.[43] Two important developments should be recorded, the first occurrence of agricultural settlements in Sumer where such an economy was only possible with irrigation, and second, the earliest unequivocal Mesopotamian evidence for buildings that can be interpreted as temples or shrines. At Eridu a sequence of religious buildings culminates in temples virtually indistinguishable in concept and design from later Sumerian temples (Figs. 4b, c).[44] Later textual evidence suggests the possibility that religious 'leaders' combined responsibility for crop fertility with more practical agricultural management, and one suspects but cannot prove that 'authority' in these 'Ubaid settlements was of this sort.

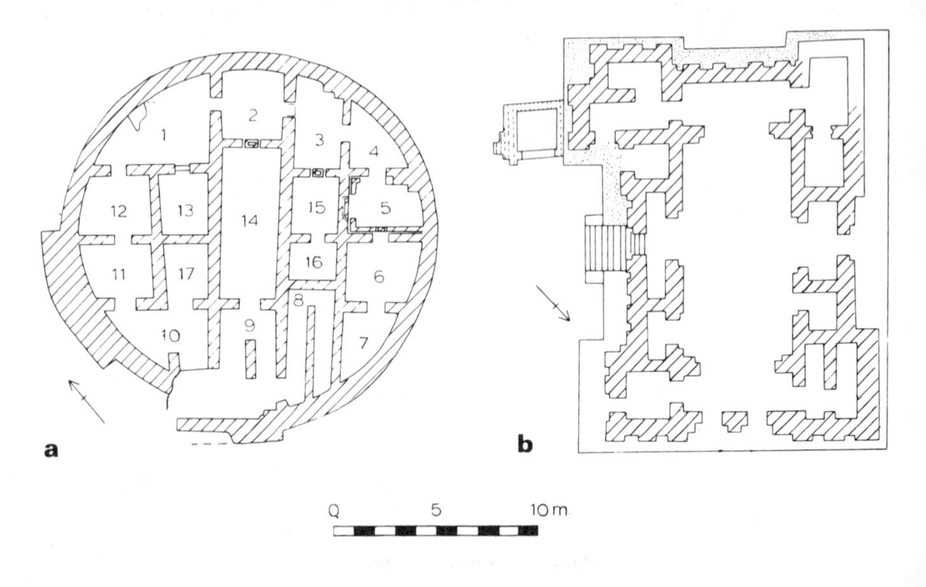

Figure 4 (*a*). Tepe Gawra, 'Round House', level XIA, after Tobler, 1950, Pl. VII.
Figure 4 (*b*). Eridu, Temple VII, after Lloyd and Safar, *Sumer*, III, 1947, Pl. 2.

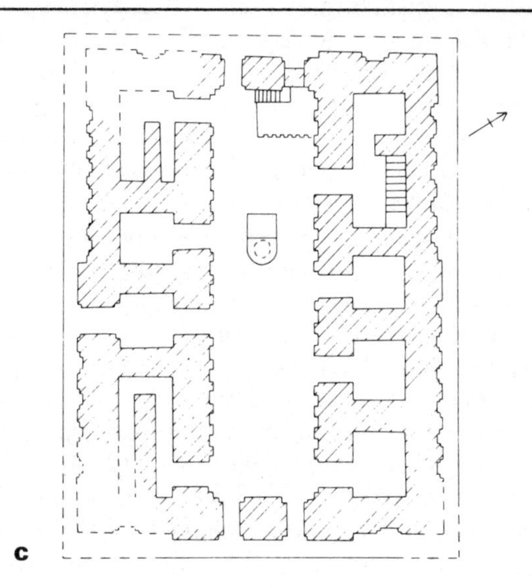

Figure 4 (*c*). Warka, 'White Temple', Anu Ziggurrat, after Heinrich, *U.V.B.*, VIII, 1937, Pl. 19.

Although significant differentiation in grave wealth is almost entirely lacking, the architectural evidence from Tepe Gawra could be interpreted as an indication of the presence of wealthier or in some way superior households; an unusual house in level XIV, for example, has an overall area of 225 m^2.[45] The first house that can reasonably be described as a 'headman's' residence, however, does not appear until the beginning of the Uruk phase at Gawra (Fig. 4a), although this could equally be interpreted as a fortified communal store. Unfortunately only one room (7) gave any clue as to its use and that contained carbonised kernels of grain. By the end of the Uruk phase (Warka IV) an enclosed area of monumental public buildings had been founded at Warka of which the 6 ha. excavated represents only a part. At the same time the earliest examples of stone sculpture depict individuals clearly of some importance though to describe them as 'priests' or 'kings' is not only to exceed the evidence but certainly to lose sight of their undoubtedly varied and complex role in Mesopotamian society.

II. Philological evidence

Our knowledge of social structure in Mesopotamia increases exponentially with the invention of writing (Warka IV, c. 3100 B.C.), but there remain major difficulties in interpretation. By the time the texts are reasonably informative – the earliest are only brief memoranda – urban civilisation had been flourishing in Mesopotamia for about 1,000 years. Thus we often see clearly only the final form of an institution and lack archaeological or textual evidence for its development. Kinship terminology is not revealing,[46] and, unfortunately, few Assyriologists have taken an interest in social organisation, with the exception of a distinguished Russian group whose approach has inevitably been in some respects Marxist.[47] The legal aspects of human relationships as reflected in the so-called law codes have been studied *in extenso*, but documentation remains unsatisfactory owing to difficulties in interpretation and the incomplete nature of the sources.

Undoubtedly the essential point to emphasise in the context of this book is that the relation of persons to property, more particularly property in land, formed the basis of Babylonian social organisation. Moreover – and this point cannot be emphasised too strongly – while it is true that Mesopotamian urban society was theocratically oriented, the role of the temple, even religion as a whole, in the daily life of the citizens has been greatly exaggerated by earlier scholars owing to the one-sided nature of the evidence. The belief in a tutelary deity for each town and city was an early development in Sumerian religious thought[48] and contributed to one of the most basic Sumerian beliefs, that the city was the actual property of its principal god to whom it was assigned on the day of creation. The temple was literally the god's home, and much of the temple ritual was concerned with the care of his person and the administration of his household. That the tripartite temple plan, known from 'Ubaid times through the Early Dynastic period, reflects simply a common house plan can be seen clearly in Fig. 3c. The fact that the city 'belonged' to the god did not mean that all land was directly owned and administered by the temple – this view has long been abandoned – but it did mean that the focus of loyalty was the city. 'People were identified as citizens of this or that city, and not with a clan or some other kin-related group.'[48]

There is textual evidence which has been interpreted to indicate that in prehistoric village society land was 'owned' by the community, but that it ultimately came under the control of an 'authority', possibly but not certainly with cultic associations, a reconstruction not seriously at variance with the archaeological evidence. Later Mesopotamian religion, however, shows hardly any features traceable to 'primitive' practices such as shamanism, nor does it exhibit any clear dependence on the fertility complex so often associated with neolithic society.[49] Nor are the functions of all temple officials in later periods overtly associated with religion in a ritual sense; even the *sanga*, often translated 'high priest' was clearly more of an administrator than a priest. We do know of one early official, the *ensi*, later a 'city governor'. Originally he was a local 'manager' or 'overseer' of agricultural activities such as ploughing, sowing and irrigating.[50] We have seen that village size alone would indicate the necessity of some authoritarian structure at least by the period of the Samarran communities in Mesopotamia, and an *ensi*-type official would have been essential to the proper maintenance of the systems of irrigation for which we have evidence at Choga Mami.

It must be re-emphasised, however, that there is little or no evidence for status distinctions among Samarran villagers or even in later 'Ubaid society. Indeed, Oppenheim asserts that even the later Mesopotamian city is characterised by 'lack of status stratification'.[51] We suspect, too, that the idea of ruling 'dynasties' comes relatively late in Sumer, possibly as late as ED II/III.[52] In Palestine, as we have already noted, there exists much earlier evidence both for status distinctions and for a preoccupation with ancestors unknown in Mesopotamia, while in historic times the city orientation of Mesopotamian society contrasts strongly with the patriarchal tribal traditions of the Old Testament. Wealth in some degree and craft specialisation there undoubtedly was among Samarran communities, but to designate these as 'chiefdoms', as has recently been proposed,[36] is to obscure perhaps significant differences between the apparently egalitarian settlements of prehistoric Mesopotamia and societies attested by ethnographic data that have almost certainly evolved under different conditions. Although neither Samarran nor 'Ubaid society can be described as 'ranked' on present archaeological data, there is undoubtedly evidence for the increasing importance of cultic activity. In later times the economic functions of some temple communities were of greater importance than their religious ones, however, though the two were inextricably mixed, and both temple and palace functioned as highly organised commercial and redistributive mechanisms. The widespread appearance of what are almost certainly ration measures, the so-called Uruk bevelled-rim bowls, not long after the end of the 'Ubaid period (Warka XII) strongly suggests some sort of economic organisation centred on the temple by the early fourth millennium B.C.[53]

Hand in hand with the theory of possible communal ownership of property in early communities is that of 'primitive democracy'[54] which is derived from traditional mythological sources but has not met with total acceptance by Assyriologists. It is suggested that political power lay in the hands of the free citizens who met in a bicameral assembly consisting of one house of 'elders' and a lower house of 'men'. This assembly was summoned in times of crisis. Its members did not 'vote' in the modern sense, but agreed by consent, indicating that the 'leader' could only propose what was generally acceptable. The assembly, *unken* (lit. 'circle of the people'), and the title *en* 'lord', appear on the earliest pictographic texts, while the 'Council of Elders' is mentioned as an administrator of temple estates in Jamdat Nasr (Warka III) times when Diakonov suggests 'the temple estates had not yet been separated from the community'.[55] In Shuruppak (Fara) the ED III documents were apparently dated by eponyms who may have been Elders presiding in turn in the Council,[56] and as late as the Old Babylonian period the dignity of *rabianum*, 'mayor' of a small community, rotated by year among the 'Elders'.[57] By then the Assembly had become merely an organ of local administration, but it could nevertheless write letters to the king, make legal decisions, sell real estate and assume corporate responsibility for robbery or murder committed within its jurisdiction.[58]

The title usually translated as 'king' does not occur in the earliest texts but both 'king' and 'palace' are found in the archaic texts from Ur (ED I, early third millennium B.C.). Jacobsen has suggested that the king was originally selected by the assembly for specific 'military' duties but that as the power and functions of the city-state grew, so grew the need for a more permanent military leader. It is perhaps significant that the earliest city walls and buildings that can be identified with reasonable certainty as 'palaces' appear in Early Dynastic II,[59] and that a number of military terms appear in the Ur texts along with *lugal* and *é-gal*, 'king' and 'palace'. Warfare is a human activity that calls for highly ramified organisation, and must have contributed to the complexity of social and political structure that emerges in the 'palace' organisation in Sumer at this time, though there is no evidence whatsoever that it was in any way a precipitating factor in the actual growth of settlements of urban proportions. Jacobsen points out a very basic difference in the development of the authority of the 'lord' (*en*), a title associated at an early period with Uruk, and 'king' (*lugal*) known from Ur. In the case of the *en* the political side of the office was originally secondary to the cult function, but in cities where the chief deity was a goddess, as in Uruk, the *en* was male and attained, because of the economic importance of his office, a position of major political importance as 'ruler'. In cities where the chief deity was male, as in Ur, the *en* was a woman who, while important in religious matters, never became a 'ruler'. Whether male and politically important or female and only cultically significant, the *en* lived in a building, the *Giparu*, which, where the *en* was male, in time took on the features of an administrative centre, a 'palace'; where the *en* was female, as in Ur, this did not happen. The *lugal*, on the other hand, was from the beginning a purely secular figure.[60]

In Mesopotamia both kings and gods were seen simply as heads of rather special households, and at least from Early Dynastic III onwards society was divided basically into two classes, persons under the authority of the head of a household and persons exercising such authority. Labourers in the 'state' sector, whether secular or religious, were conceived as under the patriarchal authority of the king or god. This group comprised a very specific class who were not in any sense 'slaves' but who lacked some of the rights of free men. Land was held by such persons on prebend in return for 'services', agricultural or 'military'. Other members of this same class were organised within the palace or temple in workshops in a variety of 'manufacturing' services for which they received payment in rations, normally oil, barley and wool. Women of this class engaged in such activities as weaving, spinning, grinding grain and looking after pigs and other domestic animals (professional pottery manufacture was a male occupation). Certain of the more responsible royal and temple servants within this class could attain a high social standing and came to constitute a sort of aristocracy.

This state sector never encompassed the whole of society, nor even a major portion of it. In the mid-third millennium, documents from Shurrupak and Bismaya record real estate sales by private individuals and records show even the king buying and selling land.[61] The approximately contemporary Lagash texts attest the presence of large patriarchal families whose land could be alienated and sold, but only by the chosen family representative, not necessarily the head, with other members of the family participating as witnesses.[62] Free men of the community were liable to certain civic obligations, including taxes in labour and possibly also in kind. The wealthier families possessed estates measuring hundreds of acres with labour performed by 'dependants' whose status resembled that of the temple or state 'dependants'.

Slavery was recognised as an institution but the effective role of slaves in the economy of most of ancient Mesopotamia was insignificant.[63] Many slaves were prisoners of war, though freemen could be reduced to slavery as punishment for certain offences and a family could sell children in times of need. Slaves performed minor tasks, for instance as household servants, but they were always much fewer in number than the *guruš* or 'dependant' class. In fact the system dominating the picture of early Mesopotamian economic history is of this semi-free class of labourers receiving prebendary land and 'rations'; it was not until c. 2000 B.C. or later that the rise of free labourers offering their services as *lú-ḫun-gá* 'hirelings' brought about a radical change in the economic and social system and with it the institution of *á*, 'wages'.[63]

Thus there existed by the end of the Early Dynastic period four classes of society: leading families including the 'king' and temple officials, ordinary free men, the *guruš* or dependant class, and slaves. In economic terms society fell into two basic groups, however, those owning the means of production and 'dependants' and slaves who did not. It would appear that status stratification was almost entirely economic and there was never a 'warrior' class nor even a standing army.[64] Moreover, in spite of intensive craft and administrative specialisation, even the highest classes of officials participated in labour or public works such as canals and irrigation, what Gelb has termed the 'everybody-works' principle.[65] All officials and free men held land in some capacity; thus society continued to be entirely 'agricultural'. Neither Sumerian nor Akkadian terminology makes any distinction as to size of settlement: *uru, ālum* signifies any settled habitation from the smallest hamlet to the largest city.

Larger kinship units such as the extended family, for which there is archaeological evidence as early as the sixth millennium, were possibly characteristic of the older historic periods,[62] but as cities grew in size and complexity the strong sense of community identity tended to minimise extended family ties so that there are no vestiges of tribal organisation in later Mesopotamian cities. On the other hand, although the term *mārē āli*, literally 'sons of the city', is often translated 'citizens', it seems unlikely that this implies a concept of citizenship in the Classical sense. Unattached individuals fell into the category of 'refugees', however,[66] and there is evidence to suggest that 'foreigners' were allowed to settle only in certain parts of the city but that foreign emissaries and traders enjoyed a special administrative, political and social status. As early as the Shuruppak texts 'visitors to the city' appear in the accounts as working for the palace; responsible for them is not the normal 'foreman' but a 'police constable'.[52] The concept of and terminology relating to hospitality are conspicuously absent.[66] Guild-like associations of craftsmen, presumably organised across social backgrounds, are common, although they were not independant entities like their counterparts in mediaeval times but functioned within the 'household' structure of the palace or temple.

Despite the changes that took place in the cities, the older form of extended family appears to have remained characteristic of country areas throughout Babylonian history, no doubt for essentially economic reasons. It must remain uncertain how far the patrilineal, patrilocal extended family pattern reflects an origin in specifically Semitic (?Akkadian) tribal organisation, still to be seen among Bedu tribes and settled village society, or whether Sumerian family groupings were in any way different. As seen in the later texts the Sumerian family was patrilinear, nuclear and monogamous, but there are tantalising and, one must emphasise, undoubtedly ambiguous hints of a perhaps different pattern in earlier times, for example a reference in the 'reform' text of Urukagina (c. 2350 B.C.) that could be interpreted as a reference to polyandry.[67] There also occur genealogies that trace descent in part through women, and we know that women held administrative posts, could own property, engage in business and qualify as witnesses. It is frustrating to know so little of Sumerian origins because it is conceivable, though one can put it no higher than that, that whatever is 'Sumerian' in the pattern we have described derives from a distinctly different ecological and technological background, and it was in Sumer that 'spontaneous' urban society arose. The antecedents of the Sumerians remain a continuing subject for controversy,[68] but archaeological evidence – in part admittedly negative – suggests strongly that they may have been an indigenous population whose way of life was in many ways comparable with that of the present-day Marsh Arabs.[69] With resources of fish, water fowl, wild pig and the date palm whose products supply many demands from architectural to gastronomic, a hunting and collecting economy would have been viable in the marsh areas that are known to have existed in prehistoric Sumer and could have supported essentially settled groups whose traces are now archaeologically undetectable. The very basic Near Eastern economic pattern of cereal agriculture would have been acquired from elsewhere; such 'southerners' could have been cultivators of the date palm but not farmers in the generally accepted sense.

Unfortunately we are unlikely ever to unravel the tangled cultural threads of the various linguistic substrata that are known to have been present in Sumer at the time of the earliest written records (there may be at least one other than Semitic Akkadian and Sumerian, whose speakers some would credit with the invention of writing). The close proximity of agricultural and grazing land in Sumer has always encouraged contact, and conflict, between settled farmers and nomadic herdsmen, but in suggesting that there may have been peculiarly 'Semitic' elements in third millennium society I do not imply that these elements derive from the social organisation of such nomadic tribes. Like many later waves of Semitic-speaking peoples the Akkadians may, at a remote period, have infiltrated into Mesopotamia from the Arabian steppe. Modern analogies suggest that in the gradual process of settling they would have shed many of the patterns of behaviour that were peculiarly adapted to life in the steppe and would have been increasingly assimilated to the economy and social structure of town and village, looking to land-owners for protection and profit. Whether their patrons were townsmen or their own shiekhs metamorphosed into landed gentry is immaterial since the sheikhs are usually among the first to adopt a settled residence and establish title to land which, unlike the psychological quality of leadership, is hereditary. In other words, the settled nomad takes on the colour of his surroundings and probably did so to an even greater extent before Islam introduced the concept of an Arab aristocracy, with its heroic mythology rooted in Bedu tradition.

It is imprudent to speculate about the ethnic composition of prehistoric populations, but one can perhaps go so far as to suggest that the Samarran settlements of Middle Mesopotamia were neither Semitic nor Sumerian, and one may assert unequivocally that the early farmers of what was later Assyria and northern Babylonia were *not* people who 'came out of the hills' and settled on the plains. The peoples of the 'Hassuna' and 'Jarmo' settlements were essentially different and at least partially contemporary groups, whose chipped stone and ceramic industries differ fundamentally, and one cannot assume that they necessarily display parallel social development.

The relationship of persons to property has already been emphasised as the crucial factor in Mesopotamian social organisaiton. This is, of course, reflected in the controls regulating inheritance and marriage. Again we are fortunate in having considerable textual documentation, in particular from the 'law codes', though these relate largely to periods of Semitic dominance. The aim of the texts was not to 'codify' existing oral tradition so much as to revise certain aspects of responsibility and liability in the light of changing social and economic conditions. Thus the law of succession is mentioned only incidentally, but by inference it would appear that sons alone (unless the word for 'sons' may conceivably include 'daughters') succeeded to whole property, although widows and daughters (?unmarried) had certain claims to inherit. The normal practice would appear to have been division into equal shares, the Old Testament preferential right of the eldest son being rare.[70] On marriage daughters received a dowry (*šeriktum*) and it would appear that daughters who were 'priestesses' who had not received the *šeriktum* were entitled to a share in the estate; provision was also made to ensure unmarried daughters' dowries and younger brothers' marriage expenses. It was common for brothers to hold inherited fields in common to prevent their division into small lots.

Professor Goody in a previous paper[71] has analysed differences in systems of inheritance on the basis of cross-cultural material in Murdock's *Ethnographic Atlas*. He has found that in major Eurasian societies property tends to be distributed directly from parents to children of both sexes, i.e. by diverging devolution. The tight control of property represented by such inheritance is seen as 'deriving from the intensive exploitation of resources which is linked to the growth of complex political institutions'. The association of diverging transmission with intensive (and plough) agriculture, with large states and with complex systems of stratification is noted. 'In such societies social differentiation, based on productive property, exists even at village level; to maintain the position of the family, man endows (and controls) his daughters as well as sons, and these ends are promoted by the tendency towards monogamous marriage. Indeed it is significant that the strongest associations of diverging devolution are with monogamy and plough agriculture.'

We cannot identify the earliest use of the plough in Mesopotamia, though draught animals would have been available from the time of the earliest farming communities in the northern plain. Archaeological evidence of 'hoes' is not helpful and does not preclude the use of the plough, as we know from the 'Farmer's Almanac' that fields continued to be hoed as well as ploughed.[72] In Mesopotamia, moreover, it is probably not so much the plough but the development of irrigation techniques that brings about the intensification of cultivation and the increasing value of land, especially that situated strategically in relation to water resources. It is no longer fashionable to suggest that irrigation *per se* played a major role in social and political development in Mesopotamia, but archaeological data for the early and extensive employment of this technique are only now forthcoming. Moreover, writers who have suggested a simple reliance on essentially natural water courses and the damming of flood waters, i.e. the lack of any need for extensive community cooperation, have failed to appreciate the major difference between the river regimes of the Tigris and Euphrates and those of the Nile and Indus, the former flooding destructively and for agricultural purposes uselessly at the time of the harvest (spring) and the latter beneficially just before the autumn planting season.

We can now demonstrate that a high level of community cooperation *was* necessary to maintain irrigation systems at the level that we have found them in Samarran, i.e. sixth millennium B.C., contexts and to guarantee an equitable distribution of the water available.[34] 'Major hydraulic schemes' are without doubt a much later phenomenon, but the scale of cooperation required even at a simple level, in particular to carry out yearly maintenance, must certainly have been a factor in the development of an increasingly complex authoritarian structure in Mesopotamian society.[73] Perhaps it is relevant that irrigation was probably employed both at Jericho and Çatal. Irrigation agriculture meant too that surpluses could for the first time be guaranteed and that mechanisms for their redistribution or other deployment became necessary, an important step in the formal organisation of trade vital to a country lacking in all essential raw materials except mud and water. Even water was a limited resource, and Sumer is unusual in that there was never a shortage of potentially cultivable land, only the water with which to irrigate it.[74] Another feature of Mesopotamian agriculture was that salination resulting from poor drainage led to the unusual phenomenon of 'shifting irrigation cultivation'.

Growth of population is a fashionable explanation of the evolution of civilisation, but in Mesopotamia at least the data are not available to enable us to assess with certainty whether the technology or the growth came first, although the appearance of 'Ubaid settlements from Saudi Arabia to northern Mesopotamia *following* the earliest stage at which we can detect the use of irrigation on more than the most minimal scale would seem to suggest at least the possibility of the former.[75] Moreover, population studies based on recent surveys show clearly both that the significant increase in size of major centres and the growth of a clustered pattern of settlement around them, reflecting a possible hierarchical ordering, occur at different points in time in different parts of the country.[76]

The role of religion in the development of society is often underestimated as the tangible evidence is often negligible and easily misunderstood, but the later economic function of the Mesopotamian temple implies an earlier importance of cultic activity not only as a possible cohesive force in the community but as a practical economic institution regulating local agricultural activities and providing a mechanism for foreign exchange. Unfortunately, archaeological data, and even to a considerable extent philogical data of the type available to us in Mesopotamia, can nowhere detect the implicit and often unexpressed ideas that regulate the way in which a society behaves and which must be of more relevance to social patterning than either environment or technology.

NOTES

1 Piggott, S. (1972), 'Conclusion', *in* Ucko, P.J., Tringham, R. and Dimbleby, G.W. (eds.), *Man, Settlement and Urbanism,* London, p. 951.

2 A fuller presentation of the archaeological evidence from Mespotamia together with a more extensive bibliography can be found in Oates, J. (1973), 'The background and development of early farming communities in Mesopotamia and the Zagros', *P.P.S.*, 39.

3 Salonen, A. (1968), *Agricultura Mesopotamica*, Helsinki, pp. 202-12; Kramer, S.N. (1963), *The Sumerians*, Chicago, pp. 340-2.

4 Wahida, G. (n.d.), 'A reconsideration of the Upper Palaeolithic in the Zagros Mountains', unpub. Cambridge dissertation; comparable evidence comes also from a survey being carried out in Luristan by Peder Mortensen (pers. comm.).

5 Braidwood, R.J. and Howe, B. (1960), 'Prehistoric investigations in Iraqi Kurdistan', *S.A.O.C.*, 31.

6 Solecki, R.L. (1964), 'Zawi Chemi Shanidar, a Post-Pleistocene village site in northern Iraq', *Rep. VIth Intern. Cong. Quatern., Warsaw.*

7 Wright, H.E. Jr. (1968), 'Natural environment of early food production', *Science*, 161. See also Braidwood, R.J. (1972), 'Prehistoric investigations in south-western Asia', Proc. Am. Phil. Soc., 116, pp. 317-18.

8 Hole, F. and Flannery, K.V. (1967), 'The prehistory of south-western Iran', *P.P.S.*, 33.

9 Flannery, K.V. (1972a), 'The origins of the village as a settlement type in Mesoamerica and the Near East', *in* Ucko, Tringham and Dimbleby (1972).

10 Perrot, J. (1966), 'Le gisement Natufien de Mallaha (Eynan), Israel', *L'Anthrop.*, 70.

11 van Loon, M. (1968), 'The Oriental Institute excavations at Mureybit, Syria: preliminary report on the 1965 campaign', *J.N.E.S.* 27; see now also report on 'Natufian' levels in J. Cauvin (1972), 'Nouvelles fouilles à Tell Mureybet (Syrie): 1971-72, rapport préliminaire', *Annales arch. arabes syriennes,* 22, pp. 105-15; Cauvin, J. (1974), in *Antiquités de l'Euphrate,* Aleppo Museum catalogue, Nov. 1974, pp. 45-50.

12 Kirkbride, D. (1966), 'Five seasons at Beidha', *P.E.Q.*; Kirkbride, D. (1967), 'Beidha 1965: an interim report', *P.E.Q.*; Kirkbride, D. (1968), 'Beidha: early Neolithic village life south of the Dead Sea', *Antiquity,* 42.

13 Flannery (1972a), p. 33.

14 See also Garrod, D.A.E. (1940), 'Notes on some decorated skeletons from the Mesolithic of Palestine', *Annual Br. Sch. Athens*, XXXVII, 1936-37.

15 Perrot, J. (1973), 'Beisamun', *I.E.J.*, 23, pl. 24; de Contenson, H. (1971), 'Tell Ramad', *Archaeology*, 24.

16 Cook and Heizer's data suggest a minimum requirement of 2 $m.^2$ per individual up to a maximum of 6 persons, floor space approaching c. 10 $m.^2$ per person only as the mean number of occupants increases over 6. Cook, S.F. and Heizer, R.F. (1968), 'Relationships among houses, settlement areas and population in Aboriginal California', *in* Chang, K.C. (ed.), *Settlement Archeology*, Palo Alto.

17 French, D. (1972), 'Settlement distribution in the Konya Plain', *in* Ucko, Tringham and Dimbleby (eds.), 1972. For the site of Çatal, see Mellaart, J. (1967), *Çatal Hüyük*, London, and reports in *Anatolian Studies*, 1962-66.

18 cf. *inter alia*, Lee, R.B. and DeVore, I. (eds.) (1968), *Man the Hunter*, Chicago.

19 Kirkbride (1968), p. 270; Kirkbride (1967), pp. 12-13.

20 Flannery (1972a), Fig. 4.

21 Kirkbride (1968), p. 270.

22 Mortensen, P. (1970), 'A preliminary study of the chipped stone industry from Beidha', *Acta Arch.*, XLI; Mortensen, P., (1973), 'On the reflection of cultural changes in artifact materials, with special regard to the study of innovation contrasted with type stability', *in* Renfrew, C. (ed.), *The Explanation of Culture Change: Models in Prehistory*, London.

23 Smith, P.E.L., 'Ganj Dareh Tepe', *Iran*, 1967 onwards.

24 Mortensen, P., Meldgaard, J. and Thrane, H. (1964), 'Excavations at Tepe Guran, Luristan', *Acta Arch.*, 34; Mortensen, P. (1972), 'Seasonal camps and early villages in the Zagros', *in* Ucko, Tringham and Dimbleby (eds.) (1972).

25 See reconstructed plan in Flannery (1972a), Fig. 5.

26 Forge, A. (1972), 'Normative factors in the settlement size of Neolithic cultivators (New Guinea)', *in* Ucko, Tringham and Dimbleby (eds.) (1972), p. 371.

27 Kirkbride, D. (1972 on), 'Umm Dabaghiyah', *Iraq* XXXIV, onwards.

28 Merpert, N.Y. and Munchaev, R.M. (1973), 'Early agricultural settlements in the Sinjar plain, northern Iraq', *Iraq*, XXXV.

29 Lloyd, S. and Safar, F. (1945), 'Tell Hassuna', *J.N.E.S.*, IV.

30 Bökönyi, S. (1972), 'Zoological evidence for seasonal or permanent occupation of prehistoric settlements', *in* Ucko, Tringham and Dimbleby (eds.) (1972).

31 De Contenson, H. (1966), 'Découvertes récentes dans le domaine du Néolithique en Syrie', *L'Anthrop.*, 70.

32 Abu al-Soof, B. *et al.*, 'Tell es-Sawwan', *Sumer* 1965 onwards.

33 Oates, J. (1969), 'Choga Mami 1967-68: a preliminary report', *Iraq*, XXXI.

34 Oates, D. and J. 1976, 'Early irrigation agriculture in Mesopotamia'.

35 Oates, J. (1972), 'Prehistoric settlement patterns in Mesopotamia', *in* Ucko, Tringham and Dimbleby (eds.) (1972), p. 306.

36 Flannery, K.V. (1972b), 'The cultural evolution of civilisations', *Ann. Rev. Ecology and Systematics*, 3, p. 403.

37 The only two possible exceptions among the graves published so far are grave 25, room 3, *Sumer* 1965, p. 25, which may have contained more than one adult, and grave 201/a, *Sumer* 1968, p. 91.

38 Naroll, R. (1956), *Amer. Anthrop.*, 58, p. 690.

39 The Choga Mami tower is illustrated in Porada, E. (1974), 'Mesopotamien und Iran', *in* Mellink, M.J. and Filip, J., *Frühe Stufen der Kunst*, Berlin, Pls. 77-8.

40 cf. the 'workshop' at Arpachiyah: Mallowan, M.E.L.M. and Rose, J.C. (1935), 'Prehistoric Assyria, the excavations at Tall Arpachiyah', *Iraq*, II, p. 17.

41 McKerrell, H. and Davidson, T., pers. comm.

42 Mallowan and Rose (1935), p. 34; Tobler, A. (1950), *Excavations at Tepe Gawra II*, p. 43; the small round structures in early Hassuna levels at Yarim Tepe I appear to be also associated with graves.

43 Lloyd, S. and Safar, F. (1943), 'Tell Uqair', *J.N.E.S.*, II; Gibson, McG. (1972), *The City and Area of Kish*, Field Research Projects, Miami, pp. 198-9.

44 Lloyd, S. and Safar, F. (1948), 'Eridu', *Sumer*, IV; see also Oates, J. (1960), 'Ur and Eridu, the prehistory', *Iraq*, XXII, p. 45.

45 Tobler (1950), p. 36, Pl. XIV.

46 cf. most recently, Sjöberg, A.W. (1967), 'Zu einigen Verwandtschaftsbezeichnungen im Sumerischen', *Heidelberger Studien zum Alten Orient*.

47 In English, see especially Diakonoff, I.M. (1972), 'Socio-economic classes in Babylonia and the Babylonian concept of social stratification', *in* Edzard, O.D. (ed.), *XVIII Rencontre assyriologique internat., Munich, Bayer, Ak.-Abh., phil. hist. Kl. Abh., N.F. 75*; also Diakonoff, I.M. (ed.) (1969), *Ancient Mesopotamia*, Moscow. Western contributions include sections on 'society' in Oppenheim, A.L. (1964), *Ancient Mesopotamia*, Chicago; and Kramer, S.N. (1963), *The Sumerians*, Chicago; also Kramer's review of R. McC. Adams' important contribution, *The Evolution of Urban Society* (in *J.N.E.S.*, 27, 1968, pp. 326-30); Oppenheim, A.L. (1967), 'A new look at

the structure of Mesopotamian society', *J.E.S.H.O.*, X; and articles by T. Jacobsen and I.J. Gelb cited elsewhere.

48 Kramer (1968), especially p. 328, notes 7-9.

49 Oppenheim (1967), p. 13, n. 1.

50 Jacobsen, T. (1957), 'Early political development in Mesopotamia, *Z.A.N.F.*, 52, p. 123.

51 Oppenheim (1967), p. 11.

52 Jacobsen (1957), pp. 121-2.

53 Nissen, H.J. (1970), 'Grabung in den Planquadraten K/L XII in Uruk-Warka', *Baghdader Mitteilungen, 5,* pp. 136 ff.; see also Johnson, G.A. (1973), 'Local exchange and early state development in south-western Iran', *Anth. Papers, Michigan,* 51, pp. 129 ff.

54 Jacobsen, T. (1943), 'Primitive democracy in ancient Mesopotamia', *J.N.E.S.*, II; Jacobsen (1957).

55 Diakonoff, I.M. (1956), 'The rise of the despotic state in ancient Mespotamia', *in* Diakonoff (ed.) (1969), p. 183.

56 Or possibly city wards, cf. Diakonoff (1956), p. 183, n. 11.

57 Landsberger, B. (1955), 'Remarks on the archive of the soldier Ubarum', *J.C.S.*, 9, p. 127, n. 44; see also Oppenheim (1967), pp. 6-7.

58. Code of Hammurapi, sections 23-4.

59 It should be noted that a considerably earlier building in the Eanna complex at Warka, originally designated 'Temple E', has now been tentatively identified as a 'palace', in the sense that it is an obviously ceremonial structure which bears little resemblance in plan to the contemporary tripartite buildings that are conventionally – though not certainly – identified as temples. On the other hand the plan of this 'palace' embodies neither the administrative nor the residential quarters that are characteristic of later Mesopotamian palaces. Its exact function – or indeed the function of the whole level IV complex – seems impossible to define on present evidence. It should be emphasised too that the city of Warka did not grow up around the Eanna 'sanctuary' (Friedman and Rowlands, this volume) but that the latter developed long after the settlement was well-established (see Nissen, H.J. (1972), 'The city wall of Uruk', *in* Ucko, Tringham and Dimbleby (eds.) (1972), esp. p. 794).

I am very much indebted to Dr. Mark Brandes for information about the level IV 'Temple E'/'Palace', as Professor Lenzen's report was not available to me in Cambridge when this paper was written. See now Lenzen, H.J. (1974), *U.V.B.*, XXV, pp. 15-22 and Pls. 30-32.

60 Jacobsen (1957), p. 107, n. 32.

61 Kramer (1963), p. 75.

62 For a discussion of Sumerian *imria/imrua*, 'extended family', ? 'clan', see Sjöberg (1967), pp. 202-9. See also Kramer (1968), and Jacobsen (1957), p. 121, n. 63. For 'clan' or 'city' totems, cf. also Jacobsen, T. (1967), 'Some Sumerian city-names', *J.C.S.*, 21, p. 101, and Biggs, R.D. (1973), 'Pre-Sargonic riddles from Lagash', *J.N.E.S.*, 32, p. 26.

63 Gelb, I.J., (1965), 'The ancient Mesopotamian ration system', *J.N.E.S.*, 24.

64 The early second millennium archive of the 'soldier' Ubarum is particularly informative in this respect; Landsberger (1955).

65 Gelb, I.J. (1967), 'Approaches to the study of ancient society', *J.A.O.S.*, 87.

66 Oppenheim (1964), p. 78.

67 Kramer (1964), p. 322.

68 See Jones, T.B. (ed.) (1969), *The Sumerian Problem*, New York.

69 Thesiger, W. (1964), *The Marsh Arabs*, London; Salim, M.S. (1962), *Marsh Arabs of the Euphrates Delta*, London.

70 Driver, G.R. and Miles, J.C. (1952), *The Babylonian Laws*, Oxford, p. 331.

71 Goody, J. (1969), 'Inheritance, property and marriage in Africa and Eurasia', *Sociology*, 3.

72 See note 3; the distinctive Hassuna hoes are *not* found in agricultural

settlements but in the context of apparently semi-nomadic society, while the finest stone hoe I have ever seen comes from an Early Dynastic context!

73 One should perhaps note that irrigation systems in Mesopotamia, which were subject to frequent flooding and heavy deposition of silt, would have demanded vastly more organised effort for their maintenance than, for example, the rice terraces of the Ifugao in the Philippines or canal systems in Ceylon, where such problems scarcely arise. Such systems, moreover, can be extended and employed over hundreds of years, in sharp contrast to the relatively limited life of canal and even river channels on the almost level Mesopotamian alluvial plain. Barton suggested that the Ifugao terraces represent 2,000 years of construction, while Leach mentions 1,400 years for the building of one Sinhalese canal system (R.F. Barton, *Ifugao Law*, Berkeley, Cal.; E.R. Leach, 'Hydraulic society in Ceylon', *Past and Present,* 15, 1959).

74 Warriner, D. (1948), *Land and Poverty in the Middle East*, London.

75 As does Flannery's population graph for Khuzistan, particularly now that the date for the introduction of irrigation must be moved back to the point at which his curve begins to change direction: (1969), 'Origins and ecological effects of early domestication in Iran and the Near East', *in* Ucko, P.J. and Dimbleby, G.W., *The Domestication and Exploitation of Plants and Animals*, London, p. 93.

76 Adams, R. McC. and Nissen, H.J. (1972), *The Uruk Countryside*, Chicago, pp. 88-90.

IVOR WILKS

Land, labour, capital and the forest kingdom of Asante: a model of early change

Introduction

The kingdom of Asante emerged, in its historic form, only in the later part of the seventeenth century. In the course of the eighteenth century it became the centre of an imperial system which extended some four hundred or so miles inland from the Atlantic seaboard on the South. In the nineteenth century the kingdom moved toward what in a European context is conveniently if ambiguously termed 'nation-statehood', and, in confrontation with imperial Britain at the end of that century, came remarkably close to maintaining its independence into the twentieth century. Asante survives today as the most historically conscious and culturally integrated of all the regions of the Republic of Ghana, within which its traditional capital, Kumase, is the second largest city. The Asante achievement has been a notable one in that the heartland of the kingdom lay in the humid forest zone, an environment not usually considered conducive to the emergence of large-scale polities.[1] It will be the central suggestion of this paper that the emergence of the political kingdom in the seventeenth century was predicated upon a major socioeconomic transformation which had occurred over the preceding two to three centuries, whereby the agrarian order was established. It is toward an understanding of the nature of the transformation that this paper is addressed.

The first part of this study describes the 'traditional' agricultural economy of the Asante region – 'traditional' in the sense of ancient, but also in a sense that distinguishes its continued existence from the 'modern' rural economy based upon production of cocoa as a cash crop. It must be emphasised, however, that the model of the 'traditional' economy developed here by design takes no account of changes already occurring in the nineteenth century, when the growth of Kumase and other towns led to changes in the organisation of production in their rural hinterlands to meet the demands of the urban population. The beginnings of rural capitalism, and the development of a system of *métayage* controlled by wealthy office-holders and others in the towns, are the subjects of a separate paper.

In the second part of this study the view is advanced that in the forestlands of the Akan people, where the Asanteman or Asante Nation was to emerge, the transformation from an economy based upon hunting and gathering activities to one based primarily upon food crop production occurred in the fifteenth to seventeenth centuries, and involved large-scale clearances of the forest. It is argued that the transformation could be effected only by the importation of labour from without the forest zone, and that this was made possible by the advantage which the Akan were able to take of the scarcity of gold in the world bullion market. And finally, it is suggested that the matriclans characteristic of the social organisation of the forest Akan are structures which evolved in the period of the transformation, as people became redistributed in ways appropriate to the new rural order.

Part I: The traditional rural economy

The bioclimatic system

The central Asante region forms part of a larger dissected peneplain composed of pre-Cambrian rocks principally of the Birrimian series, with intruded granites. Most of the land lies between 500 and 1000 feet above sea-level, but folding has left a number of ranges with peaks occasionally rising above 2000 feet. Across the northern part of the region a plateau of Voltaian sandstones extends from north-west to south-east; beyond it the humid forest gives way to wooded savannah.[2] The rainfall of the region is reliable, and shows two annual maxima in May-June and September-October. Total annual precipitation ranges between 50 and 70 inches, and there are six or seven wet months (with over 4 inches of rain) and no dry ones (with less than 1 inch). Annual mean maximum temperature is, for Kumase, 86°, and minimum, 69.6°.[3]

The soils of central Asante are predominately forest ochrosols, with some oxysols and ochrosol-oxysol intergrades.[4] Much of the forest which covers the region today is secondary regrowth,[5] though in some cases of such an age – upwards of half a century – as to approximate in floristic character to the natural climax of moist evergreen and semi-deciduous trees. The major association present is that of Celtis-Triplochiton, though in the northern part of the region this gives way to Antiaris-Chlorophora.[6] Typically, the forest forms a main canopy at about 100-120 feet, out of which emerge higher trees of up to 200 feet or more. Deciduous specimens are represented principally in these higher levels, but are not such as to shed their leaves at the same time in the year. A second and often irregular canopy is formed at around 50 to 60 feet, below which occur layers of shrubs and herbaceous plants. Throughout all levels of the forest are the lianes and creepers, extending in some cases for several hundred feet from the soil to the crowns of the highest trees.[7] The forest was such as to make a profound impression upon early European travellers to Kumase. In 1824, for example, Dupuis wrote of it as,

> magnificent as it was dense and intricate. Numerous plants and creepers of all dimensions chained tree to tree, and branch to branch, clustering the whole in entanglement . . . The opacity of this forest communicated to the atmosphere and the surrounding scenery a semblance of twilight; no ray of sunshine penetrated the cheerless gloom, and we were in idea entombed in foliage of a character novel and fanciful.[8]

The awe felt by many such travellers through the forest was appropriate, perhaps, to their encounter with what has been described as 'the most complex ecosystem on the earth'.[9] Since the concern of this paper is with the clearance of forest land for agricultural purposes, three particular determinants of the structure of the biotic system are to be stressed. First, the dense canopies and stand reduce the intensity of solar radiation to low levels, and also reduce wind velocities. Hence although the loss of water by transpiration is high, that by evaporation is correspondingly low. It has been shown that, computed over several decades, the level of evapotranspiration is more or less equivalent to the level of precipitation. Soil leaching is therefore only slight in the central Asante region so long as the forest cover is not broken.[10]

Secondly, it is a feature of the forest soils that most of the organic matter is concentrated in the top 4-6 inches, below which the nutrient value falls rapidly (and hence the roots of even the larger trees seldom extend more than 4-5 feet below ground level, stability being usually provided by the heavy plank buttresses). The nutrients in the topsoil are derived from the creation of humus, a process dependent upon the continuous return of plant material, especially leaves, to the ground surface, and upon the protection from direct solar radiation and exposure to heavy rainfall afforded to the decomposing materials by the forest cover.[11] And thirdly, the dense canopies and stand, in protecting the soil from direct exposure to heavy rainfall, also prevent soil erosion; thus even the steep slopes characteristic of the forest topography, and so susceptible to gully erosion, can remain stable.[12]

It will be apparent that the bioclimatic system is a complex one. resting upon the maintenance of a balance between the protection and sustenance of the soil provided by the heavy forest cover, and the threat to the soil, through the high levels of insolation and rainfall, presented by the climate. While the renewal cycle of the humid forest is little disturbed by the activities of human communities engaged primarily in hunting and food gathering (not least in that the environment is one more or less immune to the ravages of accidental fires), the effects upon it of those involved in agriculture are likely to be far-reaching. Phillips has referred to 'the meagre knowledge available of the fundamentals of their development and of the changes induced when the forest soils are cultivated',[13] and Ahn has commented on their 'fragility':[14] certainly when the soil is exposed for more than two or three years by removal of the forest cover, leaching occurs, levels of organic matter fall, and serious deterioration in soil fertility follows rapidly. Any form of continuous cultivation has been (and as yet remains) impossible, and the evolution of an agrarian order in the Asante forestlands has clearly involved the acquisition on the part of the cultivators, over time, of a sensitive awareness of the restraints imposed upon the exploitation of the soil by the nature of the bioclimatic system. To the rural Asante the original denizens of the forest, the monsterlike *sasabonsam* and the fairylike *mmoatia*, are still much respected, and in local lore are preserved stories which seem to recapitulate aspects of the farmers' early attempts to establish a satisfactory and productive niche within the forest environment.[15]

The farm as a unit

As late as the 1930s there was little understanding, on the part of those not directly involved, of the nature of the forest bioclimatic system and of the farming practices which it dictated. A survey of the economy of the Gold Coast, produced by the Chief Census Officer in 1931, is illustrative of the view of food crop cultivation then current. He wrote that farming

> was carried out by the system known as that of 'shifting cultivation'. The menfolk selected a small portion of the forest, cleared the undergrowth and cut the lianes. This work was carried out at the beginning of the dry season, and towards the end of that period they set fire to the dry refuse. The larger trees were left but the smaller ones usually perished. Then the womenfolk took possession, planted plantains, maize, groundnuts, yams, onions, ginger, coco-yams in a seemingly haphazard manner, according to what they considered the soil was most suited to produce. In five years or even less the patch would be abandoned and a new one selected. The old farm was exposed to the sun and became jungle so that that particular area was lost to the forest.
>
> This ruinous system of cultivation has been termed 'land robbery'...[16]

The inability to appreciate the nature of the land and crop rotational system is explicable, perhaps, on one count: by the 1930s the food farming sector of the rural economy was in a state of decline in many areas as a result of the increasing concern with the growing of cocoa as a cash crop.[17]

The farm, known in Asante as the *afuo*, was essentially a smallholding capable of supporting a single family. It consisted of two or sometimes three distinct parts, the *afuwa, mfufuwa*, and *mfufuwa-nini*. The land currently under cultivation was the *afuwa*, 'the little farm' or field, and the land under fallow was the *mfufuwa*, literally 'the non-*afuwa*'. A farmer's rights of tenure over his fallow were as secure as those over his land under cultivation. In some cases a farm may have attached to it further land – fallow that has not been brought back into cultivation at the appropriate time because, for example, of unsatisfactory yields, or of the inability of the tenants (through illnesses, deaths, or the like) to resume cropping it. Such land is known as *mfufuwa-nini*, literally 'barren fallow'. The original tenants and their heirs retain rights to the produce from it – to the fruits of palm and kola trees, for example, and to firewood and poles – but Asante law appears not to have defined with any precision the point in time at which others might acquire rights in it and recommence farming operations. Much litigation results.[18]

The size of the *afuwa*, that is, of the field under cultivation,[19] seldom exceeded more than a few acres. Bray noted food farms in Ahafo of as little as one quarter to one acre in extent;[20] Allen reported the view of Asante farmers and agronomists, that on the forest ochrosols a farm of two to three acres under cultivation adequately supports a family of five;[21] and Killick has shown that in 1963 the average farm in Asante was one of 3.3 acres under cultivation (and in Ahafo, 2.7 acres).[22] The smallness of the field seems in fact to be determined by a number of environmental factors. Regeneration of natural vegetation during fallow, for example, is in part dependent upon recolonisation of the abandoned area by species from the surrounding thicket and forest – a process the rapidity and efficacy of which will therefore be inversely correlated with the size of the former field. Again, the deleterious effects of solar radiation and rainfall on the soil are directly correlated with the extent of the area opened for cultivation; on small clearings run-off will not lead to problems of erosion since the volume of excess water is small and is in any case rapidly absorbed by the surrounding fallow and forest.[23] It is, accordingly, a matter of no surprise to find that the small field has long been characteristic of the Asante rural economy: in the early nineteenth century, for example, Hutton referred to fields of 'up to 2 acres',[24] and Dupuis to 'clearings of several acres'.[25] For the purposes of the computations which follow in this paper it is unnecessary to assume any average figure for the size of the Asante field; it will suffice and be convenient to take a field – *afuwa* – of one hectare (or just under 2.5 acres) as both paradigmatic and not atypical.

It will follow that the size of the farm, that is, of the *afuo* comprising field and fallow, is a function of the span of time a piece of land is kept under cultivation and the span it is left to fallow. On the relatively fertile forest ochrosols it appears to be the customary practice of food farmers to cultivate the field for three years before allowing it to fallow.[26] The initial stage of the fallow is one of forb regrowth, that is of the growth of annual soft-stemmed and leafy herbs which remain dominant for perhaps as little as one and a half years, perhaps as much as four. The second stage of the fallow is that of thicket regrowth; the vegetation is dominated, for up to ten years after the cessation of cultivation, by a mass of perennial shrubs, coppice shoots, climbers and young trees.[27] The thicket regrowth gives way in turn to secondary forest. Soft-wooded and light-demanding species are initially dominant, but are gradually displaced by the slow-growing shade-tolerant species characteristic of the natural climax.[28] Although adequate data are lacking, it would appear that if the fallow is not reclaimed for cultivation, the closed forest may become restored after about sixty years (though immature trees would, of course, still be preponderant).[29]

There is no clear consensus on the optimum length of fallowing on the forest soils for the maintenance of the long-term fertility of the land. It would appear that at least a ten years fallow is necessary before the level of organic matter in the soil approximates to precultivation ones,[30] and Foggie considered the minimum fallow necessary for full recovery of the soil to be fifteen years, twenty or more being preferable.[31] In fact the length of fallow will vary with the quality of the local soil but also with the demographic pressures upon land utilisation.[32] For the purposes of the present analysis, three

Table 1. Levels of exploitation of the forest

Level	Description	Fallow		Restoration of soil fertility	Approx. % of cultivated land to cultivated and fallow land*
		Stage of	Years from end of cultivation		
I	Intensive land rotation	Forb re-growth and early thicket	5–7	inadequate in short term	33
II	Less intensive land rotation	Thicket regrowth and early secondary forest	7–10	inadequate in long term	26
III	Non-intensive land rotation	Secondary forest	10–20	adequate in short and long term	17

*Based on mid-point figures for length of fallow

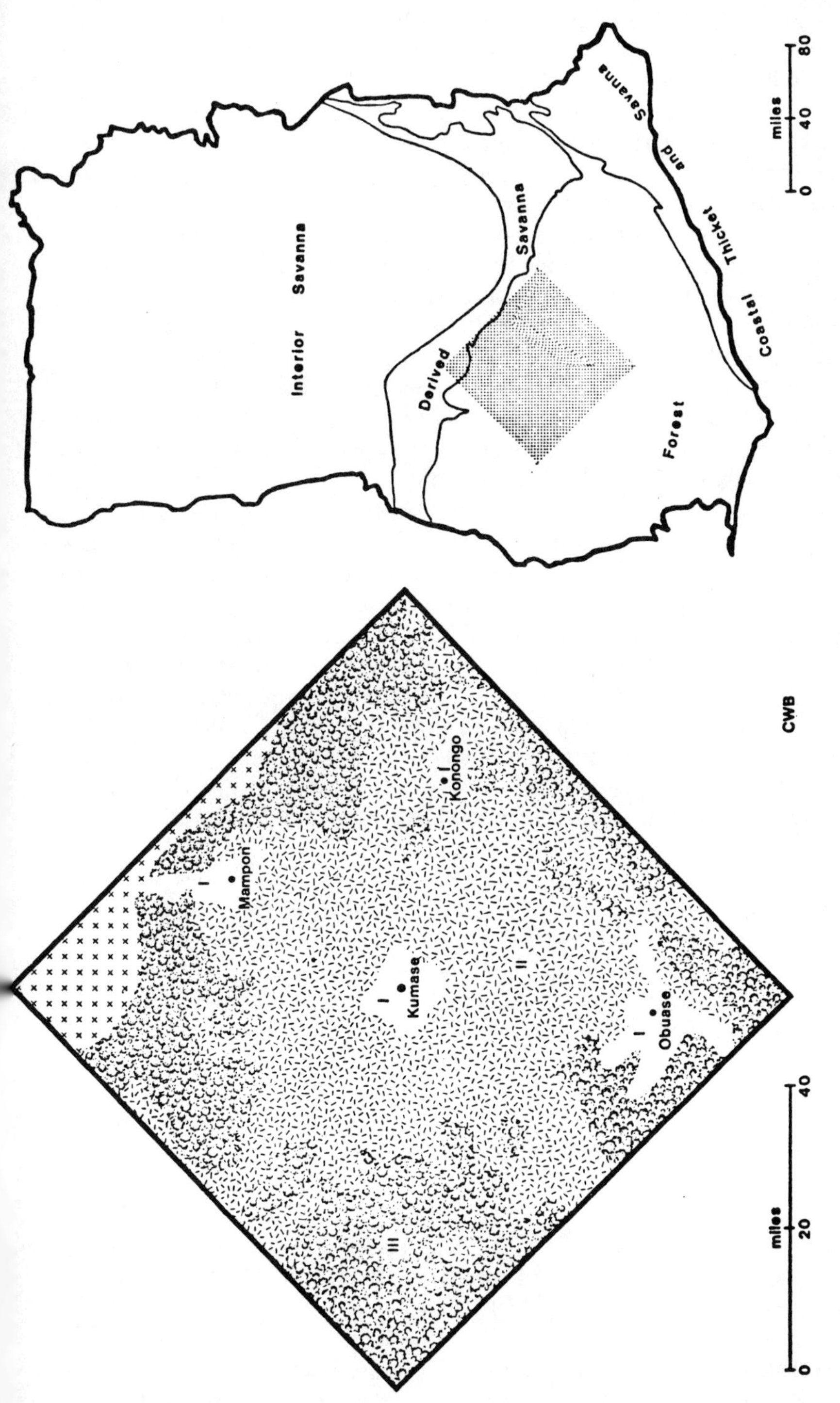

Figure 1. Land utilisation in central Asante, mid twentieth century.

broad levels in the exploitation of the forest environment for food cropping purposes may be distinguished. These are shown in Table I above, which assumes a cultivation period of three years. Reference to Fig. 1 will show the state of exploitation of the forest in central Asante in the middle of the present century.[33] Intensive land rotation (Level I) is practised in the areas immediately surrounding Kumase and other large towns where staple foodstuffs for the urban markets are grown; virtually no forest survives under such conditions. Throughout the greater part of the region less intensive land rotation (Level II) is practised, and cocoa growing is the principal activity; only a small area of natural forest survives, and secondary forest will rarely if ever develop to near climax. Towards the peripheries of the region non-intensive land rotation (Level III) is practised; much natural forest remains (often now reserved), and secondary forest not infrequently approaches near climax. Finally, in the extreme north of the region, burning has created the conditions whereby forest has given way to savannah vegetation – 'derived savannah'.[34]

It is fortunately possible to essay some comparison of the mid-twentieth century situation with that of the early nineteenth, before the introduction of cocoa as a cash crop. European visitors to Kumase were much impressed by what they observed of the rural economy. Their comments leave no doubt that the area around Kumase – then a city of around 20,000 people[35] – was already relatively densely populated and intensively farmed.[36] Bowdich, who travelled to the capital in 1817, was led to remark that 'the extent and order of the Ashantee plantations surprised us', and to comment several times upon their 'order and neatness'.[37] Of the seven miles of country between Esreso ('Sarrasou') and Kumase, he noted:

> there were continued plantations of corn, yams, ground nuts, terraboys, and encruma: the yams and ground nuts were planted with much regularity in triangular beds, with small drains around each, and carefully cleared from weeds,[38]

and of the yam fields he added that they

> had much the appearance of a hop garden well fenced in, and regularly planted in lines, with a broad walk around, and a hut at each wicker gate, where a slave and his family resided to protect the plantations.[39]

Observations made by Hutton in 1820, on farms some five miles or so south of Kumase, supported those of Bowdich. 'We passed,' he remarked,

> several plantations which were well inclosed, and in different places there was as much as two acres of ground cleared, and laid out in

> small beds not greatly dissimilar, or much inferior, to the country gardens in Europe; eschalots, ground nuts, yams, and other vegetables were plentiful. The soil is so rich, and the climate so genial, that the natives have always abundant crops.[40]

It is clear, however, that even near the capital long fallows were allowed: it was presumably of such that Dupuis remarked, in 1820, that 'the forest retained much of its characteristic gloom, and, excepting on the line of the path, its thickets and entanglements'.[41] Again, twenty years later Freeman travelled east from Kumase to Dwaben and, seemingly failing to recognise that the original forest had been felled and that he was viewing secondary regrowth, attributed the inferior stands of trees to poor soil.[42] Nevertheless, some areas of primary forest were to survive near Kumase much later in the century; in the early 1870s 'a deep forest' lay between Kumase and Kaase, only some four miles to its south,[43] and it was not until the end of the century that, for example, the forest 'finished' on the Nhenkwaadiem lands of Kwaaso, twelve miles south-east of Kumase.[44] The indications are, then, that the level of exploitation of the land around the Asante capital in the nineteenth century is to be classified as II, less intensive, rather than as I, intensive.

Correspondingly, the level of the exploitation of the central Asante lands other than those constituting the rural hinterlands of Kumase and a few other towns such as Dwaben and Mampon, must be classified as III, non-intensive, for the nineteenth century. Clearly much natural forest survived. Bowdich reported that the wealthy citizens of the capital continued to send out their labourers to create new farms 'in the more remote and stubborn tracts'.[45] There survived, moreover, communities of those who still depended, seemingly almost exclusively, upon an older mode of production: the exploitation of the food resources of the natural forest. One such was Esiankwanta, which lay on the Cape Coast road only some twenty-five miles south of the capital. It was, Dupuis remarked, a 'little dirty croom [village], inhabited by forty or fifty families, who depend for their support upon the range of the forest'.[46] Nevertheless, the farms which the visitors saw proved as impressive as those much nearer to the capital. Of Asumegya, for example, lying fifteen miles south of Kumase, Dupuis commented that 'its plantations encroach very extensively on the forest, and several large fields were, at this time, well fenced round in a state for the reception of corn and yams,'[47] and of Dompoase fifteen miles further south, that

> the plantations, which are flourishing and extensive, it would seem, are adequate to the supply of a population infinitely greater. Several large corn plats were enclosed, with tolerable fences of bamboo, to preserve the grain from the incursions of wild animals, and of pigs . . .[48]

It is, then, now possible to characterise further the structure of the paradigmatic farm for the region of non-intensive cultivation (Level III). It has been suggested that the *afuwa*, the enclosed field, might typically be about one hectare in extent, and is cropped for three years. The length of fallow will be set at fifteen years, the minimum for full recovery of soil fertility. It will follow that the *afuo* or farm will consist of the enclosed field or *afuwa* of one hectare under cultivation, and of non-cultivated land or *mfufuwa* comprising five earlier fields in various stages of fallow. The whole farm embraces, therefore, some six hectares, and the cycle of cultivation and fallow is one of eighteen years. The structure of the paradigmatic farm is shown in Fig. 2, in the first cycle of its existence and the early stages of the second cycle.

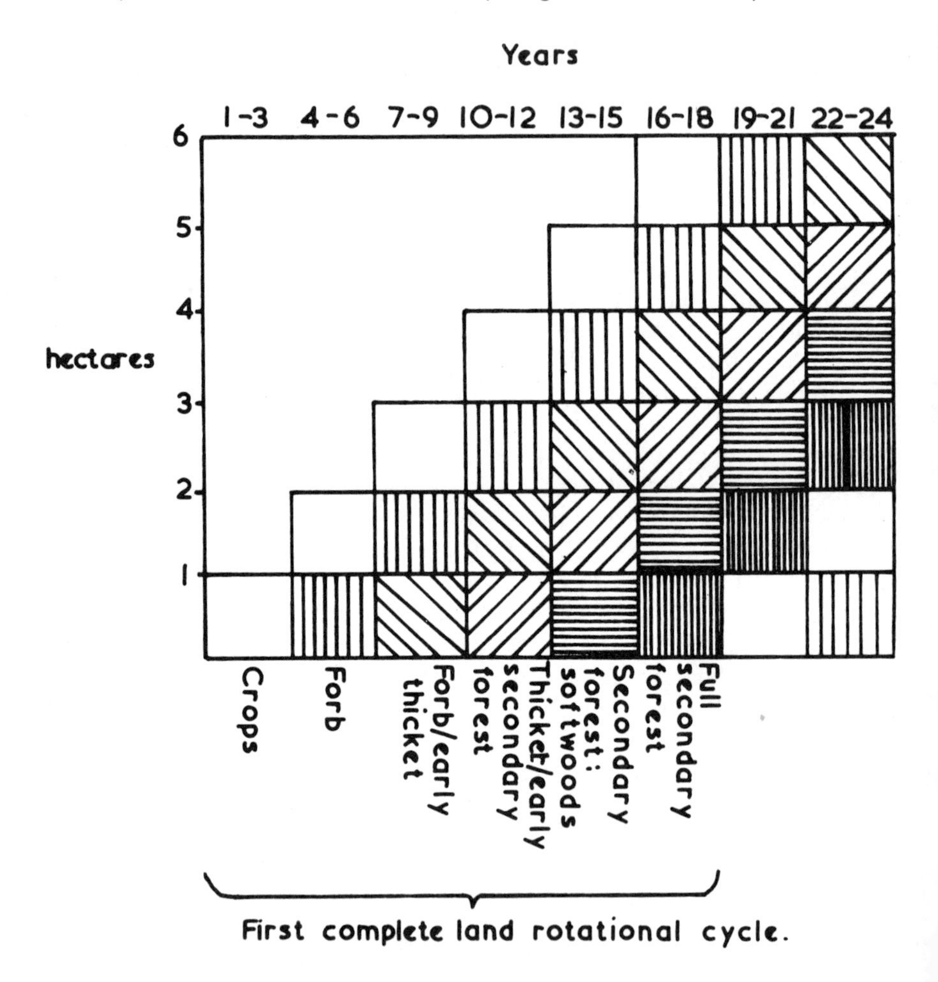

Figure 2. The Asante food farm – a paradigm.

The rural economy: the land factor

The local food production sector has recently been described as 'the Great Unknown of Ghana's economy'.[49] Little studied in the twentieth century, reconstruction of the nature of the agrarian order in former times nevertheless must rest upon extrapolation from imperfect contemporary data – subject only to the control provided by the scant reports of early travellers and by views of the matter contained in traditions orally transmitted by the Asante themselves. The figures offered here are necessarily highly imperfect: while more than merely 'decorative', their main purpose is to heighten the reality of the problems rather than to provide an adequate statistical base. It is, however, crucial to the argument of this paper that what is often described (somewhat pejoratively) as the 'traditional' farming system of Asante is recognised as indeed traditional in the sense that no major changes in the factors of production have occurred at least in the century and a half and more of recorded observation – and by implication longer. This appears to have been the case. First, the crop association is, and has been, one based upon high yielders of bulk foodstuffs, plantain, cocoyam, cassava, and yam, and upon maize which yields less but can be cropped twice in the year. It is true that in the early nineteenth century maize appears to have enjoyed a popularity which has since declined,[50] and that the popularity of cocoyam has probably increased with the introduction of the West Indian *Xanthosoma sagittifolium* in place of the older *Colocasia esculentum*.[51] Such trends, however, are unlikely to have been such as significantly to have changed the Cultivation Factor, that is, the acreage of cultivated land required to support one person. Secondly, the use of wood ash as a fertiliser has long been practised.[52] Otherwise the restoration of soil fertility has always been dependent upon the fallowing system, and indeed it has been recently remarked that 'it has yet to be shown that any form of planted fallow restores the fertility of the soil at a greater rate than the existing natural fallow system'.[53] And thirdly, the implements of husbandry have remained unchanged into this century: the axe, bill hook, hoe and cutlass representing the only investment in capital equipment.[54] Killick's remark, that 'farming embodies techniques that will maintain the fertility of the soil with large inputs of land and labour relative to the small inputs of purchased capital goods', describes not merely the state of the agrarian economy in the twentieth century, but the very nature of the system as such.[55] The factors of food crop production, then, may be taken as having been relatively constant over the span of recorded observation.

The traditional system of food farming is based not only upon land rotation (see fig. 2), but also upon crop rotation. The pattern of cropping is determined by two major considerations. First, the rapid deterioration in soil fertility over the three year cycle of a field dictates that those crops requiring the richer soil, that is, maize and yam, must be grown in the first year, and that only cassava, which grows upon almost exhausted soils, should be planted in the third year. And secondly, the necessity of protecting newly cleared land as rapidly as possible against the deleterious effects of rain and sun dictates that the broad-leaved plantains and cocoyams are established as early as possible. Thus, the maize and yam on the one hand, and plantain and cocoyam on the other, are in fact intercropped, the longer period to maturity of the latter making this practicable.[56] Hence the yam and two maize crops are harvested in the first year, the cocoyam and plaintain in the second continuing into the third, and the cassava in the third continuing if required into the fourth year after the fallow has commenced. While the individual farmer will decide the precise distribution of his land between the various crops, total yields over the three year cycle will be little affected. Table 2 suggests the magnitude of the yields from a one hectare field cultivated over three years; the acreages are simulated on the basis of typical balanced patterns of intercropping. Estimates of yields are conservative ones, made as far as is possible to discount newly introduced and improved varieties.[57] Energy values are computed with reference to the most relevant available data for Ghana.[58] The paradigmatic farm thus yields, over the three years of cultivation, of the order of twelve tons of the five principal staple crops, with an energy value of approximately fourteen and a half million calories.

Table 2. Estimated outputs of one hectare field over three years of cultivation

Year of commencing harvest	Crop	Simulated acreages with inter-cropping	Est. gross yield in tons	Inedible part as % of whole	Calories per 100 grams of edible part	Calories per edible part of gross yield (000s)
1	First maize	1	0.5	68	218	354
	Second maize	1	0.25	68	218	177
	Yam (D.spp)	1	2.5	11	160	3,617
2	Cocoyam (C.esc)	1	2.5	15	108	2,332
	Plantain	1	2.5	45	168	2,347
3	Cassava	1.5	3.75	15	180	5,830
	Totals:		12.0			14,657

The view of Asante agriculturalists, that a typical farm of between two and three acres will support a family of five, has been cited above. This observation may now be tested, and the model of the rural economy developed further. Recent investigations of the food consumption of Asante farmers indicate an average daily intake of 3.86 pounds per person, with an energy value of 1,773 calories. Of these totals, about 80 percent of the daily intake by weight is from the five staples, and about 77 percent by calorific value.[59] In Table 3 the average daily intake of each of the five staples is shown, and the total requirements for five persons over three years is computed. The assumption may reasonably be made, that patterns of food

Table 3. Average food consumption, rural Asante family of five

Staple	Lbs. per person per day	Calorie intake per person per day	Tons per 5 persons per 3 years	Calories per 5 persons per 3 years (000s)
Cassava	0.69	563	1.7	3,082
Cocoyam	1.00	490	2.4	2,683
Yam	0.14	102	0.3	558
Plantain	1.18	899	2.9	4,922
Maize	0.05	49	0.1	268
Totals	3.06	2,103	7.4	11,513

consumption at least in rural areas have not changed significantly in recent times: it has already been noted, for example, that the same staples have been grown certainly since the early nineteenth century. Table 2 and 3, computed from different sets of data, are then comparable, both being relevant to the traditional economy. Several observations may be offered. First, it would seem that the produce of a one hectare field is more than adequate to support a family of five. Secondly, however, allowances must be made for ordinary loss of crops through disease, storms, or damage from animals (whether wild or domestic). And thirdly, allowance must also be made for a fall in yields as a result of an extraordinary failure of the rains, for example, or of a drop in soil fertility through inadequacy of the fallow, or of an insufficiency of labour through death, illness, or the like. It might seem, then, that the one-hectare field is indeed appropriate to the support of a family of five, adequate even in the bad year and yielding a small surplus of food (which might either rot on the farm or be bartered locally) in the good year. The model of the Asante rural economy developed here would thus exemplify a general feature of successful ecosystems, that communities adapt not to usual but to unusual conditions.

It is suggested, then, that an Asante food farm of six hectares may be regarded as paradigmatic: with each hectare under cultivation for three years out of every eighteen, a family of five is adequately supported even in an adverse year. The central Asante region may be envisaged as comprising the block of land about eighty miles square near the centre of which lies Kumase (see fig. 1). Its area is thus some 6,400 square miles, or about 1,657,600 hectares. The proportion of cultivable land to non-cultivable (swamp, steep slope, and so forth), probably approximates to 60 percent;[60] the cultivable land, in other words, comprises some 3,840 square miles or 995,000 hectares. The implications are, then, that if all cultivable land in the region was in fact under cultivation, of the order of 166,000 farms of six hectares each would exist; that if each farm supported five persons, then a total population of about 830,000 people might be supported in the central Asante region; and that in such circumstances a critical density of population would be reached at approximately 130 persons per square mile. The writer has suggested elsewhere that on the basis of the best available data the actual population of the central (or 'metropolitan') Asante region declined in the course of the nineteenth century from about a half million to somewhat below 350,000; or that the density of population fell from about 78 to about 55 per square mile.[61] Crude though the data are, it would seem that the actual maximum density of population in the region in the nineteenth century approximated to no more than 60 percent of the critical density.

It must be stressed again, however, that the model of the rural economy developed here is one specifically of relevance to the sector of non-intensive land use (Level III), and in that sense to 'subsistence'. But by the late eighteenth century the capital, Kumase, and several other major centres of local administration – Bekwae, Dwaben, Kokofu and Mampon for example – had come to offer a wide range of employment opportunities other than farming: in court, in the civil and military administrations, in business, in crafts and so forth. In the early nineteenth century Kumase was already a town of about 20,000 people, few of whom were directly engaged in food production. Since the staple crops are not in general ones that can be transported over long periods of time (and a laden carrier would seldom travel more than ten miles a day in the forest), and since in any case portage added greatly to the sales price of the produce, areas of more intensive agricultural production (Level II) were created around Kumase and the other large towns. Fallows were shortened to permit the more intensive exploitation of the land albeit at the risk of a long-term degeneration in soil fertility, and new patterns in the organisation of the social relations of production become discernible. Lineage land purchased by wealthy townsfolk from families which had fallen into debt was parcelled out among share-croppers – often unfree – who retained a nominal third (*abusa*) of the produce for their own use and supplied the remainder to the entrepreneur. The share-cropper worked longer hours and suffered a lower standard of living than the free farmer on lineage land. A differential was thus created between dearer and cheaper labour which represented, in a sense, the social cost of feeding the urban population; urban growth depended upon agricultural growth, which in turn involved the appearance of a form of landlord tenure (though not, because of the operations of the system of death duties, of landed estates). The matter is, however, a complex one beyond the scope of the present study; the writer has treated it in some detail elsewhere.[62]

The rural economy: the labour factor

The inputs of labour necessary to the cultivation of a one hectare field are irregularly distributed over the three years cropping period. Table 4 shows the monthly variations in rainfall,[63] and identifies the principal farm tasks by season. It will be readily apparent that labour requirements are highest at the beginning of the three year period of cultivation, when the field has to be cleared for planting. Phillips has referred to the 'massive resistance to clearing and subsequent control of regrowth' of the humid forest. He writes,

> Because of the great height and volume of the trees, the frequently densely stocked woody layers, the ramifying lateral extension of many of the root systems, the plank buttresses of massive dimensions, and the tendency for many of the species to coppice, sucker and regenerate from seed, the clearing of these communities is a massive task.[64]

It is the view of Phillips that the moist weight of dead or living vegetation on average undisturbed humid forest lies towards the middle of the range 300 to 700 tons per acre. Mature secondary forest, perhaps of forty to fifty years in age, has been shown to carry about 150 tons per acre dry weight of vegetation, or about 300 tons moist weight,[65] and secondary forest of about twenty years, about 70 tons moist weight.[66] The moist weight of vegetation on secondary forest of fifteen years age – the typical length of fallow assumed in fig. 2 – would therefore be about 40 tons per acre.[67] Clearing a one hectare field from virgin forest would, in other words, involve the removal of some 1,250 tons of vegetation (using Phillips' median figure), and from a fifteen years fallow, of some 100 tons. It will be apparent that the magnitude of labour inputs in the two cases is quite different.

Some account of farming practices in the early nineteenth century was given by Dupuis, who was led to remark, 'the difficulty of clearing spots, for the reception of grain, may well be imagined, where vegetation, both above and below the surface, is knit in such indissoluble bonds'.[68] Dupuis described first the clearing of the coastal scrubland. The thicket was first removed by slaves, using the bill hook; after the upper limbs had been amputated, the larger trees were

Table 4. Major farm tasks distributed by season

Calendar	*Rainfall in inches*	*Clearing and maintenance tasks*	*Planting tasks*	*Harvest tasks*
October	7.915	Clear undergrowth; cut lianes; fell smaller trees		
November	4.325			
December	1.33	Fell larger trees; collect, heap and burn trash; spread ash	Collect planting materials; prepare yam and maize plots	
January	0.735			
February	2.455		Plant yam	
March	5.51	Fence field	Plant maize; Plant cocoyam and plantain	
April	5.69			
May	7.365			
June	9.23			
July	4.73			
August	2.635	Intensive weeding		Harvest yam and first maize
September	6.73		Plant second maize	
October	7.915			
November	4.325			Harvest second maize
December	1.33			
January	0.735			
February	2.455			
March	5.51			
April	5.69			
May	7.365			
June	9.23			Harvest major part of cocoyam and plantain
July	4.73			
August	2.635			
September	6.73	Cutlass to keep forb regrowth low without killing roots		
October	7.915			
November	4.325		Plant cassava	
December	1.33			
January	0.735			
February	2.455			
March	5.51			
April	5.69			
May	7.365			
June	9.23			
July	4.73	Little weeding or cutlassing. Forb fallow allowed to commence		Begin harvesting cassava and continue into fallow as required
August	2.635			
September	6.73			

left standing. The refuse was spread out to dry and then heaped and burned, the ash being spread as fertiliser. Although little or no stumping and rooting was carried out, Dupuis considered the clearing of such scrub as 'infinitely more arduous than in the northern [i.e., savannah] parts of the Ashantee empire'. Neither, however, in his view bore comparison with the task of clearing the humid forest:

> in the more central parts of the kingdom, the features of the land render the process of clearing it infinitely more complicated and laborious, notwithstanding the method resorted to is the same. Here trees of more than ordinary dimensions must necessarily be rooted out, or felled with the thicket . . . The cumbersome growth of fibrous stems and vines, mixed with other plants of a watery nature, requires much labour in hacking to pieces and in removing. The time they take in drying augments the expense of the operation.[69]

The observations of the early nineteenth century travellers already cited show that the cultivated fields – likened to 'the country gardens in Europe' – were clear felled; that is, that few if any trees remained on them. Adequate data on labour requirements for clearing land by traditional methods are lacking. Bray cites figures for a 'fairly heavy stand of secondary forest' which, with thirty-seven trees per acre of over two feet in diameter, may be assumed to be approaching natural climax in character;[70] twenty-nine man-days per acre were used in brushing prior to felling, fifty-nine man-days in clear felling, and ninety-four in cutting and lining the timber.[71] Cardinall gave the figure of 96 man-days – fifteen for brushing and felling small trees, sixty for felling and chopping larger trees, fifteen for burning and final clearing, and six for stumping – for secondary forest seemingly not of great age: 'felling and chopping', he commented, 'may require very much more or much less labour than the above, since those depend on the number of large trees on the selected site'.[72] Liefstingh reports a figure, of 113 man-days, for clear felling, but does not describe clearly the age of the forest cover.[73] At the other end of the scale figures of 15 to 20 man-days per acre cited for clearing refer presumably to land being brought back into cultivation from a normal fallow.[74] It is apparent, *a priori*, that the number of man-days required will bear a fairly direct relationship to the weight of vegetation which has to be removed. In Figure 3 a formula for this relationship is suggested; the figures, which are adjusted for a one hectare field, are tentative only, but are almost certainly of the right order of magnitude.

Estimates of labour requirements for the principal farm tasks other than clearing are given in Table 5. It will be apparent that very little labour is needed in the third year of cultivation, when fallow regrowth is allowed to commence once the cassava crop is well-established.[76] All figures are based upon a working day of about six hours, which includes both time spent in travelling to and from the farm and time

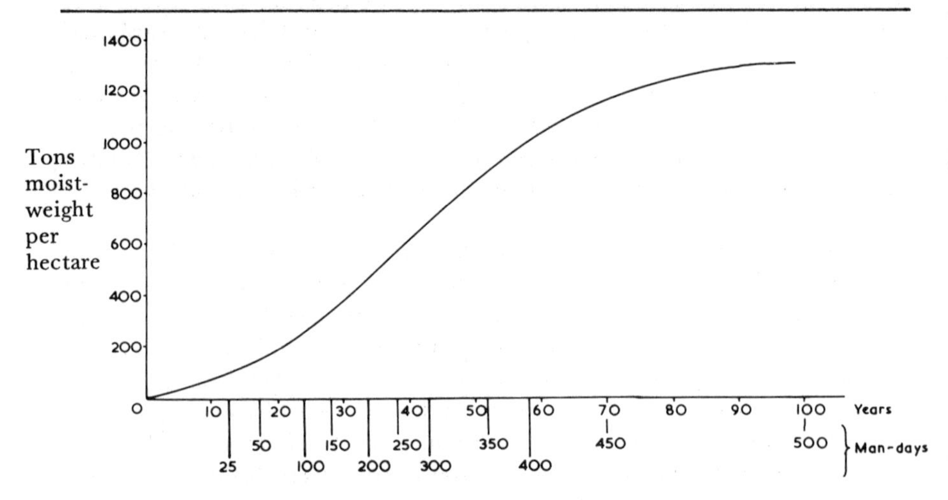

Figure 3. Increase in weight of vegetation per hectare, and approximate labour requirements for clearing by age of forest.

taken for rest, re-sharpening tools, and the like.[77] The last column offers some approximation to the energy inputs into the cultivation of a one hectare field over three years. Figures are computed for a typical male of about 120 pounds weight. It is assumed that half of the working day is spent in walking to and from the farm, resting, or undertaking very light tasks – consuming on an average about 180 calories per hour. Tasks carried out during the other half of the working day are divided into very hard, such as felling, using about 500 calories per hour; hard, such as cutlassing, using about 370; fairly hard, such as weeding and preparing crop beds, using about 270; and light, such as planting, harvesting, and fencing, using about 210.[78] All figures are reduced by 60 calories per hour – the basic expenditure during absolute rest.[79]

Reference to Tables 2 and 5 will show that within the traditional Asante food farming system, an expenditure of the order of 412,000 calories is required to produce a food bundle with a calorific value of the order of 14.5 million; the technoenvironmental advantage of the system is thus about 36. For purposes of comparison, Harris' calculations of the ratio for other systems may be cited: 9.6 for a Kalahari hunting and gathering society; 11.2 for hoe agriculture in a Gambian community; 18 for slash-and-burn agriculture among the Tsembaga of New Guinea; and 53.5 for irrigation agriculture in the Yunnan Province of China.[80]

It has been suggested that a six hectare farm, with one hectare under cultivation at any one time, is adequate only to the support of a family of about five. Nevertheless, the technoenvironmental advantage of the basic agricultural system as characterised above is such that production is sustained with relatively low inputs of human labour: only some 400 man-days are expended in the cultivation of the one

Table 5. Farm labour requirements by season and year.[75]

Year	Task	Months	Man-days per acre	Man-days for simulated one hectare field	Total calorific expenditure
1	Clear, etc. (from normal fallow)	Oct-Feb	15	38	45,296
	Collect, carry planting materials	Jan-Feb	10	25	20,250
	Prepare yam mounds	Jan-Feb	30	30	29,700
	Prepare field for maize	Feb-March	18	18	17,820
	Fence field	Feb-April	—	50	40,500
	Plant yam and stake	March-April	6	6	4,860
	Plant maize	April-May	4	4	3,360
	Plant cocoyam and plantain	April-June	12	24	19,440
	Harvest maize	Aug-Sept	4	4	3,360
	Plant second maize	Sept-Oct	4	4	3,360
	Harvest yam	Sept-Oct	6	6	4,860
	Three weedings	Through year	12	30	29,700
2	Harvest second maize	Dec-Jan	3	3	2,430
	Harvest cocoyam and plantain	April-Sept	5	10	8,100
	Three cutlassings	Through year	30	75	96,750
3	Continue cocoyam & plantain harvest	Continuing	2	4	3,240
	Plant cassava	Dec-Jan	10	15	12,150
	Harvest cassava	Aug-onward	2	3	2,430
	Two cutlassings	Through 1st part of year	20	50	64,500
			Totals	399	412,106

hectare field over three years. Since none of this advantage is derived from the utilisation of either animal or fossil fuel energy sources, it follows that the Asante farmer succeeded in establishing for himself an environmental niche within the highly complex and highly powered forest ecosystem, which enabled him to divert a significant part of its energy – ultimately solar – to the production of foodstuffs.[81]

It will be apparent from Table 5 that the labour inputs into a one hectare field are not uniformly distributed over the three years of its cultivation. The graph in Fig. 4 based upon these data, illustrates the variations in the level of labour requirements for a field cleared from a normal fallow.

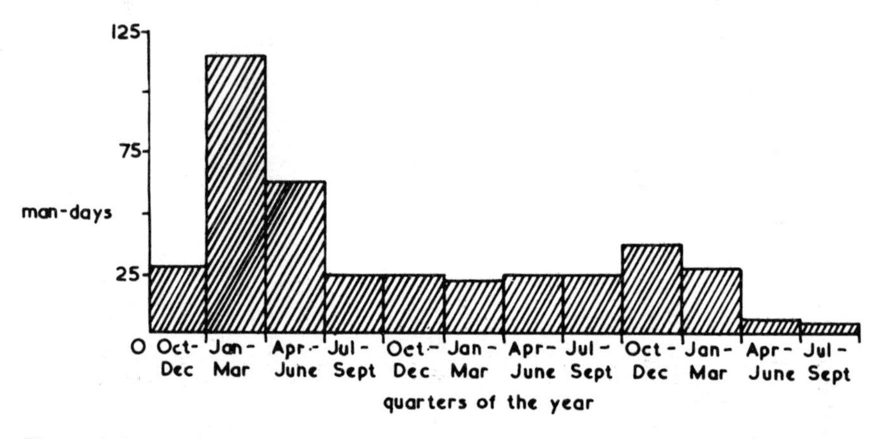

Figure 4. Seasonal variations in labour requirements on a one hectare field over three years.

Because of the complex nature of the variables, including the phasing of the domestic cycle, it is difficult to estimate the labour resources of the family to the support of which the one hectare field is adequate. For purposes of analysis, reference will be made to two simulated stages in the development of the one family, the first (Table 6a) in which the farmer still has all of his own sons and daughters in his household, and the second (Table 6b) in which the farmer's senior son has left to join his mother's brother's household, but has been replaced by a son of his sister (who will increasingly take over the running of the farm and ultimately inherit it).

Tables 6a and 6b. Simulated domestic group at five year interval

6a	*6b*
Farmer (40 years)	Farmer (45 years)
Wife, breast feeding (28 years)	Wife (33 years)
Son (11 years)	Farmer's sister's son (16 years)
Daughter (8 years)	Daughter (13 years)
Son (5 years)	Son (10 years)
	Child (6 years)

A distinction must be made between labour directly applied to the production of food, as itemised in Table 5, and labour applied to other tasks necessary to the survival of the family, such as the collection of firewood from the farm, the carrying of foodstuffs to the house, and the (time-consuming) preparation of food. In the phase of the domestic cycle simulated in Table 6a, the amount of labour effectively available for food production is one man per hectare; remaining members of the family will be almost exclusively involved in other tasks. In the phase shown in Table 6b, however, the farmer's labour will be augmented by that of his sister's son; the amount of labour may be approximated to 1.5 man-days per hectare, since as the youth moves progressively towards contributing a man-day of labour per day, so the older man progressively cuts back upon his input and gradually enters into retirement.

The labour routinely available within the domestic group for food production on the one hectare field is, then, probably within the range of 1 to 1.5 men. However, there are days in the Asante calendar when farm work is forbidden,[82] and others – the so-called 'bad' days (*dabone*) – when all enterprise is avoided.[83] There are also, of course, many days of sickness when potential working time is lost. It is doubtful whether a typical farmer would work an average of as many as five days in the week, or sixty-five days in a quarter. The available family labour per quarter may then be estimated as no higher than from 65 man-days (Table 6a) to 97.5 man-days (Table 6b). Reference to fig. 4 will suggest that the lower part of the range is more than adequate for the operation of a one hectare field throughout most of the three years under cropping, but that even the higher part of the range is inadequate in the peak period when clearing is closely followed by planting. Within the peak period, moreover, there are phases of especially intense activity: the felling of the larger trees, for example, requires the cooperation of several men, and in general the work of clearing, trashing and burning has to be accomplished within the comparatively short dry season. Reference again to fig. 4 will suggest that the level of manpower required during the peak period is such that it can easily be met through the cooperation of a neighbouring family whose field is in a different phase of the three years cultivation period. Although adequate empirical data on the basis of such cooperation are lacking, it would seem that it is most common between groups linked by marriage: that is, that a man obtains the help of his wife's brother (and thereby often procures the services of his own grown son). In other words, within the system of matriliny assistance is sought not from one's kin of the same lineage, but from one's affines of a different lineage. It should be stressed, however, that the provision of assistance does not generate any rights to participation in the harvest. The point is succinctly expressed in a lineage dirge cited by Nketia:

I ask you to help me in clearing the forest to make a farm.
Then I ask you to help me in felling the trees on the farm.
Then I ask you to help me in making mounds for the yam seeds.
But for harvesting the yams, I do not need your help,
Your subjects, male and female alike, are terrible suckers.[84]

The main features of the basic model for the agrarian economy – developed from the available data for non-intensive land rotation – may now conveniently be summarised. First, a paradigmatic farm may be conceived of as one of six hectares, each hectare being cropped for three years in rotation. Second, such a farm is adequate to the support of a family of five in even the adverse year. Third, the cropping and fallowing system preserves long-term soil fertility. Fourth, the technoenvironmental advantage of the system is relatively high. And fifth, the labour inputs into food production on an established farm are well within the capabilities of the family except at one peak period in each three years, when the assistance of a neighbouring family must be sought. It has been suggested that in the central Asante region such a subsistence system was adequate to the support of approximately 130 people per square mile.

Part II: The origins of the agrarian order

From hunting to farming: the Oyoko traditions

When the Asante kingdom emerged in its historic form in the late seventeenth century under the leadership of Obiri Yeboa and then of Osei Tutu, the new capital of Kumase was established at a location some forty or fifty miles within the humid forest zone.[1] Some twenty miles further south, and that much deeper in the forest, lies the abandoned site of Santemanso – long a protected ancient monument of the Asante people. It was visited by Rattray in the early part of this century, who referred to it as 'the Sacred Grove at Santemanso . . . which the Ashantis perhaps hold to be the most hallowed spot in all their territory'.[2] He noted that no one was allowed to clear or cultivate land there so that the impression was one of 'dense primaeval forest'; but remarked from the occupation debris revealed in cuttings, that the area must 'at some remote period, have been the site of a great settlement, larger by far than any Ashanti towns or villages of the present day'.[3] There can be no doubt that it was in fact from Santemanso that the 'founding fathers' of Asante pressed northwards, first acquiring land peacefully in the area where Kumase was soon to be built and the new nation inaugurated, and then by force of arms establishing their hegemony over the Kaase, Amakom, Tafo, Suntreso Domaa, and other peoples already settled there.[4] An early Dutch report suggests that the movement was already in progress by 1679.[5]

In the nineteenth century the historical role of Santemanso was still remembered; it was, one traveller noted, 'where in former days Kumase krom [town] stood, according to the reports of the Asantes'.[6]

Prima facie, the creation of the agrarian order in the forest would seem to be a necessary though not sufficient condition of the emergence of the political kingdom. The literary record provides little information pertinent to the problem, precisely because it becomes at all full only with the emergence of the kingdom In particular, it has remained unclear whether there was an era of massive land clearances, or whether the process was a piecemeal one extending back into remote antiquity. It is possible that the origins of agriculture in the forests of the central Asante region are to be sought in the prehistoric and not the protohistoric period. Davies has argued that fairly extensive clearings had been made around Kumase in Neolithic times,[7] and the manufacture of polished stone chisels and other such implements located near Kumase may perhaps have serviced early farming communities.[8] But Davies has also suggested, on the basis of the archaeological record, that the forest may have been virtually uninhabited until Neolithic times; that even in the early Iron Age very little of the land was cleared; that a population explosion, marked by extensive clearances and settlement, appears to have occurred in the sixteenth and seventeenth centuries; and that one of the major stimuli of the change may have been the introduction of new food crops by the Portuguese.[9] In the further resolution of the matter recourse may be made to the orally transmitted traditions of the Asante peoples, which fortunately are remarkably full for the protohistoric period. The growth of the Santemanso community is still vividly recounted in orally transmitted traditions, each group of settlers there being identified with reference to the order of its arrival, its matriclan affiliation, the name of its leader, the places of its origin and previous settlement, and the name of the ward occupied in Santemanso.[10]

The position which Santemanso holds in Asante history may be elucidated with reference to one particular branch of tradition; that preserved by the Oyoko Abohyen group of which the royal dynasty of Asante is part. It is a matter of good fortune that a recension was made in 1907 by the Asantehene Nana Agyeman Prempe I, then in exile in the Seychelles.[11] The first cycle of the tradition is entitled, 'The Story of the Hunter in the Forest'. At the beginning of the world there was a Hunter. He went into the Forest and met a Ratel.[12] The Ratel told the Hunter that people would soon be arriving from the sky at a place called Asiakwa. The Hunter went there to meet them. A herald (*esen*) appeared first, and was followed by a woman bearing a stool. Then Ankyewa Nyame, ancestress of the Oyoko Abohyen, arrived, and took possession of the stool. She then immediately departed for Santemanso, where she made a settlement. Others then flocked to join her, 'because she was the greatest of all'. Some arrived from holes in the ground at Santemanso: these became the Oyoko ne

Dako clan. Others came to settle there from the Adanse country to the south: those of the Bretuo, Atena, Agona ne Asokore, Dwum ne Asona, Ekuana, Asakyiri, and Aduana ne Atwea clans.[13] This was, then, the age of Ankyewa Nyame, greatest of all the ancestresses, who arrived in a world dominated by the denizens of the forest – the hunter and the ratel.

In the second cycle of the Oyoko Abohyen tradition, the story of the departure from Santemanso is recounted. Ankyewa Nyame and her daughter Birempomaa Piesie died at Santemanso. But a grandson of Birempomaa Piesie, Kobea Amamfi, who presided over the affairs of the Santemanso people, decided to send out a hunter with instructions to find a better place for the Oyoko Abohyen people to live. The hunter met a man named Koko, who had cleared a large farm (*afuo*) in the forest. Kobea Amamfi decided to move there with the Oyoko Abohyen, and the place was named 'Koko-afuo', that is, the present Kokofu only some three or four miles from Santemanso. In another recension of the same branch of tradition, the descendants of Ankyewa Nyame are said to have become 'hemmed in' at Santemanso, and thus forced to move.[14] In yet another recension, the influx of people to the Kokofu farms is said to have caused famine, so that it became necessary for all the immigrants to take up farming: maize was planted as being the crop which matured most rapidly.[15] The example of the Oyoko Abohyen was followed by the other groups at Santemanso, who commenced the quest for new land to settle.[16] The second cycle of the tradition, then, appears to recount, in terms of the relocation of the Oyoko Abohyen of Santemanso at Kokofu, the beginnings of the transition from dependence upon the exploitation of the resources of the forest – hunting and gathering – to one upon the cultivation of cleared lands – farming.

The third stage of the tradition narrates that another of the grandsons of Ankyewa Nyame, 'the great hunter' Okyerefo Baakuma, was first of the Oyoko Abohyen to visit the Kwaman lands (on which Kumase was later to be built). He founded a new village in the forest known as Kedwenease, 'under the *kedwene* tree' (the present Kenyase some six miles northeast of Kumase), and sent reports back to Kokofu of the availability of good land. A section of the Oyoko Abohyen, then under Kobea Amamfi's successor Oti Akenten, decided to move again. They succeeded in purchasing the land on which Kumase was later built from its female owner, Aberewa Yebetuo, for 30 peredwans (or 67.5 oz. of gold).[17] With the Kwaman purchase the protohistoric period gives way to the historic. Oti Akenten was succeeded by Obiri Yeboa, who involved the settlers from Santemanso in the struggle for political hegemony in the Kwaman region. Losing his life in battle, he was succeeded in turn by Osei Tutu – architect of the new Asante nation and first Asantehene, to whom the earliest European ambassador to Asante was accredited in 1701.[18]

Examination of the corpus of over two hundred 'stool histories' recorded in Asante by J. Agyeman-Duah between 1963 and 1967 shows that the Oyoko Abohyen branch of tradition is in no way aberrant or atypical. Though variations in the basic theme are legion, the period preceding the creation of the Asante state is consistently treated as one in which hunters located sites in the forest suitable for cultivation, after which villages were founded and the land cleared. The hunters, moreover, are attributed a central role in the demarcation of boundaries to create 'parishes' (*nkuro*, singular *kuro*): extending their operations deep into the undisturbed forest, they encountered there hunters from other settlements and agreed with them in designating the meeting place the boundary between the respective parishes. Each parish thus came to consist of a nuclear village (growing out of the first *osese* or 'cottage'), an adjacent area of farmland and fallow, and a surrounding hinterland of forest which the hunters and the gatherers of wild crops, snails and the like would continue to exploit until the expanding frontiers of the farmlands finally deprived them of a livelihood. But still in the early nineteenth century, as Bowdich noted, 'the crooms appeared insulated'.[19]

The major thrust of the Oyoko tradition is quite clear, and appears to support the arguments of Davies from the archaeological record: the period preceding the emergence of the historic kingdom of Asante was one in which intensive exploration of the forest in quest of good cultivable land was carried out, in which numerous villages were established, and in which clearance of the forest on an hitherto unprecedented scale occurred. The need for a fuller consideration of the status of the Oyoko traditions is therefore indicated.

The era of the great ancestresses

In the cosmogonic system through which the Akan in general and the Asante in particular express the nature of the social order and account for the origins of the great exogamous matriclans, the spatial frame of reference is provided by the Amansie and Adanse districts in the heartland of the forest country extending southwards by westwards of Lake Bosumtwe. It has been noted above that Santemanso, which lies on the northern edge of the area, is regarded as the place where the 'greatest' of all the ancestresses, Ankyewa Nyame of the Oyoko, settled after descending from the sky by a golden chain. Similarly, for example, Asiama Nyankopon Guahyia, ancestress of the Bretuo, descended from the sky at Ayaase in Adanse, but by a silver chain;[20] Aso Boade, the Asona ancestress, appeared from a hole in the ground at Adaboye in Adanse;[21] Amena Gyata (or otherwise Berewaa Mmosu) of the Asenie emerged from a rock at Bonabom in the same district;[22] and Seni Fontom of the Aduana emerged from the ground at Santemanso.[23] There is an urgent need for the systematic collection and collation of such materials, since each myth now occurs in a number of variant forms, branches of the original or archetypal form having arisen in the course of transmission over several centuries by groups which became spatially and sometimes politically separated from each other. Even in the absence of such a corpus, however, one major implication of the materials is unmistakably clear: that the Asante – and Akan – regard the matriclans as having originated not in the coastal scrublands, not in the northern grasslands, but in the forest heartlands which lay more or less equidistant from the Atlantic seaboard to the south and the savannah woodlands to the north.[24] It is, moreover, noteworthy that in the Akan cosmogonies there is a congruence not only in the spatial referents – that is, that the ancestresses are all associated with the one region – but also in the time referents – that is, that historically identifiable individuals of the late seventeenth or early eighteenth centuries are consistently placed in the fourth or fifth generation in descent from the ancestresses. Five pedigrees, in the female line, are shown in Table 7 in illustration of this matter.[25] Manu of the Oyoko was mother of Osei Tutu, first Asantehene who ruled from the late seventeenth century and died in 1711 or 1717.[26]

Table 7. Early descendants of the great ancestresses

Oyoko	Bretuo	Asona	Asenie	Aduana
Ankyewa Nyame	Asiama Nyankopon Guahyia	Aso Boade	Amena Gyata	Seni Fontom
Birempomaa Piesie	Agyakumaa Dufie	Nyaako Brayie	Dufie Gyampontimaa	Twabea Sanaa
Abena Gyapa	Firampon Kese	Gyaawa	Adu Twumuwaa	Abena Nwowaa
Manu			Dwirawiri Kwa	

Firampon Kese was mother both of the Mamponhene Maniampon who ruled in the late seventeenth century and of the Mamponhene Boahenantuo who died c. 1701.[27] Gyaawa of the Asona was mother of the late seventeenth-century Edwesohenes Aboagye Agyei and Asona Gyima,[28] whose successor Daako Pim fought in the Denkyera wars of 1699-1701.[29] Dwirawiri Kwa of the Asenie was mother of Okomfo Anokye, priestly adviser to Osei Tutu.[30] And finally, Abena Nwowaa of the Aduana was mother of the Kumawuhene Kwabena Kodie, who died c. 1701.[31] Since each matriclan is responsible for the transmission of its own 'charter', the consistency of the five pedigrees in terms of the temporal dimension is such as to make the possibility of chance correspondence a low one. The data are such as to suggest that, for whatever reason, the great ancestresses of the cosmogonies are all placed in a genealogical time that would appear to correspond with the sixteenth century in absolute dating.

In 1895 Reindorf commented, 'Adanse was the first seat of the

Akan nation, as they say by tradition: there God first commenced with the creation of the world.'[32] It is important, however, to appreciate the sense in which the cosmogonies relate the 'creation of the world' to the Adanse area. They do not purport to record the origins of the forest peoples as such: no Asante, that is, construes the story of the arrival of the Oyoko or Bretuo ancestresses by chains from the sky as a surviving memory of an early invasion of the forest country from outer space (such an interpretation presupposing the emergence of a peculiarly latish twentieth century brand of the untutored imagination). Indeed, there is a quite distinct body of Akan tradition which does offer an account of the early history of the forest peoples and which may incorporate folk memories of ancient migrations. The character of such traditions is quite different from those which form part of the cosmogonic cycle: names of individuals are generally absent, geographical locations are but vaguely specified, and events are not related the one to the other in any sequential form. The one common theme in them is that of the movement of people from the savannah country into the forest. The earliest literary recension of such traditions was that made by the Muslims of Kumase in the early nineteenth century. According to Dupuis, who drew upon the work of the Muslims, the Akan ('Ashantee, Gaman, Dinkera, and Akim') were driven out of the grasslands of the north as a result of the expansion of the Western Sudanese powers. In the forests, Dupuis wrote,

> they maintained their independence at the expense of much blood, and defended the country gifted with the precious metal [gold] against the most vigorous efforts that were made to bereave them of it . . . The tribes spread over the land, down to the margin of the ocean.[33]

In 1887 Ellis published a 'tradition of the Migration from the Interior' of similar content: Muslim Fula forced the ancestors of the Akan out of the grasslands and into the forest, where they 'multiplied, and built many towns and villages . . . (and) after many years always coming downwards, they reached the sea.'[34]

It is unfortunate that this second stratum of tradition has been used by writers in the present century as a basis for extravaganzas which bring the Akan to their present location from the medieval Western Sudanese kingdom of Wagadu (Ghana), and from even more remote cradles in North Africa or the Near East.[35] There is, however, no questioning the continuing existence of the underlying tradition: Rattray was aware of it,[36] Meyerowitz drew upon it,[37] and the writer can attest to its survival in present-day Asante. The veracity of such traditions of migration from the northern grasslands is, fortunately, not of concern here; what is of significance is not only that they exist, but that they can be shown already to have existed a century and a half ago. Two distinct and seemingly discrepant sets of traditions have, then, co-existed over a significant period of time. The assumption is, that they are in some way complementary. The one set, imprecise in detail and lacking in internal structure, narrates the migration of peoples into the forest from the northern savannahs, while the other, extraordinarily precise in detail and highly systematised, relates not to the origins of peoples, so it is suggested, but to the origins of the social order: that is, gives expression to the pattern of social organisation, in the more recent phase of their historical development, of the Akan of the forest country.

It is a noteworthy fact, to which Rattray drew attention in 1929, that the system of organisation into large extended matriclans characteristic of the forest Akan is one which does not extend to the peoples of the wooded savannah country to which the humid forests give way only some forty or fifty miles north of Kumase. The significance of the matter stems from the fact that many of the savannah peoples – such as the Takyiman whom Rattray described as the 'pure Brong' – are in most other respects, culturally and linguistically, Akan. Expressing his surprise that the 'pure Brong' did not use the clan names of the forest Akan, Rattray remarked that,

> their exogamous divisions seem based upon an entirely different model. In Tekiman [Takyiman] one does not ask, 'To what *abusua* (totemic clan) do you belong?' but 'In what street (*abrono*) do you reside?' There, such exogamous divisions as appear to exist apparently take their names from streets or quarters in the towns.[38]

Rattray, astute observer that he was, saw this as 'a problem of considerable interest to students of Gold Coast history'. To its resolution he found himself able only to 'hazard two tentative suggestions'. These merit quotation in full:

> One is that, in accordance with the common belief, Brong, Fanti, and Ashanti had a single origin, and that all originally had this local or 'street' organisation (in place of the totemic groups); that Fanti and Ashanti moved south, separating from the parent stock, and at a much later date, possible due to some contact with another culture, adopted their present totemic clan organisation . . . My second suggestion is that the Brong and the Ashanti were not from the same original stock; that the Ashanti were an alien race who overran the Brong, bringing with them their own clan organisation and passing southward, and settled down, ousting, or exterminating, or absorbing the local Brong inhabitants, and later, to strengthen their position, which was that of mere usurpers in the land, they encouraged the fiction of a common descent from the real proprietors, or alternatively, and again ignoring their own origin, declared that they had sprung from the ground which they had in reality appropriated.[39]

Having regard, however, for the Occamist principle, and holding constant the factor of migration, a simpler hypothesis suggests itself: that the great exogamous matriclans of the forest Akan were indeed created – as expressed in the cosmogonies – in the forest environment, and that for reasons that have to be explored, the system was never embraced by the peoples of the wooded savannahs to the north even though some of them were otherwise more or less culturally indistinguishable from the forest Akan. In fact an Asante tradition exists which even more explicitly maintains that the institution of the matrilineage or *abusua* originated in the forest country of Adanse. As early as 1895 Reindorf wrote of Abu, an Adanse ruler who 'instituted the order of family among the Tshis', and remarked, 'hence lineage is designated "abusua" i.e. imitating Abu'.[40] Another version of the story was published by Rattray in 1914:

> There lived in former times a king of Adanse who had a 'linguist' named Abu. This Abu incurred the king's anger and was heavily fined. Now, at that time children used to inherit from their father. Abu asked his children to assist him to pay the fine imposed by the king, but they refused and all went off to their mother's relatives. But Abu's sister's children rendered him assistance to pay off his debts, and Abu when he died left all his belongings to them. Other people then copied him, and willed their property to the sister's children (*abu-sua*, lit. copying Abu).[41]

Bowdich, over a hundred and fifty years ago, was the first observer to suspect that a study of the origins of the Akan matriclans would contribute to an understanding of the major economic transformation which occurred to separate 'the first race of men living on hunting' from those who followed after 'the introduction of planting and agriculture'.[42] But Bowdich regarded the matriclans as 'primaeval institutions' and believed the totemic observances to provide an index whereby clans which existed prior to the transformation might be distinguished from those created after it. An alternative view now suggests itself, that the emergence of the Asante kingdom in the late seventeenth century was indeed preceded by a period in which, on an hitherto quite unprecedented scale, the forestlands were explored and cleared, and new agrarian settlements established; that this represented a major transformation in the system of productive forces such that an economy with a primary dependence upon hunting and gathering gave way to one with a primary dependence upon the cultivation of food crops; that the social relations of production of the forest peoples were accordingly modified by the creation of the great exogamous matriclans and the redistribution of communities between them; that this socioeconomic revolution began, geographically, in the forest heartland of Amansie and Adanse, and chronologically, should probably be regarded as having reached its zenith in what is for the

Asante the immediate protohistoric period (*firi tetemu*), the sixteenth century.

In 1931 Cardinall offered a perspicuous comment upon the chronic shortage of labour in the forest country of what is now southern Ghana:

> The country at no time in its history had been able to develop by the work of its own native labour. This latter had invariably been immigrant, and there existed even in the remoter recesses of the [Western] Sudan the knowledge that a market for labour was available in this country. The news that the market was a 'bull' one soon spread and immigrants flocked to the fabled land where mere work in the fields was rewarded with wages almost incredibly high.[43]

Earlier, Rattray had remarked upon high input of human energy necessary for clearing natural forest:

> Ashanti is a country covered for the most part by dense primordial forest. To win a plot of land from these sombre unlit depths, to let in the rays of the sun, to reach its rich virgin soil beneath the tangle of lianas and living, or dead and decomposing, vegetation that covers the land, was a task that, with the applicances at the African's disposal, might have seemed almost impossible for individual effort. Gigantic trees had to be removed, huge fallen trunks over which a man could hardly climb, a few yards of whose surface alone were visible, the rest trailing away somewhere for two or three hundred feet, but completely lost to sight in the matted undergrowth – all this had to be cleared before the *nyame akuma* (stone hoe or 'axe') could reach the soil. The assistance of every able-bodied member of the family or kindred group had to be called in to give a helping hand. This assistance sounded the knell of any possible claim to individual ownership of the usufruct of the land which had been cleared by the collective efforts of the husbandman, his brother, sister, mother, and nephews and nieces . . .[44]

Rattray's apparent assumption that major clearances were accomplished in the neolithic period has already been queried. A further premise is also open to question: that the clearing of the farmlands from natural forest was possible simply by extended cooperation within the 'kindred group'. It has been suggested above that the operation of an *established* farm required assistance during the peak labour period at the beginning of every three year period of cultivation, and that the obligation to assist was more usually generated by the ties of marriage than those of descent. Comparison, however, of figs. 3 and 4 with fig. 5 will show the difference between total labour inputs into an established farm and those into one in

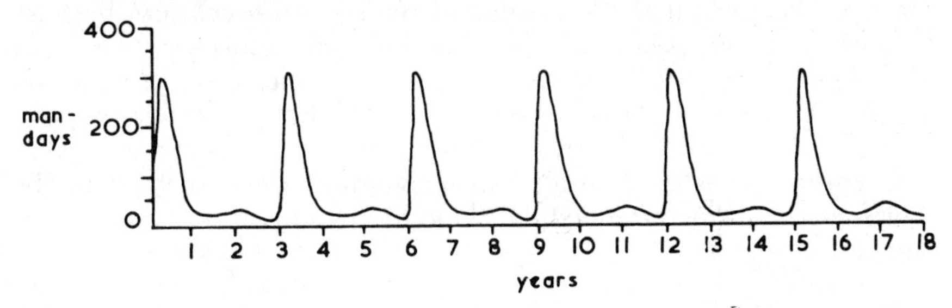

Figure 5. Fluctuations in labour requirements in the creation of a six-hectare farm from natural forest. (The seasonality of the rains operates against the levelling-out of the curves.)

process of creation out of the natural forest. If there was indeed an era of extensive land clearance of the sort indicated by the evidence from tradition, then *prima facie* it appears that the resources of labour of the local forest communities would have been incommensurate with the magnitude of the enterprise. There are strong reasons for believing that this was so; that in the fifteenth and sixteenth centuries labour was being drawn into the forest lands of the Akan from other regions both near and far, and that this labour was for the most part unfree. In the next section a broad historical reconstruction is offered, to identify the complex factors which made possible the creation of the agrarian order and the consequent expansion of food crop production.

Unfree labour in the fifteenth and sixteenth centuries

The Portuguese first commenced trading at Elmina, on the coast to the south of the Akan lands, in 1470-71. The venture proved so profitable that in 1482 the fortress of São Jorge da Mina was built. Among the commodities which the Portuguese found most readily exchangeable against the gold brought to the coast, were slaves. On his voyage of 1479, Eustache de la Fosse remarked that two of the Portuguese ships at Elmina plied for slaves to the Rio dos Escravos in the Niger Delta, and he had himself been able to sell, near Elmina, slaves purchased on the Grain Coast.[45] Following the establishment of the trading post at Gwato in or about 1486, the Portuguese began immediately to obtain slaves from Benin for sale at Elmina. De Barros gave some account of the matter:

> As this kingdom of Beny was near the Castle of S. Jorge de Mina and as the negroes who brought gold to that market place were ready to buy slaves to carry their merchandise, the King [of Portugal] ordered the building of a factory in a port of Beny, called Gato, whither there were brought for sale a great number of those slaves who were bartered very profitably at the Mina, for the merchants of gold gave twice the value obtainable for them in the Kingdom (of Beny).[46]

Pacheco Pereira, at the beginning of the sixteenth century, likewise remarked on 'our people who are sent out by the most serene King in his ships to buy slaves 200 leagues beyond the castle [of Elmina], by rivers where there is a very large city called Beny, whence they are brought thither'.[47] De Barros makes it clear that the market was, in the early sixteenth century, an expanding one, such that the Portuguese in time extended their purchasing operations even further afield:

> For a considerable time afterwards, both during the life of Don João [1481-95] and of Dom Manoel [1495-1521] this sale of slaves continued from Beny to Mina, for ordinarily the ships that left this kingdom went to Beny to buy slaves, and then carried them to the Mina, until this trade was altered on account of the great inconveniences which arose. A large caravel was wont to sail from the island of S. Thomé, where the slaves of the coast of Beny joined those from the kingdom of Congo, because all the vessels that sailed to those parts called there, and this caravel carried them from the island to Mina.[48]

Although no precise information exists on the destination of the slaves sold by the Portuguese at Elmina, it is clear that they were taken northwards by the various merchants from the interior: according to Pacheco Pereira for example, by the Abrambu ('Bremus') and Etsi ('Atis') of the immediate coastal hinterland, the Akani ('Hacanys')[49] and Adanse ('Andeses or Souzos') of the forest heartlands, and the Bron ('Boroes') and Malian Dyula ('Mandinguas') of the northern fringes of the forest.[50] Shortly before the middle of the sixteenth century there was some curtailment of Portuguese labour-contracting activities at Elmina, in circumstances outlined briefly by DeBarros:

> ... the King, Dom João the Third [1521-57], our Lord, who was then reigning, perceiving that those pagans who were in our power passed into the hands of infidels once more, so that they lost the merit of baptism, and their souls were damned eternally; accordingly as a very Christian prince, ever more mindful of the salvation of souls than of the profits of the treasury, he ordered the cessation of this trade, although he suffered great loss by this act. And by this means there were brought into the fold of the faithful more than a thousand souls, all of whom, a year before this holy precept, were in perpetual servitude to the devil . . .[51]

Nevertheless, the evidence suggests that the trade in slaves at Elmina was to continue, partly through the agency of other European interlopers, at least to the end of the sixteenth century.[52]

No adequate data exist on the volume of unfree labour which flowed northwards through the Gold Coast ports. De Barros might be read to suggest that it was of the order of one thousand a year around the middle of the sixteenth century. Birmingham has shown that two decades earlier Jorge Erbet held a concession in the São Tomé trade which obligated him to deliver five hundred best quality slaves to Elmina each year, others to be purchased from him at an agreed price.[53] Whatever the quantity, however, there can be little doubt that there was a much higher flow southwards into the forest from the savannah hinterlands. The principal agents in this trade were the Muslim Dyula, of Malian origins, who in the fifteenth and sixteenth centuries established a series of trading stations along the northern fringes of the forest. The most famous of these was at Bighu, where the Dyula had begun to settle probably by the middle of the fifteenth century.[54] Concerned with the collection of gold for despatch, via the entrepôts of the western Sudan, ultimately into the world gold markets, the Dyula like the Portuguese also became important suppliers of labour to the forest. Thus at the beginning of the sixteenth century Pacheco Pereira referred to the gold producing region of 'Toom', that is, the country of the Akan (compare modern Malinke *Tõ*, Hausa *Tonawa*, 'the Akan'), and observed that the 'merchants of Mandingua' travelled thence from Bighu and other towns ('Beetuu', 'Habanbarranaa' and 'Bahaa'), 'to purchase gold with goods and slaves which they take there'.[55] In 1513 the Governor of Elmina could complain that a shortage of slaves and other goods impeded his efforts to compete with the Dyula for the purchase of gold.[56]

The source of the slaves sold by the Dyula is nowhere documented. It must be assumed that, as in the later period, it was the acephalous societies of the Voltaic basin; that the slaves were those known to the Akan by a name borrowed, significantly enough, from the Malian traders, Twi *nnonkofo* (singular *odonko*) from Malinke *dyonko*, 'slave'.[57] It is possible that by the fifteenth century the pressure of population on the land in parts of the Voltaic region was such as to have created a ready market in human beings. However that may be, the situation appears to have changed somewhat dramatically in the middle of the sixteenth century, when cavalry groups of Malian provenance invaded the savannah hinterlands of the forest and in collaboration with the Dyula created there the framework of the Gonja state.[58] There is little doubt that the early Gonja state was organised primarily for trade; that trade consisted principally in the supply of labour to the forest in return for gold; and that the labour was procured by extensive raiding of the rural peoples.[59] Davies has remarked, that

> on the northern edge of the forest of Ghana, there flourished in central Gonja, probably in the fifteenth to seventeenth centuries an interesting culture, especially between the Black and White Volta. This land, now a poverty-stricken wilderness, waterless for half the year and suffering from soil erosion, was thickly populated. There

> are numerous hut-mounds along the few tracks which it has been possible to follow; the total number throughout this inaccessible region must be large. Water was stored in bilegas or rock-cut cisterns.[60]

In the early nineteenth century the region was known to travellers as the 'desert of Ghofe (Gbuipe)',[61] and today its density of population is as low as six persons per square mile.

The historical record, then, shows that unfree labour was being drawn into the forestlands from both north and south in the very period in which, so Asante traditions seem to indicate, massive clearances within those lands were undertaken. The argument is, that the availability of labour was a necessary precondition of the clearances and of the creation of the agrarian order. It will be apparent, however, that there is a further implication in the argument: that the availability of gold was in turn a necessary precondition of the procurement of labour.

The washing of the rivers for gold in the forest was probably of considerable antiquity,[62] but there is no clear evidence of the date of the introduction of mining. It is quite certain that by the sixteenth and early seventeenth centuries many of the major reefs in the central forestlands had been prospected and were being exploited to the lowest levels possible without the use of mechanical pumps.[63] A reference is extant from 1707, for example, to the 'deep pits underground' at 'Menason', that is, Manso (earlier Twi, *Omanaso*) Nkwanta twenty-five miles to the southwest of Kumase.[64] An account of mining operations in the Oweri Valley some thirty-five miles east of Kumase was obtained by Rømer from Akyem Kotokŭ informants probably in the 1730s; from his description it is clear that the lode was mined by a series of banks and benches to as great a depth as 200 feet.[65] Earlier still, Müller had referred to mines 'dug deeply into the hills' at 'Accaseer';[66] the site is perhaps to be identified with Kusa (or Kwisa) thirty-two miles south of Kumase, where in the early nineteenth century Dupuis saw 'a chasm or pit of great depth, said to have been excavated for gold; but latterly neglected'.[67] The weight of the evidence is such as to indicate that the development of the mining industry in the region was a fifteenth-century one,[68] and the thesis has been suggested elsewhere, that there was a direct technological input from the much more anciently exploited Bambuk and Bure goldfields of western Mali.[69] Certainly by the end of the fifteenth century reports had reached Europe of pits, 'very deeply driven into the ground', in what can only have been the Akan country.[70]

By the end of the fifteenth century the Portuguese exports of gold through Elmina appear to have been running at upwards of 20,000 ounces annually, even allowing for some exaggeration in the estimates.[71] Over the first two decades of the sixteenth century an average level of somewhat under 15,000 ounces annually was maintained,[72] the fall perhaps being a result of the adjustment of the northern Dyula competitors in the trade to the new circumstances. No satisfactory estimates can yet be made of the volume of exports through the northern markets, though it may be assumed to have been very considerably higher than through the southern.[73]

In the fifteenth and sixteenth centuries the world market for bullion was a strongly rising one; as a result of the minting of new gold currencies, of the overland trade with India and China, and of hoarding, demand persistently exceeded supply.[74] The writer has earlier suggested two major results of this situation: first, that in the mid-fifteenth century Malian gold merchants and entrepreneurs were led to extend their activities into the Akan country in an effort to increase their consignments of gold across the Sahara and thereby secure advantage of the better terms of trade, and second, that at the end of the same century the Portuguese were obliged to construct a permanent settlement at Elmina in order to compete with the northern traders for the output of the newly developed industry in the forestlands.[75] There can be no doubt that, although part of the Akan production of gold was consumed locally (whether cast into ornaments or put into circulation as currency),[76] by far the larger part was consigned to the world market via both northern and southern trade outlets, and that in the fifteenth and sixteenth centuries this represented a source of bullion probably second in importance only to that of the European mines.

The significance of the historical argument may, then, be summarised. Geographically peripheral to the major centres of world commerce, the Akan were nevertheless drawn into the world economy in the fifteenth and sixteenth centuries. Gold produced for the world bullion market was traded, both at northern outlets maintained by the Dyula and southern outlets maintained by the Portuguese, for unfree labourers drawn in part from regions as distant as Benin and beyond. The influx of labour made possible massive forest clearances, such that a society in which the dominant mode of production was hunting and gathering transformed itself into one in which the dominant mode was food crop cultivation. The creation of an efficient agrarian system, on a capital base provided by the mining industry, and within the constraints of the forest environment, is to be correlated with the emergence of a number of small-scale polities ('chiefdoms') in the region, some of which were based upon earlier organisations for the marketing or production of gold (such as Tafo, in the Kwaman or present Kumase area, and Kwadukrom, in the Oweri Valley, respectively), while others were new creations resulting from the increasing concern with the management of land and the structuring of land-rights (such as Kaase, Amakom, and Yebetuo, in Kwaman). It was these early polities which were to be unified, in the seventeenth century, into the Asante state – among the more complex systems of political control ever to evolve in the tropical forest environment.

The agrarian order and the social structure

The highest level of effective social organisation in Asante is the *abusua* (plural *mmusua*), the lineage. The lineage is territorially localised and has user-rights over land; its corporate affairs are managed by a male head (*abusua-panin*) and a female head (*obaa-panin*), assisted by a committee of elders (*abusua-mpaninfo*). All members of the lineage regard themselves as descended from a common ancestress, though 'descent' may be by some form of adoption as well as by ascription. In present day genealogies the founding ancestress is located most typically in the tenth ascendant generation from the junior living one, but the range is from as few as four or five generations to as many as fourteen.[77] Each lineage is segmented into a number of 'extended families', typically some four or five generations in depth, and each extended family comprises a number of households – small domestic groups of the kind considered earlier in this paper.

Fortes has described the *abusua* or lineage as being a 'chapter of a clan'.[78] Yet many aspects of the Asante or indeed Akan matriclan (*abusua-kese*, 'big lineage') are enigmatic. It is true that the principle of matriliny is still expressed with reference to the clan, which is generally regarded as the unit of exogamy. It is true also that a principle of fraternity and sorority is also expressed with reference to it, such that membership of the same clan is regarded as generating certain rights and duties of hospitality, mutual aid, and the like. But the matriclan, as it has survived into the present, lacks any head, whether male or female; exercises no control over user-rights in land; and the totemic avoidances to which reference was made in the early nineteenth century have become virtually extinct.[79] A matriclan, moreover, has no specific territoriality, its members being dispersed; historically, clan affiliations seem not to have been such as to transcend local political allegiances, and in various internecine struggles fellow clansmen found themselves quite naturally aligned one against the other.[80] For a quite surprising number of Asantes today, clan affiliation is a matter no longer within, or but vaguely within, the level of consciousness. In brief, the institution of the matriclan, as distinct from that of the lineage, appears in many respects vestigial.

Douglas has argued that 'matrilineal descent groups are organised to recruit members by other means additional to direct lineal descent'; that 'matrilineal descent goes with a quality of openness in the texture of effective descent groups'; and that 'because of the open texture of its descent groups and its bias towards a wide-ranging recruitment of manpower, matriliny is well adapted to any situation in which competing demands for men are higher than demands for material resources'.[81] In 1912 the missionary Lochman offered an interesting comment on the nature of the Akan matriclans, that they were 'original families . . . but not in the meaning of consanguinity, rather [they] may be described as an alliance offensive and defensive whose members have to support themselves in paying debts and defraying expenses of funeral customs, etc.'[82] While the unity of the matriclan is indeed expressed, in Asante social thought, by reference to a named founding ancestress, it is nonetheless the case that the origins of the matriclan are conceived in terms of alliance rather than of descent. The Oyoko clan, for example, is regarded as comprising the Oyoko Abohyen, the 'real descendants' by descent or adoption of the ancestress Ankyewa Nyame, but also the Oyoko Atutue, Oyoko Breman and various other groups which 'came together to' Ankyewa Nyame at Santemanso: 'there are some more Ayuku which are not families of Anchiayami'.[83] Again, the Bretuo clan is sometimes likened to the monkey genus – 'there are so many different kinds of them'.[84] It is also the case that in Asante thought a social group, created through alliance, has both a 'right and left hand'. The former – the *nifa* of the group – comprises the 'true descendants', and the latter – the *benkum* – those of alien and often unfree origins. But, in traditional thought, the matter would be explained somewhat differently: as Ankyewa Nyame is reported to have said to those who joined her at Santemanso in her Oyoko-ness (as it were), 'If you are Oyoko, then I am more Oyoko than you'![85]

One of the major thrusts in Asante social 'engineering' was towards prevention of the consolidation of a slave caste: those of unfree origins were assimilated as rapidly as possible into the class of free Asante commoners and their acquired status afforded full protection of the law.[86] 'An Ashanti slave,' wrote Rattray, 'in nine cases out of ten, possibly became an adopted member of the family, and in time his descendants so merged and intermarried with the owner's kinsmen that only a few would know their origin'.[87] But Rattray still failed to allow fully for the 'openness' in the texture of the matrilineal group. The view has been expressed to the writer on many occasions, that 'in the old days' women married at a young age and men at a relatively advanced one;[88] that a male slave might often become the third, fourth or even fifth husband of a (by them elderly) free woman, so that any children she bore by him would be free; and that female slaves were often married by free men and their children immediately adopted into the father's lineage. The thesis suggests itself, that the matriclans of the forest Akan did indeed arise in the era of the great forest clearances as the testimony of tradition indicates; that they represent the way in which people redistributed themselves in society as sets of relations appropriate to a predominantly hunting and gathering economy were superseded by ones appropriate to a predominantly agricultural one; and that the new configuration of society, in ways that remain to be fully explored, was one particularly adjusted to the incorporation and assimilation of a large immigrant and alien labour force.

Using the data base provided by Meillassoux's study of the Gouro of the Ivory Coast, Terray has argued that 'the lineage "realises" the production community based on extended cooperation, while the segment of a lineage or extended family "realises" the work-team based on restricted cooperation'.[89] For the forest Akan, the further thesis suggests itself, that the level of social organisation represented by the matriclan was commensurate with the level of the control and management of labour in the era of the great clearances, and that the level of social organisation represented by the lineage was commensurate with the level of the control and management of labour in the succeeding periods of regular food crop production. A corollary of the thesis is, that with the agrarian order firmly established in the forestlands by the late sixteenth or early seventeenth century, the size of the production community became more restricted, the demand for immigrant labour consequently dropped to lower levels, and the social relations of production were 'realised' in the lineage rather than in the matriclan. Some impression of the nature of the task forces employed in clearing land, in this case on the Gold Coast and probably not heavily forested, may be obtained from Eich's account of the three hundred slaves, divided into two or three work teams or companies, who prepared the site for the Danish trading post at Fetu in the seventeenth century.[90] It may have been similar companies which cleared the heavy forests in the interior, their members drawn from far distant regions. But the precise way in which such task forces were incorporated and assimilated into the open-textured matriclans must remain for the present a matter for speculation;[91] all that is sure is that incorporation and assimilation occurred, and that in consequence no slave caste arose within Asante society.

That the matriclan became progressively of less utility as an instrument of social organisation will, quite apparently, explain its present 'vestigial' characteristics. There is, however, evidence that there has also been a reduction over time in the number of matriclans in Asante society. In an authoritative review of the matter in 1942, by the Ashanti Confederacy Council, the existence of seven clans was recognised.[92] Some two decades earlier Rattray also listed seven,[93] but the figure of eight was given in the authoritative statement by the Asantehene Agyeman Prempe I in 1907.[94] Ninety years earlier, Bowdich had commented of the Akan in general and Asante in particular, that 'the whole of these people were originally comprehended in twelve tribes of families . . . in which they class themselves still, without any regard for national distinction'.[95] Table 8 shows the considerable discrepancy which exists not only with respect to the number of the matriclans, but even to their names.

One discrepancy in the various twentieth-century lists will be seen to be that of the Atena or Tana clan. Fortunately it is possible to elucidate the nature of the problem in this case. During the reign of his predecessor Opoku Ware [ca. 1720-1750], so the Asantehene Osei Agyeman Prempeh II informed his council in 1946, 'the Tena Clan

Table 8. Listings of the Asante matriclans

Bowdich, 1817	Prempe, 1907	Rattray, 1929	Confederacy Council, 1942
Aquonna	Ekuana	Asokore ne Ekuana	Asukore ne Kuona
Abrootoo	Bretuo	Bretuo ne Tana	Bretuo
Abbradi			
Essonna	Dwum ne Asona	Asona ne Dwum (Dwumana or Dwumina)	Asona ne Dwum
Annona			
Yoko	Oyoko ne Dako	Oyoko ne Dako	Oyoko ne Dako
Intchwa			
Abadie			
Appiadie			
Tweedam (or Etchwee)	Aduana ne Atwea	Aduana ne Atwea (Abrade?)	Aduana ne Atwea (including Asenie, Amoakare, Adaa, Nanyo and Abira)
Agoona	Agona ne Asokore	Agona ne Toa (Adome?)	Agona ne Toa
Doomina			
	Atena		
	Asakyiri		Asakyiri
		Asenie	
2	8	7	7

was abolished, if not entirely annihilated'. Clearly it did not exist in 1817. Probably in the last quarter of the nineteenth century, however, the clan was revived in Mampon for certain internal political reasons; clearly in 1907 it did exist. It was abolished again in 1946, when the Asantehene informed those claiming membership of it,

> that henceforth you shall be known as members of the Bretuo Clan i.e. you are merged into the Bretuo Clan of Mampong . . . I, as the successor of Katakyie [Opoku Ware], confirm the decision taken by him in respect of this clan and decree that there is no Tena Clan in Mampong or for that matter in the whole of Ashanti. All you who termed yourselves as Tena people are, as from today, classified as Bretuo people.[96]

It will also be apparent from Table 8 that at some period after 1817 the 'Doomina' clan was incorporated with the Asona.

It may be suggested then, that in the era of the great clearances a number of matriclans were created, among which people were in some way distributed in order to facilitate the organisation of labour, and particularly of immigrant labour, at the appropriate level; that as the level of the labour requirements of the economy subsequently fell, so the matriclans became of less and less relevance to production; that as the relevance of the matriclans diminished, so was their number reduced as exemplified with the abolition of the Atena sometime before the middle of the eighteenth century;[97] that twelve clans survived at the beginning of the nineteenth century; and that seven exist at present. The complementary argument may also be made, that in the savannah country to the north of the forest, where massive clearances had never to be undertaken, the Akan or Bron lacked reason to create instruments of social organisation of the level of the matriclan: it has been seen above that, in Rattray's words, 'their exogamous divisions seem based upon an entirely different model'.

In the first half of the eighteenth century, at the time of the great wars of expansion, the rural economy was sufficiently durable to allow the Asante government to withdraw labour temporarily from the farms at the level necessary to man the armies – frequently ones of upwards of 25,000 men. As a result of the large numbers of captives taken, Asante became for a time one of the major suppliers of labour to the growing economies of the New World. By the end of the eighteenth century, however, the agricultural expansion made necessary by the growth of the Asante urban population created new demands for labour in ways suggested above, and a constant flow, especially from the northern hinterland, was ensured through the regularisation of the tribute system.[98] Throughout the nineteenth century, and to the present, the Asante rural economy has remained dependent upon an immigrant labour force. In the early twentieth century the British colonial administration, having abolished slavery, was obliged to save the economy by introducing forced labour until such time as an effective system of wage incentives could be created.[99] To the present, nevertheless, many of the labourers within the rural economy, in both 'traditional' and 'modern' (that is, cocoa farming) sectors, remain essentially share-croppers. The vital role of the unfree workers in traditional Asante society was explained by a number of Adanse chiefs in 1906: 'Every town in this Ashanti consist of three heads and afterwards became individual. i. the real town born ii. Captives and marrying born from other places and iii. slaves born'. If the slaves were to be freed, they remarked, 'then no more towns in Ashanti . . . all our drums, blowing horns swords, elephants tail basket carrying and *farming works* are done by these'.[100] But the issues raised here are beyond those considered in this paper, which has been concerned with the creation rather than the maintenance of the agrarian order.[101]

NOTES

PART I

1 For a statement, incautious perhaps, on the 'disintegrating effect' of the humid forest environment, see Maquet, J. (1972), *Civilizations of Black Africa*, New York, pp. 85-6.

2 There is little doubt that humid forest has been retreating in this area, see e.g. Chipp, T.F. (1927), *The Gold Coast Forest: a Study in Synecology*, Oxford, pp. 67-9; Wills, J.B. (1962), 'The general pattern of land use', *in* Wills, J.B. (ed.), *Agriculture and Land Use in Ghana*, London, pp. 202, 221-2. It has not yet been possible to determine the rate of transition from forest to wooded savannah, though careful study of the historical record and of place names may in time yield results.

3 Walker, H.O. (1962), 'Weather and climate', *in* Wills (ed.) (1962), pp. 7-50.

4 Brammer, H. (1962), 'Soils', *in* Wills (ed.) (1962), pp. 92-104.

5 Lane, D.A. (1962), 'The forest vegetation', *in* Wills (ed.) (1962), p. 160.

6 *Idem.* Ahn, P.M. (1970), *West African Agriculture, I: West African Soils,* London, pp. 107-11. For an older but detailed account of the composition of the climax, see Chipp (1927), pp. 46-55 and 91-4.

7 Lane (1962), pp. 160-2; Chipp (1927), pp. 52-5; Collins, W.B. (1959), *The Perpetual Forest*, Philadelphia and New York, pp. 74-90.

8 Dupuis, J. (1824), *Journal of a Residence in Ashantee*, London, pp. 15-16.

9 Richards, P.W. (1973), 'The tropical rain forest', *Scientific American*, 229, 6 Dec., p. 59.

10 Varley, W.J. and White, H.P. (1958), *The Geography of Ghana*, London, pp. 26-9; Phillips, J. (1959), *Agriculture and Ecology in Africa*, London, p. 90; Wills (1962), p. 205; Ahn (1970), pp. 94-8.

11 Ahn (1970), pp. 118-23.

12 Ahn (1970), pp. 245-7.

13 Phillips (1959), p. 149.

14 Ahn (1970), p. 120.

15 Two such stories may conveniently be found in Brown, E.J.P. (1929), *Gold Coast and Ashanti Reader,* Book II, London, pp. 73-80. The first tells of an attempt to create a new farm which was thwarted by the *mmoatia* ('gnomes'), and the second of the discovery of the utility of palm-wine in facilitating the heavy labour of forest clearing.

16 Cardinall, A.W. (1931), *The Gold Coast, 1931,* Accra, p. 84.

17 See Bray, F.R. (1959), *Cocoa Development in Ahafo, West Ashanti*, Achimota, p. 30, for comments on the neglect of food farms.

18 See, for example, Manhyia Record Office, Kumase: proceedings in the Asantehene's Divisional Appeal Court B5, Akua Bemmah *vs.* Akua Kuntoh, 1952. It has been not uncommon for the incumbent tenants to allow newcomers to clear such fallow and only after to bring the case to court. The incidence of such litigation has increased with the rise in land values consequent upon the introduction of cocoa as a cash crop.

19 For the equivalence of the field with the farm, in the sense of unit of land under cultivation at any one time, see Killick, T. (1966), 'Agriculture and forestry', *in* Birmingham, W., Neustadt, I. and Omaboe, E.N. (eds.), *A Study of Contemporary Ghana*, Vol. I: *The Economy of Ghana*, Evanston, pp. 224-5.

20 Bray (1959), p. 26.

21 Allen (1965), *The African Husbandman*, London, pp. 63, 228.

22 Killick (1966), pp. 223-5.

23 Brammer (1962), p. 146; Quartey-Papafio, H.K. (1970), 'Problems of settled farming in Ghana', *The Ghana Farmer*, XIV, 1, p. 13.

24 Hutton, W. (1821), *A Voyage to Africa*, London, p. 202.

25 Dupuis (1824), p. 37.

26 See e.g. Chipp, T.F. (1922), *The Forest Officers' Handbook of the Gold Coast, Ashanti and the Northern Territories*, London, p. 25; Foggie, A. (1962), 'The role of forestry in the agricultural economy', *in* Wills (ed.) (1962), p. 229; Allen (1965), p. 227. See also Killick (1966) who shows that for Asante, in 1963, 74% of all land under food crops had been cultivated for three years or less, and 85% for four years or less. Even so, as Killick comments, the figures include the areas of almost continuous cultivation now existing around Kumase, which must account for most of the 15% of land in the fifth year of cultivation or above.

27 Wills (1962), p. 219; Nye, P.H. and Stephens, D. (1962), 'Soil fertility', *in* Wills (ed.), (1962), p. 135; Ahn (1970), pp. 235-6.

28 Ahn (1970), p. 236.

29 Wills (1962), p. 219; Collins (1959), p. 101, suggests a rather lower figure of 40 to 50 years. For a detailed account of the succession to secondary forest, see Chipp (1927), pp. 57-61, but see also Baker, H.G. (1962), 'The ecological study of vegetation in Ghana', *in* Wills (ed.) (1962), p. 156.

30 Ahn (1970), p. 123, Table 4.2. Ahn, p. 239, comments that 'it has been estimated that in a typical forest regrowth the weight of fresh organic material added annually to the soil may quickly reach the relatively high figure of 6 to 8 tons per acre'.

31 Foggie (1962), p. 229.

32 See e.g. Nye and Stephens (1962), p. 137.

33 Adapted from Wills (1962), pp. 202-3, Fig. 47.

34 See Wills (1962), pp. 220-2. For an account of the situation in 1912, between Kumase and Tarkwa, see Chipp (1927), pp. 91-4.

35 Wilks, I. (1975), *Asante in the Nineteenth Century: The Structure and Evolution of a Political Order*, London, p. 93.

36 See e.g. Bowdich, T.E. (1819), *Mission from Cape Coast Castle to Ashantee*, London, p. 29; Freeman, T.B. (1843), *Journal of Two Visits to the Kingdom of Ashanti*, London, p. 118.

37 Bowdich (1819), pp. 323-5.

38 Bowdich (1819), p. 31. The beds were to increase the depth of the topsoil.

39 Bowdich (1819), p. 325.

40 Hutton (1821), pp. 202-3.

41 Dupuis (1824), p. 69.

42 Freeman (1843), pp. 153, 159.

43 Ramseyer, F.A. and Kühne, J. (1875), *Four Years in Ashantee*, New York, p. 282.

44 Manhyia Record Office, Kumase: Kyidom Clan Tribunal Minute Book I. Kojo Nketia *vs.* Kwabena Domfe, case commencing 27 March 1928.

45 Bowdich, T.E. (1821a), *The British and French Expedition to Teembo*, Paris, p. 18.

46 Dupuis (1824), p. 58.

47 Dupuis (1824), p. 63. Compare Hutton (1821), p. 199.

48 Dupuis (1824), p. 57. Compare Hutton (1821), p. 192.

49 Killick (1966), p. 215.

50 See Bowdich (1819), pp. 26, 28, 31, 325; Hutton (1821), pp. 197, 205; Dupuis (1824), pp. 34, 44, 48, 57, 59, 63, 65; but see also Freeman (1843), p. 31. Allen (1965), p. 226, suggests that the present unpopularity of maize is due to its susceptibility to rodent damage – and indeed the rodent population may formerly have been better controlled by hunters. Moreover, in the nineteenth century maize was of great importance to the Asante commissariat (which provisioned armies and parties of travellers on official business) since it could be readily dried and stored. Robertson, G.A. (1819), *Notes on Africa*, London, p. 201, reported that maize had recently been introduced from central Asante into the northern hinterlands, where it was used as animal fodder.

51 Irvine, F.R. (1930), *Plants of the Gold Coast*, Oxford, p. 400. See also Reindorf, C.C. (1895), *History of the Gold Coast and Asante*, Basel, 1st ed., p. 269.

52 See, e.g., Dupuis (1824), pp. 65-6.

53 Nye and Stephens (1962), pp. 139-40.

54 See, e.g., Bowdich (1819), p. 325; Hutton (1821), p. 205. A type of chisel perhaps used for deep rooting is also mentioned by T.B. Freeman, who observed that the implement was made by local blacksmiths from imported iron, see *The Western Echo*, 6 March 1886.

55 Killick (1966), p. 217.

56 Doku, E.V. (1967), 'Are there any alternatives to the traditional bush fallow system of maintaining fertility?', *The Ghana Farmer*, XI, 1, pp. 27-9; Affran, D.K. (1968), 'Cassava and its economic importance', *The Ghana Farmer*, XII, 4, p. 174; Bray (1959), p. 29; Brammer (1962), p. 146; Nye and Stephens (1962), p. 137.

57 For yields see, e.g., *Annual Report of the Department of Agriculture for the Year 1954-55*, 1957, p. 48; Karikari, S.K. (1970), 'Problems of plantain (Musa Paradisiaca) production in Ghana', *The Ghana Farmer,* XIV, 2, pp. 55-6; Wills (ed.) (1962), pp. 371-2, 374-5, 375-6, 377-8, 381-2; May, J.M. (1965), *The Ecology of Malnutrition in Middle Africa*, New York, p. 32. Figures for maize are for mature grain on the cob, and assume about 5,000 plants per acre.

58 Watson, J.D. (1971), 'Investigations on the nutritive value of some Ghanaian foodstuffs', *Ghana Journal of Agricultural Science,* 4, pp. 95-111. The figure for cocoyam is corrected for the older variety. Comparison may be made with Nicholls, L. (1951), *Tropical Nutrition and Dietetics*, London, pp. 402-26; Welbourn, H.F. (1963), *Nutrition in Tropical Countries*, London, pp. 114-15, Table 3.

59 Ghana Central Bureau of Statistics, *Statistical and Economic Papers No. 8*, 1961, pp. 84-6. The report notes that the figures are probably a 'little low' since food actually consumed by people working on their farms is not included. See further Ghana Office of Government Statistician, *Statistical and Economic Papers No. 7*, 1960, especially pp. 102-3. For the purposes of this paper other plants which may sometimes be intercropped, for example, groundnuts, pineapples, okro, are disregarded; they constitute only a small proportion of the diet.

60 See Chipp (1922), p. 27 and note; Allen (1965), p. 228.

61 Wilks (1975), pp. 87-93.

62 Wilks, I., 'The golden stool and the elephant's tail', in G. Dalton (ed.), *Research in Economic Anthropology,* Vol. I, Greenwich (forthcoming, 1977).

63 Based on Walker (1962), p. 48, and averaged for Kumase and Bekwae.

64 Phillips (1959), p. 58.

65 Phillips (1959), pp. 160-1; Greenland, D.J. and Kowal, J.M.L. (1959), 'Nutrient content of the moist tropical forest of Ghana', *Plant and Soil*, 12, pp. 154-74.

66 Phillips (1959), pp. 160-61.

67 Computed from a projection of the data, assuming the wet weight to approach an asymptotic upper limit of about 500 tons in 100 years, and to approximate to 5 tons at the beginning of the fallow.

68 Dupuis (1824), p. 65.

69 Dupuis (1824), pp. 65-6.

70 Compare, for example, Lane, D.A. (1962), 'The forest vegetation', *in* Wills (ed.) (1962), pp. 161-2.

71 Bray (1959), pp. 62-3.

72 Cardinall (1931), pp. 86-7.

73 Liefstingh, G. (1965), 'Chemical clearing, a possibility', *The Ghana Farmer*, IX, 1, p. 13.

74 See e.g. Bray (1959), pp. 62-3; Beals, R.E. *et al.* (1966), *Labor Migration and Regional Development in Ghana*, Report of the Transportation Centre at Northwestern University, Evanston, Part II, p. 187.

75 Sources consulted in the preparation of these estimates include Wood, R.C. (1957), *A Notebook of Tropical Agriculture*, Trinidad, pp. 24-8; Urquhart, D.M. (1961), *Cocoa*, London, 2nd ed., p. 238; Wadhwa, N.D. (1965), 'Improving of efficiency on a mechanized farm', *The Ghana Farmer,* IX, 4, p. 157; Beals *et al.* (1966), Part II, pp. 186-96. No estimates have been made for lesser intercrops such as groundnuts.

76 Doku (1967), p. 28.

77 See Bray (1959), p. 64, and compare Phillips, P.G. (1954), 'The metabolic cost of common West African agricultural activities', *Journal of Tropical Medicine and Hygiene*, 57, p. 15.

78 Estimates of calorie inputs are based on Phillips (1954), *passim*. Compare also Nicholls (1951), p. 315; King, M.H. *et al.* (1972), *Nutrition for Developing Countries*, Nairobi, 6.2.

79 Nicholls (1951), p. 309.

80 Harris, M. (1971), *Culture, Man and Nature*, New York, pp. 203-16.

81 Kormondy, E.J. (1969), *Concepts of Ecology*, Englewood Cliffs, N.J., pp. 127-8, cites data on the relative 'power' of the moist tropical forest ecosystem. For example, the ratio of dead organic matter (humus) to green litter is one indicator of the rate of decomposition and of mineral recycling. For the shrubby tundra this is computed at 92:1; for boreal spruce forest, 15:1; for temperate oak forest, 4:1; and for moist tropical forest, 0.1:1.

82 Ramseyer and Kühne (1875), p. 106: 'no work is to be done in any plantation on a Thursday'.

83 See, e.g., Dupuis (1824), p. 213 note.

84 Nketia, J.H.K. (1955). *Funeral Dirges of the Akan People*. Achimota. pp. 142, 211. Nketia's version is a gloss on, rather than a literal translation of, the highly elliptical Twi original.

PART II

1 In the course of the eighteenth century Asante extended its sway far into the grasslands of its northern hinterland. There were indeed periods, and most notably that of the reign of the Asantehene Osei Kwame (1777-98), when the future of the nation might have appeared to be that of a savannah rather than a forest power, see Wilks, I. (1975), *Asante in the Nineteenth Century: the Structure and Evolution of a Political Order*, London, pp. 250-1. The seat of the court and government, however, was in fact to remain firmly based in Kumase – even after 1874 when the British had demonstrated the vulnerability of that city to invasion from the southern seaboard, the Gold Coast.

2 Rattray, R.S. (1923), *Ashanti*, Oxford, p. 121.

3 Rattray (1923), p. 122.

4 Daaku, K. (1966), 'Pre-Ashanti states', *Ghana Notes and Queries*, 9, *passim*.

5 General State Archives, the Hague, W.I.C. verspreyde stukken 848: report by Director-General Abrams, dd. Elmina, 23 November 1679.

6 General State Archives, The Hague, KvG 360: Simons' Journal of a Mission to Asante, 1831-2.

7 Davies, O. (1960), 'The neolithic revolution in tropical Africa', *Transactions of the Historical Society of Ghana*, IV, 2, p. 20; Davies, O. (1967), *West Africa before the Europeans: Archaeology and Prehistory*, London, pp. 7-8, 205, 217, 283, 313.

8 Nunoo, R. (1969). 'Buruburo factory excavations', *Actes du Premier Colloque International d'Archéologie Africaine,* Fort-Lamy, pp. 321-33. The present writer has also found stone rasps, characteristic of the more northerly 'Kintampo neolithic', near Kumase. See further Anquandah, J., 'Boyasi Hill – a Kintampo Neolithic Village site in the Forest of Ghana', *Nyame Akuma*, 8, May 1976, pp. 33-5.

9 Davies (1967), pp. 7-8, 19, 242-3, 291-2, 313.

10 One of the fullest versions recorded to date is that in Agyeman-Duah, J. (1960), 'Mampong, Ashanti: a traditional history to the reign of Nana Safo Katanka', *Transactions of the Historical Society of Ghana*, IV, 2, *passim*.

11 Manhyia Record Office, Kumase, Agyeman Prempe I, Nana (1907), *The History of the Ashanti Kings and the Whole Country Itself*, unpublished ms.; it should be noted that he had access to members of an older generation than his own, and particularly to his mother, the Asantehemaa Nana Yaa Kyaa, who was born in the 1840s.

12 Twi *sisi*, the ratel or honeybadger, *mellivora capensis*.

13 Agyeman Prempe I (1907), pp. 1-3, 27-8. In other branches of Asante tradition, the Aduana and Atwea are regarded as having also appeared from a hole in the ground at Santemanso, see e.g. Rattray (1923), pp. 123-4. Ankyewa Nyame, moreover, is also sometimes regarded as ancestress not only of the Oyoko but also of the Aduana; see Agyeman-Duah, J. (1968), 'Esumegya stool history', unpublished ms., p. 2, and compare Rattray, R.S. (1929), *Ashanti Law and Constitution*, Oxford, p. 199, n. 1.

14 Institute of African Studies, Legon, I.A.S.A.S./44: 'Kokofu stool history', recorded by J. Agyeman-Duah, 28 February 1963.

15 Institute of African Studies, Legon, I.A.S.A.S./151: 'Akokofe stool history', recorded by J. Agyeman-Duah, 24 May 1965.

16 Agyeman Prempe I (1907), pp. 4-5.

17 Agyeman Prempe I (1907), pp. 36-8. Institute of African Studies, Legon, I.A.S.A.S./110: 'Kenyase stool history', recorded by J. Agyeman-Duah, 1 March 1964; I.A.S.A.S./152: 'Kuntenase stool history', recorded by J. Agyeman-Duah, 21 February 1965.

18 For Neyendael's mission to 'the great Asjante Caboceer Zaay', see Fynn, J.K. (1971), *Asante and its Neighbours 1700-1807*, London, pp. 156-9.

19 Bowdich, T.E. (1819), *Mission from Cape Coast Castle to Ashantee*, London, p. 29.

20 See e.g. Agyeman-Duah (1960), p. 21.

21 See e.g. Denteh, A.C. (1973), 'The Asona clan', unpublished ms.

22 See e.g. Rattray (1929), p. 271, but compare Agyeman-Duah (1968), p. 5.

23 Rattray (1929), p. 217.

24 For a useful summary of this matter, with a map of the locations, see Boaten, K. (1971), 'The Asante before 1700', *Research Review*, 8, 1, Institute of African Studies, Legon, *passim*.

25 For the Oyoko, see Agyeman Prempe I (1907), pp. 2-4; the Bretuo, Agyeman-Duah (1960), pp. 21-2; the Asona, Denteh (1973) *passim*; the Asenie, Rattray (1929), Fig. 98; and the Aduana, Rattray (1929), p. 217 and Fig. 50.

26 Priestley, M. and Wilks, I. (1960), 'The Ashanti kings in the eighteenth century: revised chronology', *Journal of African History*, I, 1, pp. 84-91.

27 Agyeman-Duah (1960), p. 22.; Wilks, I. (1960), 'A note on the traditional history of Mampong', *Transactions of the Historical Society of Ghana*, IV, 2, p. 26.

28 Denteh (1973).

29 Reindorf, C.C. (n.d.), *History of the Gold Coast and Asante*, Basel, 2nd ed., p. 57.

30 Rattray (1929), p. 271 and Fig. 98.

31 Rattray (1929), pp. 219-20 and Fig. 50.

32 Reindorf, C.C. (1895), *History of the Gold Coast and Asante*, Basel, 1st ed., p. 44.

33 Dupuis, J. (1824), *Journal of a Residence in Ashantee*, London, p. 224. For a consideration of Dupuis' sources, see Wilks, I. (1961a), *The Northern Factor in Ashanti History*, Legon, pp. 30-43. Earlier, seemingly from Asante sources, Bowdich had obtained hints of the same tradition, see Bowdich (1819), p. 229.

34 Ellis, A.B. (1887), *The Tshi-speaking Peoples of the Gold Coast of West Africa*, London, pp. 331-2. See further, for example, Casely Hayford, J.E. (1903), *Gold Coast Native Institutions*, p. 24; Balmer, W.T. (1926), *A History of the Akan Peoples of the Gold Coast*, London and Cape Coast, Ch. 1.

35 For some account of this matter, see Fage, J.D. (1957), 'Ancient Ghana: a review of the evidence', *Transactions of the Historical Society of Ghana*, III, 1. pp. 92-6. The earliest such extravaganza, based upon an argument from cultural similarities, is that in Bowdich, T.E. (1821b), *An Essay on the Superstitions, Customs and Arts common to the Ancient Egyptians, Abyssinians, and Ashantees*, Paris, *passim*.

36 Rattray (1929), p. 64.

37 Meyerowitz, E.L.R. (1952), *Akan Traditions of Origin*, London, *passim*.

38 Rattray (1929), p. 64.

39 Rattray (1929), pp. 64-5.

40 Reindorf (1895), pp. 44-5.

41 Rattray, R.S. (1916), *Ashanti Proverbs*, Oxford, p. 41.

42 Bowdich (1819), pp. 230-1.

43 Cardinall, A.W. (1931), *The Gold Coast, 1931*, Accra, p. 85.

44 Rattray (1929), pp. 348-9.

45 Mauny, R. (1949), 'Eustache de la Fosse: voyage dans l'Afrique occidentale (1479-80)', *Boletim Cultural da Guine Portuguesa,* IV, 14, pp. 188, 190. Blake, J.W. (1942), *Europeans in West Africa, 1450-1560,* 2 vols, London, Vol. I, p. 240.

46 See Crone, G.R. (1937), *The Voyages of Cadamosto*, London, p. 124.

47 See Kimble, G.H.T. (1937), *Esmeraldo de Situ orbis*, London, p. 121; Mauny, R. (1956), *Esmeraldo de Situ orbis*, Bissau, pp. 126-7.

48 Crone (1937), p. 125. The accounts of one factor, Estevão Barradas, have been printed, who sold '440 head of slaves, male and female' at Elmina between August 1504 and January 1507; see Blake (1942), Vol. I, p. 107.

49 For the Akani, see Kea, R.A. (1974), *Trade, State Formation and Warfare on the Gold Coast, 1600-1826,* Ph.D. dissertation, London University, Ch. II, *passim.*

50 Kimble (1937), p. 120; Mauny (1956), pp. 122-5.

51 Crone (1937), p. 125. De Barros commented that the Portuguese were rewarded for their sacrifice by the discovery of a new gold mine near Elmina. Other reports suggest that the discovery occurred in 1551, and that the mine was some fifty leagues inland, see Blake (1942), Vol. I, p. 178.

52 See Kea (1974), pp. 142-3. For the period see also Faro, J. (1958), 'A organizacão comercial de S. Jorge da Mina em 1529 e as suas relacoes com a ilha de S. Tome', *Boletim Cultural da Guine Portuguesa*, XIII, 49; Ryder, A.F.C. (1964), 'An early Portuguese trading voyage to the Forcados River', *Journal of the Historical Society of Nigeria,* I, 4; Rodney, W. (1969), 'Gold and slaves in the Gold Coast', *Transactions of the Historical Society of Ghana,* X, pp. 13-28; Vogt, J.L. (1973), 'The early São Tome-Principe slave trade with Mina, 1500-1540', *The International Journal of African Historical Studies*, 6, 3.

53 Birmingham, D. (1970), 'The Regimento da Mina', *Transactions of the Historical Society of Ghana,* XI, pp. 4-5.

54 See Posnansky, M. (1971), *The Origins of West African Trade,* Legon, pp. 8-12; Goody, J. (1964), 'The Mande and the Akan hinterland', *in* Vansina, J., Mauny, R. and Thomas, L.V. (eds.), *The Historian in Tropical Africa*, London, *passim*; Wilks, I. (1961b), 'The northern factor in Ashanti history: Begho and the Mande', *Journal of African History,* II, 1, *passim;* Wilks, I. (1962a), 'A medieval trade route from the Niger to the Gulf of Guinea', *Journal of African History,* III, 2, *passim*; Wilks, I. (1972), 'The Mossi and Akan states 1500-1800', *in* Ajayi, J.F.A. and Crowder, M. (eds.), *History of West Africa,* Vol. I., New York, pp. 354-8. See also Bravmann, R.A. and Mathewson, R.E. (1970), 'A note on the history and archaeology of Old Bima', *International Journal of African Historical Studies*, II, 1, *passim.*

55 See Kimble (1937), p. 89; Mauny (1956), pp. 64-5.

56 Governor of Elmina to King of Portugal dd. 19 August 1513; see da Mota, A. Teixeira (1972), 'The Mande trade in Costa da Mina', unpublished paper, Conference on Manding Studies, S.O.A.S., London University, pp. 12, 20.

57 Wilks, I. (1962b), 'The Mande loan element in Twi', *Ghana Notes and Queries*, 4, pp. 26-8. Interesting evidence of the presence of *nnonkofo* in the southwestern forestlands at a date of ca. 1700 is to be found in Bellis, J.O. (1972), *Archeology and the Culture History of the Akan of Ghana*, Ph.D. dissertation, Indiana University. Excavations near Twifo Heman revealed figurines, from funerary contexts, showing the characteristic scarification patterns of the *nnonkofo.*

58 See e.g. Goody, J. (1967), 'The over-kingdom of Gonja', *in* Forde, D. and Kaberry, P.M. (eds.), *West African Kingdoms in the Nineteenth Century,* London, *passim*; Wilks (1972), pp. 362-4.

59 For a general consideration of the importance of the horse in this context, see Goody, J. (1971), *Technology, Tradition, and the State in Africa*, London, especially Chs. 2-4.

60 Davies (1967), p. 314.
61 Dupuis (1824), pp. xxxvi, cxxxi.
62 Davies (1967), pp. 24-5.
63 In 1701 the Dutch factor Bosman doubted the existence of lode mining in the interior, and surmised that 'the Negroes only ignorantly dig at random, without the least Knowledge of the Veins of the Mine', see Bosman, W. (1705), *A New and Accurate Description of the Coast of Guinea*, London, p. 86. A few years later, however, the Danish factor Rφmer was able to contradict this, pointing out that 'our good Bosman has scarcely ever seen any of the folk who dig for gold', see Rφmer, L.F. (1760), *Tilforladelig Efterretning om Kysten Guinea*, Copenhagen, p. 174.
64 General State Archives, The Hague, W.I.C. 100, Nuyts' Journal, entry for 16 April 1707.
65 Rφmer (1760), pp. 177-8.
66 Müller, W.J. (1673), *Die Africanische Landschafft Fetu*, Hamburg, pp. 272-3.
67 Dupuis (1824), p. 53. The 'Accaseer', 'Acasse', etc. of seventeenth-century European sources usually refers to the old town of Kaase immediately south of Kumase. Müller's description, however, cannot be fitted to Kaase, though he himself may have assumed 'Kusa' to be 'Kaase'.
68 See Wilks (1972), p. 358. The writer is currently preparing a more detailed study of the early mining industry in Asante.
69 Wilks (1972), p. 358.
70 Valentim Fernandes, see Cernival, P. de, and Monod, Th. (1938), *Description de la Côte d'Afrique de Ceuta au Sénégal,* Paris, pp. 86-7.
71 Wilks (1972), p. 360.
72 Godhino, V.M. (1969), *L'Economie de l'Empire Portugais aux XVe et XVIe siècles,* Paris, p. 217.
73 Valentim Fernandes reported that a prosperous Dyula ('Ungaro', that is, Wangara) merchant of Jenne, the major western Sudanese mart for gold from the Akan country, might have a business rising to 7,500 ounces – presumably gross annual turnover; see Cernival and Monod (1938), pp. 84-7. There is sufficient evidence for the continuing importance of the Western Sudanese and trans-Saharan gold trade through the seventeenth and eighteenth centuries to cast considerable doubt upon Braudel's view that the Portuguese were able to 'capture' the northern trade, see Braudel, F. (1946), 'Monnaies et civilisation: de l'or du Soudan à l'argent d'Amérique', *Annales: Economies, Sociétés, Civilisations,* I, 1, Jan.-March, pp. 12-3.
74 For a recent study of the matter, see Watson, A.M. (1967), 'Back to gold – and silver', *Economic History Review, 2nd series,* XX, 1, *passim.*
75 Wilks (1961a), pp. 5-6; Wilks (1972), pp. 354-62. For a further consideration of the issue, see Malowist, M. (1970), 'Quelques observations sur le commerce de l'or dans le Soudan occidental au Moyen Age', *Annales: Economies, Sociétés, Civilisations,* XXV, 6, Nov.-Dec., *passim.*
76 Reindorf (1895), p. 47, reports an interesting tradition, that in the period of Kobea Amamfi of Santemanso (whose *floruit* was probably a late sixteenth to early seventeenth century one, see above), iron rather than gold was the circulating medium.
77 For some observations on this matter, see Fortes, M. (1969), *Kinship and the Social Order*, Chicago, p. 167. and note.
78 Fortes, (1969), p. 163, and see pp. 158-90 for a general reconsideration of the Asante lineage.
79 Bowdich (1819), p. 230; compare Fortes (1969), p. 159.
80 Compare Fortes (1969), p. 161.
81 Douglas, M. (1971), 'Is matriliny doomed in Africa?', *in* Douglas, M. and Kaberry, P.M. (eds.), *Man in Africa*, New York, pp. 127-8, 132.
82 *West African Lands Committee: Minutes of Evidence*, Colonial Office, London, 1916: evidence of Rev. Lochman, dd. 19 Oct. 1912.
83 Agyeman Prempe I, (1907), pp. 3, 24-7.

84 Compare Rattray (1929), p. 235, note 1.

85 Agyeman Prempe I (1907), p. 24.

86 Wilks (1975), p. 86.

87 Rattray (1929), p. 42.

88 Compare Bowdich (1819), p. 302: 'Infants are as frequently wedded by adults and elderly men'.

89 Terray, E. (1972), *Marxism and 'Primitive' Societies*, London, pp. 128-9.

90 Eich, H.J. zur (1677), 'Africanische Reissbeschreibung in die Landschaft Fetu', *Vier loblicher Statt Zürich verbürgerter Reissbeschreibungen*, Part 2, pp. 91-174.

91 For an exploratory simulation of the transition, see Berberich, C. (1975), 'A simulation of Akan history', *Asante Seminar '75*, No. 1, Program of African Studies, Northwestern University, March, p. 16.

92 Asanteman Council Archives, Manhyia, Kumase: Notes on Ashanti Customs, prepared by Captain Warrington and reviewed by a Committee appointed by the Ashanti Confederacy Council, 24 July 1942.

93 Rattray (1929), pp. 66-7, and compare Rattray (1916), p. 42. It is an extraordinary fact that, after many years of research in Asante, Rattray remained uncertain about the precise listing of the clans.

94 Agyeman Prempe I (1907), pp. 1-3.

95 Bowdich (1819), pp. 229-30.

96 Asanteman Council Archives, Manhyia, Kumase: emergency session of Council, June 1946. See further, Wilks (1975), pp. 105-6.

97 In Akan Areas not subject to the political control of the Asantehene, the pattern of reduction will not have followed the same course. Hence the major differences in terminology and number between the clans of, for example, the Fante and those of Asante, see Christensen, J.B. (1954), *Double Descent among the Fante,* New Haven, pp. 23-5.

98 See Wilks (1975), pp. 66-7, 674-5.

99 Thomas, R.G. (1973), 'Forced labour in British West Africa: the case of the Northern Territories of the Gold Coast', *Journal of African History* XIV, 1, *passim.*

100 National Archives of Ghana, Kumase, D. 234: nine Adanse chiefs to Commissioner, Southern Province of Asante, dd. Fomena, 30 November 1906.

101 I am much indebted to Dr. Charles Berberich for producing the map, and to Michael Culhane of the Program of African Studies, Northwestern University, for invaluable assistance in preparing the paper for publication. Since this paper was written, G. Benneh of the University of Ghana has published a number of interesting accounts of forest agriculture, drawing attention to much the same features stressed in Part I above; see for example Benneh, G. (1974), 'The ecology of peasant farming systems in Ghana', *Environment in Africa*, I, 1, Dec., pp. 35-49. Attention is also drawn to the researches in Ghana of Dr. Kiyaga-Mulindwa, who has carried out trial excavations at a number of forest sites in the Birim valley (Akyem Kotoku), locally regarded as 'aboriginal' villages; the two radiocarbon dates so far obtained – 1465 ± 65 and 1510 ± 80 A.D. – are of obvious relevance to the argument of this paper.

JACK GOODY

Population and polity in the Voltaic region

What is the nature of the relationship between states and population, between the centralisation of the polity and the density of the inhabitants? Gordon Childe saw the agricultural revolution of the Near East as leading to population growth and the formation of the state. Ester Boserup attempts to reverse the direction of the causal arrow and sees agricultural development as the result of the pressure of people on land.[1] Both arguments assume that states are characterised by denser populations than 'tribes without rulers' (to use the phrase of Middleton and Tait).[2] While such an association undoubtedly holds for the long run (more technology = more people = more government), the correlation is not of a simple linear kind and the attempt to impose such a model on Africa contradicts what we know about its economy, its polity and its demography. It is inconsistent with the basic features of the 'African mode of production'.[3]

The assumption that African states have higher densities than the acephalous areas has been vigorously sustained by Stevenson[4] and his thesis has been pointedly used by Harris[5] not only to dispute the tentative conclusion of Fortes and Evans-Pritchard[6] that no such association was found in the societies examined by the contributors to *African Political Systems* but also as a stick to beat the functionalist horse. Whatever the general merits of this enterprise (and it is certainly far from clear that the 'cultural materialist' nag provides a better ride), the thesis seems factually wrong and theoretically misguided. To support my point I turn to an area that plays a central part in all of these discussions, namely, that part of the West African savannahs now referred to as Northern Ghana.

The pre-colonial population of this region (i.e. before 1900) can be roughly divided into those who lived in states and those who lived in acephalous communities, that is, 'tribes without rulers'. The division is a crude one; it represents the distinction that is basic to *African Political Systems*, where following Durkheim[7] the terms 'segmentary' and 'lineage' were used to characterise the non-centralised forms, and it is a distinction that has been challenged by a number of authors, some of whom try to erode it and others to complicate it.

There seems to be no case for erosion, certainly in Northern Ghana. Indeed the first agent of British rule in the area, G.E. Ferguson, himself a Fanti from Southern Ghana, clearly distinguished between 'countries with organised government' on the one hand and 'barbarous tribes' on the other. The first group consisted of the states, that is Mamprusi, Dagomba, Nanumba, Wa and Gonja. The second were made up of peoples like the Tallensi, Kusasi, the LoDagaa, Konkomba and a number of others. For Ferguson, who was attempting to negotiate treaties, the difference between these two types of social system was clear and obvious. It was equally clear to traders who had to make different types of payment in each case; they stood the chance of being raided in the acephalous areas and were often forced to pay tolls or other dues in the centralised states.[8] But while there is no reason to erode the distinction, there does seem to be a case for complication, though this undertaking is not necessary for pursuing the present argument.

Let us consider the opening question concerning the relationship between polity, economy and density, in the context of Northern Ghana, where our general interest has been in the distribution of states, their rise and fall, and the question of why we find such a patchwork distribution of political systems in the area (Fig. 1).[9] As we noted the relationship between population and states in Africa has recently been the subject of a study by R. Stevenson,[10] a work that has received much approbation from his former colleagues at Columbia. In his book on the rise of anthropological theory, M. Harris writes of the distortions introduced because of the synchronic focus of *African Political System*, which threatened to reduce our understanding of state formation to a 'shambles'. He continues: 'Apparently oblivious of, or uninterested in, the fact that for every other continent the close correspondence between state systems and high population density had been established beyond a doubt, Fortes and Evans-Pritchard reached the conclusion that, "it would be incorrect to suppose that governmental institutions are found in those societies with greatest densities. The opposite seems to be equally likely judging by our material" '. These conclusions were based upon an examination of six case studies which included the Tallensi of Northern Ghana. Harris notes that Stevenson has taken each of these cases in turn, 'applied a diachronic perspective, utilising sources available in any major library, and reversed or seriously modified every negative instance'.[11] The basic contention is that 'far from being acephalous, as Stevenson shows, the Tallensi inhabited an area which had been controlled before the advent of the British by the Mamprusi kingdom'.[12] The Tallensi case is critical to the argument because the density is much higher than in the states nearby. So if it can be considered as centralised, or at least under the control of a state, this weakens the

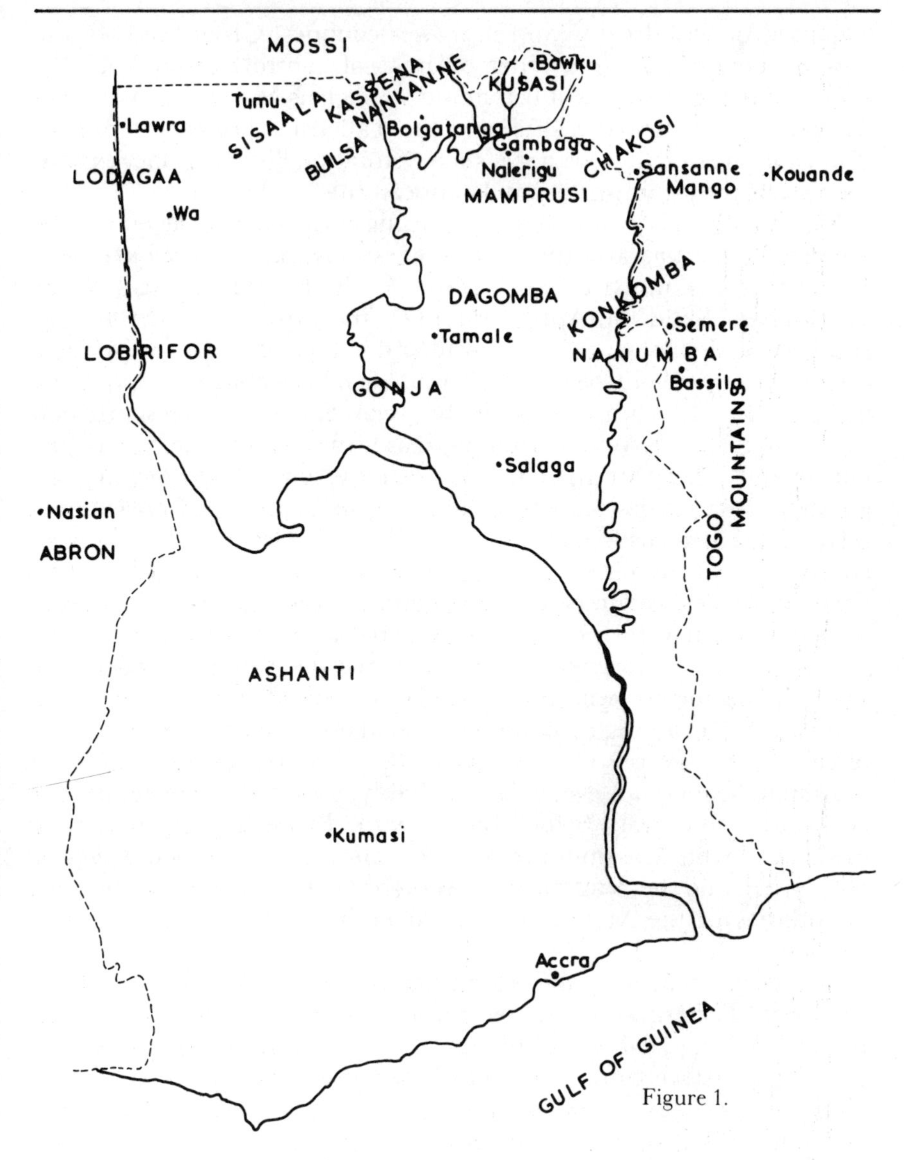

Figure 1.

suggestion that there was no observable correlation between density and polity.

Are the Tallensi in fact centralised? One element of that population, the Namoos, claims a link with chiefly lineages in neighbouring Mamprusi, having migrated from that kingdom. There are many similar traditions among the acephalous peoples of Northern Ghana. Some refer to disputes about office, which forced a particular group to leave and establish itself in an area beyond the boundaries, outside the control of that state. It may well be that the existence of such myths of origin does sometimes reflect the migration of conquerors and the establishment (or extension) of a state which later collapsed or withdrew within narrower confines. Given the ebb and flow of 'boundaries' (or rather of areas of control) throughout the region, it is certainly possible that a state such as Mamprusi may have dominated their tribal neighbours the Tallensi at an earlier period. But, from the evidence we have, such a situation did not in fact exist at the time of the establishment of European rule.

Mamprusi was not an altogether negligible power at the end of the nineteenth century and there are suggestions that it may have been larger still at a much earlier period. At the time of the visit of the Frenchman, Baud, on April 18th 1895, the capital of Nalerigu was still surrounded by an extensive wall and a ditch. Nearby the political centre was the flourishing market town of Gambaga, a 'point de passage' for the caravans going between Salaga in the south and Mossi in the north. When Baud paid his formal visit to the Nayiri (the paramount chief, Moussa) he was met by some 2,000 people; 'les guerriers sont rangés par categories, suivant qu'ils sont à cheval ou à pied; armés de fusils, d'arcs ou de lances'. Despite this show of strength, the boundaries of the kingdom were very restricted. At this time, Mamprusi made no claim to control either the trading town of Sansanne Mango to the east or the tribal area of 'Gurunshi' in the north-west (a category which often included the Tallensi). Indeed the road to the former was but sparsely populated, mainly by 'slave' cultivators. According to Baud, this weakness dated from the burning of the capital by the Chakosi when they established themselves at Sansanne Mango, an event that probably occurred in the eighteenth century. A few years before Baud's visit, Binger's party had been challenged when passing through the Frafra area (of which Taleland is a part) and he was clearly relieved to find himself within the boundaries of the Mamprusi state once he had crossed the White Volta.[13]

Shortly afterwards, and immediately before the advent of the British, G.E. Ferguson travelled throughout the region and it is clear that the Tallensi fell within his category of 'barbarous tribes', just as the Mamprusi were one of the 'organised governments'; indeed only a virginal innocence of the records could fail to recognise that at this time the Frafra fell outside the effective control of any state system.[14] Moreover the distinction between controlled and uncontrolled areas was as clear to Muslim traders as it was to the European treaty makers. At Bassila the Muslims pointed out to Baud that 'les populations sauvages qui occupent la région montaigneuse' between Sansanne Mango and Kouande, Semere, Kikiri, etc. had no relations with their neighbours. These refugee areas were plainly outside state control and constituted a threat to the trading communities. One group of 'kaffirs' challenged Baud's well-armed party and had to be pacified with a handful of beads. Such pacification, which is a kind of economic relationship, was doubtless a frequent occurrence – a cost to the traveller, a gain to the locals – since the caravan trade throughout the area was heavy, despite adverse conditions along the way from Hausaland, the destruction of the main trading town of Salaga in 1892,[15] the chaos at neighbouring Nikki,[16] the interference of the Europeans and the resistance of the Africans. Indeed the threatening of caravans resembles the kind of 'protection' the desert peoples offer to traders that pass through their midst and is one way in which the 'free' inhabitants of 'uncontrolled' areas extract wealth from the necessary transactions of the states.

These general distinctions between political systems were, then, observable both by travellers and by the actors themselves, and in the specific case of the Tallensi, Stevenson's assertion, despite the support given by Skinner, Harris and Fried,[17] tumbles to the ground. The attempt to include the Tallensi in the Mamprusi state fits all too

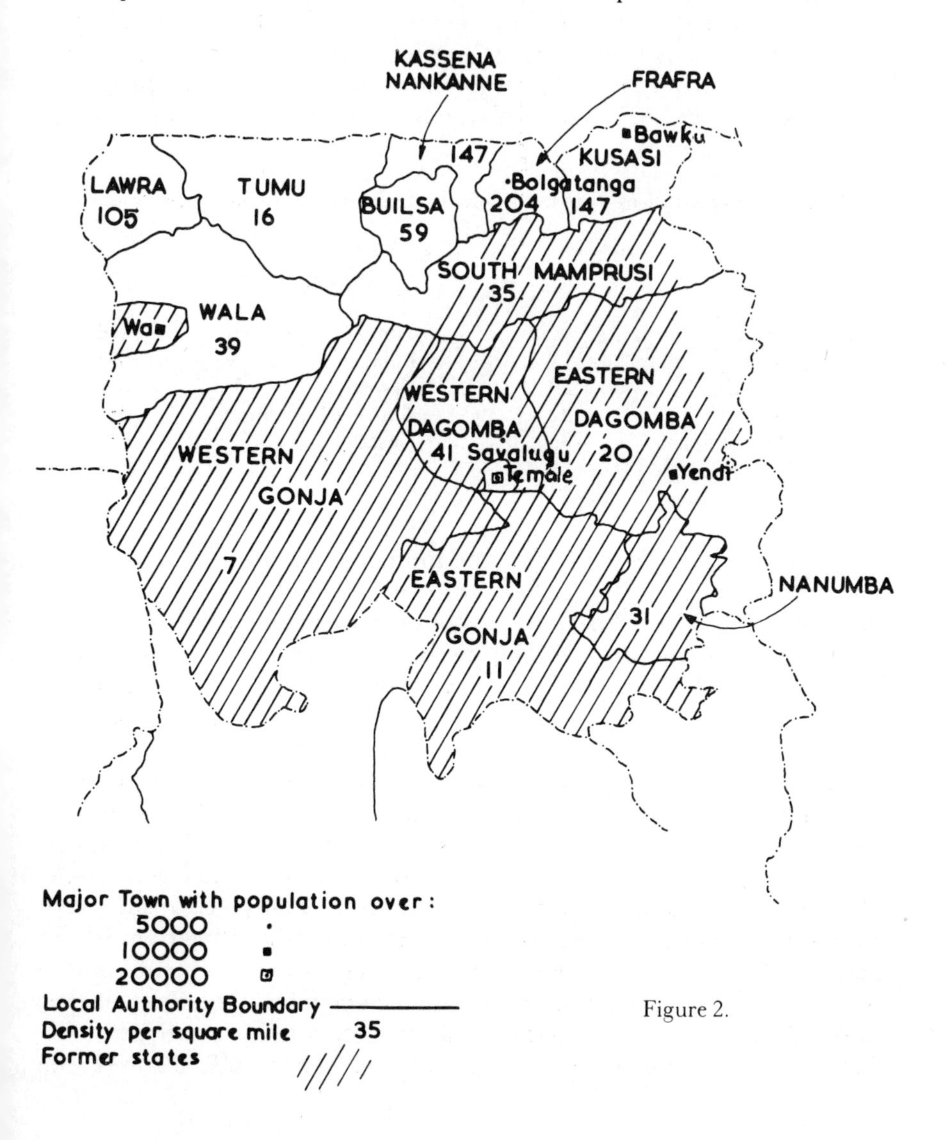

Figure 2.

neatly with the theory concerning the relation between polity and density, but it had no foundation in the period immediately before the colonial conquest. In any case, the other stateless peoples of Northern Ghana also have high densities. To extend the argument produced for the Tallensi and see all acephalous peoples with high densities as the relics of earlier states is a thesis that strains the credibility of even the most committed generaliser. Indeed it would also be necessary to apply the reverse argument to all the states since they regularly have lower densities.

Let us then accept the characterisation of the peoples of the area presented to us by Ferguson (not to mention the later work of Fortes and other scholars) and apply the thesis concerning population density. If we take the figures from the 1960 census (the most recently published) or from any previous one, we do indeed find evidence of a significant relationship (contrary to the cautious statement of Fortes and Evans-Pritchard) but it is the very opposite of the one proposed by Stevenson (Fig. 2). The table below sets out the relevant figures from the 1960 census.

Table 1. Population of Northern Ghana, 1960 census: density per square mile.

States		*Non-states*	
West Gonja	7	Tumu	16
East Gonja	11	Builsa	59
East Dagomba	20	Lawra	105
Nanumba	31	Kassena-Nankanne	147
South Mamprusi	35	Kusasi	147
Wa	39	Frafra	204
West Dagomba	41		

There was one other district, the municipal area of Tamale, which had a density of 626. This town lies within the former state of Dagomba, but it is well known (though Stevenson uses this instance as evidence for the pre-colonial picture) that in pre-colonial days it was a relatively unimportant 'fetish-town'; its present population consists almost entirely of strangers. It should also be added that the town of Bolgatanga in the Frafra district is the second largest in Northern Ghana and may somewhat swell the Frafra figures; on the other hand in this case a large percentage of the population come from the surrounding district. In considering special circumstances, undoubtedly the most disturbed area in the pre-colonial period was the Tumu and Builsa districts, from which many 'Grunshi' were despatched into slavery in other parts. Hausa writings bear witness to the great destruction wrought in this region as the result of the activities of Amrahia, Babatu and their associates, who were at first working partly for the Dagomba and later wholly for themselves. Without the attacks of freebooters and of neighbouring states, the density would undoubtedly have been much greater. Since the advent of colonial rule migration has also affected the region. But it is the non-state peoples that have tended to migrate; the percentage of persons of northern extraction living in the south of Ghana is again negatively correlated with the degree of political centralisation.

These figures refute Stevenson's suggestions, and at least for this area point to a positive association between states and low density. What is the explanation for a situation that runs so contrary to many accepted assumptions? In his recent discussion of the Kachin, Friedman[18] has examined a similar problem in the Kachin area of Burma. I cannot reproduce his argument in this context, but suffice it to say that he presents a case for 'devolution' (de-evolution) of the densely populated areas, based upon ecological considerations. He suggests that the state systems lead to exploitation, which in turn leads to inflation (because of the system of tribute and bride-wealth), overpopulation, and ultimately to a breakdown in the basic conditions which allowed for the original rise of states in the area. Hence it is in the more sparsely populated areas that one finds states, in the denser areas 'acephaly'.

It is possible that this thesis could account for some of the facts at our disposal; there may well be areas in the savannah country of West Africa that have seen this ecological degradation leading to a loss of political control. But it is difficult to see why the reversal should be so consistent and why all the states we are dealing with should be affected in the same way at the same point in time. In any case the situation here is substantially different from the Kachin area, not only because of the absence of a Shan type economy, but also because of a different organisation of 'tribute' and marriage. If there was 'de-evolution', it was not based upon over-exploitation of the environment, but of the human resources themselves.

My alternative hypothesis is directly related to the flaw in Stevenson's argument, for he is wrong for an interesting reason. In Eurasia, which he takes as his model, population growth was associated not with the state alone but with a centralised economy based upon the technical advances of the Bronze Age. If we follow the argument of Gordon Childe, the 'neolithic revolution' must have already led to a great increase in world population as compared to that under a hunting and gathering economy. The inventions of the Bronze Age, especially the plough, the wheel and irrigation, produced a further advance since they permitted a more intensive and productive agriculture, which increased the possibility of a societal saving (i.e. 'surplus'). It was in just such intensive agricultural economies that the states of the Fertile Crescent arose and expanded. But in Africa the situation was very different. Neolithic techniques spread throughout the continent; so did the much later advances of the Iron Age. But the Bronze Age inventions associated with intensive agriculture never penetrated south of the Sahara in pre-colonial times.

States were built on a very different economic base from Europe and Asia, having a system of shifting agriculture that was basically similar to that of the acephalous societies who were their neighbours, except in the more extensive use of slave labour and the greater demand for primary produce to support political, military, economic and religious specialists. Hence one should not expect any great differences in population density between states and 'tribes'. Such a hypothesis would appear to fit with the findings of Fortes and Evans-Pritchard that there was no significant relationship between density and centralisation.

In Northern Ghana, however, we find a negative correlation between centralisation and density. The stateless peoples such as the Frafra, the LoDagaa and the Tallensi, whether they had minor chiefs or not, are distinctly more crowded. Moreover, it is these groups that currently provide most of the labour migrants, so it is difficult to see that the position was any different at the end of the nineteenth century; indeed administrative records support the idea that these areas had a greater density in early colonial times. What is the reason for this difference between states and 'tribes'? First of all one must appreciate the patchwork nature of the political picture with the alternation of 'controlled' and 'uncontrolled' areas. The controlled areas were the territories of states that appear to have originated in conquest and certainly maintained themselves by their control of the means of destruction. Meanwhile these acephalous societies lay between these states whose agricultural technologies were much the same but whose military technologies were more advanced.

The ruling groups relied upon the use of horses, though this cavalry was often assisted by gunmen using imported Dane guns. To sustain this expensive weaponry, that is, the guns imported from the South and the horses from the North, the states had to provide commodities in exchange which were capable of being exported in both directions. In the savannah of West Africa the most valuable of these commodities was human beings. In search of slaves, the states raided the 'uncontrolled' populations, that is, the large 'tribal', 'acephalous' areas that lay in between, as well as capturing prisoners in inter-state wars. As a result of these raids the stateless peoples undoubtedly lost population. But raiding also made them huddle together in the safer areas so that they could better resist the invaders. One form of resistance was evasion, the tendency to seek out strategically favourable areas, high places such as the Tong Hills, the Togo mountains, the Jos plateau, the Bandiagara scarp, or the banks of rivers where they could flee to the other side and so escape the attacks of the horsemen. So it was the weak that tended to cluster together in refuge areas, while the strong controlled the emptier lands.

This strategy did not always pay off. But refuge areas were clearly attractive not only to stateless peoples but also to some of the subjects of kingdoms who wished to escape punishment, the revenge of princes, or perhaps to lead a freer life. Even where nature did not provide an adequate barrier to the aggression of others, the clustering together may itself have helped their resistance: in a report on the region in 1900, Maurice Delafosse notes how the slave raider, Babatu, avoided attacking certain areas where the villages were very populous. In other parts, such as Gwolu in Dagaba country, walls were built to provide a protected base, as well as a centre for local raiding. In many parts of the savannahs, free commoners clustered together to avoid the depradations of warrior kingdoms looking for human booty, for the market, for internal consumption, or because they were forced to provide such tribute to other states. This at any rate could be one major reason for the continuing differences in population between states and 'tribes' in Northern Ghana, leaving the latter distinctly more heavily populated than the former.

Clearly, if raiding was very severe, it could lead to a heavy loss of population, such as happened in what is now the Tumu district, inhabited by Grusi-speaking peoples.[19] Interestingly enough, it is precisely in this area of lower population that there emerged the embryonic state organised by these same free-booters, Amrahia, Babatu and their companions (some of whom were originally horse-traders from Songhai) after local resistance had been destroyed. Having devastated the country, they might also have succeeded in establishing a state. Moreover, in the course of the same process of devastation the resistance of the Sisaala and Dagaba led to the building of walled settlements and the emergence of local leaders who organised groups of men and women in a fashion that also looked like an emerging 'state', albeit a very small one. However, the process of state building would have doubtless required the destruction or incorporation of one by the other, leading to the establishment of a centralised government over an area from which may had fled or been killed.

This hypothesis is not the only one capable of accounting for the differences in population. It may be that, in other areas, invaders found it easier to conquer the more dispersed rather than the more concentrated populations.[20] However, with the invasions of Babatu and Samori in Northern Ghana, it seems to have been the process of forming or extending a state that led to the rapid reduction of population. For certainly the areas of Western Gonja into which the LoBirifor have been migrating since 1917 were heavily depopulated as the result of Samori's raids, just as the Tumu district was affected by the activities of Babatu.

Apart from these irregular wars, these 'non-processual' events, the annual raids made by established states into nearby areas inhabited by uncontrolled peoples may have reduced the population, whether by capture, death or flight, thus weakening their defences to such an extent as to lead to the incorporation of the area within the boundaries of the state (or at least within its outermost zone of control), and so providing an advanced point of departure for further raids into the more populous zone. Hence low population did not arise so much out of over-exploitation of the soil but of the people. The activities of the savannah states did not lead to greater pressure on the supply of food (indeed the reverse), but they resulted in the over-cropping of human resources on the boundary and possibly to the inclusion of these areas of devastation in the zone under centralised control. Clearly this process is related to the booty economy. While 'de-evolution' or 'ecological degradation' accounts for some aspects of the distribution of the population in the savannah zones of Africa, it is a process that operated directly on the human resources rather than through the medium of the food supply.

In discussing the relations between states and 'tribes' and their affect on the distribution of population, I have stressed the frontier as a zone than a boundary. This area was important not only for the economy of the states but also as a training ground, in a manner somewhat analogous to the internal frontier in the U.S.A., which has been discussed in the works of F.J. Turner and others.[21] In Africa the frontier provided an arena where the members of a militarily superior power could exercise dominance over their neighbours, and at the same time cultivate the values of individualism and hardiness, as well as those of harshness and violence. When Binger visited the Mossi kingdom in 1888 he found the future king in charge of a small group of horsemen carrying out frequent raids on the 'acephalous' Grunshi, seizing their men and, more especially, their women. The frontier provided both a livelihood and a training ground, at the expense of beggaring one's neighbour by captivity or driving him to take refuge in areas where either natural features or greater numbers allowed more effective resistance. Meanwhile the zones of devastation were sometimes incorporated into the states, providing a launching-pad for further forays. Such a scheme is at least consistent with the broad lines of African history and social structure, and does not depend upon the uncritical importation of models derived from Europe or the Middle East into that continent's affairs.

NOTES

1 Boserup, E. (1965), *The Conditions of Agricultural Growth: the economics of agricultural change under population pressure*, London; see discussion in *Peasant Studies Newsletter*, 1, 2, 1972.

2 Middleton, J. and Tait, D. (ed.) (1958), *Tribes without Rulers: Studies in African Segmentary Systems*, London.

3 Goody, J.R. (1971), *Technology, Tradition and the State in Africa*, London; Coquery, C. (1969), 'Recherches sur un mode de production africain', *La Pensée*, 144, pp. 61-78.

4 Stevenson, R. (1968), *Population and Political Systems in Tropical Africa*, New York.

5 Harris, M. (1969), *The Rise of Anthropological Theory*, London.

6 Fortes, M. and Evans-Pritchard, E.E. (1940), *African Political Systems*, London.

7 Durkheim, E. (1893), *De la division du travail social*, Paris.

8 Whatever may have been the case with the Abron (see Terray, E. (1973), 'Technologie, état et tradition en Afrique', *Annales E.S.C.*, 28, pp. 1331-8), parts of Gonja certainly collected taxes from traders. Binger, who travelled through the area before the advent of colonial government, had to pay for crossing rivers and passing through certain villages (Binger, L.G. (1892), *Du Niger au Golfe de Guinée*, Paris, ii, pp. 119, 122). He uses the Hausa word, *fitto*, for the payment. Captain W.G. Murray records meeting a caravan of 1,000 sheep, 300 cattle and 150 donkeys in Nassian in December, 1897, travelling from Mossi to Salaga (Gonja). He remarks: 'Up to our occupation, various towns heavily taxed the caravans, charging varying prices per head for sheep, cattle and donkeys.' Murray to Northcott, C.C.N.T., 25/7/98, Parlt. Printed Papers, P.R.O., C.O. 879/54, p. 80.

9 Goody (1971).

10 Stevenson (1968).

11 Harris (1969), p. 537.

12 Harris (1969), p. 538.

13 Binger (1892), ii, p. 25.

14 I have prepared a detailed examination of these records for publication elsewhere.

15 Braimah, J.A. and Goody, J.R. (1967), *Salaga: the Struggle for Power*, London.

16 Balloz's report on his mission to Niger, Parakou, 17/2/95; 'Le vol et le mensonge sont en honneur dans ce pays dont chaque village est un véritable repaire de bandits.'

17 Skinner, E. (1964), *The Mossi of the Upper Volta*, Stanford; Harris (1969); and Fried, M. (1967), *The Evolution of Political Society*, New York.

18 Friedman, J. (1972), *System, Structure and Contradiction in the Evolution of 'Asiatic' Social Formations*, thesis, Columbia University.

19 See Kraus, G.A. (1928), 'Hausa-Handschriften', *Mitt. Sem. für Orientalische Sprachen*, 31 – a contemporary manuscript on the Sisaala area.

20 I am indebted to Dr. N. Levtzion's seminar in African History at the Hebrew University, Jerusalem, for a useful discussion of these points.

21 Hofstadter, R. and Lipset, S.M. (1968), *Turner and the Sociology of the Frontier*, New York.

INDEX